Journeys Through Philosophy

Journeys Through Philosophy

A Classical Introduction

Edited by Nicholas Capaldi
and Luis E. Navia

℞ Prometheus Books

Buffalo, N.Y. 14215

I.C.C. LIBRARY

65681

Published 1977 by Prometheus Books
1203 Kensington Avenue, Buffalo, New York 14215

Library of Congress Card Number 76-56881
ISBN 0-87975-089-8

Printed in the United States of America

Acknowledgments

This book would not have been possible without the generous assistance, encouragement, and support of many individuals. Dr. Molly Lee, Dean of Humanities at York Institute of Technology, Dr. Chung Lee, Chairman of Social Sciences at New York Institute of Technology, and Dr. Maxim Mikulak, Dr. Gary Helfand, Dr. Maureen O'Sullivan, and Mr. Michael Zuss, also of New York Institute of Technology, have guided us in the organization and selection of some of the readings. Valuable suggestions were made by Dr. Hilail Gildin and Dr. Joseph Mullally of the Queens College Philosophy Department. We also appreciate the editorial assistance of Professor Paul Kurtz, William Ryan, Elizabeth King, Rose Schieda, Diane Malejs and Ms. Rita Wilson, of Prometheus Books. The knowledge and patience of Mrs. Alicia Navia, without which our work would have been impossible, have been invaluable.

Contents

Chapter III—Aristotle and the Aristotelian Tradition

Chapter IV—Medieval Philosophy

Chapter V—Philosophy and Modern Science

Chapter VI—Political Philosophy

Chapter VII—Philosophy in Recent Times

Chapter I—Introduction

What is Philosophy?

In the study of any discipline, the first question that should be kept in mind is the definition of its name. It is, therefore, wise to begin by attempting to give a clear, concise definition of philosophy, as a guide for our subsequent questions. Unfortunately, in the case of philosophy, there are certain initial problems which make the task of arriving at a satisfactory definition somewhat difficult. Different philosophers have given different definitions of their discipline, and in different historical times diverse understandings of its meaning have been entertained. The situation is otherwise with the sciences, which have generally accepted definitions. When, for example, we undertake the study of astronomy, we know perfectly well what it entails, what its limitations are, and what its general objectives should be. We know that the astronomer studies and investigates the positions, movements, structure, and origin of such bodies as the moon, the planets, the sun, and stars, and nebulae, and the galaxies. The methods of the astronomer are clearly understood, and the relationship between astronomy and the other physical sciences can be grasped from the very beginning, even though in the elaboration of its principles and in the organization of its data, changes may have to be introduced from time to time.

In trying to define philosophy, however, we often find ourselves in a predicament. To begin with, practically everybody has used the term "philosophy" at one time or another, as when we speak of the "philosophy of an educational institution," "the philosophy of the democratic party," "a philosophical attitude toward life," and so on. In this context, we probably have in mind the general principles on which an educational institution operates, the ideological basis of the democratic party, and the certain unemotional attitude with which this or that person faces the vicissitudes of life.

We are also aware that some of the most influential historical people of Western Civilization have been "philosophers," and although we may not be quite sure of what this means, we do not hesitate to refer to Plato, Aristotle, Descartes, and Einstein as "philosophers." The same can be said about many eminent individuals who belong to non-Western traditions. Buddha is said to have been a "great philosopher," and the moralistic sayings of Confucius are classified as "philosophical."

Lastly, we know that practically every major university has a "philosophy department" which offers courses in philosophy, and in which students study strange sounding subjects like epistemology, metaphysics, ontology, logic, ethics, cosmology, aesthetics, political philosophy, and the like. The instructors of these courses refer to themselves as "professional philosophers," which simply means that they have received a degree in philosophy which allows them to make a living by "teaching philosophy." Their degrees are usually doctoral degrees which permit them to add to their names the letters "Ph.D."

But we also know other instructors who use the same letters, and who are in no way related to philosophy. A person with a degree in economics, psychology, sociology, mathematics, or astronomy, also holds a Ph.D., which means literally *doctor philosophiae* or "doctor of philosophy." Why should other instructors have the same degree as the professional philosophers? Is economics, perhaps, a part of philosophy? In what sense can the astronomer call himself a philosopher?

In order to understand this curious circumstance in the academic world, we must briefly review some aspects of the history of the term "philosophy." Until the beginning of the twentieth century, any human activity which sought to shed light on the nature of the universe in general and man in particular was deemed to be a part of philosophy. All the theoretical sciences were seen as integral parts of one and the same human endeavor, to gain knowledge; and regardless of the specific interest of each human being involved, it was an established practice to classify them as philosophic. Philosophy was then regarded as a common name that applied to all the sciences. One example will illustrate this custom.

The name of Isaac Newton (1642-1727) is familiar to those who study the physical sciences. Indeed, Newton made so profound an impact on the development of the sciences that we can safely look upon him as one of the most decisive influences in Western Civilization. He was, above all, a mathematician, and to him we owe one of the earliest and most revealing formulations of the principles of calculus. He also was a physicist, and as such, he left us the first coherent statement of the law of gravitation. But he was an astronomer too, whose main concern was the structure of the universe, the principles of celestial mechanics, the nature of the sun, and other crucially important astronomical problems. He dealt extensively with astrology and magic through which he attempted to gain a better understanding of reality. He was concerned with the nature of time and space, and formulated an impressive system of cosmology which exercised a tremendous influence for more than a century. And yet, he regarded himself above all as a "philosopher." To him, all his varied interests were truly "philosophic," and he would have found it difficult to answer questions such as, "Are you a philosopher *or* an astronomer?" In fact, the very title of his masterpiece gave ample testimony of this. He entitled it *Mathematical Principles of Natural Philosophy,* where the term *natural philosophy* signified the investigation of the physical world.

We find a similar situation in the cases of most philosophers and men of science until the beginning of the twentieth century. The currently accepted distinction between philosophy on the one hand, and the sciences on the other, simply did not exist. Philosophy was regarded as the matrix out of which the sciences developed. This is, therefore, the origin of the custom of conferring upon economists, psychologists, sociologists, mathematicians, astronomers, and other theoretical scientists, the degree of "doctor of philosophy."

Today, however, we find ourselves in a different situation. With the overwhelming development of the sciences in the nineteenth century, scientists saw themselves compelled to become highly specialized in some limited realm of theoretical knowledge, and specialization, among other things, forced the sciences to grow increasingly apart from one another, and from what began to be known as "academic philosophy." In the twentieth century, the scientist does not refer to himself as a "philosopher," his Ph.D. notwithstanding, but neither does the academic philosopher generally call himself a scientist. As we will see later, this virtual divorce between philosophy and the sciences is both fortunate and unfortunate, as its effects are both good and bad.

It is fortunate inasmuch as it has given rise to a group of people among us who devote themselves almost exclusively to examining certain general problems of man's experience of the universe and of himself, from which some advantages have been derived. Much attention has been paid on the part of academic philosophers to issues related to the analysis of language, the overall methodology of the sciences, the nature and limits of human knowledge, the grounds for belief and disbelief in the existence of God, the general structure of the human self, the basis of moral values, the fundamental character of the universe, and other problems that are today considered to be the specific domain of philosophy. Furthermore, the separation of the sciences from philosophy has permitted scientists to become immersed in the more immediate issues of their disciplines, leaving for others the investigation of more comprehensive questions.

But, indeed, it is unfortunate, insofar as it has given birth to many academic philosophers among us who know little or nothing of what is going on in the sciences. It is possible to complete a doctoral degree in philosophy without ever having studied anything about the structure of the physical universe or about the basis of Darwinian evolution, so that often the statements made by contemporary philosophers about the universe are grounded on the most precarious foundations. Moreover, our scientists have become so preoccupied with the specific branches of their respective disciplines that they overlook the fact that all things are related. They lack, accordingly, the comprehensive vision which characterized Newton, Kant, Schopenhauer, Hume, and other earlier philosophers and scientists. They have become myopic and see the world only from the limited perspective of their limited interests, and eventually they develop into scientific technicians who think that a statistical table, a stuffed monkey, or the gadgets of a laboratory reveal at once this world in which, as St. Paul said, "we live, move, and have our being."

In order to avoid as much as possible the limited character which is inherent in many manifestations of contemporary philosophy and science, we have decided to expose students to readings of classical philosophers, that is to say, philosophers whose vision was comprehensive and penetrating. From these great thinkers we still have much to learn. It is undeniable that our technological and scientific progress has no counterpart in what pertains to man's understanding of himself and the universe. And yet, in many ways, we have not advanced one inch beyond the ancient Greeks, and the grave questions which they faced more than two thousand years ago are still unanswered. We have gone endlessly around the very same point around which they moved, but our real progress has been minimal. Perhaps this is the unavoidable predicament of human beings who find themselves in the midst of an immense universe, immense in terms of both time and space, while they are allotted only a very small time on an insignificant planet called the earth. Human reason, as Immanuel Kant (1724-1804) once said, is condemned to a most peculiar fate inasmuch as it is constantly beset with questions which it cannot avoid but which it cannot answer. The confrontation with these unavoidable and yet perhaps unanswerable questions; the perennial search for adequate and satisfying answers; the titanic struggle of the mind to reach a reasonable plateau of understanding; the necessity to introduce sense and order into the wilderness of existence; the hope that beneath the mantle of disorder and confusion, the universe is still rational and logical—this is what traditionally has been called philosophy. It is in a literal sense a collection of journeys through the strange land of ideas and speculations. It always begins, as Aristotle observed, with a disquieting feeling of wonder about the meaning of things.

This innate sense of wonder which appears to be an essential quality of every healthy human being is often crushed under the weight of dogmatism. Moved by an understandable urge to appease its questioning, the mind takes refuge in solutions that introduce supernatural explanations, acts of faith, traditional commitments, or ritualistic practices, with the support of which the mind no longer has to cope with the enigma of existence. Indeed, it is apparently better to stifle within us our tendency to question the multitude of experiences that flow daily into our consciousness. God, soul, death, time, space, moral values—all these become reduced to impertinent issues, as soon as we have accepted categorical statements and pontifical truths that others have uttered and defended.

The philosopher, however, is never at home among such statements. The very term *philosophy* clearly conveys the nature of his quest. This term appears to have been coined by the Greek mathematician Pythagoras of Samos (572-497 B.C.). It comes from two Greek words, *philos*, which means "yearning," and *sophia*, which means "wisdom." Philosophy is, then, a yearning after wisdom. The Greeks of Pythagoras' time distinguished those who claimed to know from those who were merely seeking to know. The former were called "sophists," which means simply "wise people." The latter became known as "philosophers." The former had at their disposal a finished body of knowledge which was available in the form of wise sayings, traditional beliefs, and super- stitious ideas about practically everything. They *knew* or thought they knew, and in this proud conviction, they imparted their knowledge to others. For them, all human questions were answerable in terms of gods, mythological accounts, magical incantations, socially acceptable practices, and authoritarian pronouncements.

The birth of philosophy took place when the first human being decided to liberate himself from the sages or sophists. When the first thinking-individual chose not to dance, so to speak, around the tribal fire where the others sat submissively to hear the sterile wisdom of the sophists, the initial journey of philosophy began. This must have taken place countless times among all sorts of people of antiquity, perhaps long before written records began to be made. But our knowledge of the history of mankind is so limited that we cannot speak meaningfully about these forgotten births of philosophy. This is why we must turn our attention to ancient Greece; we have sufficient historical records, and there is a direct line of intellectual continuity between the Greeks and us.

The first Greek thinker whose philosophical ideas have come down to us was a man named Thales (sixth century B.C.). We know little about his life, and none of his writings has withstood the passage of time. We do know, however, that he predicted successfully and explained correctly an eclipse of the sun that took place in the year 585 B.C. He was born in Miletus, a city on the coast of Turkey founded by the Athenians some two hundred years before his birth. He traveled extensively, and had a long sojourn in Egypt. As in the case of other Greek philosophers who visited Egypt (Pythagoras, Plato, and others), it is practically impossible to tell how much Thales learned from the Egyptians.

The importance of Thales in the history of philosophy cannot be exag- gerated. In the few fragments concerning his philosophy that have survived (fragments that are really later quotations from other writers), we discern at once a powerful mind dominated by a yearning after wisdom. The principles of his philosophy constitute a clear example of what a philosophical attitude toward the world should be. In the first place, he made every attempt to explain the universe in strictly rational and human terms, thereby avoiding any appeal to supernatural entities such as gods or invisible forces. He was convinced that nature was thoroughly explainable, that is to say, completely rational, and that its apparently mysterious character was the result of human limitations and prejudices. This led him to postulate the reality of certain inflexible laws accord- ing to which events take place. Nothing in nature happens by mere chance;

nothing in nature is the work of whimsical gods and demons who play with human beings as a child plays with worthless toys. There is, then, a universal regularity in all that happens. An eclipse of the sun, for example, is a natural event brought about by natural causes, and as such, it is both predictable and explainable. The understanding of nature is, therefore, possible if we are able to grasp the *principles* of its operation.

Here we can see how the philosophical mind is not satisfied with the apparently senseless concatenation of events and accidents that surround us daily. The philosopher goes beyond the mantle of sense impressions and experiences, and asks, What is it that underlies all events? Are there any universal principles, in compliance with which all things take place? Even if there are gods who watch over the affairs of human beings, these gods have to operate within the frame of universal principles.

Thales attempted to formulate these principles by postulating a universal substance of which all things are the manifestations. Beneath the multiplicity of things, he thought, there had to exist a primordial *element*, something basic, which gave rise to them. He arrived at the conclusion that this element was *water*. Water, he believed, turns into ice, vapor, air, earth, or fire, depending on the changes of temperature which it undergoes; but regardless of its deceptive appearance, it remains water, no more, no less. Moreover, he reasoned that if in reality the gods of religious beliefs exist, they too are made of water.

It is obvious that the philosophy of Thales presents to us a system of mechanistic materialism in which matter, or rather water, constitutes everything. We will see, in subsequent chapters, how this was revised and challenged by Thales' successors, and how within two hundred years it was fully transformed. It is important to bear in mind that in the history of philosophy there are no inflexible dogmas and no infallible masters. A text like the Bible does not have a counterpart in the world of philosophy. Accordingly, those who inherited Thales' teachings felt perfectly free to question not only his conclusions about water and his astronomical ideas, but the very principles on which his thought stood. Anaximander of Miletus (sixth century B.C.) spoke of the evolution of the species and of the multiplicity of earths in space, and rejected Thales' preference for water as the basic element. According to Anaximander, the basic element was a nameless substance, much too subtle to be observed, which he named "the boundless." Anaximenes of Miletus, a contemporary of Anaximander, replaced the boundless with ordinary air. Pythagoras, of whom we spoke earlier, maintained that numbers were the fundamental elements of things, and introduced a spiritual realm of being which would have been totally foreign to Thales. Heraclitus of Ephesus (536-470 B.C.) became convinced that the primordial substance was fire, and that the universal law was eternal change. Empedocles of Sicily (490-430 B.C.) spoke of the basic element as being fourfold: air, water, earth, and fire, and Anaxagoras (about 430 B.C.) conceived of an infinite number of elements. By the time of Socrates (469-399 B.C.), the original ideas of Thales were practically unrecognizable. They had been subjected to the merciless questioning of philosophers.

But let us return for a moment to these ideas. Indeed, to say that "everything is water" does appear to be a most unsophisticated utterance, something which only a fool could say. Don't we see many things around us that are evidently not water? How could Thales have believed that earth, fire, air, and other things are really water? It is curious to observe, however, that if our present understanding of the universe is correct, Thales' contention is almost correct. We believe that ninety percent of the observable universe is hydrogen, and that the other ten percent (helium, oxygen, nitrogen, and the rest of the elements) is the result of transformations undergone by primitive hydrogen. Our understanding of the physical processes that go on in the stars has led us to this conclusion. Now then, water itself is mostly hydrogen (two atoms of hydrogen and one atom of oxygen). Hence we must conclude that the most prevailing constituent of water is also the most prevailing constituent of the universe. Thales' mistake, if one can talk here about "mistakes," was due to his inadequate knowledge concerning the chemical composition of water. In spite of this, however, he was practically correct in his choosing water as the fundamental substance that underlies all things.

The appearance of Thales and the other early Greek philosophers constitutes an extraordinary event in the history of Western Civilization. It signals the birth of a new epoch for mankind, in which nature and the universe are approached from a rational point of view. The superstitions of darker times begin to give way to the outlook of the philosopher who searches, amid the variety of daily experiences, for basic principles, inflexible laws, and understandable patterns according to which things exist. The miracles and surprises of our ancestors, the randomness of their world, the dazzlement and fear with which they perceived the world, the mythological and religious accounts with which they attempted to make sense of the universe—all these begin to move into the background of speculation in the minds of those who call themselves "the lovers of wisdom."

Naturally, among the early Greeks it would have been unreasonable to expect to find a clear distinction between philosophy and the sciences on the one hand, and between one science and another on the other. The body of data which made up their knowledge was relatively limited, and the principles according to which they grasped their experiences were few. A philosopher in those days was what we might call a "universal scientist." We have seen how Thales was an astronomer *and* a physicist *and* a political man *and* a cartographer *and* many other things. The same can be said of Pythagoras for whom mathematics *and* physics *and* music were manifestations of philosophy. Plato, too, combined in his fabulous writings (more than twenty-four dialogues) a vast variety of subjects. He wrote on the meaning of reality, the nature of perception, the purpose of life, the significance of death, the organization of the political state, the complexity of language, the reality of the gods, the basis of moral values, the origin of mankind, and many other themes, some of which we would call today philosophical, while others would be relegated to the sciences. The example of Aristotle is indeed extraordinary. He investigated a tremendous variety of fields: the nature of the stars, the shape of the earth, the structure of the universe, the nature of man, the meaning of dreams, the political consti- tutions of Greek states, the birth of tragedy, and so on. He saw all these fields as the specific realms in which one and the same philosophical activity is at work. In Aristotle, however, we do find the first attempt to classify the sciences, and the first indication that the name "philosophy" should be reserved for that endeavor in which we seek to grasp the principles or general laws that prevail in nature.

Hence, it is not altogether inappropriate to define philosophy, following Aristotle's suggestion, as the intellectual activity in which the human mind attempts to gain some understanding of the principles, laws, concepts, and pat- terns that govern existence. In this sense, then, philosophy can be distinguished from the sciences insofar as it deals with the ideas that underlie the specific sciences. For example, concepts such as time, space, being, existence, reality, meaning, value, purpose, causality, are either taken for granted in the sciences, or are examined from a narrow point of view. These concepts constitute the very essence of the philosophical enterprise.

It is to be expected that with the great accumulation of scientific data and with the proliferation of sciences, philosophy has been compelled to separate itself from the sciences, not in the sense that it does something entirely different from what they do, but in the sense that it is called upon to do something they cannot do, namely, to examine the foundations of science in general, and there- by to shed light on human experience. Furthermore, there are many questions that contemporary scientists do not usually examine, but which, on account of their importance, must be examined. Among these problems, there is, for ex- ample, the question of the existence of God. The philosopher cannot avoid turn- ing his attention to it.

Throughout the introductions and selections of this text, the student will find a variety of examples of philosophical activity. They represent intelligent attempts to deal with problems that now, as much as in antiquity, are re- garded as the special province of the philosopher. There are few solutions, and the problems of the past remain problems for us. But before we plunge ourselves into the subject matter itself, it is important to spend some time on a prelimi- nary issue, namely, how to read and study philosophy.

How to Read Philosophy

Every discipline, no matter whether it is mathematics, poetry, history, or philosophy, has both a subject matter or content and an approach to that content which is unique. In fact, it is probably easier to understand a discipline by grasping its special techniques than it is by trying to isolate its subject matter. Philosophy is no exception. Philosophers have their own special ways of handling their subject matter, special ways of thinking about it as well as special ways of trying to communicate their thoughts to others. With increasing specialization in the academic world, these techniques have become more and more refined, and consequently require more effort on the part of novices to grasp. This is true of all fields of endeavor.

There is a special set of circumstances that makes philosophy appear formidable to the beginner. Whereas all students come to college having studied mathematics and history, or having read poetry at least in high school, very few students have had any exposure at all to philosophy. Regretably and unjustifiably, philosophy is not part of the standard high school curriculum. The language of philosophy therefore appears strange, mysterious, and even frightening to some. It would be the same if students were required to count for the first time when they entered college as freshmen, and it undoubtedly appears that way to some who study a foreign langauge for the first time. But once the student grasps and masters the techniques of a discipline, it is the content that presents the challenge and not the techniques. We believe that the content of philosophy is so important and so interesting that it is a great shame to turn

11

readers off by inadequate preparation and mystery-mongering. In short, philosophy is too important to be left to an élite or to be ignored, and that is why it must be properly introduced. We have found that there are ways of giving beginners the basic skills necessary for reading philosophy. When you finish this book, we earnestly expect that you will be able to read most philosophical works and all of the classics, and you will probably wonder at your earlier reluctance in a way similar to trying to imagine what it was like before you read at all.

There are, of course, different styles and formats for philosophers presenting their ideas to the public. In the history of philosophy, two stand out: the dialogue and the essay. Since the essay is the most common, we shall begin with it and leave the discussion of reading the dialogue for the next chapter.

Our guide to reading philosophy is in three parts. First, we shall present a brief outline for future reference. Second, we shall discuss each part of the outline. Third, we shall exemplify how the outline actually works by using it to read one of the great philosophical classics, John Stuart Mill's essay *On Liberty*, Chapter One.

I. What is the *problem?*
  A. How is the problem formulated?
  B. Why is this problem an important one?
  C. What is the history of this problem?
  D. Which prominent personalities have been interested in this problem?
II. What *solutions* to this problem are there?
  A. What conclusion is reached?
  B. By what argument(s) is the conclusion reached?
  C. What facts and assumptions serve as premises?
  D. Does the author raise objections to alternative solutions? Does he consider potential objections to his own solution?
III. *Evaluation*
  A. What are the advantages and disadvantages of the alternative formulations to the problem?
  B. Has the importance or history of the problem been misrepresented?
  C. Are the "facts" really facts? Are the assumptions acceptable? Are the objections answerable?

I. What is the *Problem?*

Every philosophical work is concerned with a particular problem, issue, or controversy. The choice of a word is not important here as long as the readers ask themselves what is the particular issue or set of issues about which the work is written. Until the reader uncovers this issue his reading is either pointless or undirected. Sometimes that issue is stated explicitly, and sometimes it is only implicit. Sometimes that issue is stated in the first paragraph and sometimes it is buried deep within the work. When the latter prevails, the reader must search for it, and perhaps even reread the work once it is found. But until you can state exactly what problem is being dealt with, your reading is merely tentative, hypothetical, and should be pursued cautiously.

Not every philosopher would win the Nobel prize for literature, anymore than every freshman essay belongs in the literary hall of fame. Some philosophers are notoriously poor writers, and this should be kept in mind so that readers do not feel that all of the problem is theirs. However, every essay in this volume has been carefully chosen for its readability.

A. *How is the problem formulated?* Law students are familiar with the old joke of the attorney who, while cross-examining a witness, asked: "Have you stopped beating your wife? Answer 'yes' or 'no.'" Either way the witness would be admitting that he had beaten his wife in the past. This, of course, may not be true, but the clever attorney will have tried to embarrass the witness by asking his question in a particular way. The moral of this story is that *how a question is asked determines the kind of answer you can expect.* When you read about Socrates you will see just how true this is. More important, you will discover that what distinguishes one philosopher from another, one philosophical style from another, is the manner in which questions are asked.

This is largely what is meant by saying that in philosophy the question is more important than the answer. It does not mean that philosophers are uninterested in the answer; on the contrary, most philosophers are passionately involved with answers. It means that the answer is implicitly structured by the question and how it is asked.

It also means that the sophisticated reader must be aware of the fact that there are alternative ways of asking a question, and the alternatives have momentous consequences. In the beginning when you have read only one or even a few philosophers, it will be difficult to think about alternatives, but after you have become familiar with several alternatives it will be easy to conceive of others. For example, after you have read Plato and Aristotle, you may read Descartes. While reading Descartes and noting how he asks questions you will automatically ask yourself, "How would Plato have viewed that question? How would Aristotle handle that issue?" and so on. The more background knowledge you accumulate, both in philosophy and in other fields, the more possibilities will occur. After a while, the only limitation will be your own imagination. By the time you are doing this, you will, in a manner of speaking be "doing philosophy."

B. *Why is this problem an important one?* Questions do not arise in a vacuum. There is a reason why, when, where, and how they occur. We say that the problem exists in a certain context, and that the context structures the problem, which is another way of saying that how the question is asked determines the answer. Knowing the background to a question is essential to understanding it. That is why we have provided sufficient background information for each essay to ensure that the reader will understand the context. It is interesting that even professional philosophers disagree with each other because they approach the same essay with different background assumptions, and that there have been major shifts in the interpretation of classical works with the discovery of more background information.

In addition to the background, there is the all-important element of how the author or philosopher sees his own problem. A clear writer will not only state the problem but he will also try to indicate just why he thinks that the problem is important enough to deserve his energies as an author, and to be worthy of the reader's attention. Spotting this element helps you to comprehend the issue and its solution. Problems are important for many reasons in philosophy, all the way from the survival of the human race (and you will be surprised at how many philosophers have this foremost in mind) to seemingly technical issues that might appear to be of interest only to specialists. Even in the latter case, these technical issues are usually related to very practical concerns. Finally, it will be interesting to see how what looks like the same problem takes on an interesting history, because in different ages the same problem may be important but for different reasons.

C. *What is the history of this problem?* Not only will the careful writer state his personal reasons for believing the problem to be important, but he will also indicate the history of the problem. Usually the same problem has appeared before, or at least has been treated by other authors. Some reference to this history or previous treatment is usually made. For the moment we are not concerned with how accurately the history of the problem has been portrayed. Rather, we are concerned with how the author "sees" the history of the problem. In some cases you might want to point out that the author "does not see." We may even grant that philosophers, especially the greatest, are frequently unfair to their predecessors and colleagues. We grant all this for the moment because what is of interest here is how the *author's personal preconceptions help structure the way in which he has asked his question.* We must always try to understand the author first from his own interior point of view. Even if we later criticize that point of view, our criticism will be fair if we have the first made a sincere attempt to see from that point of view.

D. *What prominent personalities have been interested in this problem?* Everything said above applies to this question as well. Authors will often mention other authors either explicitly or implicitly, and when they do we shall notify the reader. Knowing those other works helps to understand the work you are reading at the moment. In the beginning this is impossible, so we have provided more background information. After you have read the first few works you will be able to do this for the remaining works in this anthology.

Given the foregoing, it should be clear why in part we have chosen a historical perspective. You may address posterity but you can only answer the past. Moreover, philosophers not only read other philosophers but they react to general intellectual climates as well. You will be surprised by how much of philosophy is a response to developments in the sciences, so that not knowing the history of science is a disadvantage in trying to understand a philosophical work. The same can be said for artistic, political, social, and religious developments.

II. What *solutions* to the problem are there?

After you have identified the problem or set of problems about which the author is writing, you will be in a position to look for the answer or answers he provides. When looking for the solution, the following should be kept in mind.

A. *What are the conclusions reached?* Although we have stated matters in the form of questions and answers we should bear in mind that there are at least three possibilities.

(1) *A direct answer:* An author may have a direct answer to give to a specific problem. If so, you should look for it and state it.

(2) *Dissolving the problem:* Another possibility is the case where the author declares the problem to be a pseudo-problem; that is, no problem at all. For example, an old standby in philosophy is the question, What came first—the chicken or the egg? This question is exemplary of the Aristotelian problem of the cause of motion. In Aristotle's physics, rest is the natural state and motion is what has to be explained. The very beginning of motion, or of anything, is what an Aristotelian philosopher concerns himself with. To him, the question is important. On the contrary, in Newtonian physics, motion is a natural state, so that one can never meaningfully ask what causes motion. The very beginning of anything is not a serious issue if we take Newton's physics as our standard, and this is just exactly what Hume did. Hence, in Hume the question of most concern to an Aristotelian would be dismissed as meaningless.

It is not our purpose here to decide on the relative merits of competing theories of physics, or whether Aristotle or Hume is correct. We are concerned with pointing out how a question can seem vital to a philosopher who looks out on the world from one point of view, and how that same question can appear to be no question at all to a philosopher with another point of view. If we have prepared our ground in asking the right question about what the problem is, then we shall be able to anticipate the maneuvering that goes on in finding the solution.

(3) *Plea for recognition:* Sometimes a philosopher will not have a solution to a particular problem. Rather, it will be his purpose to point out that the problem exists. In itself this can be a great contribution since we cannot solve problems if we do not know that they exist, and even then we must be able to recognize them in time. The philosopher's penchant for seeing the forest and not just the trees gives him a unique advantage in spotting issues before others do. In a time of increasing specialization, this penchant is all the more precious.

B. *By what argument(s) is the conclusion reached?* In many ways this is the most interesting question for the philosopher. While most people think it sufficient to simply know the conclusions of this or that particular philosopher, it is much more vital to know the reasons behind the conclusion. By *reasons* here we do not mean motives, but those logical considerations which lead to the adoption of the conclusion. Why is this so?

First, we may agree with the conclusion but not with the argument behind it. A bad argument may lose support for an otherwise acceptable conclusion.

Second, we may disagree with the conclusion but find the argument powerful or useful for other purposes. Finally, by understanding the arguments we may be able to extend them to other contexts that the original author never considered. In short, we can learn from the argument more than we can from the conclusion.

Moreover, if we are to be rational men and women, then presumably we will want to defend our conclusions as rational and not merely accepted as a matter of blind faith. It is not enough to complain about the irrationality of others and then refuse to make the effort to be rational oneself.

An argument will be said to have the following structure: one or more premises and one conclusion. The *conclusion* is that which the author is trying to prove. The *premises* are those beliefs which the author gives as reason for accepting the conclusion. For our purposes it is not necessary to go into greater detail about the complexities of logic. Suffice it to say that the great philosophers, at the very least in the selections we have chosen, do not make logical mistakes. Hence, if you accept the premises you "must" accept the conclusion. If you disagree with the conclusion, then you must reject one or more of the premises.

C. *What facts or assumptions serve as the premises?* The premises are those reasons offered in support of the conclusion. Authors usually appeal to those beliefs which they think that their audience already accepts and then try to show that the favored conclusion also follows from those beliefs or is at least consistent with those beliefs.

In different historical periods and places different beliefs prevail. Many arguments are thus "dated" in the sense that what is acceptable in one time or place is not necessarily acceptable in another. Presumably, this holds for some of our own favorite beliefs as well.

There is another distinction worth making, as long as it is not made too sharply. We may distinguish between facts and assumptions. Facts are those alleged beliefs which we feel can be easily checked against experience, such as the color of an object, the temperature of a liquid, or the date of someone's birth. Assumptions are those beliefs which either cannot be checked directly, or are in principle not the sorts of things that can be checked. For example, the temperature in the center of the sun is not checkable, at least now, because no thermometer could withstand the heat. More interestingly, the belief that the future will resemble the past or the belief that mankind will one day understand everything, are not really checkable at all. Such assumptions guide our thinking about other things. Philosophers are very much concerned with the status of such *ultimate* premises. For our purposes at this stage it is only important to try to recognize when an author is stating a fact that he believes can be checked, and when he is appealing to an ultimate premise.

D. *What alternatives are considered?* Philosophers not only present arguments for their own solutions but also raise objections against alternative solutions. Frequently the case for one's conclusion is not so much its own strength but the weakness of alternative views. In line with this, the reader must learn to ask: does the author argue for or against the solutions of other authors? Does he raise objections to those solutions, and if so what are they? Does he consider objections to his own solution? A wise writer anticipates the kinds of responses he will receive and tries to meet these objections before they can ever be articulated.

A good deal of philosophical reading involves the laying out of both the author's own position and his consideration of alternative positions. Here it is important to keep asking yourself as you read, "Is the author speaking for himself or is he reporting the viewpoint of the opposition?" This is part of the dialectic of philosophical argument, and mastering it is the key to successful comprehension.

III. *Evaluation*

Students frequently ask, "Do you want us to summarize the author or do you want our opinion?" Putting the question this way presupposes that the two activities are distinct. It also presupposes a rather naive view of presenting one's own opinion. I would point out that it is impossible to "summarize" another philosopher without raising some evaluative questions. In fact, without evaluation you cannot really be said to comprehend. Then again, it is impossible to evaluate without fully comprehending. I think that if the reader makes an attempt to comprehend an author in the manner suggested by Parts I and II of the outline, then he will already have been engaged in an evaluative process. Let us spell this out.

A. Look at IA. *What are the advantages or disadvantages of the alternative formulations of the problem?* Once you have become aware of the alternative formulations, that is, once you have read at least two selections, you can at the very least use one against the other. You might even want to use each against the other in order to suggest a third possibility.

B. Look at IB and IC. *Has the importance or history of the problem been misrepresented?* Maybe the problem is no longer important, or maybe it is important for totally new reasons. Maybe a better knowledge of the history of the problem leads to a different solution. It is not only in Orwell's *1984* that history is systematically distorted. It is even possible that what a classical philosopher said many years ago caused or influenced the problem to change in the meantime. Finally, we risk pointing out that the way one interprets the history of anything is symptomatic of a particular philosophical point of view.

C. Look at IIC. *Do you agree with the facts appealed to?* As we have already pointed out, the conclusions follow from the premises. If you do not like the conclusion, then you must reject either one or more of the facts alleged or the assumptions made. Here, expressing a dissenting opinion can be a philosophically sophisticated response on your part, and not just an emotional reaction.

D. Look at IID. *Are the objections answerable?* Here there are several possibilities. If author A attacks author B, and you agree with author B, then why not try to show how author B would respond? That is, respond on his be-half. The fact that an author is attacked does not imply that the attack is a good one, and you can show how it has failed. Moreover, the fact that an author con-siders objections in advance of his solution does not mean that he has success-fully answered them. If you feel that the reply is insufficient, offer a rebuttal of your own. Finally, if you agree with an author, you may want to present addi-tional arguments in support of his case, for he may not have been in a position to consider them. By the time you have done all this, your philosophical reading will not be a mere summary or a simple-minded personal opinion but a kind of philosophy in its own right.

J. S. Mill:
On Liberty—Text and Analysis

Paragraph 1: "The subject of this essay is . . . civil, or social liberty: the nature and limits of the power which can be legitimately exercised by society over the individual." Mill immediately informs his readers of the *problem* with which he will be dealing. This corresponds to (I) in the reading guide outline. (IA) *How is the problem formulated?* The formulation of the problem involves a contrast: *society* on the one hand and the *individual* on the other. Mill thus makes a sharp distinction between the individual and society. As we shall discover later, other philosophers will not agree with this separation. As a reader of English you probably take this distinction as obvious, but that is a result of the fact that Mill represents the mainstream of Anglo-Saxon thought. It should also be noted that Mill is not asking about the present limits (a sociological question) but what *ought* to be the limits, legitimately; that is a moral question. Finally, we note that Mill does not mention the government, rather, he mentions society.

(IB) *Why is this problem an important one?* Mill notes that this problem has a long history which he will discuss shortly. But he claims that there are "new conditions" which "require a different and more fundamental treatment." What these circumstances are he does not discuss in this paragraph. See paragraphs 3, 4, and 15.

> The subject of this Essay is not the so-called Liberty of the Will, so unfortunately opposed to the misnamed doctrine of Philosophical Necessity; but Civil, or Social Liberty: the nature and limits of the power which can be legitimately exercised by

society over the individual, a question seldom stated, and hardly ever discussed, in general terms, but which profoundly influences the practical controversies of the age by its latent presence, and is likely soon to make itself recognised as the vital question of the future. It is so far from being new, that in a certain sense, it has divided mankind, almost from the remotest ages; but in the stage of progress into which the more civilized portions of the species have now entered, it presents itself under new conditions, and requires a different and more fundamental treatment.

Paragraph 2: In this paragraph, Mill gives his version of the *history of the problem* (IC). His history refers to three countries: *Greece, Rome* (of the Republican period, not the Empire), and *England*. His history is limited to those times and places relevant to the history of modern England (and the U.S. by extension) since he is writing for a specific audience. Obviously, referring to other times and places would produce a different history. In these examples, the *problems* of the individual versus society was understood in terms of an adversary relationship: "The rulers were conceived . . . as in a necessarily antagonistic position to the people whom they ruled." Some of our contemporary talk of the government as the "they" in "Washington" preserves the flavor of this history. In short, rulers were necessary evils. The individual was protected in two ways: (1) a doctrine of "rights" and (2) "constitutional checks." The U.S. Constitution with its Bill of Rights, as well as the doctrine of checks and balances, is a perfect example of this. The U.S. Constitution was the product of the eighteenth century and the previous influence upon the founding fathers of Hobbes, Locke, Hume, and Montesquieu. Mill was writing in the nineteenth century, and was an heir of that tradition. (ID)

> The struggle between Liberty and Authority is the most conspicuous feature in the portions of history with which we are earliest familiar, particularly in that of Greece, Rome, and England. But in old times this contest was between subjects, or some classes of subjects, and the government. By liberty was meant protection against the tyranny of the political rulers. The rulers were conceived (except in some of the popular governments of Greece) as in a necessarily antagonistic position to the people whom they ruled. They consisted of a governing One, or a governing tribe or caste, who derived their authority from inheritance or conquest, who, at all costs, did not hold it at the pleasure of the governed, and whose supremacy men did not venture, perhaps did not desire to contest, whatever precautions might be taken against its oppressive exercise. Their power was regarded as necessary, but also as highly dangerous; as a weapon which they would attempt to use against their subjects, no less than against external enemies. To prevent the weaker members of the community from being preyed upon by innumerable vultures, it was needful that there should be an animal of prey stronger than the rest, commissioned to keep them down. But as the king of the vultures would be no less bent upon preying on the flock, than any of the minor harpies, it was indispensable to be in a perpetual attitude of defence against his beak and claws. The aim, therefore, of patriots, was to set limits to the power which the ruler should be suffered to exercise over the community; and this limitation was what they meant by liberty. It was attempted in two ways. First, by obtaining a recognition of certain immunities, called political liberties or rights, which it was to be regarded as a breach of duty in

the ruler to infringe, and which if he did infringe, specific resistance, or general rebellion, was held to be justifiable. A second, and generally a later expedient, was the establishment of constitutional checks; by which the consent of the community or of a body of some sort, supposed to represent its interests, was made a necessary condition to some of the more important acts of the governing power. To the first of these modes of limitation, the ruling power, in most European countries, was compelled, more or less, to submit. It was not so with the second; and to attain this, or when already in some degree possessed, to attain it more completely, became everywhere the principle object of the lovers of liberty. And so long as mankind were content to combat one enemy by another, and to be ruled by a master, on condition of being guaranteed more or less efficaciously against his tyranny, they did not carry their aspirations beyond this point.

Paragraph 3: Here Mill returns to the importance of the problem (IB). What are the new circumstances that require our problem to be re-thought? As some governments became more representative, the old adversary relationship disappeared. Now instead of limiting the government's power, there grew the idea of increasing it. "The nation did not need to be protected against its own will."

The reader should compare the difference between the "old" liberal who seeks to curb government power and the "new" liberal who seeks to increase it. Which people today ask for the government to control social security, Medicare, welfare, wages and prices? Can the same government avoid fraud in public programs without resort to illegal wiretaps for example? Are we making contradictory demands?

> A time, however, came, in the progress of human affairs, when men ceased to think it a necessity of nature that their governors should be an independent power, opposed in interest to themselves. It appeared to them much better that the various magistrates of the State should be their tenants or, delegates, revocable at their pleasure. In that way alone, it seemed, could they have complete security that the powers of government would never be abused to their disadvantage. By degrees, this new demand for elective and temporary rulers became the prominent object of the exertions of the popular party, wherever any such party existed; and superseded, to a considerable extent, the previous efforts to limit the power of rulers. As the struggle proceeded for making the ruling power emanate from the periodical choice of the ruled, some persons began to think that too much importance had been attached to the limitation of the power itself. *That* (it might seem) was a resource against rulers whose interests were habitually opposed to those of the people. What was now wanted was, that the rulers should be identified with the people; that their interest and will should be the interest and will of the nation. The nation did not need to be protected against it own will. There was no fear of its tyrannizing over itself. Let the rulers be effectually responsible to it, promptly removable by it, and it could afford to trust them with power of which it could itself dictate the use to be made. Their power was but the nation's own power, concentrated, and in a form convenient for exercise. This mode of thought, or rather perhaps of feeling, was common among the last generation of European liberalism, in the Continental section of which, it still apparently predominates.

Those who admit any limit to what a government may do, except in the case of such governments as they think ought not to exist, stand out as brilliant exceptions among the political thinkers of the Continent. A similar tone of sentiment might by this time have been prevalent in our own country, if the circumstances which for a time encouraged it, had continued unaltered.

Paragraph 4: Mill continues to discuss IB. The concept he introduces to explain the new circumstances for the old problem is "the tyranny of the majority." *What is the tyranny of the majority?*
(1) the oppression of the minority or minorities by the majority;
(2) the oppression of minorities by a minority which is the "most active part of the people," that is, an active minority that speaks or claims to speak on behalf of the "people."
Does the tyranny of the majority exist? What is the position of blacks in a predominantly white society? What will the position of whites be when Rhodesia and South Africa become countries ruled by a majority of blacks? What is the position of Catholics in Protestant Northern Ireland? What is the position of Jews in a Moslem country such as Iraq, or vice versa? Do these tyrannies exist because some groups are more immoral than others, or because they are majorities? Mill borrowed the expression "tyranny of the majority" from Alexis de Tocqueville (1805-59), a French liberal politician and writer, who used it in his classic work *Democracy in America* (1835). The original meaning of the term *democracy* in Greek was mob rule.

But, in political and philosophical theories, as well as in persons, success discloses faults and infirmities which failure might have concealed from observation. The notion, that the people have no need to limit their power over themselves, might seem axiomatic, when popular government was a thing only dreamed about, or read of as having existed at some distant period of the past. Neither was that notion necessarily disturbed by such temporary aberrations as those of the French Revolution, the worst of which were the work of an usurping few, and which, in any case, belonged, not to the permanent working of popular institutions, but to a sudden and convulsive outbreak against monarchical and aristocratic despotism. In time, however, a democratic republic came to occupy a large portion of the earth's surface, and made itself felt as one of the most powerful members of the community of nations; and elective and responsible government became subject to the observations and criticisms which wait upon a great existing fact. It was now perceived that such phrases as 'self-government,' and 'the power of the people over themselves,' do not express the true state of the case. The 'people' who exercise the power, are not always the same people with those over whom it is exercised; and the 'self-government' spoken of, is not the government of each by himself, but of each by all the rest. The will of the people, moreover, practically means, the will of the most numerous or the most active *part* of the people; the majority, or those who succeed in making themselves accepted as the majority: the people, consequently, *may* desire to oppress a part of their number; and precautions are as much needed against this, as against any other abuse of power. The limitation, therefore, of the power of government over individuals, loses none of its importance when the holders of power are regularly accountable to the community, that is, to the strongest party therein. This view of things, recommending itself equally to the intelligence of thinkers and to the inclination of those important classes in European society to whose real or supposed interests democracy is adverse, has had no difficulty in establishing itself; and in political speculations 'the tyranny of the majority' is now generally included among the evils against which society requires to be on its guard.

Paragraph 5: Mill further defines the problem. The real culprit is not the government but society. "Social tyranny" is "more formidable than many kinds of political oppression." Why? Can you think of a serious social problem recently solved through political means?

Mill begins to approach the solution of his problem by formulating the question (IA) more clearly; notice the importance of "society" as opposed to government in Mill's formulation. "There is a limit to the legitimate interference of collective opinion with individual independence: and to find that limit, and maintain it against encroachment, is as indispensable to a good condition of human affairs as protection against political despotism."

> Like other tyrannies, the tyranny of the majority was at first, and is still vulgarly, held in dread, chiefly as operating through the acts of the public authorities. But reflecting persons perceived that when society is itself the tyrant—society collectively, over the separate individuals who compose it—its means of tyrannizing are not restricted to the acts which it may do by the hands of its political functionaries. Society can and does execute its own mandates: and if it issues wrong mandates instead of right, or any mandates at all in things with which it ought not to meddle, it practises a social tyranny more formidable than many kinds of political oppression, since, though not usually upheld by such extreme penalties, it leaves fewer means of escape, penetrating much more deeply into the details of life, and enslaving the soul itself. Protection, therefore, against the tyranny of the magistrate is not enough: there needs protection also against the tyranny of the prevailing opinion and feeling; against the tendency of society to impose, by other means than civil penalties, its own ideas and practices as rules of conduct on those who dissent from them; to fetter the development, and, if possible, prevent the formation, of any individuality not in harmony with its ways, and compel all characters to fashion themselves upon the model of its own. There is a limit to the legitimate interference of collective opinion with individual independence: and to find that limit, and maintain it against encroachment, is as indispensable to a good condition of human affairs, as protection against political despotism.

Paragraph 6: Before offering his own answer, Mill considers the answers we already have or have operated with. These (IID) include:
  (a) custom
  (b) personal feelings
  (c) self-interest
  (d) religious prejudice.
Note Mill's mention of women and their subservient position to men in most

societies. This is another instance of tyranny. Mill was one of the first to champion the liberation of women. His work *On the Subjection of Women* (written in 1861 and published in 1869) is still a classic. Mrs. Harriet Taylor undoubtedly influenced him on this issue, both before and after their marriage. Women are now fifty-two percent of the U.S. population. Will women's liberation eventually become a kind of tyranny?

But though this proposition is not likely to be contested in general terms, the practical question, where to place the limit—how to make the fitting adjustment between individual independence and social control—is a subject on which nearly everything remains to be done. All that makes existence valuable to any one, depends on the enforcement of restraints upon the actions of other people. Some rules of conduct, therefore, must be imposed, by law in the first place, and by opinion on many things which are not fit subjects for the operation of law. What these rules should be, is the principal question in human affairs; but if we except a few of the most obvious cases, it is one of those which least progress has been made in resolving. No two ages, and scarcely any two countries, have decided it alike; and the decision of one age or country is a wonder to another. Yet the people of any given age and country no more suspect any difficulty in it, than if it were a subject on which mankind had always been agreed. The rules which obtain among themselves appear to them self-evident and self-justifying. This all but universal illusion is one of the examples of the magical influence of custom, which is not only, as the proverb says, a second nature, but is continually mistaken for the first. The effect of custom, in preventing any misgiving respecting the rules of conduct which mankind impose on one another, is all the more complete because the subject is one on which it is not generally considered necessary that reasons should be given, either by one person to others, or by each to himself. People are accustomed to believe, and have been encouraged in the belief by some who aspire to the character of philosophers, that their feelings, on subjects of this nature, are better than reasons, and render reasons unnecessary. The practical principle which guides them to their opinions on the regulation of human conduct, is the feeling in each person's mind that everybody should be required to act as he, and those with whom he sympathizes, would like them to act. No one, indeed, acknowledges to himself that his standard of judgment is his own liking; but an opinion on a point of conduct, not supported by reasons, can only count as one person's preference; and if the reasons, when given, are a mere appeal to a similar preference felt by other people, it is still only many people's liking instead of one. To an ordinary man, however, his own preference, thus supported, is not only a perfectly satisfactory reason, but the only one he generally has for any of his notions of morality, taste, or propriety, which are not expressly written in his religious creed; and his chief guide in the interpretation even of that. Men's opinions, accordingly, on what is laudable or blameable, are affected by all the multifarious causes which influence their wishes in regard to the conduct of others, and which are as numerous as those which determine their wishes on any other subject. Sometimes their reason—at other times their prejudices or superstitions; often their social affections, not seldom their antisocial ones, their envy or jealousy, their arrogance or contemptuousness: but most commonly, their desires or fears for themselves—their legitimate or illegitimate self-interest. Wherever there is an ascendant class, a large portion of the morality of the country emanates from its class interests, and its feelings of class superiority. The morality between Spartans and Helots, between planters and negroes, between princes and subjects, between nobles and roturiers, between men and women, has been for the most part the creation of these class interests and feelings; and the sentiments thus generated, react in turn upon the moral feelings of the members of the ascendant class, in their relations among themselves. Where, on the other hand, a class, formerly ascendant, has lost its ascendancy, or where its ascendancy is unpopular, the prevailing moral sentiments frequently bear the impress of an impatient dislike of superiority. Another grand determining principle of the rules of conduct, both in act and forebearance, which have been enforced by law or opinion, has been the servility of mankind towards the supposed preferences or aversions of their temporal masters, or of their gods. This servility, though essentially selfish, is not hyprocrisy; it gives rise to perfectly genuine sentiments of abhorrence; it made men burn magicians and heretics. Among so many baser influences, the general and obvious interests of society have of course had a share, and a large one, in the direction of the moral sentiments: less, however, as a matter of reason, and on their own account, than as a consequence of the sympathies and antipathies which grew out of them: and sympathies and antipathies which had little or nothing to do with the interests of society, have made themselves felt in the establishment of moralities with quite as great force.

Paragraph 7 & 8: (IID): Mill has two objections to previous answers. First, (paragraph 7) past reformers have concentrated on substituting new dogma for old. Second, there has been (paragraph 8) a total "absence of rule or principle." That is, there has not been a consistent policy. Can you think of cases where our society has been too oppressive? Can you think of cases where our society has been too permissive? If a society can be both at the same time, how would you account for this possibility?

The likings and dislikings of society, or of some powerful portion of it, are thus the main thing which has practically determined the rules laid down for general observance, under the penalities of law or opinion. And in general, those who have been in advance of society in thought and feeling, have left this condition of things unassailed in principle, however they may have come into conflict with it in some of its details. They have occupied themselves rather in inquiring what things society ought to like or dislike, than in questioning whether its likings or dislikings should be a law to individuals. They preferred endeavouring to alter the feelings of mankind on the particular points on which they were themselves heretical, rather than make common cause in defence of freedom, with heretics generally. The only case in which the higher ground has been taken on principle and maintained with consistency, by any but an individual here and there, is that of religious belief: a case instructive in many ways, and not least so as forming a most striking instance of the fallibility of what is called the moral sense: for the *odium theologicum*, in a sincere bigot, is one of the most unequivocal cases of moral feeling. Those who first broke the yoke of what called itself the Universal Church, were in general as little willing to permit difference of religious opinion as that Church itself. But when the heat of the conflict was over, without giving a complete victory to any party, and each church or sect was reduced to limit its hopes to retaining possession of the ground it already occupied; minorities, seeing that they had no chance of becoming majorities, were under the necessity of pleading to those whom they could not convert, for permission to differ. It is accordingly on this battlefield, almost solely, that the rights of the individual against society have been asserted on broad grounds of principle, and the claim of society to exercise authority over dissentients, openly controverted. The great writers to whom the world owes what religious liberty it possesses, have mostly asserted freedom of conscience as an indefeasible right, and denied absolutely that a human being is accountable to others for his religious belief. Yet so natural to mankind is intolerance in whatever they really care about, that religious freedom has hardly anywhere been practically realized, except where religious indifference, which dislikes to have its peace disturbed by theological quarrels, has added its weight to the scale. In the minds of almost all religious persons, even in the most tolerant countries, the duty of toleration is admitted with tacit reserves. One person will bear with dissent in matters of church government, but not of dogma; another can tolerate everybody, short of a Papist or an Unitarian, another, every one who believes in revealed religion; a few extend their charity a little further, but stop at the belief in a God and in a future state. Wherever the sentiment of the majority is still genuine and intense, it is found to have abated little of its claim to be obeyed.

In England, from the peculiar circumstances of our political history, though the yoke of opinion is perhaps heavier, that of law is lighter, than in most other countries of Europe; and there is considerable jealousy of direct interference, by the legislative or the executive power, with private conduct; not so much from any just regard for the independence of the individual, as from the still subsisting habit of looking on the government as representing an opposite interest to the public. The majority have not yet learnt to feel the power of the government their power, or its opinions their opinions. When they do so, individual liberty will probably be as much exposed to invasion from the government, as it already is from public opinion. But, as yet, there is a considerable amount of feeling ready to be called forth against any attempt of the law to control individuals in things in which they have not hitherto been accustomed to be controlled by it; and this with very little discrimination as to whether the matter is, or is not, within the legitimate sphere of legal control; insomuch that the feeling, highly salutary on the whole, is perhaps quite as often misplaced as well grounded in the particular instances of its application. There is, in fact, no recognised principle by which the propriety or impropriety of government interference is customarily tested. People decide according to their personal preferences. Some, whenever they see any good to be done, or evil to be remedied, would willingly instigate the government to undertake the business; while others prefer to bear almost any amount of social evil, rather than add one to the departments of human interests amenable to governmental control. And men range themselves on one or the other side in any particular case, according to this general direction of their sentiments; or according to the degree of interest which they feel in the particular thing which it is proposed that the government should do, or according to the belief they entertain that the government would, or would not, do it in the manner they prefer; but very rarely on account of any opinion to which they consistently adhere, as to what things are fit to be done by a government. And it seems to me that in consequence of this absence of rule or principle, one side is at present as often wrong as the other; the interference of government is, with about equal frequency improperly invoked and improperly condemned.

Paragraph 9: Mill gives his answer (IIA): "The sole end for which mankind are warranted . . . in interfering with the liberty of action of any of their number is self-protection. . . . to prevent harm to others." The private area is defined by Mill as "the body and mind." Mill specifically excludes interfering when the private person's "own good, either physical or moral," is involved. This does not imply that we may not interfere with another's body when harm to others is at stake. Sufferers of contagious diseases are not at liberty to disregard their bodies.

Note as well that Mill does not advocate indifference to others in the private zone: "There are good reasons for remonstrating with him, or reasoning with him, or persuading him, or entreating him, but not for compelling him or visiting him with any evil in case he do otherwise."

> The object of this Essay is to assert one very simple principle, as entitled to govern absolutely the dealings of society with the individual in the way of compulsion and control, whether the means used be physical force in the form of legal penalties, or the moral coercion of public opinion. That principle is, that the sole end for which mankind are warranted, individually or collectively, in interfering with the liberty of action of any of their number, is self-protection. That the only purpose for which power can be rightfully exercised over any member of a civilized community, against his will, is to prevent harm to others. His own good, either physical or moral, is not a sufficient warrant. He cannot rightfully be compelled to do or forbear because it will be better for him to do so, because it will make him happier, because, in the opinions of others, to do so would be wise, or even right. These are good reasons for remonstrating with him, or reasoning with him, or persuading him, or entreating him, but not for compelling him, or visiting him with any evil in case he do otherwise. To justify that, the conduct from which it is desired to deter him, must be calculated to produce evil to some one else. The only part of the conduct of any one, for which he is amenable to society, is that which concerns others. In the part which merely concerns himself, his independence or right, is absolute. Over himself, over his own body and mind, the individual is sovereign.

Paragraph 10: Mill adds some qualifications to his answer (IIA). His theory only applies to *rational individuals.* Such individuals are defined as those with "the capacity of being guided to their own improvement by conviction or persuasion," that is, those who are "capable of being improved by free and equal discussion." According to Mill this excludes: (1) children and (2) backward states of society. It follows that "despotism is a legitimate mode of government in dealing with barbarians, provided the end be their improvement and the means justified by actually effecting that end."

It should be clear that Mill views both of these states as temporary, not permanent or inherent. Mill was very much concerned with the problems of colonialism. He and his father, by their employment in the East India Company, had great experience with the ruling of India. For J. S. Mill's views on this subject consult his *Considerations on Representative Government* (1861), chapter eighteen. There Mill debunks the economic interpretation of empires, points out that in "the subject community also there are oppressors and oppressed," and claims that no one really knows yet how to establish a benevolent and temporary despotism. Those who are concerned with introducing democracy into other countries may well ponder this difficulty.

> It is, perhaps, hardly necessary to say that this doctrine is meant to apply only to human beings in the maturity of their faculties. We are not speaking of children or of young persons below the age which the law may fix as that of manhood or womanhood. Those who are still in a state to require being taken care of by others, must be protected against their own actions as well as against external injury. For the same reason, we may leave out of consideration those backward states of society in which the race itself may be considered as in its nonage. The early difficulties in the way of spontaneous progress are so great, that there is seldom any choice of means for overcoming them; and a ruler full of the spirit of improvement is warranted in the use of any expedients that will attain an end, perhaps otherwise unattainable. Despotism is a legitimate mode of government in dealing with barbarians, provided the end be their improvement, and the means justified by actually effecting that end. Liberty, as a principle has no application to any state of things anterior to the time when mankind have become capable of being improved by free and equal discussion. Until then, there is nothing for them but implicit obedience to an Akbar or a Charlemagne, if they are so fortunate as to find one. But as soon as mankind have attained the capacity of being guided to their own improvement by conviction or persuasion (a period long since reached in all nations with whom we need here concern ourselves), compulsion, either in the direct form or in that of pains and penalties for non-compliance, is no longer admissible as a means to their own good, and justifiable only for the security of others.

Paragraph 11: Mill turns now to the defense of his answer (IIB). First, Mill avoids appealing to "rights." Why? To begin with, since there are so many rights, many of which come into conflict in specific cases, we would be left without a guiding principle in cases of conflict. Second, the theory of rights presupposes a clear conception of an unchanging and fixed human nature. Against this, Mill argues for the notion of man "as a progressive being." This will become clearer in other chapters of the essay, but Mill does not believe in a fixed human nature. His perspective is evolutionary (man grows) but not teleological; that is, we are not growing in a predetermined direction.

Let us return to the first argument, namely that rights are inadequate. Mill suggests that we need a system in which we have a principle of ultimate appeal in case of conflict. This he proposes to find in the appeal to *utility*. Mill is known as a utilitarian, and he wrote a famous work, entitled *Utilitarianism* (1863). We cannot go into that complex work here, but it is only necessary to point out that Mill defended the principle of utility because it could resolve disputes when lower level principles conflicted. His example in *On Liberty* for the application of his answer is two-tiered: First we ask, "Is an act hurtful to others?" Next we ask, "Would preventing that hurtful act produce other evils, greater than those which it would prevent?" Consider the case of Prohibition.

It is proper to state that I forgo any advantage which could be derived to my argument from the idea of abstract right, as a thing independent of utility. I regard utility as the ultimate appeal on all ethical questions; but it must be utility in the largest sense, grounded on the permanent interests of man as a progressive being. Those interests, I contend, authorize the subjection of individual spontaneity to external control, only in respect to those actions of each, which concern the interest of other people. If any one does an act hurtful to others, there is a *primâ facie* case for punishing him, by law, or, where legal penalities are not safely applicable, by general disapprobation. There are also many positive acts for the benefit of others, which he may rightfully be compelled to perform; such as, to give evidence in a court of justice; to bear his fair share in the common defence, or in any other joint work necessary to the interest of the society of which he enjoys the protection; and to perform certain acts of individual beneficence, such as saving a fellow creature's life, or interposing to protect the defenceless against ill-usage, things which whenever it is obviously a man's duty to do, he may rightfully be made responsible to society for not doing. A person may cause evil to others not only by his actions but by his inaction, and in either case he is justly accountable to them for the injury. The latter case, it is true, requires a much more cautious exercise of compulsion than the former. To make any one answerable for doing evil to others, is the rule; to make him answerable for not preventing evil, is, comparatively speaking, the exception. Yet there are many cases clear enough and grave enough to justify that exception. In all things which regard the external relations of the individual, he is *de jure* amenable to those whose interests are concerned, and if need be, to society as their protector. There are often good reasons for not holding him to the responsibility; but these reasons must arise from the special expediencies of the case: either because it is a kind of case in which he is on the whole likely to act better, when left to his own discretion, than when controlled in any way in which society have it in their power to control him; or because the attempt to exercise control would produce other evils, greater than those which it would prevent. When such reasons as these preclude the enforcement of responsibility, the conscience of the agent himself should step into the vacant judgment seat, and protect those interests of others which have no external protection; judging himself all the more rigidly, because the case does not admit of his being made accountable to the judgment of his fellow-creatures.

Paragraph 12: in this paragraph Mill does two things. First, he further clarifies what his answer implies. Second, he considers objections to his theory.

The zone of privacy has already been established in paragraph 9 as the mind and body. This means specifically: (1) freedom of thought and expression (further elaborated in Chapter Two); (2) freedom to choose one's life style (further elaborated in Chapter Three); and (3) freedom for "combination among individuals" to do the same again with the provision that it not "harm others."

The reader should note how carefully Mill's first chapter sets the stage for his later chapters. He was apparently always asking himself how his reader would respond to what he had just said. He must have also worked with an outline and asked himself, "Why write this rather than that; why put this paragraph here rather than there?"

We come now to IID. What objection against his theory does Mill consider?

He considers something that has become the standard reply: *Is there any such thing as an action which only concerns the individual?* He readily admits that "whatever affects himself may affect others through himself." His reply is to postpone a direct answer to this objection. He takes it up at length in Chapter Four. See the next paragraph.

> But there is a sphere of action in which society, as distinguised from the individual, has, if any, only an indirect interest; comprehending all that portion of a person's life and conduct which affects only himself, or if it also affects others, only with their free, voluntary, and undeceived consent and participation. When I say only himself, I mean directly, and in the first instance: for whatever affects himself, may affect others *through* himself; and the objection which may be grounded on this contingency, will receive consideration in the sequel. This, then, is the appropriate region of human liberty. It comprises, first, the inward domain of consciousness; demanding liberty of conscience, in the most comprehensive sense; liberty of thought and feeling; absolute freedom of opinion and sentiment on all subjects, practical or speculative, scientific, moral, or theological. The liberty of expressing and publishing opinions may seem to fall under a different principle, since it belongs to that part of the conduct of an individual which concerns other people; but, being almost of as much importance as the liberty of thought, itself, and resting in great part on the same reasons, is practically inseparable from it. Secondly, the principle requires liberty of tastes and pursuits; of framing the plan of our life to suit our own character; of doing as we like, subject to such consequences as may follow: without impediment from our fellow-creatures, so long as what we do does not harm them, even though they should think our conduct foolish, perverse, or wrong. Thirdly, from this liberty of each individual, follows the liberty, within the same limits, of combination among individuals; freedom to unite, for any purpose not involving harm to others; the persons combining being supposed to be of full age, and not forced or deceived.

Paragraph 13: In this paragraph Mill does indicate what his ultimate answer will be and in so doing reveals more clearly what his facts and assumptions are (IIC). He says, "Mankind are greater gainers by suffering each other to live as seems good to themselves than by compelling each to live as seems good to the rest." He goes no further here, but in Chapter Three he tries to show, through *factual historical examples,* that societies have always progressed because some individuals were courageous enough to be different.

The *assumption* behind his argument, as seen in paragraph 11, is that man does not have a fixed nature. There will always be new conditions to be faced requiring new responses, and as long as the race is free to develop alternatives, it is likely to survive. To assume that man has a fixed nature, or that no new conditions will have to be faced, are assumptions of infallible knowledge on the part of Mill's opponents. He will demolish the assumption of infallibility in Chapter Two.

> No society is which these liberties are not, on the whole, respected, is free, whatever may be its form of government; and none is completely free in which they do not exist absolute and unqualified. The only freedom which deserves the name,

is that of pursuing our own good in our own way, so long as we do not attempt to deprive others of theirs, or impede their efforts to obtain it. Each is the proper guardian of his own health, whether bodily, or mental and spiritual. Mankind are greater gainers by suffering each other to live as seems good to themselves, than by compelling each to live as seems good to the rest.

Paragraph 14: In this paragraph Mill considers the objection (IID) which would be raised by those who would formulate the problem differently (IIIA) and (IID). There are those who would argue that "the State" has "a deep interest in the whole bodily and mental discipline of every one of its citizens." Mill thinks of the individual as related to society the way a person may or may not be a member of a club. Presumably, individuals may choose and be chosen. His opponents have an *organic* conception of the individual and society. That is, they would argue that an individual is like a part of the body, a limb for example, and cannot survive or have a separate identity apart from social function. The reader must decide which of these alternatives is more plausible.

Mill attributes his opponents' views to the insecure conditions of ancient life, which no longer existed for him. Is this a correct account of why others have the organic view (IIIB)? Mill cites as an example the French thinker Comte (ID). Other examples not mentioned would be Marx, Hegel, and in England, T. H. Green.

Though this doctrine is anything but new, and, to some persons, may have the air of a truism, there is no doctrine which stands more directly opposed to the general tendency of existing opinion and practice. Society has expended fully as much effort in the attempt (according to its lights) to compel people to conform to its notions of personal, as of social excellence. The ancient commonwealths thought themselves entitled to practice, and the ancient philosophers countenanced, the regulation of every part of private conduct by public authority, on the ground that the State had a deep interest in the whole bodily and mental discipline of every one of its citizens; a mode of thinking which may have been admissible in small republics surrounded by powerful enemies, in constant peril of being subverted to foreign attack or internal commotion, and to which even a short interval of relaxed energy and self-command might so easily be fatal, that they could not afford to wait for the salutary permanent effects of freedom. In the modern world, the greater size of political communities, and above all, the separation between spiritual and temporal authority (which placed the direction of men's consciences in other hands than those which controlled their worldly affairs), prevented so great an interference by law in the details of private life; but the engines of moral repression have been wielded more strenuously against divergence from the reigning opinion in self-regarding, than even in social matters; religion, the most powerful of the elements which have entered into the formation of moral feeling, having almost always been governed either by the ambition of a hierarchy, seeking control over every department of human conduct, or by the spirit of Puritanism. And some of those modern reformers who have placed themselves in strongest opposition to the religions of the past, have been noway behind either churches or sects in their assertion of the right of spiritual domination: M. Comte, in particular, whose social system, as unfolded in his *Traité de Politique Positive*, aims at establishing (though by moral more than by legal appliances) a despotism of society over the individual, surpassing anything contemplated in the political ideal of the most rigid disciplinarian among the ancient philosophers.

Apart from the peculiar tenets of individual thinkers, there is also, in the world at large an increasing inclination to stretch unduly the powers of society over the individual, both by the force of opinion and even by that of legislation: and as the tendency of all the changes taking place in the world is to strengthen society, and diminish the power of the individual, this encroachment is not one of the evils which tend spontaneously to disappear, but, on the contrary, to grow more and more formidable. The disposition of mankind, whether as rulers or as fellow-citizens, to impose their own opinions and inclinations as a rule of conduct on others, is so energetically supported by some of the best and by some of the worst feelings incident to human nature, that it is hardly ever kept under restraint by anything but want of power; and as the power is not declining, but growing, unless a strong barrier of moral conviction can be raised against the mischief, we must expect, in the present circumstances of the world, to see it increase.

It will be convenient for the argument, if, instead of at once entering upon the general thesis, we confine ourselves in the first instance to a single branch of it, on which the principle here stated, is, if not fully, yet to a certain point, recognised by the current opinions. This one branch is the Liberty of Thought: from which it is impossible to separate the cognate liberty of speaking and of writing. Although these liberties, to some considerable amount, form part of the political morality of all countries which profess religious toleration and free institutions, the grounds, both philosophical and practical, on which they rest, are perhaps not so familiar to the general mind, nor so thoroughly appreciated by many even of the leaders of opinion, as might have been expected. Those grounds, when rightly understood, are of much wider application than to only one division of the subject, and a thorough consideration of this part of the question will be found the best introduction to the remainder. Those to whom nothing which I am about to say will be new, may therefore, I hope, excuse me, if on a subject which for now three centuries has been so often discussed, I venture on one discussion more.

Paragraph 15: Mill repeats why the problem is important for his own time. Is it important for our time?

Paragraph 16: Mill ends this chapter by indicating what he will do in the next chapter. He claims that he will take up the issue of censorship and use it as an example; if you agree with what he says about censorship, then he thinks you will agree with his argument as a whole. "Those grounds, when rightly understood, are of much wider application."

Chapter II—Plato and the Platonic Tradition

Plato and Socrates

Among all the philosophers of Western Civilization, Plato and Aristotle occupy a special position. Their influence has been so profound in the development of ideas that it can be said that they constitute the sources out of which most of our intellectual heritage has emerged. Even today, almost twenty-five centuries after their historical presence, Plato and Aristotle are indispensable elements in any study of philosophy. As we will see in this and the subsequent chapter, Platonism and Aristotelianism represent the two most powerful philosophical currents that have dominated our development since the time of the ancient Greeks. These two currents have, of course, much in common: after all, they both grew out of the same historical context, and they are both manifestations of the experiences of the same people. Yet, curiously enough, they disclose before our eyes two profoundly different concepts of reality, and the fundamental ideas on which they rest are distinctly opposed.

Plato was born in Athens in 427 B.C., during the time when the Spartan armies were challenging the supremacy of the Athenians. He came from a wealthy, aristocratic family, some of whose members held considerable power over the affairs of the city. Plato himself appears to have desired at first to devote his life to political activities. It was customary in Athens at that time for aristocratic young men to enter the political sphere, which was dominated by a long tradition of democratic practices instituted by Solon. Undoubtedly, Plato would have reached much prominence in government inasmuch as his extraordinary intelligence, his wealth, and his distinguished family would have lent him ample support.

During his lifetime, Plato witnessed many political upheavals. He was born only two years after the death of the great statesman Pericles (461-429 B.C.), the man who ruled the affairs of Athens for more than thirty years, and brought the city to its peak of cultural, military, and political power. The death of Pericles plunged the Athenian world into disarray, especially since the Spartans took advantage of his disappearance in order to devastate the whole Attic peninsula, where Athens was the chief town. Plato lived, then, through the most difficult years of the Peloponnesian War, in which Athens and Sparta fought each other with an unprecedented degree of savagery. When he was only twelve years old, he witnessed the catastrophic defeat of the Athenian fleet at the hands of the Syracuseans, and during his twenty-third year, he saw the Spartan armies march triumphantly into Athens. After the year 404 B.C., he lived in an Athens which was only a vestige of what it had been during his youth.

Sometime around the year 409 B.C., he made the acquaintance of a man about whom we will have much to say presently. His meeting Socrates became indeed the turning point of Plato's life. He abandoned all political ambitions, and devoted himself exclusively to the study of philosophy, first in a constant dialogue with Socrates, and then, after Socrates' execution in 399 B.C., in the company of a wide variety of philosophers both in Greece and elsewhere. The tribulations and trial of Socrates compelled Plato to abandon Athens for a number of years. He travelled accordingly to other neighboring Greek towns where he studied mathematics and physics, and found himself living in Italy where he made the acquaintance of the Pythagoreans. From them he learned, we will see later, a number of fundamental ideas, such as the belief in the immortality of the soul, in reincarnation, and in a spiritual world of nonphysical realities which coexists with the physical world of ordinary sense-perception. We are also told by his biographers that he spent some time in Egypt, probably in the city of Thebes, where he became an initiate of some of the mystery cults practiced by the Egyptians since the remotest times.

Sometime before 390 B.C. he returned to Athens. The political atmosphere created by Socrates' execution had already given way to a climate of tolerance and intellectual openness. He proceeded to establish an academic institution where people from all over the world could devote themselves to the study of philosophy. Its name was simply "the Academy." Here hundreds of scholars pursued mathematical, physical, and philosophical investigations. Plato, a single man throughout his life, was able to dedicate himself to his institution, and with the exception of two or three periods of absence during which he returned to Italy, he remained faithful to his post as head of the Academy.

His philosophical writings were all produced while at the Academy. These comprised about twenty-four dialogues and a few lengthy letters. The *Dialogues* of Plato cover a variety of subjects and can be divided into three groups: (1) The Socratic Dialogues, in which we are given what appears to be a rather accurate description of Socrates' philosophical activity, together with an account of Socrates' trial and death. In them, Socrates is always the main speaker, and it is safe to assume that the words of Socrates are a faithful statement of his actual ideas. The *Apology*, the *Crito*, and the *Euthyphro*, belong to this first group. (2) The *Middle Dialogues*, which were written during Plato's middle years. These include dialogues such as the *Republic*, Plato's most famous work, and in them one notices immediately that Socrates, who still remains the chief speaker, advances ideas which cannot be associated with the historical Socrates. It seems that with the passage of time, Plato outgrew the overwhelming influence of Socrates on his life. He became accordingly more independent and felt free to move far beyond the teaching of his great friend. In philosophy, unlike in religion, there is no master-disciple relationship. In the search for wisdom, the disciple, or rather the student, has to be prepared to revise, expand, or even reject some or all the ideas of the person who has introduced him to philosophy. This was precisely the case with Plato, and we should not be misguided by his *literary* practice of using the name of Socrates in his *Middle Dialogues*. When Socrates speaks in them, it is actually Plato, who is presenting his own ideas. Finally, (3) there are the *Late Dialogues*, written in Plato's last years. In them, the name of Socrates does not always appear, and when it does, the statements put into Socrates' mouth bear little relationship with Socrates' thoughts in actuality. The late dialogues reflect Plato's tendency towards mysticism. They deal with enigmatic themes, as for example when he introduces the much debated subject of a lost continent called Atlantis.

It is impossible, and indeed unwise, to insist on identifying Plato with any one of the characters of the dialogues or with any specific group of dialogues. In a sense, he is all of them and none of them. In his Seventh Letter, for example, he explicitly maintains that his philosophy is not to be found in his writings. These, he says, are mere preparatory exercises which may be of some assistance to those who, like himself, are engaged in the business of looking for the truth. It is possible that the very fact that they are *dialogues*, that is to say, conversations and discussions on human experiences, may stem from his conviction that truth has to be found by each person by himself.

And yet, it is customary to attribute some of the basic ideas expressed by the Platonic Socrates to Plato himself, especially in the context of the *Middle Dialogues*. Tradition, at any rate, has sanctioned this perhaps unfortunate practice, and the development of Platonism is precisely the outgrowth of this. For example, Plato is said to have believed in a certain type of government in which all decisions are made by "philosopher-kings," a government that is far-removed from the democratic egalitarianism in which most of us have been brought up. It is also maintained that Plato believed in the immortality of the soul, in the doctrine of reincarnation, in the existence of a world of divine realities, in the evil character of the human body, in punishments and rewards after death, in the fallibility of sense-perception, in the universal power of mathematics, and in a dualistic conception of reality. It is true that all these ideas can be found in the *Dialogues*, but it is also true that other, perhaps less acceptable notions are encountered everywhere in them. For example, in Plato's writings we are presented with countless myths, tales, and legends concerning the origin of mankind; with ideas about the magical power of numbers; with strange superstitions; with political convictions which were, even during Plato's own time, entirely out of place. Thus, the question is, What was in the mind of this extraordinary man who has determined to so great an extent the fate of Western Civilization?

The most appropriate answer is that all those ideas, indeed many others as well, were in his mind. A man of his spiritual and intellectual stature has to live, as he surely did, with a constant state of change and turmoil in his mind. It is for this reason that we look upon him as a "seminal mind." This is a mind in which there is always something new to be found, a mind that can give itself the rare luxury of contradiction with perfect impunity, a mind out of which countless schools of thought can emerge. Plato had in fact such a mind. Friedrich Nietzsche (1844-1900) once said that the gap that separates Plato from the average man is far wider than the gap that separates the average man from the chimpanzee. Whatever truth there may be in this somewhat unkind comment, we still have to admit that behind the *Dialogues* there must have lived a writer of unusual intelligence, spirituality, and dedication.

Plato died in the year 347 B.C. at the age of eighty, and his biographers tell us that he died in the midst of a wedding festivity given in honor of a student of the Academy. It is curious to observe in this context, that having a superior mind does not always prevent a man from participating in the frolicking feasts of the average human being.

Now that we talk about frolicking activities of the masses, we should introduce the person of Socrates, who was constantly engaged in the affairs of the common man. There are few historical characters as colorful, interesting, and overpowering, as Socrates. Born in the year 469 B.C., he came into this world as the son of an ordinary midwife and an ordinary Athenian citizen. He belonged to an ordinary social class, and for several years practiced a perfectly ordinary vocation: he was a brick layer. He was married to an ordinary woman named Xantippe, with whom he had two children. There was nothing in Socrates' origin, family, social position, or physical appearance, which disclosed the enormity of his intellect and the earnestness with which he viewed human existence. His biographers tell us that he disliked physical work (a common characteristic of most philosophers), and that he enjoyed simple activities such as dancing, drinking, walking, and talking.

We are told by Plato in the *Apology* and by an Athenian general named Xenophon, who wrote extensively on Socrates' life, that when he was still a young man, Socrates underwent a profound conversion as the result of an incident involving the Delphic Oracle. The Greeks of antiquity, a devotedly religious nation, placed great trust in the statements of the priests and priestesses who spoke on behalf of the gods in shrines called "oracles." In the ancient town of Delphi, one of these oracles was found: it was dedicated to Apollo, the magnificent god who "could never speak untruth." It seems that a man named Chaerophon went to Delphi to inquire from Apollo's priestess, "Who among all human beings is the wisest." The priestess replied in unmistakable terms: "Socrates of Athens is the wisest man." When given the disturbing news, Socrates was plunged into a sea of perplexities, for he was aware of his ignorance but was also conscious of the fact that Apollo could not speak except the truth.

From this point on, he felt called to follow a divinely appointed vocation, namely, that of resolving the predicament created by the priestess' utterance. In fact, he spent more than fifty years in search of anyone whose knowledge would surpass his. He questioned many Athenian workers who, like himself, knew practically nothing, politicians who claimed to know what was good for the people, wise men who spoke with authority about the world, poets who described the nature and the affairs of the gods, and philosophers who were in search of wisdom. In the process of so doing, he gained the animosity of many whose sense of security was threatened by the questioning Socrates, and whose feelings of pride were challenged by a humble brick layer who claimed to know nothing, but who consistently unveiled the inauthentic character of their assumed knowledge. At the end of his life, Socrates found himself surrounded by enemies who saw in him a busybody, an impertinent fellow and a public danger.

At the age of seventy, charges were brought against him before an Athenian court, and after a legally suicidal defense, he was convicted of high crimes and condemned to death by drinking poison. He stood before the jury as a man who had fulfilled his destiny; he knew that the only thing that he knew was that he knew nothing, and that, therefore, he knew more than his fellow citizens who only *thought* that they knew, but who in reality did not know anything either. In this sense, he knew more than they; he was, after all, the wisest man, and Apollo, always true to his divine nature, had indeed spoken the truth.

The story is itself a simple one, but beneath this mantle of simplicity there is a whole world of profound philosophical significance. Socrates, the ordinary brick layer, was able to alter the course of Western Civilization. He teaches us that the first duty of a human being is to search for the truth, and that in this sense we should all be philosophers. Pleasures, wealth, money, power, fame—all the common ambitions of human beings—are secondary in life. The search for truth should dominate a person's entire life, even if it entails the renunciation of what ordinary people cherish as indispensable. The only hope that death offers Socrates is that, if there should be another life, he may be able to spend eternity asking questions.

Truth, for Socrates, is not to be found in the external, objective world. The early philosophers like Thales and Anaximander had turned their eyes to the universe in the expectation of finding truth there. But physical investigation, according to Socrates, can only reveal the surface of reality and can only create further confusion in the questioner. Truth, he maintains, can only be found within oneself. "Know thyself" were the words engraved at the entrance of Apollo's shrine in Delphi, and they became the motivating force behind Socrates' search. This search for an understanding of the meaning of one's life is often guided by an inner voice that each one of us can hear within himself if the distractions of the external world have not entirely made him deaf. This voice, either the manifestation of one's subjective conscience, or perhaps the living link between the human self and some superior reality, constitutes the highest tribunal of personal behavior, before which human customs, traditions, beliefs, and accomplishments are of little value. It is because of this that Socrates always assumed an air of arrogance and superiority over the masses of people who acted only by reference to an external source of authority.

In the Socratic dialogues which we will read in this chapter, we will find three different examples of Socrates' activity, and his personality and philosophical significance will become abundantly clear. We will be able to understand Plato's fascination with him and with his search for knowledge. But it is important to observe at this point that Socrates was not, as it may appear at first, a man convinced of the impossibility of attaining truth. The fact that *he* was unsuccessful in his quest, the fact that he stressed his ignorance and his persistent perplexities, and the fact that he went to his death without having come to any firm conclusions about what death is, should not obscure the undeniable fact that he always remained convinced that knowledge was attainable. This conviction was inherited by Plato who, if we take some of the statements of his late dialogues literally, believed that he finally attained truth, but again an inner truth which has little to do with the revelations of the senses.

This explains the change from the Socratic uncertainty of the early dialogues (*Apology* and *Euthyphro*) to the Platonic dogmatism of some sections of the *Phaedo* which will be given in this chapter. In the development of the Platonic tradition, the presence of an even more dogmatic philosophical outlook is easily discernible. Platonism, as this tradition became known, took only certain elements of Socrates' philosophy, and extended its frontier far beyond.

The Socratic Method

Let us consider the Socratic method, the way in which Socrates engages others in philosophical discourse, from the point of view of the following questions:

I. *What are the circumstances under which philosophical analysis begins?* Are there special circumstances for the application of the Socratic method, or is it employable anywhere, anytime? Do we need a specific number of people present?

II. *How is the initial philosophical question formulated?* Try to distinguish between philosophical and non-philosophical questions, between the first question and the first philosophical question. If there is more than one philosophical question, distinguish them and try to clarify the order in which they appear.

III. *What kind of answer is sought?* Here it is important to remember that in philosophy the way the question is asked structures the kind of acceptable answer that can be given. Socrates is no exception. In fact, see if you can detect how he suggests, by the manner of his questioning, what sort of answer he is seeking.

IV. *What kind of answer to his initial philosophical question does Socrates receive? How does he deal with the received answer?* If the answer is the one he is seeking, then there is no problem. If not, then Socrates must, by some device or devices, try some other way of eliciting the kind of answer he seeks. In connection with this, pay special attention to his ironic comments and to his claim to be ignorant, that is, the alleged Socratic ignorance.

V. *How, finally, is the problem solved?* The reader must recall the different possibilities for answering a question and decide which one is applicable here. We might also raise the question, By whom is the final answer articulated, and why?

VI. *What are the aims of the method?* Aside from the obvious aim of trying to answer the major philosophical question, what other reasons could Socrates have for using his method in the way he does? Could this method be used by someone who did not share all of Socrates' beliefs?

The Socratic Method
in Euthyphro

I. The circumstances of this dialogue are fairly obvious. Socrates meets Euthyphro on the way to court and the two men engage in a conversation. There does not seem to be anything peculiar about these circumstances. Perhaps if we examined the beginning of other dialogues we might find something peculiar about the Socratic method and how it begins. Perhaps we shall find that there is nothing peculiar or distinctive. Perhaps what is distinctive about it as a method of philosophizing is that it is applicable under any set of circumstances. What is important to note is that it involves a dialogue, a give and take in conversation. It is possible to have an imaginary dialogue wherein you take both or all of the parts.

II. When Socrates asks Euthyphro why he is going to court, the question asked is not philosophical. The philosophical question is raised when Socrates asks Euthyphro, "*What is piety* [holiness]?" The question is asked in such a way that Socrates makes it clear that he is asking for a definition of the term involved. In the dialogue entitled the *Symposium*, the question is, "What is love?" In the *Republic*, as we shall see, the question is, "What is Justice?" In every case, the format is the same; Socrates asks "*What is X?*" where "X" stands for an abstract concept, frequently one dealing with a very general moral concept.

III. As Socrates makes clear by his questioning, he seeks a definition in which the common element, present in all of the different uses of the term, will be uncovered. That is, the assumption behind Socrates' way of formulating the

43

question is that every meaningful term has an essence which will allow us to determine, in every case where the term is used, whether it has been used correctly or incorrectly. Another way of putting this is to say that every use of the same term has something in common with every other correct use of that term. If we cannot state what that common element is, then we have not mastered the use of that term. It also follows that if most people do not comprehend the use of a concept, especially a moral concept, they will disagree in their respective uses of that term. This can be disastrous for individuals and for society.

> "Is not piety in every action always the same? and impiety, again—is it not always the opposite of piety, and also the same with itself. . . ?"

IV. The first answer that Socrates elicits from Euthyphro is that piety "is, *to say*, prosecuting any one who is guilty of murder, sacrilege, or of *any similar* crime. . . . " (*italics added*). That is, instead of defining the term by offering the common element, Euthyphro gives examples of pious acts. Like a child, Euthyphro offers us examples of the use of a term rather than a definition of the term. Socrates makes it clear that he is seeking something else:

> "Remember that I did not ask you to give me two or three examples of piety, but to explain the general idea which makes all pious things to be pious. Do you not recollect that there was one idea which made the impious impious, and the pious pious?"

Notice especially that Socrates does not dogmatically assert this notion of a definition. He asks, in the form of a question, if that is not what Euthyphro himself believes. He never proceeds unless the person being interrogated agrees. This makes every positive statement the property of the person being questioned.

Finally, Socrates does obtain the *type* of answer he seeks, a generalization:

> Euthyphro: "Piety, then, is that which is dear to the gods, and impiety is that which is not dear to them."

The way in which Socrates deals with this generalization is instructive and brings us to the heart of his method. By asking a further series of seemingly innocuous questions, he reveals a potential contradiction in what Euthyphro has said.

A. Piety is what the gods approve of, and impiety is what the gods disapprove of.
B. Since there are different gods, and the gods sometimes disagree, the same act may be approved of by one god and disapproved of by another.
C. If one approves of an act, the act is pious; if the same act is disapproved of by another god, the act is impious. *The same act is both pious and impious.*

Having revealed the contradiction, Socrates then permits Euthyphro to resolve it. Note that it is not Socrates but his partner who resolves the contradiction. Socrates claims to be ignorant, so that he cannot perform this function. Euthyphro, of course, claims to know. If we all admitted ignorance, we would need a different method of proceeding.

V. Socrates performs this feat again, revealing a further contradiction in Euthyphro's amended answer, and one gets the impression that Euthyphro will never get the point. Possibly he does get the point and decides to withdraw before becoming embarrassed further.

Behind the initial philosophical question is a further assumption which structures the potential answer. Socrates is really asking, "Is something right because the gods approve of it, or do the gods approve of it because it is right?" The alternatives have momentous consequences. If something is right because the gods approve of it, then there is no further rationale for why some things are right. The gods could presumably change their minds at will, and right and wrong depend upon the seemingly arbitrary will of the gods.

If the gods approve of something because it is right, then being "right" or "pious" is somehow independent of the gods, something over and above the gods, something to which even the gods are subject. Is this blasphemy on Socrates' part if he believes it?

We might point out that even in Homer the notion of *Anake*, or a necessary order, exists such that the gods themselves cannot change it. In the works of Greek playwrights such as Sophocles and Aeschylus this notion is even more apparent. Socrates makes this point in a more philosophical way, and again shows why we can say that philosophy begins with the Greeks. Behind the gods is an order or permanent structure which is knowable to man.

VI. Making our assumptions clear, or making it clear to the Greeks what their assumptions are, is one of the aims of the Socratic method. Attempting to find the answer is another. There are frequent comparisons to examples drawn from mathematics and geometry. This procedure seems to indicate that Socrates thinks analagous answers of the same permanency and certainty are attainable in other areas of human intellectual and moral concern. Finally, we might point out that it is part of Socrates' purpose to make people think for themselves. Would it have really helped Euthyphro if Socrates had supplied him with the answer? Is there an analogy between this aspect or aim of the Socratic method and the classical techniques of psychoanalysis in which the doctor strives to get the patient to articulate the "answer" rather than merely providing it for him?

Plato: Euthyphro

Persons of the Dialogue: Socrates; Euthyphro.
Scene: The Porch of the King Archon

[2] *Euthyphro.* Why have you left the Lyceum, Socrates? and what are you doing in the Porch of the King Archon? Surely you cannot be concerned in a suit before the King, like myself?

Socrates. Not in a suit, Euthyphro; impeachment is the word which the Athenians use.

Euth. What! I suppose that some one has been prosecuting you, for I cannot believe that you are the prosecutor of another.

Soc. Certainly not.

Euth. Then some one else has been prosecuting you?

Soc. Yes.

Euth. And who is he?

Soc. A young man who is little known, Euthyphro; and I hardly know him: his name is Meletus, and he is of the deme of Pitthis. Perhaps you may remember his appearance; he has a beak, and long straight hair, and a beard which is ill grown.

Euth. No, I do not remember him, Socrates. But what is the charge which he brings against you?

Soc. What is the charge? Well, a very serious charge, which shows a good deal of character in the young man, and for which he is certainly not to be despised. He says he knows how the youth are corrupted and who are their corruptors. I fancy that he must be a wise man, and seeing that I am the reverse of a wise man, he has found me out, and is going to accuse me of corrupting his young friends. And of this our mother the state is to be the judge. Of all our political men he is the only one who seems to me to begin in the right way, with the cultiva-

tion of virtue in youth; like a good husbandman, he makes the young shoots his first care, and [3] clears away us who are the destroyers of them. This is only the first step; he will afterwards attend to the elder branches; and if he goes on as he has begun, he will be a very great public benefactor.

Euth. I hope that he may; but I rather fear, Socrates, that the opposite will turn out to be the truth. My opinion is that in attacking you he is simply aiming a blow at the foundation of the state. But in what way does he say that you corrupt the young?

Soc. He brings a wonderful accusation against me, which at first hearing excites surprise: he says that I am a poet or maker of gods, and that I invent new gods and deny the existence of old ones; this is the ground of his indictment.

Euth. I understand, Socrates; he means to attack you about the familiar sign which occasionally, as you say, comes to you. He thinks that you are a neologian, and he is going to have you up before the court for this. He knows that such a charge is readily received by the world, as I myself know too well; for when I speak in the assembly about divine things, and foretell the future to them, they laugh at me and think me a madman. Yet every word that I say is true. But they are jealous of us all; and we must be brave and go at them.

Soc. Their laughter, friend Euthyphro, is not a matter of much consequence. For a man may be thought wise; but the Athenians, I suspect, do not much trouble themselves about him until he begins to impart his wisdom to others; and then for some reason or other, perhaps, as you say, from jealousy, they are angry.

Euth. I am never likely to try their temper in this way.

Soc. I dare say not, for you are reserved in your behaviour, and seldom impart your wisdom. But I have a benevolent habit of pouring out myself to everybody, and would even pay for a listener, and I am afraid that the Athenians may think me too talkative. Now if, as I was saying, they would only laugh at me, as you say that they laugh at you, the time might pass gaily enough in the court; but perhaps they may be in earnest, and then what the end will be you soothsayers only can predict.

Euth. I dare say that the affair will end in nothing, Socrates, and that you will win your cause; and I think that I shall win my own.

Soc. And what is your suit, Euthyphro? are you the pursuer or the defendant?

Euth. I am the pursuer.

Soc. Of whom?

[4] *Euth.* You will think me mad when I tell you.

Soc. Why, has the fugitive wings?

Euth. Nay, he is not very volatile at his time of life.

Soc. Who is he?

Euth. My father.

Soc. Your father! my good man?

Euth. Yes.

Soc. And of what is he accused?

Euth. Of murder, Socrates.

Soc. By the powers, Euthyphro! how little does the common herd know of the nature of right and truth. A man must be an extraordinary man, and have made great strides in wisdom, before he could have seen his way to bring such an action.

Euth. Indeed, Socrates, he must.

Soc. I suppose that the man whom your father murdered was one of your relatives—clearly he was; for if he had been a stranger you would never have thought of prosecuting him.

Euth. I am amused, Socrates, at your making a distinction between one who is a relation and one who is not a relation; for surely the pollution is the same in either case, if you knowingly associate with the murderer when you ought to clear yourself and him by proceeding against him. The real question is whether the murdered man has been justly slain. If justly, then your duty is to let the matter alone; but if unjustly, then even if the murderer lives under the same roof with you and eats at the same table, proceed against him. Now the man who is dead was a poor dependant of mine who worked for us as a field labourer on our farm in Naxos, and one day in a fit of drunken passion he got into a quarrel with one of our domestic servants and slew him. My father bound him hand and foot and threw him into a ditch, and then sent to Athens to ask of a diviner what he should do with him. Meanwhile he never attended to him and took no care about him, for he regarded him as a murderer; and thought that no great harm would be done even if he did die. Now this was just what happened. For such was the effect of cold and hunger and chains upom him, that before the messenger returned from the diviner, he was dead. And my father and family are angry with me for taking the part of the murderer and prosecuting my father. They say that he did not kill him and that if he did, the dead man was but a murderer, and I ought not to take any notice, for that a son is impious who prosecutes a father. Which shows, Socrates, how little they know what the gods think about piety and impiety.

Soc. Good heavens, Euthyphro! and is your knowledge of religion and things pious and impious so very exact, that, supposing the circumstances to be as you state them, you are not afraid lest you too may be doing an impious thing in bringing an action against your father?

Euth. The best of Euthyphro, and that which distinguishes him, Socrates, [5] from other men, is his exact knowledge of all such matters. What should I be good for without it?

Soc. Rare friend! I think that I cannot do better than be your disciple. Then before the trial with Meletus comes on I shall challenge him, and say that I have always had a great interest in religious questions, and now, as he charges me with rash imaginations and innovations in religion, I have become your disciple. You, Meletus, as I shall say to him, acknowledge Euthyphro to be a great theologian, and sound in his opinions; and if you approve of him you ought to approve of me, and not have me into court; but if you disapprove, you should begin by indicting him who is my teacher, and who will be the ruin, not of the young, but of the old; that is to say, of myself whom he instructs, and of his old father whom he admonishes and chastises. And if Meletus refuses to listen to me, but will go on, and will not shift the indictment from me to you, I cannot do better than repeat this challenge in the court.

Euth. Yes, indeed, Socrates; and if he attempts to indict me, I am mistaken if I do not find a flaw in him; the court shall have a great deal more to say to him than to me.

Soc. And I, my dear friend, knowing this, am desirous of becoming your disciple. For I observe that no one appears to notice you—not even this Meletus; but his sharp eyes have found me out at once, and he has indicted me for impiety. And therefore, I adjure you to tell me the nature of piety and impiety, which you said that you knew so well, and of murder, and of other offences against the gods. What are they? Is not piety in every action always the same? and impiety, and—is it not always the opposite of piety, and also the same with itself, having, as impiety, one notion which includes whatever is impious?

Euth. To be sure, Socrates.

Soc. And what is piety, and what is impiety?

Euth. Piety is doing as I am doing; that is to say, prosecuting any one who is guilty of murder, sacrilege, or of any similar crime—whether he be your father or mother, or whoever he may be—that makes no difference; and not to prosecute them is impiety. And please to consider, Socrates, what a notable proof I will give you of the truth of my words, a proof which I have already given to others:—of the principle, I mean, that the impious, whoever he may be, ought not to go unpunished. For do not men regard Zeus as the best and most righteous of the gods? [6]—and yet they admit that he bound his father (Cronos) because he wickedly devoured his sons, and that he too had punished his own father (Uranus) for a similar reason, in a nameless manner. And yet when I proceed against my father, they are angry with me. So inconsistent are they in their way of talking when the gods are concerned, and when I am concerned.

Soc. May not this be the reason, Euthyphro, why I am charged with impiety—that I cannot [accept] these stories about the gods? and therefore I suppose that people think me wrong. But, as you who are well informed about them approve of them, I cannot do better than assent to your superior wisdom. What else can I say, confessing as I do, that I know nothing about them? Tell me, for the love of Zeus,

whether you really believe that they are true.

Euth. Yes, Socrates; and things more wonderful still, of which the world is in ignorance.

Soc. And do you really believe that the gods fought with one another, and had dire quarrels, battles, and the like, as the poets say, and as you may see represented in the works of great artists? The temples are full of them; and notably the robe of Athene, which is carried up to the Acropolis at the great Panathenaea, is embroidered with them. Are all these tales of the gods true, Euthyphro?

Euth. Yes, Socrates; and, as I was saying, I can tell you, if you would like to hear them, many other things about the gods which would quite amaze you.

Soc. I dare say; and you shall tell me them at some other time when I have leisure. But just at present I would rather hear from you a more precise answer, which you have not as yet given, my friend, to the question, What is "piety"? When asked, you only replied, Doing as you do, charging your father with murder.

Eith. And what I said was true, Socrates.

Soc. No doubt, Euthyphro; but you would admit that there are many other pious acts?

Euth. There are.

Soc. Remember that I did not ask you to give me two or three examples of piety, but to explain the general idea which makes all pious things to be pious. Do you not recollect that there was one idea which made the impious impious, and the pious pious?

Euth. I remember.

Soc. Tell me what is the nature of this idea, and then I shall have a standard to which I may look, and by which I may measure actions, whether yours or those of any one else, and then I shall be able to say that such and such an action is pious, such another impious.

Euth. I will tell you, if you like.

Soc. I should very much like.

Euth. Piety, then, is that which is dear to the gods, and impiety is that which is not dear to them.

[7] *Soc.* Very good. Euthyphro; you have now given me the sort of answer which I wanted. But whether what you say is true or not I cannot as yet tell, although I make no doubt that you will prove the truth of your words.

Euth. Of course.

Soc. Come, then, and let us examine what we are saying. That thing or person which is dear to the gods is pious, and that thing or person which is hateful to the gods is impious, these two being the extreme opposites of one another. Was not that said?

Euth. It was.

Soc. And well said?

Euth. Yes, Socrates, I thought so; it was certainly said.

Soc. And further, Euthyphro, the gods were admitted to have enmities and hatreds and differences?

Euth. Yes, that was also said.

Soc. And what sort of difference creates enmity and anger? Suppose for example that you and I, my good friend, differ about a number; do differences of this sort make us enemies and set us at variance with one another? Do we not go at once to arithemtic, and put an end to them by a sum?

Euth. True.

Soc. Or suppose that we differ about magnitudes, do we not quickly end the differences by measuring?

Euth. Very true.

Soc. And we end a controversy about heavy and light by resorting to a weighing machine?

Euth. To be sure.

Soc. But what differences are there which cannot be thus decided, and which therefore make us angry and set us at enmity with one another? I dare say the answer does not occur to you at the moment, and therefore I will suggest that these enmities arise when the matters of difference are the just and unjust, good and evil, honourable and dishonourable. Are not these the points about which men differ, and about which when we are unable satisfactorily to decide our differences, you and I and all of us quarrel, when we do quarrel?

Euth. Yes, Socrates, the nature of the differences about which we quarrel is such as you describe.

Soc. And the quarrels of the gods, noble Euthyphro, when they occur, are of a like nature?

Euth. Certainly they are.

Soc. They have differences of opinion, as you say, about good and evil, just and unjust, honourable and dishonourable: there would have been no quarrels among them, if there had been no such differences—would there now?

Euth. You are quite right.

Soc. Does not every man love that which he deems noble and just and good, and hate the opposite of them?

Euth. Very true.

Soc. But, as you say, people regard the same things, some as just and others as unjust,— about these they dispute; and so there arise wars and fightings among them. [8]

Euth. Very true.

Soc. Then the same things are hated by the gods and loved by the gods, and are both hateful and dear to them?

Euth. True.

Soc. And upon this view the same things, Euthyphro, will be pious and also impious?

Euth. So I should suppose.

Soc. Then, my friend, I remark with surprise that you have not answered the question which I asked. For I certainly did not ask you to tell me what action is both pious and impious: but now it would seem that what is loved by the gods is also hated by them. And therefore, Euthyphro, in thus chastising your father you may very likely be doing what is agreeable to Zeus but disagreeable to Cronos or Uranus, and what is acceptable to Hephaestus but unacceptable to Here, and there may be other gods who have similar differences of opinion.

Euth. But I believe, Socrates, that all the gods would be agreed as to the propriety of punishing a murderer: there would be no difference of opinion about that.

Soc. Well, but speaking of men, Euthyphro, did you ever hear any one arguing that a murderer or any sort of evil-doer ought to be let off?

Euth. I should rather say that these are the questions which they are always arguing, especially in courts of law: they commit all sorts of crimes, and there is nothing which they will not do or say in their own defence.

Soc. But do they admit their guilt, Euthyphro, and yet say that they ought not to be punished?

Euth. No; they do not.

Soc. Then there are some things which they do not venture to say and do: for they do not venture to argue that the guilty are to be unpunished, but they deny their guilt, do they not?

Euth. Yes.

Soc. Then they do not argue that the evil-doer should not be punished, but they argue about the fact of who the evil-doer is, and what he did and when?

Euth. True.

Soc. And the gods are in the same case, if, as you assert, they quarrel about just and unjust, and some of them say while others deny that injustice is done among them. For surely neither God nor man will ever venture to say that the doer of injustice is not to be punished?

Euth. That is true, Socrates, in the main.

Soc. But they join issue about the particulars —gods and men alike; and, if they dispute at all, they dispute about some act which is called in question, and which by some is affirmed to be just, by others to be unjust. Is not that true?

Euth. Quite true.

[9] *Soc.* Well then, my dear friend Euthyphro, do tell me, for my better instruction and information, what proof have you that in the opinion of all the gods a servant who is guilty of murder, and is put in chains by the master of the dead man, and dies because he is put in chains before he who bound him can learn from the interpreters of the gods what he ought to do with him, dies unjustly; and that on behalf of such an one a son ought to proceed against his father and accuse him of murder. How would you show that all the gods absolutely agree in approving of his act? Prove to me that they do, and I will applaud your wisdom as long as I live.

Euth. It will be a difficult task; but I could make the matter very clear indeed to you.

Soc. I understand; you mean to say that I am not so quick of apprehension as the judges: for to them you will be sure to prove that the act is unjust, and hateful to the gods.

Euth. Yes indeed, Socrates; at least if they will listen to me.

Soc. But they will be sure to listen if they find that you are a good speaker. There was a notion that came into my mind while you were speaking; I said to myself: "Well, and what if Euthyphro does prove to me that all the gods regarded the death of the serf as unjust, how do I know anything more of the nature of piety and impiety? for granting that this action may be hateful to the gods, still piety and impiety are not adequately defined by these distinctions, for that which is hateful to the gods has been shown to be also pleasing and dear to them." And therefore, Euthyphro, I do not ask you to prove this; I will suppose, if you like, that all the gods condemn and abominate such an

action. But I will amend the definition so far as to say that what all the gods hate is impious, and what they love pious or holy; and what some of them love and others hate is both or neither. Shall this be our definition of piety and impiety?

Euth. Why not, Socrates?

Soc. Why not! certainly, as far as I am concerned, Euthyphro, there is no reason why not. But whether this admission will greatly assist you in the task of instructing me as you promised, is a matter for you to consider.

Euth. Yes, I should say that what all the gods love is pious and holy, and the opposite which they all hate, impious.

Soc. Ought we to enquire into the truth of this, Euthyphro, or simply to accept the mere statement on our own authority and that of others? What do you say?

Euth. We should enquire; and I believe that the statement will stand the test of enquiry.

Soc. We shall know better, my good friend, in a little while. The point which I should first wish to understand is whether the pious or holy is beloved by the gods because it is holy, [10] or holy because it is beloved of the gods.

Euth. I do not understand your meaning, Socrates.

Soc. I will endeavour to explain: we speak of carrying and we speak of being carried, of leading and being led, seeing and being seen. You know that in all such cases there is a difference, and you know also in what the difference lies?

Euth. I think that I understand.

Soc. And is not that which is beloved distinct from that which loves?

Euth. Certainly.

Soc. Well; and now tell me, is that which is carried in this state of carrying because it is carried, or for some other reason?

Euth. No; that is the reason.

Soc. And the same is true of what is led and of what is seen?

Euth. True.

Soc. And a thing is not seen because it is visible, but conversely, visible because it is seen; nor is a thing led because it is in the state of being led, or carried because it is in the state of being carried, but the converse of this. And now I think, Euthyphro, that my meaning will be intelligible; and my meaning is, that any state of action or passion implies previous action or passion. It does not become because it is becoming, but it is in a state of becoming because it becomes; neither does it suffer because it is in a state of suffering, but it is in a state of suffering because it suffers. Do you not agree?

Euth. Yes.

Soc. Is not that which is loved in some state either of becoming or suffering?

Euth. Yes.

Soc. And the same holds as in the previous instances; the state of being loved follows the act of being loved, and not the act the state.

Euth. Certainly.

Soc. And what do you say of piety, Euthyphro: is not piety, according to your definition, loved by all the gods?

Euth. Yes.

Soc. Because it is pious or holy, or for some other reason?

Euth. No, that is the reason.

Soc. It is loved because it is holy, not holy because it is loved?

Euth. Yes.

Soc. And that which is dear to the gods is loved by them, and is in a state to be loved of them because it is loved of them?

Euth. Certainly.

Soc. Then that which is dear to the gods, Euthyphro, is not holy, nor is that which is holy loved of God, as you affirm; but they are two different things.

Euth. How do you mean, Socrates?

Soc. I mean to say that the holy has been acknowledged by us to be loved of God because it is holy, not to be holy because it is loved.

Euth. Yes.

Soc. But that which is dear to the gods is dear to them because it is loved by them, not loved by them because it is dear to them.

Euth. True.

Soc. But, friend Euthyphro, if that which is holy is the same with that which is dear to God, and is loved because it is holy, then that which is dear to God would have been loved as being [*11*] dear to God; but if that which is dear to God is dear to him because loved by him, then that which is holy would have been holy becauses loved by him. But now you see that the reverse is the case, and that they are quite different from one another. For one is of a kind to be loved because it is loved, and the other

is loved because it is of a kind to be loved. Thus you appear to me, Euthyphro, when I ask you what is the essence of holiness, to offer an attribute of being loved by all the gods. But you still refuse to explain to me the nature of holiness. And therefore, if you please, I will ask you not to hide your treasure, but to tell me once more what holiness or piety really is, whether dear to the gods or not (for that is a matter about which we will not quarrel); and what is impiety?

Euth. I really do not know, Socrates, how to express what I mean. For somehow or other our arguments, on whatever ground we rest them, seem to turn round and walk away from us.

Soc. Your words, Euthyphro, are like the handiwork of my ancestor Daedalus; and if I were the sayer or propounder of them, you might say that my arguments walk away and will not remain fixed where they are placed because I am a descendant of his. But now, since these notions are your own, you must find some other gibe, for they certainly, as you yourself allow, show an inclination to be on the move.

Euth. Nay, Socrates, I shall still say that you are the Daedalus who sets arguments in motion; not I, certainly, but you make them move or go round, for they would never have stirred, as far as I am concerned.

Soc. Then I must be greater than Daedalus; for whereas he only made his own inventions to move, I move those of other people as well. And the beauty of it is, that I would rather not. For I would give the wisdom of Daedalus, and the wealth of Tantalus, to be able to detain them and keep them fixed. But enough of this. As I perceive that you are lazy, I will myself endeavor to show you how you might instruct me in the nature of piety; and I hope that you will not grudge your labour. Tell me, then,—Is not that which is pious necessarily just?

Euth. Yes.

Soc. And is, then, all which is just pious? or, is that which is pious all just, [*12*] but that which is just, only in part and not all, pious?

Euth. I do not understand you, Socrates.

Soc. And yet I know that you are as much wiser than I am, as you are younger. But, as I was saying, revered friend, the abundance of your wisdom makes you lazy. Please to exert yourself, for there is no real difficulty in understanding me. What I mean I may explain by an illustration of what I do not mean. The poet (Stasinus) sings—

Of Zeus, the author and creator of all these things. You will not tell: for where there is fear there is also reverence.

Now I disagree with this poet. Shall I tell you in what respect?

Euth. By all means.

Soc. I shall not say that where there is fear there is also reverence; for I am sure that many persons fear poverty and disease, and the like evils, but I do not perceive that they reverence the objects of their fear.

Euth. Very true.

Soc. But where reverence is, there is fear; for he who has a feeling of reverence and shame about the commission of any action, fears and is afraid of an ill reputation.

Euth. No doubt.

Soc. Then we are wrong in saying that where there is fear there is also reverence; and we should say, where there is reverence there is also fear. But there is not always reverence where there is fear; for fear is a more extended notion, and reverence is a part of fear, just as the odd is a part of number, and number is a more extended notion than the odd. I suppose that you follow me now?

Euth. Quite well.

Soc. That was the sort of question which I meant to raise when I asked whether the just is always the pious, or the pious always the just; and whether there may not be justice where there is not piety; for justice is the more extended notion of which piety is only a part. Do you dissent?

Euth. No, I think that you are quite right.

Soc. Then, if piety is a part of justice, I suppose that we should enquire what part. If you had pursued the enquiry in the previous cases; for instance, if you had asked me what is an even number, and what part of number the even is, I should have had no difficulty in replying, a number which represents a figure having two equal sides. Do you not agree?

Euth. Yes, I quite agree.

Soc. In like manner, I want you to tell me what part of justice is piety or holiness, that I may be able to tell Meletus not to do me injustice, or indict me for impiety, as I am now adequately instructed by you in the nature of piety or holiness and their opposites.

Euth. Piety or holiness, Socrates, appears to me to be that part of justice which attends to the gods, as there is the other part of justice which attends to men.

[13] *Soc.* That is good, Euthyphro; yet still there is a little point about which I should like to have further information, What is the meaning of "attention"? For attention can hardly be used in the same sense when applied to the gods as when applied to other things. For instance, horses are said to require attention, and not every person is able to attend to them; but only a person skilled in horsemanship. Is it not so?

Euth. Certainly.

Soc. I should suppose that the art of horsemanship is the art of attending to horses?

Euth. Yes.

Soc. Nor is every one qualified to attend to dogs, but only the huntsman?

Euth. True.

Soc. And I should also conceive that the art of attending to oxen?

Euth. Very true.

Soc. In like manner holiness or piety is the art of attending to the gods—that would be your meaning, Euthyphro?

Euth. Yes.

Soc. And is not attention always designed for the good or benefit of that to which the attention is given? As in the case of horses, you may observe that when attended to by the horseman's art they are benefited and improved, are they not?

Euth. True.

Soc. As the dogs are benefited by the huntsman's art, and the oxen by the art of the oxherd, and all other things are tended or attended for their good and not for their hurt?

Euth. Certainly, not for their hurt.

Soc. But for their good?

Euth. Of course.

Soc. And does piety or holiness, which has been defined to be the art of attending to the gods, benefit or improve them? Would you say that when you do a holy act you make any of the gods better?

Euth. No, no; that was certainly not what I meant.

Soc. And I, Euthyphro, never supposed that you did. I asked you the question about the nature of the attention, because I thought that you did not.

Euth. You do me justice, Socrates; that is not

the sort of attention which I mean.

Soc. Good: but I must still ask what is this attention to the gods which is called piety?

Euth. It is such, Socrates, as servants show to their masters.

Soc. I understand—a sort of ministration to the gods.

Euth. Exactly.

Soc. Medicine is also a sort of ministration or service, having in view the attainment of some object—would you say of health?

Euth. I should.

Soc. Again, there is an art which ministers to the ship-builder with a view to the attainment of some result?

Euth. Yes, Socrates, with a view to the building of a ship.

Soc. As there is an art which ministers to the housebuilder with a view to the building of a house?

Euth. Yes.

Soc. And now tell me, my good friend, about the art which ministers to the gods: what work does that help to accomplish? For you must surely know if, as you say, you are of all men living the one who is best instructed in religion.

Euth. And I speak the truth, Socrates.

Soc. Tell me then, oh tell me—what is that fair work which the gods do by the help of our ministrations?

Euth. Many and fair, Socrates, are the works which they do.

[*14*] *Soc.* Why, my friend, and so are those of a general. But the chief of them is easily told. Would you not say that victory in war is the chief of them?

Euth. Certainly.

Soc. Many and fair, too, are the works of the husbandman, if I am not mistaken; but his chief work is the production of food from the earth?

Euth. Exactly.

Soc. And of the many and fair things done by the gods, which is the chief or principal one?

Euth. I have told you already, Socrates, that to learn all these things accurately will be very tiresome. Let me simply say that piety or holiness is learning how to please the gods in word and deed, by prayers and sacrifices. Such piety is the salvation of families and states, just as the impious, which is unpleasing to the gods, is their ruin and destruction.

Soc. I think that you could have answered in much fewer words the chief question which I asked, Euthyphro, if you had chosen. But I see plainly that you are not disposed to instruct me —clearly not: else why, when we reached the point, did you turn aside? Had you only answered me I should have truly learned of you by this time the nature of piety. Now, as the asker of a question is necessarily dependent on the answerer, whither he leads I must follow; and can only ask again, what is the pious, and what is piety? Do you mean that they are a sort of science of praying and sacrificing?

Euth. Yes, I do.

Soc. And sacrificing is giving to the gods, and prayer is asking of the gods?

Euth. Yes, Socrates.

Soc. Upon this view, then, piety is a science of asking and giving?

Euth. You understand me capitally, Socrates.

Soc. Yes, my friend; the reason is that I am a votary of your science, and give my mind to it, and therefore nothing which you say will be thrown away upon me. Please then to tell me, what is the nature of this service to the gods? Do you mean that we prefer requests and give gifts to them?

Euth. Yes, I do.

Soc. Is not the right way of asking to ask of them what we want?

Euth. Certainly.

Soc. And the right way of giving is to give to them in return what they want of us. There would be no meaning in an art which gives to any one that which he does not want.

Euth. Very true, Socrates.

Soc. Then piety, Euthyphro, is an art which gods and men have of doing business with one another?

Euth. That is an expression which you may use, if you like.

Soc. But I have no particular liking for anything but the truth. I wish, however, that you would tell me what benefit accrues to the gods from our gifts. There is no doubt about what they give to us; [*15*] for there is no good thing which they do not give; but how we can give any good thing to them in return is far from being equally clear. If they give everything and we give nothing, that must be an affair of business in which we have very greatly the advantage of them.

Euth. And do you imagine, Socrates, that any benefit accrues to the gods from our gifts?

Soc. But if not, Euthyphro, what is the meaning of gifts which are conferred by us upon the gods?

Euth. What else, but tributes of honour; and, as I was just now saying, what pleases them?

Soc. Piety, then, is pleasing to the gods, but not beneficial or dear to them?

Euth. I should say that nothing could be dearer.

Soc. Then once more the assertion is repeated that piety is dear to the gods?

Euth. Certainly.

Soc. And when you say this, can you wonder at your words not standing firm, but walking away? Will you accuse me of being the Daedalus who makes them walk away, not perceiving that there is another and far greater artist than Daedalus who makes them go round in a circle, and he is yourself; for the argument, as you will perceive, comes round to the same point. Were we not saying that the holy or pious was not the same with that which is loved of the gods? Have you forgotten?

Euth. I quite remember.

Soc. And are you not saying that what is loved of the gods is holy and, is not this the same as what is dear to them—do you see?

Euth. True.

Soc. Then either we were wrong in our former assertion; or, if we were right then, we are wrong now.

Euth. One of the two must be true.

Soc. Then we must begin again and ask, What is piety? That is an enquiry which I shall never be weary of pursuing as far as in me lies; and I entreat you not to scorn me, but to apply your mind to the utmost, and tell me the truth. For, if any man knows, you are he; and therefore I must detain you, like Proteus, until you tell. If you had not certainly known the nature of piety and impiety, I am confident that you would never, on behalf of a serf, have charged your aged father with murder. You would not have run such a risk of doing wrong in the sight of the gods, and you would have had too much respect for the opinions of men. I am sure, therefore, that you know the nature of piety and impiety. Speak out then, my dear Euthyphro, and do not hide your knowledge.

Euth. Another time, Socrates; for I am in a hurry, and must go now.

Soc. Alas! my companion, and will you leave me in despair? I was hoping that you would instruct me in the nature of piety and impiety; and then I might have cleared myself of Meletus and his indictment. [16] I would have told him that I had been enlightened by Euthyphro, and had given up rash innovations and speculations, in which I indulged only through ignorance, and that now I am about to lead a better life.

Apology: Introduction

The *Apology* is one of Plato's earliest dialogues. It was probably written shortly after his return to Athens, around the year 390 B.C. The memory of Socrates was surely very alive in Plato's mind, and the influence of the Socratic impulse dominated Plato's activities. The account of the famous trial is probably fully historical in most of its aspects, even though Plato himself, as he indicates in the dialogue, was not actually present during the court proceedings. Other accounts of the trial, especially Xenophon's, lend ample support to Plato's narration.

The scene opens abruptly in the midst of an Athenian court where five hundred jurors sit in judgment. The defendant has walked into the open court room, and after the charges are read to him, he proceeds to speak on his own behalf. In ancient legal terminology, his speech was called "the apology," a term which did not have the common connotation of an apologetic excuse. Once the defendant completed his speech to the jury, a first vote was taken for the purpose of determining his guilt or innocence. A simple majority sufficed in either case. At this point, he was allowed to speak once more in order to plead for mercy or suggest the sentence which best suited his interests. Once again, a vote was taken in order to approve or reject the defendant's plea, or else one of the judges of the court asked for the customary sentence. The vote of the jury was in all cases absolutely binding, and there was no possible appeal.

In the *Apology* Socrates defends himself in the way he thinks best, namely, by merely telling the truth. He rejects the accusations brought against him as utterly false. He denies the charge of impiety and the idea that he has corrupted the Athenian youth. He points out that his entire life has been the unfolding of a divine destiny which has its roots in the Delphic Oracle. He has not taken money for his philosophical activities, and has not willingly wronged any human being; all he has done has been to act as the awakener of the Athenians. He has questioned the institutions, practices, and values of society, whenever he thought they ought to have been questioned. Occasionally, he explains, an inner voice has guided him. Now he stands accused of grave crimes. Why?

In his defense he does not appeal to the ordinary pleas for mercy, because he knows that he has done nothing wrong. He does grant that he has not behaved as most of his fellow citizens behave. He is different. He has had the unusual courage to confess his ignorance about most things, and has come to the perplexing conclusion that he only knows that he does not know anything. In his persistent search for truth, he has become aware of the emptiness and inauthenticity of most human knowledge: most people think that they know something; whereas in fact they, like him, know nothing.

He faces the guilty verdict with serenity, almost with arrogance, and when the death sentence is passed, he welcomes the coming of death as a blessing. A good man never has anything to fear, and even though he still does not know what death really is (it could be total extinction or a migration of the soul from this physical world into another), he knows that the affairs of good men are never forgotten by the gods.

In the *Apology* the character of Socrates reaches its greatest development. The ideal representation of a living philosopher is before us: he begins by confessing his ignorance, spends his life in the search for truth, acts always with a superior sense of dignity and self-respect, and, when death calls him, dies in peace and resignation.

The ideal presented to us by Plato's *Apology* has exercised a profound influence on Western Civilization. It has served as a frame of reference against which many subsequent philosophers have measured their philosophical growth, their commitment to philosophy, and their level of moral living.

Plato: Apology

[*17*] How you, O Athenians, have been affected by my accusers, I cannot tell; but I know that they almost made me forget who I was—so persuasively did they speak; and yet they have hardly uttered a word of truth. But of the many falsehoods told by them, there was one which quite amazed me;—I mean when they said that you should be upon your guard and not allow yourselves to be deceived by the force of my eloquence. To say this, when they were certain to be detected as soon as I opened my lips and proved myself to be anything but a great speaker, did indeed appear to me most shameless—unless by the force of eloquence they mean the force of truth; for if such is their meaning, I admit that I am eloquent. But in how different a way from theirs! Well, as I was saying, they have scarcely spoken the truth at all; but from me you shall hear the whole truth: not, however, delivered after their manner in a set oration duly ornamented with words and phrases. No, by heaven! but I shall use the words and arguments which occur to me at the moment; for I am confident in the justice of my cause: at my time of life I ought not to be appearing before you, O men of Athens, in the character of a juvenile orator—let no one expect it of me. And I must beg of you to grant me a favour:—If I defend myself in my accustomed manner, and you hear me using the words which I have been in the habit of using in the agora, at the tables of the money-changers, or anywhere else, I would ask you not to be surprised, and not to interrupt me on this account. For I am more than seventy years of age, and appearing now for the first time in a court of law, I am quite a stranger to the language of the place; and therefore I would have you regard me as if I were really a stranger, [*18*] whom you would excuse if he spoke in his native tongue, and after the fashion of his country:—Am I making an unfair request of you? Never mind the manner, which may or may not be good; but think only of the truth of my words, and give heed to that: let the speaker speak truly and the judge decide justly.

And first, I have to reply to the older charges and to my first accusers, and then I will go on to the later ones. For of old I have had many accusers, who have accused me falsely to you during many years; and I am more afraid of them than of Anytus and his associates, who are dangerous, too, in their own way. But far more dangerous are the others, who began when you were children, and took possession of your minds with their falsehoods, telling of one Socrates, a wise man, who speculated about the heaven above, and searched into the earth beneath, and made the worse appear the better cause. The disseminators of this tale are the accusers whom I dread; for their hearers are apt to fancy that such enquirers do not believe in the existence of the gods. And they are many, and their charges against me are of ancient date, and they were made by them in the days when you were more impressible than you are now—in childhood, or it may have been in youth—and the cause when heard went by default, for there was none to answer. And hardest of all, I do not know and cannot tell the names of my accusers; unless in the chance case of a Comic poet. All who from envy and malice have persuaded you—some of them having first convinced themselves—all this class of men are most difficult to deal with; for I cannot have them up here, and cross-examine them, and therefore I must simply fight with shadows in my own defence, and argue when there is no one who answers. I will ask you then to assume with me, as I was saying, that my opponents are of two kinds, one recent, the other ancient; and I hope that you will see the propriety of my answering the latter first, for these accusations you heard long before the others, and much oftener.

[*19*] Well, then, I must make my defence, and endeavor to clear away in a short time a slander which has lasted a long time. May I succeed, if to succeed be for my good and yours, or likely to avail me in my cause! The task is not an easy one; I quite understand the nature of it. And so leaving the event with God, in obedience to the law I will now make my defence.

I will begin at the beginning and ask what is the accusation which has given rise to the slander of me, and in fact has encourged Meletus to prefer this charge against me. Well, what do the slanderers say? They shall be my prosecutors, and I will sum up their words in an affidavit: "Socrates is an evil-doer, and a curious person, who searches into things under the earth and in heaven, and he makes the worse appear the better cause; and he teaches the aforesaid doctrines to others." Such is the nature of the accusation: it is just what you have yourselves seen in the comedy of Aristophanes, who has introduced a man whom he calls Socrates, going about and saying that he walks in air, and talking a deal of nonsense concerning matters of which I do not pretend to know either much or little—not that I mean to speak disparagingly of any one who is a student of natural philosophy. I should be very sorry if Meletus could bring so grave a charge against me. But the simple truth is, O Athenians, that I have nothing to do with physical speculations. Very many of those here present are witnesses to the truth of this, and to them I appeal. Speak then, you who have heard me, and tell your neighbours whether any of you have ever known me to hold forth in few words or in many upon such matters. . . . You hear their answer. And from what they say of this part of the charge you will be able to judge of the truth of the rest.

As little foundation is there for the report that I am a teacher, and take money; this accusation has no more truth in it than the other.

Although, if a man were really able to instruct mankind, to receive money for giving instruction would, in my opinion, be an honour to him. There is Gorgias of Leontium, and Prodicus of Ceos, and Hippias of Elis, who go the round of the cities, and are able to persuade the young men to leave their own citizens by whom they might be taught for nothing, [*20*] and come to them whom they not only pay, but are thankful if they may be allowed to pay them. There is at this time a Parian philosopher residing in Athens, of whom I have heard; and I came to hear of him in this way:—I came across a man who has spent a world of money on the Sophists, Callias, the son of Hipponicus, and knowing that he had sons, I asked him: "Callias," I said, "if your two sons were foals or calves, there would be no difficulty in finding some one to put over them; we should hire a trainer of horses, or a farmer probably, who would improve and perfect them in their own proper virtue and excellence; but as they are human beings, whom are you thinking of placing over them? Is there any one who understands human and political virtue? You must have thought about the matter, for you have sons; is there any one?" "There is," he said. "Who is he?" said I; "and of what country? and what does he charge?" "Evenus the Parian," he replied; "he is the man, and his charge is five minae." Happy is Evenus, I said to myself, if he really has this wisdom, and teaches at such a moderate charge. Had I the same, I should have been very proud and conceited; but the truth is that I have no knowledge of the kind.

I dare say, Athenians, that some one among you will reply, "Yes, Socrates, but what is the origin of these accusations which are brought against you; there must have been something strange which you have been doing? All these rumours and this talk about you would never have arisen if you had been like other men: tell us, then, what is the cause of them, for we should be sorry to judge hastily of you." Now I regard this as a fair challenge, and I will endeavour to explain to you the reason why I am called wise and have such an evil fame. Please to attend then. And although some of you may think that I am joking, I declare that I will tell you the entire truth. Men of Athens, this reputation of mine has come to a certain sort of wisdom which I possess. If you ask me what kind of wisdom, I reply, wisdom such as may perhaps be attained by man, for to that extent I am inclined to believe that I am wise; whereas the persons of whom I was speaking have a superhuman wisdom, which I may fail to describe, because I have it not myself; and he who says that I have, speaks falsely, and is taking away my character. And here, O men of Athens, I must beg you not to interrupt me, even if I seem to say something extravagant. For the word which I will speak is not mine. I will refer you to a witness who is worthy of credit; that witness shall be the God of Delphi —he will tell you about my wisdom, if I have any, and of what sort it is. You must have known Chaerephon; he was early a friend of mine, and also a friend of yours, [21] for he shared in the recent exile of the people, and returned with you. Well, Chaerephon, as you know, was very impetuous in all his doings, and he went to Delphi and boldly asked the oracle to tell him whether—as I was saying, I must beg you not to interrupt—he asked the oracle to tell him whether any one was wiser than I was, and the Pythian prophetess answered, that there was no man wiser. Chaerephon is dead himself; but his brother, who is in court, will confirm the truth of what I am saying.

Why do I mention this? Because I am going to explain to you why I have such an evil name. When I heard the answer, I said to myself, What can the god mean? and what is the interpretation of his riddle? for I know that I have no wisdom, small or great. What then can he mean when he says that I am the wisest of men? And yet he is a god, and cannot lie; that would be against his nature. After long consideration, I thought of a method of trying the question. I reflected that if I could only find a man wiser than myself, then I might go to the god with a refutation in my hand. I should say to him, "Here is a man who is wiser than I am; but you said that I was the wisest." Accordingly I went to one who had the reputation of wisdom, and observed him—his name I need not mention; he was a politician whom I selected for examination—and the result was as follows: When I began to talk with him, I could not help thinking that he was not really wise, although he was thought wise by many, and still wiser by himself; and thereupon I tried to explain to him that he thought himself wise, but was not really wise; and the consequence was that he hated me, and his enmity was shared by several who

were present and heard me. So I left him, saying to myself, as I went away: Well, though I do not suppose that either of us knows anything really beautiful and good, I am better off than he is,—for he knows nothing, and thinks that he knows: I neither know nor think that I know. In this latter particular, then, I seem to have slightly the advantage of him. Then I went to another who had still higher pretensions to wisdom, and my conclusion was exactly the same. Whereupon I made another enemy of him, and of many others besides him.

Then I went to one man after another, being not unconscious of the enmity which I provoked, and I lamented and feared this: But necessity was laid upon me,—the word of God, I thought, ought to be considered first. And I said to myself, Go I must to all who appear to know, [22] and find out the meaning of the oracle. And I swear to you, Athenians, by the dog I swear!—for I must tell you the truth— the result of my mission was just this: I found that the men most in repute were all but the most foolish; and that others less esteemed were really wiser and better. I will tell you the tale of my wanderings and of the "Herculean" labours, as I may call them, which I endured only to find at last the oracle irrefutable. After the politicians, I went to the poets; tragic, dithyrambic, and all sorts. And there, I said to myself, you will be instantly detected; now you will find out that you are more ignorant than they are. Accordingly, I took them some of the most elaborate passages in their own writings, and asked what was the meaning of them— thinking that they would teach me something. Will you believe me? I am almost ashamed to confess the truth, but I must say that there is hardly a person present who would not have talked better about their poetry than they did themselves. Then I knew that not by wisdom do poets write poetry, but by a sort of genius and inspiration; they are like diviners or soothsayers who also say many fine things, but do not understand the meaning of them. The poets appeared to me to be much in the same case; and I further observed that upon the strength of their poetry they believed themselves to be the wisest of men in other things in which they were not wise. So I departed, conceiving myself to be superior to them for the same reason that I was superior to the politicians.

At last I went to the artisans, for I was conscious that I knew nothing at all, as I may say, and I was sure that they knew many fine things; and here I was not mistaken, for they did know many things of which I was ignorant, and in this they certainly were wiser than I was. But I observed that even the good artisans fell into the same error as the poets;—because they were good workmen, they thought that they also knew all sorts of high matters, and this defect in them overshadowed their wisdom; and therefore I asked myself on behalf of the oracle, whether I would like to be as I was, neither having their knowledge nor their ignorance, or like them in both; and I made answer to myself and to the oracle that I was better off as I was.

This inquisition has led to my having many enemies of the worst and most dangerous kind, [23] and has given occasion also to many calumnies. And I am called wise, for my hearers always imagine that I myself possess the wisdom which I find wanting in others: but the truth is, O men of Athens, that God only is wise; and by his answer he intends to show that the wisdom of men is worth little or nothing; he is not speaking of Socrates; he is only using my name by way of illustration, as if he said, He, O men, is the wisest, who, like Socrates, knows that his wisdom is in truth worth nothing. And so I go about the world, obedient to the god, and search and make enquiry into the wisdom of any one, whether citizen or stranger, who appears to be wise; and if he is not wise, then in vindication of the oracle I show him that he is not wise; and my occupation quite absorbs me, and I have no time to give either to any public matter of interest or to any concern of my own, but I am in utter poverty by reason of my devotion to the god.

There is another thing:—young men of the richer classes, who have not much to do, come about me of their own accord; they like to hear the pretenders examined, and they often imitate me, and proceed to examine others; there are plenty of persons, as they quickly discover, who think that they know something, but really know little or nothing; and then those who are examined by them instead of being angry with themselves are angry with me: This confounded Socrates, they say; this villainous misleader of youth!—and then if somebody asks them, Why, what evil does he practise or teach? they do not know, and cannot tell; but in order that they

may not appear to be at a loss, they repeat the ready-made charges which are used against all philosophers about teaching things up in the clouds and under the earth, and having no gods, and making the worse appear the better cause; for they do not like to confess that their pretence of knowledge has been detected—which is the truth; and as they are numerous and ambitious and energetic, and are drawn up in battle array and have persuasive tongues, they have filled your ears with their loud and inveterate calumnies. And this is the reason why my three accusers, Meletus and Anytus and Lycon, have set upon me; Meletus, who has a quarrel with me on behalf of the poets; Anytus, on behalf of the craftsmen and politicians; [24] Lycon, on behalf of the rhetoricians: and as I said at the beginning, I cannot expect to get rid of such a mass of calumny all in a moment. And this, O men of Athens, is the truth and the whole truth; I have concealed nothing, I have dissembled nothing. And yet, I know that my plainness of speech makes them hate me, and what is their hatred but a proof that I am speaking the truth?—Hence has arisen the prejudice against me; and this is the reason of it, as you will find out either in this or in any future enquiry.

I have said enough in my defence against the first class of my accusers; I turn to the second class. They are headed by Meletus, that good man and true lover of this country, as he calls himself. Against these, too, I must try to make a defence:—Let their affidavit be read: it contains something of this kind: It says that Socrates is a doer of evil, who corrupts the youth; and who does not believe in the gods of the state, but has other new divinities of his own. Such is the charge; and now let us examine the particular counts. He says that I am a doer of evil, and corrupt the youth; but I say, O men of Athens that Meletus is a doer of evil, in that he pretends to be in earnest when he is only in jest, and is so eager to bring men to trial from a pretended zeal and interest about matters in which he really never had the smallest interest. And the truth of this I will endeavour to prove to you.

Come hither, Meletus, and let me ask a question of you. You think a great deal about the improvement of youth?

Yes, I do.

Tell the judges, then, who is their improver;

for you must know, as you have taken the pains to discover their corrupter, and are citing and accusing me before them. Speak, then, and tell the judges who their improver is.—Observe, Meletus, that you are silent, and have nothing to say. But is not this rather disgraceful, and a very considerable proof of what I was saying, that you have no interest in the matter? Speak up, friend, and tell us who their improver is.

The laws.

But that, my good sir, is not my meaning. I want to know who the person is, who, in the first place, knows the laws.

The judges, Socrates, who are present in court.

What, do you mean to say, Meletus, that they are able to instruct and improve youth?

Certainly they are.

What, all of them, or some only and not others?

All of them.

By the goddess Here, that is good news! There are plenty of improvers, [25] then. And what do you say of the audience,—do they improve them?

Yes, they do.

And the senators?

Yes, the senators improve them.

But perhaps the members of the assembly corrupt them?—or do they too improve them?

They improve them.

Then every Athenian improves and elevates them; all with the exception of myself; and I alone am their corrupter? Is that what you affirm?

That is what I stoutly affirm.

I am very unfortunate if you are right. But suppose I ask you a question: How about horses? Does one man do them harm and all the world good? Is not the exact opposite the truth? One man is able to do them good, or at least not many;—the trainer of horses, that is to say, does them good, and others who have to do with them rather injure them? Is not that true, Meletus, of horses, or of any other animals? Most assuredly it is; whether you and Anytus say yes or no. Happy indeed would be the condition of youth if they had one corrupter only, and all the rest of the world were their improvers. But you, Meletus, have sufficiently shown that you never had a thought about the young: your carelessness is seen in your not caring about the very things which you bring

against me.

And now, Meletus, I will ask you another question—by Zeus I will: Which is better, to live among bad citizens, or among good ones? Answer, friend, I say; the question is one which may be easily answered. Do not the good do their neighbours good, and the bad do them evil?

Certainly.

And is there any one who would rather be injured than benefited by those who live with him? Answer, my good friend, the law requires you to answer—does any one like to be injured?

Certainly not.

And when you accuse me of corrupting and deteriorating the youth, do you allege that I corrupt them intentionally or unintentionally?

Intentionally, I say.

But you have just admitted that the good do their neighbours good, and evil do them evil. Now, is that a truth which your superior wisdom has recognized thus early in life, and am I, at my age, in such darkness and ignorance as not to know that if a man with whom I have to live is corrupted by me, I am very likely to be harmed by him; and yet I corrupt him, and intentionally, too—so you say, although neither I nor any other human being is ever likely to be convinced by you. [26] But either I do not corrupt them, or I corrupt them unintentionally and on either view of the case you lie. If my offense is unintentional, the law has no cognizance of unintentional offences: you ought to have taken me privately, and warned and admonished me; for if I had been better advised, I should have left off doing what I only did unintentionally—no doubt I should; but you would have nothing to say to me and refused to teach me. And now you bring me up in this court, which is a place not of instruction, but of punishment.

It will be very clear to you, Athenians, as I was saying, that Meletus has no care at all, great or small, about the matter. But still I should like to know, Meletus, in what I am affirmed to corrupt the young. I suppose you mean, as I infer from your indictment, that I teach them not to acknowledge the gods which the state acknowledges, but some other new divinities or spiritual agencies in their stead. These are the lessons by which I corrupt the youth, as you say.

Yes, that I say emphatically.

Then, by the gods, Meletus, of whom we are

speaking, tell me and the court, in somewhat plainer terms, what you mean! For I do not as yet understand whether you affirm that I teach other men to acknowledge some gods, and therefore that I do believe in gods, and am not an entire atheist—this you do not lay to my charge,—but only you say that they are not the same gods which the city recognizes—the charge is that they are different gods. Or, do you mean that I am an atheist simply, and a teacher of atheism?

I mean the latter—that you are a complete atheist.

What an extraordinary statement! Why do you think so, Meletus? Do you mean that I do not believe in the godhead of the sun or moon, like other men?

I assure you, judges, that he does not: for he says that the sun is stone, and the moon earth.

Friend Meletus, you think that you are accusing Anaxagoras: and you have but a bad opinion of the judges, if you fancy them illiterate to such a degree as not to know that these doctrines are found in the books of Anaxagoras the Clazomenian, which are full of them. And so, forsooth, the youth are said to be taught them by Socrates, when there are not unfrequently exhibitions of them at the theatre (price of admission one drachma at the most); and they might pay their money, and laugh at Socrates if he pretends to father these extraordinary views. And so, Meletus, you really think that I do not believe in any god?

I swear by Zeus that you believe absolutely in none at all.

Nobody will believe you, Meletus, and I am pretty sure that you do not believe yourself. I cannot help thinking, men of Athens, that Meletus is reckless and impudent, and that he has written this indictment in a spirit of mere wantonness and youthful bravado. [27] Has he not compounded a riddle, thinking to try me? He said to himself:—I shall see whether the wise Socrates will discover my facetious contradiction, or whether I shall be able to deceive him and the rest of them. For he certainly does appear to me to contradict himself in the indictment as much as if he said that Socrates is guilty of not believing in the gods, and yet of believing in them—but this is not like a person who is in earnest.

I should like you, O men of Athens, to join me in examining what I conceive to be his incon-

sistency; and do you, Meletus, answer. And I must remind the audience of my request that they would not make a disturbance if I speak in my accustomed manner:

Did ever man, Meletus, believe in the existence of human things, and not of human beings? ... I wish, men of Athens, that he would answer, and not be always trying to get up an interruption. Did ever any man believe in horsemanship, and not in horses? or in flute-playing, and not in flute-players? No, my friend; I will answer to you and to the court, as you refuse to answer for yourself. There is no man who ever did. But now please to answer the next question: Can a man believe in spiritual and divine agencies, and not in spirits or demigods?

He cannot.

How lucky I am to have extracted that answer, by the assistance of the court! But then you swear in the indictment that I teach and believe in divine or spiritual agencies (new or old, no matter for that); at any rate, I believe in spiritual agencies,—so you say and swear in the affidavit; and yet if I believe in divine beings, how can I help believing in spirits or demigods; —must I not? To be sure I must; and therefore I may assume that your silence gives consent. Now what are spirits or demigods? are they not either gods or the sons of gods?

Certainly they are.

But this is what I call the facetious riddle invented by you: The demigods or spirits are gods, and you say first that I do not believe in gods, and then again that I do believe in gods; that is, if I believe in demigods. For if the demigods are the illegitimate sons of gods—whether by the nymphs or by any other mothers, of whom they are said to be the sons—what human being will ever believe that there are no gods if they are the sons of gods? You might as well affirm the existence of mules, and deny that of horses and asses. Such nonsense, Meletus, could only have been intended by you to make trial of me. You have put this into the indictment because you had nothing real of which to accuse me. But no one who has a particle of understanding will ever be convinced by you that the same men can believe in divine and superhuman things, and yet not believe that there are gods and demigods and heroes. [28]

I have said enough in answer to the charge of Meletus; any elaborate defence is unnecessary;

but I know only too well how many are the enmities which I have incurred, and this is what will be my destruction if I am destroyed;—not Meletus, nor yet Anytus, but the envy and detraction of the world, which has been the death of many good men, and will probably be the death of many more; there is no danger of my being the last of them.

Some one will say: And are you not ashamed, Socrates, of a course of life which is likely to bring you to an untimely end? To him I may fairly answer: There you are mistaken: a man who is good for anything ought not to calculate the chance of living or dying; he ought only to consider whether in doing anything he is doing right or wrong—acting the part of a good man or of a bad. Whereas, upon your view, the heroes who fell at Troy were not good for much, and the son of Thetis above all, who altogether despised danger in comparison with disgrace; and when he was so eager to slay Hector, his goddess mother said to him that, if he avenged his companion Patroclus and slew Hector, he would die himself—"Fate," she said, in these or the like words, "waits for you next after Hector"; he, receiving this warning, utterly despised danger and death, and instead of fearing them, feared rather to live in dishonour, and not to avenge his friend. "Let me die forthwith," he replies, "and be avenged of my enemy, rather than abide here by the beaked ships, a laughing-stock and a burden of the earth." Had Achilles any thought of death and danger? For wherever a man's place is, whether the place which he has chosen or that in which he has been placed by a commander, there he ought to remain in the hour of danger; he should not think of death or of anything but of disgrace. And this, O men of Athens, is a true saying.

Strange, indeed, would be my conduct, O men of Athens, if I who, when I was ordered by the generals whom you chose to command me at Potidaea and Amphipolis and Delium, remained where they placed me, like any other man, facing death—if now, when, as I conceive and imagine, God orders me to fulfil the philosopher's mission of searching into myself and other men, I were to desert my post through fear of death, [29] or any other fear; that would indeed be strange, and I might justly be arraigned in court for denying the existence of the gods, if I disobeyed the oracle because I was afraid of death, fancying that I was wise when I was not wise. For the fear of death is indeed the pretence of wisdom, and not real wisdom, being a pretence of knowing the unknown; and no one knows whether death, which men in their fear apprehend to be the greatest evil, may not be the greatest good. Is not this ignorance of a disgraceful sort, the ignorance which is the conceit that man knows what he does not know? And in this respect only I believe myself to differ from men in general, and may perhaps claim to be wiser than they are:—that whereas I know but little of the world below, I do not suppose that I know: but I do know that injustice and disobedience to a better, whether God or man, is evil and dishonourable, and I will never fear or avoid a possible good rather than a certain evil. And therefore if you let me go now, and are not convinced by Anytus, who said that since I had been prosecuted I must be put to death (or if not that I ought never to have been prosecuted at all); and that if I escape now, your sons will all be utterly ruined by listening to my words—if you say to me, Socrates, this time we will not mind Anytus, and you shall be let off, but upon one condition, that you are not to enquire and speculate in this way any more, and that if you are caught doing so again you shall die—if this was the condition on which you let me go, I should reply: Men of Athens, I honour and love you; but I shall obey God rather than you, and while I have life and strength I shall never cease from the practice and teaching of philosophy, exhorting any one whom I meet and saying to him after my manner: You, my friend,—a citizen of the great and mighty and wise city of Athens—are you not ashamed of heaping up the greatest amount of money and honour and reputation, and caring so little about wisdom and truth and the greatest improvement of the soul, which you never regard or heed at all? And if the person with whom I am arguing, says: Yes, but I do care; then I do not leave him or let him go at once; but I proceed to interrogate and examine and cross-examine him, and if I think that he has no virtue in him, but only says that he has, I reproach him with undervaluing the greater, and overvaluing the less. [30] And I shall repeat the same words to every one whom I meet, young and old, citizen and alien, but especially to the citizens, inasmuch as they are my brethren. For know that this is the command of

God, and I believe that no greater good has ever happened in the state than my service to the God. For I do nothing but go about persuading you all, old and young alike, not to take thought for your persons or your properties, but first and chiefly to care about the greatest improvement of the soul. I tell you that virtue is not given by money, but that from virtue comes money and every other good of man, public as well as private. This is my teaching, and if this is the doctrine which corrupts the youth, I am a mischievous person. But if any one says that this is not my teaching, he is speaking an untruth. Wherefore, O men of Athens, I say to you, do as Anytus bids or not as Anytus bids, and either acquit me or not; but whichever you do, understand that I shall never alter my ways, not even if I have to die many times.

Men of Athens, do not interrupt, but hear me; there was an understanding between us that you should hear me to the end: I have something more to say, at which you may be inclined to cry out; but I believe that to hear me will be good for you, and therefore I beg that you will not cry out. I would have you know, that if you kill such an one as I am, you will injure yourselves more than you will injure me. Nothing will injure me, not Meletus nor yet Anytus—they cannot, for a bad man is not permitted to injure a better than himself. I do not deny that Anytus may, perhaps, kill him, or drive him into exile, or deprive him of civil rights; and he may imagine, and others may imagine, that he is inflicting a great injury upon him: but there I do not agree. For the evil of doing as he is doing—the evil of unjustly taking away the life of another—is greater far.

And now, Athenians, I am not going to argue for my own sake, as you may think, but for yours, that you may not sin against the God by condemning me, who am his gift to you. For if you kill me you will not easily find a successor to me, who, if I may use such a ludicrous figure of speech, am a sort of gadfly, given to the state by God; and the state is a great and noble steed who is tardy in his motions owing to his very size, and requires to be stirred into life. [*31*] I am that gadfly which God has attached to the state, and all day long and in all places am always fastening upon you, arousing and persuading and reproaching you. You will not easily find another like me, and therefore I would advise you to spare me. I dare say that you may feel out of temper (like a person who is suddenly awakened from sleep), and you think that you might easily strike me dead as Anytus advises, and then you would sleep on for the remainder of your lives, unless God in his care of you sent you another gadfly. When I say that I am given to you by God, the proof of my mission is this:—if I had been like other men, I should not have neglected all my own concerns or patiently seen the neglect of them during all these years, and have been doing yours, coming to you individually like a father or elder brother, exhorting you to regard virtue; such conduct, I say, would be unlike human nature. If I had gained anything, or if my exhortations had been paid, there would have been some sense in my doing so; but now, as you will perceive, not even the impudence of my accusers dares to say that I have ever exacted or sought pay of any one; of that they have no witness. And I have a sufficient witness to the truth of what I say—my poverty.

Some one may wonder why I go about in private giving advice and busying myself with the concerns of others, but do not venture to come forward in public and advise the state. I will tell you why. You have heard me speak at sundry times and in divers places of an oracle or sign which comes to me, and is the divinity which Meletus ridicules in the indictment. This sign, which is a kind of voice, first began to come to me when I was a child; it always forbids but never commands me to do anything which I am going to do. This is what deters me from being a politician. And rightly, as I think. For I am certain, O men of Athens, that if I had engaged in politics, I should have perished long ago, and done no good either to you or to myself. And do not be offended at my telling you the truth: for the truth is, that no man who goes to war with you or any other multitude, honestly striving against the many lawless and unrighteous deeds which are done in a state, [*32*] will save his life; he who will fight for the right, if he would live even for a brief space, must have a private station and not a public one.

I can give you convincing evidence of what I say, not words only, but what you value far more—actions. Let me relate to you a passage of my own life which will prove to you that I should never have yielded to injustice from any fear of death, and that "as I should have refused to yield," I must have died at once. I will tell you a tale of the courts, not very interesting perhaps, but nevertheless true. The only office of state which I ever held, O men of Athens, was that of senator: the tribe Antiochis, which is my tribe, had the presidency at the trial of the generals who had not taken up the bodies of the slain after the battle of Arginusae; and you proposed to try them in a body, contrary to law, as you all thought afterwards; but at the time I was the only one of the Prytanes who was opposed to the illegality, and I gave my vote against you; and when the orators threatened to impeach and arrest me, and you called and shouted, I made up my mind that I would run the risk, having law and justice with me, rather than take part in your injustice because I feared imprisonment and death. This happened in the days of the democracy. But when the oligarchy of the Thirty was in power, they sent for me and four others into the rotunda, and bade us bring Leon the Salaminian from Salamis, as they wanted to put him to death. This was a specimen of the sort of commands which they were always giving with the view of implicating as many as possible in their crimes; and then I showed, not in word only but in deed, that, if I may be allowed to use such an expression, I cared not a straw for death, and that my great and only care was lest I should do an unrighteous or unholy thing. For the strong arm of that oppressive power did not frighten me into doing wrong; and when we came out of the rotunda the other four went to Salamis and fetched Leon, but I went quietly home. For which I might have lost my life, had not the power of the Thirty shortly afterwards come to an end. And many will witness to my words.

Now do you really imagine that I could have survived all these years, if I had led a public life, supposing that like a good man I had always maintained the right and had made justice, as I ought, the first thing? No indeed, men of Athens, neither I nor any other man. [33] But I have been always the same in all my actions, public as well as private, and never have I yielded any base compliance to those who are slanderously termed my disciples, or to any other. Not that I have any regular disciples. But if any one likes to come and hear me while I am pursuing my mission, whether he be young or old, he is not excluded. Nor do I converse only with those who pay; but any one, whether he be rich or poor, may ask and answer me and listen to my words; and whether he turns out to be a bad man or a good one, neither result can be justly imputed to me; for I never taught or professed to teach him anything. And if any one says that he has ever learned or heard anything from me in private which all the world has not heard, let me tell you that he is lying.

But I shall be asked, Why do people delight in continually conversing with you? I have told you already, Athenians, the whole truth about this matter: they like to hear the cross-examination of the pretenders to wisdom; there is amusement in it. Now this duty of cross-examining other men has been imposed upon me by God; and has been signified to me by oracles, visions, and in every way in which the will of divine power was ever intimated to any one. This is true, O Athenians; or, if not true, would be soon refuted. If I am or have been corrupting the youth, those of them who are now grown up and become sensible that I gave them bad advice in the days of their youth should come forward as accusers, and take their revenge; or if they do not like to come themselves, some of their relatives, fathers, brothers, or other kinsmen, should say what evil their families have suffered at my hands. Now is their time. Many of them I see in the court. There is Crito, who is of the same age and of the same deme with myself, and there is Critobulus his son, whom I also see. Then again there is Lysanias of Sphettus, who is the father of Aeschines—he is present, and also there is Antiphon of Cephisus, who is the father of Epigenes; and there are the brothers of several who have associated with me. There is Nicostratus, the son of Theosdotides, and the brother of Theodotus (now Theodotus himself is dead, and therefore he, at any rate, will not seek to stop him); and there is Paralus, the son of Demodocus, who had a brother Theages; and Adeimantus the son of Ariston [34] whose brother Plato is present; and Aeantodorus, who is the brother of Apollodorus, whom I also see. I might mention a great many others, some of whom Meletus should have produced as witnesses in the course of his speech; and let him still produce them, if he has forgotten—I will make way for him. And let him say, if he has any testimony of the sort which he can produce. Nay, Athenians, the very opposite is the truth.

For all these are ready to witness on behalf of the corrupter, of the injurer of their kindred, as Meletus and Anytus call me; not the corrupted youth only—there might have been a motive for that—but their uncorrupted elder relatives. Why should they too support me with their testimony? Why, indeed, except for the sake of truth and justice, and because they know that I am speaking the truth, and that Meletus is a liar.

Well, Athenians, this and the like of this is all the defence which I have to offer. Yet a word more. Perhaps there may be some one who is offended at me, when he calls to mind how he himself on a similar, or even a less serious occasion, prayed and entreated the judges with many tears, and how he produced his children in court, which was a moving spectacle, together with a host of relations and friends; whereas I, who am probably in danger of my life, will do none of these things. The contrast may occur to his mind, and he may be set against me, and vote in anger because he is displeased at me on this account. Now if there be such a person among you,—mind, I do not say that there is,—to him I may fairly reply: My friend, I am a man, and like other men, a creature of flesh and blood, and not "of wood or stone," as Homer says; and I have a family, yes, and sons, O Athenians, three in number, one almost a man, and two others who are still young; and yet I will not bring any of them hither in order to petition you for an acquittal. And why not? Not from any self-assertion or want of respect for you. Whether I am or am not afraid of death is another question, of which I will not now speak. But, having regard to public opinion, I feel that such conduct would be discreditable to myself, and to you, and to the whole state. One who has reached my years, and who has a name for wisdom, ought not to demean himself. Whether this opinion of me be deserved or not, at any rate the world has decided that Socrates is in some way superior to other men. [35] And if those among you who are said to be superior in wisdom and courage, and any other virtue, demean themselves in this way, how shameful is their conduct! I have seen men of reputation, when they have been condemned, behaving in the strangest manner: they seemed to fancy that they were going to suffer something dreadful if they died, and that they could be im-

mortal if you only allowed them to live; and I think that such are a dishonor to the state, and that any stranger coming in would have said of them that the most eminent men of Athens, to whom the Athenians themselves give honour and command, are no better than women. And I say that these things ought not to be done by those of us who have a reputation; and if they are done, you ought not to permit them; you ought rather to show that you are far more disposed to condemn the man who gets up a doleful scene and makes the city ridiculous, than him who holds his peace.

But, setting aside the question of public opinion, there seems to be something wrong in asking a favour of a judge, and thus procuring an acquittal, instead of informing and convincing him. For his duty is, not to make a present of justice, but to give judgment; and he has sworn that he will judge according to the laws, and not according to his own good pleasure; and we ought not to encourage you, nor should you allow yourself to be encouraged, in this habit of perjury—there can be no piety in that. Do not then require me to do what I consider dishonourable and impious and wrong, especially now, when I am being tried for impiety on the indictment of Meletus. For if, O men of Athens, by force of persuasion and entreaty I could overpower your oaths, then I should be teaching you to believe that there are no gods, and in defending should simply convict myself of the charge of not believing in them. But that is not so—far otherwise. For I do believe that there are gods, and in a sense higher than that in which any of my accusers believe in them. And to you and to God I commit my cause, to be determined by you as best for you and me.

There are many reasons why I am not grieved, O men of Athens, at the vote of condemnation. [36] I expected it, and am only surprised that the votes are so nearly equal; for I had thought that the majority against me would have been far larger; but now, had thirty votes gone over to the other side, I should have been acquitted. And I may say, I think, that I have escaped Meletus. I may say more; for without the assistance of Anytus and Lycon, any one may see that he would not have had a fifth part of the votes, as the law required; in which case he would have incurred a fine of a thousand drachmae.

And so he proposes death as the penalty. And what shall I propose on my part, O men of Athens? Clearly that which is my due. And what is my due? What return shall be made to the man who has never had the wit to be idle during his whole life; but has been careless of what the many care for—wealth, and family interests, and military offices, and speaking in the assembly, and magistracies, and plots, and parties. Reflecting that I was really too honest a man to be a politician and live, I did not go where I could do no good to you or to myself; but where I could do the greatest good privately to every one and to you; thither I went, and sought to persuade every man among you that he must look to himself, and seek virtue and wisdom before he looks to his private interests, and look to the state before he looks to the interests of the state; and that this should be the order which he observes in all his actions. What shall be done to such an one? Doubtless some good thing, O men of Athens, if he has his reward; and the good should be of a kind suitable to him. What would be a reward suitable to a poor man who is your benefactor, and who desires leisure that he may instruct you? There can be no reward so fitting as maintenance in the Prytaneum, O men of Athens, a reward which he deserves far more than the citizen who has won the prize at Olympia in the horse or chariot race, whether the chariots were drawn by two horses or by many. For I am in want, and he has enough; and he only gives you the appearance of happiness, and I give you the reality. And if I am to estimate the penalty fairly, I should say that maintenance in the Prytaneum is the just return. [37]

Perhaps you think that I am braving you in what I am saying now, as in what I said before about the tears and prayers. But this is not so. I speak rather because I am convinced that I never intentionally wronged any one, although I cannot convince you—the time has been too short; if there were a law at Athens, as there is in other cities, that a capital cause should not be decided in one day, then I believe that I should have convinced you. But I cannot in a moment refute great slanders; and, as I am convinced that I never wronged another, I will assuredly not wrong myself. I will not say of myself that I deserve any evil, or propose any penalty. Why should I? Because I am afraid of the penalty of death which Meletus proposes?

When I do not know whether death is a good or an evil, why should I propose a penalty which would certainly be an evil? Shall I say imprisonment? And why should I live in prison, and be the slave of the magistrates of the year—of the Eleven? Or shall the penalty be a fine, and imprisonment until the fine is paid? There is the same objection. I should have to lie in prison, for money I have none, and cannot pay. And if I say exile (and this may possibly be the penalty which you will affix), I must indeed be blinded by the love of life, if I am so irrational as to expect that when you, who are my own citizens, cannot endure my discourses and words, and have found them so grievous and odious that you will have no more of them, others are likely to endure me. No indeed, men of Athens, that is not very likely. And what a life should I lead, at my age, wandering from city to city, ever changing my place of exile, and always being driven out! For I am quite sure that wherever I go, there, as here, the young men will flock to me; and if I drive them away, their elders will drive me out at their request, and if I let them come, their fathers and friends will drive me out for their sakes.

Some one will say: Yes, Socrates, but cannot you hold your tongue, and then you may go into a foreign city, and no one will interfere with you? Now I have great difficulty in making you understand my answer to this. For if I tell you that to do as you say would be a disobedience to the God, and therefore that I cannot hold my tongue, [38] you will not believe that I am serious; and if I say again that daily to discourse about virtue, and of those other things about which you hear me examining myself and others, is the greatest good of man, and that the unexamined life is not worth living, you are still less likely to believe me. Yet I say what is true, although a thing of which it is hard for me to persuade you. Also, I have never been accustomed to think that I deserve to suffer any harm. Had I money I might have estimated the offence at what I was able to pay, and not have been much the worse. But I have none, and therefore I must ask you to proportion the fine to my means. Well, perhaps I could afford a mina, and therefore I propose that penalty: Plato, Crito, Critobulus, and Apolodorus, my friends here, bid me say thirty minae, and they will be the sureties. Let thirty minae be the penalty; for which sum they will be ample security to you.

Not much time will be gained, O Athenians, in return for the evil name which you will get from the detractors of the city, who will say that you killed Socrates, a wise man; for they will call me wise, even although I am not wise, when they want to reproach you. If you had waited a little while, your desire would have been fulfilled in the course of nature. For I am far advanced in years, as you may perceive, and not far from death. I am speaking now not to all of you, but only to those who have condemned me to death. And I have another thing to say to them: You think that I was convicted because I had no words of the sort which would have procured my acquittal—I mean, if I had thought fit to leave nothing undone or unsaid. Not so: the deficiency which led to my conviction was not of words—certainly not. But I had not the boldness or impudence or inclination to address you as you would have liked me to do, weeping and wailing and lamenting, and saying and doing many things which you have been accustomed to hear from others, and which, as I maintain, are unworthy of me. I thought at the time that I ought not to do anything common or mean when in danger: nor do I now repent of the style of my defence; I would rather die having spoken after my manner, than speak in your manner and live. For neither in war nor yet at law ought I or any man to use every way of escaping death. [39] Often in battle there can be no doubt that if a man will throw away his arms, and fall on his knees before his pursuers, he may escape death; and in other dangers there are other ways of escaping death, if a man is willing to say and do anything. The difficulty, my friends, is not to avoid death, but to avoid unrighteousness; for that runs faster than death. I am old and move slowly, and my accusers are keen and quick, and the faster runner, who is unrighteousness, has overtaken them. And now I depart hence condemned by you to suffer the penalty of death,—they too go their ways condemned by the truth to suffer the penalty of villainy and wrong; and I must abide by my award—let them abide by theirs. I suppose that these things may be regarded as fated,—and I think that they are well.

And now, O men who have condemned me, I would fain prophesy to you; for I am about to die, and in the hour of death men are gifted with prophetic power. And I prophesy to you

who are my murderers, that immediately after my departure punishment far heavier than you have inflicted on me will surely await you. Me you have killed because you wanted to escape the accuser, and not to give an account of your lives. But that will not be as you suppose: far otherwise. For I say that there will be more accusers of you than there are now; accusers whom hitherto I have restrained: and as they are younger they will be more inconsiderate with you, and you will be more offended at them. If you think that by killing men you can prevent some one from censuring your evil lives, you are mistaken; that is not a way of escape which is either possible or honourable; the easiest and the noblest way is not to be disabling others, but to be improving yourselves. This is the prophecy which I utter before my departure to the judges who have condemned me.

Friends, who would have acquitted me, I would like also to talk with you about the thing which has come to pass, while the magistrates are busy, and before I go to the place at which I must die. Stay then a little, for we may as well talk with one another while there is time. [40] You are my friends, and I should like to show you the meaning of this event which has happened to me. O my judges—for you I may truly call judges—I should like to tell you of a wonderful circumstance. Hitherto the divine faculty of which the internal oracle is the source has constantly been in the habit of opposing me even about trifles, if I were going to make a slip or error in any matter; and now as you see there has come upon me that which may be thought, and is generally believed to be, the last and worst evil. But the oracle made no sign of opposition, either when I was leaving my house in the morning, or when I was on my way to the court, or while I was speaking, at anything which I was going to say; and yet I have often been stopped in the middle of a speech, but now in nothing I either said or did touching the matter in hand has the oracle opposed me. What do I take to be the explanation of this silence? I will tell you. It is an intimation that what has happened to me is a good, and that those of us who think that death is an evil are in error. For the customary sign would surely have opposed me had I been going to evil and not to good.

Let us reflect in another way, and we shall see that there is great reason to hope that death is a good; for one of two things—either death is a state of nothingness and utter unconsciousness, or, as men say, there is a change and migration of the soul from this world to another. Now if you suppose that there is no consciousness, but a sleep like the sleep of him who is undisturbed even by dreams, death will be an unspeakable gain. For if a person were to select the night in which his sleep was undisturbed even by dreams, and were to compare with this the other days and nights of his life, and then were to tell us how many days and nights he had passed in the course of his life better and more pleasantly than this one, I think that any man, I will not say a private man, but even the great king will not find many such days or nights, when compared with the others. Now if death be of such a nature, I say that to die is gain; for eternity is then only a single night. But if death is the journey to another place, and there, as men say, all the dead abide, what good, O my friends and judges, can be greater than this? If indeed when the pilgram arrives in the world below, [41] he is delivered from the professors of justice in this world, and finds the true judges who are said to give judgment there, Minos and Rhadamanthus and Aeacus and Triptolemus, and other sons of God who were righteous in their own life, that pilgrimage will be worth making. What would not a man give if he might converse with Orpheus and Musaeus and Hesiod and Homer? Nay, if this be true, let me die again and again. I myself, too, shall have a wonderful interest in there meeting and conversing with Palamedes and Ajax, the son of Telamon, and any other ancient hero who has suffered death through an unjust judgment; and there will be no small pleasure, as I think, in comparing my own sufferings with theirs. Above all, I shall then be able to continue my search into true and false knowledge; as in this world, so also in the next; and I shall find out who is wise, and who pretends to be wise, and is not. What would not a man give, O judges, to be able to examine the leader of the great Trojan expedition; or Odysseus or Sisyphus, or numberless others, men and women too! What infinite delight would there be in conversing with them and asking them questions! In another world they do not put a man to death for asking questions: assuredly not. For besides being happier than we are, they will be immortal, if what is said is true.

Therefore, O judges, be of good cheer about death, and know of a certainty, that no evil can happen to a good man, either in life or after death. He and his are not neglected by the gods; nor has my own approaching end happened by mere chance. But I see clearly that the time had arrived when it was better for me to die and be released from trouble; wherefore the oracle gave no sign. For which reason, also, I am not angry with my condemners, or with my accusers; they have done me no harm, although they did not mean to do me any good; and for this I may gently blame them.

Still I have a favour to ask of them. When my sons are grown up, I would ask you, O my friends, to punish them; and I would have you trouble them, as I have troubled you, if they seem to care about riches, or anything, more than about virtue; or if they pretend to be something when they are really nothing—then reprove them, as I have reproved you, for not caring about that for which they ought to care, and thinking that they are something when they are really nothing. [42] And if you do this, both I and my sons will have received justice at your hands.

The hour of departure has arrived, and we go our ways—I to die, and you to live. Which is better God only knows.

Crito: Introduction

Like the *Apology*, the *Crito* is regarded as a Socratic dialogue. Once more, we are furnished with a number of details of Socrates' vicissitudes before his execution, even though we can safely assume that some of the comments made in the *Crito* are the result of Plato's imagination rather than a journalistic account of the actual events. The scene develops in the Athenian prison where Socrates has been awaiting the fulfillment of his sentence. The old man has been soundly sleeping when Crito, his friend, walks in. Nothing in Socrates' attitude gives any indication of anxiety or despair. He is prepared to face death, and has already accepted his fate. Having lived a good and moral life, and having followed, with a religious dedication, the directives of his "inner voice," Socrates has nothing to fear.

Crito, on the other hand, is agitated by anguish and sadness. How could it be possible, he asks himself, that Socrates, the human paradigm of goodness and honesty, should be condemned to death? How could he let Socrates go to a death which is the outcome of an unjust sentence? Is there anything that he can do in order to reverse the course of events?

With these thoughts in mind, Crito bribes the authorities and makes all the necessary arrangements for Socrates' escape. After all, there cannot be anything immoral in appealing to an immoral act (bribing) in order to correct an even more immoral situation (the death sentence). Furthermore, Crito has not done anything unusual; he has paid, as he says to Socrates, "the usual bribes."

Crito's designs, however, prove to be futile in the end. Socrates refuses to accept Crito's assistance unless the entire affair is examined in depth. Much to Crito's amazement, then, the old philosopher insists on reviewing a host of issues and questions before making up his mind. Socrates, unlike most human beings, thinks before he acts. Following Crito's urgent pleas, and escaping from prison, would indeed be the easy course to follow. But is this the right course? On what basis should the decision to escape be made to rest? What consequences, philosophical and practical, would it entail? Furthermore, why has Crito chosen to help his friend by bribing the authorities?

Most of the dialogue consists of the examination of the option to escape. At one point, Socrates introduces "the Laws" which, in the form of a mythological character, come to prison to question him. One gets the distinct impression that the rebellious Socrates of the *Apology*, who was always willing to follow the rulings of his own personal conscience instead of the collective injunctions embodied in the Athenian laws, has suddenly turned into an obedient and submissive citizen who kneels respectfully at the feet of the laws.

In the end, Crito is fully convinced that death is the only meaningful option left for Socrates. Crito's well-intentioned plans have finally failed. But has Socrates, as a man and as a philosopher, also failed?

Plato: Crito

Persons of the Dialogue: Socrates; Crito.
Scene: The Prison of Socrates

[43] *Socrates.* Why have you come at this hour, Crito? It must be quite early?

Crito. Yes, certainly.

Soc. What is the exact time?

Cr. The dawn is breaking.

Soc. I wonder that the keeper of the prison would let you in.

Cr. He knows me, because I often come, Socrates; moreover, I have done him a kindness.

Soc. And are you only just arrived?

Cr. No, I came some time ago.

Soc. Then why did you sit and say nothing, instead of at once awakening me?

Cr. I should not have liked myself, Socrates, to be in such great trouble and unrest as you are—indeed I should not: I have been watching with amazement your peaceful slumbers; and for that reason, I did not awake you, because I wished to minimize the pain. I have always thought you to be of a happy disposition; but never did I see anything like the easy, tranquil manner in which you bear this calamity.

Soc. Why, Crito, when a man has reached my age he ought not to be repining at the approach of death.

Cr. And yet other old men find themselves in similar misfortunes, and age does not prevent them from repining.

Soc. That is true. But you have not told me

why you come at this early hour.

Cr. I come to bring you a message which is sad and painful; not, as I believe, to yourself, but to all of us who are your friends, and saddest of all to me.

Soc. What? Has the ship come from Delos, on the arrival of which I am to die?

Cr. No, the ship has not actually arrived, but she will probably be here to-day, as persons who have come from Sunium tell me that they left her there; and therefore to-morrow, Socrates, will be the last day of your life.

Soc. Very well, Crito; if such is the will of God, I am willing; but my belief is that there will be a delay of a day.

[44] *Cr.* Why do you think so?

Soc. I will tell you. I am to die on the day after the arrival of the ship.

Cr. Yes; that is what the authorities say.

Soc. But I do not think that the ship will be here until to-morrow; this I infer from a vision which I had last night, or rather only just now, when you fortunately allowed me to sleep.

Cr. And what was the nature of the vision?

Soc. There appeared to me the likeness of a woman, fair and comely, clothed in bright raiment, who called to me and said: O Socrates,

The third day hence to fertile Phthia, shalt thou go.

Cr. What a singular dream, Socrates!

Soc. There can be no doubt about the meaning, Crito, I think.

Cr. Yes; the meaning is only too clear. But, oh! my beloved Socrates, let me entreat you once more to take my advice and escape. For if you die I shall not only lose a friend who can never be replaced, but there is another evil: people who do not know you and me will believe that I might have saved you if I had been willing to give money, but that I did not care. Now, can there be a worse disgrace than this— that I should be thought to value money more than the life of a friend? For the many will not be persuaded that I wanted you to escape, and that you refused.

Soc. But why, my dear Crito, should we care about the opinion of the many? Good men, and they are the only persons who are worth considering, will think of these things truly as they occurred.

Cr. But you see, Socrates, that the opinion of the many must be regarded, for what is now

happening shows that they can do the greatest evil to any one who has lost their good opinion.

Soc. I only wish it were so, Crito; and that the many could do the greatest evil; for then they would also be able to do the greatest good— and what a fine thing this would be! But in reality they can do neither; for they cannot make a man either wise or foolish; and whatever they do is the result of chance.

Cr. Well, I will not dispute with you; but please to tell me, Socrates, whether you are not acting out of regard to me and your other friends: are you not afraid that if you escape from prison we may get into trouble with the informers for having stolen you away, and lose either the whole or a great part of our property; or that even a worse evil may happen to us? [45] Now, if you fear on our account, be at ease; for in order ot save you, we ought surely to run this, or even a greater risk; be persuaded, then, and do as I say.

Soc. Yes, Crito, that is one fear which you mention, but by no means the only one.

Cr. Fear not—there are persons who are willing to get you out of prison at no great cost; and as for the informers, they are far from being exorbitant in their demands—a little money will satisfy them. My means, which are certainly ample, are at your service, and if you have a scruple about spending all mine, here are strangers who will give your the use of theirs; and one of them, Simmias the Theban, has brought a large sum of money for this very purpose; and Cebes and many others are prepared to spend their money in helping you to escape. I say, therefore, do not hestitate on our account, and do not say, as you did in the court, that you will have a difficulty in knowing what to do with yourself anywhere else. For men will love you in other places to which you may go, and not in Athens only; there are friends of mine in Thessaly, if you like to go to them, who will value and protect you, and no Thessalian will give you any trouble. Nor can I think that you are at all justified, Socrates, in betraying your own life when you might be saved; in acting thus you are playing into the hands of your enemies, who are hurrying on your destruction. And further I should say that you are deserting your own children; for you might bring them up and educate them; instead of which you go away and leave them, and they will have to take their chance; and if they do not meet with the usual fate of orphans, there will be small thanks to you. No man should bring children into the world who is unwilling to perserve to the end in their nurture and education. But you appear to be choosing the easier part, but the better and manlier, which would have been more becoming in one who professes to care for virtue in all his actions, like yourself. And indeed, I am ashamed not only of you, but of us who are your friends, when I reflect that the whole business will be attributed entirely to our want of courage. The trial need never have come on, or might have been managed differently; and this last act, or crowning folly, will seem to have occurred through our negligence and cowardice, who might have saved you, [46] if we had been good for anything; and you might have saved yourself, for there was no difficulty at all. See now, Socrates, how sad and discreditable are the consequences, both to us and you. Make up your mind then, or rather have your mind already made up, for the time of deliberation is over, and there is only one thing to be done, which must be done this very night, and if we delay at all will be no longer practicable or possible; I beseech you therefore, Socrates, be persuaded by me, and do as I say.

Soc. Dear Crito, your zeal is invaluable, if a right one; but if wrong, the greater the zeal the greater the danger; and therefore we ought to consider whether I shall or shall not do as you say. For I am and always have been one of those natures who must be guided by reason, whatever the reason may be which upon reflection appears to me to be the best; and now that this chance has befallen me, I cannot repudiate my own words: the principles which I have hitherto honoured and revered I still honour, and unless we can at once find other and better principles, I am certain not to agree with you; no, not even if the power of the multitude could inflict many more imprisonments, confiscations, deaths, frightening us like children with hobgoblin terrors. What will be the fairest way of considering the question? Shall I return to your old argument about the opinions of men?—we were saying that some of them are to be regarded, and others not. Now were we right in maintaining this before I was condemned? And has the argument which was once good now proved to be talk for the sake of talking—mere childish nonsense? That is what

I want to consider with your help, Crito:— whether, under my present circumstances, the argument appears to be in any way different or not; and is to be allowed by me or disallowed. That argument, which, as I believe, is maintained by many persons of authority, was to the effect, as I was saying, that the opinions of some men are to be regarded, and of other men not to be regarded. Now you, Crito, are not going to die to-morrow—at least, [47] there is no human probability of this—and therefore you are disinterested and not liable to be deceived by the circumstances in which you are placed. Tell me then, whether I am right in saying that some opinions, and the opinions of some men only, are to be valued, and that other opinions, and the opinions of other men, are not to be valued. I ask you whether I was right in maintaining this?

Cr. Certainly.

Soc. The good are to be regarded, and not the bad?

Cr. Yes.

Soc. And the opinions of the wise are good, and the opinions of the unwise are evil?

Cr. Certainly.

Soc. And what was said about another matter? Is the pupil who devotes himself to the practice of gymnastics supposed to attend to the praise and blame and opinion of every man, or of one man only—his physician or trainer, whoever he may be?

Cr. Of one man only.

Soc. And he ought to fear the censure and welcome the praise of that one only, and not of the many?

Cr. Clearly so.

Soc. And he ought to act and train, and eat and drink in the way which seems good to his single master who has understanding, rather than according to the opinion of all other men put together?

Cr. True.

Soc. And if he disobeys and disregards the opinion and approval of the one, and regards the opinion of the many who have no understanding, will he not suffer evil?

Cr. Certainly he will.

Soc. And what will the evil be, whither tending and what affecting, in the disobedient person?

Cr. Clearly, affecting the body; that is what is destroyed by the evil.

Soc. Very good; and is not this true, Crito, of other things which we need not separately enumerate? In questions of just and unjust, fair and foul, good and evil, which are the subjects of our present consultation, ought we to follow the opinion of the many and to fear them; or the opinion of the one man who has understanding? ought we not to fear and reverence him more than all the rest of the world: and if we desert him shall we not destroy and injure that principle in us which may be assumed to be improved by justice and deteriorated by injustice;—there is such a principle?

Cr. Certainly there is, Socrates.

Soc. Take a parallel instance:—if, acting under the advice of those who have no understanding, we destroy that which is improved by health and is deteriorated by disease, would life be worth having? And that which has been destroyed is—the body?

Cr. Yes.

Soc. Could we live, having an evil and corrupted body?

Cr. Certainly not.

Soc. And will life be worth having, if that higher part of man be destroyed, which is improved by justice and depraved by injustice? Do we suppose that principle, [*48*] whatever it may be in man, which has to do with justice and injustice, to be inferior to the body?

Cr. Certainly not.

Soc. More honourable than the body?

Cr. Far more.

Soc. Then, my friend, we must not regard what the many say of us: but what he, the one man who has understanding of just and unjust, will say, and what the truth will say. And therefore you begin in error when you advise that we would regard the opinion of the many about just and unjust, good and evil, honourable and dishonourable.—"Well," some one will say, "but the many can kill us."

Cr. Yes, Socrates; that will clearly be the answer.

Soc. And it is true: but still I find with surprise that the old argument is unshaken as ever. And I should like to know whether I may say the same of another proposition—that not life, but a good life, is to be chiefly valued?

Cr. Yes, that also remains unshaken.

Soc. And a good life is equivalent to a just and honourable one—that holds also?

Cr. Yes, it does.

Soc. From these premises I proceed to argue the question whether I ought or ought not to try and escape without the consent of the Athenians: and if I am clearly right in escaping, then I will make the attempt; but if not, I will abstain. The other considerations which you mention, of money and loss of character and the duty of educating one's children, are, I fear, only the doctrines of the multitude, who would be as ready to restore people to life, if they were able, as they are to put them to death—and with as little reason. But now, since the argument has thus far prevailed, the only question which remains to be considered is, whether we shall do rightly either in escaping or in suffering others to aid to our escape and paying them in money and thanks, or whether in reality we shall not do rightly; and if the latter, then death or any other calamity which may ensure on my remaining here must not be allowed to enter into the calculation.

Cr. I think that you are right, Socrates; how then shall we proceed?

Soc. Let us consider the matter together, and do you either refute me if you can, and I will be convinced; or else cease, my dear friend, from repeating to me that I ought to escape against the wishes of the Athenians: for I highly value your attempts to persuade me to do so, but I may not be persuaded against my own better judgment. [*49*] And now please to consider my first position, and try how you can best answer me.

Cr. I will.

Soc. Are we to say that we are never intentionally to do wrong, or that in one way we ought and in another we ought not to do wrong, or is doing wrong always evil and dishonourable, as I was just now saying, and as has been already acknowledged by us? Are all our former admissions which were made within a few days to be thrown away? And have we, at our age, been earnestly discoursing with one another all our life long only to discover that we are no better than children? Or, in spite of the opinion of the many, and in spite of consequences whether better or worse, shall we insist on the truth of what was then said, that injustice is always an evil and dishonour to him who acts unjustly? Shall we say so or not?

Cr. Yes.

Soc. Then we must do no wrong?

Cr. Certainly not.

Soc. Nor when injured injure in return, as the

many imagine; for we must injure no one at all?

Cr. Clearly not.

Soc. Again, Crito, may we do evil?

Cr. Surely not, Socrates.

Soc. And what of doing evil in return for evil, which is the morality of the many—is that just or not?

Cr. Not just.

Soc. For doing evil to another is the same as injuring him?

Cr. Very true.

Soc. Then we ought not to retaliate or render evil for evil to any one, whatever evil we may have suffered from him. But I would have you consider, Crito, whether you really mean what you are saying. For this opinion has never been held, and never will be held, by any considerable number or persons; and those who are agreed and those who are not agreed upon this point have no common ground, and can only despise one another when they see how widely they differ. Tell me, then, whether you agree with and assent to my first principle, that neither injury nor retaliation nor warding off evil by evil is ever right. And shall that be the premiss of our argument? Or do you decline and dissent from this? For so I have ever thought, and continue to think; but, if you are of another opinion, let me hear what you have to say. If, however, you remain of the same mind as formerly, I will proceed to the next step.

Cr. You may proceed, for I have not changed my mind.

Soc. Then I will go on the next point, which may be put in the form of a question:—Ought a man to do what he admits to be right, or ought he to betray the right?

Cr. He ought to do what he thinks right.

Soc. But if this is true, what is the application? In leaving the prison against the will of the Athenians, [*50*] do I wrong any? or rather do I not wrong those whom I ought least to wrong? Do I not desert the principles which were acknowledged by us to be just—what do you say?

Cr. I cannot tell, Socrates; for I do not know.

Soc. Then consider the matter is this way:— Imagine that I am about to play truant (you may call the proceeding by any name which you like), and the laws and the government come and interrogate me: "Tell us, Socrates," they say; "what are you about? are you not going by an act of yours to overturn us—the laws, and the whole state, as far as in you lies? Do you imagine that a state can subsist and not be overthrown, in which the decisions of law have no power, but are set aside and trampled upon by individuals?" What will be our answer, Crito, to these and the like words? Any one, and especially a rhetorician, will have a good deal to say on behalf of the law which requires a sentence to be carried out. He will argue that this law should not be set aside; and shall we reply, "Yes; but the state has injured us and given an unjust sentence." Suppose I say that?

Cr. Very good, Socrates.

Soc. "And was that our agreement with you?" the law would answer; "or were you to abide by the sentence of the state?" And if I were to express my astonishment at their words, the law would probably add: "Answer, Socrates instead of opening your eyes—you are in the habit of asking and answering questions. Tell us,—What complaint have you to make against us which justifies you in attempting to destroy us and the state? In the first place did we not bring you into existence? Your father married your mother by our aid and begat you. Say whether you have any objection to urge against those of us who regulate marriage?" None, I shall reply. "Or against those of us who after birth regulate the nurture and education of children, in which you also were trained? Were not the laws, which have the charge of education, right in commanding your father to train you in music and gymnastic?" Right, I should reply. "Well then, since you were brought into the world and nurtured and educated by us, can you deny in the first place that you are our child and slave, as your fathers were before you? And if this is true you are not on equal terms with us; nor can you think that you have a right to do to us what we are doing to you. Would you have any right to strike or revile or do any other evil to your father or your master, if you had one, because you have been struck or reviled by him, or received some other evil at his hands?—you would not say this? [*51*] And because we think right to destroy you, do you think that you have any right to destroy us in return, and your country as far as in you lies? Will you, O professor of true virtue, pretend that you are justified in this? Has a philosopher like you failed to discover that our country is more to be valued and higher and holier far than mother or father or any ancestor, and more to be regarded in the eyes of the gods and of men of understanding? also to be soothed, and gently and reverently entreated when angry, even more than a father, and either to be persuaded, or if not persuaded, to be obeyed? And when we are punished by her, whether with imprisonment or stripes, the punishment is to be endured in silence: and if she leads us to wounds or death in battle, thither we follow as is right; neither may any one yield or retreat or leave his rank, but whether in battle or in a court of law, or in any other place, he must do what his city and his country order him; or he must change their view of what is just: and if he may do no violence to his father or mother, much less may he do violence to his country." What answer shall we make to this, Crito? Do the laws speak truly, or do they not?

Cr. I think that they do.

Soc. Then the laws will say, "Consider, Socrates, if we are speaking truly that in your present attempt you are going to do us an injury. For, having brought you into the world, and nurtured and educated you, and given you and every other citizen a share in every good which we had to give, we further proclaim to any Athenian by the liberty which we allow him, that if he does not like us when he has become of age and has seen the ways of the city, and made our acquaintance, he may go where he pleases and take his goods with him. None of us laws will forbid him or interfere with him. Any one who does not like us and the city, and who wants to emigrate to a colony or to any other city, may go where he likes, retaining his property. But he who has experience of the manner in which we order justice and administer the state, and still remains, has entered into an implied contract that he will do as we command him. And he who disobeys us is, as we maintain, thrice wrong; first, because in disobeying us he is disobeying his parents; secondly, because we are the authors of his education; thirdly, because he has made an agreement with us that he will duly obey our commands; [52] and he neither obeys them nor convinces us that our commands are unjust; and we do not rudely impose them, but give him the alternative of obeying or convincing us;—that is what we offer, and he does neither.

"These are the sort of accusations to which, as we were saying, you, Socrates, will be exposed if you accomplish your intentions; you above all other Atheniams." Suppose now I ask, why I rather than anybody else? they will justly retort upon me that I above all other men have acknowledged the agreement. "There is clear proof," they will say, "Socrates, that we and the city were not displeasing to you. Of all Athenians you have been the most constant resident in the city, which, as you never leave, you may be supposed to love. For you never went out of the city either to see the games, except once when you went to the Isthmus, or to any other place unless when you were on military service; nor did you travel as other men do. Nor had you any curiosity to know other states or their laws: your affections did not go beyond us and our state; we were your special favourites, and you acquiesced in our government of you; and here in this city you begat your children, which is a proof of your satisfaction. Moreover, you might in the course of the trial, if you had liked, have fixed the penalty at banishment; the state which refuses to let you go now would have let you go then. But you pretended that you preferred death to exile, and that you were not unwilling to die. And now you have forgotten these fine sentiments, and pay no respect to us the laws, of whom you are the destroyer; and are doing what only a miserable slave would do, running away and turning your back upon the compacts and agreements which you made as a citizen. And first of all answer this very question: Are we right in saying that you agreed to be governed according to us in deed, and not in word only? Is that true or not?" How shall we answer, Crito? Must we not assent?

Cr. We cannot help it, Socrates.

Soc. Then will they not say: "You, Socrates, are breaking the covenants and agreements which you made with us at your leisure, not in any haste or under any compulsion or deception, but after you have had seventy years to think of them, during which time you were at liberty to leave the city, if we were not to your mind, or if our covenants appeared to you to be unfair. You had your choice, and might have gone either to Lacedaemon or Crete, both which states are often praised by you for their good government, [53] or to some other Hellenic or foreign state. Whereas you, above all other Athenians, seemed to be so fond of the state, or, in other words, of us her laws (and who would care about a state which has no laws?), that you never stirred out of her; the halt, the blind, the maimed were not more stationary in her than you were. And now you run away and forsake your agreements. Not so, Socrates, if you will take our advice; do not make yourself ridiculous by escaping out of the city.

"For just consider, if you transgress and err in this sort of way, what good will you do either to yourself or to your friends? That your friends will be driven into exile and deprived of citizenship, or will lose their property, is tolerably certain; and you yourself, if you fly to one of the neighbouring cities, as, for example, Thebes or Megara, both of which are well governed, will come to them as an enemy, Socrates, and their government will be against you, and all patriotic citizens will cast an evil eye upon you as a subverter of the laws, and you will confirm in the minds of the judges the justice of their own condemnation of you. For he who is a corrupter of the laws is more than likely to be a corrupter of the young and foolish portion of mankind. Will you then flee from well-ordered cities and virtuous men? and its existence worth having on these terms? Or will you go to them without shame, and talk to them, Socrates? And what will you say to them? What you say here about virtue and justice and institutions and laws being the best things among men? Would that be decent of you? Surely not. But if you go away from well-governed states to Crito's friends in Thessaly, where there is a great disorder and licence, they will be charmed to hear the tale of your escape from prison, set off with ludicrous particulars of the manner in which you were wrapped in a goatskin or some other disguise, and metamorphosed as the manner is of runaways; but will there be no one to remind you that in your old age you were not ashamed to violate the most sacred laws from a miserable desire of a little more life? Perhaps not, if you keep them in a good temper; but if they are out of temper you will hear many degrading things; you will live, but how?—as the flatterer of all men, and the servant of all men; and doing what?—eating and drinking in Thessaly, having gone abroad in order that you may get a dinner. And where will be your fine sentiments about justice and virtue? [54] Say that you wish to live for the sake of your children—you want to bring them up and educate them—will you take them into Thessaly, and deprive them of Athenian citizenship? Is this the benefit which you will confer upon them? Or are you under the impression that they will be better cared for and educated here if you are still alive, although absent from them; for your friends will take care of them? Do you fancy that if you are an inhabitant of Thessaly they will take care of them, and if you are an inhabitant of the other world that they will not take care of them? Nay; but if they who call themselves friends are good for anything, they will—to be sure they will.

"Listen, then, Socrates, to us who have brought you up. Think not of life and children first, and of justice afterwards, but of justice first, that you may be justified before the princes of the world below. For neither will you nor any that belong to you be happier or holier or juster in this life, or happier in another, if you do as Crito bids. Now you depart in innocence, a sufferer and not a doer of evil; a victim, not of the laws but of men. But if you go forth, returning evil for evil, and injury for injury, breaking the convenants and agreements which you have made with us, and wronging those whom you ought least of all to wrong, that is to say, yourself, your friends, your country, and us, we shall be angry with you while you live, and our brethren, the laws in the world below, will receive you as an enemy; for they will know that you have done your best to destroy us. Listen, then, to us and not to Crito."

This, dear Crito, is the voice which I seem to hear murmuring in my ears, like the sound of the flute in the ears of the mystic; that voice, I say, is humming in my ears, and prevents me from hearing any other. And I know that anything more which you may say will be vain. Yet speak, if you have anything to say.

Cr. I have nothing to say, Socrates.

Soc. Leave me then, Crito, to fulfil the will of God, and to follow whither he leads.

Phaedo: Introduction

Three previous dialogues have given us a clear idea of the personality and philosophy of Socrates as they were seen by Plato. In the *Euthyphro,* we found a clear example of the Socratic method, as Socrates mercilessly questioned a man who appeared to be absolutely certain of his moral convictions. In the *Apology,* we witnessed the trial in which the Athenian society asserted its rights on the rebellious philosopher who had spent almost fifty years questioning and analyzing its dogmas and institutions. Lastly, in the *Crito,* we listened to the complex conversation between Crito and Socrates in which the relationship between the individual and society was exhaustively examined. At the conclusion of the *Crito,* Socrates affirmed his intention to remain in prison and await his execution. The voice of "the Laws" has prevailed over all other voices:

> This, dear Crito, is the voice which I seem to hear murmuring in my ears, like the sound of the flute in the ears of the mystic; that voice, I say, is humming in my ears, and prevents me from hearing any other . . . Leave me then, Crito, to fulfill the will of God, and to follow whither he leads.

The divine presence, his "god," led him directly to his death, but only, he thought, to a physical death, because beyond death he expected to find eternal life. Far from him now are the uncertainties of the *Apology.* We should remember that during the trial, he had been unable to come to a firm conclusion about the meaning of death. "Either death is a state of nothing and utter unconsciousness or, as men say, there is a change and migration of the soul from this world to another," Socrates had said at the conclusion of the *Apology*. In truth, faithful to his life-long questioning, now under a death sentence, he still did not know the real meaning of death. But as the moment approached, his perplexity was replaced by a profound conviction that death can only be a migration of the soul away from the body into another world. This is, at any rate, the thought that permeates the pages of the *Phaedo*.

In this dialogue, Socrates conceives of the human being as body and soul. The body is the despicable prison where the soul is forced to live for a short time, and death is the happy moment when the soul is finally released from the fetters of the physical world. The fundamental task of the philosopher is "to dissever the soul from the communion of the body," and philosophy is defined as the preparation for dying. In the *Phaedo*, there is much talk about "purification," "a world beyond," "an eternal soul," "the evils of the body," "the judgment of the gods," and so forth. These ideas reveal an adherence to a profoundly dualistic conception of human nature: man is his soul and has a body. The Socrates of the *Phaedo* dies, then, convinced of the immortality of his soul, of the insignificance of physical existence, of the unreliability of sense-experience, and of the providential presence of God, or the gods, in the affairs of good people.

Before reading the *Phaedo*, there are, however, two points which should be kept in mind. First, let us be aware of the fact that it was written many years after Socrates' death. It does not belong, therefore, to the group of Socratic dialogues to which the three previous dialogues belong. It is, accordingly, most probable that many of the dualistic and spiritual ideas expressed by Socrates in the *Phaedo* are in reality Plato's own ideas. It is because of this circumstance that the *Phaedo* has been called the most Platonic of Plato's dialogues. As such, it served to shape the development of Platonism during many subsequent centuries, and many of its ideas can be found in the writings of religious writers even in our own times.

Secondly, it is also important to bear in mind that the historical setting of the dialogue was merely a convenient means employed by Plato to convey those thoughts which he deemed to be most essential for a philosopher. The Socrates of the *Phaedo* emerges then, as the ideal philosopher who has finally overcome the physical world and is free to surrender himself to a higher world.

The *Phaedo* takes place in the prison where Socrates has been kept for one month. Certain religious festivities of the Athenians have delayed his execution. Friends and acquaintances have gathered around the venerable old man in order to accompany him during his last moments. Crito, of course, is there. Two Pythagoreans, Cebes and Simmias, are also present. Socrates has rejected all fear, and wishes to confront reality. The conversation slowly drifts towards the subject of death. This is the point in our brief selections, where we first begin to hear Socrates' voice. The entire account of the conversation and the events is told by a man named Phaedo, who was with Socrates until the last moment. Echecrates, Phaedo's friend, is the silent listener throughout the dialogue.

Plato: Phaedo

In matters of this sort philosophers, above all other men, may be observed in every sort of way to separate the soul from the communion [65] of the body.

Very true.

Whereas, Simmias, the rest of the world are of opinion that to him who has no sense of pleasure and no part in bodily pleasure, life is not worth having; and that he who is indifferent about them is as good as dead.

That is also true.

What again shall we say of the actual acquirement of knowledge?—is the body, if invited to share in the enquiry, a hinderer or a helper? I mean to say, have sight and hearing any truth in them? Are they not as the poets are always telling us, inaccurate witnesses? and yet, if even they are inaccurate and indistinct, what is to be said of the other senses?—for you will allow that they are the best of them?

Certainly, he replied.

Then when does the soul attain truth?—for in attempting to consider anything in company with the body she is obviously deceived.

True.

Then must not true existence be revealed to her in thought, if at all?

Yes.

And thought is best when the mind is gathered into herself and none of these things trouble her—neither sounds nor sights nor pain nor any pleasure,—when she takes leave of the body, and has as little as possible to do with it, when she has no bodily sense or desire, but is aspiring after true being?

Certainly.

And in this the philosopher dishonours the body; his soul runs away from his body and desires to be alone and by herself?

That is true.

Well, but there is another thing, Simmias: Is there or is there not an absolute justice?

Assuredly there is.

And an absolute beauty and absolute good?

Of course.

But did you ever behold any of them with your eyes?

Certainly not.

Or did you ever reach them with any other bodily sense?—and I speak not of these alone, but of absolute greatness, and health, and strength, and of the essence or true nature of everything. Has the reality of them ever been perceived by you through the bodily organs? or rather, is not the nearest approach to the knowledge of their several natures made by him who so orders his intellectual vision as to have the most exact conception of the essence of each thing which he considers?

Certainly.

And he attains to the purest knowledge of them who goes to each with the mind alone, not introducing or intruding in the act of thought sight or any other sense together with reason, but with the very light of the mind in her own clearness searches into the very [66] truth of each; he who has got rid, as far as he can, of eyes and ears and, so to speak, of the whole body, these being in his opinion distracting elements which when they infect the soul hinder her from acquiring truth and knowledge—who, if not he, is likely to attain to the knowledge of true being?

What you say has a wonderful truth in it, Socrates, replied Simmias.

And when real philosophers consider all

these things, will they not be led to make a reflection which they will express in words something like the following? "Have we not found," they will say, "a path of thought which seems to bring us and our argument to the conclusion, that while we are in the body, and while the soul is infected with the evils of the body, our desire will not be satisfied? and our desire is of the truth. For the body is a source of endless trouble to us by reason of the mere requirement of food; and is liable also in the search after true being: it fills us full of lies, and lusts, and fears, and fancies of all kinds, and endless foolery, and in fact, as men say, takes away from us the power of thinking at all. Whence come wars, and fightings, and factions? whence but from the body and the lusts of the body? Wars are occasioned by the love of money, and money has to be acquired for the sake and in the service of the body; and by reason of all these impediments we have no time to give to philosophy; and, last and worst of all, even if we are at leisure and betake ourselves to some speculation, the body is always breaking in upon us causing turmoil and confusion in our enquiries, and so amazing us that we are prevented from seeing the truth. It has been proved to us by experience that if we would have pure knowledge of anything we must be quit of the body—the soul in herself must behold things in themselves: and then we shall attain the wisdom which we desire, and of which we say that we are lovers; not while we live, but after death; for if while in company with the body, the soul cannot have pure knowledge, one of two things follows—either knowledge is not to be attained at all, or, if at all, [67] after death. For then, and not till then, the soul will be parted from the body and exist in herself alone. In this present life, I reckon that we make the nearest approach to knowledge when we have the least possible intercourse or communion with the body, and are not surfeited with the bodily nature, but keep ourselves pure until the hour when God himself is pleased to release us. And thus having got rid of the foolishness of the body we shall be pure and hold converse with the pure, and know of ourselves the clear light everywhere, which is no other than the light of truth." For the impure are not permitted to approach the pure. These are the sort of words, Simmias, which the true lovers of knowledge cannot help saying to one another, and thinking. You would agree; would you not?

Undoubedly, Socrates.

But, O my friend, if this be true, there is great reason to hope that, going whither I go when I have come to the end of my journey, I shall attain that which has been the pursuit of my life. And therefore I go on my way rejoicing, and not I only, but every other man who believes that his mind has been made ready and that he is in a manner purified.

Certainly, replied Simmias.

And what is purification but the separation of the soul from the body, as I was saying before; the habit of the soul gathering and collecting herself into herself from all sides out of the body; the dwelling in her own place alone, as in another life, so also in this, as far as she can;—the release of the soul from the chains of the body?

Very true, he said.

And this separation and release of the soul from the body is termed death?

To be sure, he said.

And the true philosophers, and they only, are ever seeking to release the soul. Is not the separation and release of the soul from the body their special study?

That is true.

And, as I was saying at first, there would be a ridiculous contradiction in men studying to live as nearly as they can in a state of death, and yet repining when it comes upon them.

Clearly.

And the true philosophers, Simmias, are always occupied in the practice of dying, wherefore also to them least of all men is death terrible. Look at the matter thus:—if they have been in every way the enemies of the body, and are wanting to be alone with the soul, when this desire of theirs is granted, how inconsistent would they be if they trembled and repined, instead of rejoicing at their departure to that place where, when they arrive, they hope to gain that which in life they desired—and this was wisdom—and at the [68] same time to be rid of the company of their enemy. Many a man has been willing to go to the world below animated by the hope of seeing there an earthly love, or wife, or son, and conversing with them. And will he who is a true lover of wisdom, and is strongly persuaded in like manner that only in the world below he can worthily enjoy her, still repine at death? Will he not depart with joy? Surely he will, O my friend, if he be a true philosopher. For he will have a firm conviction that there, and there only, he can find wisdom in her purity. And if this be true, he would be very absurd, as I was saying, if he were afraid of death.

He would indeed, replied Simmias.

And when you see a man who is repining at the approach of death, is not his reluctance a sufficient proof that he is not a lover of wisdom, but a lover of the body, and probably at the same time a lover of either money or power, or both?

Quite so, he replied.

When I was young, Cebes, I had a prodigious desire to know that department of philosophy which is called the investigation of nature; to know the causes of things, and why a thing is and is created or destroyed appeared to me to be a lofty profession; and I was always agitating myself with the consideration of questions such as these:—Is the growth of animals the result of some decay which the hot and cold principle contracts, as some have said? Is the blood the element with which we think, or the air, or the fire? or perhaps nothing of the kind—but the brain may be the originating power of the perceptions of hearing and sight and smell, and memory and opinion may come from them and science may be based on memory and opinion when they have attained fixity. And then I went on to examine the corruption of them, and then to the things of heaven and earth, and at last I concluded myself to be utterly and absolutely incapable of these enquiries, as I will satisfactorily prove to you. For I was fascinated by them to such a degree that my eyes grew blind to things which I had seemed to myself, and also to others, to know quite well; I forgot what I had before thought self-evident truths; e.g. such a fact as that the growth of man is the result of eating and drinking; for when by the digestion of food flesh is added to flesh and bone to bone, and whenever there is an aggregation of congenial elements, the lesser bulk becomes larger and the small man great. Was not that a reasonable notion?

Yes, said Cebes, I think so.

Well; but let me tell you something more. There was a time when I thought that I understood the meaning of greater and less pretty well; and when I saw a great man standing by a little one, I fancied that one was taller than the other by a head; or one horse would appear to be greater than another horse: and still more clearly did I seem to perceive that ten is two more than eight, and that two cubits are more than one, because two is the double of one.

And what is now your notion of such matters? said Cebes.

I should be far enough from imagining, he replied, that I knew the cause of any of them, by heaven I should; for I cannot satisfy myself that, [97] when one is added to one, the one to which the addition is made becomes two, or that the two units added together make two by reason of the addition. I cannot understand how, when separated from the other, each of them was one and not two, and now, when they are brought together, the mere juxtaposition or meeting of them should be the cause of their becoming two: neither can I understand how the vision of one is the way to make two; for then a different cause would produce the same effect,—as in the former instance the addition and juxtaposition of one to one was the cause of two, in this the separation and subtraction of one from the other would be the cause. Nor am I any longer satisfied that I understand the reason why one or anything else is either generated or destroyed or is at all, but I have in my mind some confused notion of a new method, and can never admit the other.

Then I heard some one reading, as he said, from a book of Anaxagoras, that mind was the disposer and cause of all, and I was delighted at this notion, which appeared quite admirable, and I said to myself: If mind is the disposer, mind will dispose all for the best, and put each particular in the best place; and I argued that if any one desired to find out the cause of the generation or destruction or existence of anything, he must find out what state of being or doing or suffering was best for that thing, and therefore a man had only to consider the best for himself and others, and then he would also know the worse, since the same science comprehended both. And I rejoiced to think that I had found in Anaxagoras a teacher of the causes of existence such as I desired, and I imagined that he would tell me first whether the earth is flat or round; and whichever was true, he would proceed to explain the cause and the necessity of this being so, and then he would teach me the nature of the best and show that this was best; and if he said that the earth was in the centre, he would further explain that this position was the best, and I should be satisfied with the explanation given, and not want any other sort of cause. [*98*] And I thought that I would then go on and ask him about the sun and moon and stars, and that he would explain to me their comparative swiftness, and their returnings and various states, active and passive, and how all of them were for the best. For I could not imagine that when he spoke of mind as the disposer of them, he would give any other account of their being as they are, except that this was best; and I thought that when he had explained to me in detail the cause of each and the cause of all, he would go on to explain to me what was best for each and what was good for all. These hopes I would not have sold for a large sum of money, and I seized the books and read them as fast as I could in my eagerness to know the better and the worse.

What expectations I had formed, and how grievously was I disappointed! As I proceeded, I found my philosopher altogether forsaking mind or any other principle of order, but having recourse to air, and ether, and water, and other eccentricities. I might compare him to a person who began by maintaining generally that mind is the cause of the actions of Socrates, but who, when he endeavoured to explain the causes of my several actions in detail, went on to show that I sit here because my body is made up of bones and muscles; and the bones as he would say, are hard and have joints which divide them, and the muscles are elastic, and they cover the bones, which have also a covering or environment of flesh and skin which contains them; and as the bones are lifted at their joints by the contraction or relaxation of the muscles, I am able to bend my limbs, and this is why I am sitting here in a curved posture —that is what he would say; and he would have a similar explanation of my talking to you, which he would attribute to sound, and air, and hearing, and he would assign ten thousand other causes of the same sort, forgetting to mention the true cause, which is, that the Athenians have thought fit to condemn me; and accordingly I have thought it better and more right to remain here and undergo my sentence; [*99*] for I am inclined to think that these muscles and bones of mine would have gone off long ago to Megara or Boeotia—by the dog,

they would, if they had been moved only by their own idea of what was best, and if I had not chosen the better and nobler part, instead of playing truant and running away, of enduring any punishment which the state inflicts. There is surely a strange confusion of causes and conditions in all this. It may be said, indeed, that without bones and muscles and the other parts of the body I cannot execute my purposes. But to say that I do as I do because of them, and that this is the way in which mind acts, and not from the choice of the best, is a very careless and idle mode of speaking. I wonder that they cannot distinguish the cause from the condition, which the many, feeling about in the dark, are always mistaking and misnaming. And thus one man makes a vortex all round and steadies the earth by the heaven; another gives the air as a support to the earth, which is a sort of broad trough. Any power which in arranging them as they are arranges them for the best never enters into their minds; and instead of finding any superior strength in it, they rather expect to discover another Atlas of the world who is stronger and more everlasting and more containing than the good;—of the obligatory and containing power of the good they think nothing; and yet this is the principle which I would fain learn if any one would teach me. But as I have failed either to discover myself, or to learn of any one else, the nature of the best, I will exhibit to you, if you like, what I have found to be the second best mode of enquiring into the cause.

I should very much like to hear, he replied.

Socrates proceeded: I thought that as I had failed in the contemplation of true existence, I ought to be careful that I did not lose the eye of my soul; as people may injure their bodily eye by observing and gazing on the sun during an eclipse, unless they take the precaution of only looking at the image reflected in the water, or in some medium. So in my own case, I was afraid that my soul might be blinded altogether if I looked at things with my eyes or tried to apprehend them by the help of the senses. And I thought that I had better have recourse to the world of mind and seek there the truth of existence. [*100*] I dare say that the simile is not perfect—for I am very far from admitting that he who contemplates existences through the medium of thought, sees them only "through a glass darkly," any more than he who considers them in action and operation. However, this was the method which I adopted: I first assumed some principle which I judged to be the strongest, and then I affirmed as true whatever seemed to agree with this, whether relating to the cause or to anything else; and that which disagreed I regarded as untrue. But I should like to explain my meaning more clearly, as I do not think that you as yet understand me.

No indeed, replied Cebes, not very well.

There is nothing new, he said, in what I am about to tell you; but only what I have been always and everywhere repeating in the previous discussion and on other occasions: I want to show you the nature of that cause which has occupied my thoughts. I shall have to go back to those familiar words which are in the mouth of every one, and first of all assume that there is an absolute beauty and goodness and greatness, and the like; grant me this, and I hope to be able to show you the nature of the cause, and to prove the immortality of the soul.

Cebes said: You may proceed at once with the proof, for I grant you this.

Well, he said, then I should like to know whether you agree with me in the next step: for I cannot help thinking, if there be anything beautiful other than absolute beauty should there be such, that it can be beautiful only in so far as it partakes of absolute beauty—and I should say the same of everything. Do you agree in this notion of the cause?

Yes, he said, I agree.

He proceeded: I know nothing and can understand nothing of any other of those wise causes which are alleged; and if a person says to me that the bloom of colour, or form, or any such thing is a source of beauty, I leave all that, which is only confusing to me, and simply and singly, and perhaps foolishly, hold and am assured in my own mind that nothing makes a thing beautiful but the presence and participation of beauty in whatever way or manner obtained; for as to the manner I am uncertain, but I stoutly contend that by beauty all beautiful things become beautiful. This appears to me to be the safest answer which I can give, either to myself or to another, and to this I cling, in the persuasion that this principle will never be overthrown, and that to myself or to any one who asks the question, I may safely reply, That by beauty beautiful things become beautiful. Do you not agree with me?

I do.

And that by greatness only great things become great and greater, and by smallness the less become less?

True.

Then if a person were to remark that A is taller by a head than B, [*101*] and B less by a head than A, you would refuse to admit his statement, and would stoutly contend that what you mean is only that the greater is greater by, and by reason of, greatness, and the less is less only by, and by reason of, smallness; and thus you would avoid the danger of saying that the greater is greater and the less less by the measure of the head, which is the same in both, and would also avoid the monstrous absurdity of supposing that the greater man is greater by reason of the head, which is small. You would be afraid to draw such an inference, would you not?

Indeed, I should, said Cebes, laughing.

In like manner you would be afraid to say that ten exceeded eight by, and by reason of, two; but would say by, and by reason of, number; or you would say that two cubits exceed one cubit not by a half, but by magnitude?—for there is the same liability to error in all these cases.

Very true, he said.

Again, would you not be cautious of affirming that the addition of one to one, or the division of one, is the cause of two? And you would loudly asseverate that you know of no ways in which anything comes into existence except by participation in duality—this is the way to make two, and the participation in one is the way to make one. You would say: I will let alone puzzles of division and addition—wiser heads than mine may answer them; inexperienced as I am, and ready to start, as the proverb says, at my own shadow, I cannot afford to give up the sure ground of a principle. And if any one assails you there, you would not mind him, or answer him until you had seen whether the consequences which follow agree with one another or not, and when you are further required to give an explanation of this principle, you would go on to assume a higher principle, and a higher, until you found a resting-place in the best of the higher; but you would not confuse the principle and the consequences in your reasoning, like the Eristics—at least if you wanted to discover real existence. Not that this confusion signifies to them, who never care or think about the matter at all, for they have the wit to be well pleased with themselves however great may be the turmoil of their ideals. [*102*] But you, if you are a philosopher, will certainly do as I say.

What you say is most true, said Simmias and Cebes, both speaking at once.

But then, O my friends, he said, if the soul is really immortal, what care should be taken of her, not only in respect of the portion of time which is called life, but of eternity! And the danger of neglecting her from this point of view does indeed appear to be awful. If death had only been the end of all, the wicked would have had a good bargain in dying, for they would have been happily quit not only of their body, but of their own evil together with their souls. But now, inasmuch as the soul is manifestly immortal, there is no release or salvation from evil except the attainment of the highest virtue and wisdom. For the soul when on her progress to the world below takes nothing with her but nurture and education; and these are said greatly to benefit or greatly to injure the departed, at the very beginning of his journey thither.

For after death, as they say, the genius of each individual, to whom he belonged in life, leads him to a certain place in which the dead are gathered together, whence after judgment has been given they pass into the world below, following the guide, who is appointed to conduct them from this world to the other: and when they have there received their due and remained their time, another guide brings them back again after many revolutions of ages. Now this way to the other world is not, [*108*] as Aeschylus says in the *Telephus,* a single and straight path—if that were so no guide would be needed, for no one could miss it; but there are many partings of the road, and windings, as I infer from the rites and sacrifices which are offered to the gods below in places where three ways meet on earth. The wise and orderly soul follows in the straight path and is conscious of her surroundings; but the soul which desires the body, and which, as I was relating before, has long been fluttering about the lifeless frame and the world of sight, is after many struggles and many sufferings hardly and with violence carried away by her attendant genius; and when she arrives at the place where the other

souls are gathered, if she be impure and have done impure deeds, whether foul murders or other crimes which are the brothers of these, and the works of brothers in crime—from that soul every one flees and turns away; no one will be her companion, no one her guide, but alone she wanders in extremity of evil until certain times are fulfilled, and when they are fulfilled, she is borne irresistibly to her own fitting habitation; as every pure and just soul which has passed through life in the company and under the guidance of the gods has also her own proper home.

A man of sense ought not to say, nor will I be very confident, that the description which I have given to the soul and her mansions is exactly true. But I do say that, inasmuch as the soul is shown to be immortal, he may venture to think, not improperly or unworthily, that something of the kind is true. The venture is a glorious one, and he ought to comfort himself with words like these, which is the reason why I lengthen out the tale. Wherefore, I say, let a man be of good cheer about his soul, who having cast away the pleasures and ornaments of the body as alien to him and working harm rather than good, has sought after the pleasures of knowledge; and has arrayed the soul, not in some foreign attire, but in her own proper jewels, temperance, and justice, and courage, and nobility, [*115*] and truth—in these adorned she is ready to go on her journey to the world below, when her hour comes. You Simmias and Cebes, and all other men, will depart at some time or other. Me already, as a tragic poet would say, the voice of fate calls. Soon I must drink the poison; and I think that I had better repair to the bath first, in order that the women may not have the trouble of washing my body after I am dead. . . .

When he had done speaking, Crito said: And have you any commands for us, Socrates—anything to say about your children, or any other matter in which we can serve you?

Nothing particular, Crito, he replied: only, as I have always told you, take care of yourselves; that is a service which you may be ever rendering to me and mine and to all of us, whether you promise to do so or not. But if you have no thought for yourselves, and care not to walk according to the rule which I have prescribed for you, not now for the first time, however much you may profess or promise at the moment, it will be of no avail.

We will do our best, said Crito: And in what way shall we bury you?

In any way that you like; but you must get hold of me, and take care that I do not run away from you. Then he turned to us and added with a smile:—I cannot make Crito believe that I am the same Socrates who have been talking and conducting the argument; he fancies that I am the other Socrates whom he will soon see, a dead body—and he asks, How shall he bury me? And though I have spoken many words in the endeavour to show that when I have drunk the poison I shall leave you and go to the joys of the blessed,—these words of mine, with which I was comforting you and myself, have had, as I perceive, no effect upon Crito. And therefore I want you to be surety for me to him now, as at the trial he was surety to the judges for me: but let the promise be of another sort; for he was surety for me to the judges that I would remain, and you must be my surety to him that I shall not remain, but go away and depart; and not be grieved when he sees my body being burned or buried. I would not have him sorrow at my hard lot, or say at the burial, Thus we lay out Socrates, or, Thus we follow him to the grave or bury him; for false words are not only evil in themselves, but they infect the soul with evil. Be of good cheer then, my dear Crito, and say that you are burying my body only, [*116*] and do with that whatever is usual, and what you think best.

When he had spoken these words, he arose and went into a chamber to bathe; Crito followed him and told us to wait. So we remained behind, talking and thinking of the subject of discourse, and also of the greatness of our sorrow; he was like a father of whom we were being bereaved, and we were about to pass the rest of our lives as orphans. When he had taken the bath his children were brought to him—(he had two young sons and an elder one); and the women of his family also came, and he talked to them and gave them a few directions in the presence of Crito; then he dismissed them and returned to us.

Now the hour of sunset was near, for a good deal of time had passed while he was within. When he came out, he sat down with us again after his bath, but not much was said. Soon the jailer, who was the servant of the Eleven, entered and stood by him, saying:—To you, Socrates, whom I know to be the noblest and gentlest and best of all who ever came to this place, I will not impute the angry feelings of other men, who rage and swear at me, when, in obedience to the authorities, I bid them drink the poison—indeed, I am sure that you will not be angry with me; for others, as you are aware, and not I, are to blame. And so fare you well, and try to bear lightly what must needs be—you know my errand. Then bursting into tears he turned away and went out.

Socrates looked at him and said: I return your good wishes, and will do as you bid. Then turning to us, he said, How charming the man is: since I have been in prison he has always been coming to see me, and at times he would talk to me, and was as good to me as could be, and now see how generously he sorrows on my account. We must do as he says, Crito; and therefore let the cup be brought, if the poison is prepared: if not, let the attendant prepare some.

Yet, said Crito, the sun is still upon the hilltops, and I know that many a one has taken the draught late, and after the announcement has been made to him, he has eaten and drunk, and enjoyed the society of his beloved; do not hurry—there is time enough.

Socrates said: Yes, Crito, and they of whom you speak are right in so acting, for they think that they will be gainers by the delay; but I am right in not following their example, for I do not think that I should gain anything by drinking the poison a little later; [*117*] I should only be ridiculous in my own eyes for sparing and saving a life which is already forfeit. Please then to do as I say, and not to refuse me.

Crito made a sign to the servant, who was standing by; and he went out, and having been absent for some time, returned with the jailer carrying the cup of poison. Socrates said: You, my good friend, who are experienced in these matters, shall give me directions how I am to proceed. The man answered: You have only to walk about until your legs are heavy, and then to lie down, and the poison will act. At the same time he handed the cup to Socrates, who in the easiest and gentlest manner, without the least fear or change of colour or feature, looking at the man with all his eyes, Echecrates, as his manner was, took the cup and said: What do you say about making a libation out of this cup to any god? May I, or not? The man answered:

We only prepare, Socrates, just so much as we deem enough. I understand, he said: but I may and must ask the gods to prosper my journey from this to the other world—even so—and so be it according to my prayer. Then raising the cup to his lips, quite readily and cheerfully he drank off the poison. And hitherto most of us had been able to control our sorrow; but now when we saw him drinking, and saw too that he had finished the draught, we could no longer forbear, and in spite of myself my own tears were flowing fast; so that I covered my face and wept, not for him, but at the thought of my own calamity in having to part from such a friend. Nor was I the first; for Crito, when he found himself unable to restrain his tears, had got up, and I followed; and at that moment, Apollodorus, who had been weeping all the time, broke out in a loud and passionate cry which made cowards of us all. Socrates alone remained his calmness: What is this strange outcry? he said. I sent away the women mainly in order that they might not misbehave in this way, for I have been told that a man should die in peace. Be quiet then, and have patience. When we heard his words we were ashamed, and refrained our tears; and he walked about until, as he said, his legs began to fail, and then he lay on his back, according to the directions, and the man who gave him the poison now and then looked at his feet and legs; and after a while he pressed his foot hard, and asked him if he could feel; and he said, [*118*] No; and then his leg, and so upwards and upwards, and showed us that he was cold and stiff. And he felt them himself, and said: When the poison reaches the heart, that will be the end. He was beginning to grow cold about the groin, when he uncovered his face, for he had covered himself up, and said—they were his last words—he said: Crito, I owe a cock to Asclepius; will you remember to pay the debt? The debt shall be paid, said Crito; is there anything else? There was no answer to this question; but in a minute or two a movement was heard, and the attendents uncovered him; his eyes were set, and Crito closed his eyes and mouth.

Such was the end, Echecrates, of our friend; concerning whom I may truly say, that of all the men of his time whom I have known, he was the wisest and justest and best.

The Republic: Introduction

Plato's *Republic* ranks among the greatest works in the history of philosophy. It has been extremely influential on later thinkers, and this, combined with its great length and complexity, makes it difficult to summarize. Since we cannot do justice to it as a whole, we have selected those parts of the work which present Plato as a social scientist and which relate that aspect of his thought to his philosophy as a whole.

The ostensible theme of the *Republic* is the definition of justice. The underlying practical concern seems to be with the perennial problem of how to prevent the corruption of political leaders. In the course of dealing with these issues, Plato manages to touch upon just about every issue in the philosophical repertory.

There are those who deny the meaningfulness of the concept of justice, those who treat it merely as a legal concept, and finally, there is the Platonic attempt to present justice as both a meaningful concept and as a moral and political absolute. To establish this conclusion Plato has Socrates and his companions examine the foundations of social and political life. Society, it is argued, requires a division of labor. This division is explained in terms of the *myth of the metals*. Some individuals are motivated primarily by the desire for pleasure and pain, and as such form the bulk of the population. A second group is motivated primarily by the desire for honor and glory, what we would call status. This group will form the auxiliaries who protect the state and maintain order. A third group, comprising potential philosopher-kings, is motivated by the desire for knowledge. It is among this latter group that the best rulers, the guardians, will be found. In order to prevent corruption, Socrates describes a special system of education for the guardians, including both auxiliaries and philosopher-kings, and he prescribes a communal life style for them. That is, they are not allowed to own private property and they may not have families in the ordinary sense. Obviously no ordinary, corruptible person would even want to be a ruler under these circumstances. The remainder of society would pursue their routine activities including wealth and family ties, but they would not be permitted any power. Finally, it is made clear that being a ruler would be based upon merit, so that women and the children of the ordinary citizens would also qualify for membership in the ruling class.

Having solved the problem of corruption, Socrates returns to the definition of justice. A just society is one in which each of the parts works harmoniously with the others. A just individual is one in whom the various human needs are harmonized. In both cases the harmony is the work of reason. Of course it is a special kind of reason that grasps the ultimate "good." If we could know the ultimate good, all of our problems would be solved without friction. The existence of disagreement is symptomatic of the fact that we have not found it. Here Plato draws the ever-present analogy with mathematics. We do not argue and have clashes of opinion in mathematics; likewise, there may be one accepted answer even in the case of politics and ethics. In the example of the *divided line*, Plato draws an analogy between the axioms of mathematics and a knowledge of the ultimate good. Once we know the axioms we can prove everything. Plato seems to be an élitist in his belief that only some persons can achieve insight into the ultimate good (the *myth of the cave*), just as only some individuals are capable of discovering the great truths of the physical world. We would call such people geniuses. Our inability to duplicate their feats naturally makes us suspicious if not jealous, and this is why the philosopher-king leads a fragile existence. It may even be the case, he writes, that in a perfect society ruled by philosopher-kings, most people would not understand the reasoning behind policies, and the rulers would have to employ myths, comparable perhaps to stories we tell children: this society would certainly require strict censorship of the arts. With regard to the latter, we should recall the damage done to the reputation of Socrates by Aristophanes' play.

Was Plato serious? Did he intend his state to be a blueprint for action? Was it all done tongue in cheek? No two readers will agree. But many find more than enough evidence for interpreting the *Republic* as an *ideal* whose function it is to explain what we do have: for what we have is an imperfect manifestation of the real. At the same time, the *ideal* serves as a standard in terms of which we can judge the adequacy of what we do and what we propose to be done. Given Plato's overall view of what it means to explain, such an interpretation would be consistent with what he has done in other fields such as physical science. We close by noting that a philosophical account of society, Plato's vision of social science, in no way prevents him from making specific practical recommendations in his other works.

Plato: The Republic

PROBLEM OF JUSTICE

Once more, Socrates, I will ask you to consider another way of speaking about justice and injustice, which is not confined to the poets, [*364*] but is found in prose writers. The universal voice of mankind is always declaring that justice and virtue are honourable, but grievous and toilsome; and that the pleasures of vice and injustice are easy of attainment, and are only censured by law and opinion. They say also that honesty is for the most part less profitable than dishonesty; and they are quite ready to call wicked men happy, and to honour them both in public and private when they are rich or in any other way influential, while they despise and overlook those who may be weak and poor, even though acknowledging them to be better than the others. But most extraordinary of all is their mode of speaking about virtue and the gods: they say that the gods apportion calamity and misery to many good men, and good and happiness to the wicked. And mendicant prophets go to rich men's doors and persuade them that they have a power committed to them by the gods of making an atonement for a man's own or his ancestor's sins by sacrifices or charms, with rejoicings and feasts; and they promise to harm an enemy, whether just or unjust, at a small cost; with magic arts and incantations binding heaven, as they say, to execute their will. And the poets are the authorities to whom they appeal, now smoothing the path of vice with the words of Hesiod:

Vice may be had in abundance without trouble;
the way is smooth and her dwelling-place is near.
But before virtue the gods have set toil,

and a tedious and uphill road: then citing Homer as a witness that the gods may be influenced by men; for he also says:—

The gods, too, may be turned from their purpose; and men pray to them and avert their wrath by sacrifices and soothing entreaties, and by libations and the odour of fat, when they have sinned and transgressed.

And they produce a host of books written by Musaeus and Orpheus, who were children of the Moon and the Muses—that is what they say—according to which they perform their ritual, and persuade not only individuals, but whole cities, that expiations and atonements for sin may be made by sacrifices and amusements which fill a vacant hour, and are equally at the service of the living and the dead; [*365*] the latter sort they call mysteries, and they redeem us from the pains of hell, but if we neglect them no one knows what awaits us.

He proceeded: And now when the young hear all this said about virtue and vice, and the way in which gods and men regard them, how are their minds likely to be affected, my dear Socrates—those of them, I mean, who are quick-witted, and, like the bees on the wing, light on every flower, and from all they hear are prone to draw conclusions as to what manner of persons they should be and in what way they should walk if they would make the best of life? Probably the youth will say to himself in the words of Pindar—

Can I by justice or by crooked ways of deceit ascend a loftier tower which may be a fortress to me all my days?

For what men say is that, if I am really just and am not also thought just, profit there is none, but the pain and loss on the other hand are unmistakeable. But if, though unjust, I acquire the reputation of justice, a heavenly life is promised to me. Since then, as philosophers prove, appearance tyrannizes over truth and is lord of happiness, to appearance I must devote myself. I will describe around me a picture and shadow of virtue to be the vestibule and exterior of my house; behind I will trail the subtle and crafty fox, as Archilochus, greatest of sages, recommends. But I hear some one exclaiming that the concealment of wickedness is often difficult; to which I answer, Nothing great is easy. Nevertheless, the argument indicates this, if we would be happy, to be the path along which we should proceed. With a view to concealment we will establish secret brotherhoods and political clubs. And there are professors of rhetoric who teach the art of persuading courts and assemblies; and so, partly by persuasion and partly by force, I shall make unlawful gains and not be punished. Still I hear a voice saying that the gods cannot be deceived, neither can they be compelled. But what if there are no gods? or, suppose them to have no care of human beings—why in either case should we mind about concealment? And even if there are gods, and they do care about us, yet we know of them only from tradition and the genealogies of the poets; and these are the very persons who say that they may be influenced and turned by "sacrifices and soothing entreaties and by offerings." Let us be consistent then, and believe both or neither. If the poets speak truly, [366] why then we had better be unjust, and offer of the fruits of injustice; for if we are just, although we may escape the vengeance of heaven, we shall lose the gains of injustice; but, if we are unjust, we shall keep the gains, and by our sinning and praying, and praying and sinning, the gods will be propitiated, and we shall not be punished. "But there is a world below in which either we or our posterity will suffer for our unjust deeds." Yes, my friend, will be the reflection, but there are mysteries and atoning deities, and these have great power. That is what mighty cities declare; and the children of the gods, who were their poets and prophets, bear a like testimony.

On what principle, then, shall we any longer choose justice rather than the worst injustice?

when, if we only unite the latter with a deceitful regard to appearances, we shall fare to our mind both with gods and men, in life and after death, as the most numerous and the highest authorities tell us. Knowing all this, Socrates, how can a man who has any superiority of mind or person or rank or wealth, be willing to honour justice; or indeed to refrain from laughing when he hears justice praised? And even if there should be some one who is able to disprove the truth of my words, and who is satisfied that justice is best, still he is not angry with the unjust, but is very ready to forgive them, because he also knows that men are not just of their own free will; unless, peradventure, there be some one whom the divinity within him may have inspired with a hatred of injustice, or who has attained knowledge of the truth—but no other man. He only blames injustice who, owing to cowardice or age or some weakness, has not the power of being unjust. And this is proved by the fact that when he obtains the power, he immediately becomes unjust as far as he can be.

The cause of all this, Socrates, was indicated by us at the beginning of the argument, when my brother and I told you how astonished we were to find that of all the professing panegyrists of justice—beginning with the ancient heroes of whom any memorial has been preserved to us, and ending with the men of our own time—no one has ever blamed injustice or praised justice except with a view to the glories, honours, and benefits which flow from them. No one has ever adequately described either in verse or prose the true essential nature of either of them abiding in the soul, and invisible to any human or divine eye; or shown that of all the things of a man's soul which he has within him, justice is the greatest good, [367] and injustice the greatest evil. Had this been the universal strain, had you sought to persuade us of this from our youth upwards, we should not have been on the watch to keep one another from doing wrong, but every one would have been his own watchman, because afraid, if he did wrong, of harbouring in himself the greatest of evils. I dare say that Thrasymachus and others would seriously hold the language which I have been merely repeating, and words even stronger than these about justice and injustice, grossly, as I conceive, perverting their true nature. But I speak in this vehement manner, as I must frankly confess to you, because I want to hear from you the opposite side; and I would ask you to show not only the superiority which justice has over injustice, but what effect they have on the possessor of them which makes the one to be a good and the other an evil to him. And please, as Glaucon requested of you, to exclude reputations; for unless you take away from each of them his true reputation and add on the false, we shall say that you do not praise justice, but the appearance of it; we shall think that you are only exhorting us to keep injustice dark, and that you really agree with Thrasymachus in thinking that justice is another's good and the interest of the stronger, and that injustice is a man's own profit and interest, though injurious to the weaker. Now as you have admitted that justice is one of that highest class of goods which are desired indeed for their results, but in a far greater degree for their own sakes—like sight or hearing or knowledge or health, or any other real and natural and not merely conventional good—I would ask you in your praise of justice to regard one point only: I mean the essential good and evil which justice and injustice work in the possessors of them. Let others praise justice and injustice, magnifying the rewards and honours of the one and abusing the other; that is a manner of arguing which, coming from them, I am ready to tolerate, but from you who have spent your whole life in the consideration of this question, unless I hear the contrary from your own lips, I expect something better. And therefore, I say, not only prove to us that justice is better than injustice, but show what they either of them do to the possessor of them, which makes the one to be a good and the other an evil, whether seen or unseen by gods and men. . . .

THE INDIVIDUAL MAN; THE NATURE OF THE SOUL

[*433*] Well then, tell me, I said, whether I am right or not: You remember the original principle which we were always laying down at the foundation of the State, that one man should practise one thing only, the thing to which his nature was best adapted—now justice is this principle or a part of it.

Yes, we often said that one man should do one thing only.

Further, we affirmed that justice was doing one's own business, and not being a busybody; we said so again and again, and many others have said the same to us.

Yes, we said so. . . .

[*434*] Very true.

Think, now, and say whether you agree with me or not. Suppose a carpenter to be doing the business of a cobbler, or a cobbler of a carpenter; and suppose them to exchange their implements or their duties, or the same person to be doing the work of both, or whatever be the change; do you think that any great harm would result to the State?

Not much.

But when the cobbler or any other man whom nature designed to be a trader, having his heart lifted up by wealth or strength or the number of his followers, or any like advantage, attempts to force his way into the class of warriors, or a warrior into that of legislators and guardians, for which he is unfitted, and either to take the implements or the duties of the other; or when one man is trader, legislator, and warrior all in one, then I think you will agree with me in saying that this interchange and this meddling of one with another is the ruin of the State.

Most true.

Seeing then, I said, there are three distinct classes, any meddling of one with another, or the change of one into another, is the greatest harm to the State, and may be most justly termed evil-doing?

Precisely.

And the greatest degree of evil-doing to one's own city would be termed by you injustice?

Certainly.

Then this is injustice; and on the other hand when the trader, the auxiliary, and the guardian each do their own business, that is justice, and will make the city just.

I agree with you.

We will not, I said, be overpositive as yet; but if, on trial, this conception of justice be verified in the individual as well as in the State, there will be no longer any room for doubt; if it be not verified, we must have a fresh inquiry. First let us complete the old investigation, which we began, as you remember, under the impression that, if we could previously examine justice on the larger scale, there would be less difficulty in discerning her in the individual. That larger example appeared to be the State, and accordingly we constructed as good a one as we could, knowing well that in the good State justice would be found. Let the discovery which we made be now applied to the individual—if they agree, we shall be satisfied; or, if there be a difference in the individual, we will come back to the State and have another trial of the theory. [435] The friction of the two when rubbed together may possibly strike a light in which justice will shine forth, and the vision which is then revealed we will fix in our souls.

That will be in regular course; let us do as you say.

I proceeded to ask: When two things, a greater and less, are called by the same name, are they like or unlike in so far as they are called the same?

Like, he replied.

The just man then, if we regard the idea of justice only, will be like the just State?

He will.

And a State was thought by us to be just when the three classes in the State severally did their own business; and also thought to be temperate and valiant and wise by reason of certain other affections and qualities of these same classes?

True, he said.

And so of the individual; we may assume that he has the same three principles in his own soul which are found in the State; and he may be rightly described in the same terms, because he is affected in the same manner?

Certainly, he said.

Once more then, O my friend, we have alighted upon an easy question—whether the soul has these three principles or not?

An easy question! Nay, rather, Socrates, the proverb holds that hard is the good.

Very true, I said; and I do not think that the method which we are employing is at all adequate to the accurate solution of this question; the true method is another and a longer one. Still we may arrive at a solution not below the level of the previous enquiry.

May we not be satisfied with that? he said—under the circumstances, I am quite content.

I too, I replied, shall be extremely well satisfied.

Then faint not in pursuing the speculation, he said.

Must we not acknowledge, I said, that in each of us there are the same principles and habits which there are in the State; and that from the individual they pass into the Senate? —how else can they come there? Take the quality of passion or spirit—it would be ridiculous to imagine that this quality, when found in States, is not derived from the individuals who are supposed to possess it, e.g. the Thracians, Scythians, and in general the northern nations; and the same may be said of the love of knowledge, which is the special characteristic of our part of the world, [436] or of the love of money, which may, with equal truth, be attributed to the Phoenicians and Egyptians.

Exactly so, he said.

There is no difficulty in understanding this.

None whatever.

But the question is not quite so easy when we proceed to ask whether these principles are three or one; whether, that is to say, we learn with one part of our nature, are angry with another, and with a third part desire the satisfaction of our natural appetites; or whether the whole soul comes into play in each sort of action—to determine that is the difficulty.

Yes, he said; there lies the difficulty.

Then let us now try and determine whether they are the same or different.

How can we? he asked.

I replied as follows: The same thing clearly cannot act or be acted upon in the same part or in relation to the same thing at the same time in contrary ways; and therefore whenever this contradiction occurs in things apparently the same, we know that they are really not the same, but different.

Good.

For example, I said, can the same thing be at rest and in motion at the same time in the same part?

Impossible.

Still, I said, let us have a more precise statement of terms, lest we should hereafter fall out by the way. Imagine the case of a man who is standing and also moving his hands and his head, and suppose a person to say that one and the same person is in motion and at rest at the same moment—to such a mode of speech we should object, and should rather say that one part of him is in motion while another is at rest.

Very true.

And suppose the objector to refine still further, and to draw the nice distinction that not only parts of tops, but whole tops, when they spin round with their pegs fixed on the spot, are at rest and in motion at the same time (and he may say the same of anything which revolved in the same spot), his objection would not be admitted by us, because in such cases things are not at rest and in motion in the same parts of themselves; we should rather say that they have both an axis and a circumference; and that the axis stands still, for there is no deviation from the perpendicular; and that the circumference goes round. But if, while revolving, the axis inclines either to the right or left, forwards or backwards, then in no point of view can they be at rest.

That is the correct mode of describing them, he replied.

Then none of these objections will confuse us, or incline us to believe that the same thing at the same time, [437] in the same part or in relation to the same thing, can act or be acted upon in contrary ways.

Certainly not, according to my way of thinking.

Yes, I said, that we may not be compelled to examine all such objections, and prove at length that they are untrue, let us assume their absurdity, and go forward on the understanding that hereafter, if this assumption turn out to be untrue, all the consequences which follow shall be withdrawn.

Yes, he said, that will be the best way.

Well, I said, would you not allow that assent and dissent, desire and aversion, attraction and repulsion, are all of them opposites, whether they are regarded as active or passive (for that makes no difference in the fact of their opposition)?

Yes, he said, they are opposites.

Well, I said, and hunger and thirst, and the desires in general, and again willing and wishing—all these you would refer to the classes already mentioned. You would say—would you not?—that the soul of him who desires is seeking after the object of his desires; or that he is drawing to himself the thing which he wishes to possess: or again, when a person wants anything to be given him, his mind, longing for the realization of his desires, intimates his wish to have it by a nod of assent, as if he had been asked a question?

Very true.

And what would you say of unwillingness and dislike and the absence of desire; should not these be referred to the opposite class of repulsion and rejection?

Certainly.

Admitting this to be true of desire generally, let us suppose a particular class of desires, and out of these we will select hunger and thirst, as they are termed, which are the most obvious of them?

Let us take that class, he said.

The object of one is food, and of the other drink?

Yes.

And here comes the point: is not thirst the desire which the soul has of drink, and of drink only; not of drink qualified by anything else; for example, warm or cold, or much or little, or, in a word, drink of any particular sort: but if the thirst be accompanied by heat, then the desire is of cold drink; or, if accompanied by cold, then of warm drink, or, if the thirst be excessive, then the drink which is desired will be excessive; or, if not great, the quantity of drink will also be small: but thirst pure and simple will desire drink pure and simple, which is the natural satisfaction of thirst, as food is of hunger?

Yes, he said: the simple desire is, as you say, in every case of the simple object, and the qualified desire of the qualified object.

[438] But here a confusion may arise; and I should wish to guard against an opponent starting up and saying that no man desires drink only, but good drink, or food only, but good food; for good is the universal object of desire, and thirst being a desire, will necessarily be thirst after good drink, and the same is true of every other desire.

Yes, he replied, the opponent might have something to say.

Nevertheless I should still maintain, that of relatives some have a quality attached to either term of the relation; others are simple and have their correlatives simple.

I do not know what you mean.

Well, you know of course that the greater is relative to the less?

Certainly.

And the much greater to the much less?

Yes.

And the sometime greater to the sometime less, and the greater that is to be to the less that is to be?

Certainly, he said.

And so of more and less, and of other correlative terms, such as the double and the half, or again, the heavier and the lighter, the swifter and the slower; and of hot and cold, and of any other relatives—is not this true of all of them?

Yes.

And does not the same principle hold in the sciences? The object of science is knowledge (assuming that to be the true definition), but the object of a particular science is a particular kind of knowledge which is defined and distinguished from other kinds and is therefore termed architecture.

Certainly.

Because it has a particular quality which no other has?

Yes.

And it has this particular quality because it has an object of a particular kind; and this is true of the other arts and sciences?

Yes.

Now, then, if I have made myself clear, you will understand my original meaning in what I said about relatives. My meaning was, that if one term of a relation is taken alone, the other is taken alone; if one term is qualified, the other is also qualified. I do not mean to say that relatives may not be disparate, or that the science of health is healthy, or of disease necessarily diseased, or that the sciences of good and evil are therefore good and evil; but only that, when the term science is no longer used absolutely, but has a qualified object which in this case is the nature of health and disease, it becomes defined, and is hence called not merely science, but the science of medicine.

I quite understand, and I think as you do.

[439] Would you not say that thirst is one of these essentially relative terms, having clearly a relation—

Yes, thirst is relative to drink.

And a certain kind of thirst is relative to a certain kind of drink; but thirst taken alone is neither of much nor little, nor of good nor bad, nor of any particular kind of drink, but of drink only?

Certainly.

Then the soul of the thirsty one, in so far as he is thirsty, desires only drink; for this he yearns and tries to obtain it?

That is plain.

And if you suppose something which pulls a thirsty soul away from drink, that must be different from the thirsty principle which draws him like a beast to drink; for, as we were saying, the same thing cannot at the same time with the same part of itself act in contrary ways about the same.

Impossible.

No more than you can say that the hands of the archer push and pull the bow at the same time, but what you say is that one hand pushes and the other pulls.

Exactly so, he replied.

And might a man be thirsty, and yet unwilling to drink?

Yes, he said, it constantly happens.

And in such a case what is one to say? Would you not say that there was something in the soul bidding a man to drink, and something else forbidding him, which is other and stronger than the principle which bids him?

I should say so.

And the forbidding principle is derived from reason, and that which bids and attracts proceeds from passion and disease?

Clearly.

Then we may fairly assume that they are two, and that they differ from one another; the one with which a man reasons, we may call the rational principle of the soul, the other with which he loves and hungers and thirsts and feels the flutterings of any other desire, may be termed the irrational or appetitive, the ally of sundry pleasures and satisfactions?

Yes, he said, we may fairly assume them to be different.

Then let us finally determine that there are two principles existing in the soul. And what of passion, or spirit? Is it a third, or akin to one of the preceding?

I should be inclined to say—akin to desire.

Well, I said, there is a story which I remember to have heard, and in which I put faith. The story is, that Leonitus, the son of Aglaion coming up one day from the Piraeus, under the north wall on the outside, observed some dead bodies lying on the ground at the place of execution. He felt a desire to see them, and also a dread and abhorrence of them; [440] for a time he struggled and covered his eyes, but at length the desire got the better of him; and forcing them open he ran up to the dead bodies, saying, Look, ye wretches, take your fill of the fair sight.

I have heard the story myself, he said.

The moral of the tale is, that anger at times goes to war with desire, as though they were two distinct things.

Yes; that is the meaning, he said.

And are there not many other cases in which we observe that when a man's desires violently prevail over his reason, he reviles himself, and is angry at the violence within him, and that in this struggle, which is like the struggle of factions in a State, his spirit is on the side of his reason—but for the passionate or spirited element to take part with the desires when reason decides that she should not be opposed, is a sort of thing which I believe that you never observed occurring in yourself, nor, as I should imagine, in any one else?

Certainly not.

Suppose that a man thinks he has done a wrong to another, the nobler he is the less able is he to feel indignant at any suffering, such as hunger, or cold, or any other pain which the injured person may inflict upon him—these he deems to be just, and, as I say, his anger refuses to be excited by them.

True, he said.

But when he thinks that he is the sufferer of the wrong, then he boils and chafes, and is on the side of what he believes to be justice; and because he suffers hunger or cold or other pain he is only the more determined to persevere and conquer. His noble spirit will not be quelled until he either slays or is slain; or until he hears the voice of the shepherd, that is, reason, bidding his dog bark no more.

The illustration is perfect, he replied; and in our State, as we were saying, the auxiliaries were to be dogs, and to hear the voice of the rulers, who are their shepherds.

I perceive, I said, that you quite understand me; there is, however, a further point which I wish you to consider.

What point?

You remember that passion or spirit appeared at first sight to be a kind of desire, but now we should say quite the contrary; for in the conflict of the soul spirit is arrayed on the side of the rational principle.

Most assuredly.

But a further question arises: Is passion different from reason also, or only a kind of reason; in which latter case, instead of three principles in the soul, [441] there will only be two, the rational and the concupiscent; or rather, as

the State was composed of three classes, traders, auxiliaries, counsellors, so may there not be in the individual soul a third element which is passion or spirit, and when not corrupted by bad education is the natural auxiliary of reason?

Yes, he said, there must be a third.

Yes, I replied, if passion, which has already been shown to be different from desire, turns out also to be different from reason.

But that is easily proved:—We may observe even in young children that they are full of spirit almost as soon as they are born, whereas some of them never seem to attain to the use of reason, and most of them late enough.

Excellent, I said, and you may see passion equally in brute animals, which is a further proof of the truth of what you are saying. And we may once more appeal to the words of Homer, which have been already quoted by us,

He smote his breast, and thus rebuked his heart;

for in this verse Homer has clearly supposed the power which reasons about the better and worse to be different from the unreasoning anger which is rebuked by it.

Very true, he said.

And so, after much tossing, we have reached land, and are fairly agreed that the same principles which exist in the State exist also in the individual, and that they are three in number.

Exactly.

Must we not then infer that the individual is wise in the same way, and in virtue of the same quality which makes the State wise?

Certainly.

Also that the same quality which constitutes courage in the State constitutes courage in the individual, and that both the State and the individual bear the same relation to all the other virtues?

Assuredly.

And the individual will be acknowledged by us to be just in the same way in which the State is just?

That follows of course.

We cannot but remember that the justice of the State consisted in each of the three classes doing the work of its own class?

We are not very likely to have forgotten, he said.

We must recollect that the individual in whom the several qualities of his nature do their own work will be just, and will do his own work?

Yes, he said, we must remember that too,

And ought not the rational principle, which is wise, and has the care of the whole soul, to rule, and the passionate or spirited principle to be the subject and ally?

Certainly.

And, as we were saying, the united influence of music and gymnastic will bring them into accord, nerving and sustaining the reason with noble words and lessons, [442] and moderating and soothing and civilizing the wildness of passion by harmony and rhythm?

Quite true, he said.

And these two, thus nurtured and educated, and having learned truly to know their own functions, will rule over the concupiscent, which in each of us is the largest part of the soul and by nature most insatiable of gain; over this they will keep guard, lest, waxing great and strong with the fulness of bodily pleasures, as they are termed, the concupiscent soul, no longer confined to her own sphere, should attempt to enslave and rule those who are not her natural-born subjects, and overturn the whole life of man?

Very true, he said.

Both together will they not be the best defenders of the whole soul and the whole body against attacks from without; the one counselling, and the other fighting under his leader, and courageously executing his commands and counsels?

True.

And he is to be deemed courageous whose spirit retains in pleasure and in pain the commands of reason about what he ought or ought not to fear?

Right, he replied.

And him we call wise who has in him that little part which rules, and which proclaims these commands; that part too being supposed to have a knowledge of what is for the interest of each of three parts and of the whole?

Assuredly.

And would you not say that he is temperate who has these same elements in friendly harmony, in whom the one ruling principle of reason, and the two subject ones of spirit and desire are equally agreed that reason ought to

rule, and do not rebel?

Certainly, he said, that is the true account of temperance whether in the State or individual.

And surely, I said, we have explained again and again how and by virtue of what quality a man will be just.

That is very certain.

And is justice dimmer in the individual, and is her form different, or is she the same which we found her to be in the State?

There is no difference in my opinion, he said.

Because, if any doubt is still lingering in our minds, a few commonplace instances will satisfy us of the truth of what I am saying.

What sort of instances do you mean?

[443] If the case is put to us, must we not admit that the just State, or the man who is trained in the principles of such a State, will be less likely than the unjust to make away with a deposit of gold or silver? Would any one deny this?

No one, he replied.

Will the just man or citizen ever be guilty of sacrilege or theft, or treachery either to his friends or to his country?

Never.

Neither will he ever break faith where there have been oaths or agreements?

Impossible.

No one will be less likely to commit adultery, or to dishonour his father and mother, or to fail in his religious duties?

No one.

And the reason is that each part of him is doing its own business, whether in ruling or being ruled?

Exactly so.

Are you satisfied then that the quality which makes such men and such states is justice, or do you hope to discover some other?

Not I, indeed.

Then our dream has been realized; and the suspicion which we entertained at the beginning of our work of construction, that some divine power must have conducted us to a primary form of justice, has now been verified?

Yes, certainly.

And the division of labour which required the carpenter and the shoemaker and the rest of the citizens to be doing each his own business, and not another's, was a shadow of justice, and for that reason it was of use?

Clearly.

But in reality justice was such as we were describing, being concerned however, not with the outward man, but with the inward, which is the true self and concernment of man: for the just man does not permit the several elements within him to interfere with one another, or any of them to do the work of others,—he sets in order his own inner life, and is his own master, and his own law, and at peace with himself; and when he has bound together the three principles within him, which may be compared to the higher, lower, and middle notes of the scale, and the intermediate intervals—when he has bound all these together, and is no longer many, but has become one entirely temperate and perfectly adjusted nature, then he proceeds to act, if he has to act, whether in a matter of property, or in the treatment of the body, or in some affair of politics or private business; always thinking and calling that which preserves and co-operates with this harmonious condition, just and good action, and the knowledge which presides over it, wisdom, and that which at any time impairs this condition, [*444*] he will call unjust action, and the opinion which presides over it ignorance.

You have said the exact truth, Socrates.

Very good; and if we were to affirm that we had discovered the just man and the just State, and the nature of justice in each of them, we should not be telling a falsehood?

Most certainly not.

May we say so, then?

Let us say so.

And now, I said, injustice has to be comsidered.

Must not injustice be a strife which arises among the three principles—a meddlesomeness, and interference, and rising up of a part of the soul against the whole, an assertion of unlawful authority, which is made by a rebellious subject against a true prince, of whom he is the natural vassal—what is all this confusion and delusion but injustice, and intemperance and cowardice and ignorance, and every form of vice?

Exactly so.

And if the nature of justice and injustice be known, then the meaning of acting unjustly and being unjust, or, again, of acting justly, will also be perfectly clear?

What do you mean? he said.

Why, I said, they are like disease and health; being in the soul just what disease and health are in the body.

How so? he said.

Why, I said, that which is healthy causes health, and that which is unhealthy causes disease.

Yes.

And just actions cause justice, and unjust actions cause injustice?

That is certain.

And the creation of health is the institution of a natural order and government of one by another in the parts of the body; and the creation of disease is the production of a state of things at variance with this natural order?

True.

And is not the creation of justice the institution of a natural order and government of one by another in the parts of the soul, and the creation of injustice the production of a state of things at variance with the natural order?

Exactly so, he said.

Then virtue is the health and beauty and well-being of the soul, and vice the disease and weakness and deformity of the same?

True.

And do not good practices lead to virtue, and evil practices to vice?

Assuredly.

[*445*] Still our old question of the comparative advantage of justice and injustice has not been answered: Which is the more profitable, to be just and act justly and practise virtue, whether seen or unseen of gods and men, or to be unjust and act unjustly, if only unpunished and unreformed?

In my judgment, Socrates, the question has now become ridiculous. We know that, when the bodily constitution is gone, life is no longer endurable, though pampered with all kinds of meats and drinks, and having all wealth and all power; and shall we be told that when the very essence of the vital principle is underminded and corrupted, life is still worth having to a man, if only he be allowed to do whatever he likes with the single exception that he is not to acquire justice and virtue, or to escape from injustice and vice; assuming them both to be such as we have described?

Yes, I said, the question is, as you say, ridiculous. Still, as we are near the spot at which we may see the truth in the clearest manner with our own eyes, let us not faint by the way. . . .

THE PHILOSOPHER-KING

But still I must say, Socrates, that if you are allowed to go on in this way you will entirely forget the other question which at the commencement of this discussion you thrust aside: —Is such an order of things possible, and how, if at all? For I am quite ready to acknowledge that the plan which you propose, if only feasible, would do all sorts of good to the State. I will add, what you have omitted, that your citizens will be the bravest of warriors, and will never leave their ranks, for they will all know one another, and each will call the other father, brother, son; and if you suppose the women to join their armies, whether in the same rank or in the rear, either as a terror to the enemy, or as auxiliaries in case of need, I know that they will then be absolutely invincible; and there are many domestic advantages which might also be mentioned and which I also fully acknowledge: but, as I admit all these advantages and as many more as you please, if only this State of yours were to come into existence, we need say no more about them; assuming then the existence of the State, let us now turn to the question of possibility and ways and means—the rest may be left.

[472] If I loiter for a moment, you instantly make a raid upon me, I said, and have no mercy; I have hardly escaped the first and second waves, and you seem not to be aware that you are now bringing upon me the third, which is the greatest and heaviest. When you have seen and heard the third wave, I think you will be more considerate and will acknowledge that some fear and hesitation was natural respecting a proposal so extraordinary as that which I have now to state and investigate.

The more appeals of this sort which you make, he said, the more determined are we that you shall tell us how such a State is possible: speak out and at once.

Let me begin by reminding you that we found our way hither in the search after justice and injustice.

True, he replied; but what of that?

I was only going to ask whether, if we have discovered them, we are to require that the just man should in nothing fail of absolute justice; or may we be satisfied with an approximation, and the attainment in him of a higher degree of justice than is to be found in other men?

The approximation will be enough.

We are enquiring into the nature of absolute justice and into the character of the perfectly just, and into injustice and the perfectly unjust, that we might have an ideal. We were to look at these in order that we might judge of our own happiness and unhappiness according to the standard which they exhibited and the degree in which we resembled them, but not with any view of showing that they could exist in fact.

True, he said.

Would a painter be any the worse because, after having delineated with consummate art an ideal of a perfectly beautiful man, he was unable to show that any such man could ever have existed?

He would be none the worse.

Well, and were we not creating an ideal of a perfect State?

To be sure.

And is our theory a worse theory because we are unable to prove the possibility of a city being ordered in the manner described?

Surely not, he replied.

That is the truth, I said. But if, at your request, I am to try and show how and under what conditions the possibility is highest, I must ask you, having this in view, to repeat your former admissions.

What admissions?

[473] I want to know whether ideals are ever fully realized in language? Does not the word express more than the fact, and must not the actual, whatever a man may think, always, in the nature of things, fall short of the truth? What do you say?

I agree.

Then you must not insist on my proving that the actual State will in every respect coincide with the ideal: if we are only able to discover how a city may be governed nearly as we proposed, you will admit that we have discovered the possibility which you demand; and will be contended. I am sure that I should be contented—will not you?

Yes, I will.

Let me next endeavour to show what is that fault in States which is the cause of their present maladministration, and what is the least change which will enable a State to pass into the truer form; and let the change, if possible, be of one thing only, or, if not, of two; at any rate, let the changes be as few and slight as possible.

Certainly, he replied.

I think, I said, that there might be a reform of the State if only one change were made, which is not a slight or easy though still a possible one.

What is it? he said.

Now then, I said, I go to meet that which I liken to the greatest of the waves; yet shall the word be spoken, even though the wave break and drown me in laughter and dishonour; and do you mark my words.

Proceed:

I said: *Until philosophers are kings, or the kings and princes of this world have the spirit and power of philosophy, and political greatness and wisdom meet in one, and those commoner natures who pursue either to the exclusion of the other are compelled to stand aside, cities will never have rest from their evils—no, nor the human race, as I believe—and then only will this our State have a possibility of life and behold the light of day.* Such was the thought, my dear Glaucon, which I would fain have uttered if it had not seemed too extravagant; for to be convinced that in no other State can there be happiness private or public is indeed a hard thing.

Socrates, what do you mean? I would have you consider that the word which you have uttered is one at which numerous persons, and very respectable persons too, [474] in a figure pulling off their coats all in a moment, and seizing any weapon that comes to hand, will run at you might and main, before you know where you are, intending to do heaven knows what; and if you don't prepare an answer, and put yourself in motion, you will be "pared by their fine wits," and no mistake.

You got me into the scrape, I said.

And I was quite right; however, I will do all I can to get you out of it; but I can only give you good-will and good advice, and, perhaps, I may be able to fit answers to your questions better than another—that is all. And now, having such an auxiliary, you must do your best to show the unbelievers that you are right.

I ought to try, I said, since you offer me such invaluable assistance. And I think that, if there is to be a chance of our escaping, we must explain to them whom we mean when we say that philosophers are to rule in the State; then we shall be able to defend ourselves: There will be discovered to be some natures who ought to study philosophy and to be leaders in the State; and others who are not born to be philosophers, and are meant to be followers rather than leaders.

Then now for a definition, he said.

Follow me, I said, and I hope that I may in some way or other be able to give you a satisfactory explanation.

Proceed.

I dare say that you remember, and therefore I need not remind you, that a lover, if he is worthy of the name, ought to show his love, not to some one part of that which he loves, but to the whole.

I really do not understand, and therefore beg of you to assist my memory.

Another person, I said, might fairly reply as you do; but a man of pleasure like yourself ought to know that all who are in the flower of youth do somehow or other raise a pang or emotion in a lover's breast, and are thought by him to be worthy of his affectionate regards. Is not this a way which you have with the fair: one has a snub nose, and you praise his charming face; the hook-nose of another has, you say, a royal look; while he who is neither snub nor hooked has the grace of regularity: the dark visage is manly, the fair are children of the gods; and as to the sweet "honey pale," as they are called, what is the very name but the invention of a lover who talks in diminutives, and is not adverse to paleness if appearing on the cheek of youth? [475] In a word, there is no excuse which you will not make, and nothing which you will not say, in order not to lose a single flower that blooms in the spring-time of youth.

If you make me an authority in matters of love, for the sake of the argument, I assent.

And what do you say of lovers of wine? Do you see them doing the same? They are glad of any pretext of drinking any wine.

Very good.

And the same is true of ambitious men; if they cannot command an army, they are willing to command a file; and if they cannot be honoured by really great and important persons, they are glad to be honoured by lesser and meaner people—but honour of some kind they must have.

Exactly.

Once more let me ask: Does he who desires any class of goods, desire the whole class or a part only?

The whole.

And may we not say of the philosopher that he is a lover, not of a part of wisdom only, but of the whole?

Yes, of the whole.

And he who dislikes learning, especially in youth, when he has no power of judging what is good and what is not, such an one we maintain not to be a philosopher or a lover of knowledge, just as he who refuses his food is not hungry, and may be said to have a bad appetite and not a good one?

Very true, he said.

Whereas he who has a taste for every sort of knowledge and who is curious to learn and is never satisfied, may be justly termed a philosopher? Am I not right?

Glaucon said: If curiosity makes a philosopher, you will find many a strange being will have a title to the name. All the lovers of sights have a delight in learning, and must therefore be included. Musical amateurs, too, are a folk strangely out of place among philosophers, for they are the last persons in the world who would come to anything like a philosophical discussion, if they could help, while they run about at the Dionysiac festivals as if they had let out their ears to hear every chorus; whether the performance is in town or country—that makes no difference—they are there. Now are we to maintain that all these and any who have similar tastes, as well as the professors of quite minor acts, are philosophers?

Certainly not, I replied; they are only an imitation.

He said: Who then are the true philosophers?

Those, I said, who are lovers of the vision of truth.

That is also good, he said; but I should like to know what you mean?

To another, I replied, I might have a difficulty in explaining; but I am sure that you will admit a proposition which I am about to make.

What is the proposition?

That since beauty is the opposite of ugliness,

they are two?

Certainly.

[*476*] And inasmuch as they are two, each of them is one?

True Again.

And of just and unjust, good and evil, and of every other class, the same remark holds: taken singly, each of them is one; but from the various combinations of them with actions and things and with one another, they are seen in all sorts of lights and appear many?

Very true.

And this is the distinction which I draw between the sight-loving, art-loving, practical class and those of whom I am speaking, and who are alone worthy of the name of philosophers.

How do you distinguish them? he said.

KNOWLEDGE AND OPINION

The lovers of sounds and sights, I replied, are, as I conceive, fond of fine tones and colors and forms and all the artificial products that are made out of them, but their mind is incapable of seeing or loving absolute beauty.

True, he replied.

Few are they who are able to attain to the sight of this.

Very true.

And he who, having a sense of beautiful things has no sense of absolute beauty, or who, if another lead him to a knowledge of that beauty is unable to follow—of such an one I ask, Is he awake or in a dream only? Reflect: is not the dreamer, sleeping or waking, one who likens dissimilar things, who puts the copy in the place of the real object?

I should certainly say that such an one was dreaming.

But take the case of the other, who recognises the existence of absolute beauty and is able to distinguish the idea from the objects which participate in the idea, neither putting the objects in the place of the idea nor the idea in the place of the objects—is he a dreamer, or is he awake?

He is wide awake.

And may we not say that the mind of the one who knows has knowledge, and that the mind of the other, who opines only, has opinion?

Certainly.

But suppose that the latter should quarrel with us and dispute our statement, can we administer any soothing cordial or advice to him, without revealing to him that there is sad disorder in his wits?

We must certainly offer him some good advice, he replied.

Come, then, and let us think of something to say to him. Shall we begin by assuring him that he is welcome to any knowledge which he may have, and that we are rejoiced at his having it? But we should like to ask him a question: Does he who has knowledge know something or nothing? (You must answer for him.)

I answer that he knows something.

Something that is or is not?

Something that is; for how can that which is not ever be known?

[477] And we are assured, after looking at the matter from many points of view, that absolute being is or may be absolutely known, but that the utterly non-existent is utterly unknown?

Nothing can be more certain.

Good. But if there be anything which is of such a nature as to be and not to be, that will have a place intermediate between pure being and the absolute negation of being?

Yes, between them.

And, as knowledge corresponded to being and ignorance of necessity to not-being, for that intermediate between being and not-being there has to be discovered a corresponding intermediate between ignorance and knowledge, if there be such?

Certainly.

Do we admit the existence of opinion?

Undoubtedly.

As being the same with knowledge, or another faculty?

Another faculty.

Then opinion and knowledge have to do with different kinds of matter corresponding to this difference of faculties?

Yes.

And knowledge is relative to being and knows being. But before I proceed further I will make a division.

What division?

I will begin by placing faculties in a class by themselves: they are powers in us, and in all other things, by which we do as we do. Sight and hearing, for example, I should call faculties. Have I clearly explained the class which I mean?

Yes, I quite understand.

Then let me tell you my view about them. I do not see them, and therefore the distinctions of figure, colour, and the like, which enable me to discern the differences of some things, do not apply to them. In speaking of a faculty I think only of its sphere and its result; and that which has the same sphere and the same result I call the same faculty, but that which has another sphere and another result I call different. Would that be your way of speaking?

Yes.

And will you be so very good as to answer one more question? Would you say that knowledge is a faculty, or in what class would you place it?

Certainly knowledge is a faculty, and the mightiest of all faculties.

And is opinion also a faculty?

Certainly, he said: for opinion is that with which we are able to form an opinion.

And yet you were acknowledging a little while ago that knowledge is not the same as opinion?

[478] Why, yes, he said: how can any reasonable being ever identify that which is infallible with that which errs?

An excellent answer, proving, I said, that we are quite conscious of a distinction between them.

Yes.

Then knowledge and opinion having distinct powers have also distinct spheres or subject-matters?

That is certain.

Being is the sphere or subject-matter of knowledge, and knowledge is to know the nature of being?

Yes.

And opinion is to have an opinion?

Yes.

And do we know what we opine? or is the subject-matter of opinion the same as the subject-matter of knowledge?

Nay, he replied, that has been already disproven; if difference in faculty implies difference in the sphere or subject-matter, and if, as we were saying, opinion and knowledge are distinct faculties, then the sphere of knowledge and of opinion cannot be the same.

Then if being is the subject-matter of knowledge, something else must be the subject-matter of opinion?

Yes, something else.

Well, then, is not-being the subject-matter of opinion? or, rather, how can there be an opinion at all about not-being? Reflect: when a man has an opinion, has he not an opinion about something? Can he have an opinion which is an opinion about nothing?

Impossible.

He who has an opinion has an opinion about some one thing?

Yes.

And not-being is not one thing but, properly speaking, nothing?

True.

Of not-being, ignorance was assumed to be the necessary correlative; of being, knowledge?

True, he said.

Then opinion is not concerned either with being or with not-being?

Not with either.

And can therefore neither be ignorance nor knowledge?

That seems to be true.

But is opinion to be sought without and beyond either of them, in a greater clearness than knowledge, or in a greater darkness than ignorance?

In neither.

Then I suppose that opinion appears to you to be darker than knowledge, but lighter than ignorance?

Both; and in no small degree.

And also to be within and between them?

Yes.

Then you would infer that opinion is intermediate?

No question.

But were we not saying before, that if anything appeared to be of a sort which is and is not at the same time, that sort of thing would appear also to lie in the interval between pure being and absolute not-being; and that the corresponding faculty is neither knowledge nor ignorance, but will be found in the interval between them?

True.

And in that interval there has now been discovered something which we call opinion?

There has.

Then what remains to be discovered is the object which partakes equally of the nature of being and not-being, and cannot rightly be termed either, pure and simple; this unknown term, when discovered, we may truly call the subject of opinion, and assign each to their proper faculty—the extremes to the faculties of the extremes and the mean to the faculty of the mean.

True.

[479] This being premised, I would ask the gentleman who is of opinion that there is no absolute or unchangeable idea of beauty—in whose opinion the beautiful is the manifold—he, I say, your lover of beautiful sights, who cannot bear to be told that the beautiful is one, and the just is one, or that anything is one—to him I would appeal, saying, Will you be so very kind, sir, as to tell us whether, of all these beautiful things, there is one which will not be found ugly; or of the just, which will not be found unjust; or of the holy, which will not also be unholy?

No, he replied; the beautiful will in some point of view be found ugly; and the same is true of the rest.

And may not the many which are doubles be also halves?—doubles, that is, of one thing, and halves of another?

Quite true.

And things great and small, heavy and light, as they are termed, will not be denoted by these any more than by the opposite names?

True; both these and the opposite names will always attach to all of them.

And can any one of those many things which are called by particular names be said to be this rather than not to be this?

He replied: They are like the punning riddles which are asked at feasts or the children's puzzle about the eunuch aiming at the bat, with what he hit him, as they say in the puzzle, and upon what the bat was sitting. The individual objects of which I am speaking are also a riddle, and have a double sense: nor can you fix them in your mind, either as being or not-being, or both, or neither.

Then what will you do with them? I said. Can they have a better place than between being and not-being? For they are clearly not in greater darkness or negation than not-being, or more full of light and existence than being.

That is quite true, he said.

Thus then we seem to have discovered that the many ideas which the multitude entertain about the beautiful and about all other things are tossing about in some region which is half-way between pure being and pure not-being?

We have.

Yes: and we had before agreed that anything of this kind which we might find was to be described as matter of opinion, and not as matter of knowledge; being the intermediate flux which is caught and detained by the intermediate faculty.

Quite true.

Then those who see the many beautiful, and who yet neither see absolute beauty, nor can follow any guide who points the way thither; who see the many just, and not absolute justice, and the like— such persons may be said to have opinion but not knowledge?

That is certain.

But those who see the absolute and eternal and immutable may be said to know, and not to have opinion only?

Neither can that be denied.

The one love and embrace the subjects of knowledge, the other those of opinion? The latter are the same, as I dare say you will remember, [480] who listened to sweet sounds and gazed upon fair colours, but would not tolerate the existence of absolute beauty.

Yes, I remember.

Shall we then be guilty of any impropriety in calling them lovers of opinion rather than lovers of wisdom, and will they be very angry with us for thus describing them?

I shall tell them not to be angry; no man should be angry at what is true.

But those who love the truth in each thing are to be called lovers of wisdom and not lovers of opinion.

Assuredly. . . .

THE PHILOSOPHER, THE STATE, AND THE CROWD

[484] And thus, Glaucon, after the argument has gone a weary way, the true and the false philosophers have at length appeared in view.

I do not think, he said, that the way could have been shortened.

I suppose not, I said; and yet I believe that we might have had a better view of both of them if the discussion could have been confined to this one subject and if there were not many other questions awaiting us, which he who desires to see in what respect the life of the just differs from that of the unjust must consider.

And what is the next question? he asked.

Surely, I said, the one which follows next in order. Inasmuch as philosophers only are able to grasp the eternal and unchangeable, and those who wander in the region of the many and variable are not philosophers, I must ask you which of the two classes should be the rulers of our State?

And how can we rightly answer that question?

Whichever of the two are best able to guard the laws and institutions of our State—let them be our guardians.

Very good.

Neither, I said, can there be any question that the guardian who is to keep anything should have eyes rather than no eyes?

There can be no question of that.

And are not those who are verily and indeed wanting in the knowledge of the true being of each thing, and who have in their souls no clear pattern, and are unable as with a painter's eye to look at the absolute truth and to that original to repair, and having perfect vision of the other world to order the laws about beauty, goodness, justice in this . . . are not such persons, I ask, simply blind?

Truly. . . .

And again, if he is forgetful and retains nothing of what he learns, will he not be an empty vessel?

That is certain.

Labouring in vain, he must end in hating himself and his fruitless occupation?

Yes.

Then a soul which forgets cannot be ranked among genuine philosophic natures; we must insist that the philosopher should have a good memory?

Certainly.

And once more, the inharmonious and unseemly nature can only tend to disproportion?

Undoubtedly.

And do you consider truth to be akin to proportion or to disproportion?

To proportion.

Then, besides other qualities, we must try to find a naturally well-proportioned and gracious mind, which will move spontaneously towards the true being of everything.

Certainly.

Well, and do not all these qualities, which we have been enumerating, go together, and are they not, in a manner, necessary to a soul, which is to have a full and perfect participation of being?

[487] They are absolutely necessary, he replied.

And must not that be a blameless study which he only can pursue who has the gift of a good memory, and is quick to learn—noble, gracious, the friend of truth, justice, courage, temperance, who are his kindred?

The god of jealousy himself, he said, could find no fault with such a study.

And to men like him, I said, when perfected by years and education, and to these only you will entrust the State.

Here Adeimantus interposed and said: To these statements, Socrates, no one can offer a reply; but when you talk in this way, a strange feeling passes over the minds of your hearers: They fancy that they are led astray a little at each step in the argument, owing to their own want of skill in asking and answering questions; these littles accumulate, and at the end of the discussion they are found to have sustained a mighty overthrow and all their former notions appear to be turned upside down. And as unskilful players of draughts are at last shut up by their more skilful adversaries and have no piece to move, so they too find themselves shut up at last; for they have nothing to say in this new game of which words are the counters; and yet all the time they are in the right. The observation is suggested to me by what is now occurring. For any one of us might say, that although in words he is not able to meet you at each step of the argument, he sees as a fact that the votaries of philosophy, when they carry on the study, not only in youth as a part of education, but as the pursuit of their maturer years, most of them become strange monsters, not to say utter rogues, and that those who may be considered the best of them are made useless to the world by the very study which you extol.

Well, and do you think that those who say so are wrong?

I cannot tell, he replied; but I should like to know what is your opinion.

Hear my answer; I am of opinion that they are quite right.

Then how can you be justified in saying that cities will not cease from evil until philosophers rule in them, when philosophers are acknowledged by us to be of no use to them?

You ask a question, I said, to which a reply can only be given in a parable.

Yes, Socrates; and that is a way of speaking to which you are not at all accustomed, I suppose.

I perceive, I said, that you are vastly amused at having plunged me into such a hopeless discussion; but now hear the parable, [488] and then you will be still more amused at the meagreness of my imagination: for the manner in which the best men are treated in their own States is so grievous that no single thing on earth is comparable to it; and therefore, if I am to plead their cause, I must have recourse to fiction, and put together a figure made up of many things, like the fabulous unions of goats and stags which are found in pictures. Imagine then a fleet or a ship in which there is a captain who is taller and stronger than any of the crew, but he is a little deaf and has a similar infirmity in sight, and his knowledge of navigation is not much better. The sailors are quarreling with one another about the steering—every one is of opinion that he has a right to steer, though he has never learned the art of navigation and cannot tell who taught him or when he learned, and will further assert that it cannot be taught, and they are ready to cut in pieces any one who says the contrary. They throng about the captain, begging and praying him to commit the helm to them; and if at any time they do not prevail, but others are preferred to them, they kill the others or throw them overboard, and having first chained up the noble captain's sense with drink or some narcotic drug, they mutiny and take possession of the ship and make free with the stores; thus, eating and drinking, they proceed on their voyage in such a manner as might be expected of them. Him who is their partisan and cleverly aids them in their plot for getting the ship out of the captain's hands into their own whether by force or persuasion, they compliment with the name of sailor, pilot, able seaman, and abuse the other sort of man, whom they call a good-for-nothing; but that the true pilot must pay attention to the year and seasons and sky and stars and winds, and whatever else belongs to his art, if he intends to be really qualified for the command of a ship, and that he must and will be the steerer, whether other people like or not—the possibility of this union of authority with the steerer's art has never seriously entered into their thoughts or been made part of their calling. [489] Now in vessels which are in a state of mutiny and by sailors who are mutineers, how will the true pilot be regarded? Will he not be called by them a prater, a star-gazer, a good-for-nothing?

Of course, said Adeimantus.

Then you will hardly need, I said, to hear the interpretation of the figure, which describes the true philosopher in his relation to the State; for you understand already.

Certainly.

Then suppose you now take this parable to the gentleman who is surprised at finding that philosophers have no honour in their cities; explain it to him and try to convince him that their having honour would be far more extraordinary.

I will.

Say to him, that, in deeming the best votaries of philosophy to be useless to the rest of the world, he is right; but also tell him to attribute their uselessness to the fault of those who will not use them, and not to themselves. The pilot should not humbly beg the sailors to be commanded by him—that is not the order of nature; neither are "the wise to go to the doors of the rich"—the ingenious author of this saying told a lie—but the truth is, that, when a man is ill, whether he be rich or poor, to the physician he must go, and he who wants to be governed, to him who is able to govern. The ruler who is good for anything ought not to beg his subjects to be ruled by him; although the present governors of mankind are of a different stamp; they may be justly compared to the mutinous sailors, and the true helmsmen to those who are called by them good-for-nothings; and star-gazers.

Precisely so, he said.

For these reasons, and among men like these, philosophy, the noblest pursuit of all, is not likely to be much esteemed by those of the opposite faction; not that the greatest and most lasting injury is done to her by her opponents but by her own professing followers, the same of whom you suppose the accuser to say, that the greatest number of them are arrant rogues, and the best are useless; in which opinion I agreed.

Yes.

And the reason why the good are useless has now been explained?

True.

Then shall we proceed to show that the corruption of the majority is also unavoidable, and that this is not to be laid to the charge of philosophy any more than the other?

By all means.

And let us ask and answer in turn, first going back to the description of the gentle and noble nature. [490] Truth, as you will remember, was his leader, whom he followed always and in all things; failing in this, he was an impostor, and had no part or lot in true philosophy.

Yes, that was said.

Well, and is not this one quality, to mention no others, greatly at variance with present notions of him?

Certainly, he said.

And have we not a right to say in his defence that the true lover of knowledge is always striving after being—that is his nature; he will not rest in the multiplicity of individuals which is an appearance only, but will go on—the keen edge will not be blunted, nor the force of his desire abate until he have attained the knowledge of the true nature of every essence by a sympathetic and kindred power in the soul, and by that power drawing near and mingling and becoming incorporate with very being, having begotten mind and truth, he will have knowledge and will live and grow truly, and then and not till then, will he cease from his travel.

Nothing, he said, can be more just than such a description of him.

And will the love of a lie be any part of a philosopher's nature? Will he not utterly hate a lie?

He will.

And when truth is the captain, we cannot suspect any evil of the band which he leads?

Impossible.

Justice and health of mind will be of the company, and temperance will follow after?

True, he replied.

Neither is there any reason why I should again set in array the philosopher's virtues, as you will doubtless remember that courage, magnificence, apprehension, memory, were his natural gifts. And you objected that, although no one could deny what I then said, still, if you leave words and look at facts, the persons who are thus described are some of them manifestly useless, and the greater number utterly depraved; we were then led to enquire into the grounds of these accusations, and have now arrived at the point of asking why are the majority bad, which question of necessity brought us back to the examination and definition of the true philosopher.

Exactly.

And we have next to consider the corruptions of the philosophic nature, why so many are spoiled and so few escape spoiling—I am speaking of those who were said to be useless but not wicked—and, [491] when we have done with them, we will speak of the imitators of philosophy, what manner of men are they who aspire after a profession which is above them and of which they are unworthy, and then, by their manifold inconsistencies, bring upon philosophy, and upon all philosophers, that universal reprobation of which we speak.

What are these corruptions? he said.

I will see if I can explain them to you. Every one will admit that a nature having in perfection all the qualities which we required in a philosopher, is a rare plant which is seldom seen among men.

Rare indeed.

And what numberless and powerful causes tend to destroy these rare natures!

What causes?

In the first place there are their own virtues, their courage, temperance, and the rest of them, every one of which praiseworthy qualities (and this is a most singular circumstance) destroys and distracts from philosophy the soul which is the possessor of them.

That is very singular, he replied.

Then there are all the ordinary goods of life —beauty, wealth, strength, rank, and great connections in the State—you understand the sort of things—these also have a corrupting and distracting effect.

I understand; but I should like to know more precisely what you mean about them.

Grasp the truth as a whole, I said, in the right way; you will then have no difficulty in apprehending the preceding remarks, and they will no longer appear strange to you.

And how am I to do so? he asked.

Why, I said, we know that all germs or seeds, whether vegetable or animal, when they fail to meet with proper nutriment or climate or soil, in proportion to their vigour, are all the more sensitive to the want of a suitable environment, for evil is a greater enemy to what is good than what is not.

Very true.

There is reason in supposing that the finest natures, when under alien conditions, receive more injury than the inferior, because the contrast is greater.

Certainly.

And may we not say, Adeimantus, that the most gifted minds, when they are ill-educated, become pre-eminently bad? Do not great crimes and the spirit of pure evil spring out of a fullness of nature ruined by education rather than from any inferiority, whereas weak natures are scarcely capable of any very great good or very great evil?

There I think that you are right.

[492] And our philosopher follows the same analogy—he is like a plant which, having proper nurture, must necessarily grow and mature into all virtue, but, if sown and planted in an alien soil, becomes the most noxious of all weeds, unless he be preserved by some divine power. Do you really think, as people so often say, that our youth are corrupted by Sophists, or that private teachers of the art corrupt them in any degree worth speaking of? Are not the public who say these things the greatest of all Sophists? And do they not educate to perfection young and old, men and women alike, and fashion them after their own hearts?

When is this accomplished? he said.

When they meet together, and the world sits down at an assembly, or in a court of law, or a theatre, or a camp, or in any other popular resort, and there is a great uproar, and they praise some things which are being said or done, and blame other things, equally exaggerating both, shouting and clapping their hands, and the echo of the rocks and the place in which they are assembled redoubles the

sound of the praise or blame—at such a time
will not a young man's heart, as they say, leap
within him? Will any private training enable
him to stand firm against the overwhelming
flood of popular opinion? or will he be carried
away by the stream? Will he not have the
notions of good and evil which the public in
general have—he will do as they do, and as they
are, such will he be?

Yes, Socrates; necessity will compel him.

And yet, I said, there is a still greater necessity, which has not been mentioned.

What is that?

The gentle force of attainder or confiscation
or death, which, as you are aware, these new
Sophists and educators, who are the public,
apply when their words are powerless.

Indeed they do; and in right good earnest.

Now what opinion of any other Sophist, or of
any private person, can be expected to overcome in such an unequal contest?

None, he replied.

No, indeed, I said, even to make the attempt
is a great piece of folly; there neither is, nor has
been, nor is ever likely to be, any different type
of character which has had no other training in
virtue but that which is supplied by public
opinion—I speak, my friend, of human virtue
only; what is more than human, as the proverb
says, is not included: for I would not have you
ignorant, whatever is saved and comes to good
is saved by the power of God, [493] as we may
truly say.

I quite assent, he replied.

Then let me crave your assent also to a further observation.

What are you going to say?

Why, that all those mercenary individuals,
whom the many call Sophists and whom they
deem to be their adversaries, do, in fact, teach
nothing but the opinion of the many, that is to
say, the opinions of their assemblies; and this is
their wisdom. I might compare them to a man
who should study the tempers and desires of a
mighty strong beast who is fed by him—he
would learn how to approach and handle him,
also at what times and from what causes he is
dangerous or the reverse, and what is the meaning of his several cries, and by what sounds,
when another utters them, he is soothed or in-
furiated; and you may suppose further, that
when, by continually attending upon him, he

has become perfect in all this, he calls his
knowledge wisdom, and makes of it a system or
art, which he proceeds to teach, although he
has no real notion of what he means by the
principles or passions of which he is speaking,
but calls this honourable and that dishonourable, or good or evil, or just or unjust, all in
accordance with the tastes and tempers of the
great brute. Good he pronounces to be that in
which the beast delights and evil to be that
which he dislikes; and he can give no other
account of them except that the just and noble
are the necessary, having never himself seen,
and having no power of explaining to others the
nature of either, or the difference between
them, which is immense. By heaven, would not
such an one be a rare educator?

Indeed he would.

And in what way does he who thinks that
wisdom is the discernment of the tempers and
tastes of the motley multitude, whether in
painting or music, or, finally, in politics, differ
from him whom I have been describing? For
when a man consorts with the many, and
exhibits to them his poem or other work of art
or the service which he has done the State,
making them his judges when he is not obliged,
the so-called necessity of Diomede will oblige
him to produce whatever they praise. And yet
the reasons are utterly ludicrous which they
give in confirmation of their own notions about
the honourable and good. Did you ever hear
any of them which were not?

No, nor am I likely to hear.

You recognise the truth of what I have been
saying? Then let me ask you to consider further
whether the world will ever be induced to believe in the existence of absolute beauty rather
than of the many beautiful, [494] or of the absolute in each kind rather than of the many in
each kind?

Certainly not.

Then the world cannot possibly be a philosopher?

Impossible.

And therefore philosophers inevitably fall
under the censure of the world?

They must.

And of individuals who consort with the
mob and seek to please them?

That is evident.

Then, do you see any way in which the philosopher, can be preserved in his calling to the end? and remember what we were saying of him, that he was to have quickness and memory and courage and magnificence—these were admitted by us to be the true philosopher's gifts.

Yes.

Will not such an one from his early childhood be in all things first among all, especially if his bodily endowments are like his mental ones?

Certainly, he said.

And his friends and fellow-citizens will want to use him as he gets older for their own purposes?

No question.

Falling at his feet, they will make requests to him and do him honour and flatter him, because they want to get into their hands now, the power which he will one day possess.

That often happens, he said.

And what will a man such as he is be likely to do under such circumstances, especially if he be a citizen of a great city, rich and noble, and a tall proper youth? Will he not be full of boundless aspirations, and fancy himself able to manage the affairs of Hellenes and barbarians, and having got such notions into his head will he both dilate and elevate himself in the fulness of vain pomp and senseless pride?

To be sure he will.

Now, when he is in this state of mind, if some one gently comes to him and tells him that he is a fool and must get understanding, which can only be got by slaving for it, do you think that, under such adverse circumstances, he will be easily induced to listen?

Far otherwise.

And even if there be some one who through inherent goodness or natural reasonableness has had his eyes opened a little and is humbled and taken captive by philosophy, how will his friends behave when they think that they are likely to lose the advantage which they were hoping to reap from his companionship? Will they not do and say anything to prevent him from yielding to his better nature and to render his teacher powerless, using to this end private intrigues as well as public prosecutions?

[495] There can be no doubt of it.

And how can one who is thus circumstanced ever become a philosopher?

Impossible.

Then were we not right in saying that even the very qualities which make a man a philosopher may, if he be ill-educated, divert him from philosophy, no less than riches and their accompaniments and the other so-called goods of life?

We were quite right.

Thus, my excellent friend, is brought about all that ruin and failure which I have been describing of the natures best adapted to the best of all pursuits; they are natures which we maintain to be rare at any time; this being the class out of which come the men who are the authors of the greatest evil to States and individuals; and also the greatest good when the tide carries them in that direction; but a small man never was the doer of any great thing either to individuals or to States.

That is most true, he said.

And so philosophy is left desolate, with her marriage rite incomplete: for her own have fallen away and forsaken her, and while they are leading a false and unbecoming life, other unworthy persons, seeing that she has no kinsmen to be her protectors, enter in and dishonour her; and fasten upon her the reproaches which, as you say, her reprovers utter, who affirm of her votaries that some are good for nothing, and that the greater number deserve the severest punishment.

That is certainly what people say.

Yes; and what else would you expect, I said, when you think of the puny creatures who, seeing this land open to them—a land well stocked with fair names and showy titles—like prisoners running out of prison into a sanctuary, take a leap out of their trades into philosophy; those who do so being probably the cleverest hands at their own miserable crafts? For, although philosophy be in this evil case, still there remains a dignity about her which is not to be found in the arts. And many are thus attracted by her whose natures are imperfect and whose souls are maimed and disfigured by their meannesses, as their bodies are by their trades and crafts. Is not this unavoidable?

Yes.

Are they not exactly like a bald little tinker who has just got out of durance and come into a fortune; he takes a bath and puts on a new coat, and is decked out as a bridegroom going to marry his daughter, who is left poor and desolate?

[*496*] A most exact parallel.

What will be the issue of such marriages? Will they not be vile and bastard?

There can be no question of it.

And when persons who are unworthy of education approach philosophy and make an alliance with her who is a rank above them what sort of ideas and opinions are likely to be generated? Will they not be sophisms captivating to the ear, having nothing in them genuine, or worthy of or akin to true wisdom?

No doubt, he said.

Then, Adeimantus, I said, the worthy disciples of philosophy will be but a small remnant: perchance some noble and well educated person, detained by exile in her service, who in the absence of corrupting influences remains devoted to her; or some lofty soul born in a mean city, the politics of which he contemns and neglects; and there may be a gifted few who leave the arts, which they justly despise, and come to her—or peradventure there are some who are restrained by our friend Theages' bridle; for everything in the life of Theages conspired to divert him from philosophy; but ill-health kept him away from politics. My own case of the internal sign is hardly worth mentioning, for rarely, if ever, has such a monitor been given to any other man. Those who belong to this small class have tasted how sweet and blessed a possession philosophy is, and have also seen enough of the madness of the multitude; and they know that no politician is honest, nor is there any champion of justice at whose side they may fight and be saved. Such an one may be compared to a man who has fallen among wild beasts—he will not join in the wickedness of his fellows, but neither is he able singly to resist all their fierce natures, and therefore seeing that he would be of no use to the State or to his friends, and reflecting that he would have to throw away his life without doing any good either to himself or others, he holds his peace, and goes his own way. He is like one who, in the storm of dust and sleet which the driving wind hurries along, retires under the shelter of a wall; and seeing the rest of mankind full of wickedness, he is content, if only he can live his own life and be pure from evil or unrighteousness, and depart in peace and goodwill, with bright hopes.

Yes, he said, and he will have done a great work before he departs.

A great work—yes; but not the greatest, unless he find a State suitable to him; [*497*] for in a State which is suitable to him, he will have a larger growth and be the saviour of his country, as well as of himself.

The causes why philosophy is in such an evil name have now been sufficiently explained: the injustice of the charges against her has been shown—is there anything more which you wish to say?

Nothing more on that subject, he replied; but I should like to know which of the governments now existing is in your opinion the one adapted to her.

Not any of them, I said; and that is precisely the accusation which I bring against them—not one of them is worthy of the philosophic nature . . . what I would have you term the idea of good, and this you will deem to be the cause of science, and of truth in so far as the latter becomes the subject of knowledge; beautiful too, as are both truth and knowledge, you will be right in esteeming this other nature as more beautiful than either; [*509*] and, as in the previous instance, light and sight may be truly said to be like the sun, and yet not to the sun, so in this other sphere, science and truth may be deemed to be like the good, but not the good; the good has a place of honour yet higher.

What a wonder of beauty that must be, he said, which is the author of science and truth, and yet surpasses them in beauty; for you surely cannot mean to say that pleasure is the good?

God forbid, I replied; but may I ask you to consider the image in another point of view?

In what point of view?

You would say, would you not, that the sun is not only the author of visibility in all visible things, but of generation and nourishment and growth, though he himself is not generation?

Certainly.

In like manner the good may be said to be not only the author of knowledge to all things known, but of their being and essence, and yet the good is not essence, but far exceeds essence in dignity and power.

Glaucon said, with a ludicrous earnestness: By the light of heaven, how amazing!

Yes, I said, and the exaggeration may be set down to you; for you made me utter my fancies.

And pray continue to utter them; at any rate let us hear if there is anything more to be said about the similitude of the sun.

Yes, I said, there is a great deal more.

Then omit nothing, however slight.

I will do my best, I said; but I should think that a great deal will have to be omitted.

THE DIVIDED LINE OF KNOWLEDGE

You have to imagine, then, that there are two ruling powers, and that one of them is set over the intellectual world, the other over the visible. I do not say heaven, lest you should fancy that I am playing upon the name (ovpavos, oparos). May I suppose that you have this distinction of the visible and intelligible fixed in your mind.

I have.

Now take a line which has been cut into two unequal parts, and divide each of them again in the same proportion, and suppose the two main divisions to answer, one to the visible and the other to the intelligible, and then compare the subdivisions in respect of their clearness and want of clearness, and you will find that the first section in the sphere of the visible consists of images. [510] And by images I mean, in the first place, shadows, and in the second place reflections in water and in solid, smooth and polished bodies and the like: Do you understand?

Yes, I understand.

Imagine, now, the other section, of which this is only the resemblance, to include the animals which we see, and everything that grows or is made.

Very good.

Would you not admit that both the sections of this division have different degrees of truth, and that the copy is to the original as the sphere of opinion is to the sphere of knowledge?

Most undoubtedly.

Next proceed to consider the manner in which the sphere of the intellectual is to be divided.

In what manner?

Thus:—There are two subdivisions, in the lower of which the soul uses the figures given by the former division as images: the enquiry can only be hypothetical, and instead of going upwards to a principle descends to the other end; in the higher of the two, the soul passes out of hypotheses, and goes up to a principle which is above hypotheses, making no use of images as in the former case, but proceeding only in and through the ideas themselves.

I do not quite understand your meaning, he said.

Then I will try again; you will understand me better when I have made some preliminary remarks. You are aware that students of geometry, arithmetic, and the kindred sciences assume the odd and the even and the figures and three kinds of angles and the like in their several branches of science; these are their hypotheses, which they and everybody are supposed to know, and therefore they do not deign to give any account of them either to themselves or others; but they begin with them, and go on until they arrive at last, and in a consistent manner, at their conclusion?

Yes, he said, I know.

And do you not know also that although they make use of the visible forms and reason about them, they are thinking not of these, but of the ideals which they resemble; not of the figures which they draw, but of the absolute square and the absolute diameter, and so on—the forms which they draw or make, and which have shadows and reflections in water of their own, are converted by them into images, but they are really seeking to behold the things themselves, which can only be seen with the eye of the mind?

[511] That is true.

And of this kind I spoke as the intelligible, although in the search after it the soul is compelled to use hypotheses; not ascending to a first principle, because she is unable to rise above the region of hypothesis, but employing the objects of which the shadows below are resemblances in their turn as images, they having in relation to the shadows and reflections of them a greater distinctness, and therefore a higher value.

I understand, he said, that you are speaking of the province of geometry and the sister arts.

And when I speak of the other division of the intelligible, you will understand me to speak of that other sort of knowledge which reason herself attains by the power of dialectic, using the hypotheses not as first principles, but only as hypotheses—that is to say, as steps and points of departure into a world which is above hypotheses, in order that she may soar beyond them to the first principle of the whole; and clinging to this and then to that which depends on this, by successive steps she descends again without the aid of any sensible object, from ideas, through ideas, and in ideas she ends.

I understand you, he replied; not perfectly, for you seem to me to be describing a task which is really tremendous; but, at any rate, I understand you to say that knowledge and being, which the science of dialetic contemplates, are clearer than the notions of the arts, as they are termed, which proceed from hypotheses only: these are also contemplated by the understanding, and not by the senses: yet, because they start from hypotheses and do not ascend to a principle, those who contemplate them appear to you not to exercise the higher reason upon them, although when a first principle is added to them they are cognizable by the higher reason. And the habit which is concerned with geometry and the cognate sciences I suppose that you would term understanding and not reason, as being intermediate between opinion and reason.

You have quite conceived my meaning, I said; and now, corresponding to these four divisions, let there be four faculties in the soul—reason answering to the highest, understanding to the second, faith (or conviction) to the third, and perception of shadows to the last—and let there be a scale of them, and let us suppose that the several faculties have clearness in the same degree that their objects have truth.

I understand, he replied, and give my assent, and accept your arrangement.

THE CAVE

[514] And now, I said, let me show in a figure how far our nature is enlightened or unenlightened:—Behold! human beings living in an underground den, which has a mouth open towards the light and reaching all along the den; here they have been from their childhood, and have their legs and necks chained so that they cannot move, and can only see before them, being prevented by the chains from turning round their heads. Above and behind them a fire is blazing at a distance, and between the fire and the prisoners there is a raised way; and you will

see, if you look, a low wall built along the way, like the screen which marionette players have in front of them, over which they show the puppets.

I see.

And do you see, I said, men passing along the wall carrying all sorts of vessels, [515] and statues and figures of animals made of wood and stone and various materials, which appear over the wall? Some of them are talking, others silent.

You have shown me a strange image, and they are strange prisoners.

Like ourselves, I replied; and they see only their own shadows, or the shadows of one another, which the fire throws on the opposite wall of the cave?

True, he said: how could they see anything but the shadows if they were never allowed to move their heads?

And of the objects which are being carried in like manner they would only see the shadows?

Yes, he said.

And if they were able to converse with one another, would they not suppose that they were naming what was actually before them?

Very true.

And suppose further that the prison had an echo which came from the other side, would they not be sure to fancy when one of the passers-by spoke that the voice which they heard came from the passing shadow?

No question, he replied.

To them, I said, the truth would be literally nothing but the shadows of the images.

That is certain.

And now look again, and see what will naturally follow if the prisoners are released and disabused of their error. At first, when any of them is liberated and compelled suddenly to stand up and turn his neck round and walk and look towards the light, he will suffer sharp pains; the glare will distress him, and he will be unable to see the realities of which in his former state he had seen the shadows; and then conceive some one saying to him, that what he saw before was an illusion, but that now, when he is approaching nearer to being and his eye is turned towards more real existence, he has a clearer vision—what will be his reply? And you may further imagine that his instructor is pointing to the objects as they pass and requiring him to name them—will he not be perplexed? Will he not fancy that the shadows which he formerly saw are truer than the objects which are now shown to him?

Far truer.

And if he is compelled to look straight at the light, will he not have a pain in his eyes which will make him turn away to take refuge in the objects of vision which he can see, and which he will conceive to be in reality clearer than the things which are now being shown to him?

True, he said.

And suppose once more, that he is reluctantly dragged up a steep and rugged ascent, and held fast until he is forced into the presence of the sun himself, [516] is he not likely to be pained and irritated? When he approaches the light his eyes will be dazzled, and he will not be able to see anything at all of what are now called realities.

Not all in a moment, he said.

He will require to grow accustomed to the sight of the upper world. And first he will see the shadows best, next the reflections of men and other objects in the water, and then the objects themselves; then he will gaze upon the light of the moon and the stars and the spangled heaven; and he will see the sky and the stars by night better than the sun or the light of the sun by day?

Certainly.

Last of all he will be able to see the sun, and not mere reflections of him in the water, but he will see him in his own proper place, and not in another; and he will contemplate him as he is.

Certainly.

He will then proceed to argue that this is he who gives the season and the years, and is the guardian of all that is in the visible world, and in a certain way the cause of all things which he and his fellows have been accustomed to behold?

Clearly, he said, he would first see the sun and then reason about him.

And when he remembered his old habitation, and the wisdom of the den and his fellow-prisoners, do you not suppose that he would felicitate himself on the change, and pity them?

Certainly, he would.

And if they were in the habit of conferring honours among themselves on those who were quickest to observe the passing shadows and to

remark which of them went before, and which followed after, and which were together; and who were therefore best able to draw conclusions as to the future, do you think that he would care for such honours and glories, or envy the possessors of them? Would he not say with Homer,

Better to be the poor servant of a poor master,

and to endure anything, rather than think as they do and live after their manner?

Yes, he said, I think that he would rather suffer anything than entertain these false notions and live in this miserable manner.

Imagine once more, I said, such an one coming suddenly out of the sun to be replaced in his old situation; would he not be certain to have his eyes full of darkness?

To be sure, he said.

And if there were a contest, and he had to compete in measuring the shadows with the prisoners who had never moved out of the [517] den, while his sight was still weak, and before his eyes had become steady (and the time which would be needed to acquire this new habit of sight might be very considerable), would he not be ridiculous? Men would say of him that up he went and down he came without his eyes; and that it was better not even to think of ascending; and if any one tried to loose another and lead him up to the light, let them only catch the offender, and they would put him to death.

No question, he said.

This entire allegory, I said, you may now append, dear Glaucon, to the previous argument; the prison-house is the world of sight, the light of the fire is the sun, and you will not misapprehend me if you interpret the journey upwards to be the ascent of the soul into the intellectual world according to my poor belief, which, at your desire, I have expressed—whether rightly or wrongly God knows. But, whether true or false, my opinion is that in the world of knowledge the idea of good appears last of all, and is seen only with an effort; and, when seen, is also inferred to be the universal author of all things beautiful and right, parent of light and of the lord of light in this visible world, and the immediate source of reason and truth in the intellectual; and that this is the power upon which he who would act rationally either in public or private life must have his eye fixed.

I agree, he said, as far as I am able to understand you.

Moreover, I said, you must not wonder that those who attain to this beatific vision are unwilling to descend to human affairs; for their souls are ever hastening into the upper world where they desire to dwell; which desire of theirs is very natural, if our allegory may be trusted.

Yes, very natural.

And is there anything surprising in one who passes from divine contemplations to the evil state of man, misbehaving himself in a ridiculous manner; if, while his eyes are blinking and before he has become accustomed to the surrounding darkness, he is compelled to fight in courts of law, or in other places, about the images or the shadows of images of justice, and is endeavouring to meet the conceptions of those who have never yet seen absolute justice?

Anything but surprising, he replied.

[518] Any one who has common sense will remember that the bewilderments of the eyes are of two kinds, and arise from two causes, either from coming out of the light or from going into the light, which is true of the mind's eye, quite as much as the bodily eye; and he who remembers this when he sees any one whose vision is perplexed and weak, will not be too ready to laugh; he will first ask whether that soul of man has come out of the brighter life, and is unable to see because unaccustomed to the dark, or having turned from darkness to the day is dazzled by excess of light. And he will count the one happy in his condition and state of being, and he will pity the other; so, if he have a mind to laugh at the soul which comes from below into the light, there will be more reason in this than in the laugh which greets him who returns from above out of the light into the den.

That, he said, is a very just distinction.

But then, if I am right, certain professors of education must be wrong when they say that they can put a knowledge into the soul which was not there before, like sight into blind eyes.

They undoubtedly say this, he replied.

Whereas, our argument shows that the power and capacity of learning exists in the soul al-

ready; and that just as the eye was unable to turn from darkness to light without the whole body, so too the instrument of knowledge can only by the movement of the whole soul be turned from the world of becoming into that of being, and learn by degrees to endure the sight of being, and of the brightest and best of being, or in other words, of the good.

Very true.

And must there not be some art which will effect conversion in the easiest and quickest manner; not implanting the faculty of sight, for that exists already, but has been turned in the wrong direction, and is looking away from the truth?

Yes, he said, such an art may be presumed.

And whereas the other so-called virtues of the soul seem to be akin to bodily qualities, for even when they are not originally innate they can be implanted later by habit and exercise, the virtue of wisdom more than anything else contains a divine element which always remains, and by this conversion is rendered useful and profitable; [519] or, on the other hand, hurtful and useless. Did you never observe the narrow intelligence flashing from the keen eye of a clever rogue—how eager he is, how clearly his paltry soul sees the way to his end; he is the reverse of blind, but his keen eye-sight is forced into the service of evil, and he is mischievous in proportion to his cleverness?

Very true, he said.

But what if there had been a circumcision of such natures in the days of their youth; and they had been severed from those sensual pleasures, such as eating and drinking, which, like leaden weights, were attached to them at their birth, and which drag them down and turn the vision of their souls upon the things that are below—if, I say, they had been released from these impediments and turned in the opposite direction, the very same faculty in them would have seen the truth as keenly as they see what their eyes are turned to now.

Very likely.

Yes, I said; and there is another thing which is likely, or rather a necessary inference from what has preceded, that neither the uneducated and uninformed of the truth, nor yet those who never make an end of their education, will be able ministers of State; not the former, because they have no single aim of duty which is the rule of all their actions, private as well as public; nor the latter, because they will not act at all except upon compulsion, fancying that they are already dwelling apart in the islands of the blest.

Very true, he replied.

Then, I said, the business of us who are the founders of the State will be to compel the best minds to attain that knowledge which we have already shown to be the greatest of all—they must continue to ascend until they arrive at the good; but when they have ascended and seen enough we must not allow them to do as they do now.

What do you mean?

I mean that they remain in the upper world: but this must not be allowed; they must be made to descend again among the prisoners in the den, and partake of their labours and honours, whether they are worth having or not.

But is not this unjust? he said; ought we to give them a worse life, when they might have a better?

You have again forgotten, my friend, I said, the intention of the legislator, who did not aim at making any one class in the State happy above the rest; the happiness was to be in the whole State, and he held the citizens together by persuasion and necessity, making them benefactors of the State, [520] and therefore benefactors of one another; to this end he created them, not to please themselves, but to be his instruments in binding up the State.

True, he said, I had forgotten.

Observe, Glaucon, that there will be no injustice in compelling our philosophers to have a care and providence of others; we shall explain to them that in other States, men of their class are not obliged to share in the toils of politics and this is reasonable, for they grow up at their own sweet will, and the government would rather not have them. Being self-taught, they cannot be expected to show any gratitude for a culture which they have never received. But we have brought you into the world to be rulers of the hive, kings of yourselves and of the other citizens, and have educated you far better and more perfectly than they have been educated and you are better able to share in the double duty. Wherefore each of you, when his turn comes, must go down to the general under ground abode, and get the habit of seeing in the dark. When you have acquired the habit, you will see ten thousand times better than the inhabitants of the den, and you will know what the several images are, and what they represent because you have seen the beautiful and just and good in their truth. And thus our State which is also yours will be a reality, and not a dream only, and will be administered in a spirit unlike that of other States, in which men fight with one another about shadows only and are distracted in the struggle for power, which in their eyes is a great good. Whereas the truth is that the State in which the rulers are most reluctant to govern is always the best and most quietly governed, and the State in which they are most eager, the worst.

Quite true, he replied.

And will our pupils, when they hear this, refuse to take their turn at the toils of State, when they are allowed to spend the greater part of their time with one another in the heavenly light?

Impossible, he answered; for they are just men, and the commands which we impose upon them are just; there can be no doubt that every one of them will take office as a stern necessity, and not after the fashion of our present rulers of State.

Yes, my friend, I said; and there lies the point. You must contrive for your future rulers another and a better life than that of [521] a ruler, and then you may have a well-ordered State; for only in the State which offers this, will they rule who are truly rich, not in silver and gold, but in virtue and wisdom, which are the true blessings of life. Whereas if they go to the administration of public affairs, poor and hungering after their own private advantage, thinking that hence they are to snatch the chief good, order there can never be: for they will be fighting about office, and the civil and domestic broils which thus arise will be the ruin of the rulers themselves and of the whole State.

Most true, he replied.

And the only life which looks down upon the life of political ambition is that of true philosophy. Do you know of any other?

Indeed, I do not, he said.

And those who govern ought not to be lovers of the task? For, if they are, there will be rival lovers, and they will fight.

No question.

Who then are those whom we shall compel to be guardians? Surely they will be the men who are wisest about affairs of State, and by whom the State is best administered, and who at the same time have other honours and another and a better life than that of politics?

They are the men, and I will choose them, he replied. . . .

Platonism

Platonism is that philosophical tradition which owes it's origins to the *works* of Plato. (It is not clear whether Plato himself would have approved of being called the founder of Platonism.) The point is that Platonism is not the set of views of one person that have persisted through a long period of time, but rather, it is an attitude toward, an approach to, or better yet, a particular map charting the way through the realms of philosophy. That map has had a long and important history, and to this day it exercises a strong influence upon the minds of men. Regardless of who first made the map, its users constitute a continuous tradition whose reality is undeniable.

In describing Platonism we shall follow a format and a particular view of the history of philosophy which will help us to make sense of other philosophical traditions. As we have said before, philosophy began when man came to believe that the world was intelligible to him. In attempting to grasp that intelligible aspect of our existence, philosophers have been led to articulate rather comprehensive visions of what reality is all about. These comprehensive visions take into account what we already think we know and serve as guides for finding our way through the rest. In this latter sense they are maps. In attempting to construct these maps, philosophers take as their guide the most comprehensive and coherent body of knowledge available to them at any given time. This guide then permits the philosopher to answer all questions about what exists, *ontology*, and how to go about discovering what exists, *methodology*. But this "map-making" has never been merely a matter of incorporating the latest fashionable opinion;

for conflicts exist even within what we already claim to know. Rather, philosophers have tended to construct more stable models of rational inquiry. The obvious danger of such models is that we tend to fall in love with them, so that any intellectual pursuit which does not conform to the model is dismissed as the result of confusion. In this respect philosophers can become as dogmatic and as authoritarian as those whom they oppose. Finally, as the result of various changes in what constitutes the preeminent body of knowledge at any one time, alternative philosophical maps can be constructed. This accounts, in part, for why philosophy has a history.

1. We begin by noting that for Plato the *model science,* or example of coherent knowledge, is *geometry*. The appeal to mathematics in general and geometry in particular are incontestable elements of Plato's philosophy. Every schoolboy and girl knows about Euclid's geometry, and although Euclid formalized geometry some fifty years after Plato's death, the development of geometry as a system of proof was well known to Plato. The influence of the Pythagoreans, who were responsible for the Pythagorean theorem, upon Plato's work is well known. Platonism constructs a total vision of rational knowledge along the lines of geometry. We recall that over the door to Plato's Academy was the motto that only those who studied geometry could enter.

2. If geometry is our model science, then all good explanations must have the form of a geometrical proof. That is, all good *explanations are demonstrations* or proofs which begin with axioms or first principles such that if we accept the first principles we must, by an incontestable logic, accept the conclusion. Those who emphasize the supreme importance of deductive logic, beginning with general statements and proceeding to particulars, are Platonists.

3. *Rationality* involves beginning with self-evident axioms or *first principles known a priori.* By *self-evident* we mean that no evidence need be offered for them; they constitute their own evidence. This is necessary in order to prevent an infinite regress. If everything had to be proved we could never begin to prove anything. Therefore, there must be something which needs no proof. These are the axioms. In saying that the axioms are *a priori* we mean two things. First, *a priori* means independent of experience. *Independent* in this context means that we do not need experience to establish the truth of the axioms, and in all likelihood we could not use experience to do the job. *A priori* also means that the axioms pass a special logical test in order to qualify. One of the many ways of expressing this test is to say that axioms are such that their opposites are inconceivable. For example, it is impossible to imagine or conceive of a four-sided triangle once we understand goemetry. Platonists believe that such incontestable truths can be established in all disciplines.

4. Armed with the foregoing, Platonists can then proceed to apply their views to specific realms such as physical science and social science, and to questions of value. In the realm of *physical science,* Platonists seek those *underlying principles of permanence of which the world of our experience is but an imperfect representation.* For example, we all know that according to the laws of falling bodies, several bodies of any mass dropped simultaneously from the same

height should touch the ground at the same time. In fact, when the experiment is conducted, one of the bodies will touch before the others. Scientists readily allow that such evidence does not challenge the laws; rather, the laws hold under "ideal conditions," even if we cannot construct ideal conditions. This manner of interpreting scientific statements is Platonic. The persistent success of scientists who assume mathematical preconceptions of symmetry in the universe, even where others see chaos, would come as no surprise to a Platonist.

5. In *social science* the Platonist performs an analagous intellectual feat: that is, he seeks the basic principles of *ideal societies*. Others would call this utopianism. The Platonist would argue that just as the physical world imperfectly manifests its basic principles, so social life imperfectly manifests its own. To condemn one is necessarily to condemn the other.

6. Where questions of *value* are concerned, the Platonist draws the consistent consequence that there are first principles of value known a priori in acts of intellectual vision. Again, the same principle applies, namely, that these truths do not pretend to describe actual behavior but to make actual behavior intelligible by providing a description of what behavior would be under "ideal conditions."

Not only are there first principles for each realm, but all of these realms form an integrated system where values emerge as the central or supreme principles. When someone comprehends the system as a whole, that is, when he has a completely rational view of reality, then he automatically acts in accordance with these principles. Any failure to act consistently would indicate a failure to comprehend fully. This is the classical *faith in reason*, the belief that knowledge can solve every human problem. It is a view which does not recognize the later Christian notion of "sin," and it is certainly not a fashionable view these days.

The foregoing general outline of Platonism can be applied to subsequent philosophers in whole or in part. It will be instructive to see to what extent later philosophers can be interpreted as Platonists or to what extent they deviate from the Platonic tradition, and to determine the conditions both intellectual and social which account for that deviation.

Chapter III—Aristotle and the Aristotelian Tradition

Aristotle

With the exception of Plato, no philosopher has exercised a greater influence on the development of Western Civilization than Aristotle. His ideas have managed to survive among us for more than two thousand years, and his immense contributions to philosophy and science are still regarded as paradigms of human achievement. Like Plato, Aristotle was a seminal thinker. He has served as a source of inspiration to countless human beings who have dedicated their lives to the pursuit of wisdom. During medieval times, for example, Aristotle was referred to as "the philosopher," and his writings constituted the firm basis on which much of medieval philosophy rested. Today, even though many of his ideas and insights into the nature of the universe and man have been replaced by perhaps more adequate notions, he still remains one of the foundations of our thinking.

Aristotle was born in 384 B.C. Like many other Greek philosophers of his time, he was not an Athenian. His home was the small town of Stagira in northern Greece, and his family appears to have been devoted to the service of the Macedonian King Philip, the father of Alexander the Great. Aristotle's father, a man named Nicomachus, was the king's personal physician. The philosopher's early training was in the medical and biological sciences, and we are told by his biographers that by the age of seventeen he was already an accomplished physician.

Around the year 367 B.C., he travelled to Athens for the purpose of completing his education. Athens was the cultural capital of the Greek world, and

Plato's Academy was the place where many prominent scholars congregated. Aristotle, accordingly, entered Plato's Academy, where he remained for close to twenty years. There he functioned in the capacity of student and teacher, and it appears that the philosophy of Plato exercised a profound influence on him. We know, for example, that like Plato, he wrote philosophical dialogues, and that during his first years at the Academy he developed a system of philosophy along the lines suggested by Plato's thought. In later years, however, his relationship with Plato became somewhat strained due to the ideological differences between the two philosophers. Eventually, this led to Aristotle's leaving the Academy several years before Plato's death in 347 B.C.

Subsequently, Aristotle travelled extensively throughout the ancient Greek world, and settled down in a province of Asia Minor (Turkey) called Mycia. In 341 B.C. he was summoned by King Philip of Macedonia to serve as Alexander's tutor, and in compliance with the ancient ties of his family with the Macedonian crown, Aristotle remained close to Alexander for five years. Afterwards, he moved back to Athens, probably in the company of the invading Macedonian armies which eventually came to conquer most of the Greek world. In Athens, with the political and financial support of the Macedonians, he founded an institution of higher learning which became known as the Lyceum. Here, Aristotle taught and engaged in scientific research for thirteen years. Upon the untimely death of Alexander, who had become emperor, Aristotle was accused of impiety and treason. We can surmise, of course, that these accusations, not unlike those brought up against Socrates, were the legalistic mantle beneath which there lurked a political conspiracy against the philosopher. Unlike Socrates, however, Aristotle chose to escape from Athens even before the trial. He took refuge in the neighboring town of Chalcis, where he died one year later of natural causes.

Aristotle's writings are many and varied. Unfortunately, almost half of them perished during the Roman occupation of Greece, and there is little hope of ever finding them. But what survived is probably a sufficient basis for forming an idea of Aristotle's philosophy. Among the surviving writings, there are treatises on logic and scientific methodology, on cosmology and astronomy, on physics and biology, on dreams and psychology, on the nature of political institutions and the Athenian constitution, on poetry and drama, on ethics and history, on metaphysics, and on many other philosophical subjects. Unlike the *Dialogues* of Plato, the writings of Aristotle are designed to serve as the basis for lectures and therefore have a strictly didactic texture.

It can be safely said that no philosopher in the history of Western Civilization has made a greater attempt to systematize knowledge and to reach a more comprehensive understanding of the universe and man, than Aristotle. This is, among other things, one of the reasons for his enormous influence among us. He gave us, for the very first time, the elements for an organization of the sciences.

Aristotle held a number of ideas about the universe which are no longer accepted by the scientific orthodoxy. He believed, for example, that the earth occupied the center of the universe, and that the moon, the planets, the sun, and the stars were attached to invisible spheres which rotated daily around the earth.

The earth, of which Aristotle gave us the first recorded spherical dimensions, rested motionless at the very center of the universe. There is no reference in Aristotle's writings to the idea of development in the universe. It appears as if he thought that the universe at large was changeless.

These geocentric notions have little adequacy in the present world of astronomy. Today we are accustomed to take for granted the insignificance of our planet in the context of the Solar System, the insignificance of the sun and its system in the context of the Milky Way, and the insignificance of the Milky Way in the context of the billions of galaxies which constitute the observable universe. We are far removed from the limitations of Aristotle's geocentric cosmology. But what is curious is that this cosmology dominated the minds of human beings until the time of Copernicus (1473-1543). In medieval times, the authority of Aristotle was regarded as sufficient proof that the earth did not move in space, and even in the sixteenth century, when Galileo was prosecuted by the Catholic Inquisition, the Aristotelian ideas were quoted in the inquisitional indictment.

What the medievals and the inquisitors forgot however was, that Aristotle himself had said on repeated occasions that "experience, not authority, should be taken as the ultimate standard of judgment." If one day, said Aristotle, my ideas are found to be contrary to experience, let my ideas be forgotten. Human beings, however, feel more at ease when they can quote a distinguished authority, instead of examining their own experiences. This explains the unjustified use of Aristotle's name in order to settle controversies. As we saw in Chapter One, philosophy should have no dogmas, no final authority, no sanctified belief. In philosophy, the mind is free to explore for itself all possible regions of human experience, and to form its own judgments accordingly. All that is required is a large dose of Socratic honesty and a great deal of perseverance.

Honesty and perseverance—these are the unmistakable characteristics of Aristotle's writings, even when, from our present point of view, we are unable to agree with some of their contentions. Before examining any issue, Aristotle always begins by reviewing, in a spirit of compassion and thoroughness, most of the views held by his predecessors on the same issue. This Aristotelian habit, something which should be emulated by all philosophers and scientists, constitutes one of the major merits of his writings. In all of them, we are allowed to examine, albeit briefly, the ideas of ancient philosophers whose writings have never come to us. There are many passages in Aristotle's writings devoted to the analysis of Plato's ideas, and reading them, one becomes immediately aware of the gap that separated the two philosophers. But even when Aristotle expresses his dissatisfaction with one or another Platonic idea, he invariably displays a profound sense of respect and humility. Aristotle knew perfectly well that above the names of philosophers and their systems of ideas, the ultimate court of judgment is human experience.

His philosophy, therefore, makes a constant appeal to experience. Knowledge, he says in the *Metaphysics,* is inevitably rooted in sense experience, and ultimate knowledge has to do with individual objects of experience. In the few selections from his writings to which the student will be introduced, this will become abundantly clear.

Aristotle's Philosophy

The Problem of Change

We have identified Thales as the first philosopher, since he was the first of a long line of Greek thinkers who were concerned with defining the nature of reality. Despite giving divergent answers to the question, all of these thinkers agreed that some definitive statement could be given about the permanent nature of the real. One of the consequences of this assumption is that *change* becomes something of a problem. In our talk about things that change, we seem to be assuming that something remains permanent during the process of change. Moreover, if there is change, then there must be some permanent principles according to which change takes place. In short, Greek philosophers assumed that what was permanent was real, and they either denied the reality of what appears to change, or they interpreted change as a manifestation of what was unchanging.

Aristotle took change seriously and sought to explain it better than his predecessors had. At the same time, he never challenged their assumption that basic to this process was the existence of something unchanging.

Biology as a Guide

Since biology was the field he understood best, Aristotle sought to extend his understanding from that field to nature or to reality as a whole. In this there is nothing unusual, since if we believe that the world is intelligible there is nothing to prevent us from extending the principles of intelligibility from one discipline to another (properly qualified, of course). In fact, the demands of a total philosophical vision would seem to require this step.

There are certain principles which appear almost inescapable, or so men have thought, if we are to properly understand *life*. Life at every level seems to be characterized by growth, development, and decay—in short, by change. Moreover, that change seems to be designed to achieve certain purposes. Nutrition, growth, and reproduction seem to be fundamental to all organic activity. These functions are true of all living things, plants as well as animals. Beyond this, animals exhibit sensation, desire, and locomotion (change of place or position). And some animals exhibit the additional function or capacity for deliberate behavior (for example, beavers build dams). Beyond this, there is the purely theoretical thought of human beings. In fact, we seem to find a hierarchy wherein each level contains all that we find on the lower levels, plus something additional and peculiar to that level. Another remarkable principle discovered from the observation of animals is the persistence of the form, the species, through a changing succession of individuals. This is clear in oak trees producing acorns, which grow into other oak trees; and it is present in human reproduction, wherein certain genetic traits are preserved through the successive generations of a family.

The Causes of Change

Equipped with his knowledge of biological change, Aristotle turns to change in general. Previous thinkers had distinguished in varying and confused degrees two principles: the material constituents and the formal structure or *essence* which makes the constituent the determinate kind of thing it is. We say that the matter has the *potential* for embodying that form. Moreover, the form exists only in the succession of material objects in which it is embodied. On this crucial issue Aristotle disagrees with Plato, who had held that the forms (universals common to many objects) exist independently of the objects, which manifest the forms imperfectly. As opposed to the materialists, Aristotle insists upon the need for actual forms, because otherwise matter cannot be conceived of as actualizing its potential.

As with the animal kingdom, Aristotle conceives of the material world in general as comprising a system or hierarchy of graded existences. The simplest matter comprises the traditional four elements of earth, air, fire, and water. From these the more complex manifestations of inorganic bodies and the world of organic beings (living things) emerges. All this occurs because of the existence of more complex forms. Within this process of increasing complexity Aristotle distinguishes three kinds of change: alteration (qualitative change), quantitative change, and locomotion (change of place).

Locomotion is the most basic kind of change, but it involves more than impact. The locomotion of the four elements or primary bodies depends upon the assumption (traditional to Greek philosophy and shared by Aristotle) that each has a natural place in which it finally comes to rest. Since rest is natural, every movement requires the existence of a mover. Moreover, if the world is rational, there cannot be an infinite chain or series of movers. Hence, there must be a self-sufficient, self-explanatory, unmoved mover. In short, there must be a *first mover* or first movers. Finally, since motion is eternal, the first mover or movers must be eternal.

Unlike later Christian thought, which employs his thought, Aristotle spoke of *movers,* not one mover. Moreover, motion is eternal, otherwise a beginning to time (creation) would be needed, and such a concept would be unexplainable rationally. We also note that the need for a supreme form (unmoved mover) is part of Aristotle's biology, for the hierarchy in nature implies increasing consciousness. Even the reason by which mankind grasps the intelligibility of the world requires for its actualization a higher reason. This supreme form of intelligence is thought thinking about itself.

The Four Causes

The aim of rational inquiry is to discover the causes of a phenomenon. Aristotle finds that there are four kinds of causes: (1) material cause, (2) efficient cause, (3) formal cause, and (4) final cause. The material cause is that of which a thing is made; the efficient cause is that by which it comes into existence; the formal cause is its essence or essential nature; and the final cause is that end for which it exists. In the case of natural objects, as opposed to the products of human art, the last three causes coincide. That is, the efficient, formal, and final causes are the same.

What does this mean? Let us distinguish between the products of human art, like a statue or a house, and a natural object, like an acorn. We are concerned with natural objects. To explain an acorn we might describe the organic material of which it is made, but this is relatively unimportant. What is important are the other three causes. Where does an acorn come from? It comes from an oak tree. What happens to an acorn? It grows into an oak tree. Why does this all happen? It happens because the essence or form of an acorn is just that, namely, to become an oak tree. If we really understood or grasped the nature of the acorn, we could see that it must have come from an oak tree and that it is destined itself to become an oak tree. Such biological facts are generalized by Aristotle into a full-blown theory about how the universe works.

In Aristotelian language, the end or final cause of an object in nature is to realize its essence or formal cause. It also means that this formal cause or essence is embodied in another entity, which possesses an identical form or essence and serves as the efficient cause of its production. It is this coincidence of formal and efficient causes which permits us to infer unerringly what a cause must *necessarily* be, from mere acquaintance with the effect. The formal cause becomes in practice the basic explanatory principle, since what a thing is essentially is built into it.

The Place of Man

There is an element of Aristotle's philosophy which is difficult for some readers to grasp. As we know, most acorns do not grow into oak trees. Hence, we would say that under perfect or ideal conditions acorns grow into oaks. But note that these ideal conditions do sometimes exist in experience, unlike the Platonic ideal which need never be actualized in experience. This sense of something having an end which it does not always achieve is important for understanding Aristotle's views on man and society.

The good or end for man must be the full development of *human nature.* Human nature is understood in terms of those faculties which are distinctive of man, that separate or distinguish him from other entities. What is distinctive of us is our rational faculty, not our appetites. Our reason operates in two ways, first in the habitual subordination of appetite or passion to rational control, and second in the contemplation of truth. The first way is described as the set of moral virtues and involves the doctrine of the mean. Most moral virtues are means between extremes, as courage is the mean between being a coward and acting rashly.

In his discussion of politics, Aristotle makes it clear that a civilized community is a necessary prerequitisite for the full development of human nature. Again, for Aristotle the natural state is social life, for he finds nature only in the fully developed case. Aristotle would be appalled by the modern notion that what is natural is either what is primitive or what is usual in the statistical sense. Most acorns do not develop into oaks; but that, nevertheless, is their nature if only they get a chance to develop properly. Likewise, the highest good for man is contemplation, even though most individuals do not have the opportunity to become professional philosophers. Finally, we note that the ultimate end is not practical but theoretical.

How to Conduct a Philosophical Analysis

Every systematic science, the humblest and noblest alike, seems to admit of two distinct kinds of proficiency; one of which may be properly called scientific knowledge of the subject, while the other is a kind of educational acquaintance with it. For an educated man should be able to form a fair off-hand judgement as to the goodness or badness of the method used by a professor in his exposition. To be educated is in fact to be able to do this; and even the man of universal education we deem to be such in virtue of his having this ability. It will, however, of course, be understood that we only ascribe universal education to one who in his own individual person is thus critical in all or nearly all branches of knowledge, and not to one who has a like ability merely in some special project. For it is possible for a man to have this competence in some one branch of knowledge without having it in all.

It is plain then that, as in other sciences, so in that which inquires into nature, there must be certain canons, by reference to which a hearer shall be able to criticize the method of a professed exposition, quite independently of the question whether the statements made be true or false. Ought we, for instance (to give an illustration of what I mean), to begin by discussing each separate species—man, lion, ox, and the like—taking each kind in hand independently of the rest, or ought we rather to deal first with the attributes which they have in common in virtue of some common element of their nature, and proceed from this as a basis for the consideration of them separately? For genera that are quite distinct yet oftentimes present many identical phenomena, sleep, for instance, respiration, growth, decay, death, and other similar affections and conditions, which may be passed over for the present, as we are not prepared to treat of them with clearness and precision. Now it is plain that if we deal with each species independently of the rest, we shall frequently be obliged to repeat the same statements over and over again; for horse and dog and man present, each and all, every one of the phenomena just enumerated. A discussion therefore of the attributes of each such species separately would necessarily involve frequent repetitions as to characters, themselves identical but recurring in animals specifically distinct. (Very possibly also there may be other characters which, though they present specific differences, yet come under one and the same category. For instance, flying, swimming, walking, creeping, are plainly specifically distinct, but yet are all forms of animal progression.) We must, then, have some clear understanding as to the manner in which our investigation is to be conducted; whether, I mean, we are first to deal with the common or generic characters, and afterwards to take into consideration special peculiarities; or whether we are to start straight off with the ultimate species. For as yet no definite rule has been laid down in this matter. So also there is a likely uncertainty as to another point now to be mentioned. Ought the writer who deals with the works of nature to follow the plan adopted by the mathematicians in their astronomical demonstrations, and after considering the phenomena presented by animals, and their several parts, proceed subsequently to treat of the causes and the reason why; or ought he to follow some other method? And when these questions are answered, there yet remains another. The causes concerned in the generation of the works of nature are, as we see, more than one. There is the final cause and there is the motor cause. Now we must decide which of these two causes comes first, which second. Plainly, however, that cause is the first which we call the final one. For this is the Reason, and the Reason forms the starting-point, alike in the works of art and in works of nature. For consider how the physician or how the builder sets about his work. He starts by forming for himself a definite picture, in the one case perceptible to mind, in the other to sense, of his end—the physician of health, the builder of a house—and this he holds forward as the reason and explanation of each subsequent step that he takes, and of his acting in this or that way as the case may be. Now in the works of nature the good end and the final cause is still more dominant than in works of art such as these, nor is necessity a factor with the same significance in them all; though almost all writers, while they try to refer their origin to this cause, do so without distinguishing the various senses in which the term necessity is used. For there is absolute necessity, manifested in everything that is generated by nature as in everything that is produced by art, be it a house or what it may. For if a house or other such final object is to be realized, it is necessary that such and such material shall exist; and it is necessary that first this and then that shall be produced, and first this and then that set in motion, and so on in continuous succession, until the end and final result is reached, for the sake of which each prior thing is produced and exists. As with these productions of art, so also is it with the productions of nature. The mode of necessity, however, and the mode of ratiocination are different in natural science from what they are in the theoretical sciences; of which we have spoken elsewhere. For in the latter the starting-point is that which is; in the former that which is to be. For it is that which is yet to be—health, let us say, or a man—that, owing to its being of such and such characters, necessitates the pre-existence or previous production of this and that antecedent; and not this or that antecedent which, because it exists or has been generated, makes it necessary that health or a man is in, or shall come into, existence. Nor is it possible to trace back the series of necessary antecedents to a starting-point, of which you can say that, existing itself from eternity, it has

determined their existence as its consequent. These however, again, are matters that have been dealt with in another treatise. There too it was stated in what cases absolute and hypothetical necessity exist; in what cases also the proposition expressing hypothetical necessity is simply convertible, and what cause it is that determines this convertibility.

Another matter which must not be passed over without consideration is, whether the proper subject of our exposition is that with which the ancient writers concerned themselves, namely, what is the process of formation of each animal; or whether it is not rather, what are the characters of a given creature when formed. For there is no small difference between these two views. The best course appears to be that we should follow the method already mentioned, and begin with the phenomena presented by each group of animals, and, when this is done, proceed afterwards to state the causes of those phenomena, and to deal with their evolution. For elsewhere, as for instance in house building, this is the true sequence. The plan of the house, or the house, has this and that form; and because it has this and that form, therefore is its construction carried out in this or that manner. For the process of evolution is for the sake of the thing finally evolved, and not this for the sake of the process. Empedocles, then, was in error when he said that many of the characters presented by animals were merely the results of incidental occurrences during their development; for instance, that the backbone was divided as it is into vertebrae, because it happened to be broken owing to the contorted position of the foetus in the womb. In so saying he overlooked the fact that propagation implies a creative seed endowed with certain formative properties. Secondly, he neglected another fact, namely, that the parent animal pre-exists, not only in idea, but actually in time. For man is generated from man; and thus it is the possession of certain characters by the parent that determines the development of like characters in the child. The same statement holds good also for the operations of art, and even for those which are apparently spontaneous. For the same result as is produced by art may occur spontaneously. Spontaneity, for instance, may bring about the restoration of health. The products of art, however, require the pre-existence of an efficient cause homogeneous with themselves, such as the statuary's art, which must necessarily precede the statue; for this cannot possibly be produced spontaneously. Art indeed consists in the conception of the result to be produced before its realization in the material. As with spontaneity, so with chance; for this also produces the same result as art, and by the same process.

The fittest mode, then, of treatment is to say, a man has such and such parts, because the conception of a man includes their presence, and because they are necessary conditions of his existence, or, if we cannot quite say this, which would be best of all, then the next thing to it, namely, that it is either quite impossible for him to exist without them, or, at any rate, that it is better for him that they should be there: and their existence involves the existence of other antecedents. This we should say, because man is an animal with such and such characters, therefore is the process of his development necessarily such as it is; and therefore it is accomplished in such and such an order, this part being formed first, that next, and so on in succession; and after a like fashion should we explain the evolution of all other works of nature.

Now that with which the ancient writers, who first philosophized about Nature, busied themselves, was the material principle and the material cause. They inquired what this is, and what its character; how the universe is generated out of it, and by what motor influence, whether, for instance, by antagonism or friendship, whether by intelligence or spontaneous action, the substratum or matter being assumed to have certain inseparable properties; fire, for instance, to have a hot nature, earth a cold one; the former to be light, the latter heavy. For even the genesis of the universe is thus explained by them. After a like fashion do they deal also with the development of plants and of animals. They say, for instance, that the water contained in the body causes by its currents the formation of the stomach and the other receptacles of food or of excretion; and that the breath by its passage breaks open the outlets of the nostrils; air and water being the materials of which bodies are made; for all represent nature as composed of such or similar substances.

But if men and animals and their several parts are natural phenomena, then the natural philosopher must take into consideration not merely the ultimate substances of which they are made, but also flesh, bone, blood, and all the other homogeneous parts; not only these, but also the heterogeneous parts, such as face, hand, foot; and must examine how each of these comes to be what it is, and in virtue of what force. For to say what are the ultimate substances out of which an animal is formed, to state, for instance, that it is made of fire or earth, is no more sufficient than would be a similar account in the case of a couch or the like. For we should not be content with saying that the couch was made of bronze or wood or whatever it might be, but should try to describe its design or model of composition in preference to the material; or, if we deal with the material, it would at any rate be with the concretion of material and form. For a couch is such and such a form embodied in this or that matter, or such and such a matter with this or that form; so that its shape and structure must be included in our description. For the formal nature is of greater importance than the material nature.

Does, then, configuration and colour constitute the essence of the various animals and of their several parts? For if so, what Democritus says will be strictly correct. For such appears to have been his notion. At any rate he says that it is evident to every one what form it is that makes the man, seeing that he is recognizable by his shape and colour. And yet a dead body has exactly the same configuration as a living one; but for all that is not a man. So also no hand of bronze or wood or constituted in any but the appropriate way can possibly be a hand in more than name. For like a physician in a painting, or like a flute in a sculpture, in spite of its name it will be unable to do the office which that name implies. Precisely in the same way no part of a dead body, such I mean as its eye or its hand, is really an eye or a hand. To say, then, that shape and colour constitute the animal is an inadequate statement, and is much the same as if a woodcarver were to insist that the hand he cut out was really a hand. Yet the physiologists, when they give an account of the development and causes of the animal form, speak very much like a craftsman. What, however, I would ask, are the forces by which the hand or the body was fashioned into its shape? The woodcarver will perhaps say, by the axe or the auger; the physiologist, by air and earth. Of these two answers the artificer's is the better, but it is nevertheless insufficient. For it is not enough for him to say that by the stroke of his tool this part was formed into a concavity, that into a flat surface; but he must state the reasons why he struck his blow in such a way as to effect this, and what his final object was; namely, that the piece of wood should develop eventually into this or that shape. It is plain, then, that the teaching of the old physiologists is inadequate, and that the true method is to state what the definitive characters are that distinguish the animal as a whole; to explain what it is both in substance and in form, and to deal after the same fashion with its several organs; in fact, to proceed in exactly the same way as we should do, were we giving a complete description of a couch.

If now this something that constitutes the form of the living being be the soul, or part of the soul, or something that without the soul cannot exist; as would seem to be the case, seeing at any rate that when the soul departs, what is left is no longer a living animal, and that none of the parts remain what they were before, excepting in mere configuration, like the animals that in the fable are turned into stone; if, I say, this be so, then it will come within the province of the natural philosopher to inform himself concerning the soul, and to treat of it, either in its entirety, or, at any rate, of that part of it which constitutes the essential character of an animal; and it will be his duty to say what this soul or this part of a soul is; and to discuss the attributes that attach to this essential character, especially as nature is spoken of in two senses, and the nature of a thing is either its matter or its essence; nature as essence including both the motor cause and the final cause. Now it is the latter of these two senses that either the whole soul or some part of it constitutes the nature of an animal; and inasmuch as it is the presence of the soul that enables matter to constitute the animal nature, much more than it is the presence of matter which so enables the soul, the inquirer into nature is bound on every ground to treat of the soul rather than of the matter. For though the wood of which they are made constitutes the couch and the tripod, it only does so because it is capable of receiving such and such a form.

What has been said suggests the question, whether it is the whole soul or only some part of it, the consideration of which comes within the province of natural science. Now if it be of the whole soul that this should treat, then there is no place for any other philosophy beside it. For as it belongs in all cases to one and the same science to deal with correlated subjects—one and the same science, for instance, deals with sensation and with the objects of sense—and as therefore the intelligent soul and the objects of intellect, being correlated, must belong to one and the same science, it follows that natural science will have to include the whole universe in its province. But perhaps it is not the whole soul, nor all its parts collectively, that constitutes the source of motion; but there may be one part, identical with that in plants, which is the source of growth, another, namely the sensory part, which is the source of change of quality, while still another, and this not the intellectual part, is the source of locomotion. I say not the intellectual part; for other animals than man have the power of locomotion, but in none but him is there intellect. Thus then it is plain that it is not of the whole soul that we have to treat. For it is not the whole soul that constitutes the animal nature, but only some part or parts of it. Moreover, it is impossible that any abstraction can form a subject of natural science, seeing that everything that Nature makes is means to an end. For just as human creations are the products of art, so living objects are manifestly the products of an analogous cause or principle, not external but internal, derived like the hot and cold from the environing universe. And that the heaven, if it had an origin, was evolved and is maintained by such a cause, there is therefore even more reason to believe, than that mortal animals so originated. For order and definiteness are much more plainly manifest in the celestial bodies than in our own frame; while change and chance are characteristic of the perishable things of earth. Yet there are some who, while they allow that every animal exists and was generated by nature, nevertheless hold that the heaven was constructed to be what it is by chance and spontaneity; the heaven, in which not the faintest sign of hap-hazard or of disorder is discernible! Again, whenever there is plainly some final end, to which a motion tends should nothing stand in the way, we always say that such final end is the aim or purpose of the motion; and from this it is evident that there must be a something or other really existing, corresponding to what we call by the name of Nature. For a given germ does not give rise to any chance living being, nor spring from any chance one; but each germ springs from a definite parent and gives rise to a definite progeny. And thus it is the germ that is the ruling influence and fabricator of the offspring. For these it is by nature, the offspring being at any rate that which in nature will spring from it. At the same time the offspring is anterior to the germ; for germ and perfected progeny are related as the developmental process and the result. Anterior, however, to both germ and product is the organism from which the germ was derived. For every germ implies two organisms, the parent and the progeny. For germ or seed is both the seed of the organism from which it came, of the horse, for instance, from which it was derived and the seed of the organism that will eventually arise from it, of the mule, for example, which is developed from the seed of the horse. The same seed then is the seed both of the horse and of the mule, though in different ways as here set forth. Moreover, the seed is potentially that which will spring from it, and the relation of potentiality to actuality we know.

There are then two causes, namely, necessity and the final end. For many things are produced, simply as the results of necessity. It may, however, be asked, of what mode of necessity are we speaking when we say this. For it can be of neither of those two modes which are set forth in the philosophical treatises. There is, however, the third mode, in such things at any rate as are generated. For instance, we say that food is necessary; because an animal cannot possibly do without it. This third mode is that which may be called hypothetical necessity. Here is another example of it. If a piece of wood is to be split with an axe, the axe must of necessity be hard; and, if hard, must of necessity be made of bronze or iron. Now exactly in the same way the body, which like the axe is an instrument—for both the body as a whole and its several parts individually have definite operations for which they are made—just in the same way, I say, the body, if it is to do its work, must of necessity be of such and such a character, and made of such and such materials.

It is plain then that there are two modes of causation, and that both of these must, so far as possible, be taken into account in explaining the works of nature, or that at any rate an attempt must be made to include them both; and that those who fail in this tell us in reality nothing about nature. For primary cause constitutes the nature of an animal much more than does its matter. There are indeed passages in which even Empedocles hits upon this, and following the guidance of fact, finds himself constrained to speak of the ratio as constituting the essence and real nature of things. Such, for instance, is the case when he explains what is a bone. For he does not merely describe its material, and say it is this one element, or those two or three elements, or a compound of all the elements, but states the ratio of their combination. As with a bone, so manifestly is it with the flesh and all other similar parts.

The reason why our predecessors failed in hitting upon this method of treatment was, that they were not in possession of the notion of essence, nor of any definition of substance. The first who came near it was Democritus, and he was far from adopting it as a necessary method in natural science, but was merely brought to it, inspite of himself, by constraint of facts. In the time of Socrates a nearer approach was made to the method. But at this period men gave up inquiring into the works of nature, and philosophers diverted their attention to political science and to the virtues which benefit mankind.

Of the method itself the following is an example. In dealing with respiration we must show that it takes place for such or such a final object; and we must also show that this and that part of the process is necessitated by this and that other stage of it. By necessity we shall sometimes mean hypothetical necessity, the necessity, that is, that the requisite antecedents shall be there, if the final end is to be reached; and sometimes absolute necessity, such necessity as that which connects substances and their inherent properties and characters. For the alternate discharge and re-entrance of heat and the inflow of air are necessary if we are to live. Here we have at once a necessity in the former of the two senses. But the alternation of heat and refrigeration produces of necessity an alternate admission and discharge of the outer air, and this is a necessity of the second kind.

In the foregoing we have an example of the method which we must adopt, and also an example of the kind of phenomena, the causes of which we have to investigate.

Of things constituted by nature some are ungenerated, imperishable, and eternal, while others are subject to generation and decay. The former are excellent beyond compare and divine, but less accessible to knowledge. The evidence that might throw light on them, and on the problems which we long to solve respecting them, is furnished but scantily by sensation; whereas respecting perishable plants and animals we have abundant information, living as we do in their midst, and ample data may be collected concerning all their various kinds, if only we are willing to take sufficient pains. Both departments, however, have their special charm. The scanty conceptions to which we can attain of celestial things give us, from their excellence, more pleasure than all of our knowledge of the world in which we live; just as a half glimpse of persons that we love is more delightful than a leisurely view of other things, whatever their number and dimensions. On the other hand, in certitude and in completeness our knowledge of terrestrial things has the advantage. Moreover, their greater nearness and affinity to us balances somewhat the loftier interest of the heavenly things that are the objects of the higher philosophy. Having already treated of the celestial world, as far as our conjectures could reach, we proceed to treat of animals, without omitting, to the best of our ability any number of the kingdom, however ignoble. For if some have no graces to charm the sense, yet even these, by disclosing to intellectual perception the artistic spirit that designed them, give immense pleasure to all who can trace links of causation, and are inclined to philosophy. Indeed, it would be strange if mimic representations of them were attractive, because they disclose the mimetic skill of the painter or sculptor, and the original realities themselves were not more interesting, to all at any rate who have eyes to discern the reasons that determined their formation. We therefore must not recoil with childish aversion from the examination of the humbler animals. Every realm of nature is marvelous; and as Heraclitus, when the strangers who came to visit him found him warming himself at the furnace in the kitchen and hestitated to go in, is reported

to have bidden them not to be afraid to enter, as even in that kitchen divinities were present, so we should venture on the study of every kind of animal without distaste; for each and all will reveal to us something natural and something beautiful. Absence of haphazard and conduciveness of everything to an end are to be found in Nature's works in the highest degree, and the resultant end of her generations and combinations is a form of the beautiful.

If any person thinks the examination of the rest of the animal kingdom an unworthy task, he must hold in like disesteem the study of man. For no one can look at the primordia of the human frame—blood, flesh, bones, vessels, and the like—without much repugnance. Moreover, when any one of the parts or structures, be it which it may, is under discussion, it must not be supposed that it is its material composition to which attention is being directed or which is the object of the discussion, but the relation of such part to the total form. Similarly, the true object of architecture is not bricks, mortar, or timber, but the house; and so the principal object of natural philosophy is not the material elements, but their composition, and the totality of the form, independently of which they have no existence.

The course of exposition must be first to state the attributes common to whole groups of animals, and then to attempt to give their explanation. Many groups, as already noticed, present common attributes, that is to say, in some cases absolutely identical affections, and absolutely identical organs—feet, feathers, scales, and the like; while in other groups the affections and organs are only so far identical as that they are analogous. For instance, some groups have lungs, others have no lung, but an organ analogous to a lung in its place; some have blood, others have no blood, but a fluid analogous to blood, and with the same office. To treat of the common attributes in connexion with each individual group would involve, as already suggested, useless iteration. For many groups have common attributes. So much for this topic.

As every instrument and every bodily member subserves some partial end, that is to say, some special action, so the whole body must be destined to minister to some plenary sphere of action. Thus the saw is made for sawing, for sawing is a function, and not sawing for the soul, and each part of it for some subordinate function, to which it is adapted.

We have, then, first to describe the common functions, common, that is, to the whole animal kingdom, or to certain large groups, or to the members of a species. In other words, we have to describe the attributes common to all animals, or to assemblages, like the class of Birds of closely allied groups differentiated by gradation, or to groups like Man not differentiated into subordinate groups. In the first case the common attributes may be called analogous, in the second generic, in the third specific.

When a function is ancillary to another, a like relation manifestly obtains between the organs which discharge these functions; and similarly, if one function is prior to and the end of another, their respective organs will stand to each other in the same relation. Thirdly, the existence of these parts involves that of other things as their necessary consequents.

Instances of what I mean by functions and affections are Reproduction, Growth, Copulation, Waking, Sleep, Locomotive, and other similar vital actions. Instances of what I mean by parts are Nose, Eye, Face, and other so-called members or limbs, and also the more elementary parts of which these are made. So much for the method to be pursued. Let us now try to set forth the causes of all vital phenomena whether universal or particular, and in so doing let us follow that order of exposition which conforms, as we have indicated, to the order of nature.

The Metaphysics

All men by nature desire to know[1] and an indication of this is the love of the senses; for even, irrespective of their utility, are they loved for their own sakes, and pre-eminently above the rest, the sense of sight. For not only for practical purposes, but also when not intent on doing anything; we choose the power of vision in preference, so to say, to all the rest of the senses. And a cause of this is the following,—that this one of the senses particularly enables us to apprehend whatever knowledge it is the inlet of, and that it makes many distinctive qualities manifest.

By nature then, indeed, are animals formed endowed with sense; but in some of them memory is not innate from sense, and in others it is. And for this reason are these possessed of more foresight, as well as a greater aptitude for discipline, than those which are wanting in this faculty of memory. Those furnished with foresight, indeed, are yet without the capability of receiving instruction, whatever amongst them are unable to understand the sounds they hear; as, for instance, bees, and other similar tribes of animals; but those are capable of receiving instruction as many as, in addition to memory, are provided with this sense also.

The rest, indeed, subsist then through impressions and the operations of memory, but share experience in a slight degree; whereas the human race exists by means of art also and the powers of reasoning.

Now, experience accrues to men from memory; for repeated acts of memory about the same thing done constitute the force of a single experience: and experience seems to be a thing almost similar to science and art.

But science and art result unto men by means of experience; for experience, indeed, as Polus saith, and correctly so, has produced art, but inexperience, chance. But an art comes into being when, out of many conceptions of experience, one universal opinion is evolved with respect to similar cases. For, indeed, to entertain the opinion that this particular remedy has been of service to Callias, while labouring under this particular disease, as well as to Socrates, and so individually to many, this is an inference of experience; but that it has been conducive to the health of all,—such as have been defined according to one species,—while labouring under this disease, as, for instance, to the phlegmatic, or the choleric, or those sick of a burning fever, this belongs to the province of art.

As regards, indeed, practical purposes,[2] therefore, experience seems in no wise to differ from art; . . . experience, indeed, is a knowledge of singulars, whereas art, of universals; but all things in the doing, and all generations, are concerned about the singular: for he whose profession it is to practise medicine, does not restore man to health save by accident, but Callias, or Socrates, or any of the rest so designated, to whom it happens to be a man. If, therefore, any one without the experience is furnished with the principle, and is acquainted with the universal, but is ignorant of the singular that is involved therein, he will frequently fall into error in the case of his medical treatment; for that which is capable of cure is rather the singular.

But, nevertheless, we are of opinion that, at least, knowledge and understanding appertain to art rather than experience; and we reckon artists more wise than the experienced, inasmuch as wisdom is the concomitant of all philosophers rather in proportion to their knowledge.

But this is so because some, indeed, are aware of the cause, and some are not. For the experienced, indeed, know that a thing is so, but they do not know why it is so; but others —I mean the scientific—are acquainted with the why and the cause. Therefore, also we reckon the chief artificers in each case to be entitled to more dignity, and to the reputation of superior knowledge, and to be more wise than the handicraftsmen, because the former are acquainted with the causes of the things that are being constructed; whereas the latter produce things, as certain inanimate things do, indeed; yet these perform their functions unconsciously,—as the fire when it burns. Things indeed, therefore, that are inanimate, by a certain constitution of nature, perform each of these their functions, but the handicraftsmen through habit; inasmuch as it is not according as men are practical that they are more wise, but according as they possess the reason of a thing, and understand causes.

And, upon the whole, a proof of a person's having knowledge is even the ability to teach; and for this reason we consider art, rather than experience, to be a science; for artists can, whereas the handicraftsmen cannot, convey instruction.

And further, we regard none of the senses to be wisdom, although, at least, these are the most decisive sources of knowledge about singulars; but they make no affirmation of the why in regard of anything,—as, for example, why fire is hot, but only the fact that it is hot.

Therefore,[3] indeed, is it natural for the person who first discovers any art whatsoever, beyond the ordinary power of the senses, to be the object of human admiration, not only on account of something of the things that have been discovered being useful, but as one that is wise and superior to the rest of men. But when more arts are being discovered—both some, indeed, in relation to things that are necessary, and others for pastime—we invariably regard such more wise than those,[4] on account of their sciences not being for bare utility. Whence all things of such a sort having been already procured, those sciences have been invented which were pursued neither for purposes of pleasure nor necessity, and first in those places where

the inhabitants enjoyed leisure: wherefore, in the neighborhood of Egypt the mathematical arts were first established; for there leisure was spared unto the priestly caste. It has then, indeed, been declared in the Ethics[5] what is the difference between an art and a science, and the rest of the things of the same description.

But, at present, the reason of our producing this treatise is the fact, that all consider what is termed wisdom to be conversant about first causes and principles; so that—as has been said on a former occasion—the experienced seem to be more wise than those possessing any sense whatsoever, and the artificer than the experienced, and the master-artist than the handicraftsman, and the speculative rather than those that are productive. That, indeed, wisdom, therefore, is a science conversant about certain causes and first principles is obvious.

Now, since we are engaged in investigating this science, the following must form a subject for our consideration; namely, about what kind of causes, and what kind of first principles, is this science—I mean wisdom—conversant. If, doubtless, one would receive the opinions which we entertain concerning the wise man, perhaps from this our proposed inquiry would be evident the more.

Now, in the first place, indeed, we go on the supposition that the wise man, especially is acquainted with all things scientifically, as far as this is possible, not, however, having a scientific knowledge of them singly. In the next place, a person who is capable of knowing things that are difficult, and not easy for a man to understand, such as one we deem wise (for perception by the senses is common to all, wherefore it is a thing that is easy, and by no means wise). Further, one who is more accurate, and more competent to give instruction in the causes of things, we regard more wise about every science. And of the sciences, also, that which is desirable for its own account, and for the sake of knowledge, we consider to be wisdom in preference to that which is eligible on account of its probable results, and that which is more qualified for preeminence we regard as wisdom, rather than that which is subordinate, —for that, the wise man ought not to be dictated to, but should dictate unto others; and that this person ought not to be swayed in his opinions by another, but one less wise by this man. Respecting this wisdom and wise men[6]do we entertain such and so many suppositions.

But of these characteristics the scientific knowlege of all things must needs be found in him most especially who possesses the universal science;[7] for this person, in a manner, knows all things that are the subjects of it. But, also, the most difficult nearly for men to know are the things that are especially universal, for they are most remote from the senses. But the most accurate of the sciences are those respecting things that are primary, in the most eminent sense of the word; for those from fewer principles are more accurate than those said to be from addition, as arithmetic than geometry. But, also, that science, without doubt, is more adapted towards giving instruction, at least, which speculates about causes; for those do afford instruction who assign the causes in regard of each individual thing. Now, understanding and scientific knowledge, for their own sakes, most especially reside in the science of that which is most particularly fitted for being scientifically known. For he who selects scientific knowledge, for its own sake, will especially choose that which is preeminently science; but such is that which is the science of that which is particularly fitting as an object of scientific knowledge, and particularly fitting as objects of scientific knowledge are the first principles and causes; for on account of these, and by means of these, are the other objects of knowledge capable of being made known: but not these by means of those things that are subordinate to them. Most fit for preeminence likewise amongst the sciences, and fit for preeminence in preference to that which is subservient, is the science which communicates the knowledge of that on account of which each thing is to be done; but this constitutes the good in each particular, but, in general, that which is the best in every nature.

From all, therefore, that has been stated, the sought-for appellation lights upon the same science; for it is necessary that this be a science speculative of first principles and of causes, for the good, also, viewed as a final cause, is one from amongst our classified list of causes.

But that the science under investigation is not a science employed in producing,[8] is evident from the case of those who formed· systems of philosophy in the earliest ages. For from wonder men, both now and at the first,

began to philosophize, having felt astonishment originally at the things which were more obvious, indeed, amongst those that were doubtful; then, by degrees, in this way having advanced onwards, and, in process of time, having stated difficulties about more important subjects,—as, for example, respecting the passive conditions of the moon, and those brought to pass about the sun and stars, and respecting the generation of the universe. But he that labours under perplexity and wonder thinks that he is involved in ignorance. Therefore, also, the philosopher—that is, the lover of wisdom—is somehow a lover of fables, for the fable is made up of the things that are marvellous. Wherefore, if, for the avoidance of ignorance, men from time to time have been induced to form systems of philosophy, it is manifest that they went in pursuit of scientific knowledge for the sake of understanding it, and not on account of any utility that it might possess. But the event itself also bears witness to the truth of this statement; for on the supposition of almost all those things being in existence that are requisite towards both cause and the management of life, prudence of such a sort as this began to be in requisition. Therefore is it evident that we seek scientific knowledge from no other actual ground of utility save what springs from itself.

But as we say a free man exists who is such for his own sake, and not for the sake of another, so, also, this alone of the sciences is free, for this alone subsists for its own sake.

Wherefore, also, the acquisition of this science may be justly regarded as not human, for, in many instances, human nature is servile.

So that, according to Simonides, the Deity only should, enjoy this prerogative; yet that it is unworthy for a man not to investigate the knowledge that is in conformity with his condition. But if, in reality, the poets make any such assertion, and if the Godhead is in its nature constituted so as to envy, in this respect it is especially natural that it should happen, and that all those that are over-subtle should be unfortunate: but neither does the Divine essence admit of being affected by envy, but—according to the proverb—the bards utter many falsehoods.

Nor ought we to consider any other science more entitled to honour than such as that under investigation at present. For that which is most divine is also most worthy of honour.

But such will be so in only two ways; for that which the Deity would especially possess is a divine one amongst the sciences; and if there is any such science, this would be the case with the science of things divine. But this science, such as we have described it, alone is possessed of both of these characteristics; for to all speculators the Deity appears as a cause and a certain first principle;[9] and such a science as this, either God alone, or he principally, would possess. Therefore, indeed, may all sciences else be more requisite than this one; but none is more excellent.

It is, indeed, necessary, in a manner, to establish the order[10] of this science, in its development, in a direction contrary to the speculations that have been carried on from the beginning. For, indeed—as we have remarked—all men commence their inquiries from wonder whether a thing be so, as in the case of the spontaneous movements of jugglers' figures to those who have not as yet speculated into their cause; or respecting the solstices, or the incommensurability of the diameter; for it seems to be a thing astonishing to all, if any quantity of those that are the smallest is not capable of being measured. But it is necessary to draw our inquiry to a close in a direction the contrary to this, and towards what is better, according to the proverb. As also happens in the case of these, when they succeed in learning those points; for nothing would a geometrician so wonder at, as if the diameter of a square should be commensurable with its side. What, therefore, is the nature of the science under investigation has been declared; as, also, what the aim should be which the present inquiry and the entire treatise should strive and attain.[11]

But since it is manifest that one ought to be in possession of a science of primary causes (for then we say that we know each individual thing when we think that we are acquainted with the first cause); and since causes are denominated under four different heads,[12] the first of which we assert to be the substance and the essence of a thing (for the inquiry of the wherefore, in the first instance of a thing, is referred to the last reason,[13] but the first wherefore of a thing is a cause and first principle); and the second cause we affirm to be the matter and the subject; and the third is the source of the first principle of motion; and the fourth, the cause that is in opposition to this,—namely, both the final

cause and the good; for such is an end of every generation.[14]

But they who put forward ideas as causes, in their early investigations, indeed, to acquire the causes of these entities, in the first place have adduced other things equal in number to these;[15] as if one, desiring to have reckoned certain things, when these were less numerous, would consider this impossible, but, by creating a greater number, should succeed in counting them; for almost equal, or not less numerous, are the forms than those things respecting which, in investigating their causes, they have advanced from these to those: for, according to each individual thing, there is a certain homonymous form, and, in addition to the substances, also, of other things, there is the unity involved in the notion of plurality, both in the case of these and of things that are eternal.

Moreover,[16] in the ways in which it is demonstrated that there are forms, according to none of these the subsistence of forms becomes apparent; for, indeed, from some there is no necessity, in the sequence of the reasoning, that a syllogism arise: but from other things, also,—not of such as we should expect to find forms,—of these are there forms generated. For according to the rational principles deducible from the sciences will there be forms of all things, of as many as there are sciences; and in accordance with the argument for ideas founded on the notion of unity involved in plurality, will there also be forms or ideas of negations: and according to the ability to understand something of what has been destroyed of things liable to decay will there also be forms, for of these there is a certain phantasm. . . .

But most of all would one feel perplexed as to what at all[17] the forms contribute, either to those things that are eternal amongst sensibles, or to things that are being produced and being corrupted. For neither are they to them a cause of any motion or change whatever. But, truly, neither are they of any assistance towards the science of other things (for neither are those the substance of these, for in such a case they would be in these), nor do they contribute towards the existence of other things, inasmuch as they are not inherent in things that are their participants, at least; for so, indeed, they would perhaps be supposed as causes, just as if the white were mixed with the white it might be called the cause of a white body. But, indeed, this theory is very easily overthrown, which Anaxagoras, indeed, first and Endoxus subsequently, and certain others, advanced; for it would be easy to collect together, also, many impossibilities in reference to such an opinion; but, truly, neither do other things subsist from forms in accordance with any mode of existence of those that are wont to be mentioned.

But the assertion that these forms are exemplars, and that the rest of entities participate in them, is to speak vain words, and to utter poetic metaphors. For in what respect, may I ask does that which operates look towards the ideas as a model? for it is possible that anything whatever that is similar both should exist and be produced, and yet that it be not made like in reference to that to which it is similar. Wherefore, also, on the supposition of the existence and non-existence of Socrates, just such another one as Socrates it would be produced. And, in like manner, is it evident that this would follow, even though Socrates were eternal; and, besides, there will be many exemplars of the same thing; wherefore, also the forms—for instance, of man, such as animal and biped, and at the same time, also, ideal man—will have a subsistence. Further, not only of things sensible are forms the exemplars, but also of forms themselves; as, for example, the genus as a genus will be an exemplar of species; wherefore, an exemplar and an image will be the same thing.

Further, it would seem impossible for the substance to be separate from that of which it is the substance; therefore, in what way can the ideas, when they are substances of things, exist separately from them?

But in the *Phaedo* an assertion is made to this effect,—that the forms are causes of existence and of production. On the supposition, however, of the existence of forms, nevertheless, those things that are participants will not be produced, if there be not in existence that which is likely to be the origin of motion; and many other things are produced, such as a house and a ring, of which we do not say that there are forms. Wherefore, it is evident that it is possible, also, for other things both to exist and be produced from such causes, likewise, on account of which, also, arise those entities mentioned just now. . . .

And upon the whole,[18] seeing that wisdom investigates into the cause, in respect of things that are manifest, this consideration, indeed, have we omitted; for we say nothing regarding the cause of the origin of the principle of change: but thinking to mention the substance of these, we say that there are different substances; but in what manner those may be substances of these we ineffectually describe, for as to such being accomplished by participation—as also we have stated on a former occasion—there is no advantage gained in saying this. Neither, truly, are ideas such causes as we see to be a cause to the sciences, on account of which both every mind and every nature operate; nor that cause which we affirm to be one of the first principles do forms in any wise touch upon; but to men, in the present age, mathematics have become *the* philosophy; although they say that persons ought to cultivate these sciences for the sake of other sciences.

But, further, one may suppose the subject-substance to be as matter that is more mathematical, and rather to be converted into a predicable, and to constitute a difference of substance and of matter,—as, for instance, the great and the small,—just as, also, the natural philosophers mention the rare and the dense, saying that there are these primary differences of the subject, for these are a certain excess and defect. And respecting motion, if, indeed, these will constitute motion, it is evident that the forms will be moved; but if they are not, whence has motion originated? for thereby the entire investigation about Nature has been abolished.

And what seems to be easy—namely, the demonstration that all things are one—does not turn out to be so; for, according to the interpretation, all things do not become one, but a certain thing itself is one, if any one would grant that all things are so: and neither would he allow this, unless one would admit the existence of a universal as a genus; but this, in some cases, is impossible. . . .

But how can any one learn the elements of all things? for it is evident that it is not possible that he should be previously a person having prior knowledge thereof. For, as to one learning geometry, it is, indeed, possible to see beforehand other things; but of such things as the science consists of, and concerning which he is about to receive instruction, he can have no prior knowledge so, also, is it in the case of other things. Wherefore, if there is a certain science of all things, as some affirm, nothing could this person know beforehand. Every system of learning, however, subsists, or is attainable by means of previous knowledge, either of all things, or of certain particular things: and either by demonstration is this accomplished, or by definitions; for those things whereof the definition consists it is requisite to understand beforehand, and that they be known. In like manner is it the case with knowledge by induction. But, truly, if also it happens that there is in our possession a congenital knowledge of things, it is astonishing how we, in possession of the most excellent of the sciences, are unconscious of such a treasure.

Further, how will any one know from what particulars all things consist, and how will this be manifest? for this also involves perplexity; for one would feel a doubt, just as also concerning some syllable: for certain affirm that SMA is composed of S and M and A, but others say that it possesses a different sound from its components, and none of those that are known.

Moreover, those things of which there is perception by sense, how could any one know if he were not furnished with the capacity of perceiving by sense? although one ought, if these are the elements of all things whereof they consist, just as the compound sounds arise from their own proper elements.

That, therefore, all seem to seek the causes mentioned in our Physics, and, besides these, that we have no other to adduce, is likewise from the foregoing statements evident. But the early philosophers, I admit have treated of these causes,—obscurely, however; and, indeed, in a certain manner, all such four causes have been enumerated by speculators of an age prior to ours: and, in a certain manner, by no means has this been the case; for the earliest system of philosophy concerning all things was like unto one articulating with a stammer, inasmuch as it was new as regards, first principles, and a thing the first in its kind. For Empedocles says that a bone exists from form by the principle of composition; but this is the essence and the substance of that thing. But, truly, if this be admitted, in like manner, also, is it necessary that of both flesh, and everything else of the other things, there should subsist this principle of concretion, or that it should not subsist as a principle of anything at all; for on account of this are both flesh and bone, and each of the other things, in existence, and not on account of the matter, which he says is fire, and earth, and water, and air. But, also, with any other indeed, who would make these assertions, he would by necessity concur; but he has not expressed himself with clearness respecting them. The case regarding such points, therefore, has been made evident on a former occasion; but as many doubts as any one might indulge in respecting these same, we will a second time enumerate; for perhaps we shall thereby acquire a facility for having our difficulties resolved in reference to subsequent questions of doubt.

Since, however, that which is produced is produced[19] both by something (now, I mean that whence also originates the first principle of generation, that is, its efficient cause) and from something, (but let this be not privation, but matter, for already has it been defined in what manner we have denominated this,) also must there be that which is produced; and this is either a sphere or a circle, or whatever else of the other things that may chance to present itself; as neither the efficient cause produces the subject, (I mean, the brass,) so neither does it make the sphere, unless by accident, because a brazen sphere is a sphere; but it does not produce the sphere itself. For the production of a certain thing of this kind is the production of this particular thing from the entire subject. Now, I say, that to make the brass round is not to make the round or the sphere, but something different, such as this form in another thing. For, if the artist produces it, he would produce this from something else; for this would be the subject: as, for example, to make a brazen sphere; and this the artist makes in this manner because from this particular thing which is brass he forms this which is a sphere. If, therefore, also, he produces this very thing, it is evident that in like manner he will produce another; and the productions will go on in a process *ad infinitum.*

It is palpable, then, that neither form (or by whatever name we must needs term form, as it subsists in that which is cognisable to sense) is produced, nor is there a generation thereof, nor is this the essence or very nature of a thing; for this is that which is produced in another subject either from Art, or from Nature, or potentiality, and the efficient cause it is which produces the existence of a brazen sphere; for it produces it from brass and a sphere: for into this particular thing, which is the form, the efficient cause moulds the brass, and this constitutes a brazen sphere. And if, in short, of the being or existence of sphere there exists a generation, it will be a something that is a generation from a certain thing: for it will be necessary that what is produced always be divisible, and that this should be this particular thing, and that should be something else: now, I mean that this should be matter, and that form. Therefore, if a sphere be a figure equal from the centre to all points of its periphery, of this one part will be that in which that which produces will be inherent, and the other part that which resides in this part; but the whole is that which has been produced or generated; as, for instance, the brazen sphere. It is evident, therefore, from the statements that have been made, that what is denominated as form or as substance is not generated, but that the union which is said to take place according to this is generated, and that in everything which is being produced matter is inherent, and that one part is matter, but the other form. . . .

After these inquiries there remains for us to make our readers aware that neither matter nor form is generated. Now, I speak thus of the extremities of things; for everything that undergoes any change is changed both by something and into something—by something, of course, I mean that which is the first imparter of motion, and of something, that is, matter, and that into which the thing is changed; this is the form. Therefore, they go on in a progression to infinity, if not only the brass becomes spherical, but also the spherical or the brass is generated: therefore, must we sooner or later come to a standstill in the series.

After these inquiries we must show how each substance is generated from one synonymous with itself; for those things that are being generated by Nature, as well as other things, are substances. For things are produced either by Art, or Nature, or Chance, or Spontaneity. Art, indeed, therefore, constitutes a first principle which subsists in another subject, whereas Nature constitutes a first principle which subsists in the thing itself; for man begets man: and the remaining causes are the privations of these. Substances likewise are three in number, and one of these is matter; which is this certain

particular thing in consequence of its appearance as certain particular things in consequence of its appearance as such; for as many things as are one by contact, and not by cohesion, constitute matter and a subject: but another of these substances is Nature, which likewise is this certain particular thing, and into Nature is there the transition of a certain habit. Further, the third substance is that which subsists from these, and is ranked as a singular; for example, Socrates or Callias.

As regards some things, therefore, this certain particular thing involves no subsistence independent of a composite substance, as the form of a house, unless art constitutes this form. Neither is there any generation and corruption of these, but after a different manner they are, and are not, both the house itself, which is unconnected with matter, and health, and everything that is produced according to art; but if forms subsist, they subsist in the case of those things that are generated by Nature. Wherefore, doubtless, not injudiciously affirmed Plato that forms belong to those things as many as involve a natural subsistence, on the supposition of the existence of forms different from, or independent of, these; as, for example, fire, flesh, the head, and so forth. For all these things are matter, and belong to substance especially—I mean, such a description of matter as is ultimate.

Some causes, therefore that impart motion subsist as entities that have been previously generated, whereas other causes which subsist as the formed principle are simultaneously generated with their results; for when a man is in sound health then also is there present with him sound health, and the form of the brazen sphere subsists simultaneously with the brazen sphere.

And whether, also, there remains anything subsequently to the separation of form from the subject of form, we must examine; for in the case of some forms there is no hindrance to this taking place; as if soul were a thing of this description: not, to be sure, every soul, but the understanding; for that this should be so with every soul is not, perhaps, a thing that is possible. It is evident, therefore, that there is no necessity that on account of these, at least, ideas should have an existence; for man begets man, the singular begets a certain individual. And in like manner does the case stand with the arts; for the medicinal art is the formal principle of health.

And as regards causes and first principles in a manner are they different according as they belong to different things, and in a manner this is not the case. Supposing one to express himself universally, and according to analogy the causes and first principles of all things will be the same. For one might raise the question as to whether the first principles and elements of substances, and of things which subsist as relatives, are different or the same? and, therefore, in like manner is it the case with each of the categories. But it would be absurd if there were the same principles and elements of all things, for from the same things will relatives derive their subsistence as well as substance. What, therefore, will this be? for besides substance and the rest of the things that are predicated there is nothing that is in common. Prior, however, is the element to those things of which it is an element; but, assuredly, neither is substance an element of relatives, nor is any of these an element of substance. Further, how is it admissible that there should be the same elements of all things? for none of the elements can be the same with that which is a composite nature of the elements; as, for instance, neither B nor A can be the same with BA. Neither, therefore, is it possible that any one element of those natures that are intelligible—as, for example, unity or entity—can be the element of all things; for these are present with each of the compound natures likewise. No one of them, therefore, will have a subsistence either as substance or relation; but it will be a thing expedient, however, that they should subsist in some form or other. The elements, then, of all things are not the same.

Or, shall we say—just as we have already affirmed—that in one way this is the case, and in another that it is not? as, perhaps, in regard of sensible bodies that which is hot subsists in one way as form, and after another mode that which is cold subsists as the privation thereof; but matter subsists as that which primarily and essentially constitutes both of these in capacity; substances, however, are both these and such as consist of those things of which these are the first principles. Or, if any one thing is

generated from what is hot and from what is cold, as flesh or bone, still that which is produced from thence must needs be different from these. The first principle and elements of these, I admit, then, are the same, yet there are different elements of different things; and, without doubt, we cannot say that the case stands in this way with all things; but analogically are the elements and first principles of all things the same; just as if one should say that there are three first principles in existence—namely, form, and privation, and matter; each of these, however, is different according as it is conversant about every genus, as in colour, white, black, surface, light, darkness, air; and from these emerge forth day and night.

Since, however, not only things that are inherent are causes, but also causes of things that are external—as, for example, in the case of what imparts motion—it is evident that a first principle is a different thing from an element; yet both are causes, and into these is a first principle divided: but what subsists as that which imparts motion or rest constitutes a certain first principle and substance.

Wherefore, there are in existence three elements, indeed, according to analogy, but four causes and first principles; and a different cause subsists where the subject is different, and the first cause constitutes, as it were, that which imparts motion, and is different according as the subject is different. Thus, health is as form, disease as privation, body as matter: that which imparts motion is the medicinal art. Again, a house is as form, this certain sort of confusion [20] as privation; the bricks are as matter, and that which imparts motion, or the efficient cause, is the builder's art. And into these, therefore, is a first principle divided.

But since that which imparts motion in physical or natural things is a man, and in things springing from the understanding form, or the contrary, in one respect would there be three causes, and in another four; for the medicinal art constitutes in a manner health, and the building art the form of the house, and man begets man; further, beside these—as that which is the first of all things—is that which imparts motion, or is the efficient cause, to all things.

NOTES

1. The assertion, however, that all men desire knowledge has been objected to, on the ground that in some this desire is wholly absent; but this absence merely amounts to a suppression of the natural desire from various causes; *e.g.* want of leisure for intellectual pursuits, constitutional laziness, voluptuous habits.

2. Aristotle demonstrates that knowledge is a thing more honourable than action, in order to show that wisdom, being involved in knowledge, and not in practice, is likewise itself, on that account, more worthy of respect.

3. Aristotle here shows the paths through which men must travel into this "wisdom," or first philosophy; and for this purpose adduces the example of the Egyptian priests, who were enabled to construct the speculative sciences of geometry and mathematics by having enjoyed leisure from the laborious employments of life. They were thus allowed an opportunity of contemplating the heavenly phenomena, and, from such observations of experiences, of deducing the abstract sciences.

4. That is, that those who knew the reason of things were more wise than the artificers.

5. The objection which Aristotle imagines is tacitly implied in the foregoing remarks amounts to this,—that such are tantamount to destroying the distinction between art, science, and wisdom. Aristotle, however, repels the imputation that he is using these words in the same sense by a reference to his Ethics, book VI. chap. iii, where distinctions between them are carefully drawn.

6. Aristotle having shown, in the first chapter, that the science under investigation—which he here calls wisdom, though elsewhere by a different denomination—is conversant about causes, proceeds now to lay down what sort these causes are, their nature, and number.

7. During the first age of Greek philosophy it was styled "wisdom," and its cultivators, "wise men"; and the term philosopher was first applied to Pythagoras. This change, no doubt, betokened a corresponding change in men's mode of thought; for thereby an element hitherto undiscovered was brought into notice,—namely, the relation of our emotions to scientific investigations.

8. Aristotle shows that the science under investigation is speculative, not active, from the fact that the earliest philosophy sprang from wonder,—that wonder flows from ignorance,—that the removal of ignorance amounts to knowledge,—that this was accomplished by speculation and not practice; and that therefore wisdom, the source of the highest knowledge, was speculative and not active.

9. This is a remarkable passage to occur in the writings of Aristotle, about whose deism or atheism so much has been said and written.

10. That whereas the old philosophy originated from wonder,—that is, ignorance,—and attained unto a sort of knowledge, yet that when men reached this knowledge, knowledge, as such, became the great actuating motive in speculation. This present science under investigation, however, would set out from an opposite point in this progress, because it started from the consideration of that which is the highest object of speculative knowledge.

11. Aristotle now proceeds to examine into the labours of his predecessors; and the course he pursues is first to enumerate the opinions thereupon of the early schools of philosophy, and of individual speculators; and next, to set down arguments for or against these theories, and show how far they are true, and how far false.

12. This fourfold enumeration of causes is taken from the Physics, books I. and II. We have the same division laid down in the Posterior Analytics, book II. chap. xi.

13. "The last reason." This refers to the method of demonstration adopted by the mathematicians in their problems. . . .

14. Aristotle now proceeds to examine into another system of the supranaturalists,—namely, that of Plato: first, in respect of his theory regarding the substance of things; and secondly, respecting the first principles of things.

15. Aristotle first complains of the inconsistency of Plato; for he contends that, in proposing to assign the causes of sensibles, he should have kept the phenomena of sensibles before his eyes, and not have devised, as he has done, a theory applicable to anything else save sensibles.

16. Aristotle here details his objections against the ideal system of Plato, which he strives to overthrow by turning the reasoning of Plato against himself.

17. Aristotle now proceeds to prove the utter irrelevancy of ideas as accounting for sensible phenomena.

18. Aristotle now proceeds to argue against Plato in his theory concerning the first principles of things.

19. What Aristotle aims to establish is this, that it is not strictly true to say that naked form is generated, but that matter, in combination with a certain invariable form is. This dogma may be regarded as a necessary sequence to the reasoning that has gone before.

20. That is, the materials of the house before they are reduced by the builder to the form and shape of a house.

On Life

We regard knowledge as a good and precious thing, but we esteem one sort of knowledge more highly than another either because of the acumen required for its discovery, or because it is concerned with better and more admirable objects: for both these reasons we should rightly assign the investigation of the soul to the first rank. Further, it is supposed that a knowledge of the soul has an important bearing on all truth, and particularly on that of the natural world. For the soul is, as it were, the genetic principle in living things. Our aim is to investigate and ascertain the essential nature of the soul, and, secondly, to discover those properties which attach to it as accidents. Certain of the latter are supposed to be conditions peculiar to the soul's own nature, and others are thought to be effects produced in living beings by the soul's agency.

Now, it is altogether the most difficult problem to arrive at any fixed belief touching the soul. From the fact that the problem is one which is common to other subjects—I mean the problem of finding the essence and the real definition of a thing—it might perhaps appear to some that there is a single scientific method which applies to everything whose essence we wish to discover, as deductive proof applies to accidental properties. We shall, therefore, be obliged to make inquiry into this question of scientific method. But if there is no single and general method which applies to the ultimate nature of things, our investigation becomes in that case all the more difficult. And even if the question of method were cleaned up, whether its form be that of deductive proof, or analysis, or some other procedure, there still remains a question of great difficulty and uncertainty, viz,

from what principles are we to start our inquiry? For different principles are employed in different subjects, as *e.g.* in numbers and in plane surfaces.

The first necessity, perhaps, is to determine under what genus soul is to be classified and what its nature is—I mean by this the question whether it is an individual thing and self-subsisting entity, or whether it is a quality or a quantity or classifiable in one of the other categories already enumerated, and further, whether it is a potentiality or rather an actuality. For this makes no slight difference. We must also inquire whether the soul is divisible or whether it is without parts; whether it is an entity of one sort or not. And if it is not of one sort, we must further ask whether the differences are specific or generic. For nowadays the men who discuss and investigate the soul appear to direct their inquiries merely to the human soul. We must take pains to see whether there is a single definition that applies to the soul, just as *e.g.* there is a single definition that applies to animal, or whether a different definition is required for horse, dog, man, god, and we must further inquire whether the common notion 'animal' [1] either is nothing at all or else comes into existence only after the individual,—a question that might equally well be raised regarding any other general notion. If, however, there are not several souls, but only parts of a single soul, then the further question arises whether we should examine the soul as a whole before we examine the parts. It is also hard to determine which of these parts is in its nature different from the other and whether we should first investigate the part or the part's function, *e.g.* whether we should first investigate the process of thought or the faculty of thought, sense-perception or the organ of sense-perception; the same question applies to other cases.

Now, supposing that the functions take precedence of the faculties in the order of investigation, a further question might arise here as to whether the complements of the faculties should be investigated before the faculties themselves, *e.g.* whether the investigation of the sensible object should precede the investigation of the sense-organ, and the object of thought precede the faculty of thought. Not only does the knowledge of the essential nature of a thing seem to be helpful towards the understanding of the accidental nature and properties of substances, just as in mathematics the knowledge of the essential nature of straight or curved or of a line or surface is helpful in understanding how many right angles are contained in the angles of a triangle, but conversely, the knowledge of accidental properties contributes largely to the understanding of what a thing essentially is. For when we are able to give an account of the accidental properties of things, as we see them,—either of all these properties or of most of them,—then we are best able to speak also of their essential nature. For the essential nature is the true starting-point in all deductive proof. And so in the case of definitions where not only no knowledge of the accidental properties is furnished, but where is it not easy even to conjecture what these properties are, it is evident that all such definitions are framed after the fashion of dialectics and are void.

A further difficulty presents itself regarding the affections of the soul, viz. whether all these affections are common to the soul and to the body which contains it, or whether there is a something that is the exclusive property of the soul. And it is necessary, though not easy, to solve this difficulty. In most cases the soul apparently neither acts nor is acted upon independently of the body, *e.g.* in the feelings of anger, courage, desire, or in a word in sense-perception. Thought, however, appears to be a function which more than any other is the exclusive property of the soul. But if thought is a sort of representation in terms of a sense-image, or is impossible without this, then even thought could not exist independently of the body. If, then, there were any function or affec-

tion of the soul that were peculiar to it, it would be possible for the soul to exist separate and apart from the body.[2] If, however, there is nothing which is its exclusive property, it cannot exist apart, but the case is similar to that of a straight line, which, as straight, has many properties, *e.g.* contact with a bronze globe at a given point, although the quality 'straight,' apart from some body, does not touch the globe. For it has no abstract existence, as it is always conjoined with some body. The same thing seems to hold good of the properties of the soul: courage, gentleness, fear, pity, audacity, also joy, love, hate; they are all associated with the body. For along with these psychical conditions the body is also somewhat affected. A proof of this is the fact that sometimes when great and palpable misfortunes have befallen a man, he is not at all excited or moved to fear; on the other hand, one is sometimes aroused by slight and insignificant mishaps, and then the body swells in rage and is in the same condition as when a man is stirred in anger. But this statement receives still more support from the fact that when nothing has happened which could awaken fear, men exhibit those emotions which characterize a man in fright. And if this is true, it is evident that the emotions are ideas which find expression in the body. So that we have, for example, such definitions as the following: "Anger is a kind of movement of such and such a body, or part, or faculty, under this or that stimulus and due to this or that motive." It is for this reason that the study of the soul belongs to the province of the natural philosopher, either the soul in its entirety or such part of it as has to do with the body.

But the naturalist and the speculative philosopher would frame their definitions severally from different standpoints. For example, in reply to the question "What is anger?" the speculative philosopher says it is the desire of retaliation or something of that sort, the naturalist says it is the seething of the pericordial blood or heat; the one has furnished in his answer the matter, the other the form or reason, of the thing. For the notion is the form of a thing, and it is necessary that this notion be embodied in a particular matter, if it is to exist. For instance, the notion of a house is that of a shelter, to protect us against injury from wind and rain and heat; the natural philosopher, however, will call it stones and bricks and wood, while the other grasps the notion embodied in these things and for which they exist. Which of these now, is the real physical philosopher? Is it the one who busies himself with the matter, but is ignorant of the notion? or is it the inquirer who is occupied with the notion alone? I answer, it is rather the man who combines both of these characters. But what is the genius of each of these two men? Surely there is nobody who concerns himself merely with the properties of matter that are inseparable and merely as inseparable; but the physical philosopher has to do with all the functions and qualities of body and matter which are of such and such a kind. Such properties as are not subject-matter for the natural philosopher, are dealt with by someone else, in certain instances by a professor of one of the arts, perhaps, as *e.g.* by a builder or by a physician. But in the case of properties which are inseparable, although they attach to no particular body and may be abstractly regarded, with these the mathematician is concerned; and in so far as the qualities are regarded as abstract or transcendent entities, the metaphysician is concerned with them.

We were saying that the properties of the soul do not exist apart from the physical matter of living things, in which such qualities as courage and fear are expressed, and are not to be regarded as a line or surface.

Let the foregoing suffice as a discussion of the traditional theories of the soul; and now let us resume our subject from the start, and attempt to determine the nature of the soul and its most general definition. One class of realities we call 'substance.' This 'substance' may be regarded on the one hand as matter, which in itself is no definite thing; on the other hand, as form and idea, in terms of which definite individuality is ascribed to a thing. A third meaning of substance is the composite of matter and form. Matter is potentiality; form is actuality or realization.[3] The latter may be looked at in two ways, either as complete realization,—comparable with perfected knowledge, or as realization in process,—comparable with the activity of contemplation. The notion of substance appears to be most generally employed in the sense of body, and particularly of physical body; for this is the source of all other bodies. Some physical bodies have, and others have

not, life. By life we understand an inherent principle of nutrition, growth, and decay. So, that every natural body endowed with life would be substance, and substances in this composite sense. The body, therefore, would not be soul, since body is of such nature that life is an attribute of it. For body is not predicated of something else, but is rather itself substrate and matter. The soul must, then, be substance in this sense: it is the form of a natural body endowed with the capacity of life. In this meaning substance is the completed realization. Soul, therefore, will be the completed realization of a body such as described. Complete realization is employed in two senses. In the one sense it is comparable with perfected knowledge; in another, it is comparable with the active process of contemplation. It is evident that we mean by it here that realization which corresponds to perfected knowledge. Now, both waking and sleeping are included in the soul's existence: waking corresponds to active contemplation; sleep to attained and inactive knowledge.

In a given case science is earlier in origin than observation. Soul, then, is the first entelechy of a natural body endowed with the capacity of life. Such a body one would describe as organic. The parts of plants are also organs, although quite simple in character, *e.g.* the leaf is the covering of the pericarp, and the pericarp is covering of the fruit; the roots are analogous to mouths, both being channels of nutrition. If then we were obliged to give a general description applicable to all soul or life, we should say that it is the first entelechy of a natural organic body. It is therefore unnecessary to ask whether body and soul are one, as one should not ask whether the wax and the figure are one, or, in general, whether the matter of a particular thing and the thing composed of it are one. For although unity and being are predicted in several senses, their proper sense is that of perfect realization.

We have now given a general definition of the soul. We have defined it as an entity which realizes an idea. It is the essential notion which we ascribe to a body of a given kind. As an illustration, suppose that an instrument, *e.g.* an axe, were a natural body. Here the notion of axe constitutes its essential nature or reality, and this would be its soul. Were this taken away it would no longer be an axe, except in the sense of a homonym. It is in reality, however, merely an axe, and of a body of this sort soul is not the notional essence and the idea, but soul applies only to a natural body of a given kind, viz. a body whose principle of movement and rest is in itself.[4] The principle expressed here should be observed in its application to particular parts of the body. For if the eye were an animal, vision would be its soul, *i.e.* vision is the notional essence of the eye. The eye, however, is the matter of vision, and if the vision be wanting the eye is no longer an eye, save in the meaning of a homonym, as a stone eye or a painted eye. What applies here to a particular member, must also apply to the entire living body; for as the particular sensation is related to the particular organ of sense, so is the whole of sensation related to the entire sensitive organism, in so far as it has sensation. 'Potentiality of life' does not refer to a thing which has become dispossessed of soul, but to that which possesses it. Seed and fruit are potentially living bodies. As cutting is the realization of the axe, and vision is the realization of the eye, so is the waking state of the realization of the living body; and as vision and capacity are related to the organ, so is the soul related to the body. Body is the potential substrate. But as vision and pupil on the one hand constitute the eye, so soul and body in the other case constitute the living animal. It is, therefore, clear that the soul is not separable from the body; and the same holds good of particular parts of the soul, if its nature admits of division, for in some cases the soul is the realization of these very parts; not but that there are certain other parts where nothing forbids their possible separation, because they are not realizations of any bodily nature. And yet it is uncertain whether the soul as realization of the body is separable from it in a sense analogous to the separability of sailor, and boat. Let this suffice as a definition and outline sketch of the soul.

Inasmuch as the soul is defined mainly by means of two attributes, namely by locomotion on the one hand and by thought, judgment, and sensation on the other, it is supposed that thought and reflexion are a kind of sensation (for in both instances the soul discriminates and cognizes some reality), and even the old writers tell us that reflexion and sensation are identical, as *e.g.* Empedocles, who said: "Wisdom groweth in man in the face of a present object"; and in another verse: "Hence is given

unto them the power of reflecting ever and anon on diverse things"; and the words of Homer have the same meaning: "Such is the mind." For all of these ancient writers regard thought as something somatic, like sensation, and believe that both in sensation and thought like is apprehended by like, as we said in the beginning of this treatise. They should at the same time have spoken of error, for to animals this is more natural than truth, and their souls pass most of their existence in error. According to this theory, as some held, either all phenomena must be true or else error consists in the contact of the unlike, for this is the opinion that is opposed to the cognition of like by like. Further, in this case error and knowledge of opposite seem to be identical.

That sensation and reflexion, therefore, are not identical is evident. For all animals share in the one, but few only in the other. Neither is thought, in which right and wrong are determined *i.e.* right in the sense of practical judgment, scientific knowledge, and true opinion, and wrong in the sense of the opposite of these, —thought in this signification is not identical with sensation. For sensation when applied to its own peculiar objects is always true, and is inherent in all animals; but it is possible for discursive thoughts to be false, and it is found in no animal which is not also endowed with reason. Imagination, too, is different from sensation and discursive thought. At the same time, it is true that imagination is impossible without sensation, and conceptual thought, in turn, is impossible without imagination. That thought and conception, however, are not one and the same is evident. For imagination is under our control, and can be stimulated when we wish (for it is possible to call up before our eyes an imaginary object, as one employs images in the art of mnemonics). Conception, on the other hand, is not under our control. For it must be either false or true. Furthermore, when we conceive that something is terrible or fearful, we have at once a corresponding feeling, and the same may be said of what inspires courage. But in the case of imagination we are in the same condition as if we were to place a terrible or a courage-inspiring object before us in a picture. In conception itself there are distinct forms, such as knowledge, opinion, reflexion, and their opposites, concerning whose different meanings we shall speak later.

Since thinking differs from sense-perception, and in one signification appears to be imagination and in another signification conception, we must proceed to the treatment of the latter, after we have defined imagination. If imagination means the power whereby what we call a phantasm is awakened in us, and if our use of language here is not merely metaphorical, then imagination is one of those faculties or mental forces in us by virtue of which we judge and are capable of truth and error. And these faculties include sensation, opinion, scientific knowledge, and reasoning. That imagination is not to be confounded with sense-perception is plain from the following considerations. Sensation is either a mere power or a distinct act, like sight and seeing, but imagination is present when neither of these conditions is realized, viz. in the phantasms of dreams. Again, sensation is always present, but this is not true of imagination. If in reality it were identical with sensation, then all animals would have imagination. This does not seem to be the fact, as we find in the case of the ant, the bee, and the worm. Again, sensations are always true, while imaginations are for the most part false.

In the next place, we do not say when we are accurately observing a sense-object, that we imagine it to be a man. We say this rather when we do not clearly perceive and when the perception may be true or false, and as we said above, we see imaginary pictures even when our eyes are closed. But neither is imagination one of these faculties whose deliverances are always true, as *e.g.* scientific knowledge and reason. For imagination can also be false. It remains to be considered whether it is opinion, for opinion can be either true or false. Opinion, however, is followed by belief for no man can have an opinion and not believe what he opines, and none of the lower animals possesses belief, although imagination is found in many of them. Again every opinion is followed by belief, as belief is followed by persuasion, and persuasion by reason. Now, some of the lower animals have imagination, but none of them have reason. It is plain, then, that imagination is not opinion combined with sensation, nor mediated by sensation, nor a complex of opinion and sensation, and, for the same reason, it is clear that opinion has for its object nothing else than what sensation has for its object. I mean, *e.g.* that imagination is the complex of

an opinion of whiteness and a sensation of whiteness, and not the complex of an opinion of goodness and a sensation of whiteness. To imagine, therefore, is to opine what, strictly regarded, is a sense-object. Again, there are false appearances when we have correct conceptions, as *e.g.* in the case of the sun which appears to be a foot in diameter, whereas we believe it to be larger than the inhabited earth. The consequence is that we must either have thrown aside our true opinion which we held without the thing having changed and without any forgetfulness or change of conviction on our part; or if one still holds it, it is necessary that the same opinion be both true and false. But an opinion has become false in a case where an object, without our knowing it, has changed. Imagination, then, is not one of these faculties nor a derivative of them.

Since one thing when moved can communicate motion to another, and since imagination is held to be a form of motion which does not come into existence without sense-perception, but only in sentient creatures or in reference to objects to which sensation applies, and since motion is produced by the action of sense-perception, and this motion must be equal to the strength of the sensation, one can affirm that the motion of imagination would never be possible without sensation nor could it take place in non-sentient creatures. Further, the one who experiences it can act and be acted upon in many ways, and one's experiences may be true or false. This truth or falsehood is due to the following causes. Sense-perception is true when it concerns its own peculiar objects; at any rate, there is involved in this case, the least possible amount of error. In the second place, sense-perception may concern the accidental, and here error begins to be possible. One is not mistaken in saying that a thing is white, but if one says the white object is this or that particular thing, error arises. In the third place, error applies to common properties and concomitants of the accidental, in which peculiar properties are involved. I mean *e.g.* motion and magnitude, which are accidental properties of sensible objects, and concerning which we are especially liable to error in sense-perception. The motion set up by the activity of sensation will differ in terms of the three following forms of sense-perception. The first movement is when the sense-perception continues present, and this is true; the other two may be false whether the object is present or withdrawn, but are especially liable to error when the sense-object is removed.

If imagination contains nothing but the elements named and is what we have described it to be, it would be a movement stimulated by actualized sense-perception. Since sight is our principal sense, imagination[5] has derived its name from light, because sight is impossible without light. Because images persist and resemble sense-perceptions, animals regulate their actions to a large degree by imagination, some of them because they are incapable of reason, as the lower brutes, others because reason is sometimes veiled by passion, disease, or sleep, as is the case amongst men. Concerning imagination, what its nature is and what end it subserves, let the foregoing suffice.

Regarding that part of the soul by virtue of which one knows and reflects, whether it be a distinct part of whether it be distinct only notionally and not really, we have now to consider what its differential mark is, and by what process thinking is exercised. If thinking is like sense-perception, it would be either a kind of impression made by the object of cognition or some analogous process. It must, then, be impassive and yet receptive of the form,[6] and in its nature potentially like to the object of thought without being this object; and as the sense-organ is related to the object of sense, in a similar way thought must be related to the object of thought. Reason must, therefore, be unmixed, as Anaxagoras says, since it thinks everything, in order that it may rule, *i.e.* in order that it may know. It is the nature of thought to preclude and restrain the element that is foreign and adjacently seen. Its nature is, therefore, exclusively potentiality. What we call reason in the soul (by reason I mean the instrument by which the soul thinks and forms conceptions) is, prior to the exercise of thought, no reality at all. It is, therefore, wrong to suppose that reason itself is mixed with the body. For in that case it would have certain qualitative distinctions such as warm or cold, or it would be a sort of instrument, like a sense-organ. But in point of fact it is nothing of the kind. Certain writers[7] have happily called the soul the place of ideas, only this description does not apply to the soul as a whole, but merely to the power of thought, and it applies

to ideas only in the sense of potentiality, and not of actuality. It is evident from the sense-organ and from the nature of sensation, that the term impassivity is employed in a different meaning in sensation and in thinking. For sense-perception cannot take place when the sense-stimulus is excessive, as one does not hear sound in the midst of loud noises, neither can one see nor smell in the midst of excessively bright colours and strong odours. On the other hand, when the mind thinks a very profound thought, it thinks not in a lesser but in a deeper degree minor details. For the power of sensation is not independent of the body, while the mind is separable. When reason becomes its several objects in the sense in which an actually learned man is said to be learned (and this takes place when he can exercise knowledge through his own agency), even then reason is in a certain sense potential, although this potentiality differs from that case, potentiality signifies the capacity of thinking itself.

There is a difference between concrete magnitude and the ultimate nature of magnitude, between water and the ultimate nature of water (the same distinction can be applied to other instances, though not to all, for in some cases they are identical). Concrete flesh and the ultimate nature of flesh one judges either by a different and distinct faculty or by the same faculty under differing conditions. Flesh is not separate from matter, but like a snub-nose, it is a particular thing in a given something. By means of a sense-organ one discriminates heat and cold and those qualities of which flesh is a sort of register. On the other hand, reason judges of the essential nature of flesh either by a different and distinct faculty, or in the way in which a bent line is related to itself when straightened. We refer the straight line as we do the snub-nose to abstract entities, for they are both associated with the continuous. But the essential notion of a thing, if straightness and the straight line are different (and they are two things), is apprehended by a different power. The mind, then, judges in the two cases by means of a different power or by means of a power differently conditioned. In a word, therefore, as there are things abstracted from matter, so there are things that concern the reason. If the mind is simple and impassive, and has nothing in common with anything else, as Anaxagoras says, and if thinking means to be somehow impressed, one might ask, How will thought be possible? For it is only in so far as there is something common to two things that the one appears to act and the other to be acted upon. A further question might be raised, viz. whether the mind itself is the object of thought. If it is, mind will then either be found in other things, unless it is the object of thought in some way different from other objects, and unless the object of thought is a specific and single thing; else it will have a mixed composition which makes it like other things, the object of thought. According to our former definition, 'to be affected in reference to a common element,' means that the mind is potentially the object of thought, though perhaps not actually so until thought takes place. It must be that the case here is similar to that of the tablet on which nothing has been actually written. This is what takes place in the case of mind, and it is the object of thought as other things are. Where entities are without matter, the subject and object of thought are identical. Speculative thought and the thing speculatively known are one and the same. The reason why thought is not continuous must be investigated. On the other hand, when entities are material they are severally the object of thought only potentially; mind is not an element in them (for reason is the potentiality of such objects in abstracton from their matter), whereas it is in the reason itself that the object of thought will be found.

In the whole of nature there is on the one hand a material factor [8] for every kind of thing (and this is what all things are in their potentiality), and another factor which is causative and productive of things, by virtue of its making all objects, as art stands related to the matter it employs. These distinctions must also hold good when applied to the soul. Reason is of such character that on the one hand it becomes all things, and on the other creates all things, in this respect resembling a property like light. For light in a certain sense converts potential into actual colours, and reason, in the present meaning, is separate, impassive, and unmixed, being in its essential nature an energizing force. Now, action is always higher than passion and causal force higher than matter. Actual knowledge is identical with its object. Potential knowledge, on the other hand, pre-exists in the individual; regarded absolutely it does not so pre-exist. For mind does not at one moment think and at another not. In its separated state alone reason is what it is, immortal and eternal. We have no memory of it, because this part of reason is impassive. The passive reason, on the other hand, is perishable, and without it there can be no thought.

When thought is applied to indivisible terms, error does not arise. Where error and truth are both found is just in the combination of thoughts into a sort of unity. Empedocles *e.g.* says; "Wherefore the heads of many creatures sprang into life without necks," and later on by the attraction of Friendship they were joined together. So, too, these disjoined ideas are combined together by the reason, as *e.g.* the ideas of the incommensurable and the diagonal. If the ideas refer to the past or to the future, the element of time is added in the mind and combined with the ideas. Error is always due to the combination. For even in the case where one might think the white not to be white, one has made the combination of the 'not-white.' It is further possible to apply disjunction to everything. It is not only possible for the statement 'Cleon is fair' to be true or false, but this may be applied to the past or to the future. The unifying principle is in every case the reason. Since the simple or indivisible may be looked at from two standpoints, viz. either as potentiality or as actuality, there is nothing to prevent the mind from thinking the indivisible when it thinks of extension (which in its actual state is indivisible), and when it thinks it in an indivisible moment of time. For divisibility and indivisibility apply to time just as they do to length. It is, therefore, impossible to say what the mind thinks in each half of the time-division. For the half does not exist, except in potentiality, if the division has not been made. But in the act of thinking each half separately, the mind divides the time also, and then the time corresponds in its division to the two lengths. If, however, the mind thinks the object as a whole composed of two halves, it does this also with regard to time in its relation to the two halves.

That which is not quantitatively but only notionally indivisible, the mind thinks in an indivisible time and by an indivisible power of the soul. It does this, however, accidentally and not in so far as the factors of thought and time are divisible, but in so far as they are indivisible. And there is also in these cases an objective factor which is indivisible, although perhaps not a separate entity, that gives a unity to time and extension. And this is likewise true of everything that is continuous, whether in time or space. The point and everything obtained by division, and whatever (like a point) is no longer divisible, are explicable in terms of privation. Similar reasoning may be applied to other cases, as *e.g.* the way in which we know evil or black. For we know them somehow or other by means of their contraries. But the knowing mind must be these things potentially, and they must be reduced to unity in the mind

itself. If, however, in the case of any causal principle there is no opposite, then it knows itself, and is in actuality and is separate. A predication, as *e.g.* an affirmation, asserts something of something else, and is in every instance either true or false. This does not apply to the mind always, but when the mind asserts what a thing is in its essential nature and not what attaches to something as a predicate, then it is true. And just as sight is true when it concerns its own proper object, and on the other hand the opinion that a visible white object is or is not a man may not always be true, so it is with all immaterial entities.

NOTES

1. The question as to the nature of universals, which divided the Mediaeval Nominalists and Realists, was here clearly raised by Aristotle.

2. The difficult question as to whether the soul is capable of existing separately from the body is not very clearly or definitely answered by Aristotle. According to Aristotle's classic definition, the soul is the "entelechy of a body endowed with the capacity of life." From this definition one would conclude that the soul cannot exist apart from the body, although it is not itself corporeal. It is that which gives to a particular body its individuality and meaning, and it consists of the following elements: power of nutrition, self-movement, sensation, memory, emotion, imagination, and reason. Amongst these functions of the soul, reason is peculiar to man, although reason in its passive form is based on sensible experience and is conjoined with the life of the body. There is, however, a further form of reason, which Aristotle characterizes as active reason whose existence is entirely separable from the body, and is immortal. This form of reason is concerned with intuition or immediately apprehended truth, while the passive reason is occupied with mediated truth. There seems, however, to be no place for the former in Aristotle's definition of the soul cited above.

3. The notions here under discussion belong to the most fundamental with which the philosophy of Aristotle operates. The soul is characterized by several terms, chief of which are *form* and *entelechy*. Every individual or 'substantial' thing is a composite of form and matter. Form is that which gives a thing its character or significance. It is form, therefore, that is the object of knowledge. Becoming consists in the process of matter assuming a definite form. Matter, consequently, represents the potentiality of a thing, and form its actuality. Viewed from the standpoint of causation or process, these two notions constitute the material and formal causes; in other words, matter is the condition *sine qua non*, while the form is conceptual, efficient, and final cause. These fundamental terms in Aristotle's metaphysics are applied by him to the explanation of the soul. Man is first of all an organic whole, the living force in which is the soul, while the body is the soul's organ. Soul is that which differentiates a living from an inanimate thing, and life

signifies a process or a form of motion. Life implies, further, an active and a passive element; in other words, a moving principle and a thing moved, which in Aristotle's terminology are form and matter. Form here is equivalent to the moving or efficient cause. It is the energy or life that determines the growth of a particular body, or its transition, in Aristotelian language, from potentiality to actuality. Every living thing, then, is a composite of form and matter, or soul and body. In so far as the form is the perfected end or final cause, Aristotle describes the soul as the entelechy of a natural organic body. In so far as it is an efficient power or moving cause, he describes the soul as the actuality or actualization. It is only in the "soul that body attains its true reality." Soul is the realization of the body, apart from which the body is only formless, undeveloped, potential matter. Entelechy means the finished state of a thing or a state in which a thing's potentiality finds its complete development. Actualization, on the other hand, means the active process by which the potential thing passes over into the completed state or it is the completed state in process. Entelechy is, therefore, more ultimate than actualization, although Aristotle frequently uses the terms synonymously.

4. The meaning is that if an axe were a body with an inherent principle of movement, or in other words an animate body, then the notion of axe or axehood would constitute its soul. The soul, then, is the 'notional essence,' to use an Aristotelian phrase, of a living body.

5. It has been shown that imagination is a movement set up there by a past sensation. A sensation when past may leave an after effect in the sense-organ which again, unless some greater or cross stimulus inhibits it, may pass to the heart (the organ of the 'common sense') and there be revived as a pictorial image or phantasm, the real object being no longer present. This revival of a sense-image is imagination or phantasy, and the image thus reproduced is a phantasm. Sensation, therefore, is a prerequisite of imagination, although the revival of the residual image of sense is emancipated from the action of the sense-organ itself. Again, imagination is distinct from reason and scientific knowledge for (1) both the latter proceed by necessary steps and are consequently true, while imagination is sometimes true and sometimes false (2)

the steps in rational or scientific knowledge are not in our control, they follow from inherent necessity, while the pictures of imagination are arbitrary.

6. Sensation is described by Aristotle as the receptivity of the form or idea of a sensible thing without its matter.

7. Plato and the Academy.

8. 'Material factor' does not necessarily mean a thing constituted of crass matter, but refers to the metaphysical distinction between 'form' and 'matter,' which in other terms are 'actuality' and 'potentiality.' In this meaning sensations as containing the potentiality of ideas are their 'matters.'

Nicomachean Ethics

Every art and every scientific inquiry, and similarly every action and purpose, may be said to aim at some good. Hence the good has been well defined as that at which all things aim. But it is clear that there is a difference in the ends; for the ends are sometimes activities, and sometimes results beyond the mere activities. Also, where there are certain ends beyond the actions, the results are naturally superior to the activities.

As there are various actions, arts, and sciences, it follows that the ends are also various. Thus health is the end of medicine, a vessel of shipbuilding, victory of strategy, and wealth of domestic economy. It often happens that there are a number of such arts or sciences which fall under a single faculty, as the art of making bridles, and all such other arts as make wealth, or again by courage. As our subjects then and our premises are of this nature, we must be content to indicate the truth roughly and in outline; and as our subjects and premises are true generally *but not universally,* we must be content to arrive at conclusions which are only generally true. It is right to receive the particular statements which are made in the same spirit; for an educated person will expect accuracy in each subject only so far as the nature of the subject allows; he might as well accept probable reasoning from a mathematician as require demonstrative proofs from a rhetorician. But everybody is competent to judge the subjects which he understands, and is a good judge of them. It follows that in particular subjects it is a person of *special* education, and in general a person of universal education, who is a good judge. Hence the young[1] are not proper students of political science, as they have no

experience of the actions of life which form the premises and subjects of the reasonings. Also it may be added that from their tendency to follow their emotions they will not study the subject to any purpose or profit, as its end is not knowledge but action. It makes no difference whether a person is young in years or youthful in character; for the defect *of which I speak* is not one of time but is due to the emotional character of his life and pursuits. Knowledge is as useless to such a person as it is to an intemperate person. But where the desires and actions of people are regulated by reason the knowledge of these subjects will be extremely valuable. . . .

But having said so much by way of preface as to the students of political science, the spirit in which it should be studied, and the object which we set before ourselves, let us resume our argument as follows:

As every knowledge and moral purpose aspires to some good, what is in our view the good at which the political science aims, and what is the highest of all practical goods? As to its name there is, I may say, a general agreement. The masses and the cultured classes agree in calling it happiness, and conceive that "to live well" or "to do well" is the same thing as "to be happy." But as to the nature of happiness they do not agree, nor do the masses give the same account of it as the philosophers. The former define it as something visible and palpable, e.g. pleasure, wealth, or honour; different people give different definitions of it, and often the same person gives different definitions at different times; for when a person has been ill, it is health, when he is poor, it is wealth, and, if he is conscious of his own ignorance, he envies people who use grand language above his own comprehension. Some *philosophers* [2] on the other hand have held that, besides these various goods, there is an absolute good which is the cause of goodness in them all. It would perhaps be a waste of time to examine all these opinions, it will be enough to examine such as are most popular or as seem to be more or less reasonable.

But we must not fail to observe the distinction between the reasonings which proceed from first principles and the reasonings which lead up to first principles. For Plato was right in raising the difficult question whether the *true* way was from first principles or to first principles, as in the race-course from the judges to the goal, or *vice versa*. We must begin then with facts such as are known. But facts may be known in two ways, i.e. either relatively to ourselves or absolutely. It is probably then that *we* must begin with such facts as are known to us, *i.e. relatively*. It is necessary therefore, if a person is to be a competent student of what is noble and just and of politics in general, that he should have received a good moral training. For the fact that a thing is so is a first principle or starting-point, and, if the fact is sufficiently clear, it will not be necessary to go on to ask the reason of it. But a person who has received a good moral training either possesses first principles, or will have no difficulty in acquiring them. . . .

Perhaps, however, it seems a truth which is generally admitted, that happiness is the supreme good; what is wanted is to define its nature a little more clearly. The best way of arriving at such a definition will probably be to ascertain the function of Man. For, as with a flute-player, a statuary, or any artisan, or in fact anybody who has a definite function and action, his goodness, or excellence seems to lie in his functions, so it would seem to be with Man, if indeed he has a definite function. Can it be said then that, while a carpenter and a cobbler have definite functions and actions, Man, unlike them, is naturally functionless? The reasonable view is that, as the eye, the hand, the foot, and similarly each several part of the body has a definite function, so Man may be regarded as having a definite function apart form all these. What then, can this function be? It is not life; for life is apparently something which man shared with the plants; and it is

something peculiar to him that we are looking for. We must exclude therefore the life of nutrition and increase. There is next what may be called the life of sensation. But this too, is apparently shared by Man with horses, cattle, and all other animals. There remains what I may call the practical life of the rational part *of Man's being*. But the rational part is twofold; it is rational partly in the sense of possessing reason and intelligence. The practical life too may be conceived of in two ways, *viz., either as a moral state, or as a moral activity:* but we must understand by it the life of activity, as this seems to be the truer form of the conception.

The function of Man then is an activity of soul in accordance with reason, or not independently of reason. Again the functions of a person of a certain kind, and of such a person who is good of his kind e.g. of a harpist and a good harpist, are in our view generically the same, and this view is true of people of all kinds without exception, the superior excellence being only an addition to the function; for it is the function of a harpist to play the harp, and of a good harpist to play the harp well. This being so, if we define the function of Man as a kind of life, and this life as an activity of soul, or a course of action in conformity with reason, if the function of a good man is such activity or action of a good and noble kind, and if everything is successfully performed when it is performed in accordance with its proper excellence, it follows that the good of Man is an activity of soul in accordance with virtue or, if there are more virtues than one, in accordance with the best and most complete virtue. But it is necessary to add the words "in a complete life." For as one swallow or one day does not make a spring, so one day or a short time does not make a fortunate or happy man. . . .

In considering the first principle we must pay regard not only to the conclusion and the premisses of our argument, but also to such views as are popularly held about it. For while all experience harmonizes with the truth, it is never long before truth clashes with falsehood.

Goods have been divided into three classes, viz. external goods as they are called, goods of the soul and goods of the body. Of these three classes we consider the goods of the soul to be goods in the strictest or most literal sense. But it is to the soul that we ascribe psychical actions and activities. Thus our definition is a good one, at least according to this theory, which is not only ancient but is accepted by students of philosophy at the present time. It is right too, inasmuch as certain actions and activities are said to be the end; for thus it appears that the end is some good of the soul and not an external good. It is in harmony with this definition that the happy man should live well and do well, as happiness, it has been said, is in fact a kind of living and doing well. . . .

The question is, Do we deliberate upon everything? Is everything a matter for deliberation, or are there some things which are not subjects of deliberation?

We must presumably understand by "a matter of deliberation" not that about which a fool or a madman, but that about which a sensible person, would deliberate.

Nobody deliberates about things which are eternal, *i.e. immutable,* as e.g. the universe or the incommensurability of the diagonal and the side of a square; or about things which are in motion but always follow the same course, whether of necessity or by nature or for some other causes, as e.g. the solstices and sunrisings; or about things which are wholly irregular like droughts and showers; or about mere matters of chance such as the finding of a treasure. Nor again are all human affairs matters of deliberation; thus no Lacedaemonian will deliberate upon the best constitution for the Scythians. The reason why we do not deliberate about these things is that none of them can be effected by our action. The matters about which we deliberate are practical matters lying within our power. There is in fact no other class of matters left; for it would seem that the causes of things are nature, necessity, chance, and besides these only intelligence, and human agency in its various forms. But different classes of people deliberate about such practical matters as depend upon their several actions. Further, those sciences, which are exact and complete in themselves, do not admit of deliberation, as e.g. writing; for we are in no doubt as to the proper way of writing. But if a thing depends upon our own action and is not invariable, it is a matter of deliberation, as e.g. questions of medicine, of finance, or of navigation rather than of gymnastic, as being less exactly systematized, and similarly all other arts, and again, the arts more than the sciences, as we are more in doubt about them.

Deliberation occurs in cases which fall under a general rule, if it is uncertain what the issue will be, and in cases which do not admit of an absolute decision. We invite the help of other people in our deliberations upon matters of importance, when we distrust our own ability to decide them.

Again, we deliberate not about ends but about the means to ends. Thus a doctor does not deliberate whether he shall cure his patients, nor an orator whether he shall persuade his audience, nor a statesman whether he shall produce law and order, nor does any one else deliberate about his end. They all propose to themselves a certain end and then consider how and by what means it can be attained, and if it appears capable of attainment by several means, they consider what will be the easiest and best means of attaining it, and if there is only one means of attaining it, how it may be attained by this means, and by what means this means itself can be attained, until they come to the first cause, which in the order of discovery is last. For it seems that deliberation is a process of investigation and analysis such as this: it is like the analysis of a geometrical figure.   it appears however that, while investigation is not always deliberation, mathematical investigations, e.g. not being so, deliberation is always investigation, and that that which is last in the order of analysis is first in the order of production.

If *in a deliberation* we come upon an impossibility, we abandon our task, as e.g. if money is required and it is impossible to provide the money; but if it appears to be possible, we set about doing it. By possibilities I mean such things as may be effected by our own actions; for what is done by our friends may be said to be done by ourselves, as the origin of it lies in ourselves.   The question is sometimes what instruments are necessary, and at other times how they are to be used. Similarly in all other cases it is sometimes the means of doing a certain thing and at other times the manner or the agency that is in question.

It seems, as has been said, that a man originates his own actions. Deliberation touches such things as may be done by a man himself, and actions are done for the sake of something which lies beyond themselves. Accordingly it is not the end, but the means to the end, that will be matter of deliberation. Nor again will particular questions be matters of deliberation, as e.g. the question whether a particular thing is a loaf or has been properly baked; that is rather a matter of perception, and, if we go on deliberating for ever, we shall never come to an end.

The objects of deliberation and of moral purpose are the same, except that the object of moral purpose is already determined; for it is that which is preferred after deliberation. For everybody gives up inquiring how he shall act when he has traced back the origin of his action to himself and to the dominant part of himself, i.e. to the part which exercises moral choice or purpose. There is an illustration of this principle in the ancient polities which Homer represented, for in them the kings promulgated their purpose, whatever it might be, to the people.

But if the object of our moral purpose is that which, being in our power, is after deliberation the object of our desire, it follows that the moral purpose is a deliberate desire of something which is in our power; for we first deliberate upon a thing and, after passing judgment upon it, we desire it in accordance with our deliberation.

Let us now leave this rough sketch of the moral purpose. We have shown what are the matters with which it deals, and that it is directed to the means *rather than to the ends*. . . .

In human society, with its common life and association in words and deeds, there are some people who seem to be obsequious. They are people who try to please us by praising all that we do and never thwarting us, and who think they ought to avoid causing annoyance to anybody who comes in their way. There are others who take the contrary line of always thwarting us and never give a thought to the pain which they cause; these are called surly and contentious people.

It is clear enough then that the moral states thus described are censurable, and that the intermediate or mean state, in virtue of which a person will assent and similarly will object to the right things in the right spirit, is laudable. No special name is assigned to this mean state, but it most nearly resembles friendliness; for the person in whom it exists answers to our idea of a virtuous friend, except that friendliness implies affection as well. It differs from friendliness in being destitute of emotion or affection

for the people with whom one associates, as it is not friendship or hatred that makes such a person assent to things in a right spirit but his own character. For he will so act alike to strangers and acquaintances, and to people with whom he is or is not intimate; only in each case his action will be suitable; for it is not natural to pay the same regard to strangers as to intimate friends, or to be equally scrupulous about causing them pain.

While it is thus stated in general terms that such a person will associate with other people in a right spirit, it must be added that, in his endeavour to avoid causing pain or to cooperate in giving pleasure, he will never lose sight of what is noble and expedient. For it seems that he has to do with such pleasures and pains as occur in human society. Whenever then it is not honourable for him or is injurious to cooperate in giving pleasure, he will object to giving it, and will prefer to cause pain; or if a thing brings discredit and considerable discredit or injury upon its author, while opposition to it causes him only slight pain, he will not accept it but will raise an objection to it.

He will not associate in the same spirit with people of high position and with ordinary people, or with people whom he knows well and whom he knows only slightly, and so on as other differences may occur; but he will render to each class its proper due. Again, while he chooses the promotion of pleasure in itself, and shrinks from the infliction of pain, he will be guided by a consideration of consequences, if they are greater than the immediate pleasure or pain, i.e. of nobleness and expediency; in other words he will inflict slight pains for the sake of great subsequent pleasure.

Such is then the intermediate or mean character, although it has no proper name. But if a person tries to promote the pleasure of others, he may either aim at being pleasant without having an ulterior object, and then he will be called complaisant, or it may be his object to get some personal advantage in the way of money or of the good things which money brings with it, and then he will be called a flatterer. If a person on the other hand is disagreeable to everybody, he is a surly and contentious fellow, as has been said.

The extreme states here appear to be opposed to one another *rather than to the mean state*, because the mean state has no name. . . .

The mean state of which boastfulness is an extreme has very much the same sphere, and it also is nameless. But it will be worth while to examine these states; for we shall better understand the facts of character after discussing the moral characters severally, and shall be convinced that the virtues are mean states, by finding this to be the universal rule.

The people who in the conversation and intercourse of life make it their object to give pleasure or pain have been already described. Let us now speak of such people as are truthful and false, whether in word or in deed or in their pretensions.

It seems that the boaster is one who is fond of pretending to possess the qualities which the world esteems, although he does not possess them, or does not possess them to the extent that he pretends. The ironical person on the contrary disclaims or disparages what he possesses, the intermediate person, who is a sort of "plain dealer," is truthful both in life and in speech; he admits the fact of his possessions, he neither exaggerates nor disparages them.

It is possible to be both boastful and ironical either with or without an ulterior object. But every man speaks, acts and lives in accordance with his character, unless he has an ulterior object in view.

Falsehood in itself is base and censurable, truth is noble and laudable; so too the truthful person, as holding a mean or intermediate position, is laudable, the untruthful people are both censurable, but especially the boaster.

Let us speak of them both, beginning with the truthful person. We are not speaking of one who is truthful in legal covenants, or in all such matters as lie within the domain of justice or injustice (for these would be matters belonging to a different virtue), but where without any such important issue at stake a person is truthful both in word and in life, because his moral state is truthful. Such a person would seem to be virtuous; for he who is a lover of truth and truthful where truth is of no importance will be equally true where it is of greater importance. He will avoid falsehood in important matters as involving disgrace; for he avoided it in itself apart from its consequences; but so to avoid it is laudable. He inclines by preference to an understatement of the truth, as it appears to be in better taste than an overstatement, for all excesses are offensive.

A person who pretends to greater things than he possesses, if he has no ulterior object in doing so, seems to be a person of low character, as otherwise he would not take pleasure in a falsehood; but he looks more like a fool than a knave. Supposing he has an object, if the object be glory or honour, the pretentious person, like the boaster, is not highly censurable; but if it by money or the means of getting money, his conduct is more discreditable. It is not a particular faculty, but a particular moral purpose, which constitutes the boaster; for it is for virtue of his moral state and his character that he is a boaster, as a person is a liar, if he takes pleasure in falsehood for its own sake, or as a means of winning reputation or gain. Thus it is that boastful people, if their object is reputation, pretend to such qualities as win praise or congratulation, but if their object is gain, they pretend to such qualities as may be beneficial to their neighbours, and cannot be proved not to exist, e.g. to skill in prophesying or medicine. This is the reason why the great majority of boasters pretend to such qualities as these, and make a boast of them as they are beneficial and it is difficult to disprove them.

Ironical people, on the other hand, in depreciating themselves, show a more refined character, for it seems that their object is not to make gain but to avoid pomposity. They are particularly fond of disclaiming the same qualities as the boaster affects, the qualities which the world esteems, as was the way of Socrates.

People, whose pretensions apply to such things as are trivial and obvious, are called humbugs; they deserve nothing but contempt.

Sometimes irony itself appears to be boastfulness, as in the dress of the Lacedaemonians; for exaggerated deficiency is a form of boastfulness as well as excess. But people who employ irony with moderation, and upon such occasions as are not too obvious and palpable, present an appearance of refinement.

The boaster appears to be the opposite of the truthful man, as being worse than the ironical man.

NOTES

1. This is believed to be the passage which Shakespeare had in mind, though the reference to it is put in Hector's mouth,

"young men, whom Aristotle thought
Unfit to hear moral philosophy."

Troilus and Cressida, Act ii. Scene 2.

2. Aristotle is thinking of the Platonic "ideas."

Aristotelianism

Like Plato, Aristotle has been responsible for generating a philosophical tradition, a particular philosophical perspective, and a language with which to express its insights and respond to its critics.

1. *Model Science:* Aristotle's model science is *teleological biology*. Not only was Aristotle a great biologist and in many ways the founder of biology, but his remarkable philosophy is in large part an attempt to generalize what he found in that science into a complete vision of the universe. We should stress that his conception of biology is *teleological*: the Greek word means a study of ends or purposes. Aristotle found in life the pursuit of an end and therefore thought it meaningful to apply the category of purpose to all of reality. This kind of biology is to be contrasted with Darwinian biology or evolutionary biology. The latter does not see any purpose in nature. It sees merely struggle, survival, and development, but not development toward any specific end.

It is very easy to misunderstand and belittle the concept of teleology. Perhaps it would be more accurate to use the term *functionalism* or *structuralism* to stress the element which Aristotelianism has in view. Structures are to be understood in terms of their functions as part of a larger whole.

2. *Explanation.* Aristotle offers us the same model of what constitutes an adequate explanation as we found in Plato. That is, all adequate explanations must be demonstrations from first principles. Aristotle thus agrees with Plato that deductive explanations are the only acceptable kind. However, there is a crucial difference between Plato and Aristotle regarding how we arrive at the first principles.

3. *Rationality*. The first principles for Aristotle are abstracted from experience. Rationality thus involves an inescapable empirical or experiential element. Aristotle, therefore, rejects the Platonic conception of arriving at first principles through a priori methods. It is in this sense that we are to understand the Aristotelian insistence that intelligibility and structure are present in our experience of the world and are not a set of principles outside of our experience. We should also stress that experience is not to be understood too naively: for it involves the participation of reason in the act by which we abstract the essential features from the purely accidental features of our experience. Thus, statistically, most acorns do not become oak trees, but reason *sees* in experience that the true essence of an acorn is to become an oak. The ideal is therefore present in experience for Aristotelians, in the form of ends actually achieved at least once. The Aristotelian is contemptuous of utopian idealism, which speaks of ideals never yet realized.

For future reference, three further points might be kept in mind. Sometimes philosophers will contrast deductive reasoning, which is supposed to proceed from the general to the particular, with inductive reasoning, which proceeds from the particular to the general. Platonism stresses deductive reasoning from a priori first principles although it does recognize the need for a preparatory stage. Aristotelianism stresses the inductive process by which the examination of particulars leads us to discover the general principle contained therein. Aristotelianism recognizes, and in fact stresses, the deductive process, which follows the articulation of the general process. Aristotle's syllogistic logic is an elucidation of the rules of reasoning from general to particular, once experience has revealed the general principle. This is why every syllogism begins with at least one premise, which is a universal or general statement.

(P$_1$) All men are mortal.
(P$_2$) Socrates is a man.
_____
(C) Socrates is mortal.

The process by which we arrive at the generalization is one of the most disputed in the history of philosophy: frustrated Aristotelians frequently become Platonists on just this issue. Finally, philosophers will sometimes misleadingly speak of the difference between rationalists and empiricists and mean what we are stressing here as the difference between Platonists and Aristotelians. One must be careful to note the precise sense in which any author applies these labels.

4. *Objectivity*. Objectivity is to be understood literally as meaning in the object and not in the subject or the mind. What is merely in the subject is subjective. Aristotelians, like Platonists, are committed to the position that there is an objective reality with a permanent and absolute structure totally independent of man. Yet they believe that experience, when it is properly interpreted, reveals that structure. Another way of making this point is to say that Aristotelians are committed to the *correspondence theory of truth*, the position that a statement is true if that statement corresponds to the world outside us, and a statement

is false if it does not so correspond.

5. *Physical Science.* Given the foregoing, we should understand a serious Aristotelian interpretation of physical science to stress (a) the experiential and experimental nature of scientific methodology, (b) the necessity for testing our theories against experimental confirmation, (c) the search for the permanent structure behind the seeming irregularity of our experience, and (d) the formulation of that structure in terms of generalizations, called variously first principles, laws, or theories. Again we note that the intractable obscurity of the original process by which we move from the particular to the general will plague Aristotelians. Aristotelians see this as a technical difficulty and argue that despite disagreements we shall all agree in the end on what that objective, independent structure is.

6. *Social Science.* Just as the Aristotelian does not dwell on the individual fact but seeks to discover the general essence or the pervasive structural feature, so in social science, the Aristotelian does not dwell upon the individual but upon the general. The general in this case is the institution. Social science consists of the description of the inherent ends of institutions, whether those institutions are communities, states, nations, economic classes or races. Here again the behavior of a particular individual is irrelevant, as irrelevant as the acorn eaten by the squirrel. We are concerned with what a normal and healthy institution naturally develops into.

With regard to change, several possibilities present themselves. Sometimes it is argued that institutions follow a cyclic process like the oak-acorn-oak process. The notion appears in the guise of the theory that different forms of government follow each other in the same pattern: thus, democracy is always followed by tyranny. Sometimes the process can reconstruct a culture and the rise and fall of its institutions as a whole. Finally, it is even possible to bend this notion to argue that human social and political history as a whole is a gradual unfolding of a process with a built-in end.

7. *Values.* If healthy institutions are those that function to achieve their ends and unhealthy ones those that do not, then all questions of right and wrong conduct are answered by reference to the built-in ends of the specific institutions to which we belong. Those value judgments are treated legalistically or formally by reference to the rules of the healthy institution. There is no question of whether one ought to belong to healthy institutions, since mankind cannot achieve its full development or potential unless it does so belong.

We conclude by suggesting once more that this outline may be helpful in identifying features and interconnections in the thought of later philosophers.

Chapter IV—Medieval Philosophy

St. Augustine

The expression *Medieval Thought* may create the illusion of believing in a narrowly delimited and carefully defined set of doctrines exhibiting an unusual homogeneity. Nothing could be further from the truth. The medieval period was marked by great diversity and controversy as well as profound insight into the human predicament. Moreover, if we use the expression *medieval* to cover a time period, we must note the existence of parallel philosophical traditions within both the Jewish and Arabic communities, as well as the Christian community. Of necessity, we can only concentrate on a few major thinkers, and even then, we have chosen to emphasize those aspects of their work which reflect the continuing Platonic and Aristotelian influences in the course of Western thought. Let us keep the foregoing qualification in mind as we examine the thought of St. Augustine.

Like its predecessor, hellenistic ethical speculation, early medieval thought was marked by its concern for individual salvation. Intellectually, it expressed itself as the attempt to combine a theological tradition derived from Judaism and a philosophical vocabulary and outlook derived from the classical Greek world. A good deal of the tension of medieval thought can be understood as the attempt to rationalize these two traditions. When we speak of the relationship between faith and reason we mean, in part, this attempted synthesis. We must recall that Christianity began as an offshoot of Judaism.

We must also dispel the illusion that medieval thought was pure "rationalization" in the sense of just trying to provide a defense of what was believed independently of reason. The matter is not quite that simple; in fact, the difficulties within classical Greek philosophy demanded some new turn in thinking. The reader should recall that both Plato and Aristotle adhered to the notion that all explanation is demonstration. At the same time they recognized that not everything could be proven. That is, there must be axioms or first principles which must be known independent of proof. In the period between classical Greek thought and the medieval age, hellenistic sceptics had attacked both the Platonic and Aristotelian answers to the question of how to arrive at first principles. The burning intellectual issue was, How can we know the truth of our first premises? The answer given by St. Augustine was that we could know the truth of our first principles by the appeal to religious dogma. This idea is definitely not Aristotelian since religious dogma is not discovered in experience. It is much more of a Platonic answer, and this is especially apparent when St. Augustine goes on to identify the source of such knowledge as divine illumination. The notion of divine illumination is Augustine's analogue to Plato's myth of the cave as expressed in the *Republic.*

St. Augustine did not stop with the answer to this question but went on to construct a sophisticated intellectual framework. Consider the following argument. Augustine begins by noting that the only thing that cannot be doubted is the fact that he doubts. Anyone who doubts that he doubts is obviously doubting. Hence, no one can consistently doubt that he doubts. In the second place, if we doubt, then we think. This follows from the mere fact that doubt is a form of thought. Third, if we think, then we are acting. This follows from the fact that thought is one type of activity. Finally, if we act or are engaged in activity, then we must exist. Thus, we are led demonstratively from a first self-evident truth to the undeniable conclusion that we exist.

Augustine continues. The fact that we exist here and now (what we proved in the previous paragraph) is an eternal truth. Please note this does not mean that we shall exist for all eternity but only that the fact that we exist here an now will always be true, even when we no longer exist. The really interesting question is how to account for the source or origin of this eternal (permanent and unquestionable) truth. Surely, Augustine argues, we cannot be the cause, source, origin, or author of this truth, for we are not eternal. The assumption behind this step of the argument is that the cause of an eternal truth must be itself eternal. That is, the cause must have the same property as the effect. Eternal truth must therefore be caused in us by some thing which is eternal. Since there is only one thing which could be considered as eternal, namely God, it follows that God exists.

Augustine's proof of God's existence does not ask us to accept such a belief as a mere matter of faith. Rather, he has offered us an argument which arrives at that position by a series of seemingly unassailable steps. Moreover, the beginning of this particular argument makes no appeal to religious dogma but to purely intellectual considerations. This most famous of all philosophical arguments will reappear in Descartes.

The conclusion which St. Augustine himself drew from his efforts was that reason could be used to help us better understand what is revealed by faith. The major moral problem for Augustine was the existence of *evil*. Augustine had identified the God of the scriptures (described in the Bible as "He who is") with the Platonic form of the "Good." This meant that God was defined as all-powerful and completely good. The problem which arose was the reconciliation of the belief in such a God with the apparent existence of evil. Why would such a God create a world with evil in it? Originally, Augustine had accepted the ancient Manichean view in which the world was described as an eternal struggle between the forces of good ("God") and evil ("Satan") with the outcome unclear. He subsequently rejected this view and instead embraced the doctrine that evil is relative. That is, although individual things appear to us mortals to be evil, if we could view reality as a whole as God himself does, we could see that reality as a whole is good. Thus, if we knew the divine plan, we would not be perturbed by apparent evil. This doctrine rests upon the highly respectable logical distinction between part and whole. The properties of the parts are not necessarily the same as the properties of the whole. In fact, the whole can possess a property which is not possessed by any of its parts. For example, all of the parts of a locomotive, when dismantled, may be described as light in weight. Yet, surely when the parts are forged into a whole the locomotive is not light but heavy.

Having solved that problem, St. Augustine is immediately confronted by another. If evil is relative, how can there be such a thing as sin? This was a problem for him because he subscribed to the notion of *original sin* which had resulted from Adam's disobedience in eating the apple offered by Eve from the tree of the knowledge of good and evil. In the Hebrew tradition this was interpreted as man losing his immortality. Augustine interpreted this as mankind's loss of eternal life in paradise. To the outsider this can easily be interpreted as a kind of Platonic myth to explain how we have declined from the ideal type of life. Augustine then goes on to argue that we can only be saved by divine *grace*. God gives his grace to some but not to all individuals, but the reasons for this are knowable only to God.

The doctrines of sin, the relativity of evil, and grace have been extremely influential. Those of us who are accustomed to explaining human brutality as the result of environmental conditioning (we are all victims of circumstance) might well pay more attention to the concept of sin. How else can we account for the saintly behavior of those who exist in the most trying of circumstances (such as concentration camps) and the despicable behavior of others who have had all the advantages? An important consequence of this position is that there is no connection between merit (good works) and salvation. This was to be a great issue during the Middle Ages. Augustine's position, interestingly, was not to become the dominant position in the Catholic Church. Rather, it was to become the model for the Reformation traditions culminating in Luther and Calvin.

Finally, we note again the extent to which Augustine philosophizes within the Platonic tradition, this time with reference to the distinction between the earthly city (the declining Roman empire) and the heavenly city. This is clearly an attempt to understand human history, in part, by appeal to the way in which the Platonic "ideal" helps to explain the world of appearances, where evil is relative. The earthly city only mirrors imperfectly the idea of the heavenly city.

The City of God

CONCERNING PLATO, THE CHIEF AMONG THE DISCIPLES OF SOCRATES, AND HIS THREEFOLD DIVISION OF PHILOSOPHY

Among the disciples of Socrates, Plato was the one who shone with a glory which far excelled that of the others, and who not unjustly eclipsed them all. By birth, an Athenian of honorable parentage, he far surpassed his fellow-disciples in natural endowments, of which he was possessed in a wonderful degree. Yet, deeming himself and the Socratic discipline far from sufficient for bringing philosophy to perfection, he travelled as extensively as he was able, going to every place famed for the cultivation of any science of which he could make himself master. Thus he learned from the Egyptians whatever they held and taught as important; and from Egypt, passing into those parts of Italy which were filled with the fame of the Pythagoreans, he mastered, with the greatest facility, and under the most eminent teachers, all the Italic philosophy which was then in vogue. And, as he had a peculiar love for his master Socrates, he made him the speaker in all his dialogues, putting in his mouth whatever he had learned, either from others, or from the efforts of his own powerful intellect, tempering even his moral disputations with the grace and politeness of the Socratic style. And, as the study of wisdom consists in action and contemplation, so that one part of it may be

called active, and the other contemplative—the active part having reference to the conduct of life, that is, to the regulation of morals, and into pure truth—Socrates is said to have excelled in the active part of that study, while Pythagoras gave more attention to its contemplative part, on which he brought to bear all the force of his great intellect. To Plato is given the praise of having perfected philosophy by combining both parts into one. He then divides it into three parts—the first moral, which is chiefly occupied with action; the second natural, of which the object is contemplation; and the third rational, which discriminates between the true and the false. And though this last is necessary both to action and contemplation, it is contemplation, nevertheless, which lays peculiar claim to the office of investigating the nature of truth. Thus this tripartite division is not contrary to that which made the study of wisdom to consist in action and contemplation. Now, as to what Plato thought with respect to each of these parts—that is, what he believed to be the end of all actions, the cause of all natures, and the light of all intelligences—it would be a question too long to discuss, and about which we ought not to make any rash affirmation. For, as Plato liked and constantly affected the well-known method of his master Socrates, namely, that of dissimulating his knowledge or his opinions, it is not easy to discover clearly what he himself thought on various matters, any more than it is to discover what were the real opinions of Socrates. We must, nevertheless, insert into our work certain of those opinions which he expresses in his writings, whether he himself uttered them, or narrates them as expressed by others, and seems himself to approve of—opinions sometimes favorable to the true religion, which our faith takes up and defends, and sometimes contrary to it, as, for example, in the questions concerning the existence of one God or of many, as it relates to the truly blessed life which is to be after death. For those who are praised as having most closely followed Plato, who is justly preferred to all the other philosophers of the Gentiles, and who are said to have manifested the greatest acuteness in understanding him, do perhaps entertain such an idea of God as to admit that in Him are to be found the cause of existence, the ultimate reason for the understanding, and the end in reference to which the whole life is to be regulated. Of these three things, the first is understood to pertain to the natural, the second to the rational, and the third to the moral part of philosophy. For if man has been so created as to attain, through that which is most excellent in him, to that which excels all things—that is, to the one true and absolute good God, without whom no nature exists, no doctrine instructs, no exercise profits—let Him be sought in whom all things are secure to us, let Him be discovered in whom all truth becomes certain to us, let Him be loved in whom all becomes right to us.

THAT IT IS ESPECIALLY WITH THE PLATONISTS THAT WE MUST CARRY ON OUR DISPUTATIONS ON MATTERS OF THEOLOGY, THEIR OPINIONS BEING PREFERABLE TO THOSE OF ALL OTHER PHILOSOPHERS

If, then, Plato defined the wise man as one who imitates, knows, loves this God, and who is rendered blessed through fellowship with Him in His own blessedness, why discuss with the other philosophers? It is evident that none come nearer to us than the Platonists. To them, therefore, let that fabulous theology give place which delights the minds of men with the crimes of the gods; and that civil theology also, in which impure demons, under the name of gods, have seduced the peoples of the earth given up to earthly pleasures, desiring to be honored by the errors of men, and by filling the minds of their worshippers with impure desires, exciting them to make the representation of their crimes one of the rites of their worship, while they themselves found in the spectators of these exhibitions a most pleasing spectacle—a theology in which, whatever was honorable in the temple, was defiled by its mixture with the obscenity of the theatre, and whatever was base in the theatre was vindicated by the abominations of the temples. To these philosophers also the interpretations of Varro must give place, in which he explains the sacred rites as having reference to heaven and earth, and to the seeds and operations of perishable things; for, in the first place, those rites have not the signification which he would have men believe is attached to them, and therefore truth does not follow him in his attempt so to interpret them; and even if they had this signification, still those things ought not to be worshipped by the rational soul as its god which are placed below it in the scale of nature, nor ought the soul to prefer to itself as gods things to which the true God has given it the preference. The same must be said of those writings pertaining to the sacred rites, which Numa Pompilius took care to conceal by causing them to be buried along with himself, and which, when they were afterwards turned up by the plough, were burned by order of the senate. And, to treat Numa with all honor, let us mention as belonging to the same rank as these writings that which Alexander of Macedon wrote to his mother as communicated to him by Leo, an Egyptian high priest. In this letter not only Picus and Faunus, and Aeneas and Romulus or even Hercules, and Aesculapius and Liber, born of Semele, and the twin sons of Tyndareus, or any other mortals who have been deified, but even the principal gods themselves, to whom Cicero, in his Tusculan questions, alludes without mentioning their names, Jupiter, Juno, Saturn, Vulcan, Vesta, and many others whom Varro attempts to identify with the parts or the elements of the world, are shown to have been men. There is, as we have said, a similarity between this case and that of Numa; for the priest being afraid because he had revealed a mystery, earnestly begged to Alexander to command his mother to burn the letter which conveyed these communications to her. Let these two theologies, then, the fabulous and the civil, give place to the Platonic philosophers, who have recognized the true God as the author of all things, the source of the light of truth, and the bountiful bestower of all blessedness. And not these only, but to these great acknowledgers of so great a God, those philosophers must yield who, having their mind enslaved to their body, supposed the principles of all things to be material; as Thales, who held the first principle of all things was water; Anaximenes, that it was air; the Stoics, that it was fire; Epicurus, who affirmed that it consisted of atoms, that is to say, of minute corpuscles; and many others whom it is needless to enumerate, but who believed that bodies, simple or compound, animate or inanimate, but nevertheless bodies, were the cause and principle of all things. For some of them—as, for instance, the Epicureans—believed that living things could originate from things without life; others held that all things living or without life spring from a living principle, but that, nevertheless, all things, being material, spring from a material principle. For the Stoics thought that fire, that is, one of the four material elements of which this visible world is composed, was both living and intelligent, the maker of the world and of all things contained in it—that it was in fact God. These and others like them have only been able to suppose that which their hearts enslaved to sense have vainly suggested to them. And yet they have within themselves something which they could not see: they represented to themselves inwardly things which they had seen without, even when they were not seeing them, but only thinking of them. But this representation in thought is no longer a body, but only the similitude of a body; and that faculty of the mind by which this similitude of a body is seen is neither a body nor the similitude of a body; and the faculty which judges whether the representation is beautiful or ugly is without doubt superior to the object judged of. This principle is the understanding of man, the rational soul; and it is certainly not a body, since that similitude of a body which it beholds and judges of is itself not a body. The soul is neither earth, nor water, nor air, nor fire, of which four bodies, called the four elements, we see that this world is composed. And if the soul is not a body, how should God, its Creator, be a body? Let all those philosophers, then, give place, as we have said, to the Platonists, and those also who have been ashamed to say that God is a body, but yet have thought that our souls are of the same nature as God. They have not been staggered by the great changeableness of the soul—an attribute which it would be impious to ascribe to the divine nature—but they say it is the body which changes the soul, for in itself it is unchangeable. As well might they say, "Flesh is wounded by some body, for in itself it is invulnerable." In a word, that which is unchangeable can be changed by nothing, so that that which can be changed by the body cannot properly be said to be immutable.

CONCERNING THE MEANING OF THE PLATONISTS IN THAT PART OF PHILOSOPHY CALLED PHYSICAL

These philosophers, then, whom we see not undeservedly exalted above the rest in fame and glory, have seen that no material body is God, and therefore they have transcended all bodies in seeking for God. They have seen that whatever is changeable is not the most high God, and therefore they have transcended every soul and all changeable spirits in seeking the supreme. They have seen also that, in every changeable thing, the form which makes it that which it is, whatever be its mode or nature, can only be through Him who truly is, because He is unchangeable. And therefore, whether we consider the whole body of the world, its figure, qualities, and orderly movement, and also all the bodies which are in it; or whether we consider all life, either that which nourishes and maintains, as the life of trees, or that which, besides this, has also sensation, as the life of beasts; or that which adds to all these intelligence, as the life of man; or that which does not need the support of nutriment, but only maintains, feels, understands, as the life of angels—all can only *be* through Him who absolutely *is*. For to Him it is not one thing to *be*, and another to live, as though He could *be*, not living; nor is it to Him one thing to live, and another thing to understand, as though He could live, not understanding; nor is it to Him one thing to understand, another thing to be blessed, as though He could understand and not be blessed. But to Him to live, to understand, to be blessed, are to *be*. They have understood, from this unchangeableness and this simplicity, that all things must have been made by Him, and that He could Himself have been made by none. For they have considered that whatever *is* is either body or life, and that life is something better than body, and that the nature of body is sensible, and that of life intelligible. Therefore they have preferred the intelligible nature to the sensible. We mean by sensible things such things as can be perceived by the sight and touch of the body; by intelligible things, such as can be understood by the sight of the mind. For there is no corporeal beauty, whether in the condition of a body, as figure, or in its movement, as in music, of which it is not the mind that judges. But this could never have been, had there not existed in the mind itself a superior form of these things, without bulk, without noise of voice, without space and time. But even in respect of these things, had the mind not been mutable, it would not have been possible for one to judge better than another with regard to sensible forms. He who is clever, judges better than he who is slow, he who is skilled than he who is unskillful, he who is practised than he who is unpractised; and the same person judges better after he has gained experience than he did before. But that which is capable of more and less is mutable; whence able men, who have thought deeply on these things, have gathered that the first form is not to be found in those things whose form is changeable. Since, therefore, they saw that body and mind might be more or less beautiful in form, and that, if they wanted form, they could have no existence, they saw that there is some existence in which is the first form, unchangeable, and therefore not admitting of degrees of comparison, and in that they most rightly believed was the first principle of things which was not made, and by which all things were made. Therefore that which is known of God He manifested to them when His invisible things were seen by them, being understood by those things which have been made; also His eternal power and Godhead by whom all visible and temporal things have been created. We have said enough upon that part of theology which they call physical, that is, natural.

HOW MUCH THE PLATONISTS ARE TO BE HELD AS EXCELLING OTHER PHILOSOPHERS IN LOGIC, I.E. RATIONAL PHILOSOPHY

Then, again, as far as regards the doctrine which treats of that which they call logic, that is, rational philosophy, far be it from us to compare them with those who attributed to the bodily senses the faculty of discriminating truth, and thought, that all we learn is to be measured by their untrustworthy and fallacious rules. Such were the Epicureans, and all of the same school. Such also were the Stoics, who ascribed to the bodily senses that expertness in disputation which they so ardently love, called by them dialectic, asserting that from the senses the mind conceives the notions of those things which they explicate by definition. And hence is developed the whole plan and connection of their learning and teaching. I often wonder, with respect to this, how they can say that none are beautiful but the wise; for by what bodily sense have they perceived that beauty, by what eyes of the flesh have they seen wisdom's comeliness of form? Those, however, whom we justly rank before all others, have distinguished those things which are conceived by the mind from those which are perceived by the senses, neither taking away from the senses anything to which they are competent, nor attributing to them anything beyond their competency. And the light of our understandings, by which all things are learned by us, they affirmed to be that selfsame God by whom all things were made.

THAT THE PLATONISTS HOLD THE FIRST RANK IN MORAL PHILOSOPHY ALSO

The remaining part of philosophy is morals, or what is called by the Greeks ethics, in which is discussed the question concerning the chief good—that which will leave us nothing further to seek in order to be blessed, if only we make all our actions refer to it, and seek it not for the sake of something else, but for its own sake. Therefore it is called the end, because we wish other things on account of it, but itself only for its own sake. This beatific good, therefore, according to some, comes to a man from the body, according to others, from the mind, and, according to others, from both together. For they say that man himself consists of soul and body; and therefore they believed that from either of these two, or from both together, their well-being must proceed, consisting in a certain final good, which could render them blessed, and to which they might refer all their actions, not requiring anything ulterior to which to refer that good itself. This is why those who have added a third kind of good things, which they call extrinsic—as honor, glory, wealth, and the like—have not regarded them as part of the final good, that is, to be sought after for their own sake, but as things which are to be sought for the sake of something else, affirming that this kind of good is good to the good, and evil to the evil. Wherefore, whether they have sought the good of man from the mind or from the body, or from both together, it is still only from man they have supposed that it might be sought. But they who have sought it from the body have sought it from the inferior part of man; they who have sought it from the mind, from the superior part; and they who have sought it from both, from the whole man. Whether, therefore, they have sought it from any part, or from the whole man, still they have only sought it from man; nor have these differences, being three, given rise only to three dissentient sects of philosophers, but to many. For diverse philosophers have held diverse opinions, both concerning the good of the body, and the good of the mind, and the good of both together. Let, therefore, all these give place to those philosophers who have not affirmed that a man is blessed by the enjoyment of the body, or by the enjoyment of the mind, but by the enjoyment of God—enjoying Him, however, not as the mind does the body or itself, or as one friend enjoys another, but as the eye enjoys light, if, indeed, we may draw any comparison between these things. But what the nature of this comparison is, will, if God help me, be shown in another place, to the best of my ability. At present, it is sufficient to mention that Plato determined the final good to be to live according to virtue, and affirmed that he only can attain to virtue who knows and imitates God—which knowledge and imitation are the only cause of blessedness. Therefore he did not doubt that to philosophize is to love

God, whose nature is incorporeal. Whence it certainly follows that the student of wisdom, that is, the philosopher, will then become blessed when he shall have begun to enjoy God. For though he is not necessarily blessed who enjoys that which he loves (for many are miserable by loving that which ought not to be loved, and still more miserable when the enjoy it), nevertheless no one is blessed who does not enjoy that which he loves. For even they who love things which ought not to be loved do not count themselves blessed by loving merely, but by enjoying them. Who, then, but the most miserable will deny that he is blessed, who enjoys that which he loves, and loves the true and highest good? But the true and highest good, according to Plato, is God, and therefore he would call him a philosopher who loves God; for philosophy is directed to the obtaining of the blessed life, and he who loves God is blessed in the enjoyment of God.

THAT THE EXCELLENCY OF THE CHRISTIAN RELIGION IS ABOVE ALL THE SCIENCE OF PHILOSOPHERS

For although a Christian man instructed only in ecclesiastical literature may perhaps be ignorant of the very name of Platonists, and may not even know that there have existed two schools of philosophers speaking the Greek tongue, to wit, the Ionic and Italic, he is nevertheless not so deaf with respect to human affairs, as not to know that philosophers profess the study, and even the possession, of wisdom. He is on his guard, however, with respect to those who philosophize according to the elements of this world, not according to God, by whom the world itself was made; for he is warned by the precept of the apostle, and faithfully hears what has been said, "Beware that no one deceive you through philosophy and vain deceit, according to the elements of the world." Then, that he may not suppose that all philosophers are such as do this, he hears the same apostle say concerning certain of them, "Because that which is known of God is manifest among them, for God has manifested it to them. For His invisible things from the creation of the world are clearly seen, being understood by the things which are made, also His eternal power and Godhead." And, when speaking to the Athenians, after having spoken a mighty thing concerning God, which few are able to understand, "In Him we live, and move, and have our being," he goes on to say, "As certain also of your own have said." He knows well, too, to be on his guard against even these philosophers in their errors. For where it has been said by him that God has manifested to them by those things which are made His invisible things, that they might be seen by the understanding, there it has also been said that they did not rightly worship God Himself, because they paid divine honors, which are due to Him alone, to other things also to which they ought not to have paid them—"because, knowing God, they glorified Him not as God: neither were thankful, but became vain in their imaginations, and their foolish heart was darkened. Professing themselves to be wise, they became fools, and changed the glory of the incorruptible God into the likeness of the image of corruptible man, and of birds, and four-footed beasts, and creeping things"—where the apostle would have us understand him as meaning the Romans, and Greeks, and Egyptians, who glorified in the name of wisdom; but concerning this we will dispute with them afterwards. With respect, however, to that wherein they agree with us we prefer them to all others, namely concerning the one God, the author of this universe, who is not only above every body, being incorporeal, but also above all souls, being incorruptible—our principle, our light, our good. And though the Christian man, being ignorant of their writings, does not use in disputation words which he has not learned—not calling that part of philosophy natural (which is the Latin term), or physical (which is the Greek one), which treats of the investigation of nature; or that part rational, or logical, which deals with the question how truth may be discovered; or that part moral, or ethical, which concerns morals, and shows how good is to be sought, and evil to be shunned—he is not, therefore, ignorant that it is from the one true and supremely good God that we have that nature in which we are made in the image of God, and that doctrine by which we know Him and ourselves, and that grace through which, by cleaving to Him, we are blessed. This, therefore, is the cause why we prefer these to all the others, because, while other philosophers have

worn out their minds and powers in seeking the causes of things, and endeavoring to discover the right mode of learning and of living, these, by knowing God, have found where resides the cause by which the universe has been constituted, and the light by which truth is to be discovered, and the fountain at which felicity is to be drunk. All philosophers, then, who have had these thoughts concerning God, whether Platonists or others, agree with us. But we have thought it better to plead our cause with the Platonists, because their writings are better known. For the Greeks, whose tongue holds the highest place among the languages of the Gentiles, are loud in their praises of these writings; and the Latins, taken with their excellence, or their renown, have studied them more heartily than other writings, and, by translating them into our tongue, have given them greater celebrity and notoriety.

HOW PLATO HAS BEEN ABLE TO APPROACH SO NEARLY TO CHRISTIAN KNOWLEDGE

Certain partakers with us in the grace of Christ wonder when they hear and read that Plato had conceptions concerning God, in which they recognize considerable agreement with the truth of our religion. Some have concluded from this, that when he went to Egypt he had heard the prophet Jeremiah, or, while traveling in the same country, had read the prophetic scriptures, which opinion I myself have expressed in certain of my writings. But a careful calculation of dates, contained in chronological history, shows that Plato was born about a hundred years after the time in which Jeremiah prophesied, and, as he lived eighty-one years, there are found to have been about seventy years from his death to that time when Ptolemy, king of Egypt, requested the prophetic scriptures of the Hebrew people to be sent to him from Judea, and committed them to seventy Hebrews, who also knew the Greek tongue, to be translated and kept. Therefore, on that voyage of his, Plato could neither have seen Jeremiah, who was dead so long before, nor have read those same scriptures which had not yet been translated into the Greek language, of which he was a master, unless, indeed, we say that, as he was most earnest in the pursuit of knowledge, he also studied those writings through an interpreter, as he did those of the Egyptians—not, indeed, writing a translation of them (the facilities for doing which were only gained even by Ptolemy in return for munificent acts of kindness, though fear of his kingly authority might have seemed a sufficient motive), but learning as much as he possibly could concerning their contents by means of conversation. What warrants this supposition are the opening verses of Genesis: "In the beginning God made the heaven and earth. And the earth was invisible, and without order; and darkness was over the abyss: and the Spirit of God moved over the waters." For in the *Timaeus,* when writing on the formation of the world, he says that God first united earth and fire; from which it is evident that he assigns to fire a place in heaven. This opinion bears a certain resemblance to the statement, "In the beginning God made heaven and earth." Plato next speaks of those two intermediary elements, water and air, by which the other two extremes, namely, earth and fire, were mutually united; from which circumstance he is thought to have so understood the words, "The Spirit of God moved over the waters." For, not paying sufficient attention to the designations given by those scriptures to the Spirit of God, he may have thought that the four elements are spoken of in that place, because the air also is called spirit. Then, as to Plato's saying that the philosopher is a lover of God, nothing shines forth more conspicuously in those sacred writings. But the most striking thing in this connection, and that which most of all inclines me almost to assent to the opinion that Plato was not ignorant of those writings, is the answer which was given to the question elicited from the holy Moses when the words of God were conveyed to him by the angel; for, when he asked what was the name of the God who was commanding him to go and deliver the Hebrew people out of Egypt, this answer was given: "I am who am; and thou shalt say to the children of Israel, He who is sent me unto you," as though compared with Him that truly *is,* because He is unchangeable, those things which have been created mutable *are* not—a truth which Plato zealously held, and most diligently commended. And I know not whether this sentiment is anywhere to be found in the books of those who were before

Plato, unless in that book where it is said, "I am who am; and thou shalt say to the children of Israel, *who is* sent me unto you."

OF THE IMAGE OF THE SUPREME TRINITY, WHICH WE FIND IN SOME SORT IN HUMAN NATURE EVEN IN ITS PRESENT STATE

And we indeed recognize in ourselves the image of God, that is, of the supreme Trinity, an image which, though it be not equal to God, or rather, though it be very far removed from Him—being neither co-eternal, nor, to say all in a word, consubstantial with Him—is yet nearer to Him in nature than any other of His works, and is destined to be yet restored, that it may bear a still closer resemblance. For we both are, and know that we are, and delight in our being, and our knowledge of it. Moreover, in these three things no true-seeming illusion disturbs us; for we do not come into contact with these by some bodily sense, as we perceive the things outside of us—colors, *e.g.*, by seeing, sounds by hearing, smells by smelling, tastes by tasting, hard and soft objects by touching—of all which sensible objects it is the images resembling them, but not themselves which we perceive in the mind and hold in the memory, and which excite us to desire the objects. But, without any delusive representation of images or phantasms, I am most certain that I am, and that I know and delight in this. In respect of these truths, I am not at all afraid of the arguments of the Academicians, who say, What if you are deceived? For if I am deceived, I am. For he who is not, cannot be deceived; and if I am deceived, by this same token I am. And since I am if I am deceived, how am I deceived in believing that I am? for it is certain that I am if I am deceived. Since, therefore, I, the person deceived, should be, even if I were deceived, certainly I am not deceived in this knowledge that I am. And, consequently, neither am I deceived in knowing that I know. For, as I know that I am, so I know this also, that I know. And when I love these two things. I add to them a certain third thing, namely, my love, which is of equal moment. For neither am I deceived in this, and I love, since in those things which I love I am not deceived; though even if these were false, it would still be true that I *loved* false things. For how could I justly be blamed and prohibited from loving false things, if it were false that I loved them? But, since they are true and real, who doubts that when they are loved, the love of them is itself true and real? Further, as there is no one who does not wish to be happy, so there is no one who does not wish to be. For how can he be happy, if he is nothing?

OF EXISTENCE, AND KNOWLEDGE OF IT, AND THE LOVE OF BOTH

And truly the very fact of existing is by some natural spell so pleasant, that even the wretched are, for no other reason, unwilling to perish; and, when they feel that they are wretched, wish not that they themselves be annihilated, but that their misery be so. Take even those who, both in their own esteem, and in point of fact, are utterly wretched, and who are reckoned so, not only by wise men on account of their folly, but by those who count themselves blessed, and who think them wretched because they are poor and destitute—if any one should give these men an immortality, in which their misery should be deathless, and should offer the alternative, that if they shrank from existing externally in the same misery they might be annihilated, and exist nowhere at all, nor in any condition, on the instant they would joyfully, nay exultantly, make election to exist always, even in such a condition, rather than not exist at all. The well-known feeling of such men witnesses to this. For when we see that they fear to die, and will rather live in such misfortune than end it by death, is it not obvious enough how nature shrinks from annihilation? And, accordingly, when they know that they must die, they seek, as a great boon, that this mercy be shown them, that they may a little longer live in the same misery, and delay to end it by death. And so they indubitably prove with what glad alacrity they would accept immortality, even though it secured to them endless destruction. What! do not even all irrational animals, to whom such calculations are unknown, from the huge dragons down to the least worms, all testify that they wish to exist, and therefore shun death by every movement in their power? Nay, the very plants and shrubs, which have no such life as enables them to shun destruction by

movements we can see, do not they all seek in their own fashion to conserve their existence, by rooting themselves more and more deeply in the earth, that so they may draw nourishment, and throw out healthy branches towards the sky? In fine, even the lifeless bodies, which want not only sensation but seminal life, yet either seek the upper air or sink deep, or are balanced in an intermediate position, so that they may protect their existence in that situation where they can exist in most accordance with their nature.

And how much human nature loves the knowledge of its existence, and how it shrinks from being deceived, will be sufficiently understood from this fact, that every man prefers to grieve in a sane mind, rather than to be glad in madness. And this grand and wonderful instinct belongs to men alone of all animals; for, though some of them have keener eyesight than ourselves for this world's light, they cannot attain to that spiritual light with which our mind is somehow irradiated, so that we can form right judgments of all things. For our power to judge is proportioned to our acceptance of this light. Nevertheless, the irrational animals, though they have not knowledge, have certainly something resembling knowledge; whereas the other material things are said to be sensible, not because they have senses, but because they are the objects of our senses. Yet among plants, their nourishment and generation have some resemblance to sensible life. However, both these and all material things have their causes hidden in their nature; but their outward forms, which lend beauty to this visible structure of the world, are perceived by our senses, so that they seem to wish to compensate for their own want of knowledge by providing us with knowledge. But we perceive them by our bodily senses in such a way that we do not judge of them by these senses. For we have another and far superior sense, belonging to the inner man, by which we perceive what things are just, and what unjust—just by means of an intelligible idea, unjust by the want of it. This sense is aided in its functions neither by the eyesight, nor by the orifice of the ear, nor by the air-holes of the nostrils, nor by the palate's taste, nor by any bodily touch. By it I am assured both that I am, and that I know this; and these two I love, and in the same manner I am assured that I love them.

CONCERNING THOSE WHO CALL BY THE NAME OF FATE, NOT THE POSITION OF THE STARS, BUT THE CONNECTION OF CAUSES WHICH DEPENDS ON THE WILL OF GOD

But, as to those who call by the name of fate, not the disposition of the stars as it may exist when any creature is conceived, or born, or commences its existence, but the whole connection and train of causes which makes everything become what it does become, there is no need that I should labor and strive with them in a merely verbal controversy, since they attribute the so-called order and connection of causes to the will and power of God most high, who is most rightly and most truly believed to know all things before they come to pass, and to leave nothing unordained; from whom are all powers, although the wills of all are not from Him. Now, that it is chiefly the will of God most high, whose power extends itself irresistibly through all things which they call fate, is proved by the following verses, of which, if I mistake not, Annaeus Seneca is the author:—

> Father supreme, Thou ruler of the lofty heavens,
> Lead me where'er it is Thy pleasure; I will give
> A prompt obedience, making no delay,
> Lo! here I am. Promptly I come to do Thy sovereign will;
> If Thy command shall thwart my inclination, I will still
> Follow Thee groaning, and the work assigned,
> With all the suffering of a mind repugnant,
> Will perform, being evil; which, had I been good,
> I should have undertaken and performed, though hard,
> With virtuous cheerfulness.
> The Fates do lead the man that follows willing;
> But the man that is unwilling, him they drag.

Most evidently, in this last verse, he calls that "fate" which he had before called "the will of the Father supreme," whom, he says, he is ready to obey that he may be led, being willing, not dragged, being unwilling, since "the Fates do lead the man that follows willing, but the man that is unwilling, him they drag."

The following Homeric lines, which Cicero translates into Latin, also favor this opinion:—

> Such are the minds of men, as is the light
> Which Father Jove himself doth pour
> Illustrious o'er the fruitful earth.

Not that Cicero wishes that a poetical sentiment should have any weight in a question like this; for when he says that the Stoics, when asserting the power of fate, were in the habit of using these verses from Homer, he is not treating concerning the opinion of that poet, but concerning that of those philosophers, since by these verses, which they quote in connection with the controversy which they hold about fate, is most distinctly manifested what it is which they reckon fate, since they call by the name of Jupiter him whom they reckon the supreme god, from whom, they say, hangs the whole chain of fates.

CONCERNING THE FOREKNOWLEDGE OF GOD AND THE FREE WILL OF MAN, IN OPPOSITION TO THE DEFINITION OF CICERO

The manner in which Cicero addresses himself to the task of refuting the Stoics, shows that he did not think he could effect anything against them in argument unless he had first demolished divination. And this he attempts to accomplish by denying that there is any knowledge of future things, and maintains with all his might that there is no such knowledge of future God or man, and that there is no prediction of events. Thus he denies the foreknowledge of God, and attempts by vain arguments, and by opposing to himself certain oracles very easy to be refuted, to overthrow all prophecy. . . .

But, in refuting these conjectures of the mathematicians, his argument is triumphant, because truly these are such as destroy and refute themselves. Nevertheless, they are far more tolerable who assert the fatal influence of the stars than they who deny the foreknowledge of future events. For, to confess that God exists, and at the same time to deny that He has foreknowledge of future things, is the most manifest folly. This Cicero himself saw, and therefore attempted to assert the doctrine embodied in the words of Scripture, "The fool hath said in his heart, There is no God." That, however, he did not do in his own person, for he saw how odious and offensive such an opinion would be; and therefore, in his book on the nature of the gods, he makes Cotta dispute concerning this against the Stoics, and preferred to give his own opinion in favor of Lucilius Balbus, to whom he assigned the defence of the Stoical position, rather than in favor of Cotta, who maintained that no divinity exists. However, in his book on divination, he in his own person most openly opposes the doctrine of the prescience of future things. But all this he seems to do in order that he may not grant the doctrine of fate, and by so doing destroy free will. For he thinks that, the knowledge of future things being once conceded, fate follows as so necessary a consequence that it cannot be denied.

But, let these perplexing debatings and disputations of the philosophers go on as they may, we, in order that we may confess the most high and true God Himself, do confess His will, supreme power, and prescience. Neither let us be afraid lest, after all, we do not do by will that which we do by will, because He, whose foreknowledge is infallible, foreknew that we would do it. It was this which Cicero was afraid of, and therefore opposed foreknowledge. The Stoics also maintained that all things do not come to pass by necessity, although they contended that all things happen according to destiny. What is it, then, that Cicero feared in the prescience of future things? Doubtless it was this—that if all future things have been foreknown, they will happen in the order in which they have been foreknown; and if they come to pass in this order, there is a certain order of things foreknown by God; and if a certain order of things, then a certain order of cause, for nothing can happen which is not preceded by some efficient cause. But if there is a certain order of causes according to which everything happens which does happen, then by fate, says he, all things happen which do happen. But if this be so, then is there nothing in our own power, and there is no such thing as freedom of will; and if we grant that, says he, the whole economy of human life is subverted. In vain are laws enacted. In vain are reproaches, praises, chidings, exhortations had recourse to; and there is no justice whatever in the appointment of rewards for the good, and punishments for the wicked. And that consequences so disgraceful, and absurd, and pernicious to humanity may not follow, Cicero chooses to reject the foreknowledge of future things, and shuts up the religious mind to this alternative, to make choice between two things, either that something is in our own power, or that there is foreknowledge—both of which cannot be true; but if the one is affirmed, the other is thereby

denied. He therefore, like a truly great and wise man, and one who consulted very much and very skillfully for the good of humanity, of those two chose the freedom of the will, to confirm which he denied the foreknowledge of future things; and thus, wishing to make men free, he makes them sacrilegious. But the religious mind chooses both, confesses both, and maintains both by the faith of piety. But how so? says Cicero; for the knowledge of future things being granted, there follows a chain of consequences which ends in this, that there can be nothing depending on our own free wills. And further, if there is anything depending on our wills, we must go backwards by the same steps of reasoning till we arrive at the conclusion that there is no foreknowledge of future things. For we go backwards through all the steps in the following order:—If there is free will, all things do not happen according to fate; if all things do not happen according to fate, there is not a certain order of causes; and if there is not a certain order of causes, neither is there a certain order of things foreknown by God—for things cannot come to pass except they are preceded by efficient causes—but, if there is no fixed and certain order of causes foreknown by God, all things cannot be said to happen according as He foreknew that they would happen. And further, if it is not true that all things happen just as they have been foreknown by Him, there is not, says he, in God any foreknowledge of future events.

Now, against the sacrilegious and impious darings of reason, we assert both that God knows all things before they come to pass, and that we do by our free will whatsoever we know and feel to be done by us only because we will it. But that all things come to pass by fate, we do not say; nay we affirm that nothing comes to pass by fate; for we demonstrate that the name of fate, as it is wont to be used by those who speak of fate, meaning thereby the position of the stars at the time of each one's conception or birth, is an unmeaning word, for astrology itself is a delusion. But an order of causes in which the highest efficiency is attributed to the will of God, we neither deny nor do we designate it by the name of fate, unless, perhaps, we may understand fate to mean that which is spoken, deriving it from *fari,* to speak; for we cannot deny that it is written in the sacred Scriptures, "God hath spoken once; these two things have I heard, the power belongeth unto God. Also unto Thee, O God, belongeth mercy: for Thou wilt render unto every man according to his works." Now the expression, "Once hath He spoken," is to be understood as meaning *"immovably,"* that is, unchangeably hath He spoken, inasmuch as He knows unchangeably al! things which shall be, and all things which He will do. we might, then, use the word fate in the sense it bears when derived from fari, to speak, had it not already come to be understood in another sense, into which I am willing that the hearts of men should unconsciously slide. But it does not follow that, though there is for God a certain order of all causes, there must therefore be nothing depending on the free exercise of our own wills, for our wills themselves are included in that order of all causes which is certain to God, and is embraced by His foreknowledge, for human wills are also causes of human actions; and He who foreknew all the causes of things would certainly among those causes not have been ignorant of our wills. For even that very concession which Cicero himself makes is enough to refute him in this argument. For what does it help him to say that nothing takes place without a cause, but that every cause is not fatal, there being a fortuitous cause, a natural cause, and a voluntary cause? It is sufficient that he confesses that whatever happens must be preceded by a cause. For we say that those causes which are called fortuitous are not a mere name for the absence of causes, but are only latent, and we attribute them either to the will of the true God, or to that of spirits of some kind or other. And as to natural causes, we by no means separate them from will of Him who is the author and framer of all nature. But now as to voluntary causes. They are referable either to God, or to angels, or to men, or to animals of whatever description, if indeed those instinctive movements of animals devoid of reason, by which, in accordance with their own nature, they seek or shun various things, are to be called wills. And when I speak of the wills of angels, I mean either the wills of good angels, whom we call the angels of God, or of the wicked angels, whom we call the angels of the devil, or demons. Also by the wills of men I mean the wills either of the good or of the wicked. And from this we conclude that there are no efficient causes of all things which come

to pass unless voluntary causes, that is, such as belong to that nature which is the spirit of life. For the air or wind is called spirit, but, inasmuch as it is a body, it is not the spirit of life. The spirit of life, therefore, which quickens all things, and is the creator of every body, and of every created spirit, is God Himself, the wills of all created spirits, helping the good, judging the evil, controlling all, granting power to some, not granting it to others. For, as He is the creator of all natures, so also is He the bestower of all powers, not of all wills; for wicked wills are not from Him, being contrary to nature, which is from Him. As to bodies, they are more subject to wills: some to our wills, by which I mean the wills of all living mortal creatures, but more to the wills of men than of beasts. but all of them are most of all subject to the will of God, to whom all wills also are subject, since they have no power except what He has bestowed upon them. The cause of things, therefore, which makes but is not made, is God; but all other causes both make and are made. Such are all created spirits, and especially the rational. Material causes, therefore, which may rather be said to be made than to make, and not to be reckoned among efficient causes, because they can only do what the wills of spirits do by them. Now, then, does an order of causes which is certain to the foreknowledge of God necessitate that there should be nothing which is dependent on our wills, when our wills themselves have a very important place in the order of causes? Cicero, then, contends with those who call this order of causes fatal, or rather designate this order itself by the name of fate; to which we have an abhorrence, especially on account of the word, which men have become accustomed to understand as meaning what is not true. But, whereas he denies that the order of all causes is most certain, and perfectly clear to the prescience of God, we detest his opinion more than the Stoics do. For he either denies that God exists—which, indeed, in an assumed personage, he has labored to do, in his book *De Natura Deorum*—or if he confesses that He exists, but denies that He is prescient of future things, what is that but just the fool saying in his heart there is no God? For one who is not prescient of all future things is not God. Wherefore our wills also have just so much power as God willed and foreknew that they should have; and therefore whatever power they have, they have it within most certain limits; and whatever they are to do, they are most assuredly to do, for He whose foreknowledge is infallible foreknew that they would have the power to do it, any would do it. Wherefore, if I should choose to apply the name of fate to anything at all, I should rather say that fate belongs to the weaker of two parties, will to the stronger, who has the other in his power, than that the freedom of our will is excluded by that order of causes, which, by an unusual application of the word peculiar to themselves, the Stoics call *Fate*.

WHETHER OUR WILLS ARE RULED BY NECESSITY

Wherefore, neither is that necessity to be feared, for dread of which the Stoics labored to make such distinctions among the causes of things as should enable them to rescue certain things from the dominion of necessity, and to subject others to it. Among those things which they wished not to be subject to necessity they places our wills, knowing that they would not be free if subjected to necessity. For if that is to be called *our necessity* which is not in our power, but even though we be unwilling effects what it can effect—as, for instance, the necessity of death—it is manifest that our wills by which we live uprightly or wickedly are not under such a necessity; for we do many things which, if we were not willing, we should not do. This is primarily true of the act of willing itself—for if we will, it *is*; if we will not, it *is* not for we should not will if we were unwilling. But if we define necessity to be that according to which we say that it is necessary that anything be of such or such a nature, or be done in such and such a manner, I know not why we should have any dread of that necessity taking away the freedom of our will. For we do not put the life of God or the foreknowledge of God under necessity if we should say that it is necessary that God should live forever, and foreknow all things; as neither is His power diminished when we say that He cannot die or fall into error—for this is in such a way impossible to Him, that if it were possible for Him, He would be of less power. But assuredly He is rightly called omnipotent, though He can neither die nor fall into error. For He is called omnipotent on account of His doing what He

wills, not on account of His suffering what He wills not; for if that should befall Him, He would by no means be omnipotent. Wherefore, He cannot do some things for the very reason that He is omnipotent. So also, when we say that it is necessary that, when we will, we will by free choice, in so saying we both affirm what is true beyond doubt, and do not still subject our wills thereby to a necessity which destroys liberty. Our wills, therefore, *exist* as *wills*, and do themselves whatever we do by willing, and which would not be done if we were unwilling. But when any one suffers anything, being unwilling, by the will of another, even in that case will retains its essential validity—we do not mean the will of the party who inflicts the suffering, for we resolve it into the power of God. For if a will should simply exist, but not be able to do what it wills, it would be overborne by a more powerful will. Nor would this be the case unless there had existed will, and that not the will of the other party, but the will of him who willed, but was not able to accomplish what he willed. Therefore, whatsoever a man suffers contrary to his own will, he ought not to attribute to the will of men, or of angels, or of any created spirit, but rather to His will who gives power to wills. It is not the case, therefore, that because God foreknew what would be in the power of our wills, there is for that reason nothing in the power of our wills. For He who foreknew this did not foreknow nothing. Moreover, if He who foreknew what would be in the power of our wills did not foreknow nothing, but something, assuredly, even though He did foreknow, there is something in the power of our wills. Therefore we are by no means compelled, either, retaining the prescience of God, to take away the freedom of the will, or, retaining the freedom of the will, to deny that He is prescient of future things, which is impious. But we embrace both. We faithfully and sincerely confess both. The former, that we may believe well; the latter, that we may live well. For he lives ill who does not believe well concerning God. Wherefore, be it far from us, in order to maintain our freedom, to deny the prescience of Him by whose help we are or shall be free. Consequently, it is not in vain that laws are enacted, and that reproaches, exhortations, praises, and vituperations are had recourse to; for these also He foreknew, and they are of great avail, even as great as He foreknew that they would be of. Prayers, also, are of avail to procure those things which He foreknew that He would grant to those who offered them; and with justice have rewards been appointed for good deeds, and punishments for sins. For a man does not therefore sin because God foreknew that he would sin. Nay, it cannot be doubted but that it is the man himself who sins when he does sin, because He, whose foreknowledge is infallible, foreknew not that fate, or fortune, or something else would sin, but that the man himself would sin, who, if he wills not, sins not. But if he shall not will to sin, even this did God foreknow.

OF THE CREATION OF ANGELS AND MEN

As we promised in the immediately preceding book, this, the last of the whole work, shall contain a discussion of the eternal blessedness of the city of God. This blessedness is named eternal, not because it shall endure for many ages, though at last it shall come to an end, but because, according to the words of the gospel, "of His kingdom there shall be no end." Neither shall it enjoy the mere appearance of perpetuity which is maintained by the rise of fresh generations to occupy the place of those that have died out, as in an evergreen the same freshness seems to continue permanently, and the same appearance of dense foliage is preserved by the growth of fresh leaves in the room of those that have withered and fallen; but in that city all the citizens shall be immortal, men now for the first time enjoying what the holy angels have never lost. And this shall be accomplished by God, the most almighty Founder of the city. For He has promised it, and cannot lie, and has already performed many of His promises, and has done many unpromised kindnesses to those whom He now asks to believe that He will do this also.

For it is He who in the beginning created the world full of visible and intelligible beings, among which He created nothing better than those spirits whom He endowed with intelligence, and made capable of contemplating and enjoying Him, and united in our society, which we call the holy and heavenly city, and in which the material of their sustenance and blessedness is God Himself, as it were their common food and nourishment. It is He who gave to this intellectual nature free-will of such a kind, that if he wished to forsake God, *i.e.,* his blessedness, misery should forthwith result. It is He who, when He foreknew that certain angels would in their pride desire to suffice for their own blessedness, and would foresake their great good, did not deprive them of this power, deeming it to be more befitting His power and goodness to bring good out of evil than to prevent the evil from coming into existence. And indeed evil had never been, had not the mutable nature—mutable, though good, and created by the most high God and immutable Good, who created all things good—brought evil upon itself by sin. And this its sin is itself proof that its nature was originally good. For had it not been very good, though not equal to its Creator, the desertion of God as its light could not have been an evil to it. For as blindness is a vice of the eye, and this very fact indicates that the eye was created to see the light, and as, consequently, vice itself proves that the eye is more excellent than the other members, because it is capable of light (for on no other supposition would it be a vice of the eye to want light) so the nature which once enjoyed God teaches, even by its very vice, that it was created the best of all, since it is now miserable because it does not enjoy God. It is He who with very just punishment doomed the angels who voluntarily fell to everlasting misery, and rewarded those who continued in their attachment to the supreme good with the assurance of endless stability as the meed of their fidelity. It is He who made also man himself upright, with the same freedom of will —an earthly animal, indeed, but fit for heaven if he remained faithful to his Creator, but destined to the misery appropriate to such a nature if he forsook Him. It is He who, when He foreknew that man would in his turn sin by abandoning God and breaking His law, did not deprive him of the power of freewill, because He at the same time foresaw what good He Himself would bring out of the evil, and how from this mortal race, deservedly and justly condemned, He would by His grace collect, as now He does, a people so numerous, that He thus fills up and repairs the blank made by the fallen angels, and that thus that beloved and heavenly city is not defrauded of the full number of its citizens, but perhaps may even rejoice in a still more overflowing population.

St. Anselm of Canterbury

St. Anselm of Canterbury was born more than five hundred years after the death of St. Augustine. The changes undergone by Western Civilization during these five centuries were in many respects profound and lasting, although some of the main themes of philosophical thinking remained almost unchanged. Man's understanding of the universe was still greatly dependent on religious ideologies, and the Bible was looked upon as the chief source of knowledge. Philosophy and science were regarded as the natural complements of religious faith, and most of the philosophical problems discussed during this time were of a theological nature.

The philosophical writings of St. Anselm are a wonderful example of medieval philosophy. They express in an unmistakable way the profound spiritual devotion and the unshakable faith which characterized his time. Born in 1033, St. Anselm devoted most of his life to a religious vocation. He became a Benedictine monk in 1060 and was appointed bishop of Canterbury in 1093. He died in 1109. His major works are the *Monologium* and the *Proslogium*, both of which he completed while serving as the Benedictine abbot of a monastery in Normandy. The *Proslogium*, from which the short selection in this book is taken, is a lengthy prayer to God in which the saint asks for the gift of understanding the mystery of God. In a spirit of humility and sincerity, he acknowledges his faith in the Lord but expresses his desire to understand fully that which he has accepted on faith alone. His faith, then, is seeking understanding.

It is in the *Proslogium* that we find the famous "ontological argument" for the existence of God. But before we delve into some of the details of this argument, and before we read its text, it is important to clarify several points. The Anselmian argument is not an argument in the usual sense of the word, inasmuch as long before we arrive at its conclusion (namely, that God exists), we are already fully convinced of the undeniable reality of God. The argument can therefore be seen as an intellectual rationalization of an article of faith which precedes its reasonings. Again, St. Anselm is seeking to understand something which he, as a believer, has always accepted. Hence, the argument is apparently a circular journey in which the human mind begins by confessing its faith in God and ends by reassuring itself that such a faith is fully justified by a process of logical reasoning.

It is on account of this circularity that many serious objections can be raised against the argument, especially from a non-religious point of view. If one begins with the assumption that the existence of God is questionable, the ontological argument loses much of its initial strength. This explains the reason why so many philosophers have found the argument to be absolutely empty.

In contrast with the cosmological arguments of St. Thomas Aquinas, the Anselmian argument is called "ontological." The arguments of St. Thomas assume, or rather seek to show, that an examination of certain aspects of the cosmos or universe necessarily lead us to the conclusion that a creator must exist. All things, says St. Thomas, have a cause by virtue of which they have come into existence. Hence, he concludes, the universe as a whole must also have a cause, and this cause, he insists, is what we call God. Here, there is some attempt to begin with the facts of experience: we know through experience that things are in fact caused by other things. The Thomistic arguments for the existence of God are not entirely outside the empirical tradition that goes back to Aristotle, and can be said to be in some sense a posteriori or based on experience.

The ontological argument, on the other hand, moves on a plane in which experience (at least sense experience) is hardly pertinent. Its main purpose is to elucidate the nature of God, his essence, his real being, for which it is called "ontological." "Ontology" refers generally to the attempt to understand the ultimate nature of reality. The ontological argument is based on a series of reasonings which are apparently a priori, and its validity does not depend on this or that specific sense experience.

A careful reading of the short selection of the *Proslogium* will immediately reveal the several steps of the argument. These steps are easily identified in the following statements:

(1) God is by definition a being anything greater than which cannot be conceived.

(2) A being anything greater than which cannot be conceived is by definition a perfect being, in the sense that it would be above all other beings, and would lack nothing. It would have all possible qualities.

(3) A perfect being must of necessity exist, because if it did not exist it

would be lacking at least one quality, namely existence.

(4) Hence, God must exist.

The argument is obviously valid inasmuch as the conclusion does follow premises. The crucial question is, however, whether the premises should be left unquestioned. St. Anselm stated, echoing the biblical text, that only a fool is able to deny the existence of God; for to deny that God exists is tantamount to saying that God is not God. But we, living almost one thousand years after St. Anselm, are perhaps entitled to rehearse the perhaps foolish undertaking of examining critically the premises of the argument. Is the argument convincing?

The Ontological Argument

And so, Lord, do thou, who dost give understanding to faith, give me, so far as thou knowest it to be profitable, to understand that thou art as we believe; and that thou art that which we believe. And, indeed, we believe that thou art a being than which nothing greater can be conceived. Or is there no such nature, since the fool hath said in his heart, there is no God? (Psalms xiv. 1). But, at any rate, this very fool, when he hears of this being of which I speak—a being than which nothing greater can be conceived—understands what he hears, and what he understands is in his understanding; although he does not understand it to exist.

For, it is one thing for an object to be in the understanding, and another to understand that the object exists. When a painter first conceives of what he will afterwards perform, he has it in his understanding, but he does not yet understand it to be, because he has not yet performed it. But after he has made the painting, he both has it in his understanding, and he understands that it exists, because he has made it.

Hence, even the fool is convinced that something exists in the understanding, at least, than which nothing greater can be conceived. For,

when he hears of this, he understands it. And whatever is understood, exists in the understanding. And assuredly that, than which nothing greater can be conceived, cannot exist in the understanding alone. For, suppose it exists in the understanding alone: the it can be conceived to exist in reality; which is greater.

Therefore, if that, than which nothing greater can be conceived, exists in the understanding alone, the very being, than which nothing greater can be conceived, is one, than which a greater can be conceived. But obviously this is impossible. Hence, there is no doubt that there exists a being, than which nothing greater can be conceived, and it exists both in the understanding and in reality.

And it assuredly exists so truly, that it cannot be conceived not to exist. For, it is possible to conceive of a being which cannot be conceived not to exist; and this is greater than one which can be conceived not to exist. Hence, if that, than which nothing greater can be conceived, can be conceived not to exist, it is not that, than which nothing greater can be conceived. But this is an irreconcilable contradiction. There is, then, so truly a being than which nothing greater can be conceived to exist, that it cannot even be conceived not to exist; and this being thou art, O Lord, our God.

So truly, therefore, dost thou exist, O Lord, my God, that thou canst not be conceived not to exist; and rightly. For, if a mind could conceive of a being better than thee, the creature would rise above the Creator; and this is most absurd. And, indeed, whatever else there is, except thee alone, can be conceived not to exist. To thee alone, therefore, it belongs to exist more truly than all other beings, and hence in a higher degree than all others. For, whatever else exists does not exist so truly, and hence in a less degree it belongs to it to exist. Why, then, has the fool said in his heart, there is no God (Psalms, xiv. 1), since it is so evident, to a rational mind, that thou dost exist in the highest degree of all? Why, except that he is dull and a fool?

But how has the fool said in his heart what he could not conceive; or how is it that he could not conceive what he said in his heart? since it is the same to say in the heart, and to conceive.

But, if really, nay, since really, he both conceived, because he said in his heart; and did not say in his heart because he could not conceive. there is more than one way in which a thing is said in the heart or conceived. For, in one sense, an object is conceived, when the word signifying it is conceived; and in another, when the very entity, which the object is, is understood.

In the former sense, then, God can be conceived not to exist; but in the latter, not at all. For no one who understands what fire and water are can conceive fire to be water, in accordance with the nature of the facts themselves, although this is possible according to the words. So, then, no one who understands what God is can conceive that God does not exist; although he says these words in his heart, either without any, or with some foreign signification. For God is that than which a greater cannot be conceived. And he who thoroughly understands this, assuredly understands that this being so truly exists, that not even in concept can it be non-existent. Therefore, he who understands that God so exists, cannot conceive that he does not exist.

I thank thee, gracious Lord, I thank thee; because what I formerly believed by thy bounty, I now so understand by thine illumination, that if I were unwilling to believe that thou dost exist, I should not be able not to understand this to be true.

St. Thomas Aquinas

Between the time of Augustine and the time of Aquinas, European history was characterized by the breakdown of communications, the barbarian and Arabic invasions, and the confinement of all literacy to monasteries, and all thought to church doctrine. Later, political stability under feudalism and then economic expansion led to the reintroduction of learning. One element of this reintroduction was the rediscovery of Aristotle, whose original texts had been translated by Arabic and Jewish scholars back into Latin for use in the West. To this we might add that the increasingly social role of the Church in Western Europe necessitated a new and more realistically engaged philosophy than could be found in Platonism. Aristotle provided the needed model.

St. Thomas Aquinas, who died in 1274 but was not canonized until 1323 and whose philosophy became the official philosophy of the Catholic Church only in 1879 under Pope Leo XIII, like Augustine before him, attempted to harmonize Christian theology with Greek philosophy. However, he used Aristotle as his model. Thomas viewed his task as that of making room for reason. He argued first that *theology* rested upon faith, whereas *philosophy* rested upon the natural light of reason. Second, there is a distinction between theology and *natural theology*. Natural theology is that part of theology which could be rationalized or proved.

Like Aristotle, Aquinas found the world to be made up of individual substances which could be defined in terms of matter and form. Moreover, this world could be known through reason, by abstracting from experience. Thus,

Aquinas would reject any Platonic attempt to found our knowledge upon self-evident principles known independently of experience. That is why Thomas is adamant in his opposition to St. Anselm; for Thomas argued that we can have no clear and distinct idea of God. All of Thomas' proofs for the existence of God begin with facts about the world, namely the facts of motion; and then, using Aristotle's physics, Thomas goes on to show that our experience is unintelligible without the assumption of a first cause or prime mover, namely, God. It should be noted that (a) if one assumed the world to be rational, and (b) if one accepted Aristotle's physics as everyone did in one way or another until well into the seventeenth century, then one would have to accept the argument offered by St. Thomas.

Aquinas' discussion of God is also given within the Aristotelian framework. God is his own essence. He is intelligence, and therefore not a material being. Even creation, which is an anti-Aristotelian notion in itself, is given an Aristotelian interpretation wherein the world is viewed as a hierarchy from pure intelligence, as in God, down to inert matter. All is dependent upon the activity of God.

St. Thomas' Aristotelianism emerges best in the discussion of political and social matters. Just as Aristotle had argued for inherent growth and development, so Thomas argued that the authority of law was inherent and not dependent upon any purely human origin. The relation between human law and divine law was understood in the same way as Aristotle's argument that lower forms were intelligible only in terms of the higher manifestation of those forms. Society, like nature, is a system of ends or purposes in which the lower serves the higher and the higher directs the lower. Thus, the moral purpose of government and law is paramount. This led to the doctrine that the church's right of spiritual discipline can be a claim to legal supervision. Hierarchical and organic concepts thus predominate.

It is also interesting to contrast Augustine's notion of human behavior with that of Aquinas. Aquinas provides for a genuine element of human freedom or contingency and at the same time provides for the notion of a divine plan. That is, he rejected Augustinian predestination. This distinction is sometimes difficult to grasp and easily misunderstood. Try to recall Aristotle's discussion of the acorn and the oak. Not all acorns grow into oaks; they are not predetermined. Yet the nature ("plan") of acorns is such that if they develop properly at all, they can only develop into oak trees. God's plan is like the inherent pattern of nature, and human freedom is the contingent possibility of fitting ourselves into that plan. That all of us do not fit no more invalidates the plan than the acorn eaten by the squirrel invalidates biology. Here the element of good works parallels Aristotle's discussion of habits, for we are in a sense free to follow the plan by practicing it.

Reason and Faith

CHAPTER I—*The Function of the Wise Man*

My mouth shall discuss truth, and my lips shall detest the ungodly (Prov. viii, 7).

According to established popular usage, which the Philosopher considers should be our guide in the naming of things, they are called 'wise' who put things in their right order and control them well. Now, in all things that are to be controlled and put in order to an end, the measure of control and order must be taken from the end in view; and the proper end of everything is something good. Hence we see in the arts that art A governs and, as it were, lords it over art B, when the proper end of art B belongs to A. Thus the art of medicine lords it over the art of the apothecary, because health, the object of medicine, is the end of all drugs that the apothecary's art compounds. These arts that lord it over others are called 'master-building,' or 'masterful arts'; and the 'master-builders' who practise them arrogate to themselves the name of 'wise men.' But because these persons deal with the ends in view of certain particular things, without attaining to the general end of all things, they are called 'wise in this or that particular thing,' as it is said, *As a wise architect I have laid the foundation* (I Cor. iii, 10); while the name of 'wise' without qualification is reserved for him alone who deals with the last end of the universe, which is also the first beginning of the order of the universe. Hence, according to the Philosopher, it is proper to the wise man to consider the highest causes.

Now the last end of everything is that which is intended by the prime author or mover thereof. The prime author and mover of the universe is intelligence, as will be shown later (B. II, Chap. XXIII, XXIV). Therefore the last end of the universe must be the good of the intelligence, and that is truth. Truth then must be the final end of the whole universe; and about the consideration of that end wisdom must primarily be concerned. And therefore the Divine Wisdom, clothed in flesh, testifies that He came into the world for the manifestation of truth: *For this was I born, and unto this I came into the world, to give testimony to the truth* (John xviii, 37). The Philosopher also rules that the first philosophy is the science of truth, not of any and every truth, but of that truth which is the origin of all truth, and appertains to the first principle of the being of all things; hence its truth is the principle of all truth, for things are in truth as they are in being.

It is one and the same function to embrace either of two contraries and to repel the other. Hence, as it is the function of the wise man to discuss truth, particularly of the first beginning, so it is his also to impugn the contrary error. Suitably therefore is the double function of the wise man displayed in the words above quoted from the Sapiential Book, namely, to study, and upon study to speak out the truth of God, which of all other is most properly called truth, and this is referred to in the words, *My mouth shall discuss truth*, and to impugn error contrary to truth, as referred to in the words, *And my lips shall detest the ungodly.*

CHAPTER II—*Of the Author's Purpose*

Of all human pursuits, the pursuit of wisdom is the more perfect, the more sublime, the more useful, and the more agreeable. The more perfect, because in so far as a man gives himself up to the pursuit of wisdom, to that extent he enjoys already some portion of true happiness. *Blessed is the man that shall dwell in wisdom* (Ecclus xiv, 22). The more sublime, because thereby man comes closest to the likeness of God, who *hath made all things in wisdom* (Ps. ciii, 24). The more useful, because by this same wisdom we arrive at the realm of immortality. *The desire of wisdom shall lead to an everlasting kingdom* (Wisd. vi, 21). The more agreeable, because *her conversation hath no bitterness, nor her company any weariness, but gladness and joy* (Wisd. viii, 16).

But on two accounts it is difficult to proceed against each particular error: first, because the sacrilegious utterances of our various erring opponents are not so well known to us as to enable us to find reasons, drawn from their own words, for the confutation of their errors: for such was the method of the ancient doctors in confuting the errors of the Gentiles, whose tenets they were readily able to know, having either been Gentiles themselves, or at least having lived among Gentiles and been instructed in their doctrines. Secondly, because some of them, as Mohammedans and Pagans, do not agree with us in recognising the authority of any scripture, available for their conviction, as we can argue against the Jews from the Old Testament, and against heretics from the New. But these receive neither: hence it is necessary to have recourse to natural reason, which all are obliged to assent to. But in the things of God natural reason is often at a loss.

CHAPTER III—*That the Truths which we confess concerning God fall under two Modes or Categories*

Because not every truth admits of the same mode of manifestation, and "a well-educated man will expect exactness in every class of subject, according as the nature of the thing admits," as is very well remarked by the Philosopher (*Eth. Nicom.* I, 1094b), we must first show what mode of proof is possible for the truth that we have now before us. The truths that we confess concerning God fall under two modes. Some things true of God are beyond all the competence of human reason, as that God is Three and One. Other things there are to which

even human reason can attain, as the existence and unity of God, which philosophers have proved to a demonstration under the guidance of the light of natural reason. That there are points of absolute intelligibility in God altogether beyond the compass of human reason, most manifestly appears. For since the leading principle of all knowledge of any given subject-matter is an understanding of the thing's innermost being, or substance—according to the doctrine of the Philosopher, that the essence is the principle of demonstration—it follows that the mode of our knowledge of the substance must be the mode of knowledge of whatever we know about the substance. Hence if the human understanding comprehends the substance of anything, as of a stone or triangle, none of the points of intelligibility about that thing will exceed the capacity of human reason. But this is not our case with regard to God. The human understanding cannot go so far of its natural power as to grasp His substance, since under the conditions of the present life the knowledge of our understanding commences with sense; and therefore objects beyond sense cannot be grasped by human understanding except so far as knowledge is gathered of them through the senses. But things of sense cannot lead our understanding to read in them the essence of the Divine Substance, inasmuch as they are effects inadequate to the power that caused them. Nevertheless our understanding is thereby led to some knowledge of God, namely, of His existence and of other attributes that must necessarily be attributed to the First Cause. There are, therefore, some points of intelligibility in God, accessible to human reason, and other points that altogether transcend the power of human reason.

The same thing may be understood from consideration of degrees of intelligibility. Of two minds, one of which has a keener insight into truth than the other, the higher mind understands much that the other cannot grasp at all, as is clear in the 'plain man' (*in rustico*), who can in no way grasp the subtle theories of philosophy. Now the intellect of an angel excels that of a man more than the intellect of the ablest philosopher excels that of the plainest of plain men (*r dissimi idiotae*). The angel has a higher standpoint in creation than man as a basis of his knowledge of God, inasmuch as the substance of the angel whereby he is led to know God by a process of natural knowledge, is nobler and more excellent than the things of sense, and even than the soul itself whereby the human mind rises to the knowledge of God. But the Divine Mind exceeds the angelic much more than the angelic the human. For the Divine Mind of its own comprehensiveness covers the whole extent of its substance, and therefore perfectly understands its own essence, and knows all that is knowable about itself; but an angel of his natural knowledge does not know the essence of God, because the angel's own substance, whereby it is led to acknowledge a God, is an effect inadequate to the power of the cause that animated it. Hence not all things that God understands in Himself can be grasped by the natural knowledge of an angel; nor is human reason competent to take in all that an angel understands of his own natural ability. As therefore it would be the height of madness in a 'plain man' to declare a philosopher's propositions false, because he could not understand them, so and much more would a man show exceeding folly if he suspected of falsehood a divine revelation given by the ministry of angels, on the mere ground that it was beyond the investigation of reason.

The same thing manifestly appears from the incapacity which we daily experience in the observation of nature. We are ignorant of very many properties of the things of sense; and of the properties that our senses do apprehend, in most cases we cannot perfectly discover the reason. Much more is it beyond the competence of human reason to investigate all the points of intelligibility in that supreme excellent and transcendent substance of God. Consonant with this is the saying of the Philosopher, that "as the eyes of bats are to the light of the sun, so is the intelligence of our soul to the things most manifest by nature" (Aristotle, *Metaphysics* I, min. 1).

To this truth Holy Scripture also bears testimony. For it is said: *Perchance thou wilt seize upon the traces of God, and fully discover the Almighty* (Job xi, 7). And *Lo, God is great, and surpassing our knowledge* (Job xxxvi, 26). And, *We know in part* (I Cor. xiii, 9). Not everything, therefore, that is said of God, even though it be beyond the power of reason to investigate, is at once to be rejected as false.

CHAPTER IV—*That it is an advantage for the Truths of God known by Natural Reason to be proposed to men to be believed on Faith*

If a truth of this nature were left to the sole enquiry of reason, three disadvantages would follow. One is that the knowledge of God would be confined to few. The discovery of truth is the fruit of studious enquiry. From this very many are hindered. Some are hindered by a constitutional unfitness, their natures being ill-disposed to the acquisition of knowledge. They could never arrive by study to the highest grade of human knowledge, which consists in the knowledge of God. Others are hindered by the needs of business and the ties of the management of property. There must be in human society some men devoted to temporal affairs. These could not possibly spend time enough in the learned lessons of speculative enquiry to arrive at the highest point of human enquiry, the knowledge of God. Some again are hindered by sloth. The knowledge of the truths that reason can investigate concerning God presupposes much previous knowledge. Indeed almost the entire study of philosophy is directed to the knowledge of God. Hence, of all parts of philosophy, that part stands over to be learnt last, which consists of metaphysics dealing with points of Divinity. Thus, only with great labour of study is it possible to arrive at the searching out of the aforesaid truth; and this labour few are willing to undergo for sheer love of knowledge.

Another disadvantage is that such as did arrive at the knowledge or discovery of the aforesaid truth would take a long time over it, on account of the profundity of such truth, and the many prerequisites to the study, and also because in youth and early manhood, the soul, tossed to and fro on the waves of passion, is not fit for the study of such high truth: only in settled age does the soul become prudent and scientific, as the Philosopher says. Thus, if the only way open to the knowledge of God were the way of reason, the human race would dwell long in thick darkness of ignorance: as the knowledge of God, the best instrument for making men perfect and good, would accrue only to a few, and to those few after a considerable lapse of time.

A third disadvantage is that, owing to the

infirmity of our judgment and the perturbing force of imagination, there is some admixture of error in most of the investigations of human reason. This would be a reason to many for continuing to doubt even of the most accurate demonstrations, not perceiving the force of the demonstration, and seeing the divers judgements of divers persons who have the name of being wise men. Besides, in the midst of much demonstrated truth there is sometimes an element of error, not demonstrated but asserted on the strength of some plausible and sophistic reasoning that is taken for a demonstration. And therefore it was necessary for the real truth concerning divine things to be presented to men with fixed certainty by way of faith. Wholesome therefore is the arrangement of divine clemency, whereby things even that reason can investigate are commanded to be held on faith, so that all might easily be partakers of the knowledge of God, and that without doubt and error.

Hence it is said: *Now ye walk not as the Gentiles walk in the vanity of their own notions, having the understanding darkened* (Eph. iv, 17, 18); and, *I will make all thy sons taught of the Lord* (Isa. liv, 15).

CHAPTER V—*That it is an advantage for things that cannot be searched out by Reason to be proposed as Tenets of Faith*

Some may possibly think that points which reason is unable to investigate ought not to be proposed to man to believe, since Divine Wisdom provides for every being according to the measure of its nature; and therefore we must show the necessity of things even that transcend reason being proposed by God to man for his belief.

1. One proof is this. No one strives with any earnestness of desire after anything, unless it be known to him beforehand. Since, then, as will be traced out in the following pages (B. III, Chap. CXLVIII), Divine Providence directs men to a higher good than human frailty can experience in the present life, the mental faculties ought to be evoked and led onward to something higher than our reason can attain at present, learning thereby to desire something and earnestly to tend to something that transcends the entire state of the present life. And such is the special function of the Christian religion, which stands alone in its promise of spiritual and eternal goods, whereas the Old Law, carrying temporal promises, proposed few tenets that transcended the enquiry of human reason.

2. Also another advantage is thence derived, to wit, the repression of presumption, which is the mother of error. For there are some so presumptuous of their own genius as to think that they can measure with their understanding the whole nature of the Godhead, thinking all that to be true which seems true to them, and that to be false which does not seem true to them. In order then that the human mind might be delivered from this presumption, and attain to a modest style of enquiry after truth, it was necessary for certain things to be proposed to man from God that altogether exceeded his understanding.

3. There is also another evident advantage in this, that any knowledge, however imperfect, of the noblest objects confers a very high perfection on the soul. And therefore, though human reason cannot fully grasp truths above reason, nevertheless it is much perfected by holding such truths after some fashion at least by faith. And therefore it is said: *Many things beyond the understanding of man are shown to thee* (Ecclus iii, 23). And, *The things that are of God, none knoweth but the Spirit of God: but to us God hath revealed them through his Spirit* (I Cor. ii, 10, 11).

CHAPTER VI—*That there is no lightmindedness in assenting to Truths of Faith, although they are above Reason*

The Divine Wisdom, that knows all things most fully, has deigned to reveal these her secrets to men, and in proof of them has displayed works beyond the competence of all natural powers, in the wonderful cure of diseases in the raising of the dead, and what is more wonderful still, in such inspiration of human minds as that simple and ignorant persons, filled with the gift of the Holy Ghost, have gained in an instant the height of wisdom and eloquence. By force of the aforesaid proof, without violence of arms, without promise of pleasures, and, most wonderful thing of all, in the midst of the violence of persecutors, a countless multitude, not only of the uneducated but of the wisest men, flocked to the Christian faith, wherein doctrines are preached that transcend all human understanding, pleasures of sense are restrained, and a contempt is taught of all worldly possessions. That mortal minds should assent to such teaching is the greatest of miracles, and a manifest work of divine inspiration leading men to despise the visible and desire only invisible goods. Nor did this happen suddenly nor by chance, but by a divine disposition, as is manifest from the fact that God foretold by many oracles of His prophets that He intended to do this. The books of those prophets are still venerated amongst us, as bearing testimony to our faith. This argument is touched upon in the text: *Which* (salvation) *having begun to be uttered by the Lord, was confirmed by them that heard him even unto us, God joining in the testimony by signs and portents and various distributions of the Holy Spirit* (Heb. ii, 3, 4). This so wonderful conversion of the world to the Christian faith is so certain a sign of past miracles, that they need no further reiteration, since they appear evidently in their effects. It would be more wonderful than all other miracles, if without miraculous signs the world had been induced by simple and low-born men to believe truths so arduous, to do works so difficult, to hope for reward so high. And yet even in our times God ceases not through His saints to work miracles for the confirmation of the faith.

CHAPTER VII—*That the Truth of Reason is not contrary to the Truth of Christian Faith*

The natural dictates of reason must certainly be quite true: it is impossible to think of their being otherwise. Nor again is it permissible to believe that the tenets of faith are false, being so evidently confirmed by God. Since therefore falsehood alone is contrary to truth, it is impossible for the truth of faith to be contrary to principles known by natural reason.

2. Whatever is put into the disciple's mind by the teacher is contained in the knowledge of the teacher, unless the teacher is teaching dishonestly, which would be a wicked thing to say of God. But the knowledge of principles naturally known is put into us by God. Therefore these principles also are contained in the Divine Wisdom. Whatever therefore is contrary to these principles is contrary to Divine Wisdom, and cannot be of God.

3. Contrary reasons fetter our intellect fast, so that it cannot proceed to the knowledge of the truth. If therefore contrary informations were sent us by God, our intellect would be thereby hindered from knowledge of the truth: but such hindrance cannot be of God.

4. What is natural cannot be changed while nature remains. But contrary opinions cannot be in the same mind at the same time: therefore no opinion or belief is sent to man from God contrary to natural knowledge.

And therefore the Apostle says: *The word is near in thy heart and in thy mouth, that is, the word of faith which we preach* (Rom. x, 8). But because it surpasses reason it is counted by some as contrary to reason, which cannot be. To the same effect is the authority of Augustine (*Gen. ad litt.* ii, 18): "What truth reveals can nowise be contrary to the holy books either of the Old or of the New Testament." Hence the conclusion is evident, that any arguments against the teachings of faith do not proceed logically from first principles of nature, and so do not amount to a demonstration; but are either probable reasons or sophistical; hence room is left for refuting them.

CHAPTER VIII—*Of the Relation of Human Reason to the first Truth of Faith*

The things of sense, from whence human reason takes its beginning of knowledge, retain in themselves some trace of imitation of God, inasmuch as they *are,* and are *good;* yet so imperfect is this trace that it proves wholly insufficient to declare the substance of God Himself. Since every agent acts to the producing of its own likeness, effects in their several ways bear some likeness to their causes: nevertheless the effect does not always attain to the perfect likeness of the agent that produces it. In regard then to knowledge of the truth of faith, which can only be thoroughly known to those who behold the substance of God, human reason stands so conditioned as to be able to argue some true likenesses to it: which likenesses however are not sufficient for any sort of demonstrative or intuitive comprehension of the aforesaid truth. Still it is useful for the human mind to exercise itself in such reasonings, however feeble, provided there be no presumptuous hope of perfect comprehension or demonstration. With this view the authority of Hilary agrees, who says (*De Trinitate,* ii, 10), speaking of such truth: "In this belief start, run, persist; and though I know that you will not reach the goal, still I shall congratulate you as I see you making progress. But intrude not into that sanctuary, and plunge not into the mystery of infinite truth; entertain no presumptuous hope of comprehending the height of intelligence, but understand that it is incomprehensible."

CHAPTER IX—*The Order and Mode of Procedure in this Work*

There is then a twofold sort of truth in things divine for the wise man to study: one that can be attained by rational enquiry, another that transcends all the industry of reason. This truth of things divine I do not call twofold on the part of God, who is one simple Truth, but on the part of our knowledge, as our cognitive faculty has different aptitudes for the knowledge of divine things. To the declaration therefore of the first sort of truth we must proceed by demonstrative reasons that may serve to convince the adversary. But because such reasons are not forthcoming for truth of the second sort, our aim ought not to be to convince the adversary by reasons, but to refute his reasonings against the truth, which we may hope to do, since natural reason cannot be contrary to the truth of faith. The special mode of refutation to be employed against an opponent of this second sort of truth is by alleging the authority of Scripture confirmed from heaven by miracles. There are however some probable reasons available for the declaration of this truth, to the exercise and consolation of the faithful, but not to the convincing of opponents, because the mere insufficiency of such reasoning would rather confirm them in their error, they thinking that we assented to the truth of faith for reasons so weak.

According then to the manner indicated we will bend our endeavour, first, to the manifestation of that truth which faith professes and reason searches out, alleging reasons demonstrative and probable, some of which we have gathered from the books of philosophers and

saints, for the establishment of the truth and the confutation of the opponent. Then, to proceed from what is more to what is less manifest in our regard, we will pass to the manifestation of that truth which transcends reason, solving the arguments of opponents, and by probable reasons and authorities, so far as God shall enable us, declaring the truth of faith.

Taking therefore the way of reason to the pursuit of truths that human reason can search out regarding God, the first consideration that meets us is of the attributes of God in Himself; secondly of the coming forth of creatures from God; thirdly of the order of creatures to God as to their last end.

CHAPTER X—*Of the Opinion of those who say that the Existence of God cannot be proved, being a Self-evident Truth*

This opinion rests on the following grounds:

1. Those truths are self-evident which are recognized at once, as soon as the terms in which they are expressed are known. Such a truth is the assertion that God exists: for by the name 'God' we understand something greater than which nothing can be thought. This notion is formed in the understanding by whoever hears and understands the name 'God,' so that God must already exist at least in the mind. Now He cannot exist in the mind only: for what is in the mind and in reality is greater than that which is in the mind only; but nothing is greater than God, as the very meaning of the name shows: it follows that the existence of God is a self-evident truth, being evidenced by the mere meaning of the name.

2. The existence of a being is conceivable, that could not be conceived not to exist; such a being is evidently greater than another that could be conceived not to exist. Thus then something greater than God is conceivable if He could be conceived not to exist; but anything 'greater than God' is against the meaning of the name 'God.' It remains then that the existence of God is a self-evident truth.

3. Those propositions are most self-evident which are either identities, as 'Man is man,' or in which the predicates are included in the definitions of the subjects, as 'Man is an animal.' But in God of all beings this is found true, that His existence is His essence, as will

be shown later (Chap. XXII); and thus there is one and the same answer to the question 'What is He?' and 'Whether He is.' Thus, then, when it is said 'God is,' the predicate is either the same with the subject or at least is included in the definition of the subject; and thus the existence of God will be a self-evident truth.

4. Things naturally known are self-evident: for the knowledge of them is not attained by enquiry and study. But the existence of God is naturally known, since the desire of man tends naturally to God as to his last end, as will be shown further on (B. III, Chap. XXV).

5. That must be self-evident whereby all other things are known; but such is God; for as the light of the sun is the principle of all visual perception, so the divine light is the principle of all intellectual cognition.

CHAPTER XI—*Rejection of the aforesaid Opinion, and Solution of the aforesaid Reasons*

The above opinion arises partly from custom, men being accustomed from the beginning to hear and invoke the name of God. Custom, especially that which is from the beginning, takes the place of nature; hence notions wherewith the mind is imbued from childhood are held as firmly as if they were naturally known and self-evident. Partly also it owes its origin to the neglect of a distinction between what is self-evident *of itself absolutely* and what is self-evident *relatively to us.* Absolutely indeed the existence of God is self-evident, since God's essence is His existence. But since we cannot mentally conceive God's essence, his existence is not self-evident relatively to us.

1. Nor is the existence of God necessarily self-evident as soon as the meaning of the name 'God' is known. First, because it is not evident, even to all who admit the existence of God, that God is something greater than which nothing can be conceived, since many of the ancients said that this world was God. Then granting that universal usage understands by the name 'God' something greater than which nothing can be conceived, it will not follow that there exists *in rerum natura* something greater than which nothing can be conceived. For 'thing' and "notion implied in the name of the thing" must answer to one another. From the conception in the mind of what is declared by this name 'God' it does not follow that God exists otherwise than in the mind. Hence there will be no necessity either of that something, greater than which nothing can be conceived, existing otherwise than in the mind; and from this it does not follow that there is anything *in rerum natura* greater than which nothing can be conceived. And so the supposition of the non-existence of God goes untouched. For the possibility of our thought outrunning the greatness of any given object, whether of the actual or of the ideal order, has nothing in it to vex the soul of any one except of him alone who already grants the existence *in rerum natura* of something than which nothing can be conceived greater.

2. Nor is it necessary for something greater than God to be conceivable, if His non-existence is conceivable. For the possibility of conceiving Him not to exist does not arise from the imperfection or uncertainty of His Being, since His Being is of itself most manifest, but from the infirmity of our understanding, which cannot discern Him as He is of Himself, but only by the effects which He produces; and so it is brought by reasoning to the knowledge of Him.

3. As it is self-evident to us that the whole is greater than its part, so the existence of God is most self-evident to them that see the divine essence, inasmuch as His essence is His existence. But because we cannot see His essence, we are brought to the knowledge of His existence, not by what He is in Himself but by the effects which He works.

4. Man knows God naturally as he desires Him naturally. Now man desires Him naturally inasmuch as he naturally desires happiness, which is a certain likeness to the divine goodness. Thus it is not necessary that God, considered in Himself, should be naturally known to man, but a certain likeness of God. Hence man must be led to a knowledge of God through the likenesses of Him that are found in the effects which He works.

5. God is that wherein all things are known, not as though other things could not be known without His being known first, as happens in the case of self-evident principles, but because through His influence all knowledge is caused in us.

CHAPTER XII—*Of the Opinion of those who say that the Existence of God is a Tenet of Faith alone and cannot be demonstrated*

The falseness of this opinion is shown to us as well by the art of demonstration, which teaches us to argue causes from effects, as also by the order of the sciences,—for if there be no knowable substance above sensible substances, there will be no science above physical science; as also by the efforts of philosophers, directed to the proof of the existence of God; as also by apostolic truth asserting: *The invisible things of God are clearly seen, being understood by the things that are made* (Rom. i, 20).

The axiom that in God essence and existence are the same is to be understood of the existence whereby God subsists in Himself, the manner of which is unknown to us, as also is His essence; not of the existence which signifies an affirmative judgement of the understanding. For in the form of such affirmative judgement the fact that *there is a God* falls under demonstration; as our mind is led by demonstrative reasons to form such a proposition declaratory of the existence of God. In the reasonings whereby the existence of God is demonstrated it is not necessary to assume for a premise the essence or *quiddity* of God: but instead of the quiddity the effect is taken for a premise, as is done in demonstrations *a posteriori* from effect to cause. All the names of God are imposed either on the principle of denying of God Himself certain effects of His power, or from some habitude of God towards those effects. Although God transcends sense and the objects of sense, nevertheless sensible effects are the basis of our demonstration of the existence of God. Thus the origin of our own knowledge is in sense, even of things that transcend sense.

CHAPTER XIII—*Reasons in Proof of the Existence of God*

We will put first the reasons by which Aristotle proceeds to prove the existence of God from the consideration of motion as follows. Everything that is in motion is put and kept in motion by some other thing. It is evident to sense that there are beings in motion. A thing is in motion because something else puts and keeps it in motion. That mover therefore either is itself in motion or not. If it is not in motion, our point is gained which we proposed to prove, namely, that we must posit something which moves other things without being itself in motion, and this we call God. But if the mover is itself in motion, then it is moved by some other mover. Either then we have to go on to infinity, or we must come to some mover which is motionless; but it is impossible to go on to infinity, therefore we must posit some motionless prime mover. In this argument there are two propositions to be proved; that everything which is motion is put and kept in motion by something else; and that in the series of movers and things moved it is impossible to go on to infinity.

The Philosopher also goes about in another way to show that it is impossible to proceed to infinity in the series of efficient causes, but we must come to one first cause, and this we call God. The way is more or less as follows. In every series of efficient causes, the first term is cause of the intermediate, and the intermediate is cause of the last. But if in efficient causes there is a process to infinity, none of the causes will be the first: therefore all the others will be taken away which are intermediate. But that is manifestly not the case; therefore we must posit the existence of some first efficient cause, which is God.

Another argument is brought by St. John Damascene (*De Fid. Orthod.* I, 3), thus: It is impossible for things contrary and discordant to fall into one harmonious order always or for the most part, except under some one guidance, assigning to each and all a tendency to a fixed end. But in the world we see things of different natures falling into harmonious order, not rarely and fortuitously, but always or for the most part. Therefore there must be some Power by whose providence the world is governed; and that we call God.

CHAPTER XIV—*That in order to a Knowledge of God we must use the Method of Negative Differentiation*

After showing that there is a First Being, whom we call God, we must enquire into the conditions of His existence. We must use the method of negative differentiation, particularly in the consideration of the divine substance. For the divine substance, by its immensity, transcends every form that our intellect can realize; and thus we cannot apprehend it by knowing what it is, but we have some sort of knowledge of it by knowing what it is not. The more we can negatively differentiate it, or the more attributes we can strike off from it in our mind, the more we approach to a knowledge of it: for we know each thing more perfectly, the fuller view we have of its differences as compared with other things; for each thing has in itself a proper being, distinct from all others. Hence in dealing with things that we can define, we first place them in some genus, by which we know in general what the thing is, and afterwards we add the differentias whereby the thing in distinguished from other things; and thus iş achieved a complete knowledge of the substance of the thing. But because in the study of the divine substance we cannot fix upon anything for a genus (Chap. XXV), nor can we mark that substance off from other things by affirmative differentias, we must determine it by negative differentias. In affirmative differentias one limits the extension of another, and brings us nearer to a complete designation of the thing under enquiry, inasmuch as it makes that thing differ from more and more things. And the same holds good also of negative differentias. For example, we may say that God is not an *accident*, in that He is distinguished from all accidents; then if we add that He is not a *body*, we shall further distinguish Him from some substances; and so in order by such negations He will be further distinguished from everything besides Himself; and there will be a proper notion of His substance, when He shall be known as distinct from all. Still it will not be a perfect knowledge, because He will not be known for what He is in Himself.

To proceed therefore in the knowledge of God by way of negative differentiation, let us take as a principle what has been shown in a previous chapter, that God is altogether immovable, which is confirmed also by the authority of Holy Scripture. For it is said: *I am the Lord and change not* (Mal. iii, 6); *With whom there is no change* (James i, 17); *God is not as man, that he should change* (Num. xxiii, 19).

CHAPTER XV — *That God is Eternal*

The beginning of anything and its ceasing to be is brought about by motion or change. But it has been shown that God is altogether unchangeable: He is therefore eternal, without beginning or end.

2. Those things alone are measured by time which are in motion, inasmuch as time is an enumeration of motion. But God is altogether without motion, and therefore is not measured by time. Therefore in Him it is impossible to fix any *before or after*: He has no *being* after *not being*, nor can He have any *not being* after *being*, nor can any succession be found in His being, because all this is unintelligible without time. He is therefore without beginning and without end, having all His being at once, wherein consists the essence of eternity.

3. If at some time God was not, and afterwards was, He was brought forth by some cause from not being to being. But not by Himself, because what is not cannot do anything. But if by another, that other is prior to Him. But it has been shown that God is the First Cause; therefore He did not begin to be: hence neither will He cease to be; because what always has been has the force of being always.

4. We see in the world some things which are possible to be and not to be. But everything that is possible to be has a cause: for seeing that of itself it is open to two alternatives, being and not being; if being is to be assigned to it, that must be from some cause. But we cannot proceed to infinity in a series of causes: therefore we must posit something that necessarily is. Now everything necessary either has the cause of its necessity from elsewhere, or not from elsewhere, but is of itself necessary. But we cannot proceed to infinity in the enumeration of things necessary that have the cause of their necessity from elsewhere: therefore we must come to some first thing necessary, that is of itself necessary; and that is God. Therefore God is eternal, since everything that is of itself necessary is eternal.

Hence the Psalmist: *But thou, O Lord, abidest for ever: thou art the self-same, and thy years shall not fail* (Ps. ci, 13-28).

Chapter V—Philosophy and Modern Science

Introduction

The remarkable growth of scientific knowledge in the sixteenth and seventeenth centuries has led some to describe it as a revolution in science or as the age of genius. Seeking an explanation for this period of great productivity, some have been led to emphasize the renewed application of mathematics as the language of science; others have stressed the importance of observation and experimentation. In retrospect it now seems as if we have been slightly misled by our enthusiasm. The scientific advances of the sixteenth and seventeenth centuries clearly have their roots in the work of medieval theorists. Patient scholarship has revealed the presence of keen minds continually occupied during the medieval period with scientific problems. Moreover, there was nothing new in the empiricism of the modern age; for since the time of Plato, physical science has aimed at "saving the phenomena," that is, explaining our experience. Moreover, the scientific revolution did not consist in the application of mathematics; for there has always been a mathematical tradition since the time of the Pythagoreans. It is doubtful whether one can find a single or simple explanation for the growth of science, and it is probable that social and economic forces are as relevant to this growth as are intellectual currents.

It might be more profitable to explore how scientific developments led to philosophical developments, rather than vice versa. It is our thesis that a radical reorientation in Western thinking was introduced by Copernicus, developed by Galileo and Descartes, and philosophically explicated by Hume and Kant. In fact, it was not until the time of Hume and Kant that the full implications of the

Copernican revolution were realized.

It is often true that the winners write history, and this is true in the history of ideas as well as in politics and military affairs. We have been taught that Copernicus was "right"; that Kepler, Galileo, and Newton saw immediately that Copernicus was right; and that the history of science has been one continuous march of progress since then. What is overlooked is that the work of Copernicus created more problems than it solved. (We think of this as a compliment, for it was fertile in generating further scientific developments.) We are not made aware that for a century at least, it was an open question as to whether Copernicus would prevail; that Galileo was intellectually embarrassed at his trial because he defended Copernicus without reflecting on the difficulties involved; and that it was not until the nineteenth century that we even *could* provide answers to all of the objections to the views of Copernicus. We leave open the question whether or not the answers are adequate.

The fact of the matter is that both the Ptolemaic theory, in which the earth was the center of the universe, and the Copernican theory, in which the sun was the center, were capable of accounting for all of the known phenomena. Every line-of-sight observation in the one theory could be found in the other. We thus had the peculiar intellectual problem of the existence of alternative hypotheses for saving the phenomena. The very existence of viable alternatives led to the challenge of the Aristotelian insistence upon the reliability of everyday experience. It was the growth of a more subtle empiricism that was to prove most influential.

Copernicus' position was characterized by three theses. (1) He claimed that his hypothesis had greater *simplicity* in the qualitative sense of giving a unified explanation for some planetary phenomena, which in Ptolemy's system were connected only arbitarily. The appeal to this kind of simplicity was not original to Copernicus but was part of a long tradition, a fact which made Copernicus' theory attractive to men such as Kepler and Galileo. Here, philosophical and aesthetic prejudices played a key part in the acceptance of the theory. However, Copernicus drew two additional implications from his simplicity appeal. (2) A simpler hypothesis could lead us to recognize the unreliability of everyday experience as ordinarily understood. For example, the sun may appear to move, to rise in the east and to set in the west, but the same phenomenon could be explained by hypothesizing the motion of the earth. (3) A simpler hypothesis could lead us to change in perspective. The earth need not be the center of the universe.

Having challenged Ptolemy directly and Aristotle indirectly, especially on the notion of the role of observation, it was but a short step to challenging Aristotelian physics in other problematic areas. Let us take one important example and give a somewhat simplified explanation. The basic assumption of Aristotelian physics, the physics which dominated the Western world until the seventeenth century, was that rest is the natural state. It followed that what had to be explained was motion, and that motion implied or necessitated a mover. Thus, without a mover there would be no motion. But various phenomena seemed to defy explanation from this point of view. For example, an arrow shot from a bow should stop moving as soon as it leaves the bow, for it has lost contact with its mover. To account for the continued motion of the arrow, Aristotelians postulated that the air in front of the arrow came around to the back of the arrow and pushed it. The air was originally disturbed by the initial motion of the arrow as it left the bow. Now suppose we wanted to test the truth of this contention. We could put a streamer on the back of the arrow (near the feathers) and then as the air pushed the arrow, the streamer should be pushed forward or point toward the front of the arrow. In fact, we all know that the streamer would point backward. Instances like this led to the rejection of the simplified Aristotelian view of the universe. In fact, it led Galileo, Descartes, and Newton, to the rejection of the view that rest was natural and to the view that motion was the natural state.

No doubt Galileo was sustained by his faith that the geometrical patterns so essential to Copernicus' and to his own theories about the world were real; but it was also true of Aristotelian physics and common sense views of the world which he accepted. It was still necessary to "save the phenomena." On one hand, Galileo praised Copernicus for setting mathematics over the evidence of the senses, but at the same time he proposed the distinction between primary and secondary qualities. The latter distinction between the world that could be measured and the world as experientially confronted (secondary qualities—what could not be measured) became the basis for all modern philosophy, both its triumphs and its tribulations.

The question now became, Is there one set of phenomena with alternative descriptions, or are there two worlds, the phenomenal and the intelligible, with two radically different descriptions? Descartes played a decisive role in answering this question. Encouraged by his studies of vision, Descartes attempted to carry out the Galilean proposal of explaining the world of sensory appearance (described in Aristotelian terms) as effects of causes described in mathematical terms. The philosophical implications of this dichotomy are drawn in the famous Cartesian dualism of mind and body.

The universe of modern philosophy now consisted of the following:

The causal connection between (O) and (E) was taken to be a scientific fact. For example, objects in themselves, independent of man, have neither color nor taste. They consist, at least for Galileo, of small particles in motion. The mathematical properties of objects—size, shape, speed—are real, *objective* in the sense of being "in the object." The color of an object is not in the object itself but only exists when a human nervous system comes into contact with the object. The color is secondary, *subjective* in the sense of being "in the subject." The problems of dealing with a world so conceived were monumental, challenging, and perhaps insuperable. We shall see this better when we turn to individual philosophers.

Francis Bacon

Bacon was once considered the father of modern science; unfortunately, his reputation as a scientist and as a philosopher has waned. Some historians of science now speak of the Baconian myth. Nevertheless, Bacon was a useful critic of the past and a prophet for the future in many ways. He symbolizes the new spirit of his time: the desire to use human technological gains to foster human welfare. In retrospect this may have been his most important contribution. If we recall that for the classical traditions of both Plato and Aristotle practice was for the sake of theory, we shall better appreciate how totally new, modern, and radical is the idea that *theory is for the sake of practice*. We take such a view for granted, forgetting that it is not an obvious belief but one of recent vintage, and that Bacon more than any other writer was responsible for both the articulation of this view and its initial defense.

Francis Bacon (1561-1626) was born the son of Sir Nicholas Bacon, Lord Keeper of the Great Seal for Queen Elizabeth. He studied at Cambridge and took up law at Gray's Inn. Later, he became a member of Parliament. When James I succeeded Elizabeth, Bacon's fortunes rose. He was knighted, and in the following years held numerous important posts at court. However, in 1621 he was found guilty of accepting bribes and dismissed from his posts.

In 1620 he published The *Great Instauration* including the *Novum Organum*, in which he dealt with a method that he thought would revolutionize the sciences. Previously, in 1605 he had published *The Advancement of Learning*. It is in this work that Bacon first formulated the distinction between the speculative study of nature and the practical philosophy of nature. He argued that no technological innovations were possible without adequate causal knowledge, and he argued as well that there would be no perfect speculation until a practical application could be found. The linking of experimentation with practical concerns was a novel idea. At the same time, the early work shows the extent to which Bacon was still an Aristotelian; for in it he introduced the Aristotelian doctrine of the four causes. Bacon rejected only the notion of a final cause, and in his detailed handling of issues he treats the formal causes as an instance of the material cause. (This will prove to be highly influential in Locke's treatment of substance.) Metaphysics, says Bacon, deals with immutable causes such as the formal cause. Physics deals with mutable causes such as the efficient cause.

In discussing the barriers to human learning, Bacon enumerates seven major sources of error: pessimism about human capabilities, an inferiority complex with regard to antiquity, the appeal to authority, the inadequacies of syllogistic logic, the irresponsible use of hypotheses, disregard for the utility of knowledge, and the infamous "idols." Bacon's critique of the syllogism is very instructive. As we have already seen, a syllogism is an argument with two premises and a conclusion. If a syllogism has true premises and is constructed according to the rules of valid deductive argumentation, then the conclusion must be true. The entire syllogism turns upon the truth of the premises, especially the truth of the major premise. For example:

> All men are mortal. (Major premise)
> Socrates is a man. (minor premise)
> _____
> Socrates is mortal. (conclusion)

There is nothing wrong with the syllogism per se, claims Bacon; but it does not reveal any new information. It simply allows you to draw the consequences from information you already possess. The trouble with the medieval schoolmen is that they obtained their premises either from scripture or from the classics. What Bacon wants is a way of arriving at new truths. This is called *induction* since it is concerned with the process of establishing premises, not drawing conclusions from premises already established. Bacon proposed that experimentation would provide a new and more useful source of first principles or premises. In the end we can say that Bacon really agrees with Aristotle's logic but dissents from its medieval restrictions on the derivation of first principles.

In his scientific methodology Bacon distinguished between *natures,* finite in number, which were either simple and referred to sensations, or complex and referred to combinations (such as gold which is made up of the simple natures of yellowness, malleability, and so on). The changes we perceive in natures is due to the *forms* or fixed laws underlying the natures. Strictly speaking, says Bacon, only the natures really exist. Bacon had to explain how we moved from the observation of natures to a knowledge of "underlying" forms. He rejected the naive view of induction by enumeration, which assumes that we merely collect instances and then generalize. He also rejected the notion of highly speculative hypotheses, such as one found in Copernicus and in Gilbert's work on magnetism. Bacon believed that somehow the facts would suggest hypotheses of a responsible sort, but he never explained how. In this respect, Bacon reveals the weakness of Aristotelian science: a lack of a clear conception of how one abstracts the forms from experience. This weakness was to plague later "empiricist" philosophies of science down through Locke and even into the twentieth century. The contemporary "empiricist-Aristotelian" view is to accept the notion that hypotheses can come from anywhere or any source, and that the real emphasis should be on the verification of the results.

$$(facts) \xrightarrow{(1)} (hypothesis) \xrightarrow{(2)} (deduce\ consequences) \xrightarrow{(3)} check\ the\ new\ facts\ (4)$$

Bacon was concerned with (1); the syllogism or any type of deductive logic operates at (2); the contemporary Baconian would be concerned with the relation of (4) to (3).

Scientific Method

Being convinced that the human intellect makes its own difficulties, not using the true helps which are at man's disposal soberly and judiciously; whence follows manifold ignorance of things, and by reason of that ignorance mischiefs innumerable; he thought all trial should be made, whether that commerce between the mind of man and the nature of things, which is more precious than anything on earth, or at least than anything that is of the earth, might by any means be restored to its perfect and original condition, or if that may not be, yet reduced to a better condition than that in which it now is. Now that the errors which have hitherto prevailed, and which will prevail forever, should (if the mind be left to go its own way), either by the natural force of the understanding or by help of the aids and instruments of logic, one by one correct themselves, was a thing not

to be hoped for: because the primary notions of things which the mind readily and passively imbibes, stores up, and accumulates (and it is from them that all the rest flow) are false, confused, and overhastily abstracted from the facts; nor are the secondary and subsequent notions less arbitrary and inconstant: whence it follows that the entire fabric of human reason which we employ in the inquisition of nature, is badly put together and built up, and like some magnificent structure without any foundation. For while men are occupied in admiring and applauding the false powers of the mind, they pass by and throw away those true powers, which, if it be supplied with the proper aids and can itself be content to wait upon nature instead of vainly affecting to overrule her, are within its reach. There was but one course left, therefore,—to try the whole thing anew upon a

better plan, and to commence a total recon-
struction of sciences, arts, and all human
knowledge, raised upon the proper foundations. And this, though in the project and
undertaking it may seem a thing infinite and
beyond the powers of man, yet when it comes to
be dealt with it will be found sound and sober,
more so than what has been done hitherto. For
of this there is some issue; whereas in what is
now done in the matter of science there is only a
whirling round about, and perpetual agitation,
ending where it began. And although he was
well aware how solitary an enterprise it is, and
how hard a thing to win faith and credit for;
nevertheless he was resolved not to abandon
either it or himself, nor to be deterred from
trying and entering upon that one path which is
alone open to the human mind. For better it is
to make a beginning of that which may lead to
something, than to engage in a perpetual struggle and pursuit in courses which have no exit.
And certainly the two ways of contemplation
are much like those two ways of action, so much
celebrated, in this—that the one, arduous and
difficult in the beginning, leads out at last into
the open country; while the other, seeming at
first sight easy and free from obstruction, leads
to pathless and precipitous places.

Moreover, because he knew not how long it
might be before these things would occur to
anyone else, judging especially from this, that
he has found no man hitherto who has applied
his mind to the like, he resolved to publish at
once so much as he has been able to complete.
The cause of which haste was not ambition for
himself, but solicitude for the work; that in case
of his death there might remain some outline
and project of that which he had conceived, and
some evidence likewise of his honest mind and
inclination towards the benefit of the human
race. Certain it is that all other ambition whatsoever seemed poor in his eyes compared with
the work which he had in hand; seeing that the
matter at issue is either nothing, or a thing so
great that it may well be content with its own
merit, without seeking other recompense.

Preface

*That the state of knowledge is not prosperous
nor greatly advancing; and that a way must be
opened for the human understanding entirely
different from any hitherto known, and other*
*helps provided, in order that the mind may
exercise over the nature of things the authority
which properly belongs to it.*

It seems to me that men do not rightly understand either their store or their strength, but
overrate the one and underrate the other.
Hence it follows, that either from an extravagant estimate of the value of the arts which
they possess, they seek no further; or else from
too mean an estimate of their own powers, they
spend their strength in small matters and never
put it fairly to the trial in those which go to the
main. These are as the pillars of fate set in the
path of knowledge; for men have neither desire
nor hope to encourage them to penetrate
further. And since opinion of store is one of the
chief causes of want, and satisfaction with the
present induces neglect of provision for the
future, it becomes a thing not only useful, but
absolutely necessary, that the excess of honor
and admiration with which our existing stock of
inventions is regarded be in the very entrance
and threshold of the work, and that frankly and
without circumlocution, stripped off, and men
be duly warned not to exaggerate or make too
much of them. For let a man look carefully into
all that variety of books with which the arts and
sciences abound, he will find everywhere
endless repetitions of the same thing, varying in
the method of treatment, but not new in substance, insomuch that the whole stock, numerous as it appears at first view, proves on
examination to be but scanty. And for its value
and utility it must be plainly avowed that that
wisdom which we have derived principally from
the Greeks is but like the boyhood of knowledge, and has the characteristic property of
boys: it can talk, but it cannot generate; for it is
fruitful of controversies but barren of works. So
that the state of learning as it now is appears to
be represented to the life in the old fable of
Scylla, who had the head and face of a virgin,
but her womb was hung round with barking
monsters, from which she could not be delivered. For in like manner the sciences to which
we are accustomed have certain general positions which are specious and flattering; but as
soon as they come to particulars, which are as
the parts of generation, when they should
produce fruit and works, then arise contentions
and barking disputations, which are the end of
the matter and all the issue they can yield.

Observe also, that if sciences of this kind had any life in them, that could never have come to pass which has been the case now for many ages—that they stand almost at a stay, without receiving any augmentations worthy of the human race; insomuch that many times not only what was asserted once is asserted still, but what was a question once is a question still, and instead of being resolved by discussion is only fixed and fed; and all the tradition and succession of schools is still a succession of masters and scholars, not of inventions and those who bring to further perfection the things invented. In the mechanical arts we do not find it so; they, on the contrary, as having in them some breath of life, are continually growing and becoming more perfect. As originally invented they are commonly rude, clumsy, and shapeless; afterwards they acquire new powers and more commodious arrangements and constructions; in so far that men shall sooner leave the study and pursuit of them and turn to something else, than they arrive at the ultimate perfection of which they are capable. Philosophy and the intellectual sciences, on the contrary, stand like statues, worshiped and celebrated, but not moved or advanced. Nay, they sometimes flourish most in the hands of the first author, and afterwards degenerate. For when men have once made over their judgments to others' keeping, and (like those senators whom they called *Pedarii*) have agreed to support some one person's opinion, from that time they make no enlargement of the sciences themselves, but fall to the servile office of embellishing certain individual authors and increasing their retinue.

And let it not be said that the sciences have been growing gradually till they have at last reached their full stature, and so (their course being completed) have settled in the works of a few writers; and that there being now no room for the invention of better, all that remains is to embellish and cultivate those things which have been invented already. Would it were so! But the truth is that this appropriating of the sciences has its origin in nothing better than the confidence of a few persons and the sloth and indolence of the rest. For after the sciences had been in several parts perhaps cultivated and handled diligently, there has risen up some man of bold disposition, and famous for methods and short ways which people like, who

has in appearance reduced them to an art, while he has in fact only spoiled all that the others had done. And yet this is what posterity like, because it makes the work short and easy, and saves further inquiry, of which they are weary and impatient. And if anyone take this general acquiescence and consent for an argument of weight, as being the judgment of Time, let me tell him that the reasoning on which he relies is most fallacious and weak. For, first, we are far from knowing all that in the matter of sciences and arts has in various ages and places been brought to light and published; much less, all that has been by private persons secretly attempted and stirred; so neither the births nor the miscarriages of Time are entered in our records. Nor, secondly, is the consent itself and the time it has continued a consideration of much worth. For however various are the forms of civil politics, there is but one form of polity in the sciences; and that always has been and always will be popular. Now the doctrines which find most favor with the populace are those which are either contentious and pugnacious, or specious and empty; such, I say, as either entangle assent or tickle it. And therefore no doubt the greatest wits in each successive age have been forced out of their own course; men of capacity and intellect above the vulgar having been fain, for reputation's sake, to bow to the judgment of the time and the multitude; and thus if any contemplations of a higher order took light anywhere, they were presently blown out by the winds of vulgar opinions. So that Time is like a river, which has brought down to us things light and puffed up, while those which are weighty and solid have sunk. Nay, those very authors who have usurped a kind of dictatorship in the sciences and taken upon them to lay down the law with such confidence, yet when from time to time they came to themselves again, they fall to complaints of the subtlety of nature, the hiding-places of truth, the obscurity of things, the entanglement of causes, the weakness of the human mind; wherein nevertheless they show themselves never the more modest, seeing that they will rather lay the blame upon the common condition of men and nature than upon themselves. And then whatever any art fails to attain, they ever set it down upon the authority of that art itself as impossible of attainment; and how can art be found guilty when it is judge in its own cause? So it is but a device for exempting ignorance from ignominy.

Now for those things which are delivered and received, this is their condition: barren of works, full of questions; in point of enlargement slow and languid; carrying a show of perfection in the whole, but in the parts ill filled up; in selection popular, and unsatisfactory even to those who propound them; and therefore fenced round and set forth with sundry artifices. And if there be any who have determined to make trial for themselves, and put their own strength to the work of advancing the boundaries of the sciences; yet have they not ventured to cast themselves completely loose from received opinions or to seek their knowledge at the fountain; but they think they have done some great thing if they do but add and introduce into the existing sum of science something of their own; prudently considering with themselves that by making the addition they can assert their liberty, while they retain the credit of modesty by assenting to the rest. But these mediocrities and middle ways so much praised, in deferring to opinions and customs, turn to the great detriment of the sciences. For it is hardly possible at once to admire an author and to go beyond him; knowledge being as water, which will not rise above the level from which it fell. Men of this kind, therefore, amend some things, but advance little; and improve the condition of knowledge, but do not extend its range. Some, indeed, there have been who have gone more boldly to work, and taking it all for an open matter and giving their genius full play, have made a passage for themselves and their own opinions by pulling down and demolishing former ones; and yet all their stir has but little advanced the matter; since their aim has been not to extend philosophy and the arts in substance and value, but only to change doctrines and transfer the kingdom of opinions to themselves; whereby little has indeed been gained, for though the error be the opposite of the other, the causes of erring are the same in both. And if there have been any who, not binding themselves either to other men's opinions or to their own, but loving liberty, have desired to engage others along with themselves in search, these, though honest in intention, have been weak in endeavor. For they have been content

to follow probable reasons, and are carried round in a whirl of arguments, and in the promiscuous liberty of search have relaxed the severity of inquiry.

There is none who has dwelt upon experience and the facts of nature as long as is necessary. Some there are indeed who have committed themselves to the waves of experience, and almost turned mechanics; yet these again have in their very experiments pursued a kind of wandering inquiry, without any regular system of operations. And besides they have mostly proposed to themselves certain petty tasks, taking it for a great matter to work out some single discovery;—a course of proceeding at once poor in aim and unskillful in design. For no man can rightly and successfully investigate the nature of anything in the thing itself; let him vary his experiments as laboriously as he will, he never comes to a resting place, but still finds something to seek beyond. And there is another thing to be remembered: namely, that all industry in experimenting has begun with proposing to itself certain definite works to be accomplished, and has pursued them with premature and unseasonable eagerness; it has sought, I say, experiments of Fruit, not experiments of Light; not imitating the divine procedure, which in its first day's work created light only and assigned to it one entire day; on which day it produced no material work, but proceeded to that on the days following. As for those who have given the first place to Logic, supposing that the surest helps to the sciences were to be found in that, they have indeed most truly and excellently perceived that the human intellect left to its own course is not to be trusted; but then the remedy is altogether too weak for the disease, nor is it without evil in itself. For the Logic which is received, though it be very properly applied to civil business and to those arts which rest in discourse and opinion, is not nearly subtle enough to deal with nature; and in offering at what it cannot master, has done more to establish and perpetuate error than to open the way to truth.

Upon the whole therefore, it seems that men have not been happy hitherto either in the trust which they have placed in others or in their own industry with regard to the sciences; especially as neither the demonstrations nor the experiments as yet known are much to be relied upon. But the universe to the eye of the human understanding is framed like a labyrinth; presenting as it does on every side so many ambiguities of way, such deceitful resemblances of objects and signs, natures so irregular in their lines, and so knotted and entangled. And then the way is still to be made by the uncertain light of the sense, sometimes shining out, sometimes clouded over, through the woods of experience and particulars; while those who offer themselves for guides are (as was said) themselves also puzzled and increase the number of errors and wanderers. In circumstances so difficult, neither the natural force of man's judgment nor even any accidental felicity offers any chance of success. No excellence of wit, no repetition of chance experiments, can overcome such difficulties as these. Our steps must be guided by a clue, and the whole way from the very first perception of the senses must be laid out upon a sure plan. Not that I would be understood to mean that nothing whatever has been done in so many ages by so great labors. We have no reason to be ashamed of the discoveries which have been made, and no doubt the ancients proved themselves in everything that turns on wit and abstract meditation, wonderful men. But as in former ages when men sailed only by observation of the stars, they could indeed coast along the shores of the old continent or cross a few small and mediterranean seas; but before the ocean could be traversed and the new world discovered, the use of the mariner's needle, as a more faithful and certain guide, had to be found out: in like manner the discoveries which have been hitherto made in the arts and sciences are such as might be made by practice, meditation, observation, argumentation—for they lay near to the senses, and immediately beneath common notions; but before we can reach the remoter and more hidden parts of nature; it is necessary that a more perfect use and application of the human mind and intellect be introduced.

For my own part at least, in obedience to the everlasting love of truth, I have committed myself to the uncertainties and difficulties and solitudes of the ways, and relying on the divine assistance have upheld my mind both against the shocks and embattled ranks of opinion, and against my own private and inward hesitations and scruples, and against the fogs and clouds of nature, and the phantoms flitting about on every side; in the hope of providing at last for the present and future generations guidance more faithful and secure. Wherein if I have made any progress, the way has been opened to me by no other means than the true and legitimate humiliation of the human spirit. For all those who before me have applied themselves to the invention of arts have but cast a glance or two upon facts and examples and experience, and straightway proceeded, as if invention were nothing more than an exercise of thought, to invoke their own spirits to give them oracles. I, on the contrary, dwelling purely and constantly among the facts of nature, withdraw any intellect from them no further than may suffice to let the images and rays of natural objects meet in a point, as they do in the sense of vision; whence it follows that the strength and excellency of the wit has but little to do in the matter. And the same humility which I use in inventing I employ likewise in teaching. For I do not endeavor either by triumphs of confutation, or pleading of antiquity, or assumption of authority, or even by the veil of obscurity, to invest these inventions of mine with any majesty; which might easily be done by one sought to give luster to his own name rather than light to other men's minds. I have not sought (I say) nor do I seek either to force or ensnare men's judgments; but I lead them to things themselves and the concordance of things, that they may see for themselves what they have, what they can dispute, what they can add and contribute to the common stock. And for myself, if in anything I have been either too credulous or too little awake and attentive, or if I have fallen off by the way and left the inquiry incomplete, nevertheless I so present these things naked and open, that my errors can be marked and set aside before the mass of knowledge be further infected by them; and it will be easy also for others to continue and carry on my labors. And by these means I suppose that I have established for ever a true and lawful marriage between the empirical and the rational faculty, the unkind and ill-starred divorce and separation of which has thrown into confusion all the affairs of the human family. . . .

And now having said my prayers, I turn to men; to whom I have certain salutary admonitions to offer and certain fair requests to make. My first admonition (which was also my prayer) is that men confine the sense within the limits of duty in respect of things divine: for the sense is like the sun, which reveals the face of earth, but seals and shuts up the face of heaven. My next, that in flying from this evil they fall not into the opposite error, which they will surely do if they think that the inquisition of nature is in any part interdicted or forbidden. For it was not that pure and uncorrupted natural knowledge whereby Adam gave names to the creatures according to their propriety, which gave occasion to the fall. It was the ambitious and proud desire of moral knowledge to judge of good and evil, to the end that man may revolt from God and give laws to himself, which was the form and manner of the temptation. Whereas of the sciences which regard nature, the divine philosopher declares that "it is the glory of God to conceal a thing, but it is the glory of the King to find a thing out." Even as though the divine nature took pleasure in the innocent and kindly sport of children playing a hide and seek, and vouchsafed to his kindness and goodness to admit the human spirit for his playfellow at that game. Lastly, I would address one general admonition to all: that they consider what are the true ends of knowledge, and that they seek it not either for pleasure of the mind, or for contention, or for superiority to others, or for profit, or fame, or power, or any of these inferior things; but for the benefit and use of life; and that they perfect and govern it in charity. For it was from lust of power that the angels fell, from lust of knowledge that man fell; but of charity there can be no excess, neither did angel or man ever come in danger by it.

The requests I have to make are these. Of myself I say nothing; but in behalf of the business which is in hand I entreat men to believe that it is not an opinion to be held, but a work to be done; and to be well assured that I am laboring to lay the foundation, not of any sect or doctrine, but of human utility and power. Next, I ask them to deal fairly by their own interests, and laying aside all emulations and prejudices in favor of this or that opinion, to join in consultation for the common good; and being now freed and guarded by the securities and helps which I offer from the errors and impediments of the way, to come forward themselves and take part in that which remains to be done. Moreover, to be of good hope, nor to imagine that this *Instauration* of mine is a

thing infinite and beyond the power of man, when it is in fact the true end and termination of infinite error; and seeing also that it is by no means forgetful of the conditions of mortality and humanity (for it does not suppose that the work can be altogether completed within one generation, but provides for its being taken up by another); and finally that it seeks for the sciences not arrogantly in the little cells of human wit, but with reverence in the greater world. But it is the empty things that are vast: things solid are most contracted and lie in little room. And now I have only one favor more to ask (else injustice to me may perhaps imperil the business itself)—that men will consider well how far, upon that which I must needs assert (if I am to be consistent with myself); they are entitled to judge and decide upon these doctrines of mine; inasmuch as all that premature human reasoning which anticipates inquiry, and is abstracted from the facts rashly and sooner than is fit, is by me rejected (so far as the inquisition of nature is concerned) as a thing uncertain, confused, and ill built up; and I cannot be fairly asked to abide by the decision of a tribunal which is itself on its trial.

xlviii

The human understanding is unquiet; it cannot stop or rest, and still presses onward, but in vain. Therefore it is that we cannot conceive of any end or limit to the world; but always as of necessity it occurs to us that there is something beyond. Neither again can it be conceived how eternity has flowed down to the present day: for that distinction which is commonly received of infinity in time past and in time to come can by no means hold; for it would thence follow that one infinity is greater than another, and that infinity is wasting away and tending to become finite. The like subtlety arises touching the infinite divisibility of lines, from the same inability of thought to stop. But this inability interferes more mischievously in the discovery of causes: for although the most general principles in nature ought to be held merely positive, as they are discovered, and cannot with truth be referred to a cause; nevertheless the human understanding being unable to rest still seeks something prior in the order of nature. And then it is that in struggling towards that which is further off it falls back upon that which is more nigh at hand,—namely, on final causes; which have relation clearly to the nature of man rather than to the nature of the universe, and from this source have strangely defiled philosophy. But he is no less an unskilled and shallow philosopher who seeks causes of that which is most general, than he who in things subordinate and subaltern omits to do so.

xlix

The human understanding is no dry light, but receives an infusion from the will and affections; whence proceed sciences which may be called "sciences as one would." For what a man had rather were true he more readily believes. Therefore he rejects difficult things from impatience of research; sober things, because they narrow hope; the deeper things of nature, from superstition; the light of experience, from arrogance and pride, lest his mind should seem to be occupied with things mean and transitory; things not commonly believed, out of deference to the opinion of the vulgar. Numberless in short are the ways, and sometimes imperceptible, in which the affections color and infect the understanding.

l

But by far the greatest hindrance and aberration of the human understanding proceeds from the dullness, incompetency, and deceptions of the senses; in that things which strike the sense outweigh things which do not immediately strike it, though they be more important. Hence it is that speculation commonly ceases where sight ceases, insomuch that of things invisible there is little or no observation. Hence all the working of the spirits inclosed in tangible bodies lies hid and unobserved of men. So also all the more subtle changes of form in the parts of coarser substances (which they commonly call alteration, though it is in truth local motion through exceedingly small spaces) is in like manner unobserved. And yet unless these two things just mentioned be searched out and brought to light, nothing great can be achieved in nature, as far as the production of works is concerned. So again the essential nature of our common air, and of all bodies less dense than air (which are very many), is almost

unknown. For the sense by itself is a thing infirm and erring; neither can instruments for enlarging or sharpening the senses do much: but all the truer kind of interpretation of nature is effected by instances and experiments fit and apposite; wherein the sense decides touching the experiment only, and the experiment touching the point in nature and the thing itself.

li

The human understanding is of its own nature prone to abstractions and gives a substance and reality to things which are fleeting. But to resolve nature into abstractions is less to our purpose than to dissect her into parts; as did the school of Democritus, which went further into nature than the rest. Matter rather than forms should be the object of our attention, its configurations and changes of configuration, and simple action, and law of action or motion; for forms are figments of the human mind, unless you will call those laws of action forms.

lii

Such then are the idols which I call *Idols of the Tribe*; and which take their rise either from the homogeneity of the substance of the human spirit, or from its preoccupation, or from its narrowness, or from its restless motion, or from an infusion of the affections, or from the incompetency of the senses, or from the mode of impression.

liii

The *Idols of the Cave* take their rise in the peculiar constitution, mental or bodily, of each individual; and also in education, habit, and accident. Of this kind there is a great number and variety; but I will instance those the pointing out of which contains the most important caution, and which have most effect in disturbing the clearness of the understanding.

liv

Men become attached to certain particular sciences and speculations, either because they fancy themselves the authors and inventors thereof, or because they have bestowed the greatest pains upon them and become most habituated to them. But men of this kind, if they betake themselves to philosophy and contemplations of a general character, distort and color them in obedience to their former fancies; a thing especially to be noticed in Aristotle, who made his natural philosophy a mere bondservant to his logic, thereby rendering it contentious and well nigh useless. The race of chemists again out of a few experiments of the furnace have built up a fantastic philosophy, framed with reference to a few things; and Gilbert also, after he had employed himself most laboriously in the study and observation of the lodestone, proceeded at once to construct an entire system in accordance with his favorite subject.

lv

There is one principal and as it were radical distinction between different minds, in respect of philosophy and the sciences; which is this: that some minds are stronger and apter to mark the differences of things, others to mark their resemblances. The steady and acute mind can fix its contemplations and dwell and fasten on the subtlest distinctions; and lofty and discursive mind recognizes and puts together the finest and most general resemblances. Both kinds however easily err in excess, by catching the one at gradations the other at shadows.

lvi

There are found some minds given to an extreme admiration of antiquity, others to an extreme love and appetite for novelty; but few so duly tempered that they can hold the mean, neither carping at what has been well laid down by the ancients, nor despising what is well introduced by the moderns. This however turns to the great injury of the sciences and philosophy: since these affectations of antiquity and novelty are the humors of partisans rather than judgments; and truth is to be sought for not in the felicity of any age, which is an unstable thing, but in the light of nature and experience, which is eternal. These factions therefore must be abjured, and care must be taken that the intellect be not hurried by them into assent.

lvii

Contemplations of nature and of bodies in their simple form break up and distract the understanding, while contemplations of nature and bodies in their composition and configuration overpower and dissolve the understanding: a distinction well seen in the school of Leucippus and Democritus as compared with the other philosophies. For that school is so busied with the particles that it hardly attends to the structure; while the others are so lost in admiration of the structure that they do not penetrate to the simplicity of nature. These kinds of contemplation should therefore be alternated and taken by turns; that so the understanding may be rendered at once penetrating and comprehensive, and the inconveniences above mentioned, with the idols which proceed from them, may be avoided.

lviii

Let such then be our provision and contemplative prudence for keeping off and dislodging the Idols of the Cave, which grow for the most part either out of the predominance of a favorite subject, or out of an excessive tendency to compare or to distinguish, or out of partiality for particular ages, or out of the largeness or minuteness of the objects contemplated. And generally let every student of nature take this as a rule,—that whatever his mind seizes and dwells upon with peculiar satisfaction is to be held in suspicion, and that so much the more care is to be taken in dealing with such questions to keep the understanding even and clear.

lix

But the *Idols of the Market-place* are the most troublesome of all: idols which have crept into the understanding through the alliances of words and names. For men believe that their reason governs words; but it is also true that words react on the understanding; and this it is that has rendered philosophy and the sciences sophistical and inactive. Now words, being commonly framed and applied according to the capacity of the vulgar, follow those lines of division which are most obvious to the vulgar understanding. And whenever an understanding of greater acuteness or a more diligent observation would alter those lines to suit the true divisions of nature, words stand in the way and resist the change. Whence it comes to pass that the high and formal discussions of learned men end oftentimes in disputes about words and names; with which (according to the use and wisdom of the mathematicians) it would be more prudent to begin, and so by means of definitions reduce them to order. Yet even definitions cannot cure this evil in dealing with natural and material things; since the definitions themselves consist of words, and those words beget others: so that it is necessary to recur to individual instances, and those in due series and order; as I shall say presently when I come to the method and scheme for the formation of notions and axioms.

lx

The idols imposed by words on the understanding are of two kinds. They are either names of things which do not exist (for as these are things left unnamed through lack of observation, so likewise are there names which result from fantastic suppositions and to which nothing in reality corresponds), or they are names of things which exist, but yet confused and ill-defined, and hastily and irregularly derived from realities. Of the former kind are Fortune, the Prime Mover, Planetary Orbits, Elements of Fire, and like fictions which owe their origin to false and idle theories. And this class of idols is more easily expelled, because to get rid of them it is only necessary that all theories should be steadily rejected and dismissed as obsolete. . . .

lxii

Idols of the Theater, or of Systems, are many, and there can be and perhaps will be yet many more. For were it not that now for many ages men's minds have been busied with religion and theology; and were it not that civil governments, especially monarchies, have been averse to such novelties, even in matters speculative; so that men labor therein to the peril and harming of their fortunes,—not only unrewarded, but exposed also to contempt and envy: doubtless there would have arisen many other phil-

osophical sects like to those which in great variety flourished once among the Greeks. For as on the phenomena of the heavens many hypotheses may be constructed, so likewise (and more also) many various dogmas may be set up and established on the phenomena of philosophy. And in the plays of this philosophical theater you may observe the same thing which is found in the theater of the poets, that stores invented for the stage are more compact and elegant, and more as one would wish them to be, than true stories out of history.

In general however there is taken for the material of philosophy either a great deal out of a few things, or a very little out of many things; so that on both sides philosophy is based on too narrow a foundation of experiment and natural history, and decides on the authority of too few cases. For the rational school of philosophers snatches from experience a variety of common instances, neither duly ascertained nor diligently examined and weighed, and leaves all the rest to meditation and agitation of wit.

There is also another class of philosophers, who having bestowed much diligent and careful labor on a few experiments, have thence made bold to educe the construct systems; wresting all other facts in a strange fashion to conformity therewith.

And there is yet a third class, consisting of those who out of faith and veneration mix their philosophy with theology and traditions; among whom the vanity of some has gone so far aside as to seek the origin of science among spirits and genii. So that this parent stock of errors—this false philosophy—is of three kinds; the *sophistical*, the *empirical*, and the *superstitious*.

lxiii

The most conspicuous example of the first class was Aristotle, who corrupted natural philosophy by his logic; fashioning the world out of categories; assigning to the human soul, the noblest of substances, a genus from words of the second intention; doing the business of density and rarity (which is to make bodies of greater or less dimensions, that is, occupy greater or less spaces), by the frigid distinction of act and power; asserting that single bodies have each a single and proper motion, and that if they participate in any other, then this results from an external cause; and imposing countless other arbitrary restrictions on the nature of things: being always more solicitous to provide an answer to the question and affirm something positive in words, than about the inner truth of things; a failing best shown when his philosophy is compared with other systems of note among the Greeks. For the *homoeomera* of Anaxagoras; the atoms of Leucippus and Democritus; the Heaven and Earth of Parmenides; the Strife and Friendship of Empedocles; Heraclitus's doctrine how bodies are resolved into the indifferent nature of fire, and remolded into solids; have all of them some taste of the natural philosopher,—some savor the nature of things, and experience, and bodies; whereas in the physics of Aristotle you hear hardly anything but the words of logic; which in his metaphysics also, under a more imposing name, and more forsooth as a realist than a nominalist, he has handled over again. Nor let any weight be given to the fact that in his books on animals, and his *Problems,* and other of his treatises, there is frequent dealing with experiments. For he had come to his conclusion before: he did not consult experience, as he should have done, in order to the framing of his decisions and axioms; but having first determined the question according to his will, he then resorts to experience, and bending her into conformity with his placets leads her about like a captive in a procession; so that even on this count he is more guilty than his modern followers, the schoolmen, who have abandoned experience altogether.

lxiv

But the empirical school of philosophy gives birth to dogmas more deformed and monstrous than the sophistical or rational school. For it has its foundations not in the light of common notions (which, though it be a faint and superficial light, is yet in a manner universal, and has reference to many things) but in the narrowness and darkness of a few experiments. To those therefore who are daily busied with these experiments, and have infected their imagination with them, such a philosophy seems probable and all but certain; to all men else incredible and vain. Of this there is a notable instance in

the alchemists and their dogmas; though it is hardly to be found elsewhere in these times, except perhaps in the philosophy of Gilbert. Nevertheless with regard to philosophies of this kind there is one caution not to be omitted; for I foresee that if ever men are roused by my admonitions to betake themselves seriously to experiment and bid farewell to sophistical doctrines, then indeed through the premature hurry of the understanding to leap or fly to universals and principles of things, great danger may be apprehended from philosophies of this kind; against which evil we ought even now to prepare.

lxv

But the corruption of philosophy by superstition and an admixture of theology is far more widely spread, and does the greatest harm, whether to entire systems or to their parts. For the human understanding is obnoxious to the influence of the imagination no less than to the influence of common notions. For the contentious and sophistical kind of philosophy ensnares the understanding; but this kind, being fanciful and tumid and half-poetical, and misleads it more by flattery. For there is in man an ambition of the understanding, no less than of the will, especially in high and lofty spirits.

Of this kind we have among the Greeks a striking example of Pythagoras, though he united with it a coarser and more cumbrous superstition; another in Plato and his school, more dangerous and subtle. It shows itself likewise in parts of other philosophies, in the introduction of abstract forms and final causes and first causes, with the omission in most cases of causes intermediate, and the like. Upon this point the greatest caution should be used. For nothing is so mischievous as the apotheosis of error; and it is a very plague of the understanding for vanity to become the object of veneration. Yet in this vanity some of the moderns have with extreme levity indulged so far as to attempt to found a system of natural philosophy on the first chapters of Genesis, on the book of Job, and other parts of the sacred writings; seeking for the dead among the living: which also makes the inhibition and repression of it the more important, because from this unwholesome mixture of things human and divine there arises not only a fantastic philosophy but also an heretical religion. Very meet it is therefore that we be sober-minded, and give to faith that only which is faith's.

René Descartes

Descartes was a seventeenth century French scientist and philosopher. Among his many achievements was the invention of analytic geometry. His importance in the history of thought is that he turned the procedures and results of Galileo into a comprehensive philosophy of nature. Descartes was born in 1596 at Touraine and died in 1650 in Sweden. He spent a good deal of his life in the Netherlands because of the intellectually free climate of that nation. He studied at the University of Poitiers and included among his areas of expertise, law and medicine. His interest in medicine led to one of the early formulations of a mechanistic biology.

After his formal education, Descartes became a soldier of fortune, joining different military expeditions. While in winter quarters near Ulm, Germany, he had a series of dreams on the night of December 10, 1619. In these dreams, Descartes was visited by an angel who showed him how he must unite all the sciences and solve all philosophical problems with one grand method. Inspired by such a vision, Descartes set about writing his *Rules for the Direction of the Mind*. He completed the work in 1628, but it remained unpublished until 1701. Later, he wrote a work entitled *The World or Treatise on Light*, but in 1633 upon hearing the news of Galileo's trial, he put the work aside, and it was not published until 1664.

In 1637, having decided that he had already exceeded normal life expectancy, Descartes published his *Discourse on Method,* a work on *Dioptrics, Meteors*, and *Geometry*. All four of these works were intended to introduce the reader to Descartes' thought and to prepare the way for the more radical views he hesitated to publish. His *Meditations on First Philosophy* appeared in 1641; the *Principles of Philosophy* was published in 1644. He died in 1650 after having given one of his frequent 5:00 a.m. lessons in philosophy to the Queen of Sweden.

Scientific Work

In the *Principles of Philosophy*, Descartes presented the first comprehensive theory of the universe. Everything, with the exception of man's rational soul, is given a *mechanical* explanation. All physical phenomena are explainable in terms of motion, and motion is explained by reference to space and time. The world that Descartes envisages may be described as follows: Space is infinite, but space is never empty. Every point of space is occupied by matter. This is called a *plenum.* The essence of matter is extension. Matter is uniform, impenetrable, and infinitely divisible. It is also either at rest or in motion. To explain motion Descartes appeals to direct contact, for he does not accept the existence of action at a distance (gravity). Since every point of the system is occupied by some matter, movement in one part of the system implies movement in all other parts of the system. The first cause of motion in the system is God, but after that the system runs on its own.

Descartes' plenum is opposed to the atomism of the ancient Greek thinker Democritus and to the modern atomism of Gassendi and Newton. What Descartes is describing is more similar to the world of Plato's *Timaeus*; it is called a *corpuscular* theory. The idea that all nature must be filled with some medium, however fine, had a long history, and this medium later came to be known as *ether.* Descartes' insistence on this view is a derivation of his belief that geometry, both in its Euclidean form and in his own analytic geometry, was the whole truth somehow embedded in our mind, and nature must conform to that truth. We can easily recognize this as Platonism. If the atomists were correct, then physics would have to be supplemented with other concepts, dynamic ones for example, which are not found in geometry, and it would become a matter of debatable, empirical fact to discover the properties of atoms.

In astronomy, Descartes attempted a compromise between Copernicus and the older Aristotelian physics. All the motions of the planets are explained by *vortices* (similar to the celestial spheres of the ancients in which the planets were attached and it was really the spheres that moved). All motion then becomes relative to the surrounding medium. Thus, on the one hand the earth could be said to move around the sun, although only within its own vortex, and on the other, the earth could be said to be stationary in relation to other bodies.

In the case of man, Descartes offered a purely mechanical view of the human body, but he traced all the movements of the body through the nervous system to the pineal gland. It was "within" the pineal gland that he found room for man's soul, including his rational faculties and his will. Needless to add, Descartes failed to explain exactly how an unextended thing like the soul could interact with an extended (space-occupying) thing like the brain.

Philosophy

Descartes' philosophy may be briefly *summarized* as follows: his model science is geometry; his notion of explanation is proof. Every proof involves two parts, an original analysis or discovery and a subsequent demonstration. The analysis has two parts, the methodical use of *doubt* designed as a road to intuition, and an intuitive stage in which we grasp simple natures. The simple natures are either material or spiritual. The criterion for truth in Descartes' system is whether our ideas are *clear and distinct.* In his proofs Descartes first establishes the existence of a finite thinking self; then an infinitely powerful and veracious God; and finally, an extended, material universe. His universe may thus be described as having four kinds of entities: an absolute substance (God); relative substances (minds and bodies); attributes (the mind's attribute is thought; the body's attribute is extension); and modes (the mind knows and wills; the body has the modes of figure and movement).

Descartes is easy to identify as a classic Platonic philosopher. To begin with, he describes physics as founded upon metaphysics in the same way as the trunk of a tree is founded upon its roots. The other sciences are like branches of the tree. Thus we are to understand knowledge as forming a formal deductive system like geometry, but the axioms are metaphysical. The metaphysical axioms or first principles are thus crucial in Descartes' philosophy. First principles are not themselves capable of being proved; they must be self-evident. Descartes proposes to find a basic principle that could never be doubted. He argues, like Augustine, that we can never doubt that we doubt. Thus, the one thing we can know for sure is the existence of a thinking self which is finite and immaterial. This is known as the *cogito* (from the Latin "I think"). Not only is this first principle indubitable, but all other principles such as the law of contradiction, the principle of causality, and the notion of substance are guaranteed by it. Thus the cogito is both a first principle and a test to determine if other principles can serve as axioms.

Intuition, for Descartes, springs from the light of reason alone, not from the senses. In fact, intuition is only possible when the mind has been freed from dependence on the senses. The purpose of the analysis of the piece of wax is in part to show how this freedom from the senses is both possible and necessary. Further, Descartes' dualism between the mind and body reflects the more fundamental metaphysical dualism between knowing and existence, wherein existence is but a reflection of knowledge itself. Even probability is interpreted this way, for according to Descartes the evidence in probability is not itself probable, and the decision on how to use it is not made by the senses, but by reason.

Descartes' discussion of God is very instructive. To begin with, the proof of the existence of God is based upon the principle of efficient causality. But the principle itself is supposed to be guaranteed by the cogito. According to Descartes, every effect must have a cause. Moreover, any property of that effect must be the result of a similar property in the cause. We have an idea of a perfect being; but being imperfect ourselves we cannot be the cause of the idea of something perfect. Only something perfect can be the cause of something perfect—even an idea. Hence there must be at least one perfect being. That being is God. What is curious and significant about this principle of efficient causality is that it derives ultimately from Aristotle's physics. However, instead of arguing that we derive this principle from experience, as any Aristotelian would argue, Descartes first makes the principle a metaphysical, not a physical one, and then argues that it is a self-evident principle guaranteed by the cogito. According to Descartes the principle of efficient causality (every property of an effect is the result of a similar property in the cause) is clear and distinct and cannot be doubted. Descartes' proof for God is Platonic in that it flows from the cogito, not from the order of the world.

When Descartes comes to explain human error, he offers us the typical Platonic contrast between reason and passion. Our reason is finite but our will is infinite. This creates a tension which sometimes leads the passions to overcome our reason. When this happens we are led into error. As long as reason prevails we cannot be in error.

There are, of course, some unresolved difficulties in Descartes' philosophy. We mention just one. According to Descartes, the basic truths are contingent upon God's will. But for a consistent Platonist, if he be one, this is not possible. Recall the Socratic question: Is it right because the gods want it, or do the gods want it because it is right? Platonists would seem to require the latter. This, in fact, is what the great philosopher Leibniz will urge, against Descartes, who appeared to argue for the former possibility.

Meditations on the First Philosophy

IN WHICH

THE EXISTENCE OF GOD, AND THE
REAL DISTINCTION OF MIND AND
BODY, ARE DEMONSTRATED

MEDITATION I

OF THE THINGS ON WHICH WE MAY DOUBT

Several years have now elapsed since I first became aware that I had accepted, even from my youth, many false opinions for true, and that consequently what I afterward based on such principles was highly doubtful; and from that time I was convinced of the necessity of undertaking once in my life to rid myself of all the opinions I had adopted, and of commencing anew the work of building from the foundation, if I desired to establish a firm and abiding superstructure in the sciences. But as this enterprise appeared to me to be one of great magnitude, I waited until I had attained an age so mature as to leave me no hope that at any stage of life more advanced I should be better able to execute my design. On this account, I have delayed so long that I should henceforth consider I was doing wrong were I still to consume in deliberation any of the time that now remains for action. To-day, then, since I have opportunely freed my mind from all cares [and am happily disturbed by no passions], and since I am in the secure possession of leisure in a peaceable retirement, I will at length apply myself earnestly and freely to the general overthrow of all my former opinions.

But, to this end, it will not be necessary for me to show that the whole of these are false—a point, perhaps, which I shall never reach; but as even now my reason convinces me that I ought not the less carefully to withhold belief from what is not entirely certain and indubitable, than from what is manifestly false, it will be sufficient to justify the rejection of the whole if I shall find in each some ground for doubt. Nor for this purpose will it be necessary even to deal with each belief individually, which would be truly an endless labor; but, as the removal from below of the foundation necessarily involves the downfall of the whole edifice, I will at once approach the criticism of the principles on which all my former beliefs rested.

All that I have, up to this moment, accepted as possessed of the highest truth and certainty, I received either from or through the senses. I observed, however, that these sometimes misled us; and it is the part of prudence not to place absolute confidence in that by which we have even once been deceived.

But it may be said, perhaps, that, although the senses, occasionally mislead us respecting minute objects, and such as are so far removed from us as to be beyond the reach of close observation, there are yet many other of their informations (presentations), of the truth of which it is manifestly impossible to doubt; as for example, that I am in this place, seated by the fire, clothed in a winter dressing gown, that I hold in my hands this piece of paper, with other intimations of the same nature. But how could I deny that I possess these hands and this body, and withal escape being classed with persons in a state of insanity, whose brains are so disordered and clouded by dark bilious vapors as to cause them pertinaciously to assert that they are monarchs when they are in the greatest poverty; or clothed [in gold] and purple when destitute of any covering; or that their head is made of clay, their body of glass, or that they are gourds? I should certainly be not less insane than they, were I to regulate my procedure according to examples so extravagant.

Though this be true, I must nevertheless here consider that I am a man, and that, consequently, I am in the habit of sleeping, and representing to myself in dreams those same things, or even sometimes others less probable, which the insane think are presented to them in their waking moments. How often have I dreamt that I was in these familiar circumstances, that I was dressed, and occupied this place by the fire, when I was lying undressed in bed? At the present moment, however, I certainly look upon this paper with eyes wide awake; the head which I now move is not asleep; I extend this hand consciously and with express purpose, and I perceive it; the occurrences in sleep are not so distinct as all this. But I cannot forget that, at other times I have been deceived in sleep by similar illusions; and, attentively considering those cases, I perceive too clearly that there exist no certain marks by which the state of waking can ever be distinguished from sleep, that I feel greatly astonished; and in amazement I almost persuade myself that I am now dreaming.

Let us suppose, then, that we are dreaming, and that all these particulars—namely, the opening of the eyes, the motion of the head, the forth-putting of the hands—are merely illusions; and even that we really possess neither an entire body nor hands such as we see. Nevertheless it must be admitted at least that the objects which appear to us in sleep are, as it were, painted representations which could not have been formed unless in the likeness of realities; and, therefore, that those general objects, at all events, namely, eyes, a head, hands, and an entire body, are not simply imaginary, but really existent. For, in truth, painters themselves, even when they study to represent sirens and satyrs by forms the most fantastic and extraordinary, cannot bestow upon them natures absolutely new, but can only make a certain medley of the members of different animals; or if they chance to imagine something so novel that nothing at all similar

has ever been seen before, and such as is, therefore, purely fictitious and absolutely false, it is at least certain that the colors of which this is composed are real.

And on the same principle, although these general objects, viz, eyes, a head, hands, and the like, be imaginary, we are nevertheless absolutely necessitated to admit the reality at least of some other objects still more simple and universal than these, of which, just as of certain real colors, all those images of things, whether true and real, or false and fantastic, that are found in our consciousness (*cogitatio*), are formed.

To this class of objects seem to belong corporeal nature in general and its extension; the figure of extended things, their quantity or magnitude, and their number, as also the place in, and the time during, which they exist, and other things of the same sort. We will not, therefore, perhaps reason illegitimately if we conclude from this that Physics, Astronomy, Medicine, and all the other sciences that have for their end the consideration of composite objects, are indeed of a doubtful character; but that Arithmetic, Geometry, and the other sciences of the same class, which regard merely the simplest and most general objects, and scarcely inquire whether or not these are really existent, contain somewhat that is certain and indubitable: for whether I am awake or dreaming, it remains true that two and three make five, and that a square has but four sides; nor does it seem possible that truths so apparent can ever fall under a suspicion of falsity [or incertitude].

Nevertheless, the belief that there is a God who is all powerful, and who created me, such as I am, has, for a long time, obtained steady possession of my mind. How, then, do I know that he has not arranged that there should be neither earth, nor sky, nor any extended thing, nor figure, nor magnitude, nor place, providing at the same time, however, for [the rise in me of the perceptions of all these objects, and] the persuasion that these do not exist otherwise than as I perceive them? And further, as I sometimes think that others are in error respecting matters of which they believe themselves to possess a perfect knowledge, how do I know that I am not also deceived each time I add together two and three, or number the sides of a square, or form some judgment still more simple, if more simple indeed can be imagined? But perhaps God has not been willing that I should be thus deceived, for he is said to be supremely good. If, however, it were repugnant to the goodness of God to have created me subject to constant deception, it would seem likewise to be contrary to his goodness to allow me to be occasionally deceived; and yet it is clear that this is permitted. Some, indeed, might perhaps be found who would be disposed rather to deny the existence of a Being so powerful than to believe that there is nothing certain. But let us for the present refrain from opposing this opinion, and grant that all which is here said of a God is fabulous: nevertheless, in whatever way it be supposed that I reach the state in which I exist, whether by fate, or chance, or by an endless series of antecedents and consequents, or by any other means, it is clear (since to be deceived and to err is a certain defect) that the probability of my being so imperfect as to be the constant victim of deception, will be increased exactly in proportion as the power possessed by the cause, to which they assign my origin, is lessened. To these reasonings I have assuredly nothing to reply, but am constrained at last to avow that there is nothing of all that I formerly believed to be true of which it is impossible to doubt, and that not through thoughtlessness or levity, but from cogent and maturely considered reasons; so that henceforward, if I desire to discover anything certain, I ought not the less carefully to refrain from assenting to those same opinions than to what might be shown to be manifestly false.

But it is not sufficient to have made these observations; care must be taken likewise to keep them in remembrance. For those old and customary opinions perpetually recur—long and familiar usage giving them the right of occupying my mind, even almost against my will, and subduing my belief; nor will I lose the habit of deferring to them and confiding in them so long as I shall consider them to be what in truth they are, viz, opinions to some extent doubtful, as I have already shown, but still highly probable, and such as it is much more reasonable to believe than deny. It is for this reason I am persuaded that I shall not be doing wrong, if, taking an opposite judgment of deliberate design, I become my own deceiver, by supposing, for a time, that all those opinions are entirely false and imaginary, until at length, having thus balanced my old by my new prejudices, my judgment shall no longer be turned aside by perverted usage from the path that may conduct to the perception of truth. For I am assured that, meanwhile, there will arise neither peril nor error from this course, and that I cannot for the present yield too much to distrust, since the end I now seek is not action but knowledge.

I will suppose, then, not that God, who is sovereignly good and the fountain of truth, but that some malignant demon, who is at once exceedingly potent and deceitful, has employed all his artifice to deceive me; I will suppose that the sky, the air, the earth, colors, figures, sounds, and all external things, are nothing better than the illusions of dreams, by means of which this being has laid snares for my credulity; I will consider myself as without hands, eyes, flesh, blood, or any of the senses, and as falsely believing that I am possessed of these; I will continue resolutely fixed in this belief, and if indeed by this means it be not in my power to arrive at the knowledge of truth, I shall at least do what is in my power, viz [suspend my judgment], and guard with settled purpose against giving my assent to what is false, and being imposed upon by this deceiver, whatever be his power and artifice.

But this undertaking is arduous, and a certain indolence insensibly leads me back to my ordinary course of life; and just as the captive, who, perchance, was enjoying in his dreams an imaginary liberty, when he begins to suspect that it is but a vision, dreads awakening, and conspires with the agreeable illusions that the deception may be prolonged; so I, of my own accord, fall back into the train of my former beliefs, and fear to arouse myself from my slumber, lest the time of laborious wakefulness that would succeed this quiet rest, in place of bringing any light of day, should prove inadequate to dispel the darkness that will arise from the difficulties that have now been raised.

MEDITATION II

OF THE NATURE OF THE HUMAN MIND; AND THAT IT IS MORE EASILY KNOWN THAN THE BODY

The Meditation of yesterday has filled my

mind with so many doubts, that it is no longer in my power to forget them. Nor do I see, meanwhile, any principle on which they can be resolved; and, just as if I had fallen all of a sudden into very deep water, I am so greatly disconcerted as to be unable either to plant my feet firmly on the bottom or sustain myself by swimming on the surface. I will, nevertheless, make an effort, and try anew the same path on which I had entered yesterday, that is, proceed by casting aside all that admits of the slightest doubt, not less than if I had discovered it to be absolutely false; and I will continue always in this track until I shall find somethng that is certain, or at least, if I can do nothing more, until I shall know with certainty that there is nothing certain. Archimedes, that he might transport the entire globe from the place it occupied to another, demanded only a point that was firm and immovable; so, also, I shall be entitled to entertain the highest expectations, if I am fortunate enough to discover only one thing that is certain and indubitable.

I suppose, accordingly, that all the things which I see are false (fictitious); I believe that none of those objects which my fallacious memory represents ever existed; I suppose that I possess no senses; I believe that body, figure, extension, motion, and place are merely fictions of my mind. What is there, then, that can be esteemed true? Perhaps this only, that there is absolutely nothing certain.

But how do I know that there is not something different altogether from the objects I have now enumerated, of which it is impossible to entertain the slightest doubt? Is there not a God, or some being, by whatever name I may designate him, who causes these thoughts to arise in my mind? But why suppose such a being, for it may be I myself am capable of producing them? Am I, then, at least not something? But I before denied that I possessed senses or a body; I hesitate, however, for what follows from that? Am I so dependent on the body and the senses that without these I cannot exist? But I had the persuasion that there was absolutely nothing in the world, that there was no sky and no earth, neither minds nor bodies; was I not, therefore, at the same time, persuaded that I did not exist? Far from it; I assuredly existed, since I was persuaded. But there is I know not what being, who is possessed at once of the highest power and the deepest

cunning, who is constantly employing all his ingenuity in deceiving me. Doubtless, then, I exist, since I am deceived; and, let him deceive me as he may, he can never bring it about that I am nothing, so long as I remain conscious that I am something. So that it must, in fine, be maintained, all things being maturely and carefully considered, that this proposition (*pronunciatum*) I am, I exist, is necessarily true each time it is expressed by me, or conceived in my mind.

But I do not yet know with sufficient clearness what I am, though assured that I am; and hence, in the next place, I must take care, lest perchance I inconsiderately substitute some other object in room of what is properly myself, and thus wander from truth, even in that knowledge (cognition) which I hold to be of all others the most certain and evident. For this reason, I will now consider anew what I formerly believed myself to be, before I entered on the present train of thought; and of my previous opinion I will retrench all that can in the least be invalidated by the grounds of doubt I have adduced, in order that there may at length remain nothing but what is certain and indubitable. What then did I formerly think I was? Undoubtedly I judged that I was a man. But what is a man? Shall I say a rational animal? Assuredly not; for it would be necessary forthwith to inquire into what is meant by animal, and what by rational, and thus, from a single question, I should insensibly glide into others, and these more difficult than the first; nor do I now possess enough of leisure to warrant me in wasting my time amid subtleties of this sort. I prefer here to attend to the thoughts that sprung up of themselves in my mind, and were inspired by my own nature alone, when I applied myself to the consideration of what I was. In the first place, then, I thought that I possessed a countenance, hands, arms, and all the fabric of members that appears in a corpse, and which I called by the name of body. It further occurred to me that I was nourished, that I walked, perceived, and thought, and all those actions I referred to the soul; but what the soul itself was I either did not stay to consider, or, if I did, I imagined that it was something extremely rare and subtile, like wind, or flame, or ether, spread through my grosser parts. As regarded the body, I did not even doubt of its nature, but thought I distinctly knew it, and if I had wished to describe it according to the notions I then entertained, I should have explained myself in this manner: By body I understand all that can be terminated by a certain figure; that can be comprised in a certain place, and so fill a certain space as therefrom to exclude every other body; that can be perceived either by touch, sight, hearing, taste, or smell; that can be moved in different ways, not indeed of itself, but by something foreign to it by which it is touched and from which it receives the impression; for the power of self-motion, as likewise that of perceiving and thinking, I held as by no means pertaining to the nature of body; on the contrary, I was somewhat astonished to find such faculties existing in some bodies.

But as to myself, what can I now say that I am, since I suppose there exists an extremely powerful, and, if I may so speak, malignant being, whose whole endeavors are directed toward deceiving me? Can I affirm that I possess any one of all those attributes of which I have lately spoken as belonging to the nature of body? After attentively considering them in my own mind, I find none of them that can properly be said to belong to myself. To recount them were idle and tedious. Let us pass, then, to the attributes of the soul. The first mentioned were the powers of nutrition and walking; but, if it be true that I have no body, it is true likewise that I am capable neither of walking nor of being nourished. Perception is another attribute of the soul; but perception too is impossible without the body; besides, I have frequently, during sleep, believed that I perceived objects which I afterward observed I did not in reality perceive. Thinking is another attribute of the soul; and here I discover what properly belongs to myself. This alone is inseparable from me. I am—I exist: this is certain; but how often? As often as I think; for perhaps it would even happen, if I should wholly cease to think, that I should at the same time altogether cease to be. I now admit nothing that is not necessarily true. I am therefore, precisely speaking, only a thinking thing, that is, a mind (*mens sive animus*), understanding, or reason, terms whose signification was before unknown to me. I am, however, a real thing, and really existent; but what thing? The answer was, a thinking thing. The question now arises, am I something besides? I will stimulate my imagina-

tion with a view to discover whether I am not still something more than a thinking being. Now it is plain I am not the assemblage of members called the human body; I am not a thin and penetrating air diffused through all these members, or wind, or flame, or vapor, or breath, or any of all the things I can imagine; for I supposed that all these were not, and, without changing the supposition, I find that I still feel assured of my existence.

But it is true, perhaps, that those very things which I suppose to be non-existent, because they are unknown to me, are not in truth different from myself whom I know. This is a point I cannot determine, and do not now enter into any dispute regarding it. I can only judge of things that are known to me: I am conscious that I exist, and I who know that I exist inquire into what I am. It is, however, perfectly certain that the knowledge of my existence, thus precisely taken, is not dependent on things, the existence of which is as yet unknown to me: and consequently it is not dependent on any of the things I can feign in imagination. Moreover, the phrase itself, I frame an image (*effingo*), reminds me of my error; for I should in truth frame one if I were to imagine myself to be anything, since to imagine is nothing more than to contemplate the figure or image of a corporeal thing; but I already know that I exist, and that it is possible at the same time that all those images, and in general all that relates to the nature of body, are merely dreams or chimeras. From this I discover that it is not more reasonable to say, I will excite my imagination that I may know more distinctly what I am, than to express myself as follows: I am now awake, and perceive something real; but because my perception is not sufficiently clear, I will of express purpose go to sleep that my dreams may represent to me the object of my perception with more truth and clearness. And, therefore, I know that nothing of all that I can embrace in imagination belongs to the knowledge which I have of myself, and that there is need to recall with the utmost care the mind from this mode of thinking, that it may be able to know its own nature with perfect distinctness.

But what, then, am I? A thinking thing, it has been said. But what is a thinking thing? It is a thing that doubts, understands, conceives, affirms, denies, wills, refuses; that imagines also, and perceives. Assuredly it is not little, if all these properties belong to my nature. But why should they not belong to it? Am I not that very being who now doubts of almost everything; who, for all that, understands and conceives certain things; who affirms one alone as true, and denies the others; who desires to know more of them, and does not wish to be deceived; who imagines many things, sometimes even despite his will; and is likewise percipient of many, as if through the medium of the senses. Is there nothing of all this as true as that I am, even although I should be always dreaming, and although he who gave me being employed all his ingenuity to deceive me? Is there also any one of these attributes that can be properly distinguished from my thought, or that can be said to be separate from myself? For it is of itself so evident that it is I who doubt, I who understand, and I who desire, that it is here unnecessary to add anything by way of rendering it more clear. And I am as certainly the same being who imagines; for although it may be (as I before supposed) that nothing I imagine is true, still the power of imagination does not cease really to exist in me and to form part of my thought. In fine, I am the same being who perceives, that is, who apprehends certain objects as by the organs of sense, since, in truth, I see light, hear a noise, and feel heat. But it will be said that these presentations are false, and that I am dreaming. Let is be so. At all events it is certain that I seem to see light, hear a noise, and feel heat; this cannot be false, and this is what in me is properly called perceiving (*sentire*), which is nothing else than thinking. From this I begin to know what I am with somewhat greater clearness and distinctness than heretofore.

But, nevertheless, it still seems to me, and I cannot help believing, that corporeal things, whose images are formed by thought which fall under the senses, and are examined by the same, are known with much greater distinctness than that I know not what part of myself which is not imaginable; although, in truth, it may seem strange to say that I know and comprehend with greater distinctness things whose existence appears to me doubtful, that are unknown, and do not belong to me, than others of whose reality I am persuaded, that are known to me, and appertain to my proper nature; in a word, than myself. But I see clearly what is the state of the case. My mind is apt to wander, and will not yet submit to be restrained within the limits of truth. Let us therefore leave the mind to itself once more, and, according to it every kind of liberty permit it to consider the objects that appear to it from without, in order that, having afterward withdrawn it from these gently and opportunely and fixed it on the consideration of its being and the properties it finds in itself, it may then be the more easily controlled.

Let us now accordingly consider the objects that are commonly thought to be the most easily, and likewise *the most distinctly known,* viz, the bodies we touch and see; not, indeed, bodies in general, for these general notions are usually somewhat more confused, but one body in particular. Take, for example, this piece of wax; it is quite fresh, having been but recently taken from the beehive; it has not yet lost the sweetness of the honey it contained; it still retains somewhat of the odor of the flowers from which it was gathered; its color, figure, size, are apparent (to the sight); it is hard, cold, easily handled; and sounds when struck upon with the finger. In fine, all that contributes to make a body as distinctly known as possible, is found in the one before us. But, while I am speaking, let it be placed near the fire—what remained of the taste exhales, the smell evaporates, the color changes, its figure is destroyed, its size increases, it becomes liquid, it grows hot, it can hardly be handled, and, although struck upon, it emits no sound. Does the same wax still remain after this change? It must be admitted that it does remain; no one doubts it, or judges otherwise. What then was it I knew with so much distinctness in the piece of wax? Assuredly, it could be nothing of all that I observed by means of the senses, since all the things that fell under taste, smell, sight, touch, and hearing are changed, and yet the same wax remains. It was perhaps what I now think, viz, that this wax was neither the sweetness of honey, the pleasant odor of flowers, the whiteness, the figure, nor the sound, but only a body that a little before appeared to me conspicuous under these forms, and which is now perceived under others. But, to speak precisely, what is it that I imagine when I think of it in this way? Let it be attentively considered, and, retrenching all that does not belong to the wax, let us see what remains. There certainly remains nothing, except something extended, flexible, and movable. But what is meant by flexible and movable? Is it not that I imagine that the piece of wax, being round, is capable of becoming square, or of passing from a square into a triangular figure? Assuredly such is not the case, because I conceive that it admits of an infinity of similar changes; and I am, moreover, unable to compass this infinity by imagination, and consequently this conception which I have of the wax is not the product of the faculty of imagination. But what now is this extension? Is it not also unknown? for it becomes greater when the wax is melted, greater when it is boiled, and greater still when the heat increases; and I should not conceive clearly and according to truth, the wax as it is, if I did not suppose that the piece we are considering admitted even of a wider variety of extension than I ever imagined. I must, therefore, admit that I cannot even comprehend by imagination what the piece of wax is, and that it is the mind alone which perceives it. I speak of one piece in particular; for as to wax in general, this is still more evident. But what is the piece of wax that can be perceived only by the understanding or mind? It is certainly the same which I see, touch, imagine. But (and this it is of moment to observe) the perception of it is neither an act of sight, of touch, nor of imagination, and never was either of these, though it might formerly seem so, but is simply an intuition (*inspectio*) of the mind, which may be imperfect and confused, as it formerly was, or very clear and distinct, as it is at present, according as the attention is more or less directed to the elements which it contains, and of which it is composed.

But, meanwhile, I feel greatly astonished when I observe the weakness of my mind, and its proneness to error. For although,. without at all giving expression to what I think, I consider all this in my own mind, words yet occasionally impede my progress, and I am almost led into error by the terms of ordinary language. We say, for example, that we see the same wax when it is before us, and not that we judge it to be the same from its retaining the same color and figure: whence I should forthwith be disposed to conclude that the wax is known by the act of sight, and not by the intuition of the mind alone, were it not for the analogous instance of human beings passing on in the street below, as observed from a window. In this case

I do not fail to say that I see the men themselves, just as I say that I see the wax; and yet what do I see from the window beyond hats and cloaks that might cover artificial machines, whose motions might be determined by springs? But I judge that there are human beings from these appearances, and thus I comprehend, by the faculty of judgment alone which is in the mind, what I believed I saw with my eyes.

The man who makes it his aim to rise to knowledge superior to the common, ought to be ashamed to seek occasions of doubting from the vulgar forms of speech: instead, therefore, of doing this, I shall proceed with the matter in hand, and inquire whether I had a clearer and more perfect perception of the piece of wax when I first saw it, and when I thought I knew it by means of the external sense itself, or, at all events, by the common sense (*sensus communis*), as it is called, that is, by the imaginative faculty; or whether I rather apprehend it more clearly at present, after having examined with greater care, both what it is, and in what way it can be known. It would certainly be ridiculous to entertain any doubt on this point. For what, in that first perception, was there distinct? What did I perceive which any animal might not have perceived? But when I distinguish the wax from its exterior forms, and when, as if I had stripped it of its vestments, I consider it quite naked, it is certain, although some error may still be found in my judgment, that I cannot, nevertheless, thus apprehend it without possessing a human mind.

But, finally, what shall I say of the mind itself, that is, of myself? for as yet I do not admit that I am anything but mind. What, then! I who seem to possess so distinct an apprehension of the piece of wax, do I not know myself, both with greater truth and certitude, and also much more distinctly and clearly? For if I judge that the wax exists because I see it, it assuredly follows, much more evidently, that I myself am or exist, for the same reason: for it is possible that what I see may not in truth be wax, and that I do not even possess eyes with which to see anything; but it cannot be that when I see, or, which comes to the same thing, when I think I see, I myself who think am nothing. So likewise, if I judge that the wax exists because I touch it, it will also follow that I am; and if I determine that my imagination, or any other cause, whatever it be, persuades me of the exist-ence of the wax, I will still draw the same con-clusion. And what is here remarked of the piece of wax, is applicable to all the other things that are external to me. And further, if the (notion or) perception of wax appeared to me more pre-cise and distinct, after that not only sight and touch, but many other causes besides, ren-dered it manifest to my apprehension, with how much greater distinctness must I now know my-self, since all the reasons that contribute to the knowledge of the nature of wax, or of any body whatever, manifest still better the nature of my mind? And there are besides so many other things in the mind itself that contribute to the illustration of its nature, that those dependent on the body, to which I have here referred, scarcely merit to be taken into account.

But, in conclusion, I find I have insensibly reverted to the point I desired; for, since it is now manifest to me that bodies themselves are not properly perceived by the senses nor by the faculty of imagination, but by the intellect alone; and since they are not perceived because they are seen and touched, but only because they are understood (or rightly comprehended by thought), I readily discover that there is nothing more easily or clearly apprehended than my own mind. But because it is difficult to rid one's self so promptly of an opinion to which one has been long accustomed, it will be desirable to tarry for some time at this stage, that, by long continued meditation, I may more deeply impress upon my memory this new knowledge.

MEDITATION III

OF GOD: THAT HE EXISTS

I will now close my eyes, I will stop my ears, I will turn away my senses from their objects, I will even efface from my consciousness all the images of corporeal things; or at least, because this can hardly be accomplished, I will con-sider them as empty and false; and thus, hold-ing converse only with myself, and closely ex-amining my nature, I will endeavor to obtain by degrees a more intimate and familiar knowl-edge of myself. I am a thinking (conscious) thing, that is, a being who doubts, affirms, denies, knows a few objects, and is ignorant of many,—(who loves, hates), wills, refuses, who

imagines likewise, and perceives; for, as I be-fore remarked, although the things which I per-ceive or imagine are perhaps nothing at all apart from me (and in themselves), I am never-theless assured that those modes of conscious-ness which I call perceptions and imaginations, in as far only as they are modes of conscious-ness, exist in me. And in the little I have said I think I have summed up all that I really know, or at least all that up to this time I was aware I knew. Now, as I am endeavoring to extend my knowledge more widely, I will use circumspec-tion, and consider with care whether I can still discover in myself anything further which I have not yet hitherto observed. I am certain that I am a thinking thing; but do I not there-fore likewise know what is required to render me certain of a truth? In this first knowledge, doubtless, there is nothing that gives me as-surance of its truth except the clear and dis-tinct perception of what I affirm, which would not indeed be sufficient to give me the assur-ance that what I say is true, if it could ever hap-pen that anything I thus clearly and distinctly perceived should prove false; and accordingly it seems to me that I may now take as a general rule, that all that is very clearly and distinctly apprehended (conceived) is true.

Nevertheless I before received and admitted many things as wholly certain and manifest, which yet I afterward found to be doubtful. What, then, were those? They were the earth, the sky, the stars, and all the other objects which I was in the habit of perceiving by the senses. But what was it that I clearly and dis-tinctly perceived in them? Nothing more than that the ideas and the thoughts of those objects were presented to my mind. And even now I do not deny that these ideas are found in my mind. But there was yet another thing which I af-firmed, and which, from having been accus-tomed to believe it, I thought I clearly per-ceived, although, in truth, I did not perceive it at all; I mean the existence of objects external to me, from which those ideas proceeded, and to which they had a perfect resemblance; and it was here I was mistaken, or if I judged correct-ly, this assuredly was not to be traced to any knowledge I possessed.

But when I considered any matter in arith-metic and geometry, that was very simple and easy, as, for example, that two and three added together make five, and things of this sort, did I not view them with at least sufficient clearness to warrant me in affirming their truth? Indeed, if I afterward judged that we ought to doubt of these things, it was for no other reason than because it occurred to me that a God might perhaps have given me such a nature as that I should be deceived, even respecting the matters that appeared to me the most evidently true. But as often as this preconceived opinion of the sovereign power of a God presents itself to my mind, I am constrained to admit that it is easy for him, if he wishes it, to cause me to err, even in matters where I think I possess the highest evidence; and, on the other hand, as often as I direct my attention to things which I think I apprehend with great clearness, I am so persuaded of their truth that I naturally break out into expressions such as these: Deceive me who may, no one will yet ever be able to bring it about that I am not, so long as I shall be conscious that I am, or at any future time cause it to be true that I have never been, it being now true that I am, or make two and three more or less than five, in supposing which, and other like absurdities, I discover a manifest contradiction.

And in truth, as I have no ground for believing that God is deceitful, and as, indeed, I have not even considered the reasons by which the existence of God of any kind is established, the ground of doubt that rests only on this supposition is very slight, and, so to speak, metaphysical. But, that I may be able wholly to remove it, I must inquire whether there is a God, as soon as an opportunity of doing so shall present itself; and if I find that there is a God, I must examine likewise whether he can be a deceiver; for, without the knowledge of these two truths, I do not see that I can ever be certain of anything. And that I may be enabled to examine this without interrupting the order of meditation I have proposed to myself which is, to pass by degrees from the notions that I shall find first in my mind to those I shall afterward discover in it, it is necessary at this stage to divide all my thoughts into certain classes, and to consider in which of these classes truth and error are, strictly speaking, to be found.

Of my thoughts some are, as it were, images of things, and to these alone properly belong the name ideas; as when I think [represent to my mind] a man, a chimera, the sky, an angel or God. Others, again, have certain other forms; as when I will, fear, affirm, or deny, I always, indeed, apprehend something as the object of my thought, but I also embrace in thought something more than the representation of the object; and of this class of thoughts some are called volitions or affections, and others judgments.

Now, with respect to ideas, if these are considered only in themselves, and are not referred to any object beyond them, they cannot, properly speaking, be false; for, whether I imagine a goat or chimera, it is not less true that I imagine the one than the other. Nor need we fear that falsity may exist in the will or affections; for, although I may desire objects that are wrong, and even that never existed, it is still true that I desire them. There thus only remain our judgments, in which we must take diligent heed that we be not deceived. But the chief and most ordinary error that arises in them consists in judging that the ideas which are in us are conformed to the things that are external to us; for assuredly, if we but considered the ideas themselves as certain modes of our thought (consciousness), without referring them to anything beyond, they could hardly afford any occasion of error.

But among these ideas, some appear to me to be innate, others adventitious, and others to be made by myself (factitious); for, as I have the power of conceiving what is called a thing, or a truth, or a thought, it seems to me that I hold this power from no other source than my own nature; but if I now hear a noise, if I see the sun, or if I feel heat, I have all along judged that these sensations proceeded from certain objects existing out of myself; and, in fine, it appears to me that sirens, hippogryphs, and the like, are inventions of my own mind. But I may even perhaps come to be of opinion that all my ideas are of the class which I call adventitious, or that they are all innate, or that they are all factitious; for I have not yet clearly discovered their true origin; and what I have here principally to do is to consider, with reference to those that appear to come from certain objects without me, what grounds there are for thinking them like these objects.

The first of these grounds is that it seems to me I am so taught by nature; and the second that I am conscious that those ideas are not dependent on my will, and therefore not in myself, for they are frequently presented to me against my will, as at present, whether I will or not, I feel heat; and I am thus persuaded that this sensation or idea (*sensum vel ideam*) of heat is produced in me by something different from myself, viz., by the heat of the fire by which I sit. And it is very reasonable to suppose that this object impresses me with its own likeness rather than any other thing.

But I must consider whether these reasons are sufficiently strong and convincing. When I speak of being taught by nature in this matter, I understand by the word nature only a certain spontaneous impetus that impels me to believe in a resemblance between ideas and their objects, and not a natural light that affords a knowledge of its truth. But these two things are widely different; for what the natural light shows to be true can be in no degree doubtful, as, for example, that I am because I doubt, and other truths of the like kind; inasmuch as I possess no other faculty whereby to distinguish truth from error, which can teach me the falsity of what the natural light declares to be true, and which is equally trustworthy; but with respect to seemingly natural impulses, I have observed, when the question related to the choice of right or wrong in action, that they frequently led me to take the worse part; nor do I see that I have any better ground for following them in what relates to truth and error. Then, with respect to the other reason, which is that because these ideas do not depend on my will, they must arise from objects existing without me, I do not find it more convincing than the former; for just as those natural impulses, of which I have lately spoken, are found in me, notwithstanding that they are not always in harmony with my will, so likewise it may be that I possess some power not sufficiently known to myself capable of producing ideas without the aid of external objects, and, indeed, it has always hitherto appeared to me that they are formed during sleep, by some power of this nature, without the aid of something external. And, in fine, although I should grant that they proceeded from those objects, it is not a necessary consequence that they must be like them. On the contrary, I have observed, in a number of instances, that there was a great difference between the object and its idea. Thus, for example, I find in my mind two wholly diverse ideas of the sun; the one, by which it appears to me extremely small draws its origin from the senses; and should be placed in the class of

adventitious ideas; the other, by which it seems to be many times larger than the whole earth, is taken up on astronomical grounds, that is, elicited from certain notions born with me, or is framed by myself in some other manner. These two ideas cannot certainly both resemble the same sun; and reason teaches me that the one which seems to have immediately emanated from it is the most unlike. And these things sufficiently prove that hitherto it has not been from a certain and deliberate judgment, but only from a sort of blind impulse, that I believe in the existence of certain things different from myself, which, by the organs of sense, or by whatever other means it might be, conveys their ideas or images into my mind and impressed it with their likenesses.

But there is still another way of inquiring whether, of the objects whose ideas are in my mind, there are any that exist out of me. If ideas are taken in so far only as they are certain modes of consciousness, I do not remark any difference or inequality among them, and all seem, in the same manner, to proceed from myself; but, considering them as images, of which one represents one thing and another a different, it is evident that a great diversity obtains among them. For, without doubt, those that represent substances are something more, and contain in themselves, so to speak, more objective reality [that is, participate by representation in higher degrees of being or perfection], than those that represent only modes or accidents; and again, the idea by which I conceive a God sovereign, eternal, infinite, immutable, all-knowing, all-powerful, and the creator of all things that are out of himself, this, I say, has certainly in it more objective reality than those ideas by which finite substances are represented.

Now, it is manifest by the natural light that there must at least be as much reality in the efficient and total cause as in its effect; for whence can the effect draw its reality if not from its cause? And how could the cause communicate to it this reality unless it possessed it in itself? And hence it follows, not only that what is cannot be produced by what is not, but likewise that the more perfect, in other words, that which contains in itself more reality, cannot be the effect of the less perfect; and this is not only evidently true of those effects, whose reality is actual or formal, but likewise of ideas, whose reality is only considered as objective. Thus, for example, the stone that is not yet in existence, not only cannot now commence to be, unless it be produced by that which possesses in itself, formally or eminently, all that enters into its composition, [in other words, by that which contains in itself the same properties that are in the stone, or others superior to them]; and heat can only be produced in a subject that was before devoid of it, by a cause that is of an order, degree or kind, at least as perfect as heat; and so of the others. But further, even the idea of the heat, or of the stone, cannot exist in me unless it be put there by a cause that contains, at least, as much reality as I conceive existent in the heat or in the stone: for although that cause may not transmit into my idea anything of its actual or formal reality, we ought not on this account to imagine that it is less real; but we ought to consider, that, as every idea is a work of the mind, its nature is such as of itself to demand no other formal reality than that which it borrows from our consciousness, of which it is but a mode [that is, a manner or way of thinking]. But in order that an idea may contain this objective reality rather than that, it must doubtless derive it from some cause in which is found at least as much formal reality as the idea contains of objective; for, if we suppose that there is found in an idea anything which was not in its cause, it must of course derive this from nothing.

But, however, imperfect may be the mode of existence by which a thing is objectively [or by representation] in the understanding by its idea, we certainly cannot, for all that, allege that this mode of existence is nothing, nor, consequently, that the idea owes its origin to nothing. Nor must it be imagined that, since the reality which is considered in these ideas is only objective, the same reality need not be formally (actually) in the causes of these ideas, but only objectively: for, just as the mode of existing objectively belongs to ideas by their peculiar nature, so likewise the mode of existing formally appertains to the causes of these ideas (at least to the first and principal), by their peculiar nature. And although an idea may give rise to another idea, this regress cannot, nevertheless, be infinite; we must in the end reach a first idea, the cause of which is, as it were, the archetype in which all the reality [or

perfection] that is found objectively in these ideas is contained formally. I am thus clearly taught by the natural light that ideas exist in me as pictures or images, which may, in truth, readily fall short of the perfection of the objects from which they are taken, but can never contain anything greater or more perfect.

And in proportion to the time and care with which I examine all those matters, the conviction of their truth brightens and becomes distinct. But, to sum up, what conclusion shall I draw from it all? It is this: if the objective reality [or perfection] of any one of my ideas be such as clearly to convince me, that this same reality exists in me neither formally nor eminently, and if, as follows from this, I myself cannot be the cause of it, it is a necessary consequence that I am not alone in the world, but that there is besides myself some other being who exists as the cause of that idea; while, on the contrary, if no such idea be found in my mind, I shall have no sufficient ground of assurance of the existence of any other being besides myself; for, after a most careful search, I have, up to this moment, been unable to discover any other ground.

But, among these my ideas, besides that which represents myself, respecting which there can be here no difficulty, there is one that represents a God; others that represent corporeal and inanimate things; others angels; other animals; and, finally, there are some that represent men like myself. But with respect to the ideas that represent other men, or animals, or angels, I can easily suppose that they were formed by the mingling and composition of the other ideas which I have of myself, of corporeal things, and of God, although they were, apart from myself, neither men, animals, nor angels. And with regard to the ideas of corporeal objects, I never discovered in them anything so great or excellent which I myself did not appear capable of originating; for, by considering these ideas closely and scrutinizing them individually, in the same way that I yesterday examined the idea of wax, I find that there is but little in them that is clearly and distinctly perceived. As belonging to the class of things that are clearly apprehended, I recognize the following, viz, magnitude or extension in length, breadth, and depth; figure, which results from the termination of extension; situation, which bodies of diverse figures preserve with reference to each other; and motion or the change of situation; to which may be added substance, duration, and number. But with regard to light, colors, sounds, odors, tastes, heat, cold, and the other tactile qualities, they are thought with so much obscurity and confusion, that I cannot determine even whether they are true or false; in other words, whether or not the ideas I have of these qualities are in truth the ideas of real objects. For although I before remarked that it is only in judgments that formal falsity, or falsity properly so called, can be met with, there may nevertheless be found in ideas a certain material falsity, which arises when they represent what is nothing as if it were something.

Thus, for example, the ideas I have of cold and heat are so far from being clear and distinct, that I am unable from them to discover whether cold is only the privation of heat, or heat the privation of cold; or whether they are or are not real qualities; and since, ideas being as it were images there can be none that does not seem to us to represent some object, the idea which represents cold as something real and positive will not improperly be called false, if it be correct to say that cold is nothing but a privation of heat; and so in other cases. To ideas of this kind, indeed, it is not necessary that I should assign any author besides myself: for if they are false, that is, represent objects that are unreal, the natural light teaches me that they proceed from nothing; in other words, that they are in me only because something is wanting to the perfection of my nature; but if these ideas are true, yet because they exhibit to me so little reality that I cannot even distinguish the object represented from non-being, I do not see why I should not be the author of them.

With reference to those ideas of corporeal things that are clear and distinct, there are some which, as appears to me, might have been taken from the idea I have of myself, as those of substance, duration, number, and the like. For when I think that a stone is a substance, or a thing capable of existing of itself, and that I am likewise a substance, although I conceive that I am a thinking and non-extended thing, and that the stone, on the contrary, is extended and unconscious, there being thus the greatest diversity between the two concepts, yet these two ideas seem to have this in common that they both represent substances. In the same way, when I think of myself as now existing, and recollect besides that I existed some time ago, and when I am conscious of various thoughts whose number I know, I then acquire the ideas of duration and number, which I can afterward transfer to as many objects as I please. With respect to the other qualities that go to make up the ideas of corporeal objects, viz, extension, figure, situation, and motion, it is true that they are not formally in me, since I am merely a thinking being; but because they are only certain modes of substance, and because I myself am a substance, it seems possible that they may be contained in me eminently.

There only remains, therefore, the idea of God, in which I must consider whether there is anything that cannot be supposed to originate with myself. By the name God, I understand a substance infinite, eternal, immutable, independent, all-knowing, all-powerful, and by which I myself, and every other thing that exists, if any such there be, were created. But these properties are so great and excellent, that the more attentively I consider them the less I feel persuaded that the idea I have of them owes its origin to myself alone. And thus it is absolutely necessary to conclude, from all that I have before said, that God exists: for though the idea of substance be in my mind owing to this, that I myself am a substance, I should not, however, have the idea of an infinite substance, seeing I am a finite being, unless it were given me by some substance in reality infinite.

And I must not imagine that I do not apprehend the infinite by a true idea, but only by the negation of the finite, in the same way that I comprehend repose and darkness by the negation of motion and light: since, on the contrary, I clearly perceive that there is more reality in the infinite substance than in the finite, and therefore that in some way I possess the perception (notion) of the infinite before that of the finite, that is, the perception of God before that of myself, for how could I think that I doubt, desire, or that something is wanting to me, and that I am not wholly perfect, if I possessed no idea of a being more perfect than myself, by comparison of which I knew the deficiencies of my nature?

And it cannot be said that this idea of God is

perhaps materially false, and consequently that it may have arisen from nothing [in other words, that it may exist in me from my imperfection], as I before said of the ideas of heat and cold, and the like: for, on the contrary, as this idea is very clear and distinct, and contains in itself more objective reality than any other, there can be no one of itself more true, or less open to the suspicion of falsity.

The idea, I say, of a being supremely perfect, and infinite, is in the highest degree true; for although, perhaps, we may imagine that such a being does not exist, we cannot, nevertheless, suppose that his idea represents nothing real, as I have already said of the idea of cold. It is likewise clear and distinct in the highest degree, since whatever the mind clearly and distinctly conceives as real or true, and as implying any perfection, is contained entire in this idea. And this is true, nevertheless, although I do not comprehend the infinite, and although there may be in God an infinity of things that I cannot comprehend, nor perhaps even compass by thought in any way; for it is of the nature of the infinite that it should not be comprehended by the finite; and it is enough that I rightly understand this, and judge that all which I clearly perceive, and in which I know there is some perfection, and perhaps also an infinity of properties of which I am ignorant, are formally or eminently in God, in order that the idea I have of him may become the most true, clear, and distinct of all the ideas in my mind.

But perhaps I am something more than I suppose myself to be, and it may be that all those perfections which I attribute to God, in some way exist potentially in me, although they do not yet show themselves, and are not reduced to act. Indeed, I am already conscious that my knowledge is being increased and perfected by degrees; and I see nothing to prevent it from thus gradually increasing to infinity, nor any reason why, after such increase and perfection, I should not be able thereby to acquire all the other perfections of the Divine nature; nor, in fine, why the power I possess of acquiring those perfections, if it really now exist in me, should not be sufficient to produce the ideas of them. Yet in looking more closely into the matter, I discover that this cannot be; for, in the first place, although it were true that my knowledge daily acquired new degrees of per-

fection, and although there were potentially in my nature much that was not as yet actually in it, still all these excellences make not the slightest approach to the idea I have of God in whom there is no perfection merely potentially [but all actually] existent; for it is even an unmistakable token of imperfection in my knowledge, that it is augmented by degrees. Further, although my knowledge increase more and more, nevertheless I am not, therefore, induced to think that it will ever be actually infinite, since it can never reach that point beyond which it shall be incapable of further increase. But I conceive God as actually infinite, so that nothing can be added to his perfection. And, in fine, I readily perceive that the objective being of an idea cannot be produced by a being that is merely potentially existent, which, properly speaking, is nothing, but only by a being existing formally or actually.

And, truly, I see nothing in all that I have now said which it is not easy for anyone, who shall carefully consider it, to discern by the natural light; but when I allow my attention in some degree to relax, the vision of my mind being obscured, and, as it were, blinded by the images of sensible objects, I do not readily remember the reason why the idea of a being more perfect than myself, must of necessity have proceeded from a being in reality more perfect. On this account I am here desirous to inquire further, whether I, who possess this idea of God, could exist supposing there were no God. And I ask, from whom could I, in that case, derive my existence? Perhaps from myself, or from my parents, or from some other causes less perfect than God; for anything more perfect, or even equal to God, cannot be thought or imagined. But if I were independent of every other existence, and were myself the author of my being, I should doubt of nothing, I should desire nothing, and, in fine, no perfection would be awanting to me; for I should have bestowed upon myself every perfection of which I possess the idea, and I should thus be God.

And it must not be imagined that what is now wanting to me is perhaps of more difficult acquisition than that of which I am already possessed; for, on the contrary, it is quite manifest that it was a matter of much higher difficulty that I, a thinking being, should arise from nothing, than it would be for me to acquire the knowledge of many things of which I am ignorant, and which are merely the accidents of a thinking substance; and certainly, if I possessed of myself the greater perfection of which I have now spoken [in other words, if I were the author of my own existence], I would not at least have denied to myself things that may be more easily obtained [as that infinite variety of knowledge of which I am at present destitute]. I could not, indeed, have denied to myself any property which I perceive is contained in the idea of God, because there is none of these that seems to me to be more difficult to make or acquire; and if there were any that should happen to be more difficult to acquire, they would certainly appear so to me because I should discover in them a limit to my power. And though I were to suppose that I always was as I now am, I should not, on this ground, escape the force of these reasonings, since it would not follow, even on this supposition, that no author of my existence needed to be sought after. For the whole time of my life may be divided into an infinity of parts, each of which is in no way dependent on any other; and, accordingly, because I was in existence a short time ago, it does not follow that I must now exist, unless in this moment some cause create me anew as it were, that is, conserve me. In truth, it is perfectly clear and evident to all who will attentively consider the nature of duration, that the conservation of a substance, in each moment of its duration, requires the same power and act that would be necessary to create it, supposing it were not yet in existence; so that it is manifestly a dictate of the natural light that conservation and creation differ merely in respect of our mode of thinking and not in reality. All that is here required, therefore, is that I interrogate myself to discover whether I possess any power by means of which I can bring it about that I, who now am, shall exist a moment afterward: for, since I am merely a thinking thing (or since, at least, the precise question, in the meantime, is only of that part of myself), if such a power resided in me, I should, without doubt, be conscious of it; but I am conscious of no such power, and thereby I manifestly know that I am dependent upon some being different from myself.

But perhaps the being upon whom I am dependent is not God, and I have been produced either by my parents, or by some causes less perfect than God. This cannot be: for, as I before said, it is perfectly evident that there must at least be as much reality in the cause as in its effect; and accordingly, since I am a thinking thing and possess in myself an idea of God, whatever in the end be the cause of my existence, it must of necessity be admitted that it is likewise a thinking being, and that it possesses in itself the idea and all the perfections I attribute to God. Then it may again be inquired whether this cause owes its origin and existence to itself, or to some other cause. For if it be self-existent, it follows, from what I have before laid down, that this cause is God; for since it possesses the perfection of self-existence, it must likewise, without doubt, have the power of actually possessing every perfection of which it has the idea—in other words, all the perfections I conceive to belong to God. But if it owe its existence to another cause than itself, we demand again, for a similar reason, whether this second cause exists of itself or through some other, until, from stage to stage, we at length arrive at an ultimate cause, which will be God. And it is quite manifest that in this matter there can be no infinite regress of causes, seeing that the question raised respects not so much the cause which once produced me, as that by which I am at this present moment conserved.

Nor can it be supposed that several causes concurred in my production, and that from one I received the idea of one of the perfections I attribute to God, and from another the idea of some other, and thus that all those perfections are indeed found somewhere in the universe, but do not all exist together in a single being who is God; for, on the contrary, the unity, the simplicity, or inseparability of all the properties of God, is one of the chief perfections I conceive him to possess; and the idea of this unity of all the perfections of God could certainly not be put into my mind by any cause from which I did not likewise receive the ideas of all the other perfections; for no power could enable me to embrace them in an inseparable unity, without at the same time giving me the knowledge of what they were and of their existence in a particular mode.

Finally, with regard to my parents [from whom it appears I sprung], although all that I believed respecting them be true, it does not, nevertheless, follow that I am conserved by them, or even that I was produced by them, in so far as I am a thinking being. All that, at the most, they contributed to my origin was the giving of certain dispositions (modifications) to the matter in which I have hitherto judged that I or my mind, which is what alone I now consider to be myself, is inclosed; and thus there can here be no difficulty with respect to them, and it is absolutely necessary to conclude from this alone that I am, and possess the idea of a being absolutely perfect, that is, of God, that his existence is most clearly demonstrated.

There remains only the inquiry as to the way in which I received this idea from God; for I have not drawn it from the senses, nor is it even presented to me unexpectedly, as is usual with the ideas of sensible objects, when these are presented or appear to be presented to the external organs of the senses; it is not even a pure production or fiction of my mind, for it is not in my power to take from or add to it; and consequently there but remains the alternative that it is innate, in the same way as is the idea of myself. And, in truth, it is not to be wondered at that God, at my creation, implanted this idea in me, that it might serve, as it were, for the mark of the workman impressed on his work; and it is not also necessary that the mark should be something different from the work itself; but considering only that God is my creator, it is highly probable that he in some way fashioned me after his own image and likeness, and that I perceive this likeness, in which is contained the idea of God, by the same faculty by which I apprehend myself, in others words, when I make myself the object of reflection, I only find that I am an incomplete, [imperfect] and dependent being, and one who unceasingly aspires after something better and greater than he is. At the same time, I am assured likewise that he upon whom I am dependent possesses in himself all the goods after which I aspire [and the ideas of which I find in my mind], and they not merely indefinitely and potentially, but infinitely and actually, and that he is thus God. And the whole force of the argument of which I have here availed myself to establish the existence of God, consists in this, that I perceive I could not possibly be of such a nature as I am, and yet have in my mind the idea of a God, if God did not in reality exist— this same God, I say, whose idea is in my mind

—that is, a being who possesses all those lofty perfections, of which the mind may have some slight conception, without, however, being able fully to comprehend them, and who is wholly superior to all defect [and has nothing that marks imperfection]: whence it is sufficiently manifest that he cannot be a deceiver, since it is a dictate of the natural light that all fraud and deception spring from some defect.

But before I examine this with more attention, and pass on to the consideration of other truths that may be evolved out of it, I think it proper to remain here for some time in the contemplation of God himself—that I may ponder at leisure his marvelous attributes—and behold, admire, and adore the beauty of this light so unspeakably great, as far, at least, as the strength of my mind, which is to some degree dazzled by the sight, will permit. For just as we learn by faith that the supreme felicity of another life consists in the contemplation of the Divine majesty alone, so even now we learn from experience that a like meditation, though incomparably less perfect, is the source of the highest satisfaction of which we are susceptible in this life. . . .

MEDITATION V

OF THE ESSENCE OF MATERIAL THINGS; AND, AGAIN, OF GOD; THAT HE EXISTS

Several other questions remain for consideration respecting the attributes of God and my own nature or mind. I will, however, on some other occasion perhaps resume the investigation of these. Meanwhile, as I have discovered what must be done and what must be avoided to arrive at the knowledge of truth, what I have chiefly to do is to essay to emerge from the state of doubt in which I have for some time been, and to discover whether anything can be known with certainty regarding material objects. But before considering whether such objects as I conceive exist without me, I must examine their ideas in so far as these are to be found in my consciousness, and discover which of them are distinct and which confused.

In the first place, I distinctly imagine that quantity which the philosophers commonly call continuous, or the extension in length, breadth, and depth that is in this quantity, or rather in the object to which it is attributed. Further, I can enumerate in it many diverse parts, and attribute to each of these all sorts of sizes, figures, situations, and local motions; and, in fine, I can assign to each of these motions all degrees of duration. And I not only distinctly know these things when I thus consider them in general; but besides, by a little attention, I discover innumerable particulars respecting figures, numbers, motion, and the like, which are so evidently true, and so accordant with my nature, that when I now discover them I do not so much appear to learn anything new, as to call to remembrance what I before knew, or for the first time to remark what was before in my mind, but to which I had not hitherto directed my attention. And what I here find of most importance is, that I discover in my mind innumerable ideas of certain objects, which cannot be esteemed pure negations, although perhaps they possess no reality beyond my thought, and which are not framed by me though it may be in my power to think, or not to think them, but possess true and immutable natures of their own. As, for example, when I imagine a triangle, although there is not perhaps and never was in any place in the universe apart from my thought one such figure, it remains true nevertheless that this figure possesses a certain determinate nature, form, or essence, which is immutable and eternal, and not framed by me, nor in any degree dependent on my thought; as appears from the circumstance, that diverse properties of the triangle may be demonstrated, viz, that its three angles are equal to two right, that its greatest side is subtended by its greatest angle, and the like, which, whether I will or not, I now clearly discern to belong to it, although before I did not at all think of them, when, for the first time, I imagined a triangle, and which accordingly cannot be said to have been invented by me. Nor is it a valid objection to allege, that perhaps this idea of a triangle came into my mind by the medium of the senses, through my having seen bodies of a trianglar figure; for I am able to form in thought an innumerable variety of figures with regard to which it cannot be supposed that they were ever objects of sense, and I can nevertheless demonstrate diverse properties of their nature no less than of the triangle, all of which are assuredly true since I clearly conceive them; and they are therefore something, and not mere negations;

for it is highly evident that all that is true is something, [truth being identical with existence]; and I have already fully shown the truth of the principle, that whatever is clearly and distinctly known is true. And although this had not been demonstrated, yet the nature of my mind is such as to compel me to assert to what I clearly conceive while I so conceive it; and I recollect that even when I still strongly adhered to the objects of sense, I reckoned among the number of the most certain truths those I clearly conceived relating to figures, numbers, and other matters that pertain to arithmetic and geometry, and in general to the pure mathematics.

But now if because I can draw from my thought the idea of an object, it follows that all I clearly and distinctly apprehend to pertain to this object, does in truth belong to it, may I not from this derive an argument for the existence of God? It is certain that I no less find the idea of a God in my consciousness, that is the idea of a being supremely perfect, than that of any figure or number whatever: and I know with not less clearness and distinctness that an [actual and] eternal existence pertains to his nature than that all which is demonstrable of any figure or number really belongs to the nature of that figure or number; and, therefore, although all the conclusions of the preceding Meditations were false, the existence of God would pass with me for a truth at least as certain as I ever judged any truth of mathematics to be, although indeed such a doctrine may at first sight appear to contain more sophistry than truth. For, as I have been accustomed in every other matter to distinguish between existence and essence, I may believe that the existence can be separated from the essence of God, and that thus God may be conceived as not actually existing. But, nevertheless, when I think of it more attentively, it appears that the existence can no more be separated from the essence of God, than the idea of a mountain from that of a valley, or the equality of its three angles to two right angles, from the essence of a [rectilineal] triangle; so that it is not less impossible to conceive a God, that is, a being supremely perfect, to whom existence is awanting, or who is devoid of a certain perfection, than to conceive a mountain without a valley.

But though, in truth, I cannot conceive a

God unless as existing, any more than I can a mountain without a valley, yet, just as it does not follow that there is any mountain in the world merely because I conceive a mountain with a valley, so likewise, though I conceive God as existing, it does not seem to follow on that account that God exists; for my thought imposes no necessity on things; and as I may imagine a winged horse, though there be none such, so I could perhaps attribute existence to God, though no God existed. But the cases are not analogous, and a fallacy lurks under the semblance of this objection: for because I cannot conceive a mountain without a valley, it does not follow that there is any mountain or valley in existence, but simply that the mountain or valley, whether they do or do not exist, are inseparable form each other; whereas, on the other hand, because I cannot conceive God unless as existing, it follows that existence is inseparable from him, and therefore that he really exists: not that this is brought about by my thought, or that it imposes any necessity on things, but, on the contrary, the necessity which lies in the thing itself, that is, the necessity of the existence of God, determines me to think in this way: for it is not in my power to conceive a God without existence, that is, a being supremely perfect, and yet devoid of an absolute perfection, as I am free to imagine a horse with or without wings.

Nor must it be alleged here as an objection, that it is in truth necessary to admit that God exists, after having supposed him to possess all perfections, since existence is one of them, but that my original supposition was not necessary. This objection is, I say, incompetent; for although it may not be necessary that I shall at any time entertain the notion of God, yet each time I happen to think of a first and sovereign being, and to draw, so to speak, the idea of him from the storehouse of the mind, I am necessitated to attribute to him all kinds of perfections, though I may not then enumerate them all, nor think of each of them in particular. And this necessity is sufficient, as soon as I discover that existence is a perfection, to cause me to infer the existence of this first and sovereign being; just as it is not necessary that I should ever imagine any triangle, but whenever I am desirous of considering a rectilineal figure composed of only three angles, it is absolutely necessary to attribute those properties to it from which it is cor-

rectly inferred that its three angles are not greater than two right angles, although perhaps I may not then advert to this relation in particular. But when I consider what figures are capable of being inscribed in the circle, it is by no means necessary to hold that all quadrilateral figures are of this number; on the contrary, I cannot even imagine such to be the case, so long as I shall be unwilling to accept in thought something that I do not clearly and distinctly conceive; and consequently there is a vast difference between false suppositions, as is the one in question, and the true ideas that were born with me, the first and chief of which is the idea of God. For indeed I discern on many grounds that this idea is not factitious depending simply on my thought, but that it is the representation of a true and immutable nature: in the first place because I can conceive no other being, except God, to whose essence existence [necessarily] pertains; in the second, because it is impossible to conceive two or more gods of this kind; and it being supposed that one such God exists, I clearly see that he must have existed from all eternity, and will exist to all eternity; and finally, because I apprehend many other properties in God, none of which I can either diminish or change.

But, indeed, whatever mode of probation I in the end adopt, it always returns to this, that it is only the things I clearly and distinctly conceive which have the power of completely persuading me. And although, of the objects I conceive in this manner, some indeed, are obvious to every one, while others are only discovered after close and careful investigation; nevertheless after they are once discovered, the latter are not esteemed less certain than the former. Thus, for example, to take the case of a right-angled triangle, although it is not so manifest at first that the square of the base is equal to the squares of the other two sides, as that the base is opposite to the greatest angle; nevertheless, after it is once apprehended, we are as firmly persuaded of the truth of the former as of the latter. And, with respect to God, if I were not pre-occupied by prejudices, and my thought beset on all sides by the continual presence of the images of sensible objects, I should know nothing sooner or more easily than the fact of his being. For is there any truth more clear than the existence of a Supreme Being, or of God, seeing it is to his essence alone that [necessary and eternal] existence pertains? And although the right conception of this truth has cost me much close thinking, nevertheless at present I feel not only as assured of it as of what I deem most certain, but I remark further that the certitude of all other truths is so absolutely dependent on it that without this knowledge it is impossible ever to know anything perfectly.

For although I am of such a nature as to be unable, while I have a very clear and distinct apprehension of a matter, to resist the conviction of its truth, yet because my constitution is also such as to incapacitate me from keeping my mind continually fixed on the same object, and as I frequently recollect a past judgment without at the same time being able to recall the grounds of it, it may happen meanwhile that other reasons are presented to me which would readily cause me to change my opinion, if I did not know that God existed; and thus I should possess no true and certain knowledge, but merely vague and vacillating opinions. Thus, for example, when I consider the nature of the [rectilineal] triangle, it most clearly appears to me, who have been instructed in the principles of geometry, that its three angles are equal to two right angles, and I find it impossible to believe otherwise, while I apply my mind to the demonstration; but as soon as I cease from attending to the process of proof, although I still remember that I had a clear comprehension of it, yet I may readily come to doubt of the truth demonstrated, if I do not know that there is a God: for I may persuade myself that I have been so constituted by nature as to be sometimes deceived, even in matters which I think I apprehend with the greatest evidence and certitude, especially when I recollect that I have considered many things to be true and certain which other reasons afterward constrained me to reckon as wholly false.

But after I have discovered that God exists, seeing I also at the same time observed that all things depend on him, and that he is no deceiver, and thence inferred that all which I clearly and distinctly perceive is of necessity true: although I no longer attend to the grounds of a judgment, no opposite reason can be alleged sufficient to lead me to doubt of its truth, provided only I remember that I once possessed a clear and distinct comprehension of it. My knowledge of it thus becomes true and certain. And this same knowledge extends like-wise to whatever I remember to have formerly demonstrated, as the truths of geometry and the like: for what can be alleged against them to lead me to doubt of them? Will it be that my nature is such that I may be frequently deceived? But I already know that I cannot be deceived in judgments of the grounds of which I possess a clear knowledge. Will it be that I formerly deemed things to be true and certain which I afterward discovered to be false? But I had no clear and distinct knowledge of any of those things, and, being as yet ignorant of the rule by which I am assured of the truth of a judgment, I was led to give my assent to them on grounds which I afterward discovered were less strong than at the time I imagined them to be. What further objection, then, is there? Will it be said that perhaps I am dreaming (an objection I lately myself raised), or that all the thoughts of which I am now conscious have no more truth than the reveries of my dreams? But although, in truth, I should be dreaming, the rule still holds that all which is clearly presented to my intellect is indisputably true.

And thus I very clearly see that the certitude and truth of all science depends on the knowledge alone of the true God, insomuch that, before I knew him, I could have no perfect knowledge of any other thing. And now that I know him, I possess the means of acquiring a perfect knowledge respecting innumerable matters, as well relative to God himself and other intellectual objects as to corporeal nature.

MEDITATION VI

OF THE EXISTENCE OF MATERIAL THINGS, AND OF THE REAL DISTINCTION BETWEEN THE MIND AND BODY OF MAN

There now only remains the inquiry as to whether material things exist. With regard to this question, I at least know with certainty that such things may exist, in as far as they constitute the object of the pure mathematics, since, regarding them in this aspect, I can conceive them clearly and distinctly. For there can be no doubt that God possesses the power of producing all the objects I am able distinctly to conceive, and I never considered anything impossible to him, unless when I experienced a contradiction in the attempt to conceive it aright.

Further, the faculty of imagination which I possess, and of which I am conscious that I make use when I devote myself to the consideration of material things, is sufficient to persuade me of their existence: for, when I attentively consider what imagination is, I find that it is simply a certain application of the cognitive faculty (*facultas cognoscitiva*) to a body which is immediately present to it, and which therefore exists.

And to render this quite clear, I remark, in the first place, the difference that subsists between imagination and pure intellection [or conception]. For example, when I imagine a triangle I not only conceive that it is a figure comprehended by three lines, but at the same time also I look upon these three lines as present by the power and internal application of my mind and this is what I call imagining. But if I desire to think of a chiliogen, I indeed rightly conceive that it is a figure composed of a thousand sides, as easily as I conceive that a triangle is a figure composed of only three sides; but I cannot imagine the thousand sides of a chiliogon as I do the three sides of a triangle, nor, so to speak, view them as present with the eyes of my mind. And although, in accordance with the habit I have of always imagining something when I think of corporeal things, it may happen that, in conceiving a chiliogon, I confusedly represent some figure to myself, yet it is quite evident that this is not a chiliogon, since it in no wise differs from that which I would represent to myself, if I were to think of a myriogon, or any other figure of many sides; nor would this representation be of any use in discovering and unfolding the properties that constitute the difference between a chiliogon and other polygons. But if the question turns on a pentagon, it is quite true that I can conceive its figure, as well as that of a chiliogon, without the aid of imagination; but I can likewise imagine it by applying the attention of my mind to its five sides, and at the same time to the area which they contain. Thus I observe that a special effort of mind is necessary to the act of imagination, which is not required to conceiving or understanding; and this special exertion of mind clearly shows the difference between imagination and pure intellection (*imaginatio et intellectio pura*). I remark, besides, that this power of imagination which I possess, in as far

as it differs from the power of conceiving, is in no way necessary to my nature or essence, that is, to the essence of my mind; for although I did not possess it, I should still remain the same that I now am, from which it seems we may conclude that it depends on something different from the mind.

And I easily understand that, if some body exists, with which my mind is so conjoined and united as to be able, as it were, to consider it when it chooses, it may thus imagine corporeal objects; so that this mode of thinking differs from pure intellection only in this respect, that the mind in conceiving turns in some way upon itself, and considers someone of the ideas it possesses within itself; but in imagining it turns toward the body, and contemplates in it some object conformed to the idea which it either of itself conceived or apprehended by sense. I easily understand, I say, that imagination may be thus formed, if it is true that there are bodies; and because I find no other obvious mode of explaining it, I hence, with probability, conjecture that they exist, but only with probability; and although I carefully examine all things, nevertheless I do not find that, from the distinct idea of corporeal nature I have in my imagination, I can necessarily infer the existence of any body.

But I am accustomed to imagine many other objects besides that corporeal nature which is the object of the pure mathematics, as, for example, colors, sounds, tastes, pain, and the like, although with less distinctness; and, inasmuch as I perceive these objects much better by the senses, through the medium of which and of memory, they seem to have reached the imagination, I believe that, in order the more advantageously to examine them, it is proper I should at the same time examine what sense-perception is, and inquire whether from those ideas that are apprehended by this mode of thinking (consciousness), I cannot obtain a certain proof of the existence of corporeal objects.

And, in the first place, I will recall to my mind the things I have hitherto held as true, because perceived by the senses, and the foundations upon which my belief in their truth rested; I will, in the second place, examine the reasons that afterward constrained me to doubt of them; and finally, I will consider what of them I ought now to believe.

Firstly, then, I perceived that I had a head, hands, feet, and other members composing that body which I considered as part, or perhaps even as the whole, of myself. I perceived further, that that body was placed among many others, by which it was capable of being affected in diverse ways, both beneficial and hurtful; and what was beneficial I remarked by a certain sensation of pleasure, and what was hurtful by a sensation of pain. And besides this pleasure and pain, I was likewise conscious of hunger, thirst, and other appetites, as well as certain corporeal inclinations toward joy, sadness, anger, and similar passions. And, out of myself, besides the extension, figure, and motions of bodies, I likewise perceived in them hardness, heat, and the other tactile qualities, and, in addition, light, colors, odors, tastes, and sounds, the variety of which gave me the means of distinguishing the sky, the earth, the sea, and generally all the other bodies, from one another. And certainly, considering the ideas of all these qualities, which were presented to my mind, and which alone I properly and immediately perceived, it was not without reason that I thought I perceived certain objects wholly different from my thought, namely, bodies from which those ideas proceeded; for I was conscious that the ideas were presented to me without my consent being required, so that I could not perceive any object, however desirous I might be, unless it were present to the organ of sense; and it was wholly out of my power not to perceive it when it was thus present. And because the ideas I perceived by the senses were much more lively and clear, and even, in their own way, more distinct than any of those I could of myself frame by meditation, or which I found impressed on my memory, it seemed that they could not have proceeded from myself, and must therefore have been caused in me by some other objects; and as of those objects I had no knowledge beyond what the ideas themselves gave me, nothing was so likely to occur to my mind as the supposition that the objects were similar to the ideas which they caused. And because I recollected also that I had formerly trusted to the senses, rather than to reason, and that the ideas which I myself formed were not so clear as those I perceived by sense, and that they were even for the most part composed of parts of the latter, I was readily persuaded that I had no idea in my intellect which had not

formerly passed through the senses. Nor was I altogether wrong in likewise believing that that body which, by a special right, I called my own, pertained to me more properly and strictly than any of the others; for in truth, I could never be separated from it as from other bodies; I felt in it and on account of it all my appetites and affections, and in fine I was affected in its parts by pain and the titillation of pleasure, and not in the parts of the other bodies, that were separated from it. But when I inquired into the reason why, from this I know not what sensation of pain, sadness of mind should follow, and why from the sensation of pleasure, joy should arise, or why this indescribable twitching of the stomach, which I call hunger, should put me in mind of taking food, and the parchedness of the throat of drink, and so in other cases, I was unable to give any explanation, unless that I was so taught by nature; for there is assuredly no affinity, at least none that I am able to comprehend, between this irritation of the stomach and the desire of food, any more than between the perception of an object that causes pain and the consciousness of sadness which springs from the perception. And in the same way it seemed to me that all the other judgments I had formed regarding the objects of sense, were dictates of nature; because I remarked that those judgments were formed in me, before I had leisure to weigh and consider the reasons that might constrain me to form them.

But, afterward, a wide experience by degrees sapped the faith I had reposed in my senses; for I frequently observed that towers, which at a distance seemed round, appeared square, when more closely viewed, and that colossal figures, raised on the summits of these towers, looked like small statues, when viewed from the bottom of them; and, in other instances without number, I also discovered error in judgments founded on the external senses; and not only in those founded on the external, but even in those that rested on the internal senses; for is there anything more internal than pain? And yet I have sometimes been informed by parties whose arm or leg had been amputated, that they still occasionally seemed to feel pain in that part of the body which they had lost,—a circumstance that led me to think that I could not be quite certain even that any one of my members was affected when I felt pain in it. And to these grounds of doubt I shortly afterward also added two others of very wide generality: the first of them was that I believed I never perceived anything when awake which I could not occasionally think I also perceived when asleep; and as I do not believe that the ideas I seem to perceive in my sleep proceed from objects external to me, I did not any more observe any ground for believing this of such as I seem to perceive when awake; the second was that since I was as yet ignorant of the author of my being or at least supposed myself to be so, I saw nothing to prevent my having been so constituted by nature as that I should be deceived even in matters that appeared to me to possess the greatest truth. And, with respect to the grounds on which I had before been persuaded of the existence of sensible objects, I had no great difficulty in finding suitable answers to them; for as nature seemed to incline me to many things from which reason made me averse, I thought that I ought not to confide much in its teachings. And although the perceptions of the senses were not dependent on my will, I did not think that I ought on that ground to conclude that they proceeded from things different from myself, since perhaps there might be found in me some faculty, though hitherto unknown to me, which produced them.

But now that I begin to know myself better, and to discover more clearly the author of my being, I do not, indeed, think that I ought rashly to admit all which the senses seem to teach, nor, on the other hand, is it my conviction that I ought to doubt in general of their teachings.

And, firstly, because I know that all which I clearly and distinctly conceive can be produced by God exactly as I conceive it, it is sufficient that I am able clearly and distinctly to conceive one thing apart from another, in order to be certain that the one is different from the other, seeing they may at least be made to exist separately, by the omnipotence of God; and it matters not by what power this separation is made, in order to be compelled to judge them different; and, therefore, merely because I know with certitude that I exist, and because, in the meantime, I do not observe that anything necessarily belongs to my nature or essence beyond my being a thinking thing, I rightly conclude that my essence consists only in my being a thinking thing [or a substance whose whole essence or nature is merely thinking].

And although I may, or rather, as I will shortly say, although I certainly do possess a body with which I am very closely conjoined; nevertheless, because, on the other hand, I have a clear and distinct idea of myself, in as far as I am only a thinking and unextended thing, and as, on the other hand, I have a distinct idea of body, in as far as it is only an extended and unthinking thing, it is certain that I, [that is, my mind, by which I am what I am], is entirely and truly distinct from my body, and may exist without it.

Moreover, I find in myself diverse faculties of thinking that have each their special mode: for example, I find I possess the faculties of imagining and perceiving, without which I can indeed clearly and distinctly conceive myself as entire, but I cannot reciprocally conceive them without conceiving myself, that is to say, without an intelligent substance in which they reside, for [in the notion we have of them, or to use the terms of the schools] in their formal concept, they comprise some sort of intellection; whence I perceive that they are distinct from myself as modes are from things. I remark likewise certain other faculties, as the power of changing place, of assuming diverse figures, and the like, that cannot be conceived and cannot therefore exist, any more than the proceeding, apart from a substance in which they inhere. It is very evident, however, that these faculties, if they really exist, must belong to some corporeal or extended substance, since in their clear and distinct concept there is contained some sort of extension, but no intellection at all. Further, I cannot doubt but that there is in me a certain passive faculty of perception, that is, of receiving and taking knowledge of the ideas of sensible things; but this would be useless to me, if there did not also exist in me, or in some other thing, another active faculty capable of forming and producing those ideas. But this active faculty cannot be in me [in as far as I am but a thinking thing], seeing that it does not presuppose thought, and also that those ideas are frequently produced in my mind without my contributing to it in any way, and even frequently contrary to my will. This faculty must therefore exist in some substance different from me, in which all the objective reality of the ideas that are produced by this faculty, is contained formally or eminently, as I before remarked: and this substance is either a body, that is to say, a corporeal nature in which is contained formally [and in effect] all that is objectively [and by representation] in those ideas; or it is God himself, or some other creature, of a rank superior to body, in which the same is contained eminently. But as God is no deceiver, it is manifest that he does not of himself and immediately communicate those ideas to me, nor even by the intervention of any creature in which their objective reality is not formally, but only eminently, contained. For as he has given me no faculty whereby I can discover this to be the case, but on the contrary, a very strong inclination to believe that those ideas arise from corporeal objects, I do not see how he could be vindicated from the charge of deceit, if in truth they proceed from any other source, or were produced by other causes than corporeal things: and accordingly it must be concluded, that corporeal objects exist. Nevertheless, they are not perhaps exactly such as we perceive by the senses, for their comprehension by the senses is, in many instances, very obscure and confused; but it is at least necessary to admit that all which I clearly and distinctly conceive as in them, that is, generally speaking, all that is comprehended in the object of speculative geometry, really exists external to me.

But with respect to other things which are either only particular, as, for example, that the sun is of such a size and figure, etc., or are conceived with less clearness and distinctness, as light, sound, pain, and the like, although they are highly dubious and uncertain, nevertheless on the ground alone that God is no deceiver, and that consequently he has permitted no falsity in my opinions which he has not likewise given me a faculty of correcting, I think I may with safety conclude that I possess in myself the means of arriving at the truth. And, in the first place, it cannot be doubted that in each of the dictates of nature there is some truth: for by nature, considered in general, I now understand nothing more than God himself, or the order and disposition established by God in created things; and by my nature in particular I understand the assemblage of all that God has given me.

But there is nothing which that nature teaches me more expressly [or more sensibly] than that I have a body which is ill affected when I feel pain, and stands in need of food and drink when I experience the sensations of hunger and thirst, etc. And therefore, I ought not to doubt but that there is some truth in these informations.

Nature likewise teaches me by these sensations of pain, hunger, thirst, etc., that I am not only lodged in my body as a pilot in a vessel, but that I am besides so intimately conjoined, and as it were intermixed with it, that my mind and body compose a certain unity. For if this were not the case, I should not feel pain when my body is hurt, seeing I am merely a thinking thing, but should perceive the wound by the understanding alone, just as a pilot perceives by sight when any part of his vessel is damaged; and when my body has need of food or drink, I should have a clear knowledge of this, and not be made aware of it by the confused sensations of hunger and thirst, pain, etc., which are nothing more than certain confused modes of thinking, arising from the union and apparent fusion of mind and body.

Besides this, nature teaches me that my own body is surrounded by many other bodies, some of which I have to seek after, and others to shun. And indeed, as I perceive different sorts of colors, sounds, odors, tastes, heat, hardness, etc., I safely conclude that there are in the bodies from which the diverse perceptions of the senses proceed, certain varieties corresponding to them, although, perhaps, not in reality like them; and since, among these diverse perceptions of the senses, some are agreeable, and others disagreeable, there can be no doubt that my body, or rather my mind, may be variously affected, both beneficially and hurtfully, by surrounding bodies.

But there are many other beliefs which though seemingly the teaching of nature, are not in reality so, but which obtained a place in my mind through a habit of judging inconsiderately of things. It may thus easily happen that such judgments shall contain error: thus, for example, the opinion I have that all space in which there is nothing to affect [or make an impression on] my senses is void: that in a hot body there is something in every respect similar to the idea of heat in my mind; that in a white or green body there is the same whiteness or greeness which I perceive; that in a bitter or sweet body there is the same taste, and so in other instances; that the stars, towers, and all distant bodies, are of the same size and figure as they appear to our eyes, etc., But that I may avoid everything like indistinctness of conception, I must accurately define what I properly understand by being taught by nature. For nature is here taken in a narrower sense than when it signifies the sum of all the things which God has given me; seeing that in that meaning the notion comprehends much that belongs only to the mind [to which I am not here to be understood as referring when I use the term nature]; as, for example, the notion I have of the truth, that what is done cannot be undone, and all the other truths I discern by the natural light [without the aid of the body]; and seeing that it comprehends likewise much besides that belongs only to body, and is not here any more contained under the name nature, as the quality of heaviness, and the like, of which I do not speak, the term being reserved exclusively to designate the things which God has given to me as a being composed of mind and body. But nature, taking the term in the sense explained, teaches me to shun what causes in me the sensation of pain, and to pursue what affords me the sensation of pleasure, and other things of this sort; but I do not discover that it teaches me, in addition to this, from these diverse perceptions of the senses, to draw any conclusions respecting external objects without a previous [careful and mature] consideration of them by the mind: for it is, as appears to me, the office of the mind alone, and not of the composite whole of mind and body, to discern the truth in those matters. Thus, although the impression a star makes on my eye is not larger than that from the flame of a candle, I do not, nevertheless, experience any real or positive impulse determining me to believe that the star is not` greater than the flame; the true account of the matter being merely that I have so judged from my youth without any rational ground. And, though on approaching the fire I feel heat, and even pain on approaching it too closely, I have, however, from this no ground for holding that something resembling the heat I feel is in the fire, any more than that there is something similar to the pain; all that I have ground for believing is, that there is something in it, whatever it may be, which excites in me those sensations of heat or pain. So also, although there are spaces in which I find nothing to excite and affect my senses, I must not therefore conclude that those spaces contain in them no body; for I see that in this, as in many other similar matters, I have been accustomed to pervert the order of nature, because these perceptions of the senses, although given me by nature merely to signify to my mind what things are beneficial and hurtful to the composite whole of which it is a part, and being sufficiently clear and distinct for that purpose, are nevertheless used by me as infallible rules by which to determine immediatley the essence of the bodies that exist out of me, of which they can of course afford me only the most obscure and confused knowledge.

But I have already sufficiently considered how it happens that, notwithstanding the supreme goodness of God, there is falsity in my judgments. A difficulty, however, here presents itself, respecting the things which I am taught by nature must be pursued or avoided, and also respecting the internal sensations in which I seem to have occasionally detected error, [and thus to be directly deceived by nature]: thus, for example, I may be so deceived by the agreeable taste of some viand with which poison has been mixed, as to be induced to take the poison. In this case, however, nature may be excused, for it simply leads me to desire the viand for its agreeable taste, and not the poison, which is unknown to it; and thus we can infer nothing from this circumstance beyond that our nature is not omniscient; at which there is assuredly no ground for surprise, since, man being of a finite nature, his knowledge must likewise be of a limited perfection. But we also not unfrequently err in that to which we are directly impelled by nature, as is the case with invalids who desire drink or food that would be hurtful to them.

It will here, perhaps, be alleged that the reason why such persons are deceived is that their nature is corrupted; but this leaves the difficulty untouched, for a sick man is not less really the creature of God than a man who is in full health; and therefore it is as repugnant to the goodness of God that the nature of the former should be deceitful as it is for that of the latter to be so. And as a clock, composed of wheels and counter weights, observes not the less accurately all the laws of nature when it is ill made, and points out the hours incorrectly, than when it satisfies the desire of the maker in every respect; so likewise if the body of man be considered as a kind of machine, so made up and composed of bones, nerves, muscles, veins, blood, and skin, that although there were in it no mind, it would still exhibit the same motions which it at present manifests involuntarily, and therefore without the aid of the mind, [and simply by the dispositions at its organs], I easily discern that it would also be as natural for such a body, supposing it dropsical, for example, to experience the parchedness of the throat that is usually accompanied in the mind by the sensation of thirst, and to be disposed by this parchedness to move its nerves and its other parts in the way required for drinking, and thus increase its malady and do itself harm, as it is natural for it, when it is not indisposed to be stimulated to drink for its good by a similar cause; and although looking to the use for which a clock was destined by its maker, I may say that it is deflected from its proper nature when it incorrectly indicates the hours, and on the same principle, considering the machine of the human body as having been formed by God for the sake of the motions which it usually manifests, although I may likewise have ground for thinking that it does not follow the order of its nature when the throat is parched and drink does not tend to its preservation, nevertheless I yet plainly discern that this latter acceptation of the term nature is very different from the other: for this is nothing more than a certain denomination, depending entirely on my thought, and hence called extrinsic, by which I compare a sick man and an imperfectly constructed clock with the idea I have of a man in good health and a well made clock; while by the other acceptation of nature is understood something which is truly found in things, and therefore possessed of some truth.

But certainly, although in respect of a dropsical body, it is only by way of exterior denomination that we say its nature is corrupted, when, without requiring drink, the throat is parched; yet, in respect of the composite whole, that is, of the mind in its union with the body, it is not a pure denomination, but really an error of nature, for it to feel thirst when drink would be hurtful to it: and, accordingly, it still remains to be considered why it is that the goodness of God does not prevent the nature of man thus taken from being fallacious.

To commence this examination accordingly, I here remark, in the first place, that there is a vast difference between mind and body, in respect that body, from its nature, is always divisible, and that mind is entirely indivisible. For in truth, when I consider the mind, that is, when I consider myself in so far only as I am a thinking thing, I can distinguish in myself no parts, but I very clearly discern that I am somewhat absolutely one and entire; and although the whole mind seems to be united to the whole body, yet, when a foot, an arm, or any other part is cut off, I am conscious that nothing has been taken from my mind; nor can the faculties of willing, perceiving, conceiving, etc., properly be called its parts, for it is the same mind that is exercised [all entire] in willing, in perceiving, and in conceiving etc. But quite the opposite holds in corporeal or extended things; for I cannot imagine any one of them [how small soever it may be]; which I cannot easily sunder in thought, and which, therefore, I do not know to be divisible. This would be sufficient to teach me that the mind or soul of man is entirely different from the body, if I had not already been apprised of it on other grounds.

I remark, in the next place, that the mind does not immediately receive the impression from all the parts of the body, but only from the brain, or perhaps even from one small part of it, viz, that in which the common sense (*sensus communis*) is said to be, which as often as it is affected in the same way gives rise to the same perception in the mind, although meanwhile the other parts of the body may be diversely disposed, as is proved by innumerable experiments. . . .

I remark, finally, that as each of the movements that are made in the part of the brain by which the mind is immediately affected, impresses it with but a single sensation, the most likely supposition in the circumstances is, that this movement causes the mind to experience, among all the sensations which it is capable of impressing upon it, that one which is the best fitted, and generally the most useful for the preservation of the human body when it is in full health. But experience shows us that all the perceptions which nature has given us are of such a kind as I have mentioned; and accordingly, there is nothing found in them that does not manifest the power and goodness of God. Thus, for example, when the nerves of the foot are violently or more than usually shaken, the motion passing through the medulla of the spine to the innermost parts of the brain affords a sign to the mind on which it experiences a sensation, viz., of pain, as if it were in the foot, by which the mind is admonished and excited to do its utmost to remove the cause of it as dangerous and hurtful to the foot. It is true that God could have so constituted the nature of man as that the same motion in the brain would have informed the mind of something altogether different: the motion might, for example, have been the occasion on which the mind became conscious of itself, in so far as it is in the brain, or in so far as it is in some place intermediate between the foot and the brain, or, finally, the occasion on which it perceived some other object quite different, whatever that might be; but nothing of all this would have so well contributed to the preservation of the body as that which the mind actually feels. In the same way, when we stand in need of drink, there arises from this want a certain parchedness in the throat that moves its nerves, and by means of them the internal parts of the brain; and this movement affects the mind with the sensation of thirst, because there is nothing on that occasion which is more useful for us than to be made aware that we have need of drink for the preservation of our health; and so in other instances.

Whence it is quite manifest that, notwithstanding the sovereign goodness of God, the nature of man, in so far as it is composed of mind and body, cannot but be sometimes fallacious. For, if there is any cause which excites, not in the foot, but in some one of the parts of the nerves that stretch from the foot to the brain, or even in the brain itself, the same movement that is ordinarily created when the foot is ill affected, pain will be felt, as it were, in the foot, and the sense will thus be naturally deceived; for as the same movement in the brain can but impress the mind with the same sensation, and as this sensation is much more frequently excited by a cause which hurts the foot than by one acting in a more different quarter, it is reasonable that it should lead the mind to feel pain in the foot rather than in any other part of the body. And if it sometimes happens that the parchedness of the throat does not arise, as is usual, from drink being necessary for the health of the body, but from quite the opposite cause, as is the case with the dropsical, yet it is much better that it should be deceitful in that instance, than if, on the contrary, it were continually fallacious when the body is well-disposed; and the same holds true in other cases.

And certainly this consideration is of great service, not only in enabling me to recognize the errors to which my nature is liable, but likewise in rendering it more easy to avoid or correct them: for, knowing that all my senses more usually indicate to me what is true than what is false, in matters relating to the advantage of the body, and being able almost to make use of more than a single sense in examining the same object, and besides this, being able to use my memory in connecting present with past knowledge, and my understanding which has already discovered all the causes of my errors, I ought no longer to fear that falsity may be met with in what is daily presented to me by the senses. And I ought to reject all the doubts of those bygone days, as hyperbolical and ridiculous, especially the general uncertainty respecting sleep, which I could not distinguish from the waking state: for I now find a very marked difference between the two states, in respect that our memory can never connect our dreams with each other and with the course of life, in the way it is in the habit of doing with events that occur when we are awake. And, in truth, if some one, when I am awake, appeared to me all of a sudden and as suddenly disappeared, as do the images I see in sleep, so that I could not observe either whence he came or whither he went, I should not without reason esteem it either a specter formed in my brain, rather than a real man. But when I perceive objects with regard to which I can distinctly determine both the place whence they come, and that in which they are, and the time at which they appear to me, and when, without interruption, I can connect the perception I have of them with the whole of the other parts of my life, I am perfectly sure that what I thus perceive occurs while I am awake and not during sleep. And I ought not in the least degree to doubt of the truth of these presentations, if, after having called together all my senses, my memory, and my understanding for the purpose of examining them, no deliverance is given by any one of these faculties which is repugnant to that of any other: for since God is no deceiver, it follows that I am not herein deceived. But because the necessities of action frequently oblige us to come to a determination before we have had leisure for careful examination, it must be confessed that the life of man is frequently obnoxious to error with respect to individual objects; and we must, in conclusion, acknowledge the weakness of our nature.

John Locke

It is customary to classify modern European philosophers as either *empiricists* or *rationalists*. The latter are supposed to favor reason over the senses, and the former, the senses over reason. Locke, Berkeley, and Hume are supposed to be the empiricists, being British besides. Descartes, Spinoza, and Leibniz are supposed to be the rationalists, being from the continent besides. We find this classification too restricting. It obscures important differences among empiricists or among rationalists and important similarities between members of the alleged opposing schools.

Some other classification or general points might be more helpful. All of the philosophers in the modern period were united in their opposition to the scientific views embodied in Aristotle's physics. But this united front did not prevent some modern philosophers from adopting Aristotle's metaphysics in order to interpret new developments in science. In addition, some Aristotelian physical notions reappear in a new guise, as in Descartes, who makes them metaphysical principles with a Platonic justification. Bacon criticized the syllogism but his suggestion for an improvement was only a slightly more sophisticated restatement of Aristotle's own theory. In addition, there were conflicting scientific theories as well as conflicting metaphysical views. The major opponents were Cartesian science (corpuscular) and Newtonian science (atomistic). Hence it might be more useful to ask first, what view of science is being defended, and second, what metaphysical interpretation is being given to that science. From this point of view, it will emerge that Locke is defending Newtonian science from an Aristotelian point of view.

Locke was born in 1632. He received strict Puritan training as a youth and was then sent to Oxford. At Oxford he received a thorough grounding in "scholastic" philosophy, which he later dismissed as unintelligible; but the Aristotelianism of that training remained a permanent feature of his thought. At Oxford he also worked with Robert Boyle, famous for formulating one of the gas laws, who imparted to Locke the doctrine of the distinction between primary and secondary qualities.

After some medical training, Locke became a friend of the Shaftesbury family who headed the Protestant opposition to James II. At one point Locke was forced to flee to Holland and probably became the only philosopher ever to appear on the ten most wanted list. Fortunately for Locke his side won the "Glorious Revolution" of 1688 which put William and Mary on the throne. In 1690 he published *Two Treatises of Government,* which challenged the divine right theory of government and offered a defense of the Whig position in English government. In the same year he published *An Essay Concerning Human Understanding*. He died in 1704 having left a permanent mark on British thought.

Locke, like Descartes, argued that no intellectual issue could be settled until we had a clear conception of what role reason could play in our life. What is the scope of our understanding? Locke begins with the modern standpoint which argues that our experience is caused in our minds by external physical objects. These experiences he denotes as *ideas.* He sees two sources of ideas: sensation and reflection (what we might call introspection). These ideas are either simple or complex. Simple ideas might come from one sense (such as color), several senses (extension, figure, rest, motion), reflection (thinking, volition), or from both sensation and reflection (pleasure and pain, power). Complex ideas are either modes (such as space), substances (something like the matter which holds the qualities of objects together), or relations (such as causality, identity, or even morality). In opposition to Descartes, Locke argues against the existence of innate ideas such as the cogito and instead claims that the mind is originally like a blank tablet (tabula rasa) on which nature writes. In addition, the mind has the power of abstracting complex ideas from experience.

As opposed to Cartesian science (named after Descartes), Locke believed in Newtonian science. This meant a belief that the world was made up of discrete bodies (separate atoms) in motion in an otherwise empty space. This explains why Locke insisted that solidity must be added to the list of primary qualities, for solidity was an empirically discoverable way of gaining access to discrete bodies. Extension was not enough to characterize such bodies.

Locke opposed Descartes not only on scientific grounds but on philosophical grounds as well. To begin with, Locke opposed the notion of self-evident truths and argued instead that all knowledge is abstracted from experience. His was the classic Aristotelian position in which ideas were said to be "in" the things themselves; ideas were the intelligible aspect of things. Moreover, Locke insisted that the idea in the human mind was identical with the idea in things.

This is why he insisted that primary qualities at the very least truly represent the object itself. Even secondary qualities are caused in us by the presence of the primary qualities. Like all Aristotelians, Locke defended the notion of demonstrative science. Of course Platonists also have a demonstrative conception of science but they differ from the Aristotelians on the source of first principles. Locke, of course, faces the seemingly insuperable problems of explaining just how we know that our ideas conform to objects in reality and explaining just how the "abstracting" power of the mind works. But in the end he asserts that the "subatomic" world is a certain world, and if we could but gain access to it, we would know with unerring certainty why things happen. This is necessary for Locke to say because he maintains that knowledge must be of universal truths, "the being of things themselves" (I, iii, 25). In the end, his defense of his position is to challenge the Platonists by asserting that they (Descartes) cannot show exactly how the laws of physics could be derived from the law of contradiction.

Many specific problems are generated in Locke's philosophy. The central one concerns substance. In defending a Newtonian view of mass and forces, Locke must believe in powers and substances. This is why, as we have seen, he insisted that solidity, which is not reducible to extension, must be a primary quality. But Locke cannot really justify his insistence upon the distinction of primary and secondary qualities because he agrees that we never have direct access to objects, only to the ideas objects cause in us. The problem of substance leads to the problems with causation, identity, and the existence of abstract ideas. Even Locke recognized them and tried to solve the causation problem by arguing that while we do not perceive it per se in objects, we know from reflection on our selves (as when we raise our arm) what causation would be like in objects. Throughout his philosophy, Locke defends the Aristotelian notion of causation in which a property of the effect necessitates a corresponding property in the cause.

Essay Concerning Human Understanding

INTRODUCTION

1. *An inquiry into the understanding, pleasant and useful.*—Since it is the *understanding* that sets man above the rest of sensible beings, and gives him all the advantage and dominion which he has over them, it is certainly a subject, even for its nobleness, worth our labor to inquire into. The understanding, like the eye, whilst it makes us see and perceive all other things, takes no notice of itself; and it requires art and pains to set it at a distance, and make it its own object. But whatever be the difficulties that lie in the way of this inquiry, whatever it be that keeps us so much in the dark to ourselves, sure I am that all the light we can let in upon our own minds, all the acquaintance we can make with our own understandings, will not only be very pleasant, but bring us great advantage in directing our thoughts in the search of other things.

2. *Design.*—This, therefore, being my purpose, to inquire into the original, certainty, and extent of *human knowledge*, together with the grounds and degrees of *belief, opinion,* and *assent,* I shall not at present meddle with the physical consideration of the mind, or trouble myself to examine wherein its essence consists or by what motions of our spirits, or alteration of our bodies, we come to have any sensation by our organs, or any *ideas* in our understandings; and whether those ideas do, in their formation, any or all of them, depend on matter or not. These are speculations, which, however curious and entertaining, I shall decline, as lying out of my way in the design I am now upon. It shall suffice to my present purpose, to consider the discerning faculties of a man, as they are employed about the objects which they have to do with. And I shall imagine I have not wholly misemployed myself in the thoughts I shall have on this occasion, if, in this historical, plain method, I can give any account of the ways whereby our understandings come to attain those notions of things we have, and can set down any measures of the certainty of our knowledge, or the grounds of those persuasions which are to be found amongst men, so various, different, and wholly contradictory; and yet asserted somewhere or other with such assurance and confidence, that he that shall take a view of the opinions of mankind, observe their opposition, and at the same time consider the fondness and devotion wherewith they are embraced, the resolution and eagerness wherewith they are maintained, may perhaps have reason to suspect that either there is no such thing as truth at all or that mankind hath no sufficient means to attain a certain knowledge of it.

3. *Method.*—It is therefore worth while to search out the bounds between opinions and knowledge, and examine by what measures, in things whereof we have no certain knowledge, we ought to regulate our assent, and moderate our persuasions. In other whereunto, I shall pursue this following method:—

First, I shall inquire into the original of those *ideas,* notions, or whatever else you please to call them, which a man observes, and is conscious to himself he has in his mind; and the ways whereby the understanding comes to be furnished with them.

Secondly, I shall endeavor to show what *knowledge* the understanding hath by those ideas, and the certainty, evidence, and extent to it.

Thirdly, I shall make some inquiry into the nature and grounds of *faith* or *opinion*; whereby I mean, that assent which we give to any proposition as true, of whose truth yet we have no certain knowledge and here we shall have occasion to examine the reasons and degrees of assent.

4. *Useful to know the extent of our comprehension.*—If by this inquiry into the nature of the understanding, I can discover the powers thereof, how far they reach, to what things they are in any degree proportionate, and where they fail us, I suppose it may be of use to prevail with the busy mind of man to be more cautious in meddling with things exceeding its comprehension, to stop when it is at the utmost extent of its tether, and to sit down in a quiet ignorance of those things which, upon examination, are found to be beyond the reach of our capacities. We should not then, perhaps, be so forward, out of an affectation of an universal knowledge, to raise questions, and perplex ourselves and others with disputes, about things to which our understandings are not suited, and of which we cannot frame in our minds any clear or distinct perceptions, or whereof (as it has, perhaps, too often happened) we have not any notions at all. If we can find out how far the understanding can extend its view, how far it has faculties to attain certainty, and in what cases it can only judge and guess, we may learn to content ourselves with what is attainable by us in this state.

5. *Our capacity suited to our state and concerns.*—For though the comprehension of our understandings comes exceeding short of the vast extent of things, yet we shall have cause enough to magnify the bountiful Author of our being for that proportion and degree of knowledge He has bestowed on us, so far above all the rest of the inhabitants of this our mansion. Men have reason to be well satisfied with what God hath thought fit for them, since He has given them, as St. Peter says, whatsoever is necessary for the conveniences of life, and information of virtue; and has put within the reach of their discovery, the comfortable provision for this life and the way that leads to a better. How short soever their knowledge may come of an universal or perfect comprehension of whatsoever is, it yet secures their great concernments that they have light enough to lead them to the knowledge of their Maker, and the sight of their own duties. Men may find matter suffi-

cient to busy their heads and employ their hands with variety, delight, and satisfaction, if they will not boldly quarrel with their own constitution, and throw away the blessings their hands are filled with, because they are not big enough to grasp everything. We shall not have much reason to complain of the narrowness of our minds, if we will but employ them about what may be of use to us; for of that they are very capable; and it will be an unpardonable as well as childish peevishness, if we undervalue the advantages of our knowledge, and neglect to improve it to the ends for which it was given us, because there are some things that are set out of the reach of it. It will be no excuse to an idle and untoward servant, who would not attend his business by candlelight, to plead that he had not broad sunshine. The candle that it set up in us shines bright enough for all our purposes. The discoveries we can make with this ought to satisfy us; and we shall then use our understandings right, when we entertain all objects in that way and proportion that they are suited to our faculties, and upon those grounds they are capable of being proposed to us; and not peremptorily or intemperately require demonstration, and demand certainty, where probability only is to be had, and which is sufficient to govern all our concernments. If we will disbelieve everything because we cannot certainly know all things, we shall do much-what as wisely as he who would not use his legs, but sit still and perish because he had no wings to fly.

6. *Knowledge of our capacity a cure of scepticism and idleness.*—When we know our own strength, we shall the better know what to undertake with hopes of success; and when we have well surveyed the *powers* of our own minds, and made some estimate what we may expect from them, we shall not be inclined either to sit still, and not set our thoughts on work at all, in despair of knowing anything; nor, on the other side, question everything and disclaim all knowledge, because some things are not to be understood. It is of great use to the sailor to know the length of his line, though he cannot with it fathom all the depths of the ocean; it is well he knows that it is long enough to reach the bottom at such places as are necessary to direct his voyage, and caution him against running upon shoals that may ruin him. Our business here is not to know all things, but

those which concern our conduct. If we can find out those measures whereby a rational creature, put in that state which man is in this world, may and ought to govern his opinions and actions depending thereon, we need not be troubled that some other things escape our knowledge. . . .

8. *What 'idea' stands for.*—I must here, in the entrance, beg pardon of my reader for the frequent use of the word 'idea' which he will find in the following treatise. It being that term which, I think, serves best to stand for whatsoever is the *object* of the understanding when a man thinks, I have used it to express whatever is meant by phantasm, notion, species, or whatever it is which the mind can be employed about in thinking; and I could not avoid frequently using it.

I presume it will be easily granted me, that there are such *ideas* in men's minds. Everyone is conscious of them in himself; and men's words and actions will satisfy him that they are in others.

Our first inquiry, then, shall be, how they come into the mind. . . .

NO INNATE SPECULATIVE PRINCIPLES

1. It is an established opinion amongst some men, that there are in the understanding certain *innate principles*; some primary notions, Kolivoci evvoloci, characters, as it were stamped upon the mind of man; which the soul receives in its very first being, and brings into the world with it. It would be sufficient to convince unprejudiced readers of the falseness of this supposition, if I should only show (as I hope I shall in the following parts of this Discourse) how men, barely by the use of their natural faculties, may attain to all the knowledge they have, without the help of any innate impressions; and may arrive at certainty, without any such original notions or principles. For I imagine any one will easily grant that it would be impertinent to suppose the ideas of colours innate in a creature to whom God hath given sight, and a power to receive them by the eyes from external objects: and no less unreasonable would it be to attribute several truths to the impressions of nature, and innate characters, when we may observe in ourselves faculties fit to attain as easy and certain knowledge of them as if they were originally imprinted on the mind.

But because a man is not permitted without censure to follow his own thoughts in the search of truth, when they lead him ever so little out of the common road, I shall set down the reasons that made me doubt of the truth of that opinion, as an excuse for my mistake, if I be in one; which I leave to be considered by those who, with me, dispose themselves to embrace truth wherever they find it.

2. There is nothing more commonly taken for granted than that there are certain *principles,* both *speculative* and *practical,* (for they speak of both), universally agreed upon by all mankind: which therefore, they argue, must needs be the constant impressions which the souls of men receive in their first beings, and which they bring into the world with them, as necessarily and really as they do any of their inherent faculties.

3. This argument, drawn from universal consent, has this misfortune in it, that if it were true in matter of fact, that there were certain truths wherein all mankind agreed, it would not prove them innate, if there can be any other way shown how men may come to that universal agreement, in the things they do consent in, which I presume may be done.

4. But, which is worse, this argument of universal consent, which is made use of to prove innate principles, seems to me a demonstration that there are none such: because there are none to which all mankind give an universal assent. I shall begin with the speculative, and instance in those magnified principles of demonstration, 'Whatsoever is, is,' and 'It is impossible for the same thing to be and not to be'; which, of all others, I think have the most allowed title to innate. These have so settled a reputation of maxims universally received, that it will no doubt be thought strange if any one should seem to question it. But yet I take liberty to say, that these propositions are so far from having an universal assent, that there are a great part of mankind to whom they are not so much as known.

5. For, first, it is evident, that all children and idiots have not the least apprehension or thought of them. And the want of that is enough to destroy that universal assent which must needs be the necessary concomitant of all innate truths: it seeming to me near a contradiction to say, that there are truths imprinted

on the soul, which it perceives or understands not: imprinting, if it signify anything, being nothing else but the making certain truths to be perceived. For to imprint anything on the mind without the mind's perceiving it, seems to me hardly intelligible. If therefore children and idiots have souls, have minds, with those impressions upon them, *they* must unavoidably perceive them, and necessarily know and assent to these truths; which since they do not, it is evident that there are no such impressions. For if they are not notions naturally imprinted, how can they be innate? and if they are notions imprinted, how can they be unknown? To say a notion is imprinted on the mind, and yet at the same time to say, that the mind is ignorant of it, and never yet took notice of it, is to make this impression nothing. No proposition can be said to be in the mind which it never yet knew, which it was never yet conscious of. For if any one may, then, by the same reason, all propositions that are true, and the mind is capable ever of assenting to, may be said to be in the mind, and to be imprinted: since, if any one can be said to be in the mind, which it never yet knew, it must be only because it is capable of knowing it; and so the mind is of all truths it ever shall know. Nay, thus truths may be imprinted on the mind which it never did, nor ever shall now; for a man may live long, and die at last in ignorance of many truths which his mind was capable of knowing, and that with certainty. So that if the capacity of knowing be the natural impression contended for, all the truths a man ever comes to know will, by this account, be every one of them innate; and this great point will amount to no more, but only to a very improper way of speaking; which, whilst it pretends to assert the contrary, says nothing different from those who deny innate principles. For nobody, I think, ever denied that the mind was capable of knowing several truths. The capacity, they say, is innate; the knowledge acquired. But then to what end such contest for certain innate maxims? If truths can be imprinted on the understanding without being perceived, I can see no difference there can be between any truths the mind is *capable* of knowing in respect of their original: they must all be innate or all adventitious: in vain shall a man go about to distinguish them. He therefore that talks of innate notions in the understanding, cannot (if he intend thereby any distinct sort of

truths) mean such truths to be in the understanding as it never perceived, and is yet wholly ignorant of. For if these words 'to be in the understanding' have any propriety, they signify to be understood. So that to be in the understanding, and not to be understood; to be in the mind and never to be perceived, is all one as to say anything is and is not in the mind or understanding. If therefore these two propositions, 'Whatsoever is, is,' and 'It is impossible for the same thing to be and not to be,' are by nature imprinted, children cannot be ignorant of them: infants, and all that have souls, must necessarily have them in their understandings, know the truth of them, and assent to it.

6. To avoid this, it is usually answered, that all men know and assent to them, *when they come to the use of reason*; and this is enough to prove them innate, I answer:

7. Doubtful expressions, that have scarce any significance, go for clear reasons to those who, being prepossessed, take not the pains to examine even what they themselves say. For, to apply this answer with any tolerable sense to our present purpose, it must signify one of these two things: either that as soon as men come to the use of reason these supposed native inscriptions come to be known and observed by them; or else, that the use and exercise of men's reason, assists them in the discovery of these principles, and certainly makes them known to them.

8. If they mean, that by the use of reason men may discover these principles, and that this is sufficient to prove them innate; their way of arguing will stand thus, viz. that whatever truths reason can certainly discover to us, and make us firmly assent to, those are all naturally imprinted on the mind; since that universal assent, which is made the mark of them, amounts to no more but this,—that by the use of reason we are capable to come to a certain knowledge of and assent to them; and, by this means, there will be no difference between the maxims of the mathematicians, and theorems they deduce from them: all must be equally allowed innate; they being all discoveries made by the use of reason, and truths that a rational creature may certainly come to know, if he apply his thoughts rightly that way.

9. But how can these men think the use of reason necessary to discover principles that are supposed innate, when reason (if we may

believe them) is nothing else but the faculty of deducing unknown truths from principles or propositions that are already known? That certainly can never be thought innate which we have need of reason to discover; unless as I have said, we will have all the certain truths that reason ever teaches us, to be innate. We may as well think the use of reason necessary to make our eyes discover visible objects, as that there should be need of reason, or the exercise thereof, to make the understanding see what is originally engraven on it, and cannot be in the understanding before it be perceived by it. So that to make reason discover those truths thus imprinted, is to say, that the use of reason discovers to a man what he knew before: and (if men have those innate impressed truths originally, and before the use of reason, and yet are always ignorant of them till they come to the use of reason, it is in effect to say, that men know and know them not at the same time). . . .

15. The senses at first let in *particular ideas*, and furnish the yet empty cabinet, and the mind by degrees growing familiar with some of them, they are lodged in the memory, and names got to them. Afterwards, the mind proceeding further, abstracts them, and by degrees learns the use of general names. In this manner the mind comes to be furnished with ideas, and language, the *materials* about which to exercise its discursive faculty. And the use of reason becomes daily more visible, as these materials that give it employment increase. But though the having of general ideas and the use of general words and reason usually grow together, yet I see not how this any way proves them innate. The knowledge of some truths, I confess, is very early in the mind; but in a way that shows them not to be innate. For, if we will observe, we shall find it still to be about ideas, not innate, but acquired; it being about those first which are imprinted by external things, with which infants have earliest to do, which make the most frequent impressions on their senses. In ideas thus got, the mind discovers that some agree and others differ, probably as soon as it has any use of memory; as soon as it is able to retain and perceive distinct ideas. But whether it be then or no, this is certain, it does so long before it has the use of words; or comes to that which we commonly call 'the use of reason.' For a child knows as certainly before it can speak the difference between the ideas of

sweet and bitter (i.e. that sweet is not bitter), as it knows afterwards (when it comes to speak; that wormwood and sugarplums are not the same thing. . . .

BOOK II: OF IDEAS

CHAPTER I

OF IDEAS IN GENERAL, AND THEIR ORIGINAL

1. *Idea is the object of thinking.*—Every man being conscious to himself that he thinks, and that which his mind is applied about whilst thinking being the ideas that are there, it is past doubt that men have in their mind several ideas, such as are those expressed by the words whiteness, hardness, sweetness, thinking, motion, man, elephant, army, drunkenness, and others: it is in the first place then to be inquired, How he comes by them? I know it is a received doctrine, that men have native ideas and original characters stamped upon their minds in their very first being. This opinion I have at large examined already; and, I suppose, what I have said in the foregoing book will be much more easily admitted, when I have shown whence the understanding may get all the ideas it has, and by what ways and degrees they may come into the mind; for which I shall appeal to everyone's own observation and experience.

2. *All ideas come from sensation or reflection.*—Let us then suppose the mind to be, as we say, white paper, void of all characters, without any ideas; how comes it to be furnished? Whence comes it by that vast store, which the busy and boundless fancy of man has painted on it with an almost endless variety? Whence has it all the materials of reason and knowledge? To this I answer, in one word, from experience. In that all our knowledge is founded, and from that it ultimately derives itself. Our observation, employed either about external sensible objects, or about the internal operations of our minds, perceived and reflected on by ourselves, is that which supplies our understandings with all the materials of thinking. These two are the fountains of knowledge, from whence all the ideas we have, or can naturally have, do spring.

3. *The object of sensation one source of ideas.*— First, our senses, conversant about

particular sensible objects, do convey into the mind several distinct perceptions of things, according to those various ways wherein those objects do affect them; and thus we come by those ideas we have of yellow, white, heat, cold, soft, hard, bitter, sweet, and all those which we call sensible qualities; which when I say the senses convey into the mind, I mean, they from external objects convey into the mind what produces these those perceptions. This great source of most of the ideas we have, depending wholly upon our senses, and derived by them to the understanding, I call *sensation*.

4. *The operations of our minds the other source of them.*—Secondly, the other fountain, from which experience furnisheth the understanding with ideas, is the perception of the operations of our own mind within us, as it is employed about the ideas it has got; which operations when the soul comes to reflect on and consider, do furnish the understanding with another set of ieas which could not be had from things without; and such are perception, thinking, doubting, believing, reasoning, knowing, willing, and all the different actings of our own minds; which we, being conscious of, and observing in ourselves, do from these receive into our understandings as distinct ideas, we do from bodies affecting our senses. This source of ideas every man has wholly in himself; and though it be not sense as having nothing to do with external objects, yet it is very like it, and might properly enough be called *internal sense.* But as I call the other sensation, so I call this *reflection,* the ideas it affords being such only as the mind gets by reflecting on its own operations within itself. By reflection, then, in the following part of this discourse, I could be understood to mean that notice which the mind takes of its own operations, and the manner of them, by reason whereof there come to be ideas of these operations in the understanding. These two, I say, viz., external material things as the object of sensation, and the operations of our own minds within as the objects of sensation, and, to me, the only originals from whence all our ideas take their beginnings. The term *operations* here, I use in a large sense, as comprehending not barely the actions of the mind about its ideas, but some sort of passions arising sometimes from them, such as is the satisfaction or uneasiness arising from any thought.

5. *All our ideas are of the one or the other of these.*—The understanding seems to me not to have the least glimmering of any ideas which it doth not receive from one of these two. *External objects* furnish the mind with the ideas of sensible qualities, which are all those different perceptions they produce in us; and *the mind* furnishes the understanding with ideas of its own operations.

These, when we have taken a full survey of them, and their several modes, [combinations, and relations,] we shall find to contain all our whole stock of ideas; and that we have nothing in our minds which did not come in one of these two ways. Let anyone examine his own thoughts, and thoroughly search into his understanding, and then let him tell me, whether all the original ideas he has there, are any other than of the objects of his senses, or of the operations of his mind considered as objects of his reflection; and how great a mass of knowledge soever he imagines to be lodged there, he will, upon taking a strict view, see that he has not any idea in his mind but what one of these two have imprinted, though perhaps with infinite variety compounded and enlarged by the understanding, as we shall see hereafter. . . .

CHAPTER II

OF SIMPLE IDEAS

1. *Uncompounded appearances.*—The better to understand the nature, manner, and extent of our knowledge, one thing is carefully to be observed concerning the ideas we have; and that is, that some of them are *simple*, and some *complex*.

Though the qualities that affect our senses are, in the things themselves, so united and blended that there is no separation, no distance between them; yet it is plain the ideas they produce in the mind enter by the senses simple and unmixed. For though the sight and touch often take in from the same object, at the same time, different ideas—as a man sees at once motion and color, the hand feels softness and warmth in the same piece of wax—yet the simple (ideas thus united in the same subjects are as perfectly distinct as those that come in by different senses; the coldness and hardness which a man feels in a piece of ice being as distinct ideas in the mind as the smell and whiteness of a lily, or as the taste of sugar and smell of a rose: and there is nothing can be plainer to a man than the clear and distinct perception he has of those simple ideas; which, being each in itself uncompounded, contains in it nothing but *one uniform appearance or conception in the mind,* and is not distinguishable into different ideas.

2. *The mind can neither make nor destroy them.*—These simple ideas, the materials of all our knowledge, are suggested and furnished to the mind only by those two ways above mentioned, viz., sensation and reflection. When the understanding is once stored with these simple ideas, it has the power to repeat, compare, and unite them, even to an almost infinite variety, and so can make at pleasure new complex ideas. But it is not in the power of the most exalted wit or enlarged understanding, by any quickness or variety of thought, to *invent* or *frame* one new simple idea in the mind, not taken in by the ways before mentioned; nor can any force of the understanding *destroy* those that are there: the dominion of man in this little world of his own understanding, being muchwhat the same as it is in the great world of visible things; wherein his power, however managed by art and skill, reaches no farther than to compound and divide the materials that are made to his hand but can do nothing towards the making the least particle of new matter, or destroying one atom of what is already in being. The same inability will everyone find in himself, who shall go about to fashion in his understanding any simple idea not received in by his senses from external objects, or by reflection from the operations of his own mind about them. I would have anyone try to fancy any taste which had never affected his palate, or frame the idea of a scent he had never smelt; and when he can do this, I will also conclude that a blind man hath *ideas* of colors, and a deaf man true, distinct notions of sounds.

3. *Only the qualities that affect the senses are imaginable.*—This is the reason why, though we cannot believe it impossible to God to make a creature with other organs, and more ways to convey into the understanding the notice of corporeal things than those five as they are usually counted, which He has given to man; yet I think it is not possible for anyone to imagine any other qualities in bodies, howsoever constituted, whereby they can be taken

notice of, besides sounds, tastes, smells, visible and tangible qualities. . . .

CHAPTER IV

IDEA OF SOLIDITY

1. *We receive this idea from touch.*—The idea of *solidity* we receive by our touch; and it arises from the resistance which we find in body to the entrance of any other body into the place it possesses, till it has left it. There is no idea which we receive more constantly from sensation than solidity. Whether we move or rest, in what posture soever we are, we always feel something under us that supports us, and hinders our farther sinking downwards; and the bodies which we daily handle make us perceive that whilst they remain between them, they do, by an insurmountable force, hinder the approach of the parts of our hands that press them. *That which thus hinders the approach of two bodies, when they are moving one towards another, I call solidity.* I will not dispute whether this acceptation of the word solid be nearer to its original signification than that which mathematicians use it in; it suffices that, I think, the common notion of solidity, will allow, if not justify, this use of it; but if any one think it better to call it *impenetrability*, he has my consent. Only I have thought the term solidity the more proper to express this idea, not only because of its vulgar use in that sense, but also because it carried something more of positive in it than impenetrability, which is negative, and is, perhaps, more a consequence of solidity than solidity itself. This of all others, seems the idea most intimately connected with and essential to body, so as nowhere else to be found or imagined but only in matter and though our senses take notice of it but in masses of matter, of a bulk sufficient to cause a sensation in us; yet the mind, having once got this idea from such grosser sensible bodies, traces it farther and considers it, as well as figure, in the minutest particle of matter that can exist, and finds it inseparably inherent in body, wherever or however modified.

2. *Solidity fills space.*—This is the idea which belongs to body, whereby we conceive it to fill space. The idea of which filling of space is, that where we imagine any space taken up by a solid substance, we conceive it so to possess it

that it excludes all other solid substances, and will for ever hinder any two other bodies, that move towards one another in a straight line, from coming to touch one another, unless it removes from between them in a line not parallel to that which they move in. This idea of it, the bodies which we ordinarily handle sufficiently furnish us with.

3. *Distinct from space.*—This resistance, whereby it keeps other bodies out of the space which it possesses, is so great that no force, how great soever, can surmount it. All the bodies in the world, pressing a drop of water on all sides, will never be able to overcome the resistance which it will make, as soft as it is, to their approaching one another, till it be removed out of their way: whereby our idea of solidity is distinguished both from pure space, which is capable neither of resistance nor motion, and from the ordinary idea of hardness. For a man may conceive two bodies at a distance so as they may approach one another without touching or displacing any solid thing till their superficies come to meet; whereby, I think, we have the clear idea of space without solidity. For (not to go so far as annihilation of any particular body), I ask, whether a man cannot have the idea of the motion of one single body alone, without any other succeeding immediately into its place? I think it is evident he can: the idea of motion in one body no more including the idea of motion in another, than the idea of a square figure in one body includes the idea of a square figure in another. I do not ask, whether bodies do so *exist,* that the motion of one body cannot really be without the motion of another. To determine this either way is to beg the question for or against a *vacuum.* But my question is, whether one cannot have the idea of one body moved, whilst others are at rest? And I think this no one will deny. If so, then the place it deserted gives us the idea of pure space without solidity, whereinto another body may enter without either resistance or protrusion of anything. When the sucker in a pump is drawn, the space it filled in the tube is certainly the same, whether any other body follows the motion of the sucker or not; nor does it imply a contradiction that upon the motion of one body, another that is only contiguous to it should not follow it. The necessity of such a motion is built only on the supposition that the world is full, but not on the distinct ideas of

space and solidity; which are as different as resistance and not-resistance, protrusion and not-protrusion. And that men have ideas of space without body, their very disputes about a vacuum plainly demonstrate, as is showed in another place.

5. *On solidity depend impulse, resistance, and protrusion.*—By this idea of solidity is the extension of body distinguished from the extension of space: the extension of body being nothing but the cohesion or continuity of solid, separable, movable parts; and the extension of space, the continuity of unsolid, inseparable, and immovable parts. Upon the solidity of bodies also depend their mutual impulse, resistance, and protrusion. Of pure space, then, and solidity, there are several (amongst which I confess myself one) who persuade themselves they have clear and distinct ideas; and that they can think on space without anything in it that resists or is protruded by body. This is the idea of pure space, which they think they have as clear as any idea they can have of the extension of body: the idea of the distance between the opposite parts of a concave superficies being equally as clear without as with the idea of any solid parts between; and on the other side they persuade themselves that they have, distinct from that of pure space, the idea of something that fills space, that can be protruded by the impulse of other bodies, or resist their motion. If there be others that have not these two ideas distinct, but confound them, and make but one of them, I know not how men who have the same idea under different names, or different ideas under the same name, can in that case talk with one another, any more than a man who, not being blind or deaf, has distinct ideas of the color of scarlet and the sound of a trumpet, would discourse concerning scarlet color with the blind man I mention in another place, who fancied that the idea of scarlet was like the sound of a trumpet. . . .

CHAPTER VIII

8. Whatsoever the mind perceives in itself, or is the immediate object of perception, thought, or understanding, that I call *idea;* and the power to produce any idea in our mind, I call *quality* of the subject wherein that power is. Thus a snowball having the power to produce in us the ideas of white, cold, and round, the

powers to produce those ideas in us as they are in the snowball, I call qualities; and as they are sensations or perceptions in our understandings, I call them ideas; which ideas, if I speak of them sometimes as the things themselves, I would be understood to mean those qualities in the objects which produce them in us.

9. *Primary qualities.*—[Qualities thus considered in bodies are: *First* such as are utterly inseparable from the body, in what estate soever it be;] and such as, in all the alterations and changes it suffers, all the force can be used upon it, it constantly keeps; and such as sense constantly finds in every particle of matter which has bulk enough to be perceived, and the mind finds inseparable from every particle of matter, though less than to make itself singly be perceived by our senses: v.g., take a grain of wheat, divide it into two parts, each part has still solidity, extension, figure, and mobility, divide it again, and it retains still the same qualities: and so divide it on till the parts become insensible, they must retain still each of them all those qualities. For, division (which is all that a mill or pestle or any other body does upon another, in reducing it to insensible parts) can never take away either solidity, extension, figure, or mobility from any body, but only makes two or more distinct separate masses of matter of that which was but one before; all which distinct masses, reckoned as so many distinct bodies, after division, make a certain number. [These I call *original* or *primary qualities* of body, which I think we may observe to produce simple ideas in us, viz., solidity, extension, figure, motion or rest, and number.

10. *Secondary qualities.*—*Secondly,* such qualities, which in truth are nothing in the objects themselves, but powers to produce various sensations in us by their primary qualities, i.e., by the bulk, figure, texture, and motion of their insensible parts, as colors, sounds, tastes, etc., these I call *secondary* qualities. To these might be added a third sort, which are allowed to be barely powers, though they are as much real qualities in the subject as those which I, to comply with the common way of speaking, call qualities, but, for distinction, *secondary* qualities. For, the power in fire to produce a new color or consistency in wax or clay, by its primary qualities, is as much a quality in fire as the power it has to produce in

me a new idea or sensation of warmth or burning, which I felt not before, by the same primary qualities, viz., the bulk, texture, and motion of its insensible parts.]

11. [*How primary qualities produce ideas in us.*—The next thing to be considered is, how bodies produce ideas in us; and that is manifestly by impulse, the only way which we can conceive bodies to operate in.]

12. If, then, external objects be not united to our minds when they produce ideas herein, and yet we perceive these original qualities in such of them as singly fall under our senses, it is evident that some motion must be thence continued by our nerves, or animal spirits, by some parts of our bodies, to the brain or the seat of sensation, there to produce in our minds the particular ideas we have to them. And since the extension, figure, number, and motion of bodies of an observable bigness, may be perceived at a distance by the sight, it is evident some singly imperceptible bodies must come from them to the eyes, and thereby convey to the brain some motion which produces these ideas which we have of them in us.

13. *How secondary.*—After the same manner that the ideas of these original qualities are produced in us, we may conceive that the ideas of secondary qualities are also produced, viz., by the operation of insensible particles on our senses. For it being manifest that there are bodies, and good store of bodies, each whereof are so small that we cannot by any of our senses discover either their bulk, figure, or motion (as is evident in the particles of the air and water, and others extremely smaller than those, perhaps as much smaller than the particles of air or water as the particles of air or water are smaller than peas or hailstones): let us suppose at present that the different motions and figures, bulk and number, of such particles, affecting the several organs of our senses, produce in us these different sensations which we have from the colors and smells of bodies, v.g., that a violet, by the impulse of such insensible particles of matter of peculiar figures and bulks, and in different degrees and modifications of their motions, causes the ideas of the blue color and sweet scent of that flower to be produced in our minds; it being no more impossible to conceive that God should annex such ideas to such motions, with which they

have no similitude, than that He should annex the idea of pain to the motion of a piece of steel dividing our flesh, with which the idea hath no resemblance.

14. What I have said concerning colors and smells may be understood also of tastes and sounds, and other the like sensible qualities; which, whatever reality we by mistake attribute to them, are in truth nothing in the objects themselves, but powers to produce various sensations in us, and depend on those primary qualities, viz., bulk figure, texture, and motion of parts [as I have said].

15. *Ideas of primary qualities are resemblances; of secondary, not.*—From whence I think it is easy to draw this observation, that the ideas of primary qualities of bodies are resemblances of them, and their patterns do really exist in the bodies themselves; but the ideas produced in us by these secondary qualities have no resemblance of them at all. There is nothing like our ideas existing in the bodies themselves. They are, in the bodies we denominate from them, only a power to produce those sensations in us; and what is sweet, blue, or warm in idea, is but the certain bulk, figure, and motion of the insensible parts of the bodies themselves, which we call so.

16. Flame is denominated hot and light; snow, white, and cold; and manna, white and sweet, from the ideas they produce in us, which qualities are commonly thought to be the same in those bodies that those ideas are in us, the one the perfect resemblance of the other, as they are in a mirror; and it would by most men be judged very extravagant, if one should say otherwise. And yet he that will consider that the same fire that at one distance produces in us the sensation of warmth, does at a nearer approach produce in us the far different sensation of pain, ought to bethink himself what reason he has to say, that this idea of warmth which was produced in him by the fire, is actually in the fire, and his idea of pain which the same fire produced in him the same way is not in the fire. Why are whiteness and coldness in snow and pain not, when it produces the one and the other idea in us, and can do neither but by the bulk, figure, number, and motion of its solid parts?

17. The particular bulk, number, figure, and motion of the parts of fire or snow are really in them, whether anyone's senses perceive them or no; and therefore they may be called *real* qualities, because they really exist in those bodies. But light, heat, whiteness, or coldness, are no more really in them than sickness or pain is in manna. Take away the sensation of them; let not the eyes see light or colors, nor the ears hear sounds; let the palate not taste, nor the nose smell; and all colors, tastes, odors, and sounds, as they are such particular ideas, vanish and cease, and are reduced to their causes, i.e., bulk, figure, and motion of parts. . . .

19. Let us consider the red and white colors in porphyry; hinder light but from striking on it, and its colors vanish; it no longer produces any such ideas in us. Upon the return of light, it produces these appearances on us again. Can anyone think any real alterations are made in the porphyry by the presence or absence of light, and that those ideas of whiteness and redness are really in porphyry in the light, when it is plain it has no color in the dark? It has indeed such a configuration of particles, both night and day, as are apt, by the rays of light rebounding from some parts of that hard stone, to produce in us the idea of redness, and from others the idea of whiteness. But whiteness or redness are not in it at any time, but such a texture that hath the power to produce such a sensation in us. . . .

22. I have, in what just goes before, been engaged in physical inquiries a little farther than perhaps I intended. But it being necessary to make the nature of sensation a little understood, and to make the difference between the qualities in bodies, and the ideas produced by them in the mind, to be distinctly conceived, without which it were impossible to discourse intelligibly of them, I hope I shall be pardoned this little excursion into natural philosophy, it being necessary in our present inquiry to distinguish the primary and real qualities of bodies, which are always in them (viz., solidity, extension, figure, number, and motion on rest, and are sometimes perceived by us, viz., when the bodies they are in are big enough singly to be discerned), from those secondary and imputed qualities, which are but the powers of several combinations of those primary ones, when they operate without being distinctly discerned; whereby we also may come to know what ideas

are, and what are not, resemblances of something really existing in the bodies we denominate from them. . . .

CHAPTER XII

OF COMPLEX IDEAS

1. *Made by the mind out of simple ones.*— We have hitherto considered those ideas, in the reception whereof the mind is only passive, which are those simple ones received from sensation and reflection before mentioned, whereof the mind cannot make one to itself, nor have any ideas which does not wholly consist of them. [But as the mind is wholly passive in the reception of all its simple ideas, so it exerts several acts of its own, whereby out of its simple ideas, as the materials and foundations of the rest, the others are framed. The acts of the mind wherein its exerts its power over its simple ideas are chiefly these three: (1) Combining several simple ideas into one compound one; and thus all *complex ideas* are made. (2) The second is bringing two ideas, whether simple or complex, together, and setting them by one another, so as to take a view of them at once, without uniting them into one; by which way it gets all its *ideas of relations*. (3) The third is separating them from all other ideas that accompany them in their real existence; this is called abstraction: and thus all its *general ideas* are made. This shows man's power and its way of operation to be much the same in the material and intellectual world. For, the materials in both being such as he had no power over, either to make or destroy, all that man can do is either to unite them together, or to set them by one another, or wholly separate them. I shall here begin with the first of these in the consideration of complex ideas, and come to the other two in their due places.] As simple ideas are observed to exist in several combinations united together so the mind has a power to consider several of them united together as one idea; and that not only as they are united in external objects, but as itself has joined them. Ideas thus made up of several simple ones put together I call *complex*; such as are beauty, gratitude, a man, an army, the universe; which, though complicated of various simple ideas or complex ideas made up of simple ones, yet are, when the mind pleases, considered each by itself as one entire thing, and signified by one name.

2. *Made voluntarily.*—In this faculty of repeating and joining together its ideas, the mind has great power in varying and multiplying the objects of its thoughts infinitely beyond what sensation or reflection furnished it with; but all this still confined to those simple ideas which it received from those two sources, and which are the ultimate materials of all its compositions. For, simple ideas are all from things themselves; and of these the mind can have no more nor other than what are suggested to it. It can have no other ideas of sensible qualities than what come from without by the senses, nor any ideas of other kind of operations of a thinking substance than what it finds in itself. But when it has once got these simple ideas, it is not confined barely to observation, and what offers itself from without; it can, by its own power, put together those ideas it has, and make new complex ones which it never received so united.

3. *Complex ideas are either of modes, substances, or relations.*—Complex ideas, however compounded and decompounded, though their number be infinite, and the variety endless wherewith they fill and entertain the thoughts of men, yet I think they may be all reduced under these three heads: (1) Modes. (2) Substances. (3) Relations.

4. *Ideas of modes.*—First, *modes* I call such complex ideas which, however compounded, contain not in them the supposition of subsisting by themselves, but are considered as dependences on, or affections of, substances; such are the ideas signified by the words, triangle, gratitude, murder, etc. And if in this I use the word mode in somewhat a different sense from its ordinary signification, I beg pardon; it being unavoidable in discourses differing from the ordinary received notions, either to make new words or to use old words in somewhat a new signification: the latter whereof, in our present case, is perhaps the more tolerable of the two. . . .

6. *Ideas of substances, single or collective.*— Secondly, the ideas of *substances* are such combinations of simple ideas as are taken to represent distinct *particular* things subsisting by themselves, in which the supposed or confused idea of substance, such as it is, is always the first and chief. Thus, if to substance be joined the simple idea of a certain dull, whitish color,

with certain degrees of weight, hardness, ductility, and fusibility, we have the idea of lead; and a combination of the ideas of a certain sort of figure, with the powers of motion, thought, and reasoning, joined to substance, make the ordinary idea of a man. Now of substances also there are two sorts of ideas, one of single substances, as they exist separately, as of a man or a sheep; the other of several of those put together, as an army of men or flock of sheep; which collective ideas of several substances thus put together, are as much each of them one single idea as that of a man or an unit.

7. *Relation.*—Thirdly, the last sort of complex ideas is that we call *relation*, which consists in the consideration and comparing one idea with another. Of these several kinds we shall treat in their order.

8. *The abstrusest ideas are from the two sources.*—If we trace the progress of our minds, and with attention observe how it repeats, adds together, unites its simple ideas received from sensation or reflection, it will lead us further than at first perhaps we should have imagined. And I believe we shall find, if we warily observe the originals of our notions, that even the most abstruse ideas, how remote soever they may seem from sense, or from any operation of our own minds, are yet only such as the standing frames to itself, by repeating and joining together ideas that it had either from objects of sense, or from its own operations about them: so that those even large and abstract ideas are derived from sensation or reflection, being no other than what the mind, by the ordinary use of its own faculties, employed about ideas received from objects of sense, or from the operations it observes in itself about them, may and does attain unto. This I shall endeavor to show in the ideas we have of space, time, and infinity, and some few other that seem the most remote from those originals. . . .

CHAPTER XXIII

OF OUR COMPLEX IDEAS OF SUBSTANCES

1. *Ideas of particular substances, how made.*—The mind being, as I have declared, furnished with a great number of the simple ideas conveyed in by the senses, as they are found in exterior things, or by reflection on its own oper-

ations, takes notice, also, that a certain number of these simple ideas go constantly together; which being presumed to belong to one thing, and words being suited to common apprehensions, and made use of for quick despatch, are called, so united in one subject, by one name; which, by inadvertency, we are apt afterward to talk of and consider as one simple idea, which indeed is a complication of many ideas together: because, as I have said, not imagining how these simple ideas can subsist by themselves, we accustom ourselves to suppose some *substratum* wherein they do subsist, and from which they do result; which therefore we call *substance*.

2. *Our obscure idea of substance in general.*—So that if anyone will examine himself concerning his notion of pure substance in general, he will find he has no other idea of it at all, but only a supposition of he knows not what support of such qualities which are capable of producing simple ideas in us; which qualities are commonly called accidents. If anyone should be asked, what is the subject wherein color or weight inheres, he would have nothing to say, but, the solid extended parts. And if he were demanded, what is that solidity and extension inhere in, he would not be in a much better case than the Indian before mentioned, who, saying that the world was supported by a great elephant, was asked, what the elephant rested on; to which his answer was, a great tortoise; but being again pressed to know what gave support to the broad-backed tortoise, replied —something, he knew not what. And thus here, as in all other cases where we use words without having clear and distinct ideas, we talk like children: who, being questioned what such a thing is which they know not, readily give this satisfactory answer, that it is *something*; which in truth signifies no more, when so used either by children or men, but that they know not what; and that the thing they pretend to know and talk of, is what they have no distinct idea of at all, and so are perfectly ignorant of it, and in the dark. The idea, then, we have, to which we give the *general* name substance, being nothing but the supposed, but unknown, support of those qualities we find existing, which we imagine cannot subsist *sine re substante*, "without something to support them," we call that support *substantia;* which, according to the true import of the word, is, in plain

English, standing under, or upholding.

3. *Of the sorts of subtances.*—An obscure and relative idea of substance in general being thus made, we come to have the ideas of particular sorts of substances, by collecting such combinations of simple ideas as are by experience and observation of men's senses taken notice of to exist together, and are therefore supposed to flow from the particular internal constitution or unknown essence of that substance. Thus we come to have the ideas of a man, horse, gold, water, etc., of which substances, whether anyone has any other clear idea, farther than of certain simple ideas coexistent together, I appeal to everyone's own experience. It is the ordinary qualities observable in iron or a diamond, put together, that make the true complex idea of those substances, which a smith or a jeweler commonly knows better than a philosopher; who, whatever substantial forms he may talk of, has no other idea of those substances than what is framed by a collection of those simple ideas which are to be found in them. Only we must take notice that our complex ideas of substances, besides all these simple ideas they are made up of, have always the confused idea of something to which they belong, and in which they subsist: and therefore when we speak of any sort of substance, we say it is a thing having such or such qualities; as, body is a thing, that is extended, figured, and capable of motion; spirit, a thing capable of thinking; and so hardness, friability, and power to draw iron, we say, are qualities to be found in a loadstone. These and the like fashions of speaking, intimate that the substance is supposed always something, besides the extension, figure, solidity, motion, thinking, or other observable ideas, though we know not what it is.

4. *No clear or distinct idea of substance in general.*—Hence, when we talk or think of any particular sort of corporeal substances, as horse, stone, etc., though the idea we have of either of them be but the complication or collection of those several simple ideas of sensible qualities which we used to find united in the thing called horse or stone; yet because we cannot conceive how they should subsist alone, nor one in another, we suppose them existing in, and supported by, some common subject; which support we denote by the name substance, though it be certain we have no clear or distinct idea of that thing we suppose a support.

5. *As clear an idea of spirit as body.*—The same happens concerning the operations of the mind; viz., thinking, reasoning, fearing, etc., which we, concluding not to subsist of themselves, nor apprehending how they can belong to body, or be produced by it, we are apt to think these the actions of some other substance, which we call *spirit*; whereby yet it is evident, that having no other idea or notion of matter but something wherein those many sensible qualities which affect our senses do subsist; by supposing a substance wherein thinking knowing, doubting, and a power of moving, etc., do subsist, we have as clear a notion of the substance of spirit as we have of body: the one being supposed to be (without knowing what it is) the *substratum* to those simple ideas we have from without; and the other supposed (with a like ignorance of what it is) to be the *substratum* to those operations which we experiment in ourselves within. It is plain, then, that the idea of *corporeal substance* in matter is as remote from our conceptions and apprehensions as that of *spiritual substance,* or spirit; and therefore, from our not having any notion of the substance of spirit, we can no more conclude its non-existence than we can, for the same reason, deny the existence of body: it being as rational to affirm there is no body, because we have no clear and distinct idea of the substance of matter, as to say there is no spirit, because we have no clear and distinct idea of the substance of a spirit.

6. *Our ideas of particular sorts of substances.*—Whatever therefore be the secret and abstract nature of substance in general, all the ideas we have of particular, distinct sorts of substances, are nothing but several combinations of simple ideas coexisting in such, though unknown, cause of their union, as makes the whole subsist of itself. It is by such combinations of simple ideas, and nothing else, that we represent particular sorts of substances to ourselves, such are the ideas we have of their several species in our minds; and such only do we, by their specific names, signify to others, v.g., man, horse, sun, water, iron; upon hearing which words everyone who understands the language, frames in his mind a combination of

those several simple ideas which he has usually observed or fancied to exist together under that denomination; all which he supposed to rest in, and be, as it were, adherent to, that unknown common subject, which inheres not in anything else. Though in the meantime it be manifest, and everyone upon inquiry into his own thoughts will find, that he has no other ideas of any substance, v.g., let it be gold, horse, iron, man, vitriol, bread, but what he has barely of those sensible qualities which he supposes to inhere with a supposition of such a *substratum* as gives, as it were, a support to those qualities, or simple ideas, which he has observed to exist united together. Thus, the idea of the sun,—what is it but an aggregate of those several simple ideas—bright, hot, roundish, having a constant regular motion, at a certain distance from us, and perhaps some other: as he who thinks and discourses of the sun has been more or less accurate in observing those sensible qualities, ideas, or properties which are in that thing which he calls the sun. . . .

11. *The now secondary qualities of bodies would disappear, if we could discover the primary ones of their minute parts.*—Had we senses acute enough to discern the minute particles of bodies, and the real constitution on which their sensible qualities depend, I doubt not but they would produce quite different ideas in us, and that which is now the yellow color of gold would then disappear, and instead of it we should see an admirable texture of parts of a certain size and figure. This microscopes plainly discover to us; for, what to our naked eyes produces a certain color is, by thus augmenting the acuteness of our senses, discovered to be quite a different thing; and the thus altering, as it were, the proportion of the bulk of the minute parts of a colored object to our usual sight, produces different ideas from what it did before. Thus sand, or pounded glass, which is opaque and white to the naked eye, is pellucid in a microscope; and a hair seen this way loses its former color, and is in a great measure pellucid, with a mixture of some bright sparkling colors, such as appear from the refraction of diamonds and other pellucid bodies. Blood to the naked eye appears all red; but by a good microscope, wherein its lesser parts appear, shows only some few globules of red, swimming in a pellucid liquor; and how

these red globules would appear, if glasses could be found that yet could magnify them one thousand or ten thousand times more, is uncertain. . . .

15. *Idea of spiritual substances as clear as of bodily substances.*—Besides the complex ideas we have of material sensible substances, of which I have last spoken, by the simple ideas we have taken from those operations of our own minds, which we experiment daily in ourselves, as thinking, understanding, willing, knowing, and power of beginning motion, etc., co-existing in some substance, we are able to frame the *complex idea of an immaterial spirit*. And thus, by putting together the ideas of thinking, perceiving, liberty, and power of moving themselves and other things, we have as clear a perception and notion of immaterial substances as we have of material. For putting together the ideas of thinking willing, or the power of moving or quieting corporeal motion, joined to substance, of which we have no distinct idea, we have the idea of an immaterial spirit; and by putting together the ideas of coherent, solid parts, and a power of being moved, joined with substance, of which, likewise we have no positive idea, we have the idea of matter. The one is as clear and distinct an idea as the other: the idea of thinking and moving a body being as clear and distinct ideas as the ideas of extension, solidity, and begin moved. For our idea of substance is equally obscure, or none at all, in both; it is but a supposed I-know-not-what, to support those ideas we call accidents. [It is for want of reflection that we are apt to think that our senses show us nothing but material things. Every act of sensation, when duly considered, gives us an equal view of both parts of nature, the corporeal and spiritual. For whilst I know, by seeing or hearing, etc., that there is some corporeal being without me, the object of that sensation, I do more certainly know that there is some spiritual being within me that sees and hears. This I must be convinced cannot be the action of bare insensible matter, nor ever could be without an immaterial thinking being.]

16. *No idea of abstract substance.*—By the complex idea of extended, figured, colored, and all other sensible qualities, which is all that we know of it, we are as far from the idea of the substance of body as if we knew nothing at all; nor after all the acquaintance and familiarity

which we imagine we have with matter, and the many qualities men assure themselves they perceive and know in bodies, will it, perhaps, upon examination be found that they have any more or clearer primary ideas belonging to body than they have belonging to immaterial spirit.

17. *The cohesion of solid parts and impulse, the primary ideas of body.*—The primary ideas we have peculiar to body, as contradistinguished to spirit, are the *cohesion of solid and consequently separable parts,* and a *power of communicating motion by impulse.* These, I think, are the original ideas proper and peculiar to body; for figure is but the consequence of finite extension.

18. *Thinking and motivity, the primary ideas of spirit.*—The ideas we have belonging and peculiar to spirit are *thinking,* and *will,* or a *power of putting body into motion by thought,* and, which is consequent to it, *liberty.* For as body cannot but communicate its motion by impulse to another body, which it meets with at rest; so the mind can put bodies into motion, or forbear to do so, as it pleases. The ideas of existence, duration, and mobility are common to them both. . . .

29. To conclude: Sensation convinces us that there are solid, extended substances; and reflection, that there are thinking ones; experience assures us of the existence of such beings; and that the one hath a power to move body by impulse, the other by thought; this we cannot doubt of. Experience, I say, every moment furnishes us with the clear ideas both of the one and the other. But beyond these ideas, as received from their proper sources, our faculties will not reach. If we would inquire farther into their nature, causes, and manner, we perceive not the nature of extension clearer than we do of thinking. If we would explain them any farther, one is as easy as the other; and there is no more difficulty to conceive how a substance we know not should by impulse set body into motion. So that we are no more able to discover wherein the ideas belonging to body consist, than those belonging to spirit. From whence it seems probable to me that the simple ideas we receive from sensation and reflection are the boundaries of our thoughts; beyond which, the mind, whatever efforts it would make, is not able to advance one jot; nor can it make any discoveries, when it would pry into

the nature and hidden causes of those ideas. . . .

33. *Idea of God.*—For if we examine the idea we have of the incomprehensible Supreme Being, we shall find that we come by it the same way; and that the complex ideas we have both of God and separate spirits are made of the simple ideas we receive from reflection: v.g., having, from what we experiment in ourselves, got the ideas of existence and duration, of knowledge and power, of pleasure and happiness, and of several other qualities and powers which it is better to have than to be without; when we would frame an idea the most suitable we can to the Supreme Being, we enlarge every one of these with our idea of infinity; and so, putting them together, make our complex idea of God For that the mind has such a power of enlarging some of its ideas, received from sensation and reflection, has been already showed.

34. If I find that I know some few things, and some of them, or all, perhaps, imperfectly; I can frame an idea of knowing twice as many, which I can double again as often as I can add to number; and thus enlarge my idea of knowledge, by extending its comprehension to all things existing or possible. The same also I can do of knowing them more perfectly, i.e., all their qualities, powers, causes, consequences, and relations, etc., till all be perfectly known that is in them, or can any way relate to them; and thus frame the idea of infinite or boundless knowledge. The same may also be done of power, till we come to that we call infinite; and also of the duration of existence without beginning or end; and so frame the idea of an eternal being. The degrees or extent, wherein we ascribe existence, power, wisdom, and all other perfections (which we can have any ideas of), to that Sovereign Being which we call God, being all boundless and infinite, we frame the best idea of Him our minds are capable of: all which is done, I say, by enlarging those simple ideas we have taken from the operations of our own minds by reflection, or by our senses from exterior things, to that vastness to which infinity can extend them.

35. For it is infinity which, joined to our ideas of existence, power, knowledge, etc., makes that complex idea whereby we represent to ourselves, the best we can, the Supreme Being. For though in His own essence, which certainly we do not know (not knowing the real essence of a

pebble, or a fly, or of our own selves), God be simple and uncompounded; yet, I think, I may say we have no other idea of Him but a complex one of existence, knowledge, power, happiness, etc., infinite and eternal: which are all distinct ideas, and some of them being relative are again compounded of others; all which, being, as has been shown, originally got from sensation and reflection, go to make up the idea or notion we have of God. . . .

37. *Recapitulation.*—And thus we have seen what kind of ideas we have of substances of all kinds, wherein they consist, and how we came by them. From whence, I think, it is very evident:—

First, that all our ideas of the several sorts of substances are nothing but collections of simple ideas, with a supposition of something to which they belong, and in which they subsist; though of this supposed something we have no clear distinct idea at all.

Secondly, that all the simple ideas that, thus united in one common substratum, make up our complex ideas of several sorts of substances, are no other but such as we have received from sensation or reflection. So that even in those which we think we are most intimately acquainted with, and that come nearest the comprehension of our most enlarged conceptions, we cannot reach beyond those simple ideas. And even in those which seem most remote from all we have to do with, and do infinitely surpass anything we can perceive in ourselves by reflection, or discover by sensation in other things, we can attain to nothing but those simple ideas which we originally received from sensation or reflection; as is evident in the complex ideas we have of angels, and particularly of God Himself.

Thirdly, that most of the simple ideas that make up our complex ideas of substances, when truly considered, are only powers, however we are apt to take them for positive qualities: v.g., the greatest part of the ideas that make our complex idea of gold are yellowness, great weight, ductility, fusibility, and solubility in *aqua regia,* etc., all united together in an unknown substratum; all which ideas are nothing else but so many relations to other substances, and are not really in the gold considered barely in itself, though they depend on those real and primary qualities of its internal constitution, whereby it has a fitness differently

to operate and be operated on by several other substances.

CHAPTER XXV

OF RELATION

1. *Relation, what.*—Besides the ideas, whether simple or complex, that the mind has of things as they are in themselves, there are others it gets from their comparison one with another. The understanding, in the consideration of anything, is not confined to that precise object: it can carry any idea, as it were, beyond itself, or at least look beyond it to see how it stands in conformity to any other. When the mind so considers one thing, that it does, as it were, bring it to and set it by another, and carries its view from one to the other: this is, as the words import, *relation* and *respect*; and the denominations given to positive things, intimating that respect, and serving as marks to lead the thoughts beyond the subject itself denominated to something distinct from it, are what we call *relatives*; and the things so brought together, *related*. Thus, when the mind considers Caius as such a positive being, it takes nothing into that idea, but what really exists in Caius; v.g., when I consider him as man, I have nothing in my mind but the complex idea of the species man. So likewise, when I say, "Caius is a white man," I have nothing but the bare consideration of man who hath that white color. But when I give Caius the name 'husband,' I intimate some other person; and when I give him the name 'whiter,' I intimate some other thing; in both cases my thought is led to something beyond Caius, and there are two things brought into consideration. And since any idea, whether simple or complex, may be the occasion why the mind thus brings two things together, and as it were, takes a view of them at once, though still considered as distinct; therefore any of our ideas may be the foundation of relation. As in the above-mentioned instance, the contract and ceremony of of marriage with Sempronia, is the occasion of the denomination or relation of husband; and the color white, the occasion why he is said to be whiter than freestone. . . .

4. *Relation different from the things related.* —This farther may be observed, that the ideas of relation may be the same in men who have

far different ideas of the things, that are related, or that are thus compared: v.g., those who have far different ideas of a man, may yet agree in the notion of a father: which is a notion superinduced to the substance, or man, and refers only to an act of that thing called man, whereby he contributed to the generation of one of his own kind, let man be what it will. . . .

9. *Relations all terminate in simple ideas.*— Thirdly, though there be a great number of considerations wherein things may be compared, and so a multitude of relations; yet they all terminate in, and are concerned about, those simple ideas either of sensation or reflection, which I think to be the whole materials of all our knowledge. To clear this, I shall show it in the most considerable relations that we have any notion of; and in some that seem to be remote from sense or reflection: which yet will appear to have their ideas from thence, and leave it past doubt, that the notions we have of them are but certain simple ideas, and so originally derived from sense or reflection. . . .

11. *Conclusion.*—Having laid down these premises concerning relation in general, I shall now proceed to show in some instances how all the ideas we have of relation are made up, as the others are, only of simple ideas; and that they all, how refined or remote from sense soever they seem, terminate at last in simple ideas. I shall begin with the most comprehensive relation, wherein all things that do or can exist are concerned; and that is the relation of cause and effect. The idea whereof, how derived from the two fountains of all our knowledge, sensation and reflection, I shall next consider.

CHAPTER XXVI

OF CAUSE AND EFFECT AND OTHER RELATIONS

1. *Whence their ideas got.*—In the notice that our senses take of the constant vicissitude of things, we cannot but observe that several particular both qualities and substances begin to exist; and that they receive this their existence from the due application and operation of some other being. From this observation we get our ideas of cause and effect. *That which produces any simple or complex ideas*, we denote by the general name *cause;* and *that which is produced, effect.* Thus finding that in that substance which we call 'wax' fluidity, which is a simple idea that was not in it before, is constantly produced by the application of a certain degree of heat, we call the simple idea of heat, in relation to fluidity in wax, the cause of it, and fluidity the effect. So also finding that the substance, wood, which is a certain collection of simple ideas so called, by the application of fire is turned into another substance called ashes, i.e., another complex idea, consisting of a collection of simple ideas, quite different from that complex idea which we call wood, we consider fire, in relation to ashes, as cause, and the ashes, as effect. So that whatever is considered by us to conduce or operate to the producing any particular simple idea, or collection of simple ideas, whether substance or mode, which did not before exist, hath thereby in our minds the relation of a cause, and so is denominated by us. . . .

George Berkeley

The influence of George Berkeley (1685-1753) on the development of ideas in Western Civilization is undeniable. Born in an age in which an increasingly mechanistic and materialistic philosophy was becoming the prevailing intellectual mood, he had the courage to stand in opposition to it in the name of a philosophical outlook which subjected the ordinary idea of matter to a devastating critique. Berkeley's famous statement *"esse est percipi,"* or "to be is to be perceived," came to serve as the slogan of a philosophy which became known as "subjective idealism." According to Berkeley, the entire physical world is real only insofar as there is a consciousness which perceives it. In the absence of the knowing subject or consciousness, the physical or material world reduces itself to nothing: no object can exist unless there is a knowing subject.

The religious tendencies of Berkeley, however, prevented him from falling into the philosophical position known as solipsism, which maintains that only the subject itself (I myself) exists, and that the whole world of experience is merely my mental representation. A solipsist rejects the substantial existence of anything outside of his own mind and affirms that the real world is coextensive with his awareness of the world. It seems that some of the ideas of Berkeley moved in this solipsistic direction, for, after all, he reduced matter to the category of a mental representation or idea.

But Berkeley was unwilling to accept the solipsistic conclusions that could have easily emerged from his philosophical outlook. He insisted on affirming the existence of his consciousness or spirit, and the existence of other consciousnesses or spirits as well. The material world is, therefore, not merely a private hallucination or an individual illusion, but the collective world of experiences in which all conscious beings participate. Furthermore, underneath the world of physical reality and the world of spiritual existence, there was, for Berkeley, the permeating presence of an omnipresent and omnipotent God who is in fact the only genuine reality.

Berkeley's philosophy is, accordingly, supported by the most fervent religious faith, and his own life was a living testimony to his faith. He became a clergyman in 1709 and in 1724 was appointed bishop of Cloyne in Ireland. The dream of his life was the conversion of the American Indians to Christianity, and to pave the way for the realization of such a dream, he travelled to the American continent, where he spent three years waiting for the financial support that his enterprise required. In 1731 he returned to Ireland, after becoming convinced of the impracticality of his project.

As a philosopher, Berkeley delved into questions pertaining to the nature of vision and light, the structure of the process of knowledge, and the general metaphysical meaning of reality. His most important work is *A Treatise Concerning the Principles of Human Knowledge* (1710, 1734). We have chosen to include in our book the last section of his *Three Dialogues Between Hylas and Philonous* (1713). As in the case of Plato's *Dialogues*, in Berkeley's dialogues there is a constant battle of ideas. Unquestionably, Philonous speaks on behalf of the philosophical bishop of Cloyne, and Hylas defends a materialistic point of view.

Does the Material World Exist?

Philonous. Tell me, Hylas, what are the fruits of yesterday's meditation? Hath it confirmed you in the same mind you were in at parting? or have you since seen cause to change your opinion?

Hylas. Truly my opinion is, that all our opinions are alike vain and uncertain. What we approve to-day, we condemn tomorrow. We keep a stir about knowledge, and spend our lives in the pursuit of it, when, alas! we know nothing all the while: nor do I think it possible for us ever to know anything in this life. Our faculties are too narrow and too few. Nature certainly never intended us for speculation.

Phil. What! say you we can know nothing, Hylas?

Hyl. There is not that single thing in the world, whereof we can know the real nature, or what it is in itself.

Phil. Will you tell me I do not really know what fire or water is?

Hyl. You may indeed know that fire appears

hot, and water fluid: but this is no more than knowing what sensations are produced in your own mind, upon the application of fire and water to your organs of sense. Their internal constitution, their true and real nature, you are utterly in the dark as to that.

Phil. Do I not know this to be a real stone that I stand on, and that which I see before my eyes to be a real tree?

Hyl. Know? No, it is impossible you or any man alive should know it. All you know is, that you have such a certain idea or appearance in your own mind. But what is this to the real tree or stone? I tell you, that colour, figure, and hardness, which you perceive, are not the real natures of those things, or in the least like them. The same may be said of all other real things or corporeal substances which compose the world. They have none of them any thing in themselves, like those sensible qualities by us perceived. We should not therefore pretend to affirm or know anything of them, as they are in their own nature.

Phil. But surely, Hylas, I can distinguish gold, for example, from iron: and how could this be, if I knew not what either truly was?

Hyl. Believe me, Philonous, you can only distinguish between your own ideas. That yellowness, that weight, and other sensible qualities, think you they are really in the gold? They are only relative to the senses, and have no absolute existence in nature. And in pretending to distinguish the species of real things, by the appearances in your mind, you may perhaps act as wisely as he that should conclude two men were of a different species, because their clothes were not of the same colour.

Phil. It seems then we are altogether put off with the appearances of things, and those false ones too. The very meat I eat, and the cloth I wear, have nothing in them like what I see and feel.

Hyl. Even so.

Phil. But is it not strange the whole world should be thus imposed on and so foolish as to believe their senses? And yet I know not how it is, but men eat, and drink, and sleep, and perform all the offices of life as comfortably and conveniently, as if they really knew the things they are conversant about.

Hyl. They do so: but you know ordinary practice does not require a nicety of speculative knowledge. Hence the vulgar retain their mis-

takes, and for all that, make a shift to bustle through the affairs of life. But philosophers know better things.

Phil. You mean, they know that they *know nothing.*

Hyl. That is the very top and perfection of human knowledge.

Phil. But are you all this while in earnest, Hylas; and are you seriously persuaded that you know nothing real in the world? Suppose you are going to write, would you not call for pen, ink, and paper, like another man; and do you not know what it is you call for?

Hyl. How often must I tell you, that I know not the real nature of any one thing in the universe? I may, indeed, upon occasion, make use of pen, ink, and paper. But what any one of them is in its own true nature, I declare positively I know not. And the same is true with regard to every other corporeal thing. And, what is more, we are not only ignorant of the true and real nature of things, but even of their existence. It cannot be denied that we perceive such certain appearances or ideas; but it cannot be concluded from thence that bodies really exist. Nay, now I think on it, I must, agreeably to my former concessions, further declare, that it is impossible any real corporeal thing should exist in nature.

Phil. You amaze me. Was ever any thing more wild and extravagant than the notion you now maintain: and is it not evident you are led into all these extravagancies by the belief of *material substance?* This makes you dream of those unknown natures in every thing. It is this occasions your distinguishing between the reality and sensible appearances of things. It is to this you are indebted for being ignorant of what every body else knows perfectly well. Nor is this all: you are not only ignorant of the true nature of every thing, but you know not whether any thing really exists, or whether there are any true natures at all; forasmuch as you attribute to your material beings an absolute or external existence, wherein you suppose their reality consists. And as you are forced in the end to acknowledge such an existence means either a direct repugnancy, or nothing at all, it follows that you are obliged to pull down your own hypothesis of material substance, and positively to deny the real existence of any part of the universe. And so you are plunged into the deepest and most deplorable *scepticism* that ever man was. Tell me. Hylas, is it not as I say?

Hyl. I agree with you. *Material substance* was no more than an hypothesis, and a false and groundless one too. I will no longer spend my breath in defence of it. But whatever hypothesis you advance, or whatsoever scheme of things you introduce in its stead, I doubt not it will appear every whit as false: let me but be allowed to question you upon it. That is, suffer me to serve you in your own kind, and I warrant it shall conduct you through as many perplexities and contradictions, to the very same state of scepticism that I myself am in at present.

Phil. I assure you, Hylas, I do not pretend to frame any hypothesis at all. I am of a vulgar cast, simple enough to believe my senses, and leave things as I find them. To be plain, it is my opinion, that the real things are those very things I see and feel, and perceive by my senses. These I know, and finding they answer all the necessities and purposes of life, have no reason to be solicitous about any other unknown beings. A piece of sensible bread, for instance, would stay my stomach better than ten thousand times as much of that insensible, unintelligible, real bread you speak of. It is likewise my opinion, that colours and other sensible qualities are on the objects. I cannot for my life help thinking that snow is white, and fire hot. You indeed, who by *snow* and *fire* mean certain external, unperceived, unperceiving substances are in the right to deny whiteness or heat to be affections inherent in them. But I, who understand by those words the things I see and feel, am obliged to think like other folks. And as I am no sceptic with regard to the nature of things, so neither am I as to their existence. That a thing should be really perceived by my senses, and at the same time not really exist, is to me a plain contradiction; since I cannot prescind or abstract, even in thought, the existence of a sensible thing from its being perceived. Wood, stones, fire, water, flesh, iron, and the like things, which I name and discourse of, are things that I know. And I should not have known them, but that I perceived them by my senses; and things perceived by the senses are immediately perceived; and things immediately perceived are ideas; and ideas cannot exist without the mind; their existence therefore consists in being perceived; when therefore they are actually perceived, there can be no doubt of

their existence. Away then with all that scepticism, all those ridiculous philosophical doubts. What a jest is it for a philosopher to question the existence of sensible things, till he hath it proved to him from the veracity of God; or to pretend our knowledge in this point falls short of intuition or demonstration! I might as well doubt of my own being, as of the being of those things I actually see and feel.

Hyl. Not so fast, Philonous: you say you cannot conceive how sensible things should exist without the mind. Do you not?

Phil. I do.

Hyl. Supposing you were annihilated, cannot you conceive it possible that things perceivable by sense may still exist?

Phil. I can; but then it must be in another mind. When I deny sensible things an existence out of the mind, I do not mean my mind in particular, but all minds. Now it is plain they have an existence exterior to my mind, since I find them by experience to be independent of it. There is therefore some other mind wherein they exist, during the intervals between the times of my perceiving them: as likewise they did before my birth, and would do after my supposed annihilation. And as the same is true with regard to all other finite created spirits, it necessarily follows, there is an *omnipresent, eternal Mind,* which knows and comprehends all things, and exhibits them to our view in such a manner, and according to such rules as he himself hath ordained, and are by us termed the *laws of nature.*

Hyl. Answer me, Philonous. Are all our ideas perfectly inert beings? Or have they any agency included in them?

Phil. They are altogether passive and inert.

Hyl. And is not God an agent, a being purely active?

Phil. I acknowledge it.

Hyl. No idea therefore can be like unto, or represent the nature of God.

Phil. It cannot.

Hyl. Since therefore you have no idea of the mind of God, how can you conceive it possible, that things should exist in his mind? Or, if you can conceive the mind of God without having an idea of it, why may not I be allowed to conceive the existence of matter, notwithstanding that I have no idea of it?

Phil. As to your first question: I own I have

properly no idea, either of God or any other spirit; for these being active, cannot be represented by things perfectly inert, as our ideas are. I do nevertheless know, that I, who am a spirit or thinking substance, exist as certainly, as I know my ideas exist. Further, I know what I mean by the terms *I* and *myself*; and I know this immediately, or intuitively, though I do not perceive it as I perceive a triangle, a colour, or a sound. The mind, spirit, or soul, is that indivisible, unextended thing, which thinks, acts, and perceives. I say *indivisible*, because unextended; and *unextended*, because extended, figured, moveable things, are ideas; and that which perceives ideas, which thinks and wills, is plainly itself no idea, nor like an idea. Ideas are things inactive, and perceived; and spirits a sort of beings altogether different from them. I do not therefore say my soul is an idea, or like an idea. However, taking the word *idea* in a large sense, my soul may be said to furnish me with an idea, that is, an image, or likeness of God, though indeed extremely inadequate. For all the notion I have of God, is obtained by reflecting on my own soul, heightening its powers, and removing its imperfections. I have therefore, though not an inactive idea, yet in myself some sort of an active thinking image of the Deity. And though I perceive him not by sense, yet I have a notion of him, or know him by reflection and reasoning. My own mind and my own ideas I have an immediate knowledge of; and by the help of these, do mediately apprehend the possibility of the existence of other spirits and ideas. Further, from my own being, and from the dependency I find in myself and my ideas, I do by an act of reason necessarily infer the existence of a God, and of all created things in the mind of God. So much for your first question. For the second: I suppose by this time you can answer it yourself. For you neither perceive matter objectively, as you do an inactive being or idea, nor know it, as you do yourself, by a reflex act: neither do you mediately apprehend it by similitude of the one or the other: nor yet collect it by reasoning from that which you know immediately. All which makes the case of *matter* widely different from that of the *Deity*.

Hyl. You say your own soul supplies you with some sort of an idea or image of God. But at the same time you acknowledge you have, properly speaking, no idea of your own soul. You even affirm that spirits are a sort of beings altogether different from ideas. Consequently that no idea can be like a spirit. We have therefore no idea of any spirit. You admit nevertheless that there is spiritual substance, although you have no idea of it; while you deny there can be such a thing as material substance, because you have no notion or idea of it. Is this fair dealing? To act consistently, you must either admit matter or reject spirit. What say you to this?

Phil. I say in the first place, that I do not deny the existence of material substance merely because I have no notion of it, but because the notion of it is inconsistent, or in other words, because it is repugnant that there should be a notion of it. Many things, for aught I know, may exist, whereof neither I nor any other man hath or can have any idea or notion whatsoever. But then those things must be possible, that is, nothing inconsistent must be included in their definition. I say secondly, that although we believe things to exist which we do not perceive; yet we may not believe that any particular thing exists, without some reason for such belief: but I have no reason for believing the existence of matter. I have no immediate intuition thereof: neither can I mediately from my sensations, ideas, notions, actions, or passions, infer an unthinking, unperceiving, inactive substance, either by probable deduction, or necessary consequence. Whereas the being of myself, that is, my own soul, mind, or thinking principle, I evidently know by reflection. You will forgive me if I repeat the same things in answer to the same objections. In the very notion or definition of material substance, there is included a manifest repugnance and inconsistency. But this cannot be said of the notion of spirit. That ideas should exist in what doth not perceive, or be produced by what doth not act, is repugnant. But it is no repugnancy to say, that a perceiving thing should be the subject of ideas, or an active thing the cause of them. It is granted we have neither an immediate evidence nor a demonstrative knowledge of the existence of other finite spirits; but it will not thence follow that such spirits are on a foot with material substances: if to suppose the one be inconsistent, and it be not inconsistent to suppose the other; if the one can be inferred by no argument, and there is a probability for the other; if we see signs and effects indicating distinct finite agents like ourselves, and see no sign or symptom whatever that leads to a rational belief of matter. I say lastly, that I have a notion of spirit, though I have not, strictly speaking, an idea of it. I do not perceive it as an idea or by means of an idea, but know it by reflection.

Hyl. Notwithstanding all you have said, to me it seems, that according to your own way of thinking, and in consequence of your own principles, it should follow that you are only a system of floating ideas, without any substance to support them. Words are not to be used without a meaning. And as there is no more meaning in spiritual substance than in material substance, the one is to be exploded as well as the other.

Phil. How often must I repeat, that I know or am conscious of my own being; and that I myself am not my ideas, but somewhat else, a thinking, active principle that perceives, knows, wills, and operates about ideas? I know that I, one and the same self, perceive both colours and sounds: that a colour cannot perceive a sound, nor a sound a colour: that I am therefore one individual principle distinct from colour and sound; and, for the same reason, from all other sensible things and inert ideas. But I am not in like manner conscious either of the existence or essence of matter. On the contrary, I know that nothing inconsistent can exist, and that the existence of matter implies an inconsistency. Further, I know what I mean, when I affirm that there is a spiritual substance or support of ideas, that is, that a spirit knows and perceives ideas. But I do not know what is meant, when it is said, that an unperceiving substance hath inherent in it and supports either ideas or the archetypes of ideas. There is therefore upon the whole no parity of case between spirit and matter.

Hyl. I own myself satisfied in this point. But do you in earnest think, the real existence of sensible things consists in their being actually perceived? If so, how comes it that all mankind distinguish between them? Ask the first man you meet, and he shall tell you, to *be perceived* is one thing, and *to exist* is another.

Phil. I am content, Hylas, to appeal to the common sense of the world for the truth of my notion. Ask the gardener, why he thinks yonder cherry-tree exists in the garden, and he shall tell you, because he sees and feels it; in a word, because he perceives it by his senses. Ask him, why he thinks an orange-tree not to be there, and he shall tell you, because he does not perceive it. What he perceives by sense, that he terms a real being, and saith it *is*, or *exists*; but that which is not perceivable, the same, he saith, hath no being.

Hyl. Yes, Philonous, I grant the existence of a sensible thing consists in being perceivable, but not in being actually perceived.

Phil. And what is perceivable but an idea? And can an idea exist without being actually perceived? These are points long since agreed between us.

Hyl. But be your opinion never so true, yet surely you will not deny it is shocking, and contrary to the common sense of men. Ask the fellow, whether yonder tree hath an existence out of his mind: what answer, think you, he would make?

Phil. The same that I should myself, to wit, that it doth exist out of his mind. But then to a Christian it cannot surely be shocking to say, the real tree existing without his mind is truly known and comprehended by (that is, *exists in*) the infinite mind of God. Probably he may not at first glance be aware of the direct and immediate proof there is of this, inasmuch as the very being of a tree, or any other sensible thing, implies a mind wherein it is. But the point itself he cannot deny. The question between the materialists and me is not, whether things have a real existence out of the mind of this or that person, but whether they have an absolute existence, distinct from being perceived by God, and exterior to all minds. This indeed some heathens and philosophers have affirmed, but whoever entertains notions of the Deity suitable to the holy scriptures, will be of another opinion.

Hyl. But according to your notions, what difference is there between real things, and chimeras formed by the imagination, or the visions of a dream, since they are all equally in the mind?

Phil. The ideas formed by the imagination are faint and indistinct; they have besides an entire dependence on the will. But the ideas perceived by sense, that is, real things, are more vivid and clear, and being imprinted on the mind by a spirit distinct from us, have not a like dependence on our will. There is therefore no danger of confounding these with the foregoing: and there is as little of confounding them with the visions of a dream, which are dim, irregular, and confused. And though they should happen to be never so lively and natural, yet by their not being connected, and of a piece with the preceding and subsequent transactions of our lives, they might easily be distinguished from realities. In short, by whatever method you distinguish *things* from *chimeras* on your own scheme, the same, it is evident, will hold also upon mine. For it must be, I presume, by some perceived difference, and I am not for depriving you of any one thing that you perceive.

Hyl. But still, Philonous, you hold, there is nothing in the world but spirits and ideas. And this, you must needs acknowledge, sounds very oddly.

Phil. I own the word *idea*, not being commonly used for *thing*, sounds something out of the way. My reason for using it was, because a necessary relation to the mind is understood to be implied by that term; and it is now commonly used by philosophers, to denote the immediate objects of the understanding. But however oddly the proposition may sound in words, yet it includes nothing so very strange or shocking in its sense, which in effect amounts to no more than this, to wit, that there are only things perceiving, and things perceived; or that every unthinking being is necessarily, and from the very nature of its existence, perceived by some mind; if not by any finite created mind, yet certainly by the infinite mind of God, in whom "we live, and move, and have our being." Is this as strange as to say, the sensible qualities are not on the objects: or, that we cannot be sure of the existence of things, or know any thing of their real natures, though we both see and feel them, and perceive them by all our senses?

Hyl. And in consequence of this, must we not think there are no such things as physical or corporeal causes; but that a spirit is the immediate cause of all the phenomena in nature? Can there be any thing more extravagant than this?

Phil. Yes, it is infinitely more extravagant to say, a thing which is inert, operates on the mind, and which is unperceiving, is the cause of our perceptions. Besides, that which to you, I know not for what reason, seems so extravagant, is no more than the holy scriptures assert in a hundred places. In them God is represented as the sole and immediate author of all those effects, which some heathens and philosophers are wont to ascribe to nature,

matter, fate, or the like unthinking principle. This is so much the constant language of scripture, that it were needless to confirm it by citations.

Hyl. You are not aware, Philonous, that in making God the immediate author of all the motions in nature, you make him the author of murder, sacrilege, adultery, and the like heinous sins.

Phil. In answer to that, I observe first, that the imputation of guilt is the same, whether a person commits an action with or without an instrument. In case therefore you suppose God to act by the mediation of an instrument, or occasion, called *matter*, you as truly make him the author of sin as I, who think him the immediate agent in all those operations vulgarly ascribed to nature. I further observe, that sin or moral turpitude doth not consist in the outward physical action or motion, but in the internal deviation of the will from the laws of reason and religion. This is plain, in that the killing an enemy in a battle, or putting a criminal legally to death, is not thought sinful, though the outward act be the very same with that in the case of murder. Since therefore sin doth not consist in the physical action, the making God an immediate cause of all such actions, is not making him the author of sin. Lastly, I have no where said that God is the only agent who produces all the motions in bodies. It is true, I have denied there are any other agents beside spirits: but this is very consistent with allowing to thinking, rational beings, in the production of motions, the use of limited powers, ultimately indeed derived from God, but immediately under the direction of their own wills, which is sufficient to entitle them to all the guilt of their actions.

Hyl. But the denying matter, Philonous, or corporeal substance; there is the point. You can never persuade me that this is not repugnant to the universal sense of mankind. Were our dispute to be determined by most voices, I am confident you would give up the point, without gathering the votes.

Phil. I wish both our opinions were fairly stated and submitted to the judgment of men who had plain common sense, without the prejudices of a learned education. Let me be represented as one who trusts his senses, who thinks he knows the things he sees and feels, and entertains no doubts of their existence; and you fairly set forth with all your doubts, your paradoxes, and your scepticism about you, and I shall willingly acquiesce in the determination of any indifferent person. That there is no substance wherein ideas can exist beside spirit, is to me evident. And that the objects immediately perceived are ideas, is on all hands agreed. And that sensible qualities are objects immediately perceived, no one can deny. It is therefore evident there can be no *substratum* of those qualities but spirit, in which they exist, not by way of mode or property, but as a thing perceived in that which perceives it. I deny therefore that there is any unthinking *substratum* of the objects of sense, and in that acceptation that there is any material substance. But if by *material substance* is meant only sensible body, that which is seen and felt (and the unphilosophical part of the world, I dare say, mean no more), then I am more certain of matter's existence than you, or any other philosopher, pretend to be. If there be any thing which makes the generality of mankind averse from the notions I espouse, it is a misapprehension that I deny the reality of sensible things: but as it is you who are guilty of that and not I, it follows that in truth their aversion is against your notions, and not mine. I do therefore assert that I am as certain as of my own being, that there are bodies or corporeal substances (meaning the things I perceive by my senses); and that granting this, the bulk of mankind will take no thought about, nor think themselves at all concerned in the fate of those unknown natures, and philosophical quiddities, which some men are so fond of.

Hyl. What say you to this? Since, according to you, men judge of the reality of things by their senses, how can a man be mistaken in thinking the moon a plain lucid surface, about a foot in diameter; or a square tower, seen at a distance, round; or an oar, with one end in the water, crooked?

Phil. He is not mistaken with regard to the ideas he actually perceives; but in the inferences he makes from his present perceptions. Thus in the case of the oar, what he immediately perceives by sight is certainly crooked; and so far he is in the right. But if he thence conclude, that upon taking the oar out of the water he shall perceive the same crookedness, or that it would affect his touch as crooked things are wont to do, in that he is mistaken. In like manner, if he should conclude

from what he perceives in one station, that in case he advances toward the moon or tower, he should still be affected with the like ideas, he is mistaken. But his mistake lies not in what he perceives immediately and at present (it being a manifest contradiction to suppose he should err in respect of that), but in the wrong judgment he makes concerning the ideas he apprehends to be connected with those immediately perceived: or concerning the ideas that, from what he perceives at present, he imagines would be perceived in other circumstances. The case is the same with regard to the Copernican system. We do not here perceive any motion of the earth: but it were erroneous thence to conclude, that in case we were placed at as great a distance from that, as we are now from the other planets, we should not then perceive its motion.

Hyl. I understand you; and must needs own you say things plausible enough: but give me leave to put you in mind of one thing. Pray, Philonous, were you not formerly as positive that matter existed, as you are now that it does not?

Phil. I was. But here lies the difference. Before, my positiveness was founded without examination, upon prejudice; but now, after inquiry, upon evidence.

Hyl. After all, it seems our dispute is rather about words than things. We agree in the thing, but differ in the name. That we are affected with ideas from without is evident; and it is no less evident, that there must be (I will not say archetypes, but) powers without the mind, corresponding to those ideas. And as these powers cannot subsist by themselves, there is some subject of them necessarily to be admitted, which I call *matter,* and you call *spirit.* This is all the difference.

Phil. Pray, Hylas, is that powerful being, or subject of powers, extended?

Hyl. It hath not extension; but it hath the power to raise in you the idea of extension.

Phil. It is therefore itself unextended.

Hyl. I grant it.

Phil. Is it not also active?

Hyl. Without doubt: otherwise, how could we attribute powers to it?

Phil. Now let me ask you two questions: first, whether it be agreeable to the usage either of philosophers or others, to give the name *matter* to an unextended active being? And secondly, whether it be not ridiculously absurd to misapply names contrary to the common use of language?

Hyl. Well, then, let it not be called matter, since you will have it so, but some *third nature* distinct from matter and spirit. For, what reason is there why you should call it spirit? Does not the notion of spirit imply, that it is thinking as well as active and unextended?

Phil. My reason is this: because I have a mind to have some notion or meaning in what I say; but I have no notion of any action distinct from volition, neither can I conceive volition to be any where but in a spirit: therefore when I speak of an active being, I am obliged to mean a spirit. Beside, what can be plainer than that a thing which hath no ideas in itself, cannot impart them to me; and if it hath ideas, surely it must be a spirit. To make you comprehend the point still more clearly, if it be possible: I assert as well as you, that since we are affected from without, we must allow powers to be without in a being distinct from ourselves. So far we are agreed. But then we differ as to the kind of this powerful being. I will have it to be spirit, you matter, or I know not what (I may add too, you know not what) third nature. Thus I prove it to be spirit. From the effects I see produced, I conclude there are actions; and because actions, volitions; and because there are volitions, there must be a will. Again, the things I perceive must have an existence, they or their archetypes, out of my mind: but being ideas, neither they nor their archetypes can exist otherwise than in an understanding: there is therefore an understanding. But will and understanding constitute in the strictest sense a mind or spirit. The powerful cause therefore of my ideas, is in strict propriety of speech a *spirit.*

Hyl. And now I warrant you think you have made the point very clear, little suspecting that what you advance leads directly to a contradiction. Is it not an absurdity to imagine any imperfection in God?

Phil. Without doubt.

Hyl. To suffer pain is an imperfection.

Phil. It is.

Hyl. Are we not sometimes affected with pain and uneasiness by some other being?

Phil. We are.

Hyl. And have you not said that being is a spirit, and is not that spirit God?

Phil. I grant it.

Hyl. But you have asserted, that whatever ideas we perceive from without, are in the mind which affects us. The ideas therefore of pain and uneasiness are in God; or in other words, God suffers pain: that is to say, there is an imperfection in the divine nature, which you acknowledged was absurd. So you are caught in a plain contradiction.

Phil. That God knows or understands all things, and that he knows among other things what pain is, even every sort of painful sensation, and what it is for his creatures to suffer pain, I make no question. But that God, though he knows and sometimes causes painful sensations in us, can himself suffer pain, I positively deny. We who are limited and dependent spirits, and liable to impressions of sense, the effects of an external agent, which being produced against our wills, are sometimes painful and uneasy. But God, who, no external being can affect, who perceives nothing by sense as we do, whose will is absolute and independent, causing all things, and liable to be thwarted or resisted by nothing; it is evident, such a being as this can suffer nothing, nor be affected with any painful sensation, or indeed any sensation at all. We are chained to a body, that is so say, our perceptions are connected with corporeal motions. By the law of our nature we are affected upon every alteration in the nervous parts of our sensible body: which sensible body rightly considered, is nothing but a complexion of such qualities or ideas, as have no existence distinct from being perceived by a mind; so that this connexion of sensations with corporeal motions, means no more than a correspondence in the order of nature between two sets of ideas, or things immediately perceivable. But God is a pure spirit, disengaged from all such sympathy or natural ties. No corporeal motions are attended with the sensations of pain or pleasure in his mind. To know every thing knowable is certainly a perfection; but to endure, or suffer, or feel any thing by sense, is an imperfection. The former, I say, agrees to God, but not the latter. God knows or hath ideas: but his ideas are not conveyed to him by sense, as ours are. Your not distinguishing where there is so manifest a difference, makes you fancy you see an absurdity where there is none.

Hyl. But all this while you have not considered, that the quantity of matter hath been demonstrated to be proportioned to the gravity of bodies. And what can withstand demonstration?

Phil. Let me see how you demonstrate that point?

Hyl. I lay it down for a principle, that the moments or quantities of motion in bodies, are in a direct compounded reason of the velocities and quanitites of matter contained in them. Hence, where the velocities are equal, it follows, the moments are directly as the quantity of matter in each. But it is found by experience, that all bodies (bating the small inequalities arising from the resistance of the air) descend with an equal velocity; the motion therefore of descending bodies, and consequently their gravity, which is the cause or principle of that motion, is proportional to the quantity of matter: which was to be demonstrated.

Phil. You lay it down as a self-evident principle, that the quantity of motion in any body is proportional to the velocity and *matter* taken together: and this is made use of to prove a proposition, from whence the existence of *matter* is inferred. Pray is not this arguing in a circle?

Hyl. In the premise I only mean, that the motion is proportional to the velocity, jointly with the extension and solidity.

Phil. But allowing this to be true, yet it will not thence follow, that gravity is proportional to *matter*, in your philosophic sense of the word; except you take it for granted, that unknown *substratum*, or whatever else you call it, is proportional to those sensible qualities; which to suppose is plainly begging the question. That there is magnitude, and solidity, or resistance, perceived by sense, I readily grant; as likewise that gravity may be proportional to those qualities, I will not dispute. But that either these qualities as perceived by us, or the powers producing them, do exist in a *material substratum*; this is what I deny, and you indeed affirm, but notwithstanding your demonstration, have not yet proved.

Hyl. I shall insist no longer on that point. Do you think, however, you shall persuade me that natural philosophers have been dreaming all this while? pray what becomes of all their hypotheses and explications of the phenomena, which suppose the existence of matter?

Phil. What mean you, Hylas, by the phenomena?

Hyl. I mean the appearances which I perceive by my senses.

Phil. And the appearances perceived by sense, are they not ideas?

Hyl. I have told you so a hundred times.

Phil. Therefore, to explain the phenomena, is to show how we come to be affected with ideas, in that matter and order wherein they are imprinted on our senses. Is it not?

Hyl. It is.

Phil. Now if you can prove, that any philosopher hath explained the production of any one idea in our minds by the help of *matter*, I shall for ever acquiesce, and look on all that hath been said against it as nothing: but if you cannot, it is in vain to urge the explication of phenomena. That a being endowed with knowledge and will, should produce or exhibit ideas, is easily understood. But that a being which is utterly destitute of these faculties should be able to produce ideas, or in any sort to affect an intelligence, this I can never understand. This I say, though we had some positive conception of matter, though we knew its qualities, and could comprehend its existence, would yet be so far from explaining things, that it is itself the most inexplicable thing in the world. And yet for all this, it will not follow, that philosophers have been doing nothing; for by observing and reasoning upon the connexion of ideas, they discover the laws and methods of nature, which is a part of knowledge both useful and entertaining.

Hyl. After all, can it be supposed God would deceive all mankind? Do you imagine, he would have induced the whole world to believe the being of matter, if there was no such thing?

Phil. That every epidemical opinion arising from prejudice, or passion, or thoughtlessness, may be imputed to God, as the author of it, I believe you will not affirm. Whatsoever opinion we father on him, it must be either because he has discovered it to us by supernatural revelation, or because it is so evident to our natural faculties, which were framed and given us by God, that it is impossible we should withhold our assent from it. But where is the revelation, or where is the evidence that extorts the belief of matter? Nay, how does it appear that matter, taken for something distinct from what we perceive by our senses, is thought to exist by all mankind, or indeed by any except a few philosophers, who do not know what they would be at? Your question supposes these points are clear; and when you have cleared them, I shall think myself obliged to give you another answer. In the mean time let it suffice that I tell you, I do not suppose God has deceived mankind at all.

Hyl. But the novelty, Philonous, the novelty! There lies the danger. New notions should always be discountenanced; they unsettle men's minds, and nobody knows where they will end.

Phil. Why the rejecting a notion that hath no foundation either in sense, or in reason, or in divine authority, should be thought to unsettle the belief of such opinions as are grounded on all or any of these, I cannot imagine. That innovations in government and religion are dangerous, and ought to be discountenanced, I freely own. But is there the like reason why they should be discouraged in philosophy? The making any thing known which was unknown before, is an innovation in knowledge: and if all such innovations had been forbidden, men would [not] have made a notable progress in the arts and sciences. But it is none of my business to plead for novelties and paradoxes. That the qualities we perceive are not on the objects: that we must not believe our senses: that we know nothing of the real nature of things, and can never be assured even of their existence: that real colours and sounds are nothing but certain unknown figures and motions: that motions are in themselves neither swift nor slow: that there are in bodies absolute extensions, without any particular magnitude or figure: that a thing stupid, thoughtless, and inactive, operates on a spirit: that the least particle of a body contains innumerable extended parts. These are the novelties, these are the strange notions which shock the genuine uncorrupted judgment of all mankind; and being once admitted, embarrass the mind with endless doubts and difficulties. And it is against these and the like innovations, I endeavour to vindicate common sense. It is true, in doing this, I may perhaps be obliged to use some *ambages,* and ways of speech not common. But if my notions are once thoroughly understood, that which is most singular in them will in effect be found to amount to no more than this: that it is absolutely impossible, and a plain contradiction to suppose, any unthinking being should exist without being perceived by a mind. And if this notion be singular, it is a shame it should be so at this time of day, and in a Christian country.

Hyl. As for the difficultes other opinions may be liable to, those are out of the question. It is your business to defend your own opinion. Can any thing be plainer, than that you are for changing all things into ideas? You, I say, who are not ashamed to charge me with *scepticism.* This is so plain, there is no denying it.

Phil. You mistake me. I am not for changing things into ideas, but rather ideas into things; since those immediate objects of perception, which, according to you, are only appearances of things, I take to be the real things themselves.

Phil. What you call the empty forms and outside of things, seems to me the very things themselves. Nor are they empty or incomplete otherwise, than upon your supposition, that matter is an essential part of all corporeal things. We both therefore agree in this, that we perceive only sensible forms: but herein we differ, you will have them to be empty appearances, I real beings. In short you do not trust your senses, I do.

Hyl. You say you believe your senses; and seem to applaud yourself that in this you agree with the vulgar. According to you therefore, the true nature of a thing is discovered by the senses. If so, whence comes that disagreement? Why is not the same figure, and other sensible qualities, perceived all manner of ways? and why should we use a microscope, the better to discover the true nature of a body, if it were discoverable to the naked eye?

Phil. Strictly speaking, Hylas, we do not see the same object that we feel; neither is the same object perceived by the microscope, which was by the naked eye. But in case every variation was thought sufficient to constitute a new kind or individual, the endless number or confusion of names would render language impracticable. Therefore to avoid this as well as other inconveniences which are obvious upon a little thought, men combine together several ideas, apprehended by divers senses, or by the same sense at different times, or in different circumstances, but observed however to have some connexion in nature, either with respect to coexistence or succession; all which they refer to one name, and consider as one thing. Hence it follows that when I examine by my other senses a thing I have seen, it is not in order to understand better the same object which I had perceived by sight, the object of one sense not being perceived by the other senses. And when I look through a microscope, it is not that I may perceive more clearly what I perceived already with my bare eyes, the object perceived by the glass being quite different from the former. But in both cases my aim is only to know what ideas are connected together; and the more a man knows of the connexion of ideas, the more he is said to know of the nature of things. What therefore if our ideas are variable? What if our senses are not in all circumstances affected with the same appearances? It will not thence follow, they are not to be trusted, or that they are inconsistent either with themselves or any thing else, except it be with your preconceived notion of (I know not what) one single, unchanged, unperceivable, real nature, marked by each name: which prejudice seems to have taken its rise from not rightly understanding the common language of men speaking of several distinct ideas, as united into one thing by the mind. And indeed there is cause to suspect several erroneous conceits of the philosophers are owing to the same original: while they began to build their schemes, not so much on notions as words, which were framed by the vulgar, merely for conveniency and despatch in the common actions of life, without any regard to speculation.

Hyl. Methinks I apprehend your meaning.

Phil. It is your opinion, the ideas we perceive by our senses are not real things, but images, or copies of them. Our knowledge therefore is no further real, than as our ideas are the true representations of those originals. But as these supposed originals are in themselves unknown, it is impossible to know how far our ideas resemble them; or whether they resemble them at all. We cannot therefore be sure we have any real knowledge. Further, as our ideas are perpetually varied, without any change in the supposed real things, it necessarily follows they cannot all be true copies of them; or if some are, and others are not, it is impossible to distinguish the former from the latter. And this plunges us yet deeper in uncertainty. Again, when we consider the point, we cannot conceive how any idea, or any thing like an idea, should have an absolute existence out of a mind; nor consequently, according to you, how there should be any real thing in nature. The result of all which is, that we are thrown into the most

hopeless and abandoned *scepticism*. Now give me leave to ask you, first, whether your referring ideas to certain absolutely existing unperceived substances, as their originals, be not the source of all this *scepticism?* Secondly, whether you are informed, either by sense or reason, of the existence of those unknown originals? And in case you are not, whether it be not absurd to suppose them? Thirdly, whether upon inquiry, you find there is anything distinctly conceived or meant by the *absolute or external existence of unperceiving substances?* Lastly, whether, the premises considered, it be not the wisest way to follow nature, trust your senses, and laying aside all anxious thought about unknown natures or substances, admit with the vulgar those for real things, which are perceived by the senses?

Hyl. For the present, I have no inclination to the answering part. I would much rather see how you can get over what follows. Pray are not the objects perceived by the senses of one, likewise perceivable to others present? If there were a hundred more here, they would all see the garden, the trees, and flowers as I see them. But they are not in the same manner affected with the ideas I frame in my imagination. Does not this make a difference between the former sort of objects and the latter?

Phil. I grant it does. Nor have I ever denied a difference between the objects of sense and those of imagination. But what would you infer from thence? You cannot say that sensible objects exist unperceived, because they are perceived by many.

Hyl. I own, I can make nothing of that objection, but it hath led me into another. Is it not your opinion that by our senses we perceive only the ideas existing in our minds?

Phil. It is.

Hyl. But the same idea which is in my mind, cannot be in yours, or in any other mind. Doth it not therefore follow from your principles, that no two can see the same thing? And is not this highly absurd?

Phil. If the term *same* be taken in the vulgar acceptation, it is certain (and not at all repugnant to the principles I maintain) that different persons may perceive the same thing; or the same thing or idea exist in different minds. Words are of arbitrary imposition; and since men are used to apply the word *same* where no distinction or variety is perceived, and I do not pretend to alter their perceptions, it follows, that as men have said before, *several saw the same thing*, so they may upon like occasions still continue to use the same phrase, without any deviation either from propriety of language, or the truth of things. But if the term *same* be used in the acceptation of philosophers, who pretend to an abstracted notion of identity, then, according to their sundry definitions of this notion (for it is not yet agreed wherein that philosophic identity consists), it may or may not be possible for divers persons to perceive the same thing. But whether philosophers shall think fit to call a thing the *same* or no, is, I conceive, of small importance. Let us suppose several men together, all endowed with the same faculties, and consequently affected in like sort by their senses, and who had yet never known the use of language; they would without question agree in their perceptions. Though perhaps, when they came to the use of speech, some regarding the uniformness of what was perceived, might call it the *same* thing: others especially regarding the diversity of persons who perceived, might choose the denomination of different things. But who sees not that all the dispute is about a word; to wit, whether what is perceived by different persons, may yet have the term *same* applied to it? Or suppose a house, whose walls or outward shell remaining unaltered, the chambers are pulled down, and new ones built in their place; and that you should call this the *same*, and I should say it was not the *same* house: would we not for all this perfectly agree in our thoughts of the house, considered in itself? And would not all the difference consist in a sound? If you should say, we differ in our notions; for that you superadded to your idea of the house the simple abstracted idea of identity, whereas I did not; I would tell you I know not what you mean by that *abstracted idea of identity;* and should desire you to look into your own thoughts, and be sure you understood yourself.—Why so silent, Hylas? Are you not yet satisfied, men may dispute about identity and diversity, without any real difference in their thoughts and opinions, abstracted from names? Take this further reflection with you: that whether matter be allowed to exist or no, the case is exactly the same as to the point in hand. For the materialists themselves acknowledge what we immediately perceive by our senses to be our own ideas. Your difficulty therefore, that no two see the same thing, makes equally against the materialists and me.

Hyl. But they suppose an external archetype, to which referring their several ideas, they may truly be said to perceive the same thing.

Phil. And (not to mention your having discovered those archetypes) so may you suppose an external archetype on my principles: *external*, I mean, to your own mind; though indeed it must be supposed to exist in that mind which comprehends all things; but then this serves all the ends of identity, as well as if it existed out of a mind. And I am sure you yourself will not say, it is less intelligible.

Hyl. You have indeed clearly satisfied me, either that there is no difficulty at bottom in this point; or if there be, that it makes equally against both opinions.

Phil. But that which makes equally against two contradictory opinions, can be a proof against neither.

Hyl. I acknowledge it. But after all, Philonous, when I consider the substance of what you advance against scepticism, it amounts to no more than this. We are sure that we really see, hear, feel; in a word, that we are affected with sensible impressions.

Phil. And how are we concerned any further? I see this *cherry*, I feel it, I taste it: and I am sure *nothing* cannot be seen, or felt, or tasted: it is therefore *real*. Take away the sensations of softness, moisture, redness, tartness, and you take away the *cherry*. Since it is not a being distinct from sensations; a *cherry*, I say, is nothing but a congeries of sensible impressions, or ideas perceived by various senses; which ideas are united into one thing (or have one name given them) by the mind; because they are observed to attend each other. Thus when the palate is affected with such a particular taste, the sight is affected with a red colour, the touch with roundness, softness, &c. Hence, when I see, and feel, and taste, in sundry certain manners, I am sure the *cherry* exists, or is real; its reality being in my opinion nothing abstracted from those sensations. But if by the word *cherry* you mean an unknown nature distinct from all those sensible qualities, and by its existence something distinct from its being perceived; then indeed I own, neither you, nor I, nor any one else can be sure it exists.

Hyl. But what would you say, Philonous, if I

should bring the very same reasons against the existence of sensible things in a mind, which you have offered against their existing in a material *substratum*?

Phil. When I see your reasons, you shall hear what I have to say to them.

Hyl. Is the mind extended or unextended?

Phil. Unextended, without doubt.

Hyl. Do you say the things you perceive are in your mind?

Phil. They are.

Hyl. Again, have I not heard you speak of sensible impressions?

Phil. I believe you may.

Hyl. Explain to me now, O Philonous! how it is possible there should be room for all those trees and houses to exist in your mind. Can extended things be contained in that which is unextended? or are we to imagine impressions made on a thing void of all solidity? You cannot say objects are in your mind, as books in your study: or that things are imprinted on it, as the figure of a seal upon wax. In what sense therefore are we to understand those expressions? Explain me this if you can: and I shall then be able to answer all those queries you formerly put to me about my substratum.

Phil. Look you, Hylas, when I speak of objects as existing in the mind or imprinted on the senses, I would not be understood in the gross literal sense, as when bodies are said to exist in a place, or a seal to make an impression upon wax. My meaning is only that the mind comprehends or perceives them; and that it is affected from without, or by some being distinct from itself. This is my explication of your difficulty; and how it can serve to make your tenet of an unperceiving material substratum intelligible, I would fain know.

Hyl. Nay, if that be all, I confess I do not see what use can be made of it. But are you not guilty of some abuse of language in this?

Phil. None at all: it is no more than common custom, which you know is the rule of language, hath authorized: nothing being more usual, than for philosophers to speak of the immediate objects of the understanding as things existing in the mind. Nor is there any thing in this, but what is conformable to the general analogy of language; most part of the mental operations being signified by words borrowed from sensible things; as is plain in the terms *comprehend, reflect, discourse,* &c., which being

applied to the mind, must not be taken in their gross original sense.

Hyl. You have, I own, satisfied me in this point; but there still remains one great difficulty, which I know not how you will get over. And, indeed, it is of such importance, that if you could solve all others, without being able to find a solution for this, you must never expect to make me a proselyte to your principles.

Phil. Let me know this mighty difficulty.

Hyl. The scripture account of the creation is what appears to me utterly irreconcilable with your notions. Moses tells us of a creation: a creation of what? of ideas? No, certainly, but of things, of real things, solid corporeal substances. Bring your principles to agree with this, and I shall perhaps agree with you.

Phil. Moses mentions the sun, moon, and stars, earth and sea, plants and animals: that all these do really exist, and were in the beginning created by God, I make no question. If by *ideas* you mean fictions and fancies of the mind, then these are no ideas. If by *ideas* you mean immediate objects of the understanding, or sensible things which cannot exist unperceived, or out of a mind, then these things are ideas. But whether you do or do not call them *ideas,* it matters little. The difference is only about a name. And whether that name be retained or rejected, the sense, the truth, and reality of things continues the same. In common talk, the objects of our senses are not termed *ideas,* but *things.* Call them so still; provided you do not attribute to them any absolute external existence, and I shall never quarrel with you for a word. The creation, therefore, I allow to have been a creation of things, of *real* things. Neither is this in the least inconsistent with my principles, as is evident from what I have now said; and would have been evident to you without this, if you had not forgotten what had been so often said before. But as for solid corporeal substances, I desire you to show where Moses makes any mention of them; and if they should be mentioned by him, or any other inspired writer, it would still be incumbent on you to show those words were not taken in the vulgar acceptation, for things falling under our senses, but in the philosophic acceptation, for matter, or an unknown quiddity, with an absolute existence. When you have proved these points, then (and not till then) may you bring the authority of Moses into our dispute.

Hyl. It is in vain to dispute about a point so clear. I am content to refer it to your own conscience. Are you not satisfied there is some peculiar repugnancy between the Mosaic account of the creation and your notions?

Phil. If all possible sense, which can be put on the first chapter of Genesis, may be conceived as consistently with my principles as any other, then it has no peculiar repugnancy with them. But there is no sense you may not as well conceive, believing as I do. Since, besides spirits, all you conceive are ideas, and the existence of these I do not deny. Neither do you pretend they exist without the mind.

Hyl. Pray let me see any sense you can understand it in.

Phil. Why I imagine that if I had been present at the creation, I should have seen things produced into being; that is, become perceptible, in the order described by the sacred historian. I ever before believed the Mosaic account of the creation, and now find no alteration in my manner of believing it. When things are said to begin or end their existence, we do not mean this with regard to God, but his creatures. All objects are eternally known by God, or, which is the same thing, have an eternal existence in his mind: but when things before imperceptible to creatures, are by a decree of God, made perceptible to them; then are they said to begin a relative existence with respect to created minds. Upon reading therefore the Mosaic account of the creation, I understand that the several parts of the world became gradually perceivable to finite spirits, endowed with proper faculties; so that, whoever such were present, they were in truth perceived by them. This is the literal, obvious sense suggested to me by the words of the holy scripture: in which is included no mention or no thought, either of substratum, instrument, occasion, or absolute existence. And upon inquiry, I doubt not it will be found, that most plain, honest men, who believe the creation, never think of those things any more than I. What metaphysical sense you may understand it in, you only can tell.

Hyl. But, Philonous, you do not seem to be aware, that you allow created things in the beginning only a relative, and, consequently, hypothetical being; that is to say, upon supposition there were men to perceive them, without

which they have no actuality of absolute existence, wherein creation might terminate. Is it not, therefore, according to you plainly impossible, the creation of any inanimate creatures should precede that of man? And is not this directly contrary to the Mosaic account?

Phil. In answer to that I say, first, created beings might begin to exist in the mind of other created intelligences, beside men. You will not therefore be able to prove any contradiction between Moses and my notions, unless you first show, there was no other order of finite created spirits in being before man. I say further, in case we conceive the creation, as we should at this time a parcel of plants or vegetables of all sorts, produced by an invisible power, in a desert where nobody was present: that this way of explaining or conceiving it, is consistent with my principles, since they deprive you of nothing, either sensible or imaginable: that it exactly suits with the common, natural, undebauched notions of mankind: that it manifests the dependence of all things on God; and consequently hath all the good effect or influence, which it is possible that important article of our faith should have in making men humble, thankful, and resigned to their Creator. I say, moreover, that in this naked conception of things, divested of words, there will not be found any notion of what you call the *actuality of absolute existence*. You may indeed raise a dust with those terms, and so lengthen our dispute to no purpose. But I entreat you calmly to look into your own thoughts, and then tell me if they are not a useless and unintelligible jargon.

Hyl. I own I have no very clear notion annexed to them. But what say you to this? Do you not make the existence of sensible things consist in their being in a mind? and were not all things eternally in the mind of God? Did they not therefore exist from all eternity, according to you? And how could that which was eternal be created in time? Can any thing be clearer or better connected than this?

Phil. And are not you too of opinion, that God knew all things from eternity?

Hyl. I am.

Phil. Consequently they always had a being in the divine intellect.

Hyl. This I acknowledge.

Phil. By your own confession therefore, nothing is new, or begins to be, in respect of the mind of God. So we are agreed in that point.

Hyl. What shall we make then of the creation?

Phil. May we not understand it to have been entirely in respect of finite spirits; so that things, with regard to us, may properly be said to begin their existence, or be created, when God decreed they should become perceptible to intelligent creatures, in that order and manner which he then established, and we now call the laws of nature? You may call this a *relative,* or *hypothetical existence* if you please. But so long as it supplies us with the most natural, obvious, and literal sense of the Mosaic history of the creation; so long as it answers all the religious ends of that great article; in a word, so long as you can assign no other sense or meaning in its stead; why should we reject this? Is it to comply with a ridiculous sceptical humour of making every thing nonsense and unintelligible? I am sure you cannot say it is for the glory of God. For allowing it to be a thing possible and conceivable, that the corporeal world should have an absolute subsistence extrinsical to the mind of God, as well as to the minds of all created spirits: yet how could this set forth either the immensity or omniscience of the Deity, or the necessary and immediate dependence of all things on him? Nay, would it not rather seem to derogate from those attributes?

Hyl. Well, but as to this decree of God's, for making things perceptible: what say you, Philonous, is it not plain, God did either execute that decree from all eternity, or at some certain time began to will what he had not actually willed before, but only designed to will? If the former, then there could be no creation or beginning of existence in finite things. If the latter, then we must acknowledge something new to befall the Deity; which implies a sort of change; and all change argues imperfection.

Phil. Pray consider what you are doing. Is it not evident, this objection concludes equally against a creation in any sense; nay, against every other act of the Deity, discoverable by the light of nature? None of which can we conceive, otherwise than as performed in time, and having a beginning. God is a being of transcendent and unlimited perfections: his nature therefore is incomprehensible to finite spirits. It is not therefore to be expected, that any man, whether *materialist* or *immaterialist*, should have exactly just notions of the Deity, his attributes, and ways of operation. If then you would infer any thing against me, your difficulty must not be drawn from the inadequateness of our conceptions of the divine nature, which is unavoidable on any scheme: but from the denial of matter, of which there is not one word, directly or indirectly, in what you have now objected.

Hyl. I must acknowledge the difficulties you are concerned to clear, are such only as arise from the non-existence of matter, and are peculiar to that notion. So far you are in the right. But I cannot by any means bring myself to think there is no such peculiar repugnancy between the creation and your opinion; though indeed where to fix it, I do not distinctly know.

Phil. What would you have? Do I not acknowledge a twofold state of things, the one ectypal or natural, the other archetypal and eternal? The former was created in time; the latter existed from everlasting in the mind of God. Is not this agreeable to the common notions of divines? or is any more than this necessary in order to conceive the creation? But you suspect some peculiar repugnancy, though you know not where it lies. To take away all possibility of scruple in the case, do but consider this one point. Either you are not able to conceive the creation on any hypothesis whatsoever; and if so, there is no ground for dislike or complaint against my particular opinion on that score: or you are able to conceive it; and if so, why not on my principles, since thereby nothing conceivable is taken away? You have all along been allowed the full scope of sense, imagination, and reason. Whatever therefore you could before apprehend, either immediately or mediately by your senses, or by ratiocination from your senses; whatever you could perceive, imagine, or understand, remains still with you. If therefore the notion you have of the creation by other principles be intelligible, you have it still upon mine; if it be not intelligible, I conceive it to be no notion at all; and so there is no loss of it. And indeed it seems to me very plain, that the supposition of matter, that is, a thing perfectly unknown and inconceivable, cannot serve to make us conceive any thing. And I hope, it need not be proved to you, that if the existence of matter doth not make the creation conceivable, the creation's being without it inconceivable, can be no objection against its non-existence.

Hyl. I confess, Philonous, you have almost satisfied me in this point of the creation.

Phil. I would fain know why you are not quite satisfied. You tell me indeed of a repugnancy between the Mosaic history and immaterialism: but you know not where it lies. Is this reasonable, Hylas? Can you expect I should solve a difficulty without knowing what it is? But to pass by all that, would not a man think you were assured there is no repugnancy between the received notions of materialists and the inspired writings?

Hyl. And so I am.

Phil. Ought the historical part of scripture to be understood in a plain, obvious sense, or in a sense which is metaphysical and out of the way?

Hyl. In the plain sense, doubtless.

Phil. When Moses speaks of herbs, earth, water, &c., as having been created by God; think you not the sensible things, commonly signified by those words, are suggested to every unphilosophical reader?

Hyl. I cannot help thinking so.

Phil. And are not all ideas, or things perceived by sense, to be denied a real existence by the doctrine of the materialists?

Hyl. This I have already acknowledged.

Phil. The creation therefore, according to them, was not the creation of things sensible, which have only a relative being, but of certain unknown natures, which have an absolute being, wherein creation might terminate.

Hyl. True.

Phil. Is it not therefore evident, the asserters of matter destroy the plain obvious sense of Moses, with which their notions are utterly inconsistent; and instead of it obtrude on us I know not what, something equally unintelligible to themselves and me.

Hyl. I cannot contradict you.

Phil. Moses tells us of a creation. A creation of what? of unknown qualities, of occasions, or substratums? No, certainly; but of things obvious to the senses. You must first reconcile this with your notions, if you expect I should be reconciled to them.

Hyl. I see you can assault me with my own weapons.

Phil. Then as to *absolute existence;* was there ever known a more jejune notion that that? Something it is, so abstracted and unintelligible, that you have frankly owned you could not conceive it, much less explain any thing by

it. But allowing matter to exist, and the notion of absolute existence to be as clear as light, yet was this ever known to make the creation more credible? Nay, hath it not furnished the atheists and infidels of all ages with the most plausible argument against a creation? That a corporeal substance, which hath an absolute existence without the minds of spirits, should be produced out of nothing by the mere will of a spirit, hath been looked upon as a thing so contrary to all reason, so impossible and absurd, that not only the most celebrated among the ancients, but even divers modern and Christian philosophers, have thought matter co-eternal with the Deity. Lay these things together, and then judge you whether materialism disposes men to believe the creation of things.

Hyl. I own, Philonous, I think it does not. This of the *creation* is the last objection I can think of; and I must needs own it hath been sufficiently answered as well as the rest. Nothing now remains to be overcome, but a sort of unaccountable backwardness that I find in myself toward your notions.

Phil. When a man is swayed, he knows not why, to one side of a question, can this, thank you, be any thing else but the effect of prejudice, which never fails to attend old and rooted notions? And indeed in this respect I cannot deny the belief of matter to have very much the advantage over the contrary opinion, with men of a learned education.

Hyl. I confess it seems to be as you say.

Phil. As a balance therefore to this weight of prejudice, let us throw into the scale the great advantages that arise from the belief of immaterialism, both in regard to religion and human learning. The being of a God, and incorruptibility of the soul, those great articles of religion, are they not proved with the clearest and most immediate evidence? When I say the being of a *God*, I do not mean an obscure, general cause of things, whereof we have no conception, but *God*, in the strict and proper sense of the word. A being whose spirituality, omnipresence, providence, omniscience, infinite power, and goodness, are as conspicuous as the existence of sensible things, of which (notwithstanding the fallacious pretences and affected scruples of sceptics) there is no more reason to doubt than of our own being. Then with relation to human sciences; in natural philosophy, what intricacies, what obscurities, what contradictions, hath the belief of matter led men into! To say nothing of the numberless disputes about its extent, continuity, homogeneity, gravity, divisibility, &c., do they not pretend to explain all things by bodies operating on bodies, according to the laws of motion? and yet, are they able to comprehend how any one body should move another? Nay, admitting there was no difficulty in reconciling the notion of an inert being with a cause; or in conceiving how an accident might pass from one body to another; yet by all their strained thoughts and extravagant suppositions, have they been able to reach the mechanical production of any one animal or vegetable body? Can they account by the laws of motion, for sounds, tastes, smells, or colours, or for the regular course of things? Have they accounted by physical principles for the aptitude and contrivance, even of the most inconsiderable parts of the universe? But laying aside matter and corporeal causes, and admitting only the efficiency of an all-perfect mind, are not all the effects of nature easy and intelligible? If the phenomena are nothing else but *ideas;* God is a *spirit*, but matter an unintelligent, unperceiving being. If they demonstrate an unlimited power in their cause; God is active and omnipotent, but matter an inert mass. If the order, regularity, and usefulness of them can never be sufficiently admired; God is infinitely wise and provident, but matter destitute of all contrivance and design. These surely are great advantages in *physics*. Not to mention that the apprehension of a distant Deity naturally disposes men to a negligence in their *moral* actions, which they would be more cautious of in case they thought him immediately present, and acting on their minds without the interposition of matter, or unthinking second causes. Then in *metaphysics;* what difficulties concerning entity in abstract, substantial forms, hylarchic principles, plastic natures, substance and accident, principle of individuation, possibility of matter's thinking, origin of ideas, the manner how two independent substances, so widely different as *spirit* and *matter,* should mutually operate on each other! what difficulties, I say, and endless disquisitions concerning these and innumerable other like points, do we escape by supposing only spirits and ideas? Even the *mathematics* themselves, if we take away the absolute existence of extended things, become much more clear and easy; the most shocking paradoxes and intricate speculations in those sciences, depending on the infinite divisibility of finite extension, which depends on that supposition. But what need is there to insist on the particular sciences? Is not that opposition to all science whatsoever, that frenzy of the ancient and modern sceptics, built on the same foundation? Or can you produce so much as one argument against the reality of corporeal things, or in behalf of that avowed utter ignorance of their natures, which doth not suppose their reality to consist in an external absolute existence. Upon this supposition indeed, the objections from the change of colours in a pigeon's neck, or the appearances of a broken oar in the water, must be allowed to have weight. But those and the like objections vanish, if we do not maintain the being of absolute external originals, but place the reality of things in ideas, fleeting indeed, and changeable; however not changed at random, but according to the fixed order of nature. For herein consists that constancy and truth of things, which secures all the concerns of life, and distinguishes that which is *real* from the irregular visions of the fancy.

Hyl. I agree to all you have now said, and must own that nothing can incline me to embrace your opinion, more than the advantages I see it is attended with. I am by nature lazy, and this would be a mighty abridgment in knowledge. What doubts, what hypotheses, what labyrinths of amusement, which fields of disputation, what an ocean of false learning, may be avoided by that single notion of *immaterialism!*

Phil. After all, is there any thing further remaining to be done? You may remember you promised to embrace that opinion which upon examination should appear most agreeable to common sense, and remote from scepticism. This, by your own confession, is that which denies matter, or the absolute existence of corporeal things. Nor is this all; the same notion has been proved several ways, viewed in different lights, pursued in its consequences, and all objections against it cleared. Can there be a greater evidence of its truth? or is it possible it should have all the marks of a true opinion, and yet be false?

Hyl. I own myself entirely satisfied for the present in all respects. But what security can I have that I shall still continue the same full assent to your opinion, and that no unthought-of objection or difficulty will occur hereafter?

Phil. Pray, Hylas, do you in other cases, when a point is once evidently proved, withhold your assent on account of objections or difficulties it may be liable to? Are the difficulties that attend the doctrine of incommensurable quantities, of the angle of contact, of the asymptotes to curves, or the like, sufficient to make you hold out against mathematical demonstration? Or will you disbelieve the providence of God, because there may be some particular things which you know not how to reconcile with it? If there are difficulties attending immaterialism, there are at the same time direct and evident proofs for it. But for the existence of matter there is not one proof, and far more numerous and insurmountable objections lie against it. But where are those mighty difficulties you insist on? Alas! you know not where or what they are; something which may possibly occur hereafter. If this be a sufficient pretence for withholding your full assent, you should never yield it to any proposition, how free soever from exceptions, how clearly and solidly soever demonstrated.

Hyl. You have satisfied me, Philonous.

Phil. But to arm you against all future objections, do but consider, that which bears equally hard on two contradictory opinions, can be a proof against neither. Whenever therefore any difficulty occurs, try if you can find a solution for it on the hypothesis of the *materialists*. Be not deceived by words; but sound your own thoughts. And in case you cannot conceive it easier by the help of *materialism*, it is plain it can be no objection against *immaterialism*. Had you proceeded all along by this rule, you would probably have spared yourself abundance of trouble in objecting; since of all your difficulties I challenge you to show one that is explained by matter; nay, which is not more unintelligible with, than without that supposition, and consequently makes rather *against* than *for* it. You should consider in each particular, whether the difficulty arises from the *non-existence* of matter. If it doth not, you might as well argue from the infinite divisibility of extension against the divine prescience, as from such a difficulty against *immaterialism*. And yet upon recollection I believe you will find this to have been often, if not always the case. You should likewise take heed not to argue on a *petitio principii*. One is apt to say, the un-

known substances ought to be esteemed real things, rather than the ideas in our minds: and who can tell but the unthinking external substance may concur as a cause or instrument in the production of our ideas? But is not this proceeding on a supposition that there are such external substances? And to suppose this, is it not begging the question? But above all things you should beware of imposing on yourself by that vulgar sophism, which is called *ignoratio elenchi*. You talked often as if you thought I maintained the non-existence of sensible things: whereas in truth no one can be more thoroughly assured of their existence than I am, and it is you who doubt; I should have said, positively deny it. Every thing that is seen, felt, heard, or any way perceived by the senses, is on the principles I embrace, a real being, but not on yours. Remember the matter you contend for is an unknown somewhat (if indeed it may be termed *somewhat*), which is quite stripped of all sensible qualites, and can neither be perceived by sense, nor apprehended by the mind. Remember, I say, that it is not any object which is hard or soft, hot or cold, blue or white, round or square, &c. For all these things I affirm do exist. Though indeed I deny they have any existence distinct from being perceived; or that they exist out of all minds whatsoever. Think on these points; let them be attentively considered and still kept in view. Otherwise you will not comprehend the state of the question; without which your objections will always be wide of the mark, and instead of mine, may possibly be directed (as more than once they have been) against your own notions.

Hyl. I must needs own, Philonous, nothing seems to have kept me from agreeing with you more than this same *mistaking the question*. In denying matter, at first glimpse I am tempted to imagine you deny the things we see and feel; but upon reflection find there is no ground for it. What think you therefore of retaining the name *matter*, and applying it to sensible things? This may be done without any change in your sentiments: and believe me it would be a means of reconciling them to some persons, who may be more shocked at an innovation in words than in opinion.

Phil. With all my heart: retain the word *matter*, and apply it to the objects of sense, if you please, provided you do not attribute to them any subsistence distinct from their being perceived. I shall never quarrel with you for an expression. *Matter,* or *material substance,* are terms introduced by philosophers; and as used by them, imply a sort of independency, or a subsistence distinct from being perceived by a mind: but are never used by common people; or if ever, it is to signify the immediate objects of sense. One would think therefore, so long as the names of all particular things, with the terms *sensible, substance, body, stuff,* and the like, are retained, the word *matter* should be never missed in common talk. And in philosophical discourses it seems the best way to leave it quite out; since there is not perhaps any one thing that hath more favoured and strengthened the depraved bent of the mind toward *atheism,* than the use of that general confused term.

Hyl. Well but, Philonous, since I am content to give up the notion of an unthinking substance exterior to the mind, I think you ought not to deny me the privilege of using the word *matter* as I please, and annexing it to a collection of sensible qualities subsisting only in the mind. I freely own there is no other substance in a strict sense, than *spirit.* but I have been so long accustomed to the term *matter,* that I know not how to part with it. To say, there is no *matter* in the world, is still shocking to me. Whereas to say, there is no *matter,* if by that term be meant an unthinking substance existing without the mind; but if by matter is meant some sensible thing, whose existence consists in being perceived, then there is *matter*: this distinction gives it quite another turn: and men will come into your notions with small difficulty, when they are proposed in that manner. For after all, the controversy about matter, in the strict acceptation of it, lies altogether between you and the philosophers, whose principles, I acknowledge, are not near so natural, or so agreeable to the common sense of mankind, and holy scripture, as yours. There is nothing we either desire or shun, but as it makes, or is apprehended to make some part of our happiness or misery. But what hath happiness or misery, joy or grief, pleasure or pain, to do with absolute existence, or with unknown entities, abstracted from all relation to us? It is evident, things regard us only as they are pleasing or displeasing: and they can please or displease only so far forth as they are perceived. Further therefore we are not concerned; and thus far you leave things as you found them. Yet still there is something new in this doctrine. It is plain, I do not now think with the philosophers, nor yet altogether with the vulgar. I would know how the case stands in that respect: precisely, what you have added to, or altered in my former notions.

Phil. I do not pretend to be a setter-up of *new notions.* My endeavours tend only to unite and place in a clearer light that truth, which was before shared between the vulgar and the philosophers: the former being of opinion, that *those things they immediately perceive are the real things*: and the latter, that *the things immediately perceived are ideas which exist only in the mind.* Which two notions put together, do in effect constitute the substance of what I advance.

Hyl. I have been a long time distrusting my senses; me-thought I saw things by a dim light, and through false glasses. Now the glasses are removed, and a new light breaks in upon my understanding. I am clearly convinced that I see things in their native forms; and am no longer in pain about their unknown natures or absolute existence. This is the state I find myself in at present: though indeed the course that brought me to it I do not yet thoroughly comprehend. You set out upon the same principles that Academics, Cartesians, and the like sects, usually do; and for a long time it looked as if you were advancing their philosophical scepticism; but in the end your conclusions are directly oppcsite to theirs.

Phil. You see, Hylas, the water of yonder fountain, how it is forced upwards, in a round column, to a certain height; at which it breaks and falls back into the basin from whence it rose: its ascent, as well as descent, proceeding from the same uniform law or principle of *gravitation.* Just so, the same principles which at first view lead to scepticism, pursued to a certain point, bring men back to common sense.

David Hume

Depending upon your point of view, David Hume is the most celebrated or the most infamous philosopher ever produced by the British Isles. He was born in Edinburgh in 1711 and later attended the University of Edinburgh but without taking a degree. He later studied law there but again without completing the work for a degree. What he did acquire at Edinburgh was a thorough grounding in the new Newtonian science which was to prove so influential on his philosophy. From 1735 to 1737 he lived in La Fleche, France, where Descartes had gone to school, and completed the *Treatise of Human Nature* by the age of 26. Although the work was not a publishing success, it was later to prove to be one of the greatest works of modern philosophy.

Because of his religious reputation, Hume was unable to obtain a teaching post. He spent some time as a tutor, as a librarian, and as a bureaucrat in various capacities. Yet Hume did become a success as a man of letters by writing some highly popular essays on morals, politics, and economics. From 1754-62 Hume published a history of England which brought him instant fame and which remained the standard work on the subject for well over a century. Hume was taken seriously in France by the philosophers; he was taken seriously by his close friend Adam Smith, the founder of modern economic theory; and he was taken seriously as a historian by the public. But he was not taken seriously where it most mattered to him, in the field of philosophy. He was bitterly opposed by clergymen who could not understand him and by some philosophers who would not see the point of his philosophy. He died in 1776 having made significant and permanent contributions in history, economics, and philosophy; having made friends with the great men of the eighteenth century, including Benjamin Franklin; and even having defended the American colonists in their opposition to the policies of King George III. To this day Hume's philosophy is a focal point of controversy.

We have selected the *Enquiry Concerning Human Understanding,* originally published in 1748, because it presents the major themes of his philosophy in a brief way. To begin with, it will be clear that Hume sides with Newton's physics, and that it is the avowed purpose of Hume's philosophy to do for the study of mankind what Newton had done for the study of nature. That is, Hume attempted to analyze the human thinking process along the same lines Newton had used to analyze the phenomena of nature. This point alone has led to great misunderstanding. It is Hume's assumption, along with most philosophers in the modern period, that external physical objects cause us to have experiences, some of which are not physical in the sense that they do not occupy space. That is, Hume works with the dualism we have already encountered in Descartes and Locke. Hume then attempts to explain the operations of the mind. Unfortunately, some readers have been led to think that Hume, like Berkeley, denies the existence of the external world. This is partly the result of not reading him carefully, and partly the result of interpreting Hume as an empiricist who follows Locke and Berkeley.

Moreover, this misunderstanding has rebounded to obscure Hume's analysis of causation. There are two dimensions to Hume's analysis. First, Hume shows the philosophical implications of Newtonian physics and its opposition to Aristotelian physics. More about this is discussed below. Second, Hume offers a psychological account of how some thinkers have been misled into giving the wrong account of our thinking process. Hume does not confuse the two accounts as his readers sometimes do; rather he sees them as symmetrical.

The radical new dimension which Hume adds to philosophy can be seen here. In opposition to both Platonists and Aristotelians, Hume denies that the human thinking process can be understood according to traditional rationalistic models. One example will show this. We all believe in regularity, that the future will somehow be consistent with the past. This is nowadays referred to as the principle of *induction.* Hume asks why do we believe this? The Platonist would have to argue that it is an a priori truth. Hume argues that this cannot be the case because we can conceive of or imagine the future not resembling the past. The Aristotelian would argue that we have abstracted this truth from experience. Hume argues that this cannot be true because our experience is of the past, and what is being questioned is whether we should believe that the experience of the future will conform to the experience of the past. In short, we do not derive this principle from experience but bring the principle to our interpretation of our experience. Hume's answer is that the principle is a contribution of the human mind, that this contribution is psychological and biological, that it is necessary for our survival, and that no logical analysis can be adequate unless it is supplemented by this kind of psychological analysis. This is *the Copernican element in Hume's philosophy.*

The important point to note is that Hume's own Copernican hypothesis is given only after Hume has shown on logical grounds and through an analysis of Newtonian physics that the alternative accounts are incorrect. Let us now turn to Hume's Newtonian analysis of causation. The reader is advised to review what was said earlier about Aristotle's four causes before proceeding.

The Newtonian Analysis of Causation

The crucial element in Aristotle's analysis of causation is the license it gives to infer that a property of the effect must result from a similar property in the cause. This follows from the identity of the final, formal, and efficient causes. Further, this identity leads to three kinds of proofs for God's existence, and to the fact that all three proofs or combinations thereof will emerge in the same writer. Not only does Aristotle's analysis of causation lead to the inference that there must be a first cause, but God is by definition (ontological proof) the only being self-sufficient enough to be considered the first cause. It further follows from our definition of God that He is benevolent, so that what He causes to happen (teleological proof) must ultimately be good. Later, Kant was to argue that all three proofs depend upon the ontological proof. But it could just as easily be argued that all three depend upon the cosmological proof, especially if one stresses the Aristotelian or Thomistic way into the arguments.

It is now easy to see that even after giving up some of the preconceptions of the so-called rationalists, both Locke and Berkeley still argue for a first cause. That is, both Locke and Berkeley still employ the Aristotelian notion of causation even though they are familiar with Newton. Locke maintained that primary qualities really do reflect something permanent in the object, and Berkeley argued that an "idea" must be caused by a mind, hence the necessity for an all-encompassing mind. Only Hume was to see the real implications of Newton.

This brings us to the crucial question of what revolution was introduced by Newton's physics. Newton's first law of motion states that: "Every body continues in its state of rest or of uniform motion in a right line unless it is compelled to change that state by forces impressed upon it." The revolutionary idea was that uniform motion in a straight line is as natural a state as rest. If uniform rectilinear motion is a natural state, then it is no longer either necessary or meaningful to ask for the original cause of motion. It is not motion but a change in motion that has to be explained. Moreover, a change in motion results from the action of a force, for example, another independent body which collides with the body whose change of motion is to be explained. In short, change of motion can be explained in the Newtonian system by impact alone (or by gravity in the case of a falling object). The relation between the two colliding bodies can only be discovered empirically and can never be discovered by the mere examination of just one of the bodies. In conclusion, there is no reason to believe that anything is built-in.

If a philosopher were to grasp this new Newtonian framework, then he would derive five philosophical consequences.

1. There is no need for a first cause or a cause for something to exist or begin to exist.

2. Since change of motion is produced by an external body, no examination can reveal a potential to be moved. There is no built-in necessity, or essence. In short, there are no formal causes.

3. Since change of motion is produced by an external body, no examination of an isolated individual object can reveal its potential or power to be a mover, to move another object. In short, efficient causes can only be discovered empirically and after the fact.

4. If (3) is true, then there is no ground for the assumption that an efficient cause must embody the same essence as the effect. In other words, no observation of the effect alone can justify any assertion about the nature of the cause.

5. If rest is not universally natural, then there is no end to be realized; in short, there is no final cause.

The only kind of causation Hume recognizes is efficient causation. The denial of a formal cause, the denial of the identity of the formal-efficient-final causes, is extended into a full-scale attack on the concept of necessary causation. Hume's claim that we cannot observe a cause is not intended as a denial of the fact that we observe causation in nature. What Hume is denying is that we can observe formal causes or essences. Having established this point by an examination of Newtonian physics and by a logical analysis of its consequences, Hume then and only then suggests a psychological account of why people mistakenly believe in necessity.

If we examine the *Enquiry* beyond the first section, which reasserts the same program of the introduction to the *Treatise,* and the brief reintroduction to the theory of the origin and the association of ideas, what we find in the rest of the book is a clear working out of the implications of the Newtonian analysis of causation. Here Hume argues against the demonstrative conception of causality, against the notion of a necessary connection among events, against the Lockean argument that we have an internal idea of power, and finally discusses the theological aspect of Newton's conception of causality. Not content with these implications, Hume draws the further implication that causality as thus understood applies to human behavior as well.

There is one dramatically serious problem in Hume's philosophy, and interestingly enough, it is a problem to which he personally calls our attention. Previous philosophers had solved the problem of the relationship between our experience and the external physical world by using the Aristotelian theory of efficient causality in one way or another. Descartes had used it to prove God's existence and then to show that God would not deceive us in our belief about the external world. Locke had used it in his notion that primary qualities really represent the object in itself. Even Berkeley had used the theory of arguing that God maintains a regularity in our experience of ideas. But Hume argued that once we surrender the Aristotelian theory of causation, then we cannot make any such inference. Hume then proceeded to supplement his critique with the positive theory that the mind causes us to believe in the external world, and this belief is not explainable by the older rationalistic philosophies, including those of Locke and Berkeley. At the same time, it is the case that Hume took the existence of the external world as something real and given, hence the reason that the Newtonian analysis could be extended from it to the mind. But Hume felt increasingly uncomfortable with this as a bare assumption. This problem continued to plague later philosophers even more after Hume's devastating critique.

Hume's Copernicanism

So much is said about Hume's alleged empiricism that it is sometimes difficult to realize to what degree he was not an empiricist. Certainly Hume was not a Platonic rationalist, and the critique of innate ideas which he follows Locke in giving is meant to reinforce this denial. The assertion that all of our ideas come from experience is again designed as a critical weapon against rationalism of the Cartesian variety. At the same time, Hume's request that an idea be related to its impression is used against Aristotelian rationalists, including Locke, to show that these Aristotelians cannot justify their views by an appeal to experience. But much more important is Hume's positive contention, found in the section on association, that what is really important in the reasoning process is the contribution made by the mind. The mind *associates* ideas that come from experience, but association is not given in the ideas themselves. This is a nonempirical element. We experience the association of the mind but the association is not itself one of the items given; rather it is our contribution. Thus, Hume is not a strict empiricist. At the same time, the contribution of the mind does not consist of self-evident a priori truths as the Platonic rationalists would have it. Rather, Hume argues that the activity of the mind is ultimately contingent; that is, there is nothing permanent about the way the mind operates. We cannot show that the first principles of the mind, association, are a priori; we cannot show that these principles are derived from experience. All we can show is the psychological, historical, or biological origin of the principles. This represented an entirely new way of philosophizing.

Hume's new philosophical method could be called his Copernican metaphysics. He himself was aware of the Copernican origin of modern science. He himself stressed the mind's contribution to the knowing process. In our discussion of Kant, we shall see this point again. Once we admit the mind's contribution to the knowing process, we are free from the narrowly intellectualistic constraints of previous philosophers. We have already seen, in the discussion of Bacon, how the practical relevance of science was emerging in the modern period. Hume's Copernicanism can incorporate this by showing how practicality is part of the mind's contribution. This is why we can ignore skeptical arguments in *practice*. It is why Hume stresses in the introduction to the *Enquiry* that amidst all of our philosophizing we not forget that we are men, that is, creatures who act as well as think.

An Enquiry Concerning Human Understanding

SECTION I

OF THE DIFFERENT SPECIES OF PHILOSOPHY

Moral philosophy, or the science of human nature, may be treated after two different manners; each of which has its peculiar merit, and may contribute to the entertainment, instruction, and reformation of mankind. The one considers man chiefly as born for action; and as influenced in his measures by taste and sentiment; pursuing one object, and avoiding another, according to the value which these objects seem to possess, and according to the light in which they present themselves. As virtue, of all objects, is allowed to be the most valuable, this species of philosophers paint her in the most amiable colors; borrowing all helps from poetry and eloquence, and treating their subject in an easy and obvious manner, and such as is best fitted to please the imagination, and engage the affections. They select the most striking observations and instances from common life; place opposite characters in a proper contrast; and alluring us into the paths of virtue by the views of glory and happiness, direct our steps in these paths by the soundest precepts and most illustrious examples. They make us *feel* the difference between vice and virtue; they excite and regulate our sentiments; and so they can but bend our hearts to the love of probity and true honor, they think, that they have fully attained the end of all their labors.

The other species of philosophers consider man in the light of a reasonable rather than an active being, and endeavor to form his understanding more than cultivate his manners. They

regard human nature as a subject of speculation; and with a narrow scrutiny examine it, in order to find those principles, which regulate our understanding, excite our sentiments, and make us to approve or blame any particular object, action, or behavior. They think it a reproach to all literature, that philosophy should not yet have fixed, beyond controversy, the foundation of morals, reasoning, and criticism; and should for ever talk of truth and falsehood, vice and virtue, beauty and deformity, without being able to determine the source of these distinctions. While they attempt this arduous task, they are deterred by no difficulties; but proceeding from particular instances to general principles, they still push on their inquiries to principles more general, and rest not satisfied till they arrive at those original principles, by which, in every science, all human curiosity must be bounded. Though their speculations seem abstract, and even unintelligible to common readers, they aim at the approbation of the learned and the wise; and think themselves sufficiently compensated for the labor of their whole lives, if they can discover some hidden truths, which may contribute to the instruction of posterity.

It is certain that the easy and obvious philosophy will always, with the generality of mankind, have the preference above the accurate and abstruse; and by many will be recommended, not only as more agreeable, but more useful than the other. It enters more into common life; molds the heart and affections; and, by touching those principles which actuate men, reforms their conduct, and brings them nearer to that model of perfection which it describes. On the contrary, the abstruse philosophy, being founded on a turn of mind, which cannot enter into business and action, vanishes when the philosopher leaves the shade, and comes into open day; nor can its principles easily retain any influence over our conduct and behavior. The feelings of our heart, the agitation of our passions, the vehemence of our affections, dissipate all its conclusions, and reduce the profound philosopher to a mere plebeian.

This also must be confessed, that the most durable, as well as justest fame, has been acquired by the easy philosophy, and that abstract reasoners seem hitherto to have enjoyed only a momentary reputation, from the caprice or ignorance of their own age, but have not been able to support their renown with more equitable posterity. It is easy for a profound philosopher to commit a mistake in his subtle reasonings; and one mistake is the necessary parent of another, while he pushes on his consequences, and is not deterred from embracing any conclusion, by its unusual appearance, or its contradiction to popular opinion. But a philosopher, who purposes only to represent the common sense of mankind in more beautiful and more engaging colors, if by accident he falls into error, goes no farther; but renewing his appeal to common sense, and the natural sentiments of the mind, returns into the right path, and secures himself from any dangerous illusions. The fame of Cicero flourishes at present; but that of Aristotle is utterly decayed. La Bruyere passes the seas, and still maintains his reputation: But the glory of Malebranche is confined to his own nation, and to his own age. Addison, perhaps, will be read with pleasure, when Locke shall be entirely forgotten.

The mere philosopher is a character, which is commonly but little acceptable in the world, as being supposed to contribute nothing either to the advantage or pleasure of society; while he lives remote from communication with mankind, and is wrapped up in principles and notions equally remote from their comprehension. On the other hand, the mere ignorant is still more despised; nor is anything deemed a surer sign of an illiberal genius in an age and nation where the sciences flourish, than to be entirely destitute of all relish for those noble entertainments. The most perfect character is supposed to lie between those extremes; retaining an equal ability and taste for books,

company, and business; preserving in conversation that discernment and delicacy which arise from polite letters; and in business, that probity and accuracy which are the natural result of a just philosophy. In order to diffuse and cultivate so accomplished a character, nothing can be more useful than compositions of the easy style and manner, which draw not too much from life, require no deep application or retreat to be comprehended, and send back the student among mankind full of noble sentiments and wise precepts, applicable to every exigence of human life. By means of such compositions, virtue becomes amiable, science agreeable, company instructive, and retirement entertaining.

Man is a reasonable being; and as such, receives from science his proper food and nourishment: But so narrow are the bounds of human understanding, that little satisfaction can be hoped for in this particular, either from the extent or security of his acquisitions. Man is a sociable, no less than a reasonable being: But neither can he always enjoy company agreeable and amusing, or preserve the proper relish for them. Man is also an active being; and from that disposition, as well as from the various necessities of human life, must submit to business and occupation: But the mind requires some relaxation, and cannot always support its bent to care and industry. It seems, then, that nature has pointed out a mixed kind of life as most suitable to the human race, and secretly admonished them to allow none of these biases to *draw* too much, so as to incapacitate them for other occupations and entertainments. Indulge your passion for science, says she, but let your science be human, and such as may have a direct reference to action and society. Abstruse thought and profound researches I prohibit, and will severely punish, by the pensive melancholy which they introduce, by the endless uncertainty in which they involve you, and by the cold reception which your pretended discoveries shall meet with, when communicated. Be a philosopher; but, amidst all your philosophy, be still a man.

Were the generality of mankind contented to prefer the easy philosophy to the abstract and profound, without throwing any blame or contempt on the latter, it might not be improper, perhaps, to comply with this general opinion, and allow every man to enjoy, without opposition, his own taste and sentiment. But as the matter is often carried farther, even to the absolute rejecting of all profound reasonings, or what is commonly called *metaphysics,* we shall now proceed to consider what can reasonably be pleaded in their behalf.

We may begin with observing, that one considerable advantage, which results from the accurate and abstract philosophy, is, its subserviency to the easy and humane, which, without the former, can never attain a sufficient degree of exactness in its sentiments, precepts, or reasonings. All polite letters are nothing but pictures of human life in various attitudes and situations; and inspire us with different sentiments, of praise or blame, admiration or ridicule, according to the qualities of the object, which they set before us. An artist must be better qualified to succeed in this undertaking, who, besides a delicate taste and a quick apprehension, possesses an accurate knowledge of the internal fabric, the operations of the understanding, the workings of the passions, and the various species of sentiment which discriminate vice and virtue. How painful soever this inward search or inquiry may appear, it becomes, in some measure, requisite to those, who would describe with success the obvious and outward appearances of life and manners. The anatomist presents to the eye the most hideous and disagreeable objects; but his science is useful to the painter in delineating even a Venus or an Helen. While the latter employs all the richest colors of his art, and gives his figures the most graceful and engaging airs; he must still carry his attention to the inward structure of the human body, the position of the muscles, the fabric of the bones, and the use and figure of every part or organ. Accuracy is, in every case, advantageous to beauty,and just reasoning to delicate sentiment. In vain would we exalt the one by depreciating the other.

Besides, we may observe, in every art or profession, even those which most concern life or action, that a spirit of accuracy, however acquired, carries all of them nearer their perfection, and renders them more subservient to the interests of society. And though a philosopher may live remote from business, the genius of philosophy, if carefully cultivated by several, must gradually diffuse itself throughout the whole society, and bestow a similar correctness on every art and calling. The politician will ac-

quire greater foresight and subtlety, in the subdividing and balancing of power; the lawyer more method and finer principles in his reasonings; and the general more regularity in his discipline, and more caution in his plans and operations. The stability of modern governments above the ancient, and the accuracy of modern philosophy, have improved, and probably will still improve, by similar gradations.

Were there no advantage to be reaped from these studies, beyond the gratification of an innocent curiosity, yet ought not even this to be despised; as being one accession to those few safe and harmless pleasures, which are bestowed on the human race. The sweetest and most inoffensive path of life leads through the avenues of science and learning; and whoever can either remove any obstructions in this way, or open up any new prospect, ought so far to be esteemed a benefactor to mankind. And though these researches may appear painful and fatiguing, it is with some minds as with some bodies, which being endowed with vigorous and florid health, require severe exercise, and reap a pleasure from what, to the generality of mankind, may seem burdensome and laborious. Obscurity, indeed, is painful to the mind as well as to the eye; but to bring light from obscurity, by whatever labor, must needs be delightful and rejoicing.

But this obscurity in the profound and abstract philosophy, is objected to, not only as painful and fatiguing, but as the inevitable source of uncertainty and error. Here indeed lies the justest and most plausible objection against a considerable part of metaphysics, that they are not properly a science; but arise either from the fruitless efforts of human vanity, which would penetrate into subjects utterly inaccessible to the understanding, or from the craft of popular superstitions, which, being unable to defend themselves on fair ground, raise these entangling brambles to cover and protect their weakness. Chased from the open country, these robbers fly into the forest, and lie in wait to break in upon every unguarded avenue of the mind, and overwhelm it with religious fears and prejudices. The stoutest antagonist, if he remit his watch a moment, is oppressed. And many, through cowardice and folly, open the gates to the enemies, and willingly receive them with reverence and submission, as their legal sovereigns.

But is this a sufficient reason, why philosophers should desist from such reseachers, and leave superstition still in possession of her retreat? Is it not proper to draw an opposite conclusion, and perceive the necessity of carrying the war into the most secret recesses of the enemy? In vain do we hope, that men, from frequent disappointment, will at last abandon such airy sciences, and discover the proper province of human reason. For, besides, that many persons find too sensible an interest in perpetually recalling such topics; besides this, I say, the motive of blind despair can never reasonably have place in the sciences; since, however unsuccessful former attempts may have proved, there is still room to hope, that the industry, good fortune, or improved sagacity of succeeding generations may reach discoveries unknown to former ages. Each adventurous genius will leap at the arduous prize, and find himself stimulated, rather than discouraged, by the failures of his predecessors; while he hopes that the glory of achieving so hard an adventure is reserved for him alone. The only method of freeing learning, at once, from these abstruse questions, is to inquire seriously into the nature of human understanding, and show, from an exact analysis of its powers and capacity, that it is by no means fitted for such remote and abstruse subjects. We must submit to this fatigue, in order to live at ease ever after: And must cultivate true metaphysics with some care, in order to destroy the false and adulterate. Indolence, which, to some persons, affords a safeguard against this deceitful philosophy, is, with others, over-balanced by curiosity; and despair, which, at some moments, prevails, may give place afterwards to sanguine hopes and expectations. Accurate and just reasoning is the only catholic remedy, fitted for all persons and all dispositions; and is alone able to subvert that abstruse philosophy and metaphysical jargon, which, being mixed up with popular superstition, renders it in a manner impenetrable to careless reasoners, and gives it the air of science and wisdom.

Besides this advantage of rejecting, after deliberate inquiry, the most uncertain and disagreeable part of learning, there are many positive advantages, which result from an accurate scrutiny into the powers and faculties of human nature. It is remarkable concerning the operations of the mind, that, though most intimately present to us, yet, whenever they become the object of reflection, they seem involved in obscurity; nor can the eye readily find those lines and boundaries, which discriminate and distinguish them. The objects are too fine to remain long in the same aspect or situation; and must be apprehended in an instant, by a superior penetration, derived from nature, and improved by habit and reflection. It becomes, therefore, no inconsiderable part of science barely to know the different operations of the mind, to separate them from each other, to class them under their proper heads, and to correct all that seeming disorder, in which they lie involved, when made the object of reflection and inquiry. This talk of ordering and distinguishing, which has no merit, when performed with regard to external bodies, the objects of our senses, rises in its value, when directed towards the operations of the mind, in proportion to the difficulty and labor, which we meet with in performing it. And if we can go no farther than this mental geography, or delineation of the distinct parts and powers of the mind, it is at least a satisfaction to go so far; and the more obvious this science may appear (and it is by no means obvious) the more contemptible still must the ignorance of it be esteemed, in all pretenders to learning and philosophy.

Nor can there remain any suspicion, that this science is uncertain and chimerical; unless we should entertain such a scepticism as is entirely subversive of all speculation, and even action. It cannot be doubted, that the mind is endowed with several powers and faculties, that these powers are distinct from each other, that what is really distinct to the immediate perception may be distinguished by reflection; and consequently, that there is a truth and falsehood in all propositions on this subject, and a truth and falsehood, which lie not beyond the compass of human understanding. There are many obvious distinctions of this kind, such as those between the will and understanding, the imagination and passions, which fall within the comprehension of every human creature; and the finer and more philosophical distinctions are no less real and certain, though more difficult to be comprehended. Some instances, especially late ones, of success in these inquiries, may give us a juster notion of the certainty and solidity of this branch of learning. And shall we esteem is worthy the labor of a philosopher to give us a true system of the planets, and adjust the position and order of those remote bodies; while we affect to overlook those, who, with so much success, delineate the parts of the mind, in which we are so intimately concerned?

But may we not hope, that philosophy, it cultivated with care, and encouraged by the attention of the public, may carry its researches still farther, and discover, at least in some degree, the secret springs and principles, by which the human mind is actuated in its operations? Astronomers had long contented themselves with proving, from the phenomena, the true motions, order, and magnitude of the heavenly bodies: Till a philosopher, at last arose, who seems, from the happiest reasoning, to have also determined the laws and forces, by which the revolutions of the planets are governed and directed. The like has been performed with regard to other parts of nature. And there is no reason to despair of equal success in our inquiries concerning the metal powers and economy, if prosecuted with equal capacity and caution. It is probable, that one operation and principle of the mind depends on another; which, again, may be resolved into one more general and universal: And how far these researches may possibly be carried, it will be difficult for us, before, or even after, a careful trial, exactly to determine. This is certain, that attempts of this kind are every day made even by those who philosophize the most negligently: And nothing can be more requisite than to enter upon the enterprise with thorough care and attention; that, if it lie within the compass of human understanding, it may at last be happily achieved; if not, it may, however, be rejected with some confidence and security. This last conclusion, surely, is not desirable; nor ought it to be embraced too rashly. For how much must we diminish from the beauty and value of this species of philosophy, upon such a supposition? Moralists have hitherto been accustomed, when they considered the vast multitude and diversity of those actions that excite our approbation or dislike, to search for some common principle, on which this variety of sentiments might depend. And though they have sometimes carried the matter too far, by their passion for some one general principle; it must, however, be confessed, that they are excusable in expecting to find some

general principles, into which all the vices and virtues were justly to be resolved. The like has been the endeavor of critics, logicians, and even politicians: Nor have their attempts been wholly unsuccessful; though perhaps longer time, greater accuracy, and more ardent application may bring these sciences still nearer their prefection. To throw up at once all pretensions of this kind may justly be deemed more rash, precipitate, and dogmatical, than even the boldest and most affirmative philosophy, that has ever attempted to impose its crude dictates and principles on mankind.

What though these reasonings concerning human nature seem abstract, and of difficult comprehension? This affords no presumption of their falsehood. On the contrary, it seems impossible, that what has hitherto escaped so many wise and profound philosophers can be very obvious and easy. And whatever pains these researches may cost us, we may think ourselves sufficiently rewarded, not only in point of profit but of pleasure, if, by that means, we can make any addition to our stock of knowledge, in subjects of such unspeakable importance.

But as, after all, the abstractedness of these speculations is no recommendation, but rather a disadvantage to them, and as this difficulty may perhaps be surmounted by care and art, and the avoiding of all unnecessary detail, we have, in the following inquiry, attempted to thrown some light upon subjects, from which uncertainty has hitherto deterred the wise, and obscurity the ignorant. Happy, if we can unite the boundaries of the different species of philosophy, by reconciling profound inquiry with clearness, and truth with novelty! And still more happy, if reasoning in this easy manner, we can undermine the foundations of an abstruse philosophy, which seems to have hitherto served only as a shelter to superstition, and a cover to absurdity and error!

SECTION II

OF THE ORIGIN OF IDEAS

Everyone will readily allow that there is a considerable difference between the perceptions of the mind, when a man feels the pain of excessive heat, or the pleasure of moderate warmth, and when he afterwards recalls to his memory this sensation, or anticipates it by his imagintion. These faculties may mimic or copy the perceptions of the senses; but they never can entirely reach the force and vivacity of the original sentiment. The utmost we say of them, even when they operate with greatest vigor, is, that they represent their object in so lively a manner, that we could *almost* say we feel or see it: But, except the mind be disordered by disease or madness, they never can arrive at such a pitch of vivacity, as to render these perceptions altogether undistinguishable. All the colors of poetry, however splendid, can never paint natural objects in such a manner as to make the description be taken for a real landscape. The most lively thought is still inferior to the dullest sensation.

We may observe a like distinction to run through all the other perceptions of the mind. A man in a fit of anger, is actuated in a very different manner from one who only thinks of that emotion. If you tell me, that any person is in love, I easily understand your meaning, and form a just conception of his situation; but never can mistake that conception for the real disorders and agitations of the passion. When we reflect on our past sentiments and affections, our thought is a faithful mirror, and copies its objects truly; but the colors which it employs are faint and dull, in comparison of those in which our original perceptions were clothed. It requires no nice discernment or metaphysical head to mark the distinction between them.

Here therefore we may divide all the perceptions of the mind into two classes or species, which are distinguished by their different degrees of force and vivacity. The less forcible and lively are commonly denominated *thoughts* or *ideas*. The other species want a name in our language, and in most others; I suppose, because it was not requisite for any, but philosophical purposes, to rank them under a general term or appellation. Let us, therefore, use a little freedom, and call them *impressions;* employing that word in a sense somewhat different from the usual. By the term *impression,* then, I mean all our more lively perceptions, when we hear, or see, or feel, or love, or hate, or desire, or will. And impressions are distinguished from ideas, which are the less lively perceptions, of which we are conscious, when we reflect on any of those sensations or movements above mentioned.

Nothing, at first view, may seem more unbounded than the thought of man, which not only escapes all human power and authority, but is not even restrained within the limits of nature and reality. To form monsters, and join incongruous shapes and appearances, costs the imagination no more trouble than to conceive the most natural and familiar objects. And while the body is confined to one planet, along which it creeps with pain and difficulty; the thought can in an instant transport us into the most distant regions of the universe; or even beyond the universe, into the unbounded chaos, where nature is supposed to lie in total confusion. What never was seen, or heard of, may yet be conceived; nor is anything beyond the power of thought, except what implies an absolute contradiction.

But though our thought seems to possess this unbounded liberty, we shall find, upon a nearer examination, that it is really confined within very narrow limits, and that all this creative power of the mind amounts to no more than the faculty of compounding, transposing, augmenting, or diminishing the materials afforded us by the senses and experience. When we think of a golden mountain, we only join two consistent ideas, *gold,* and *mountain,* with which we were formerly acquainted. A virtuous horse we can conceive; because, from our own feeling, we can conceive virtue; and this we may unite to the figure and shape of a horse, which is an animal familiar to us. In short, all the materials of thinking are derived either from our outward or inward sentiment: the mixture and composition of these belongs alone to the mind and will. Or, to express myself in philosophical language, all our ideas or more feeble perceptions are copies of our impressions or more lively ones.

To prove this, the two following arguments will, I hope, be sufficient. First, when we analyze our thoughts or ideas, however compounded or sublime, we always find that they resolve themselves into such simple ideas as were copied from a precedent feeling or sentiment. Even those ideas, which, at first view, seem the most wide of this origin, are found, upon a nearer scrutiny, to be derived from it. The idea of God, as meaning an infinitely intelligent, wise, and good Being, arises from reflecting on the operations of our own mind, and augmenting, without limit, those qualities of goodness and wisdom. We may prosecute this inquiry to what length we please; where we shall always find, that every idea which we examine is copied from a similar impression. Those who would assert that this position is not universally true nor without exception, have only one, and that an easy method of refuting it; by producing that idea, which, in their opinion, is not derived from this source. It will then be incumbent on us, if we would maintain our doctrine, to produce the impression, or lively perception, which corresponds to it.

Secondly. If it happen, from a defect of the organ, that a man is not susceptible of any species of sensation, we always find that he is as little susceptible of the correspondent ideas. A blind man can form no notion of colors; a deaf man of sounds. Restore either of them that sense in which he is deficient; by opening this new inlet for his sensations, you also open an inlet for the ideas; and he finds no difficulty in conceiving these objects. The case is the same, if the object, proper for exciting any sensation, has never been applied to the organ. A Laplander or Negro has no notion of the relish of wine. And though there are few or no instances of a like deficiency in the mind, where a person has never felt or is wholly incapable of a sentiment or passion that belongs to his species; yet we find the same observation to take place in a less degree. A man of mild manners can form no idea of inveterate revenge or cruelty; nor can a selfish heart easily conceive the heights of friendship and generosity. It is readily allowed, that other beings may possess many senses of which we can have no conception; because the ideas of them have never been introduced to us in the only manner by which an idea can have access to the mind, to wit, by the actual feeling and sensation.

There is, however, one contradictory phenomenon, which may prove that it is not absolutely impossible for ideas to arise, independent of their correspondent impressions. I believe it will readily be allowed, that the several distinct ideas of color, which enter by the eye, or those of sound, which are conveyed by the ear, are really different from each other; though, at the same time, resembling. Now if this be true of different colors, it must be no less so of the different shades of the same color; and each shade produces a distinct idea, independent of the rest. For if this should be denied, it is possible, by the continual gradation of shades, to run a

color insensibly into what is most remote from it; and if you will not allow any of the means to be different, you cannot, without absurdity, deny the extremes to be the same. Suppose, therefore, a person to have enjoyed his sight for thirty years, and to have become perfectly acquainted with colors of all kinds except one particular shade of blue, for instance, which it never has been his fortune to meet with. Let all the different shades of that color, except that single one, be placed before him, descending gradually from the deepest to the lightest; it is plain that he will perceive a blank, where that shade is wanting, and will be sensible that there is a greater distance in that place between the contiguous colors than in any other. Now I ask, whether it be possible for him, from his own imagination, to supply this deficiency, and raise up to himself the idea of that particular shade, though it had never been conveyed to him by his senses? I believe there are few but will be of opinion that he can: and this may serve as a proof that the simple ideas are not always, in every instance, derived from the correspondent impressions; though this instance is so singular, that it is scarcely worth our observing, and does not merit that for it alone we should alter our general maxim.

Here, therefore, is a proposition, which not only seems, in itself, simple and intelligible; but, if a proper use were made of it, might render every dispute equally intelligible, and banish all that jargon, which has so long taken possession of metaphysical reasonings, and drawn disgrace upon them. All ideas, especially abstract ones, are naturally faint and obscure: the mind has but a slender hold of them: they are apt to be confounded with other resembling ideas; and when we have often employed any term, though without a distinct meaning, we are apt to imagine it has a determinate idea annexed to it. On the contrary, all impressions, that is, all sensations, either outward or inward, are strong and vivid: the limits between them are more exactly determined: nor is it easy to fall into any error or mistake with regard to them. When we entertain, therefore, any suspicion that a philosophical term is employed without any meaning or idea (as is but too frequent), we need but inquire, *from what impression is that supposed idea derived?* And if it be impossible to assign any, this will serve to confirm our suspicion. By bringing ideas into so clear a light we may reasonably hope to remove all dispute, which may arise, concerning their nature and reality.

SECTION III

OF THE ASSOCIATION OF IDEAS

It is evident that there is a principle of connection between the different thoughts or ideas of the mind, and that, in their appearance to the memory or imagination, they introduce each other with a certain degree of method and regularity. In our more serious thinking or discourse this is so observable that any particular thought, which breaks in upon the regular tract or claim of ideas, is immediately remarked and rejected. And even in our wildest and most wandering reveries, nay in our very dreams, we shall find, if we reflect, that the imagination ran not altogether at adventures, but that there was still a connection upheld among the different ideas, which succeeded each other. Were loosest and freest conversation to be transcribed, there would immediately be observed something which connected it in all its transitions. Or where this is wanting, the person who broke the thread of discourse might still inform you, that there had secretly revolved in his mind a sucession of thought, which had gradually led him from the subject of conversation. Among different languages, even where we cannot suspect the least connection or communication, it is found, that the words, expressive of ideas, the most compounded, do yet nearly correspond to each other: a certain proof that the simple ideas, comprehended in the compound ones, were bound together by some universal principle, which had an equal influence on all mankind.

Though it be too obvious to escape observation, that different ideas are connected together; I do not find that any philosopher has attempted to enumerate or class all the principles of association; a subject, however, that seems worthy of curiosity. To me, there appear to be only three principles of connection among ideas, namely, *resemblance, contiguity* in time or place, and *cause* or *effect*.

That these principles serve to connect ideas will not, I believe, be much doubted. A picture naturally leads our thoughts to the original: the mention of one apartment in a building

naturally introduces an inquiry or discourse concerning the others; and if we think of a wound, we can scarcely forbear reflecting on the pain which follows it. But that this enumeration is complete, and that there are no other principles of association except these, may be difficult to prove to the satisfaction of the reader, or even to a man's own satisfaction. All we can do, in such cases, is to run over several instances, and examine carefully the principle which binds the different thoughts to each other, never stopping till we render the principle as general as possible. The more instances we examine, and the more care we employ, the more assurance shall we acquire, that the enumeration, which we form from the whole, is complete and entire.

SECTION IV

SCEPTICAL DOUBTS CONCERNING THE OPERATIONS OF THE UNDERSTANDING

Part I

All the objects of human reason or inquiry may naturally be divided into two kinds, to wit, *relations of ideas,* and *matters of fact.* Of the first kind are the sciences of geometry, algebra, and arithmetic; and in short, every affirmation which is either intuitively or demonstratively certain. *That the square of the hypothenuse is equal to the squares of the two sides,* is a proposition which expressed a relation between these figures. *That three times five is equal to the half of thirty*, expresses a relation between these numbers. Propositions of this kind are discoverable by the mere operation of thought, without dependence on what is anywhere existent in the universe. Though there never was a circle or triangle in nature, the truths demonstrated by Euclid would for ever retain their certainty and evidence.

Matters of fact, which are the second objects of human reason, are not ascertained in the same manner; nor is our evidence of their truth, however great, of a like nature with the foregoing. The contrary of every matter of fact is still possible; because it can never imply a contradiction, and is conceived by the mind with the same facility and distinctness, as if ever so comfortable to reality. *That the sun will not rise tomorrow* is no less intelligible a proposition, and implies no more contradiction than the affirmation, *that it will rise.* We should in vain, therefore, attempt to demonstrate its falsehood. Were it demonstratively false, it would imply a contradiction, and could never be distinctly conceived by the mind.

It may, therefore, be a subject worthy of curiosity, to inquire what is the nature of that evidence which assures us of any real existence and matter of fact, beyond the present testimony of our senses, or the records of our memory. This part of philosophy, it is observable, has been little cultivated, either by the ancients or moderns; and therefore our doubts and errors, in the prosecution of so important an inquiry, may be the more excusable; while we march through such difficult paths without any guide or direction. They may even prove useful, by exciting curiosity, and destroying that implicit faith and security, which is the bane of all reasoning and free inquiry. The discovery of defects in the common philosophy, if any such there be, will not, I presume, be a discouragement, but rather an incitment, as is usual, to attempt something more full and satisfactory than has yet been proposed to the public.

All reasonings concerning matter of fact seem to be founded on the relation of *cause* and *effect.* By means of that relation alone we can go beyond the evidence of our memory and senses. If you were to ask a man, why he believes any matter of fact, which is absent; for instance, that his friend is in the country, or in France; he would give you a reason; and this reason would be some other fact; as a letter received from him, or the knowledge of his former resolutions and promises. A man finding a watch or any other machine in a desert island, would conclude that there had once been men in that island. All our reasonings concerning fact are of the same nature. And here it is constantly supposed that there is a connection between the present fact and that which is inferred from it. Were there nothing to bind them together, the inference would be entirely precarious. The hearing of an articulate voice and rational discourse in the dark assures us of the presence of some person: Why? because these are the effects of the human make and fabric, and closely connected with it. If we anatomize all the other reasonings of this nature, we shall find that they are

founded on the relation of cause and effect, and that this relation is either near or remote, direct or collateral. Heat and light are collateral effects of fire, and the one effect may justly be inferred from the other.

If we would satisfy ourselves, therefore, concerning the nature of that evidence, which assures us of matters of fact, we must inquire how we arrive at the knowledge of cause and effect.

I shall venture to affirm, as a general proposition, which admits of no exception, that the knowledge of this relation is not, in any instance, attained by reasonings a priori; but arises entirely from experience, when we find that any particular objects are constantly conjoined with each other. Let an object be presented to a man of ever so strong natural reason and abilities; if that object be entirely new to him, he will not be able, by the most accurate examination of its sensible qualities, to discover any of its causes or effects. Adam, though his rational faculties be supposed, at the very first, entirely pefect, could not have inferred from the fluidity and transparency of water that it would suffocate him, or from the light and warmth of fire that it would consume him. No object ever discovers, by the qualities which appear to the senses, either the causes which produced it, or the effects which will arise from it; nor can our reason, unassisted by experience, ever draw any inference concerning real existence and matter of fact.

This proposition, *that causes and effects are discoverable, not by reason but by experience,* will readily be admitted with regard to such objects, as we remember to have once been altogether unknown to us; since we must be conscious of the utter inability, which we then lay under, of foretelling what would arise from them. Present two smooth pieces of marble to a man who has no tincture of natural philosophy; he will never discover that they will adhere together in such a manner as to require great force to separate them in a direct line, while they make so small a resistance to a lateral pressure. Such events, as bear little analogy to the common course of nature, are also readily confessed to be known only by experience; nor does any man imagine that the explosion of gunpowder, or the attraction of a loadstone, could ever be discovered by arguments a priori. In like manner, when an effect is supposed to depend upon an intricate machinery or secret structure of parts, we make no difficulty in attributing all our knowledge of it to experience. Who will assert that he can give the ultimate reason, why milk or bread is proper nourishment for a man, not for a lion or a tiger?

But the same truth may not appear, at first sight, to have the same evidence with regard to events, which have become familiar to us from our first appearance in the world, which bear a close analogy to the whole course of nature, and which are supposed to depend on the simple qualities of objects, without any secret structure of parts. We are apt to imagine that we could discover these effects by the mere operation of our reason, without experience. We fancy, that were we brought on a sudden into this world, we could at first have inferred that one billiard ball would communicate motion to another upon impulse; and that we needed not to have waited for the event, in order to pronounce with certainty concerning it. Such is the influence of custom, that, where it is strongest, it not only covers our natural ignorance, but even conceals itself, and seems not to take place, merely because it is found in the highest degree.

But to convince us that all the laws of nature, and all the operations of bodies without exception, are known only by experience, the following reflections may, perhaps, suffice. Were any object presented to us, and were we required to pronounce concerning the effect, which will result from it, without consulting past observation; after what manner, I beseech you, must the mind proceed in this operation? It must invent or imagine some event, which it ascribes to the object as its effect; and it is plain that this invention must be entirely arbitrary. The mind can never possibly find the effect in the supposed cause, by the most accurate scrutiny and examination. For the effect is totally different from the cause, and consequently can never be discovered in it. Motion in the second billiard ball is a quite distinct event from motion in the first: nor is there anything in the one to suggest the smallest hint of the other. A stone or piece of metal raised into the air, and left without any support, immediately falls: but to consider the matter *a priori*, is there anything we discover in this situation which can beget the idea of a downward, rather than an upward, or any other motion, in the stone or metal?

And as the first imagination or invention of a particular effect, in all natural operations, is arbitrary, where we consult not experience; so must we also esteem the supposed tie or connection between the cause and effect, which binds them together, and renders it impossible that any other effect could result from the operation of that cause. When I see, for instance, a billiard ball moving in a straight line towards another; even suppose motion in the second ball should by accident be suggested to me, as the result of their contact or impulse; may I not conceive, that a hundred different events might as well follow from that cause? May not both these balls remain at absolute rest? May not the first ball return in a straight line, or leap off from the second in any line or direction? All these suppositions are consistent and conceivable. Why then should we give the preference to one, which is no more consistent or conceivable than the rest? All our reasonings *a priori* will never be able to show us any foundation for this preference.

In a word, then, every effect is a distinct event from its cause. It could not, therefore, be discovered in the cause, and the first invention or conception of it, *a priori*, must be entirely arbitrary. And even after it is suggested, the conjunction of it with the cause must appear equally arbitrary; since there are always many other effects, which, to reason, must seem fully as consistent and natural. In vain, therefore, should we pretend to determine any single event, or infer any cause or effect, without the assistance of observation and experience.

Hence we may discover the reason why no philosopher, who is rational and modest, has ever pretended to assign the ultimate cause of any natural operation, or to show distinctly the action of that power, which produces any single effect in the universe. It is confessed, that the utmost effort of human reason is to reduce the principles, productive of natural phenomena, to a greater simplicity, and to resolve the many particular effects into a few general causes, by means of reasonings from analogy, experience, and observation. But as to the causes of these general causes, we should in vain attempt their discovery; nor shall we ever be able to satisfy ourselves, by any particular explication of them. These ultimate springs and principles are totally shut up from human curiosity and inquiry. Elasticity, gravity, cohesion of parts, communication of motion by impulse; these are probably the ultimate causes and principles which we ever discover in nature; and we may esteem ourselves sufficiently happy, if, by accurate inquiry and reasoning, we can trace up the particular phenomena to, or near to, these general principles. The most perfect philosophy of the natural kind only staves off our ignorance a little longer: as perhaps the most perfect philosophy of the moral or metaphysical kind serves only to discover larger portions of it. Thus the observation of human blindness and weakness is the result of all philosophy, and meets us at every turn, in spite of our endeavors to elude or avoid it.

Nor is geometry, when taken into the assistance of natural philosophy, ever able to remedy this defect, or lead us into the knowledge of ultimate causes, by all that accuracy of reasoning for which it is so justly celebrated. Every part of mixed mathematics proceeds upon the supposition that certain laws are established by nature in her operations; and abstract reasonings are employed, either to assist experience in the discovery of these laws, or to determine their influence in particular instances, where it depends upon any precise degree of distance and quantity. Thus, it is a law of motion, discovered by experience, that the moment or force of any body in motion is in the compound ratio or proportion of its solid contents and its velocity; and consequently, that a small force may remove the greatest obstacle or raise the greatest weight, if, by any contrivance or machinery, we can increase the velocity of that force, so as to make it an overmatch for its antagonist. Geometry assists us in the application of this law, by giving us the just dimensions of all the parts and figures which can enter into any species of machine; but still the discovery of the law itself is owing merely to experience, and all the abstract reasonings in the world could never lead us one step towards the knowledge of it. When we reason *a priori*, and consider merely any object or cause, as it appears to the mind, independent of all observation, it never could suggest to us the notion of any distinct object, such as its effects; much less, show us the inseparable and inviolable connection between them. A man must be very sagacious who could discover by reasoning that crystal is the effect of heat, and ice of cold,

without being previously acquainted with the operation of these qualities.

Part II

But we have not yet attained any tolerable satisfaction with regard to the question first proposed. Each solution still gives rise to a new question as difficult as the foregoing, and leads us on to farther inquiries. When it is asked, *What is the nature of all our reasonings concerning matter of fact?* the proper answer seems to be, that they are founded on the relation of cause and effect. When again it is asked, *What is the foundation of all our reasonings and conclusions concerning that relation?* it may be replied in one word, *experience.* But if we still carry on our sifting humor, and ask, *What is the foundation of all conclusions from experience?* this implies a new question, which may be of more difficult solution and explication. Philosophers, that give themselves airs of superior wisdom and sufficiency, have a hard task when they encounter persons of inquisitive dispositions, who push them from every corner to which they retreat, and who are sure at last to bring them to some dangerous dilemma. The best expedient to prevent this confusion, is to be modest in our pretensions; and even to discover the difficulty ourselves before it is objected to us. By this means, we may make a kind of merit of our very ignorance.

I shall content myself, in this section, with an easy task, and shall pretend only to give a negative answer to the question here proposed. I say then, that, even after we have experience of the operations of cause and effect, our conclusions from that experience are *not* founded on reasoning, or any process of the understanding. This answer we must endeavor both to explain and to defend.

It must certainly be allowed, that nature has kept us at a great distance from all her secrets, and has afforded us only the knowledge of a few superficial qualities of objects; while she conceals from us those powers and principles on which the influence of those objects entirely depends. Our senses inform us of the color, weight, and consistence of bread; but neither sense nor reason can ever inform us of those qualities which fit it for the nourishment and support of a human body. Sight or feeling conveys an idea of the actual motion of bodies; but as to that wonderful force or power, which would carry on a moving body for ever in a continued change of place, and which bodies never lose but by communicating it to others; of this we cannot form the most distant conception. But notwithstanding this ignorance of natural powers and principles, we always presume, when we see like sensible qualities, that they have like secret powers, and expect that effects, similar to those which we have experienced, will follow from them. If a body of like color and consistence with that bread, which we have formerly eat, be presented to us, we make no scruple of repeating the experiment, and foresee, with certainty, like nourishment and support. Now this is a process of the mind or thought, of which I would willingly know the foundation. It is allowed on all hands that there is no known connection between the sensible qualities and the secret powers; and consequently, that the mind is not led to form such a conclusion concerning their constant and regular conjunction, by anything which it knows of their nature. As to past *experience,* it can be allowed to give *direct* and *certain* information of those precise objects only, and that precise period of time, which fell under its cognizance: but why this experience should be extended to future times, and to other objects, which, for aught we know, may be only in appearance similar; this is the main question on which I would insist. The bread, which I formerly eat, nourished me; that is, a body of such sensible qualities was, at that time, endued with such secret powers: but does it follow, and that like sensible qualities must always be attended with like secret powers? The consequence seems no wise necessary. At least, it must be acknowledged that there is here a consequence drawn by the mind; that there is a certain step taken; a process of thought, and an inference, which wants to be explained. These two propositions are far from being the same, *I have found that such an object has always been attended with such an effect,* and *I foresee, that other objects, which are, in appearance, similar, will be attended with similar effects.* I shall allow, if you please, that the one proposition may justly be inferred from the other; I know, in fact, that is always inferred. But if you insist that the inference is made by a chain of reasoning, I desire you to produce that reasoning. The connection between these propositions is not intuitive. There is required a medium, which may enable the mind to draw such an inference, if indeed it be drawn by reasoning and argument. What that medium is, I must confess, passes my comprehension; and it is incumbent on those to produce it, who assert that it really exists, and is the origin of all our conclusions concerning matter of fact.

This negative argument must certainly, in process of time, become altogether convincing, if many penetrating and able philosophers shall turn their inquiries this way and no one be ever able to discover any connecting proposition or intermediate step, which supports the understanding in this conclusion. But as the question is yet new, every reader may not trust so far to his own penetration, as to conclude, because an argument escapes his inquiry, that therefore it does not really exist. For this reason it may be requisite to venture upon a more difficult task; and enumerating all the branches of human knowledge, endeavor to show that none of them can afford such an argument.

All reasonings may be divided into two kinds, namely demonstrative reasoning, or that concerning relations of ideas, and moral reasoning, or that concerning matter of fact and existence. That there are no demonstrative arguments in the case seems evident; since it implies no contradiction that the course of nature may change, and that an object, seemingly like those which we have experienced, may be attended with different or contrary effects. May I not clearly and distinctly conceive that a body, falling from the clouds, and which, in all other respects, resembles snow, has yet the taste of salt or feeling of fire? Is there any more intelligible proposition than to affirm, that all the trees will flourish in December and January, and decay in May and June? Now whatever is intelligible, and can be distinctly conceived, implies no contradiction, and can never be proved false by any demonstrative argument or abstract reasoning *a priori.*

If we be, therefore, engaged by arguments to put trust in past experience, and make it the standard of our future judgment, these arguments must be probable only, so such as regard matter of fact and real existence, according to the division above mentioned. But that there is no argument of this kind, must appear, if our explication of that species of reasoning be admitted as solid and satisfactory. We have said that all arguments concerning existence are founded on the relation of cause and effect; that our knowledge of that relation is derived entirely from experience; and that all our experimental conclusions proceed upon the supposition by probable arguments, or arguments regarding existence, must be evidently going in a circle, and taking that for granted, which is the very point in question.

In reality, all arguments from experience are founded on the similiarity which we discover among natural objects, and by which we are induced to expect effects similar to those which we have found to follow from such objects. And though none but a fool or madman will ever pretend to dispute the authority of experience, or to reject that great guide of human life, it may surely be allowed a philosopher to have so much curiosity at least as to examine the principle of human nature, which gives this mighty authority to experience, and makes us draw advantage from that similarity which nature has placed among different objects. From causes which appear *similar* we expect similar effects. This is the sum of all our experimental conclusions. Now it seems evident that, if this conclusion were formed by reason, it would be as perfect at first, and upon one instance, as after ever so long a course of experience. But the case is far otherwise. Nothing so like as eggs; yet no one, on account of this appearing similarity, expects the same taste and relish in all of them. It is only after a long course of uniform experiments in any kind, that we attain a firm reliance and security with regard to a particular event. Now where is that process of reasoning which, from one instance, draws a conclusion, so different from that which it infers from a hundred instances that are nowise different from that single one? This question I propose as much for the sake of information, as with an intention of raising difficulties. I cannot find, I cannot imagine any such reasoning. But I keep my mind still open to instruction, if anyone will vouchsafe to bestow it on me.

Should it be said that, from a number of uniform experiments, we *infer* a connection between the sensible qualities and the secret powers; this, I must confess, seems the same difficulty, couched in different terms. The question still recurs, on what process of argument this *inference* is founded? Where is the

medium, the interposing ideas, which join propositions so very wide of each other? It is confessed that the color, consistence, and other sensible qualities of bread appear not, of themselves, to have any connection with the secret powers of nourishment and support. For otherwise we could infer these secret powers from the first appearance of these sensible qualities, without the aid of experience; contrary to the sentiment of all philosophers, and contrary to plain matter of fact. Here, then, is our natural state of ignorance with regard to the powers and influence of all objects. How is this remedied by experience? It only shows us a number of uniform effects, resulting from certain objects, and teaches us that those particular objects, at that particular time, were endowed with such powers and forces. When a new object, endowed with similar sensible qualities, is produced, we expect similar powers and forces, and look for a like effect. From a body of like color and consistence with bread we expect like nourishment and support. But this surely is a step or progress of the mind, which wants to be explained. When a man says, *I have found, in all past instances, such sensible qualities conjoined with such secret powers*: And when he says, *Similar sensible qualities will always be conjoined with similar secret powers*, he is not guilty of a tautology, nor are these propositions in any respect the same. You say that the one proposition is an inference from the other. But you must confess that the inference is not intuitive; neither is it demonstrative: Of what nature is it, then? To say it is experimental, is begging the question. For all inferences from experience suppose, as their foundation, that the future will resemble the past, and that similar powers will be conjoined with similar sensible qualities. If there be any suspicion that the course of nature may change, and that the past may be no rule for the future, all experience becomes useless, and can give rise to no inference or conclusion. It is impossible, therefore, that any arguments from experience can prove this resemblance of the past to the future; since all these arguments are founded on the supposition of that resemblance. Let the course of things be allowed hitherto ever so regular; that without some new argument or inference, proves not that, for the future, it will continue so. In vain do you pretend to have learned the nature of bodies from your past experience.

Their secret nature, and consequently all their effects and influence, may change, without any change in their sensible qualities. This happens sometimes, and with regard to some objects: Why may it not happen always, and with regard to all objects? What logic, what process of argument secures you against this supposition? My practice, you say, refutes my doubts. But you mistake the purport of my question. As an agent, I am quite satisfied in the point; but as a philosopher, who has some share of curiosity, I will not say scepticism, I want to learn the foundation of this inference. No reading, no inquiry has yet been able to remove my difficulty, or give me satisfaction in a matter of such importance. Can I do better than propose the difficulty to the public, even though, perhaps, I have small hopes of obtaining a solution? We shall, at least, by this means, be sensible of our ignorance, if we do not augment our knowledge.

I must confess that a man is guilty of unpardonable arrogance who concludes, because an argument has escaped his own investigation, that therefore it does not really exist. I must also confess that, though all the learned, for several ages, should have employed themselves in fruitless search upon any subject, it may still, perhaps, be rash to conclude positively that the subject must, therefore, pass all human comprehension. Even though we examine all the sources of our knowledge, and conclude them unfit for such a subject, there may still remain a suspicion, that the enumeration is not complete, or the examination not accurate. But with regard to the present subject, there are some considerations which seem to remove all this accusation of arrogance or suspicion of mistake.

It is certain that the most ignorant and stupid peasants—nay infants, nay even brute beasts—improve by experience, and learn the qualities of natural objects, by observing the effects which result from them. When a child has felt the sensation of pain from touching the flame of a candle, he will be careful not to put his hand near any candle; but will expect a similar effect from a cause which is similar in its sensible qualities and appearance. If you assert, therefore, that the understanding of the child is led into this conclusion by any process of argument or ratiocination, I may justly require you to produce that argument; nor have you any

pretense to refuse so equitable a demand. You cannot say that the argument is abstruse, and may possibly escape your inquiry; since you confess that it is obvious to the capacity of a mere infant. If you hesitate, therefore, a moment, or if, after reflection, you produce any intricate or profound argument, you, in a manner, give up the question, and confess that it is not reasoning which engages us to suppose the past resembling the future, and to expect similar effects from causes which are, to appearance, similar. This is the proposition which I intended to enforce in the present section. If I be right, I pretend not to have made any mighty discovery. And if I be wrong, I must acknowledge myself to be indeed a very backward scholar; since I cannot now discover an argument which, it seems, was perfectly familiar to me long before I was out of my cradle.

SECTION V

SCEPTICAL SOLUTION OF THESE DOUBTS

Part I

The passion for philosophy, like that for religion, seems liable to this inconvenience, that, thought it aims at the correction of our manners, and extirpation of our vices, it may only serve, by imprudent management, to foster a predominant inclination, and push the mind, with more determined resolution, towards that side which already *draws* too much, by the bias and propensity of the natural temper. It is certain that, while we aspire to the magnanimous firmness of the philosophic sage, and endeavor to confine our pleasures altogether within our own minds, we may, at last, render our philosophy like that of Epictetus, and other *stoics*, only a more refined system of selfishness, and reason ourselves out of all virtue as well as social enjoyment. While we study with attention the vanity of human life, and turn all our thoughts towards the empty and transitory nature of riches and honors, we are, perhaps, all the while flattering our natural indolence, which, hating the bustle of the world, and drudgery of business, seeks a pretense of reason to give itself a full and uncontrolled indulgence. There is, however, one species of philosophy which seems little liable to this inconvenience, and that because it strikes in with no disorderly passion of the human mind, nor can mingle itself with any natural affection or propensity; and that is the *academic* or *sceptical* philosophy. The academics always talk of doubt and suspense of judgment, of danger in hasty determinations, of confining to very narrow bounds the inquiries of the understanding, and of renouncing all speculations which lie not within the limits of common life and practice. Nothing, therefore, can be more contrary than such a philosophy to the supine indolence of the mind, its rash arrogance, its lofty pretensions, and its superstitious credulity. Every passion is mortified by it, except the love of truth; and that passion never is, nor can be, carried to too high a degree. It is surprising, therefore, that this philosophy, which, in almost every instance, must be harmless and innocent, should be the subject of so much groundless reproach and obloquy. But, perhaps, the very circumstance which renders it so innocent is what chiefly exposes it to the public hatred and resentment. By flattering no irregular passion, it gains few partisans: By opposing so many vices and follies, it raises to itself abundance of enemies, who stigmatize it as libertine, profane, and irreligious.

Nor need we fear that this philosophy, while it endeavors to limit our inquiries to common life, should ever undermine the reasonings of common life, and carry its doubts so far as to destroy all action, as well as speculation. Nature will always maintain her rights, and prevail in the end over any abstract reasoning whatsoever. Though we should conclude, for instance, as in the foregoing section, that, in all reasonings from experience, there is a step taken by the mind which is not supported by any argument or process of the understanding; there is no danger that these reasonings, on which almost all knowledge depends, will ever be affected by such a discovery. If the mind be not engaged by argument to make this step, it must be induced by some other principle of equal weight and authority; and that principle will preserve its influence as long as human nature remains the same. What that principle is may well be worth the pains of inquiry.

Suppose a person, though endowed with the strongest faculties of reason and reflection, to be brought on a sudden into this world; he would, indeed, immediately observe a continual succession of objects, and one event following another; but he would not be able to discover anything farther. He would not, at first, by any reasoning, be able to reach the idea of cause and effect; since the particular powers, by which all natural operations are performed, never appear to the senses; nor is it reasonable to conclude, merely because one event, in one instance, precedes another, that therefore the one is the cause, the other the effect. Their conjunction may be arbitrary and casual. There may be no reason to infer the existence of one from the appearance of the other. And in a word, such a person, without more experience, could never employ his conjecture or reasoning concerning any matter of fact, or be assured of anything beyond what was immediately present to his memory and senses.

Suppose, again, that he has acquired more experience, and has lived so long in the world as to have observed familiar objects or events to be constantly conjoined together; what is the consequence of this experience? He immediately infers the existence of one object from the appearance of the other. Yet he has not, by all his experience, acquired any idea or knowledge of the secret power by which the one object produces the other; nor is it, by any process of reasoning, he is engaged to draw this inference. But still he finds himself determined to draw it: And though he should be convinced that his understanding has no part in the operation, he would nevertheless continue in the same course of thinking. There is some other principle which determines him to form such a conclusion.

This principle is *custom* or *habit*. For wherever the repetition of any particular act or operation produces a propensity to renew the same act or operation, without being impelled by any reasoning or process of the understanding, we always say, that this propensity is the effect of *custom*. By employing the word, we pretend not to have given the ultimate reason of such a propensity. We only point out a principle of human nature, which is universally acknowledged, and which is well known by its effects. Perhaps we can push our inquiries no farther, or pretend to give the cause of this cause; but must rest contented with it as the ultimate principle, which we can assign, of all our conclusions from experience. It is sufficient satisfaction, that we can go so far, without repining at the narrowness of our faculties because they will carry us no farther. And it is certain we here advance a very intelligible proposition at least, if not a true one, when we assert that, after the constant conjunction of two objects—heat and flame, for instance, weight and solidity—we are determined by custom alone to expect the one from the appearance of the other. This hypothesis seems even the only one which explains the difficulty, why we draw, from a thousand instances, an inference which we are not able to draw from one instance, that is, in no respect, different from them. Reason is incapable of any such variation. The conclusions which it draws from considering one circle are the same which it would form upon surveying all the circles in the universe. But no man, having seen only one body move after being impelled by another, could infer that every other body will move after a like impulse. All inferences from experience, therefore, are effects of custom, not of reasoning.

Custom, then, is the great guide of human life. It is that principle alone which renders our experience useful to us, and makes us expect, for the future, a similar train of events with those which have appeared in the past. Without the influence of custom, we should be entirely ignorant of every matter of fact beyond what is immediately present to the memory and senses. We should never know how to adjust means to ends, or to employ our natural powers in the production of any effect. There would be an end at once of all action, as well as of the chief part of speculation.

But here it may be proper to remark, that though our conclusions from experience carry us beyond our memory and senses, and assure us of matters of fact which happened in the most distant places and most remote ages, yet some fact must always be present to the senses or memory, from which we may first proceed in drawing these conclusions. A man, who should find in a desert country the remains of pompous buildings, would conclude that the country had, in ancient times, been cultivated by civilized inhabitants; but did nothing of this nature occur to him, he could never form such an inference. We learn the events of former ages from history; but then we must peruse the volumes in which this instruction is contained, and thence carry up our inferences from one testimony to another, till we arrive at the eye-witnesses and spectators of these distant events. In a word, if we proceed not upon some fact, present to the memory or senses, our reasonings would be merely hypothetical; and however the particular links might be connected with each other, the whole chain of inferences would have nothing to support it, nor could we ever, by its means, arrive at the knowledge of any real existence. If I ask why you believe any particular matter of fact, which you relate, you must tell me some reason; and this reason will be some other fact, connected with it. But as you cannot proceed after this manner, *in infinitum*, you must at last terminate in some fact, which is present to your memory or senses; or must allow that your belief is entirely without foundation. . . .

Here, then, is a kind of pre-established harmony between the course of nature and the succession of our ideas; and though the powers and forces, by which the former is governed, be wholly unknown to us; yet our thoughts and conceptions have still, we find, gone on in the same train with the other works of nature. Custom is that principle, by which this correspondence has been effected; so necessary to the subsistence of our species, and the regulation of our conduct, in every circumstance and occurrence of human life. Had not the presence of an object, instantly excited the idea of those objects, commonly conjoined with it, all our knowledge must have been limited to the narrow sphere of our memory and senses; and we should never have been able to adjust means to ends, or employ our natural powers, either to the producing of good, or avoiding of evil. Those, who delight in the discovery and contemplation of *final causes*, have here ample subject to employ their wonder and admiration.

I shall add, for a further confirmation of the foregoing theory, that, as this operation of the mind, by which we infer like effects from like causes, and *vice versa*, is so essential to the subsistence of all human creatures, it is not probable, that it could be trusted to the fallacious deductions of our reason, which is slow in its operations; appears not, in any degree, during the first years of infancy; and at best is, in every age and period of human life, extremely liable to error and mistake. It is more conformable to the ordinary wisdom of nature to secure so necessary an act of the mind, by some instinct or mechanical tendency, which may be infallible in its operations, may discover itself at the first appearance of life and thought, and may be independent of all the labored deductions of the understanding. As nature has taught us the use of our limbs, without giving us the knowledge of the muscles and nerves, by which they are actuated; so has she implanted in us an instinct, which carries forward the thought among external objects; though we are ignorant of those powers and forces, on which this regular course and succession of objects totally depends.

SECTION VI

OF PROBABILITY

Mr. Locke divides all arguments into demonstrative and probable. In this view, we must say, that it is only probable all men must die, or that the sun will rise tomorrow. But to conform our language more to common use, we ought to divide arguments into *demonstrations, proofs,* and *probabilities*. By proofs meaning such arguments from experience as leave no room for doubt or opposition.

. . . There is certainly a probability, which arises from a superiority of chances on any side; and according as this superiority increases, and surpasses the opposite chances, the probability receives a proportionable increase, and begets still a higher degree of belief or assent to that side, in which we discover the superiority. If a die were marked with one figure or number of spots on four sides, and with another figure or number of spots on the two remaining sides, it would be more probable, that the former would turn up than the latter; though, if it had a thousand sides marked in the same manner, and only one side different, the probability would be much higher, and our belief or expectation of the event more steady and secure. This process of the thought or reasoning may seem trivial and obvious; but to those who consider it more narrowly, it may, perhaps, afford matter for curious speculation.

It seems evident, that, when the mind looks forward to discover the event, which may result from the throw of such a die, it considers the turning up of each particular side as alike probable; and this is the very nature of chance, to render all the particular events, comprehended in it, entirely equal. But finding a greater num-

ber of sides concur in the one event than in the other, the mind is carried more frequently to that event, and meets it oftener, in revolving the various possibilities or chances, on which the ultimate result depends. This concurrence of several views in one particular event begets immediately, by an inexplicable contrivance of nature, the sentiment of belief, and gives that event the advantage over its antagonist, which is supported by a smaller number of views, and recurs less frequently to the mind. If we allow, that belief is nothing but a firmer and stronger conception of an object than what attends the mere fictions of the imagination, this operation may, perhaps, in some measure, be accounted for. The concurrence of these several views or glimpses imprints the idea more strongly on the imagination; gives it superior force and vigor; renders its influence on the passions and affections more sensible; and in a word, begets that reliance or security, which constitutes the nature of belief and opinion.

The case is the same with the probability of causes, as with that of chance. There are some causes, which are entirely uniform and constant in producing a particular effect; and no instance has ever yet been found of any failure or irregularity in their operation. Fire has always burned, and water suffocated every human creature: the production of motion by impulse and gravity is an universal law, which has hitherto admitted of no exception. But there are other causes which have been found more irregular and uncertain; nor has rhubarb always proved a purge, or opium a soporific to everyone, who has taken these medicines. It is true, when any cause fails of producing its usual effect, philosophers ascribe not this to any irregularity in nature; but suppose, that some secret causes, in the particular structure of parts, have prevented the operation. Our reasonings, however, and conclusions concerning the event are the same as if this principle had no place. Being determined by custom to transfer the past to the future, in all our inferences; where the past has been entirely regular and uniform, we expect the event with the greatest assurance, and leave no room for any contrary supposition. But where different effects have been found to follow from causes, which are to *appearance* exactly similar, all these various effects must occur to the mind in transferring the past to the future, and enter into our consideration, when we determine the probability of the event. Though we give the preference to that which has been found most usual, and believe that this effect will exist, we must not overlook the other effects, but must assign to each of them a particular weight and authority, in proportion as we have found it to be more or less frequent. It is more probable, in almost every country of Europe, that there will be frost sometime in January, than that the weather will continue open throughout the whole month; though this possibility varies according to the different climates, and approaches to a certainty in the more northern kingdoms. Here then it seems evident, that, when we transfer the past to the future, in order to determine the effect, which will result from any cause, we tranfer all the different events, in the same proportion as they have appeared in the past, and conceive one to have existed a hundred times, for instance, another ten times, and another once. As a great number of views do here concur in one event, they fortify and confirm it to the imagination, beget that sentiment which we call *belief*, and give its object the preference above the contrary event, which is not supported by an equal number of experiments, and recurs not so frequently to the thought in transferring the past to the future. Let anyone try to account for this operation of the mind upon any of the received systems of philosophy, and he will be sensible of the difficulty. For my part, I shall think it sufficient, if the present hints excite the curiosity of philosophers, and make them sensible how defective all common theories are in treating of such curious and such sublime subjects.

SECTION VII

OF THE IDEA OF NECESSARY CONNECTION

Part I

The great advantage of the mathematical sciences above the moral consists in this, that the ideas of the former, being sensible, are always clear and determinate, the smallest distinction between them is immediately perceptible, and the same terms are still expressive of the same ideas, without ambiguity or variation.

An oval is never mistaken for a circle, nor an hyperbola for an ellipsis. The isosceles and scalenum are distinguished by boundaries more exact than vice and virtue, right and wrong. If any term be defined in geometry, the mind readily, of itself, substitutes, on all occasions, the definition for the term defined: or even when no definition is employed, the object itself may be presented to the senses, and by that means be steadily and clearly apprehended. But the finer sentiments of the mind, the operations of the understanding, the various agitations of the passions, though really in themselves distinct, easily escape us, when surveyed by reflection; nor is it in our power to recall the original object, as often as we have occasion to contemplate it. Ambiguity, by this means, is gradually introduced into our reasonings: similar objects are readily taken to be the same: and the conclusion becomes at last very wide of the premises.

One may safely, however, affirm, that, if we consider these sciences in a proper light, their advantages and disadvantages nearly compensate each other, and reduce both of them to a state of equality. If the mind, with greater facility, retains the ideas of geometry clear and determinate, it must carry on a much longer and more intricate chain of reasoning, and compare ideas much wider of each other, in order to reach the abstruser truths of that science. And if moral ideas are apt, without extreme care, to fall into obscurity and confusion, the inferences are always much shorter in these disquisitions, and the intermediate steps, which lead to the conclusion, much fewer than in the sciences which treat of quantity and number. In reality, there is scarcely a proposition in Euclid so simple, as not to consist of more parts, than are to be found in any moral reasoning which runs not into chimera and conceit. Where we trace the principles of the human mind through a few steps, we may be very well satisfied with our progress; considering how soon nature throws a bar to all our inquiries concerning causes, and reduces us to an acknowledgement of our ignorance. The chief obstacle, therefore, to our improvement in the moral or metaphysical sciences is the obscurity of the ideas, and ambiguity of the terms. The principal difficulty in the mathematics is the length of inferences and compass of thought, requisite to the forming of any conclusion. And, perhaps, our progress in natural philosophy is chiefly retarded by the want of proper experiments and phenomena, which are often discovered by chance, and cannot always be found, when requisite, even by the most diligent and prudent inquiry. As moral philosophy seems hitherto to have received less improvement than either geometry or physics, we may conclude, that, if there be any difference in this respect among these sciences, the difficulties, which obstruct the progress of the former, require superior care and capacity to be surmounted.

There are no ideas, which occur in metaphysics more obscure and uncertain, than those of *power, force, energy* or *necessary connection,* of which it is every moment necessary for us to treat in all our disquisitions. We shall, therefore; endeavor, in this section, to fix, if possible, the precise meaning of these terms, and thereby remove some part of that obscurity, which is so much complained of in this species of philosophy.

It seems a proposition, which will not admit of much dispute, that all our ideas are nothing but copies of our impressions, or, in other words, that it is impossible for us to *think* of anything, which we have not antecedently *felt,* either by external or internal senses. I have endeavored to explain and prove this proposition, and have expressed my hopes, that, by a proper application of it, men may reach a greater clearness and precision in philosophical reasonings, than what they have hitherto been able to attain. Complex ideas may, perhaps, be well known by definition, which is nothing but an enumeration of those parts or simple ideas, that compose them. But when we have pushed up definitions to the most simple ideas, and find still some ambiguity and obscurity; what resource are we then possessed of? By what invention can we throw light upon these ideas, and render them altogether precise and determinate to our intellectual view! Produce the impressions or original sentiments, from which the ideas are copied. These impressions are all strong and sensible. They admit not of ambiguity. They are not only placed in a full light themselves, but may throw light on their correspondent ideas, which lie in obscurity. And by this means, we may, perhaps, attain a new microscope or species of optics, by which, in the moral sciences, the most minute, and most simple ideas may be so enlarged as to fall readily under our apprehension, and be equally known with the grossest and most sensible ideas, that can be the object of our inquiry.

To be fully acquainted, therefore, with the idea of power or necessary connection, let us examine its impression; and in order to find the impression with greater certainty, let us search for it in all the sources, from which it may possibly be derived.

When we look about us towards external objects, and consider the operation of causes, we are never able, in a single instance, to discover any power or necessary connection; any quality, which binds the effect to the cause, and renders the one an infallible consequence of the other. We only find, that the one does actually, in fact, follow the other. The impulse of one billiard ball is attended with motion in the second. This is the whole that appears to the *outward* senses. The mind feels no sentiment or *inward* impression from this succession of objects: consequently there is not, in any single, particular instance of cause and effect, anything which can suggest the idea of power or necessary connection.

From the first appearance of an object, we never can conjecture what effect will result from it. But were the power or energy of any cause discoverable by the mind, we could foresee the effect, even without experience; and might, at first, pronounce with certainty concerning it, by mere dint of thought and reasoning.

In reality, there is no part of matter, that does ever, by its sensible qualities, discover any power or energy, or give us ground to imagine, that it could produce anything, or be followed by any other object, which we could denominate its effect. Solidity, extension, motion; these qualities are all complete in themselves, and never point out any other event which may result from them. The scenes of the universe are continually shifting, and one object follows another in an uninterrupted succession; but the power of force, which actuates the whole machine, is entirely concealed from us, and never discovers itself in any of the sensible qualities of body. We know, that, in fact, heat is a constant attendant of flame; but what is the connection between them, we have no room so much as to conjecture or imagine. It is impossible, therefore, that the idea of power can be derived from the contemplation of bodies, in single instances of their operation; because no bodies ever discover any power, which can be the original of this idea. Mr. Locke, in his chapter on power says, that, finding from experience, that there are several new productions in matters, and concluding that there must somewhere be a power capable of producing them, we arrive at last by this reasoning at the idea of power. But no reasoning can ever give us a new original, simple idea; as this philosopher himself confesses. This, therefore, can never be the origin of that idea.

Since, therefore, external objects as they appear to the senses, give us no idea of power or necessary connection, by their operation in particular instances, let us see, whether this idea be derived from reflection on the operations of our own minds, and be copied from any internal impression. It may be said, that we are every moment conscious of internal power; while we feel, that, by the simple command of our will, we can move the organs of our body, or direct the faculties of our mind. An act of volition produces motion in our limbs, or raises a new idea in our imagination. This influence of the will we know by consciousness. Hence we acquire the idea of power or energy; and are certain, that we ourselves and all other intelligent beings are possessed of power. This idea, then, is an idea of reflection, since it arises from reflecting on the operations of our own mind, and on the command which is exercised by will, both over the organs of the body and faculties of the soul.

We shall proceed to examine this pretension; and first with regard to the influence of volition over the organs of the body. This influence, we may observe, is a fact, which, like all other natural events, can be known only by experience, and can never be foreseen from any apparent energy or power in the cause, which connects it with the effect, and renders the one an infallible consequence of the other. The motion of our body follows upon the command of our will. Of this we are every moment conscious. But the means, by which this is effected; the energy, by which the will performs so extraordinary an operation; of this we are so far from being immediately conscious, that it must for ever escape our most diligent inquiry. . . .

I cannot perceive any force in the arguments on which this theory is founded. We are ignorant, it is true, of the manner in which bodies operate on each other: their force or energy is entirely incomprehensible: but are we not equally ignorant of the manner or force by which a mind, even the supreme mind, operates either on itself or on body? Whence, I beseech you, do we acquire any idea of it? We have no sentiment or consciousness of this power in ourselves. We have no idea of the Supreme Being but what we learn from reflection on our own faculties. Were our ignorance, therefore, a good reason for rejecting anything, we should be led into that principle of denying all energy in the Supreme Being as much as in the grossest matter. We surely comprehend as little the operations of one as of the other. Is it more difficult to conceive that motion may arise from impulse than that it may arise from volition? All we know is our profound ignorance in both cases.

I need not examine at length the *vis inertiae,* which is so much talked of in the new philosophy, and which is ascribed to matter. We find by experience, that a body at rest or in motion continues forever in its present state, till put from it by some new cause; and that a body impelled takes as much motion from the impelling body as it acquires itself. These are facts. When we call this a *vis inertiae,* we only mark these facts, without pretending to have any idea of the inert power; in the same manner as, when we talk of gravity, we mean certain effects, without comprehending that active power. It was never the meaning of Sir Isaac Newton to rob second causes of all force or energy; though some of his followers have endeavored to establish that theory upon his authority. On the contrary, that great philosopher had recourse to an etherial active fluid to explain his universal attraction; though he was so cautious and modest as to allow, that it was a mere hypothesis, not to be insisted on, without more experiments. I must confess, that there is something in the fate of opinions a little extraordinary. Descartes insinuated that doctrine of the universal and sole efficiency of the Deity, without insisting on it. Malebranche and other Cartesians made it the foundation of all their philosophy. It had, however, no authority in England. Locke, Clarke, and Cudworth, never so much as take notice of it, but suppose all along, that matter has a real, though subordinate and derived power. By what means has it become so prevalent among our modern metaphysicians?

Part II

But to hasten to a conclusion of this argument, which is already drawn out to too great a length: we have sought in vain for an idea of power or necessary connection in all the sources from which we could suppose it to be derived. It appears that, in single instances of the operation of bodies, we never can, by our utmost scrutiny, discover anything but one event following another, without being able to comprehend any force or power by which the cause operates, or any connection between it and its supposed effect. The same difficulty occurs in contemplating the operations of mind on body—where we observe the motion of the latter to follow upon the volition of the former, but are not able to observe or conceive the tie which binds together the motion and volition, or the energy by which the mind produces this effect. The authority of the will over its own faculties and ideas is not a whit more comprehensible: so that, upon the whole, there appears not, throughout all nature, any one instance of connection which is conceivable by us. All events seem entirely loose and separate. One event follows another; but we never can observe any tie between them. They seem *conjoined,* but never *connected.* And as we can have no idea of anything which never appeared to our outward sense or inward sentiment, the necessary conclusion *seems* to be that we have no idea of connection or power at all, and that these words are absolutely without any meaning, when employed either in philosophical reasonings or common life.

But there still remains one method of avoiding this conclusion, and one source which we have not yet examined. When any natural object or event is presented, it is impossible for us, by any sagacity or penetration, to discover, or even conjecture, without experience, what event will result from it, or to carry our foresight beyond that object which is immediately present to the memory and senses. Even after one instance or experiment where we have observed a particular event to follow upon another, we are not entitled to form a general rule, or foretell what will happen in like cases; it being justly esteemed an unpardonable temerity to judge of the whole course of nature from one single experiment, however accurate or certain. But when one particular species of event has always, in all instances, been conjoined with another, we make no longer any scruple of foretelling one upon the appearance of the other, and of employing that reasoning which can alone assure us of any matter of fact or existence. We then call the one object, *cause;* the other, *effect.* We suppose that there is some connection between them; some power in the one, by which it infallibly produces the other, and operates with the greatest certainty and strongest necessity.

It appears, then, that this idea of a necessary connection among events arises from a number of similar instances which occur of the constant conjunction of these events; nor can that idea ever be suggested by any one of these instances, surveyed in all possible lights and positions. But there is nothing in a number of instances, different from every single instance, which is supposed to be exactly similar; except only, that after a repetition of similar instances, the mind is carried by habit, upon the appearance of one event, to expect its usual attendant, and to believe that it will exist. This connection, therefore, which we *feel* in the mind, this customary transition of the imagination from one object, to its usual attendant, is the sentiment or impression from which we form the idea of power or necessary connection. Nothing farther is in the case. Contemplate the subject on all sides; you will never find any other origin of that idea. This is the sole difference between one instance, from which we can never receive the idea of connection, and a number of similar instances, by which it is suggested. The first time a man saw the communication of motion by impulse, as by the shock of two billiard balls, he could not pronounce that the one event was *connected;* but only that it was *conjoined* with the other. After he has observed several instances of this nature, he then pronounces them to be *connected.* What alteration has happened to give rise to this new idea of *connection?* Nothing but that he now *feels* these events to be *connected* in his imagination, and can readily foretell the existence of one from the appearance of the other. When we say, therefore, that one object is connected with another, we mean only that they have acquired a connection in our thought, and give rise to this inference, by which they become proofs of each other's existence: a conclusion which is somewhat extraordinary, but which seems founded on sufficient evidence. Nor will its evidence be weakened by any general diffidence of the understanding, or sceptical suspicion concerning every conclusion which is new and extraordinary. No conclusions can be more agreeable to scepticism than such as make discoveries concerning the weakness and narrow limits of human reason and capacity.

And what stronger instance can be produced of the surprising ignorance and weakness of the understanding than the present? For surely, if there be any relation among objects which it imports to us to know perfectly, it is that of cause and effect. On this are founded all our reasonings concerning matter of fact or existence. By means of it alone we attain any assurance concerning objects which are removed from the present testimony of our memory and senses. The only immediate utility of all sciences, is to teach us, how to control and regulate future events by their causes. Our thoughts and inquiries are, therefore, every moment, employed about this relation: yet so imperfect are the ideas which we form concerning it, that it is impossible to give any just definition of cause, except what is drawn from something extraneous and foreign to it. Similar objects are always conjoined with similar. Of this we have experience. Suitably to this experience, therefore, we may define a cause to be *an object, followed by another, and where all the objects similar to the first are followed by objects similar to the second.* Or in other words *where, if the first object had not been, the second never had existed.* The appearance of a cause always conveys the mind, by a customary transition, to the idea of the effect. Of this also we have experience. We may, therefore, suitably to this experience, form another definition of cause, and call it, *an object followed by another, and whose appearance always conveys the thought to that other.* But though both these definitions be drawn from circumstances foreign to the cause, we cannot remedy, this inconvenience, or attain any more perfect definition, which may point out those circumstances in the cause, which gives it a connection with its effect. We have no idea of this connection, nor even any distinct notion what it is we desire to know, when we endeavor a conception of it. We say,

for instance, that the vibration of this string is the cause of this particular sound. But what do we mean by that affirmation? We either mean *that this vibration is followed by this sound, and that all similar vibrations have been followed by similar sounds: Or, that this vibration is followed by this sound, and that upon the appearance of one the mind anticipates the senses, and forms immediately an idea of the other.* We may consider the relation of cause and effect in either of these two lights; but beyond these, we have no idea of it.

To recapitulate, therefore, the reasonings of this section: every idea is copied from some preceding impression or sentiment; and where we cannot find any impression, we may be certain that there is no idea. In all single instances of the operation of bodies or minds, there is nothing that produces any impression, nor consequently can suggest any idea of power or necessary connection. But when many uniform instances appear, and the same object is always followed by the same event; we then begin to entertain the notion of cause and connection. We then feel a new sentiment or impression, to wit, a customary connection in the thought or imagination between one object and its usual attendant; and this sentiment is the original of that idea which we seek for. For as this idea arises from a number of similar instances, and not from any single instance, it must arise from that circumstance, in which the number of instances differ from every individual instance. But this customary connection or transition of the imagination is the only circumstance in which they differ. In every other particular they are alike. The first instance which we saw of motion communicated by the shock of two billiard balls (to return to this obvious illustration) is exactly similar to any instance that may, at present, occur to us; except only that we could not, at first, *infer* one event from the other which we are enabled to do at present, after so long a course of uniform experience. I know not whether the reader will readily apprehend this reasoning. I am afraid that, should I multiply words about it, or throw it into a greater variety of lights, it would only become more obscure and intricate. In all abstract reasonings there is one point of view which, if we can happily hit, we shall go farther towards illustrating the subject than by all the eloquence in the world. This point of view we should endeavor to reach, and reserve the flowers of rhetoric for subjects which are more adapted to them.

SECTION VIII

OF LIBERTY AND NECESSITY

Part I

It might reasonably be expected in questions which have been convassed and disputed with great eagerness, since the first origin of science and philosophy, that the meaning of all the terms, at least, should have been agreed upon among the disputants; and our inquiries, in the course of two thousand years, been able to pass from words to the true and real subject of the controversy. For how easy may it seem to give exact definitions of the terms employed in reasoning, and make these definitions, not the mere sound of words, the object of future scrutiny and examination? But if we consider the matter more narrowly, we shall be apt to draw a quite opposite conclusion. From this circumstance alone, that a controversy has been long kept on foot, and remains still undecided, we may presume that there is some ambiguity in the expression, and that the disputants affix different ideas to the terms employed in the controversy. For as the faculties of the mind are supposed to be naturally alike in every individual; otherwise nothing could be more fruitless than to reason or dispute together; it were impossible, if men affix the same ideas to their terms, that they could so long form different opinions of the same subject; especially when they communicate their views, and each party turn themselves on all sides, in search of arguments which may give them the victory over their antagonists. It is true, if men attempt the discussion of questions which lie entirely beyond the reach of human capacity, such as those concerning the origin of worlds, or the economy of the intellectual system or region of spirits, they may long beat the air in their fruitless contests, and never arrive at any determinate conclusion. But if the question regard any subject of common life and experience, nothing, one would think, could preserve the dispute so long undecided but some ambiguous expressions, which keep the antagonists still at a distance, and hinder them from grappling with each other.

This has been the case in the long disputed question concerning liberty and necessity; and to so remarkable a degree that, if I be not much mistaken; we shall find, that all mankind, both learned and ignorant, have always been of the same opinion with regard to this subject, and that a few intelligible definitions would immediately have put an end to the whole controversy. I own that this dispute has been so much canvassed on all hands, and has led philosophers into such a labyrinth of obscure sophistry, that it is no wonder, if a sensible reader indulge his ease so far as to turn a deaf ear to the proposal of such a question, from which he can expect neither instruction nor entertainment. But the state of the argument here proposed may, perhaps, serve to renew his attention; as it has more novelty, promises at least some decision of the controversy, and will not much disturb his ease by any intricate or obscure reasoning.

I hope, therefore, to make it appear that all men have ever agreed in the doctrine both of necessity and of liberty, according to any reasonable sense, which can be put on these terms; and that the whole controversy has hitherto turned merely upon words. We shall begin with examining the doctrine of necessity.

It is universally allowed that matter, in all its operations, is actuated by a necessary force, and that every natural effect is so precisely determined by the energy of its cause that no other effect, in such particular circumstances, could possibly have resulted from it. The degree and direction of every motion is, by the laws of nature, prescribed with such exactness that a living creature may as soon arise from the shock of two bodies as motion in any other degree or direction than what is actually produced by it. Would we, therefore, form a just and precise idea of *necessity*, we must consider whence the idea arises when we apply it to the operation of bodies.

It seems evident that, if all the scenes of nature were continually shifted in such a manner that no two events bore any resemblance to each other, but every object was entirely new, without any similitude to whatever had been seen before, we should never, in that case, have attained the least idea of necessity, or of a connection among these objects. We might say, upon such a supposition, that one object or event has followed another; not that one was produced by the other. The relation of cause and effect must be utterly unknown to mankind. Inference and reasoning concerning the operations of nature would, from that moment, be at an end; and the memory and senses remain the only canals, by which the knowledge of any real existence could possibly have access to the mind. Our ideas, therefore, of necessity and causation arises entirely from the uniformity observable in the operation of nature, where similar objects are constantly conjoined together, and the mind is determined by custom to infer the one from the appearance of the other. These two circumstances form the whole of that necessity, which we ascribe to matter. Beyond the constant *conjunction* of similar objects, and the consequent *inference* from one to the other, we have no notion of any necessity or connection.

If it appear, therefore, that all mankind have ever allowed, without any doubt or hesitation, that these two circumstances take place in the voluntary actions of men, and in the operations of mind; it must follow, that all mankind have ever agreed in the doctrine of necessity, and that they have hitherto disputed, merely for not understanding each other.

As to the first circumstance, the constant and regular conjunction of similar events, we may possibly satisfy ourselves by the following considerations. It is universally acknowledged that there is a great uniformity among the actions of men, in all nations and ages, and that human nature remains still the same, in its principles and operations. The same motives always produce the same actions; the same events follow the same causes. Ambition, avarice, self-love, vanity, friendship, generosity, public spirit: these passions, mixed in various degrees, and distributed through society, have been, from the beginning of the world, and still are, the source of all the actions and enterprises, which have ever been observed among mankind. Would you know the sentiments, inclinations, and course of life of the Greeks and Romans? Study well the temper and actions of the French and English: you cannot be much mistaken in transferring to the former *most* of the observations which you have made with regard to the latter. Mankind are so much the same, in all times and places, that history informs us of nothing new or strange in this particular. Its chief use is only to discover the constant and

universal principles of human nature, by showing men in all varieties of circumstances and situations, and furnishing us with materials from which we may form our observations and become acquainted with the regular springs of human action and behavior. These records of wars, intrigues, factions, and revolutions, are so many collections of experiments, by which the politician or moral philosopher fixes the principles of his science, in the same manner as the physician or natural philosopher becomes acquainted with the nature of plants, minerals, and other external objects, by the experiments which he forms concerning them. Nor are the earth, water, and other elements, examined by Aristotle, and Hippocrates, more like to those which at present lie under our observation than the men described by Polybius and Tacitus are to those who now govern the world.

... We must not, however, expect that this uniformity of human actions should be carried to such a length as that all men, in the same circumstances, will always act precisely in the same manner, without making any allowance for the diversity of characters, prejudices, and opinions. Such a uniformity in every particular, is found in no part of nature. On the contrary, from observing the variety of conduct in different men, we are enabled to form a greater variety of maxims, which still suppose a degree of uniformity and regularity. . . .

Part II

There is no method of reasoning more common, and yet none more blamable, than, in philosophical disputes, to endeavor the refutation of any hypothesis, by a pretense of its dangerous consequences to religion and morality. When any opinion leads to absurdities, it is certainly false; but it is not certain that an opinion is false, because it is of dangerous consequence. Such topics, therefore, ought entirely to be foreborne; as serving nothing to the discovery of truths, but only to make the person of an antagonist odious. This I observe in general, without pretending to draw any advantage from it. I frankly submit to an examination of this kind, and shall venture to affirm that the doctrines, both of necessity and of liberty, as above explained, are not only consistent with morality, but are absolutely essential to its support.

Necessity may be defined two ways, conformably to the two definitions of *cause,* of which it makes an essential part. It consists either in the constant conjunction of like objects, or in the inference of the understanding from one object to another. Now necessity, in both these senses (which, indeed, are at bottom the same), has universally, though tacitly, in the schools, in the pulpit, and in common life, been allowed to belong to the will of man; and no one has ever pretended to deny that we can draw inferences concerning human actions, and that those inferences are founded on the experienced union of like actions, with like motives, inclinations, and circumstances. The only particular in which anyone can differ, is, that either, perhaps, he will refuse to give the name of necessity to this property of human actions: but as long as the meaning is understood, I hope the word can do no harm; or that he will maintain it possible to discover something farther in the operations of matter. But this, it must be acknowledged, can be of no consequence to morality or religion, whatever it may be to natural philosophy or metaphysics. We may here be mistaken in asserting that there is no idea of any other necessity or connection in the actions of body; but surely we ascribe nothing to the actions of the mind, but what everyone does, and must readily allow of. We change no circumstance in the received orthodox system with regard to the will, but only in that with regard to material objects and causes. Nothing, therefore, can be more innocent, at least, than this doctrine.

All laws being founded on rewards and punishments, it is supposed as a fundamental principle, that these motives have a regular and uniform influence on the mind, and both produce the good and prevent the evil actions. We may give to this influence what name we please; but, as it is usually conjoined with the action, it must be esteemed a *cause,* and be looked upon as an instance of that necessity, which we would here establish.

The only proper object of hatred or vengeance is a person or creature, endowed with thought and consciousness; and when any criminal or injurious actions excite that passion, it is only by their relation to the person, or connection with him. Actions are, by their very nature, temporary and perishing; and where they proceed not from some *cause* in the character and disposition of the person who per-

formed them, they can neither redound to his honor, if good; nor infamy, if evil. The actions themselves may be blamable; they may be contrary to all the rules of morality and religion. But the person is not answerable for them; and as they proceeded from nothing in him that is durable and constant, and leave nothing of that nature behind them, it is impossible he can, upon their account, become the object of punishment or vengeance. According to the principle, therefore, which denied necessity, and consequently causes, a man is as pure and untainted, after having committed the most horrid crime, as at the first moment of his birth, nor is his character anywise concerned in his actions, since they are not derived from it, and the wickedness of the one can never be used as a proof of the depravity of the other.

Men are not blamed for such actions as they perform ignorantly and casually, whatever may be the consequences. Why? but because the principles of these actions are only momentary, and terminate in them alone. Men are less blamed for such actions as they perform hastily and unpremeditately than for such as proceed from deliberation. For what reason? but because a hasty temper, though a constant cause or principle in the mind, operates only by intervals, and infects not the whole character. Again, repentance wipes off every crime, if attended with a reformation of life and manners. How is this to be accounted for? but by asserting that actions render a person criminal merely as they are proofs of criminal principles in the mind; and when, by an alteration of these principles, they cease to be just proofs, they likewise cease to be criminal. But, except upon the doctrine of necessity, they never were just proofs, and consequently never were criminal.

It will be equally easy to prove, and from the same arguments, that *liberty,* according to that definition above mentioned, in which all men, agree, is also essential to morality, and that no human actions, where it is wanting, are susceptible of any moral qualities, or can be the objects either of approbation or dislike. For as actions are objects of our moral sentiment, so far only as they are indications of the internal character, passions, and affections; it is impossible that they can give rise either to praise or blame, where they proceed not from these principles, but are derived altogether from external violence.

I pretend not to have obviated or removed all objections to this theory, with regard to necessity and liberty. I can foresee other objections, derived from topics which have not here been treated of. It may be said, for instance, that, if voluntary actions be subjected to the same laws of necessity with the operations of matter, there is a continued chain of necessary causes, pre-ordained and pre-determined, reaching from the original cause of all to every single volition of every human creature. No contingency anywhere in the universe; no difference; no liberty. While we act, we are, at the same time, acted upon. The ultimate Author of all our volitions is the Creator of the world, who first bestowed motion on this immense machine, and placed all beings in that particular position, whence every subsequent event, by an inevitable necessity, must result. Human actions, therefore, either can have no moral turpitude at all, as proceeding from so good a cause; or if they have any turpitude, they must involve our Creator in the same guilt, while he is acknowledged to be their ultimate cause and author. For as a man, who fired a mine, is answerable for all the consequences whether the train he employed be long or short; or wherever a continued chain of necessary causes is fixed, that Being, either finite or infinite, who produces the first, is likewise the author of all the rest, and must both bear the blame and acquire the praise which belong to them. Our clear and unalterable ideas of morality establish this rule, upon unquestionable reasons, when we examine the consequences of any human action; and these reasons must still have greater force when applied to the volitions and intentions of a Being infinitely wise and powerful. Ignorance or impotence may be pleaded for so limited a creature as man; but these imperfections have no place in our Creator. He foresaw, he ordained, he intended all those actions of men, which we so rashly pronounce criminal. And we must therefore conclude, either that they are not criminal, or that the Deity, not man, is accountable for them. But as either of these positions is absurd and impious, it follows, that the doctrine from which they are deduced cannot possibly be true, as being liable to all the same objections. An absurd consequence, if necessary, proves the original doctrine to be absurd in the same manner as criminal actions render criminal the original

cause, if the connection between them be necessary and inevitable.

This objection consists of two parts, which we shall examine separately. *First,* that, if human actions can be traced up, by a necessary chain, to the Deity, they can never be criminal; on account of the infinite perfection of that Being from whom they are derived, and who can intend nothing but what is altogether good and laudable. Or, *Secondly,* if they be criminal, we must retract the attribute of perfection, which we ascribe to the Deity, and must acknowledge him to be the ultimate author of guilt and moral turpitude in all his creatures.

The answer to the first objection seems obvious and convincing. There are many philosophers who, after an exact scrutiny of all the phenomena of nature, conclude, that the *whole,* considered as one system, is, in every period of its existence, ordered with perfect benevolence; and that the utmost possible happiness will, in the end, result to all created beings, without any mixture of positive or absolute ill or misery. Every physical ill, say they, makes an essential part of this benevolent system, and could not possibly be removed, even by the Deity himself considered as a wise agent, without giving entrance to greater ill, or excluding greater good, which will result from it. From this theory, some philosophers, and the ancient Stoics among the rest, derived a topic of consolation under all afflictions, while they taught their pupils that those ills under which they labored were, in reality, goods to the universe; and that to an enlarged view, which could comprehend the whole system of nature, every event became an object of joy and exultation. But though this topic be specious and sublime, it was soon found in practice weak and ineffectual. You would surely more irritate than appease a man lying under the racking pains of the gout by preaching up to him the rectitude of those general laws, which produced the malignant humors in his body, and led them through the proper canals, to the sinews and nerves, where they now excite such acute torments. These enlarged views may, for a moment, please the imagination of a speculative man, who is placed in ease and security; but neither can they dwell with constancy on his mind, even though undisturbed by the emotions of pain or passions; much less can they maintain their ground when attacked by such powerful antagonists. The affections take a narrower and more natural survey of their object; and by an economy, more suitable to the infirmity of human minds, regard alone the beings around us, and are actuated by such events as appear good or ill to the private system.

The case is the same with *moral* as with *physical* ill. It cannot reasonably be supposed, that those remote considerations, which are found of so little efficacy with regard to one, will have a more powerful influence with regard to the other. The mind of man is so formed by nature, that, upon the appearance of certain characters dispositions, and actions, it immediatley feels the sentiment of approbation or blame; nor are there any emotions more essential to its frame and constitution. The characters which engage our approbation are chiefly such as contribute to the peace and security of human society; as the characters which excite blame are chiefly such as tend to public detriment and disturbance: whence it may reasonably be presumed, that the moral sentiments arise, either mediately or immediately, from a reflection of these opposite interests. What though philosophical meditations establish a different opinion or conjecture; that everything is right with regard to the *whole,* and that the qualities, which disturb society, are, in the main, as beneficial, and are as suitable to the primary intention of nature as those which more directly promote its happiness and welfare? Are such remote and uncertain speculations able to counterbalance the sentiments which arise from the natural and immediate view of the objects? A man who is robbed of a considerable sum; does he find his vexation for the loss anywise diminished by these sublime reflections? Why then should his moral resentment against the crime be supposed incompatible with them? Or why should not the acknowledgement of a real distinction between vice and virtue be reconcilable to all speculative systems of philosophy, as well as that of a real distinction between personal beauty and deformity? Both these distinctions are founded in the natural sentiments of the human mind; and these sentiments are not to be controlled or altered by any philosophical theory or speculation whatsoever.

The *second* objection admits not so easy and satisfactory an answer; nor is it possible to explain distinctly, how the Deity can be the mediate cause of all the actions of men, without being the author of sin and moral turpitude. These are mysteries, which were natural and unassisted reason is very unfit to handle; and whatever system she embraces, she must find herself involved in inextricable difficulties, and even contradictions, at every step which she takes with regard to such subjects. To reconcile the indifference and contingency of human actions with prescience; or to defend absolute decrees, and yet free the Deity from being the author of sin, has been found hitherto to exceed all the power of philosophy. Happy, if she be thence sensible of her temerity, when she pries into these sublime mysteries; and leaving a scene so full of obscurities and perplexities, return, with suitable modesty, to her true and proper province, the examination of common life; where she will find difficulties enough to employ her inquiries, without launching into so boundless an ocean of doubt, uncertainty and contradiction!

SECTION IX

OF THE REASON OF ANIMALS

All our reasonings concerning matter of fact are founded on a species of *analogy*, which leads us to expect from any cause the same events, which we have observed to result from similar causes. Where the causes are entirely similar, the analogy is perfect, and the inference, drawn from it, is regarded as certain and conclusive: nor does any man ever entertain a doubt, when he sees a piece of iron, that it will have weight and cohesion of parts; as in all other instances, which have ever fallen under his observation. But where the objects have not so exact a similarity, the analogy is less perfect, and the inference is less conclusive; though still it has some force, in proportion to the degree of similarity and resemblance. The anatomical observations, formed upon one animal, are, by this species of reasoning, extended to all animals; and it is certain, that when the circulation of the blood, for instance, is clearly proved to have place in one creature, as a frog, or fish, it forms a strong presumption. that the same principle has placed in all. These analogical observations may be carried farther, even to this science, of which we are now treating; and any theory, by which we explain the operations of the understanding, or the origin and connection of the passions in man, will acquire additional authority, if we find, that the same theory is requisite to explain the same phenomena in all other animals. We shall make trial of this, with regard to the hypothesis, by which we have, in the foregoing discourse, endeavored to account for all experimental reasonings; and it is hoped, that this new point of view will serve to confirm all our former observations.

First, It seems evident, that animals as well as men learn many things from experience, and infer, that the same events will always follow from the same causes. By this principle they become acquainted with the more obvious properties of external objects, and gradually, from their birth, treasure up a knowledge of the nature of fire, water, earth, stones, heights, depths, etc., and of the effects which result from their operation. The ignorance and inexperience of the young are here plainly distinguishable from the cunning and sagacity of the old, who have learned, by long observation, to avoid what hurt them and to pursue what gave ease or pleasure. A horse, that has been accustomed to the field, becomes acquainted with the proper height which he can leap, and will never attempt what exceeds his force and ability. An old greyhound will trust the more fatiguing part of the chase to the younger, and will place himself so as to meet the hare in her doubles; nor are the conjectures, which he forms on this occasion, founded in anything but his observation and experience.

This is still more evident from the effects of discipline and education on animals, who, by the proper application of rewards and punishments, may be taught any course of action, and most contrary to their natural instincts and propensities. Is it not experience, which renders a dog apprehensive of pain, when you menace him, or lift up the whip to beat him? Is it not even experience, which makes him answer to his name, and infer, from such an arbitrary sound, that you mean him rather than any of his fellows, and intend to call him, when you pronounce it in a certain manner, and with a certain tone and accent.

In all these cases, we may observe, that the animal infers some fact beyond what immediately strikes his senses; and that this inference is altogether founded on past experience, while the creature expects from the present object the same consequences, which it has always found in its observation to result from similar objects.

Secondly, It is impossible, that this inference of the animal can be founded on any process of argument or reasoning, by which he concludes, that like events must follow like objects, and that the course of nature will always be regular in its operations. For if there be in reality any arguments of this nature, they surely lie too abstruse for the observation of such imperfect understandings; since it may well employ the utmost care and attention of a philosophic genius to discover and observe them. Animals, therefore, are not guided in these inferences by reasoning; neither are children; neither are the generality of mankind, in their ordinary actions and conclusions; neither are philosophers themselves, who, in all the active parts of life, are, in the main, the same with the vulgar, and are governed by the same maxims. Nature must have provided some other principle, of more ready, and more general use and application; nor can an operation of such immense consequence in life, as that of inferring effects from causes, be trusted to the uncertain process of reasoning and argumentation. Were this doubtful with regard to men, it seems to admit of no question with regard to the brute creation; and the conclusion being once firmly established in the one, we have a strong presumption, from all the rules of analogy, that it ought to be universally admitted, without any exception or reserve. It is custom alone, which engages animals, from every object, that strikes their senses, to infer its usual attendant, and carries their imagination, from the appearance of the one, to conceive the other, in that particular manner, which we denominate *belief.* No other explication can be given of this operation, in all the higher, as well as lower classes of sensitive beings, which call under our notice and observation.

But though animals learn many parts of their knowledge from observation, there are also many parts of it, which they derive from the original hand of nature; which much exceed the share of capacity they possess on ordinary occasions; and in which they improve, little or nothing, by the longest practice and experience.

These we denominate *instincts,* and are so apt to admire as something very extraordinary, and inexplicable by all the disquisitions of human understanding. But our wonder will, perhaps, cease or diminish, when we consider, that the experimental reasoning itself, which we possess in common with beasts, and on which the whole conduct of life depends, is nothing but a species of instinct or mechanical power, that acts in us unknown to ourselves; and in its chief operations, is not directed by any such relations or comparisons of ideas, as are the proper objects of our intellectual faculties. Though the instinct be different, yet still it is an instinct, which teaches a man to avoid the fire; as much as that, which teaches a bird, with such exactness, the art of incubation, and the whole economy and order of its nursery.

SECTION X
OF MIRACLES

PART I

. . . A miracle is a violation of the laws of nature; and as a firm and unalterable experience has established these laws, the proof against a miracle, from the very nature of the fact, is as entire as any argument from experience can possibly be imagined. Why is it more than probable, that all men must die; that lead cannot, of itself, remain suspended in the air; that fire consumes wood, and is extinguished by water; unless it be, that these events are found agreeable to the laws of nature, and there is required, a violation of these laws, or in other words, a miracle to prevent them? Nothing is esteemed a miracle, if it ever happen in the common course of nature. It is no miracle that a man, seemingly in good health, should die on a sudden: because such a kind of death, though more unusual than any other, has yet been frequently observed to happen. But it is a miracle, that a dead man should come to life; because that has never been observed in any age or country. There must, therefore, be a uniform experience against every miraculous event, otherwise the event would not merit that appellation. And as a uniform experience amounts to a proof, there is here a direct and full *proof,* from the nature of the fact, against the existence of any miracle; nor can such a

proof be destroyed, or the miracle rendered credible, but by an opposite proof, which is superior. Sometimes an event may not, *in itself,* seem to be contrary to the laws of nature, and yet, if it were real, it might, by reason of some circumstances, be denominated a miracle; because, *in fact,* it is contrary to these laws. Thus if a person, claiming a divine authority, should command a sick person to be well, a healthful man to fall down dead, the clouds to pour rain, the winds to blow, in short, should order many natural events, which immediately follow upon his command; these might justly be esteemed miracles, because they are really, in this case, contrary to the laws of nature. For if any suspicion remain, that the event and command concurred by accident, there is no miracle and no transgression of the laws of nature. If this suspicion be removed, there is evidently a miracle, and a transgression of these laws; because nothing can be more contrary to nature than that the voice or command of a man should have such an influence. A miracle may be accurately defined, *a transgression of a law of nature by a particular volition of the Deity, or by the interposition of some invisible agent.* A miracle may either be discoverable by men or not. This alters not its nature and essence. The raising of a house or ship into the air is a visible miracle. The raising of a feather, when the wind wants ever so little of a force requisite for that purpose, is as real a miracle, though not so sensible with regard to us.

The plain consequence is (and it is a general maxim worthy of our attention), 'That no testimony is sufficient to establish a miracle, unless the testimony be of such a kind, that its falsehood would be more miraculous, than the fact, which it endeavors to establish; and even in that case there is a mutual destruction of arguments, and the superior only gives us an assurance suitable to that degree of force, which remains, after deducting the inferior.' When anyone tells me, that he saw a dead man restored to life, I immediately consider with myself, whether it be more probable, that this person should either deceive or be deceived, or that the fact, which he relates should really have happened. I weigh the one miracle against the other; and according to the superiority, which I discover, I pronounce my decision, and always reject the greater miracle. If the falsehood of his testimony would be more miraculous, than the event which he relates; then, and not till then, can he pretend to command my belief or opinion.

Part II

In the foregoing reasoning we have supposed, that the testimony, upon which a miracle is founded, may possibly amount to an entire proof, and that the falsehood of that testimony would be a real prodigy. But it is easy to show, that we have been a great deal too liberal in our concession, and that there never was a miraculous event established on so full an evidence.

For *first*, there is not to be found, in all history, any miracle attested by a sufficient number of men, of such unquestioned good sense, education, and learning, as to secure us against all delusion in themselves; of such undoubted integrity, as to place them beyond all suspicion of any design to deceive others; of such credit and reputation in the eyes of mankind, as to have a great deal to lose in case of their being detected in any falsehood; and at the same time, attesting facts performed in such a public manner and in so celebrated a part of the world, as to render the detection unavoidable: all which circumstances are requisite to give us a full assurance in the testimony of men.

Secondly. We may observe in human nature a principle which, if strictly examined, will be found to diminish extremely the assurance, which we might, from human testimony, have in any kind of prodigy. The maxim, by which we commonly conduct ourselves in our reasonings, is, that the objects, of which we have no experience, resemble those, of which we have; that what we have found to be most usual is always most probable; and that where there is an opposition of arguments, we ought to give the preference to such as are founded on the greatest number of past observations. But though, in proceeding by this rule, we readily reject any fact which is unusual and incredible in an ordinary degree; yet in advancing farther, the mind observes not always the same rule; but when anything is affirmed utterly absurd and miraculous, it rather the more readily admits of such a fact, upon account of that very circumstance, which ought to destroy all its authority. The passion of *surprise* and *wonder,* arising from miracles, being an agreeable emotion,

gives a sensible tendency towards the belief of those events, from which it is derived. And this goes so far, that even those who cannot enjoy this pleasure immediately, nor can believe those miraculous events, of which they are informed, yet love to partake of the satisfaction at second hand or by rebound, and place a pride and delight in exciting the admiration of others. . . .
. . . The many instances of forged miracles, and prophecies, and supernatural events, which, in all ages, have either been detected by contrary evidence, or which detect themselves by their absurdity, prove sufficiently the strong propensity of mankind to the extraordinary and marvellous, and ought reasonably to beget a suspicion against all relations of this kind. This is our natural way of thinking, even with regard to the most common and most credible events. For instance: there is no kind of report which rises so easily, and spreads so quickly, especially in country places and provincial towns, as those concerning marriages; insomuch that two young persons of equal condition never see each other twice, but the whole neighborhood immediately join them together. The pleasure of telling a piece of news so interesting, of propagating it, and of being the first reporters of it, spreads the intelligence. And this is so well known, that no man of sense gives attention to these reports, till he find them confirmed by some greater evidence. Do not the same passions, and others still stronger, incline the generality of mankind to believe and report, with the greatest vehemence and assurance, all religious miracles?

Thirdly. It forms a strong presumption against all supernatural and miraculous relations, that they are observed chiefly to abound among ignorant and barbarous nations; or if a civilized people has ever given admissions to any of them, that people will be found to have received them from ignorant and barbarous ancestors, who transmitted them with that inviolable sanction and authority, which always attend received opinions. When we peruse the first histories of all nations, we are apt to imagine ourselves transported into some new world; where the whole frame of nature is disjointed, and every element performs its operations in a different manner, from what it does at present. Battles, revolutions, pestilence, famine and death, are never the effect of those natural causes, which we experience. Prodigies, omens, oracles, judgments, quite obscure the few natural events, that are intermingled with them. But as the former grow thinner every page, in proportion as we advance nearer the enlightened ages, we soon learn, that there is nothing mysterious or supernatural in the case, but that all proceeds from the usual propensity of mankind towards the marvellous, and that, though this inclination may at intervals receive a check from sense and learning, it can never be thoroughly extirpated from human nature. . . .

. . . I may add a *fourth* reason, which diminishes the authority of prodigies, that there is no testimony for any, even those which have not been expressly detected, that is not opposed by an infinite number of witnesses; so that not only the miracle destroys the credit of testimony, but the testimony destroys itself. To make this the better understood, let us consider, that, in matters of religion, whatever is different is contrary; and that it is impossible the religions of ancient Rome, of Turkey, of Siam, and of China should, all of them, be established on any solid foundation. Every miracle, therefore, pretended to have been wrought in any of these religions (and all of them abound in miracles), as its direct scope is to establish the particular system to which it is attributed; so has it the same force, though more indirectly, to overthrow every other system. In destroying a rival system, it likewise destroys the credit of those miracles, on which that system was established; so that all the prodigies of different religions are to be regarded as contrary facts, and the evidences of these prodigies, whether weak or strong, as opposite to each other. According to this method of reasoning, when we believe any miracle of Mahomet or his successors, we have for our warrant the testimony of a few barbarous Arabians. And on the other hand, we are to regard the authority and witnesses, Grecian, Chinese, and Roman Catholic, who have related any miracle in their particular religion; I say, we are to regard their testimony in the same light as if they had mentioned that Mohammedan miracle, and had in express terms contradicted it, with the same certainty as they have for the miracle they relate. This argument may appear oversubtle and refined; but is not in reality different from the reasoning of a judge, who supposes, that the credit of two witnesses, maintaining a crime against anyone,

is destroyed by the testimony of two others, who affirm him to have been two hundred leagues distant, at the same instant when the crime is said to have been committed. . . .

Upon the whole, then, it appears, that no testimony for any kind of miracle has ever amounted to a probability, much less to a proof; and that, even supposing it amounted to a proof, it would be opposed by another proof; derived from the very nature of the fact, which it would endeavor to establish. It is experience only, which gives authority to human testimony; and it is the same experience, which assures us of the laws of nature. When, therefore, these two kinds of experience are contrary, we have nothing to do but substract the one from the other, and embrace an opinion, either on one side or the other, with that assurance which arises from the remainder. But according to the principle here explained, this substraction, with regard to all popular religions, amounts to an entire annihilation; and therefore we may establish it as a maxim, that no human testimony can have such force as to prove a miracle, and make it a just foundation for any such system of religion.

I beg the limitations here made may be remarked, when I say, that a miracle can never be proved, so as to be the foundation of a system of religion. For I own, that otherwise, there may possibly be miracles, or violations of the usual course of nature, of such a kind as to admit of proof from human testimony; though, perhaps, it will be impossible to find any such in all the records of history. Thus, suppose, all authors, in all languages, agree, that, from the first of January 1600, there was a total darkness over the whole earth for eight days: suppose that the tradition of this extraordinary event is still strong and lively among the people: that all travelers, who return from foreign countries, bring us accounts of the same tradition, without the least variation or contradiction: it is evident, that our present philosophers, instead of doubting the fact, ought to receive it as certain, and ought to search for the causes whence it might be derived. The decay, corruption, and dissolution of nature, is an event rendered probable by so many analogies, that any phenomenon, which seems to have a tendency towards that catastrophe, comes within the reach of human testimony, if that testimony be very extensive and uniform.

SECTION XI

OF A PARTICULAR PROVIDENCE AND OF A FUTURE STATE

I was lately engaged in conversation with a friend who loves sceptical paradoxes; where, though he advanced many principles, of which I can by no means approve, yet as they seem to be curious, and to bear some relation to the chain of reasoning carried on throughout this inquiry, I shall here copy them from my memory as accurately as I can, in order to submit them to the judgment of the reader.

Our conversation began with my admiring the singular good fortune of philosophy, which, as it requires entire liberty above all other privileges, and chiefly flourishes from the free opposition of sentiments and argumentation, received its first birth in an age and country of freedom and toleration, and was never cramped, even in its most extravagant principles, by any creeds, concessions, or penal statutes. For, except the banishment of Protagoras, and the death of Socrates, which last event proceeded partly from other motives, there are scarcely any instances to be met with, in ancient history, of this bigoted jealousy, with which the present age is so much infested. Epicurus lived at Athens to an advanced age, in peace and tranquillity; Epicureans were even admitted to receive the sacerdotal character, and to officiate at the altar, in the most sacred rites of the established religion. And the public encouragement of pensions and salaries was afforded equally, by the wisest of all the Roman emperors, to the professors of every sect of philosophy. How requisite such kind of treatment was to philosophy, in her early youth, will easily be conceived, if we reflect, that, even at present, when she may be supposed more hardy and robust, she bears with much difficulty the inclemency of the seasons, and those harsh winds of calumny and persecution, which blow upon her.

You admire, says my friend, as the singular good fortune of philosophy, what seems to result from the natural course of things, and to be unavoidable in every age and nation. This pertinacious bigotry, of which you complain, as so fatal to philosophy, is really her offspring, who, after allying with superstition, separates himself entirely from the interest of his parent, and becomes her most inveterate enemy and persecutor. Speculative dogmas of religion, the present occasions of such furious dispute, could not possibly be conceived or admitted in the early ages of the world; when mankind, being wholly illiterate, formed an idea of religion more suitable to their weak apprehension, and composed there sacred tenets of such tales chiefly as were the objects of traditional belief, more than of argument or disputation. After the first alarm, therefore, was over, which arose from the new paradoxes and principles of the philosophers; these teachers seem ever after, during the ages of antiquity, to have lived in great harmony with the established superstition, and to have made a fair partition of mankind between them; the former claiming all the learned and wise, the latter possessing all the vulgar and illiterate.

It seems then, say I, that you leave politics entirely out of the question, and never suppose, that a wise magistrate can justly be jealous of certain tenets of philosophy, such as those of Epicurus, which, denying a divine existence, and consequently a providence and a future state, seem to loosen, in a great measure, the ties of morality, and may be supposed, for that reason, pernicious to the peace of civil society.

I know, replied he, that in fact these persecutions never, in any age, proceeded from calm reason, or from experience of the pernicious consequences of philosophy; but arose entirely from passion and prejudice. But what if I should advance farther, and assert, that if Epicurus had been accused before the people, by any of the *sycophants* or informers of those days, he could easily have defended his cause, and proved his principles of philosophy to be as salutary as those of his adversaries, who endeavored, with such zeal, to expose him to the public hatred and jealousy?

I wish, said I, you would try your eloquence upon so extraordinary a topic, and make speech for Epicurus, which might satisfy, not the mob of Athens, if you will allow that ancient and polite city to have contained any mob, but the more philosophical part of his audience, such as might be supposed capable of comprehending his arguments.

The matter would not be difficult, upon such conditions, replied he. And if you please, I shall suppose myself Epicurus for a moment, and make you stand for the Athenian people, and shall deliver you such an harangue as will fill all the urn with white beans, and leave not a black one to gratify the malice of my adversaries.

Very well: pray proceed upon these suppositions.

I come hither, O ye Athenians, to justify in your assembly what I maintained in my school, and I find myself impeached by furious antagonists, instead of reasoning with calm and dispassionate inquirers. Your deliberations, which of right should be directed to questions of public good, and the interest of the commonwealth, are diverted to the disquisitions of speculative philosophy; and these magnificent, but perhaps fruitless inquiries, take place of your more familiar but more useful occupations. But so far as in me lies, I will prevent this abuse. We shall not here dispute concerning the origin and government of worlds. We shall only inquire how far such questions concern the public interest. And if I can persuade you, that they are entirely indifferent to the peace of society and security of government, I hope that you will presently send us back to our schools, there to examine, at leisure, the question the most sublime, but at the same time, the most speculative of all philosophy.

The religious philosophers, not satisfied with the tradition of your forefathers, and doctrine of your priests (in which I willingly acquiesce), indulge a rash curiosity, in trying how far they can establish religion upon the principles of reason; and they thereby excite, instead of satisfying, the doubts which naturally arise from a diligent and scrutinous inquiry. They paint, in the most magnificent colors, the order, beauty, and wise arrangement of the universe; and then ask, if such a glorious display of intelligence could proceed from the fortuitous concourse of atoms, or if chance could produce what the greatest genius can never sufficiently admire. I shall not examine the justness of this argument. I shall allow it to be as solid as my antagonists and accusers can desire. It is sufficient, if I can prove, from this very reasoning, that the question is entirely speculative, and that, when, in my philosophical disquisitions, I deny a providence and a future state, I undermine not the foundations of society, but advance principles, which they themselves, upon their own topics, if they argue consistently, must allow to be solid and satisfactory.

You then, who are my accusers, have ac-

knowledged, that the chief or sole argument for a divine existence (which I never questioned) is derived from the order of nature, where there appear such marks of intelligence and design, that you think it extravagant to assign for its cause, either chance, or the blind and unguided force of matter. You allow, that this is an argument drawn from effects to causes. From the order of the work, you infer, that there must have been project and forethought in the workman. If you cannot make out this point, you allow, that your conclusion fails; and you pretend not to establish the conclusion in a greater latitude than the phenomena of nature will justify. These are your concessions. I desire you to mark the consequences.

When we infer any particular cause from an effect, we must proportion the one to the other, and can never be allowed to ascribe to the cause any qualities, but what are exactly sufficient to produce the effect. A body of ten ounces raised in any scale may serve as a proof, that the counterbalancing weight exceeds ten ounces; but never afford a reason that it exceeds a hundred. If the cause, assigned for any effect, be not sufficient to produce it, we must either reject that cause, or add to it such qualities as will give it a just proportion to the effect. But if we ascribe to it further qualities, or affirm it capable of producing other effects, we can only indulge the license of conjecture, and arbitrarily suppose the existence of qualities and energies, without reason or authority.

The same rule holds, whether the cause assigned be brute unconscious matter, or a rational intelligent being. If the cause be known only by the effect, we never ought to ascribe to it any qualities, beyond what are precisely requisite to produce the effect; nor can we, by any rules of just reasoning, return back from the cause, and infer other effects from it, beyond those by which alone it is known to us. No one, merely from the sight of one of Zeuxis's pictures, could know, that he was also a statuary or architect, and was an artist no less skillful in stone and marble than in colors. The talents and taste, displayed in the particular work before us; these we may safely conclude the workman to be possessed of. The cause must be proportioned to the effect; and if we exactly and precisely proportion it, we shall never find in it any qualities, that point farther, or afford an inference concerning any other design or performance. Such qualities must be somewhat beyond what is merely requisite for producing the effect, which we examine.

Allowing, therefore, the gods to be the authors of the existence or order of the universe; it follows, that they possess that precise degree of power, intelligence, and benevolence, which appears in their workmanship; but nothing farther can ever be proved, except we call in the assistance of exaggeration and flattery to supply the defects of argument and reasoning. So far as the traces of any attributes, at present appear, so far may we conclude these attributes to exist. The supposition of farther attributes is mere hypothesis; much more the supposition, that, in distant regions of space or periods of time, there has been, or will be, a more magnificent display of these attributes, and a scheme of administration more suitable to such imaginary virtues. We can never be allowed to mount up from the universe, the effect, to Jupiter, the cause; and then descend downwards, to infer any new effect from that cause; as if the present effects alone were not entirely worthy of the glorious attributes, which we ascribe to that deity. The knowledge of the cause being derived solely from the effect, they must be exactly adjusted to each other; and the one can never refer to anything farther, or be the foundation of any new inference and conclusion.

You find certain phenomena in nature. You seek a cause or author. You imagine that you have found him. You afterwards become so enamored of this offspring of your brain, that you imagine it impossible, but he must produce something greater and more perfect than the present scene of things, which is so full of ill and disorder. You forget, that this superlative intelligence and benevolence are entirely imaginary, or, at least, without any foundation in reason; and that you have no ground to ascribe to him any qualities, but what you see he has actually exerted and displayed in his productions. Let your gods, therefore, O philosophers, be suited to the present appearances of nature: and presume not to alter these appearances by arbitrary suppositions, in order to suit them to the attributes, which you so fondly ascribe to your deities.

When priests and poets, supported by your authority, O Athenians, talk of a golden or silver age, which preceded the present state of vice and misery, I hear them with attention and with reverence. But when philosophers, who pretend to neglect authority, and to cultivate reason, hold the same discourse, I pay them not, I own, the same obsequious submission and pious deference. I ask, who carried them into the celestial regions, who admitted them into the councils of the gods, who opened to them the book of fate, that they thus rashly affirm, that their deities have executed, or will execute, any purpose beyond what has actually appeared? If they tell me, that they have mounted on the steps or by the gradual ascent of reason, and by drawing inferences from effects to causes, I still insist, that they have aided the ascent of reason by the wings of imagination; otherwise they could not thus change their manner of inference, and argue from causes to effects; presuming, that a more perfect production than the present world would be more suitable to such perfect beings as the gods, and forgetting that they have no reason to ascribe to these celestial beings any perfection or any attribute, but what can be found in the present world.

Hence all the fruitless industry to account for the ill appearances of nature, and save the honor of the gods; while we must acknowledge the reality of that evil and disorder, with which the world so much abounds. The obstinate and intractable qualities of matter, we are told, or the observance of general laws, or some such reason, is the sole cause, which controlled the power and benevolence of Jupiter, and obliged him to create mankind and every sensible creature so imperfect and so unhappy. These attributes then, are, it seems, beforehand, taken for granted, in their greatest latitude. And upon that supposition, I own that such conjectures may, perhaps, be admitted as plausible solutions of the ill phenomena. But still I ask, Why take these attributes for granted, or why ascribe to the cause any qualities but what actually appear in the effect? Why torture your brain to justify the course of nature upon suppositions, which, for aught you know, may be entirely imaginary, and of which there are to be found no traces in the course of nature?

The religious hypothesis, therefore, must be considered only as a particular method of accounting for the visible phenomena of the universe: but no just reasoners will ever presume to infer from it any single fact, and alter or add to the phenomena, in any single particular. If you think, that the appearances of things prove such causes, it is allowable for you to draw an inference concerning the existence of these causes. In such complicated and sublime subjects, everyone should be indulged in the liberty of conjecture and argument. But here you ought to rest. If you come backward, and arguing from your inferred causes, conclude, that any other fact has existed, or will exist, in the course of nature, which may serve as a fuller display of particular attributes; I must admonish you, that you have departed from the method of reasoning, attached to the attributes of the cause, beyond what appears in the effect; otherwise you could never, with tolerable sense or propriety, add anything to the effect, in order to render it more worthy of the cause.

Where, then, is the odiousness of that doctrine, which I teach in my school, or rather, which I examine in my gardens? Or what do you find in this whole question, wherein the security of good morals, or the peace and order of society, is in the least concerned?

I deny a providence, you say, and supreme governor of the world, who guides the course of events, and punishes the vicious with infamy and disappointment, and rewards the virtuous with honor and success, in all their undertakings. But surely, I deny not the course itself of events, which lies open to everyone's inquiry and examination. I acknowledge, that, in the present order of things, virtue is attended with more peace of mind than vice, and meets with a more favorable reception from the world. I am sensible, that, according to the past experience and mankind, friendship is the chief joy of human life, and moderation the only source of tranquillity and happiness. I never balance between the virtuous and the vicious course of life; but am sensible, that, to a well-disposed mind, every advantage is on the side of the former. And what can you say more, allowing all your suppositions and reasonings? You tell me, indeed, that the disposition of things proceeds from intelligence and design. But whatever it proceeds from, the disposition itself, on which depends our happiness or misery, and consequently our conduct and deportment in life, is still the same. It is still open for me, as well as you, to regulate my behavior, by my

experience of past events. And if you affirm, that, while a divine providence is allowed, and a supreme distributive reward of the good, and punishment of the bad, beyond the ordinary course of events; I here find the same fallacy, which I have before endeavored to detect. You persist in imagining, that if, we grant that divine existence, for which you so earnestly contend, you may safely infer consequences from it, and add something to the experienced order of nature, by arguing from the attributes which you ascribe to your gods. You seem not to remember, that all your reasonings on this subject can only be drawn from effects to causes; and that every argument, deducted from causes to effects, must of necessity be a gross sophism; since it is impossible for you to know anything of the cause, but what you have antecedently, not inferred, but discovered to the full, in the effect.

But what must a philosopher think of those vain reasoners, who, instead of regarding the present scene of things as the sole object of their contemplation, so far reverse the whole course of nature, as to render this life merely a passage to something farther; a porch, which leads to a greater, and vastly different building; a prologue, which serves only to introduce the piece, and give it more grace and propriety? Whence, do you think, can such philosophers derive their idea of the gods? From their own conceit and imagination surely. For if they derived it from the present phenomena, it would never point to anything farther, but must be exactly adjusted to them. That the divinity may *possibly* be endowed with attributes, which we have never seen exerted; may be governed by principles of action, which we cannot discover to be satisfied: all this will freely be allowed. But still this is mere *possibility* and hypothesis. We never can have reason to *infer* any attributes, or any principles of action in him, but so far as we know them to have been exerted and satisfied.

Are there any marks of distributive justice in the world? If you answer in the affirmative, I conclude, that, since justice here exerts itself, it is satisfied. If you reply in the negative, I conclude, that you have then no reason to ascribe justice, in our sense of it, to the gods. If you hold a medium between affirmation and negation, by saying, that the justice of the gods, at present, exerts itself in part, but not in its full extent; I answer, that you have no reason to give it any particular extent, but only so far as you see it, *at present,* exert itself.

Thus I bring the dispute, O Athenians, to a short issue with my antagonists. The course of nature lies open to my contemplation as well as to theirs. The experienced train of events is the great standards, by which we all regulate our conduct. Nothing else can be appealed to in the field, or in the senate. Nothing else ought ever to be heard of in the school, or in the closet. In vain would our limited understanding break through those boundaries, which are too narrow for our fond imagination. While we argue from the course of nature, and infer a particular intelligent cause, which first bestowed, and still preserves order in the universe, we embrace a principle, which is both uncertain and useless. It is uncertain; because the subject lies entirely beyond the reach of human experience. It is useless; because our knowledge of this cause being derived entirely from the course of nature, we can never, according to the rules of just reasoning, return back from the cause with any new inference, or making additions to the common and experienced course of nature, establish any new principles of conduct and behavior.

I observe (said I, finding he had finished his harangue) that you neglect not the artifice of the demagogues of old; and as you were pleased to make me stand for the people, you insinuated yourself into my favor by embracing those principles, to which, you know, I have always expressed a particular attachment. But allowing you to make experience (as indeed I think you ought) the only standards of our judgment concerning this, and all other questions of fact; I doubt not but, from the very same experience, to which you appeal, it may be possible to refute this reasoning, which you have put into the mouth of Epicurus. If you saw, for instance, a half-finished building, surrounded with heaps of brick and stone and mortar, and all the instruments of masonry; could you not *infer* from the effect, that it was a work of design and contrivance? And could you not return again, from this inferred cause, to infer new additions to the effect, and conclude, that the building would soon be finished, and receive all the further improvements, which art could bestow upon it? If you saw upon the seashore the print of one human foot, you would

conclude, that a man had passed that way, and that he had also left the traces of the other foot, though effaced by the rolling of the sands or inundation of the waters. Why then do you refuse to admit the same method of reasoning with regard to the order of nature? Consider the world and the present life only as an imperfect building, from which you can infer a superior intelligence; and arguing from that superior intelligence, which can leave nothing imperfect; why may you not infer a more finished scheme or plan, which will receive its completion in some distant point of space or time? Are not these methods of reasoning exactly similar? And under what pretense can you embrace the one, while you reject the other?

The infinite difference of the subjects, replied he, is a sufficient foundation for this difference in my conclusions. In works of *human* art and contrivance, it is allowable to advance from the effect to the cause, and returning back from the cause, to form new inferences concerning, the effect, and examine the alterations, which it has probably undergone, or may still undergo. But what is the foundation of this method of reasoning? Plainly this: that man is a being, whom we know by experience, whose motives and designs we are acquainted with, and whose projects and inclinations have a certain connection and coherence, according to the laws which nature has established for the government of such a creature. When, therefore, we find, that any work has proceeded from the skill and industry of man; as we are otherwise acquainted with the nature of the animal, we can draw a hundred inferences concerning what may be expected from him; and these inferences will all be founded in experience and observation. But did we know man only from the single work or production which we examine, it were impossible for us to argue in this manner; because our knowledge of all the qualities, which we ascribe to him, being in that case derived from the production, it is impossible they could point to anything further, or be the foundation of any new inference. The print of a foot in the sand can only prove, when considered alone, that there was some figure adapted to it, by which it was produced: but the print of a human foot proves likewise, from our other experience, that there was probably another foot, which also left its impression, though effaced by time or other accidents. Here we mount from the effect to the cause; and descending again from the cause, infer alterations in the effect; but this is not a continuation of the same simple chain of reasoning. We comprehend in this case a hundred other experiences and observations, concerning the usual figure and members of that species of animal, without which this method of argument must be considered as fallacious and sophistical.

The case is not the same with our reasonings from the works of nature. The Deity is known to us only by his productions, and is a single being in the universe, not comprehended under any species or genus, from whose experienced attributes or qualities, we can, by analogy, infer any attribute or quality in him, As the universe shows wisdom and goodness, we infer wisdom and goodness. As it shows a particular degree of these perfections, we infer a particular degree of them, precisely adapted to the effect which we examine. But further attributes or further degrees of the same attributes, we can never be authorized to infer or suppose, by any rules of just reasoning. Now, without some such license of supposition, it is impossible for us to argue from the cause, or infer any alteration in the effect, beyond what has immediately fallen under our observation. Greater good produced by this Being must still prove a greater degree of goodness; a more impartial distribution of rewards and punishments must proceed from a greater rewards to justice and equity. Every supposed addition to the works of nature makes an addition to the attributes of the Author of nature; and consequently, being entirely unsupported by any reason or argument, can never be admitted but as mere conjecture and hypothesis.

The great source of our mistake in this subject, and of the unbounded license of conjecture, which we indulge, is, that we tacitly consider ourselves, as in the place of the Supreme Being, and conclude, that he will, on every occasion, observe the same conduct, which we ourselves, in his situation, would have embraced as reasonable and eligible. But, besides that the ordinary course of nature may convince us, that almost everything is regulated by principles and maxims very different from ours; besides this, I say, it must evidently appear contrary to all rules of analogy to reason, from the intentions and project of men, to those of a

Being so different, so that when, from any fact, we have discovered one intention of any man, it may often be reasonable, from experience, to infer another, and draw a long chain of conclusions concerning his past or future conduct. But this method of reasoning can never have place with regard to a Being, so remote and incomprehensible, who bears much less analogy to any other being in the universe than the sun to a waxen taper, and who discovers himself only by some faint traces or outlines, beyond which we have no authority to ascribe to him any attribute or perfection. What we imagine to be a superior perfection, may really be a defect. Or were it ever so much a perfection, the ascribing of it to the Supreme Being, where it appears not to have been really exerted, to the full, in his works, savors more of flattery and panegyric, than of just reasoning and sound philosophy. All the philosophy, therefore, in the world, and all the religion, which is nothing but a species of philosophy, will never be able to carry us beyond the usual course of experience, or give us measures of conduct and behavior different from those which are furnished by reflections on common life. No new fact can ever be inferred from the religious hypothesis; no event foreseen or foretold; no reward or punishment expected or dreaded, beyond what is already known by practice and observation. So that my apology for Epicurus will still appear solid and satisfactory; nor have the political interests of society any connection with the philosophical disputes concerning metaphysics and religion.

There is still one circumstance, replied I, which you seem to have overlooked. Though I should allow your premises, I must deny your conclusion. You conclude, that religious doctrines and reasonings can have no influence on life, because they *ought* to have no influence; never considering, that men reason not in the same manner you do, but draw many consequences from the belief of a divine existence, and suppose that the Deity will inflict punishments on vice, and bestow rewards on virtue, beyond what appear in the ordianry course of nature. Whether this reasoning of theirs be just or not, is no matter. Its influence on their life and conduct must still be the same And, those, who attempt to disabuse them of such prejudices, may, for aught I know, be good reasoners, but I cannot allow them to be good citizens and politicians; since they free men from one restraint upon their passions, and make the infringement of the laws of society, in one respect, more easy and secure.

After all, I may, perhaps, agree to your general conclusion in favor of liberty, though upon different premises from those, on which you endeavor to found it. I think, that the state ought to tolerate every principle of philosophy; nor is there an instance, that any government has suffered in its political interests by such indulgence. There is no enthusiasm among philosophers; their doctrines are not very alluring to the people; and no restraint can be put upon their reasonings, but what must be of dangerous consequence to the sciences, and even to the state, by paving the way for persecution and oppression in points, where the generality of mankind are more deeply interested and concerned.

But there occurs to me (continued I) with regard to your main topic, a difficulty, which I shall just propose to you without insisting on it; lest it lead into reasonings of too nice and delicate a nature. In a word, I much doubt whether it be possible for a cause to be known only by its effect (as you have all along supposed) or to be of so singular and particular a nature as to have no parallel and no similiarity with any other cause or object, that has ever fallen under our observation. It is only when two *species* or objects are found to be constantly conjoined, that we can infer the one from the other; and were an effect presented, which was entirely singular, and could not be comprehended under any known *species,* I do not see, that we could form any conjecture or inference at all concerning its cause. If experience and observation and analogy be, indeed, the only guides which we can reasonably follow in inferences of this nature; both the effect and cause must bear a similarity and resemblance to other effects and causes, which we know, and which we have found, in many instances, to be conjoined with each other. I leave it to your own reflection to pursue the consequences of this principle. I shall just observe, that, as the antagonists of Epicurus always suppose the universe, an effect quite singular and unparalleled, to be the proof of a Deity, a cause no less singular and unparalleled; your reasonings, upon that supposition, seem, at least, to merit our attention. There is, I own, some difficulty,

how we can ever return from the cause to the effect, and, reasoning from our ideas of the former, infer any alteration on the latter, or any addition to it.

SECTION XII

OF THE ACADEMICAL OR SCEPTICAL PHILOSOPHY

Part I

There is not a greater number of philosophical reasonings, displayed upon any subject, than those, which prove the existence of a Deity, and refute the fallacies of *atheists;* and yet the most religious philosophers still dispute whether any man can be so blinded as to be a speculative atheist. How shall we reconcile these contradictions? The knights-errant, who wandered about to clear the world of dragons and giants, never entertained the least doubt with regard to the existence of these monsters.

The *sceptic* is another enemy of religion, who naturally provokes the indignation of all divines and graver philosophers; though it is certain, that no man ever met with any such absurd creature, or conversed with a man, who had no opinion or principle concerning any subject, either of action or speculation. This begets a very natural question; What is meant by a sceptic? And how far is it possible to push these philosophical principles of doubt and uncertainty?

There is a species of scepticism, *antecedent* to all study and philosophy, which is much inculcated by Descartes and others, as a sovereign preservative against error and precipitate judgement. It recommends an universal doubt, not only of all our former opinions and principles, but also of our very faculties; of whose veracity, say they, we must assure ourselves, by a chain of reasoning, deduced from some original principle, which cannot possibly be fallacious or deceitful. But neither is there any such original principle, which has a prerogative above others, that are self-evident and convincing: or if there were, could we advance a step beyond it, but by the use of those very faculties, of which we are supposed to be already diffident. The Cartesian doubt, therefore, were it ever possible to be attained by any human creature (as it plainly is not) would be entirely incurable; and no reasoning could ever bring us to a state of assurance and conviction upon any subject.

It must, however, be confessed, that this species of scepticism, when more moderate, may be understood in a very reasonable sense, and is a necessary preparative to the study of philosophy, by preserving a proper impartiality in our judgments, and weaning our mind from all those prejudices, which we may have imbibed from education or rash opinion. To begin with clear and self-evident principles, to advance by timorous and sure steps, to review frequently our conclusions, and examine accurately all their consequences; though by these means we shall make both a slow and a short progress in our systems; are the only methods, by which we can ever hope to reach truths, and attain a proper stability and certainty in our determinations.

There is another species of scepticism, *consequent* to science and inquiry, when men are supposed to have discovered either the absolute fallaciousness of their mental faculties, or their unfitness to reach any fixed determination in all those curious subjects of speculation, about which they are commonly employed. Even our very senses are brought into dispute, by a certain species of philosophers; and the maxims of common life are subjected to the same doubt as the most profound principles or conclusions of metaphysics and theology. As these paradoxical tenets (if they may be called tenets) are to be met with in some philosophers, and the refutation of them in several, they naturally excite our curiosity, and make us inquire into the arguments, on which they may be founded.

I need not insist upon the more trite topics, employed by the sceptics in all ages, against the evidence of *sense;* such as those which are derived from the imperfection and fallaciousness of our organs, on numberless occasions; the crooked appearance of an oar in water; the various aspects of objects, according to their different distances; the double images which arise from the pressing one eye; with many other appearances of a like nature. These sceptical topics, indeed, are only sufficient to prove, that the senses alone are not implicitly to be depended on; but that we must correct their evidence by reason, and by considerations, derived from the nature of the medium, the distance of the object, and the disposition of the organ, in order to render them, within their sphere, the proper *criteria* of truth and falsehood. There are other more profound arguments against the senses, which admit not of so easy a solution.

It seems evident, that men are carried, by a natural instinct or pre-possession, to repose faith in their senses; and that, without any reasoning, or even almost before the use of reason, we always suppose an external universe, which depends not on our preception, but would exist, though we and every sensible creature were absent or annihilated. Even the animal creation are governed by a like opinion, and preserve this belief of external objects, in all their thoughts, designs, and actions.

It seems also evident, that, when men follow this blind and powerful instinct of nature, they always suppose the very images, presented by the senses, to be the external objects, and never entertain any suspicion, that the one are nothing but representations of the other. This very table, which we see white, and which we feel hard, is believed to exist, independent of our perception, and to be something external to our mind, which perceives it. Our presence bestows not being on it; our absence does not annihilate it. It preserves its existence uniform and entire, independent of the situation of intelligent beings, who perceive or contemplate it.

But this universal and primary opinion of all men is soon destroyed by the slightest philosophy, which teaches us, that nothing can ever be present to the mind but an image or perception, and that the senses are only the inlets, through which these images are conveyed, without being able to produce any immediate intercourse between the mind and the object. The table, which we see, seems to diminish, as we remove farther from it; but the real table, which exists independent of us, suffers no alteration: it was, therefore, nothing but its image, which was present to the mind. These are the obvious dictates of reason; and no man, who reflects, ever doubted, that the existences, which we consider, when we say, *this house* and *that tree*, are nothing but perceptions in the mind, and fleeting copies or representations of other existences, which remain uniform and independent.

So far, then, are we necessitated by reasoning to contradict or depart from the primary instincts of nature, and to embrace a new system with regard to the evidence of our senses. But here philosophy finds herself extremely embarrassed, when she would justify this new system, and obviate the cavils and objections to the sceptics. She can no longer plead the infallible and irresistible instinct of nature: for that led us to a quite different system, which is acknowledged fallible and ever erroneous. And to justify this pretended philosophical system, by a chain of clear and convincing argument, or even any appearance of argument, exceeds the power of all human capacity.

By what argument can it be proved, that the perceptions of the mind must be caused by external objects, entirely different from them, though resembling them (if that be possible) and could not arise either from the energy of the mind itself, or from the suggestion of some invisible and unknown spirit, or from some other cause still more unknown to us? It is acknowledged, that, in fact, many of these perceptions arise not from anything external, as in dreams, madness, and other diseases. And nothing can be more inexplicable than the manner, in which body should so operate upon mind as ever to convey an image of itself to a substance, supposed of so different, and even contrary a nature.

It is a question of fact, whether the perceptions of the senses be produced by external objects, resembling them: how shall this question be determined? By experience surely; as all other questions of a like nature. But here experience is, and must be entirely silent. The mind has never anything present to it but the perceptions, and cannot possibly reach any experience of their connection with objects. The supposition of such a connection is, therefore, without any foundation in reasoning.

To have recourse to the veracity of the supreme Being, in order to prove the veracity of our senses, is surely making a very unexpected circuit. If this veracity were at all concerned in this matter, our senses would be entirely infallible; because it is not possible that he can ever deceive. Not to mention, that, if the external world be once called in question, we shall be at a loss to find arguments, by which we may prove the existence of that Being or any of his attributes.

This is a topic, therefore, in which the profounder and more philosophical sceptics will

always triumph, when they endeavor to introduce an universal doubt into all subjects of human knowledge and inquiry. Do you follow the instincts and propensities of nature, may they say, in assenting to the veracity of senses? But these lead you to believe that the very perception or sensible image is the external object. Do you disclaim this principle, in order to embrace a more rational opinion, that the perceptions are only representations of something external? You here depart from your natural propensities and more obvious sentiments; and yet are not able to satisfy your reason, which can never find any convincing argument from experience to prove, that the perceptions are connected with any external objects.

There is another sceptical topic of a like nature, derived from the most profound philosophy; which might merit our attention, were it requisite to dive so deep, in order to discover arguments and reasonings, which can so little serve to any serious purpose. It is universally allowed by modern inquirers, that all the sensible qualities of objects, such as hard, soft, hot, cold, white, black, etc. are merely secondary, and exist not in the objects themselves, but are perceptions of the mind, without any external archetype or model, which they represent. If this be allowed, with regard to secondary qualities, it must also follow, with regard to the supposed primary qualities of extension and solidity; nor can the latter be any more entitled to that denomination than the former. The idea of extension is entirely acquired from the senses of sight and feeling; and if all the qualities, perceived by the senses, be in the mind, not in the object, the same conclusion must reach the idea of extension, which is wholly dependent on the sensible ideas or the ideas of secondary qualities. Nothing can save us from this conclusion, but the asserting, that the ideas of those primary qualities are attained by *abstraction*, an opinion, which, if we examine it accurately, we shall find to be unintelligible, and even absurd. An extension, that is neither tangible nor visible, cannot possibly be conceived; and a tangible or visible extension, which is neither hard nor soft, black or white, is equally beyond the reach of human conception. Let any man try to conceive a triangle in general, which is neither *isosceles* nor *scalenum*, nor has any particular length or proportion of sides; and he will soon perceive the absurdity of all the scholastic notions with regard to abstraction and general ideas.

Thus the first philosophical objection to the evidence of sense or to the opinion of external existence consists in this, that such an opinion, if rested on natural instinct, is contrary to reason, and if referred to reason, is contrary to natural instinct, and at the same time carries no rational evidence with it, to convince an impartial inquirer. The second objection goes farther, and represents this opinion as contrary to reason, at least, if it be a principle of reason, that all sensible qualities are in the mind, not in the object. Bereave matter of all its intelligible qualities, both primary and secondary, you in a manner annihilate it, and leave only a certain unknown, inexplicable *something*, as the cause of our perceptions; a notion so imperfect, that no sceptic will think it worth while to contend against it.

Part II

It may seem a very extravagant attempt of the sceptics to destroy *reason* by argument and ratiocination; yet is this the grand scope of all their inquiries and disputes. They endeavor to find objections, both to our abstract reasonings, and to those which regard matter of fact and existence.

The chief objection against all *abstract* reasonings is derived from the ideas of space and time; ideas, which in common life and to a careless view, are very clear and intelligible, but when they pass through the scrutiny of the profound sciences (and they are the chief object of these sciences) afford principles, which seem full of absurdity and contradiction. No priestly *dogmas*, invented on purpose to tame and subdue the rebellious reason of mankind, ever shocked common sense more than the doctrine of the infinite divisibility of extension, with its consequences; as they are pompously displayed by all geometricians and metaphysicians, with a kind of triumph and exultation. A real quantity, infinitely less than any finite quantity, containing quantities, infinitely less than itself, and so on *in infinitum;* this is an edifice so bold and prodigious, that it is too weighty for any pretended demonstration to support, because it shocks the clearest and most natural principles of human reason. But what renders the matter

more extraordinary, is, that these seemingly absurd opinions are supported by a chain of reasoning, the clearest and most natural; nor is it possible for us to allow the premises without admitting the consequences. Nothing can be more convincing and satisfactory than all the conclusions concerning the properties of circles and triangles; and yet, when these are once received, how can we deny, that the angle of contact between a circle and its tangent is infinitely less than any rectilineal angle, that as you may increase the diameter of the circle *in infinitum*, this angle of contact becomes still less, even *in infinitum*, and that the angle of contact between other curves and their tangents may be infinitely less than those between any circle and its tangent, and so on, *in infinitum*? The demonstration of these principles seems as unexceptionable as that which proves the three angles of a triangle to be equal to two right ones, though the latter opinion be natural and easy, and the former big with contradiction and absurdity. Reason here seems to be thrown into a kind of amazement and suspense, which, without the suggestions of any sceptic, gives her a diffidence of herself, and of the ground, on which she treads, she sees a full light, which illuminates certain places; but that light borders upon the most profound darkness. And between these she is so dazzled and confounded, that she scarcely can pronounce with certainty and assurance concerning any one object.

The absurdity of these bold determinations of the abstract sciences seems to become, if possible, still more palpable with regard to time than extension. An infinite number of real parts of time, passing in succession, and exhausted one after another, appears so evident a contradiction, that no man, one should think, whose judgment is not corrupted, instead of being improved, by the sciences, would ever be able to admit of it.

Yet still reason must remain restless, and unquiet, even with regard to that scepticism, to which she is driven by these seeming absurdities and contradictions. How any clear, distinct idea can contain circumstances, contradictory to itself, or to any other clear, distinct idea, is absolutely incomprehensible; and is, perhaps, as absurd as any proposition, which can be formed. So that nothing can be more sceptical, or more full of doubt and hesitation, than this scepticism itself, which arises from some of the paradoxical conclusions of geometry or the science of quantity.

The sceptical objections to *moral* evidence, or to the reasonings concerning matter of fact, are either *popular* or *philosophical*. The popular objections are derived from the natural weakness of human understanding; the contradictory opinions, which have been entertained in different ages and nations; the variations of our judgment in sickness and health, youth and old age, prosperity and adversity; the perpetual contradiction of each particular man's opinions and sentiments; with many other topics of that kind. It is needless to insist farther on this head. These objections are but weak. For as, in common life, we reason every moment concerning fact and existence, and cannot possibly subsist, without continually employing this species of argument, any popular objections, derived from thence, must be insufficient to destroy that evidence. The great subverter of *Pyrrhonism* or the excessive principles of scepticism is action, and employment, and the occupations of common life. These principles may flourish and triumph in the schools; where it is, indeed, difficult, if not impossible, to refute them. But as soon as they leave the shade, and by the presence of the real objects, which actuate our passions and sentiments, are put in opposition to the more powerful principles of our nature, they vanish like smoke, and leave the most determined sceptic in the same condition as other mortals.

The sceptic, therefore, had better keep within his proper sphere, and display those *philosophical* objects, which arise from more profound researches. Here he seems to have ample matter of triumph; while he justly insists, that all our evidence for any matter of fact, which lies beyond the testimony of sense or memory, is derived entirely from the relation of cause and effect; that we have no other idea of this relation than that of two objects, which have been frequently *conjoined* together, that we have no argument to convince us, that objects, which have, in our experience, been frequently conjoined, will likewise, in other instances, be conjoined in the same manner; and that nothing leads us to this inference but custom or a certain instinct of our nature; which it is indeed difficult to resist, but which, like other instincts, may be fallacious and

deceitful. While the sceptic insists upon these topics, he shows his force, or rather, indeed, his own and our weakness; and seems, for the time at least, to destroy all assurance and conviction. These arguments might be displayed at greater length, if any durable good or benefit to society could ever be expected to result from them.

For here is the chief and most confounding objection to *excessive* scepticism, that no durable good can ever result from it; while it remains in its full force and vigor. We need only ask such a sceptic. *What his meaning is? And what he proposes by all these curious researches?* He is immediately at a loss, and knows not what to answer. A Copernican or Ptolemaic, who supports each his different system of astronomy, may hope to produce a conviction, which will remain constant and durable, with his audience. A Stoic or Epicurean displays principles, which may not be durable, but which have an effect on conduct and behavior. But a Pyrrhonian cannot expect, that his philosophy will have any constant influence on the mind: or if it had, that its influence would be beneficial to society. On the contrary, he must acknowledge, if he will acknowledge anything, that all human life must perish, were his principles universally and steadily to prevail. All discourse, all action would immediately cease; and men remain in a total lethargy, till the necessities of nature, unsatisfied, put an end to their miserable existence. It is true; so fatal an event is very little to be dreaded. Nature is always too strong for principle. And though a Pyrrhonian may throw himself or others into a momentary amazement and confusion by his profound reasonings; the first and most trivial event in life will put to flight all his doubts and scruples, and leave him the same, in every point of action and speculation, with the philosophers of every other sect, or with those who never concerned themselves in any philosophical researches. When he awakes from his dream, he will be the first to join in the laugh against himself, and to confess, that all his objections are mere amusement, and can have no other tendency than to show the whimsical condition of mankind, who must act and reason and believe; though they are not able, by their most diligent inquiry, to satisfy themselves concerning the foundation of these operations, or to remove the objections, which may be raised against them.

Part III

There is, indeed, a more *mitigated* scepticism or *academical* philosophy, which may be both durable and useful, and which may, in part, be the result of this Pyrrhonism, or *excessive* scepticism, when its undistinguished doubts are, in some measure, corrected by common sense and reflection. The greater part of mankind are naturally apt to be affirmative and dogmatical in their opinions; and while they see objects only on one side, and have no idea of any counterposing argument, they throw themselves precipitately into the principles, to which they are inclined; nor have they any indulgence for those who entertain opposite sentiments. To hesitate or balance perplexes their understanding, checks their passion, and suspends their action. They are, therefore, impatient till they escape from a state, which to them is so uneasy: and they think, that they could never remove themselves far enough from it, by the violence of their affirmations and obstinacy of their belief. But could such dogmatical reasoners become sensible of the strange infirmities of human understanding, even in its most perfect state, and when most accurate and cautious in its determinations; such a reflection would naturally inspire them with more modesty and reserve, and diminish their fond opinion of themselves, and their prejudice against antagonists. The illiterate may reflect on the disposition of the learned, who, amidst all the advantages of study and reflection, are commonly still diffident in their determinations: and if any of the learned be inclined, from their natural temper, to haughtiness and obstinacy, a small tincture of Pyrrhonism might abate their pride, by showing them, that the few advantages, which they may have attained over their fellows, are but inconsiderable, if compared with the universal perplexity and confusion, which is inherent in human nature. In general, there is a degree of doubt, and caution, and modesty, which, in all kinds of scrutiny and decision, ought forever to accompany a just reasoner.

Another species of *mitigated* scepticism which may be of advantage to mankind, and which may be the natural result of the Pyrrhonian doubts and scruples, is the limitation of our inquiries to such subjects as are best adapted to the narrow capacity of human understanding.

The *imagination* of man is naturally sublime, delighted with whatever is remote and extraordinary, and running, without control, into the most distant parts of space and time in order to avoid the objects, which custom has rendered too familiar to it. A correct *judgment* observes a contrary method, and avoiding all distant and high inquiries, confines itself to common life, and to such subjects as fall under daily practice and experience; leaving the more sublime topics to the embellishment of poets and orators, or to the arts of priests and politicians. To bring us to so salutary a determination, nothing can be more serviceable, than to be once thoroughly convinced of the force of the Pyrrhonian doubt, and of the impossibility, that anything, but the strong power of natural instinct, could free us from it. Those who have a propensity to philosophy, will still continue their researches; because they reflect, that, besides the immediate pleasure, attending such an occupation, philosophical decisions are nothing but the reflections of common life, methodized and corrected. But they will never be tempted to go beyond common life, so long as they consider the imperfection of those faculties which they employ, their narrow reach, and their inaccurate operations. While we cannot give a satisfactory reason, why we believe, after a thousand experiments, that a stone will fall, or fire burn; can we ever satisfy ourselves concerning any determination, which we may form, with regard to the origin of worlds, and the situation of nature, from, and to eternity?

This narrow limitation, indeed, of our inquiries, is, in every respect, so reasonable, that it suffices to make the slightest examination into the natural powers of the human mind and to compare them with their objects, in order to recommend it to us. We shall then find what are the proper subjects of science and inquiry.

It seems to me, that the only objects of the abstract science or of demonstration are quantity and number, and that all attempts to extend this more perfect species of knowledge beyond these bounds are mere sophistry and illusion. As the component parts of quantity and number are entirely similar, their relations become intricate and involved; and nothing can be more curious, as well as useful, than to trace, by a variety of mediums, their equality or inequality, through their different appearances. But as all other ideas are clearly distinct and different from each other, we can never advance farther, by our utmost scrutiny, than to observe this diversity, and, by an obvious reflection, pronounce one thing not to be another. Or if there be any difficulty in these decisions, it proceeds entirely from the undeterminate meaning of words, which is corrected by juster definitions. That *the square of the hypothenuse is equal to the squares of the other two sides,* cannot be known, let the terms be ever so exactly defined, without a train of reasoning and inquiry. But to convince us of this proposition, *that where there is no property, there can be no injustice,* it is only necessary to define the terms, and explain injustice to be a violation of property. This proposition is, indeed, nothing but a more imperfect definition. It is the same case with all those pretended syllogistical reasonings, which may be found in every other branch of learning, except the sciences of quantity and number; and these may safely, I think, be pronounced the only proper objects of knowledge and demonstration.

All other inquiries of men regard only matter of fact and existence; and these are evidently incapable of demonstration. Whatever *is* may *not be.* No negation of a fact can involve a contradiction. The non-existence of any being, without exception, is as clear and distinct an idea as its existence. The proposition, which affirms it not to be, however false, is no less conceivable and intelligible, than that which affirms it to be. The case is different with the sciences, properly so called. Every proposition, which is not true, is there confused and unintelligible. That the cube root of 64 is equal to the half of 10, is a false proposition, and can never be distinctly conceived. But that Caesar, or the angel Gabriel, or any being never existed, may be a false proposition, but still is perfectly conceivable, and implies no contradiction.

The existence, therefore, of any being can only be proved by arguments from its cause or its effect; and these arguments are founded entirely on experience. If we reason, *a priori,* anything may appear able to produce anything. The falling of a pebble may, for aught we know, extinguish the sun; or the wish of a man, control the planets in their orbits. It is only experience, which teaches us the nature and bounds of cause and effect, and enables us to infer the existence of one object from that of another. Such is the foundation of moral reasoning, which forms the greater part of human knowledge, and is the source of all human action and behavior.

Moral reasonings are either concerning particular or general facts. All deliberations in life regard the former; as also all disquisitions in history, chronology, geography, and astronomy.

The sciences, which treat of general facts, are politics, natural philosophy, physics, chemistry, etc., where the qualities, causes and effects of a whole species of objects are inquired into.

Divinity or Theology, as it proves the existence of a Deity, and the immortality of souls, is composed partly of reasonings concerning particular, partly concerning general facts. It has a foundation in *reason,* so far as it is supported by experience. But its best and most solid foundation is *faith* and divine revelation.

Morals and criticism are not so properly objects of the understanding as of taste and sentiment. Beauty, whether moral or natural, is felt, more properly than perceived. Or if we reason concerning it, and endeavor to fix its standard, we regard a new fact, to wit, the general tastes of mankind, or some such fact, which may be the object of reasoning and inquiry.

When we run over libraries, persuaded of these principles, what havoc must we make? If we take in our hand any volume; of divinity or school metaphysics, for instance; let us ask, *Does it contain any abstract reasoning concerning quantity or number?* No. *Does it contain any experimental reasoning concerning matter of fact and existence?* No. Commit it then to the flames: for it can contain nothing but sophistry and illusion.

Immanuel Kant

Immanuel Kant (1724-1804) was a German philosopher who exercised a profound influence on the development of philosophy and science in the eighteenth and nineteenth centuries. This influence has remained powerful, even in our own time. Born in the small Prussian town of Konigsberg, Kant lived a quiet and uneventful life in close association with the university activities of Konigsberg. He was a living example of dedication and devotion to his intellectual endeavors, and as a professor and a writer he became the center of philosophical attraction in the European continent. In his early career he was deeply immersed in strictly scientific activities, and in 1755 he published a monumental work in which he advanced a number of cosmological and astronomical ideas which have significantly changed man's understanding of the universe.

In this work of 1755, *Universal Natural Theory and History of the Heavens*, Kant attempted to give a cogent explanation of the formation of the solar system. His thorough knowledge of astronomy led him to the conclusion that the sun and the planets were born as the result of the condensation of a huge cloud of gas and dust, a nebula, which gave rise to a nucleus and a series of rings. The nucleus became the sun, and the rings finally turned into the planets and their satellites. Today we believe that Kant's explanation of the formation of our solar system is probably the most adequate hypothesis of solar and planetary astronomy. The importance of Kant's nebular theory consists in the fact that it does not force us to postulate any kind of catastrophic hypothesis (stellar collisions, unique spatial situations, and so on) in order to account for the reality of the solar system. The solar system, of which the earth is an insignificant member, is, according to Kant's views, a perfectly common and ordinary phenomenon in the universe; it is logical to postulate the existence of billions of similar systems in which intelligent life is probably a common development.

Just as Copernicus relegated the earth to the category of one planet among other planets, Kant relegated the entire solar system (the sun and the planets) to the category of a system among countless other systems. After Kant, then, it is no longer possible to attribute anything special or unique to the earth or to the solar system.

Still more important than his nebular hypothesis, however, was Kant's conviction that the Milky Way is by no means the totality of the universe. By means of one of the most brilliant intuitions in the history of mankind, and in absolute defiance of the scientific orthodoxy of his time, Kant advanced the view that most of the nebulae observed by astronomers through their telescopes were not merely clouds of dust and gas within the confines of the Milky Way, but true "island-universes" made up of billions of stars and planets. Thus, just as the earth is not unique among the planets, or the solar system is not unique among other systems, the Milky Way is not a unique galaxy. The universe, according to Kant, is made up of billions of galaxies.

Kant's almost unbelievable astronomical speculations were finally verified by the American astronomer Edwin Hubble, in 1924, almost two hundred years after the publication of Kant's astronomical work. Hubble showed that the nebular cloud known as M31 (Andromeda) is not a nebula and is not a part of the Milky Way. M31 is a galaxy, in fact bigger than the Milky Way, that lies at a distance of more than two million light years from our own galaxy.

Kant's early scientific work taught him a number of lessons which were later decisive in the formulation of his philosophical system:

(1) Philosophy and science are intimately related inasmuch as they both seek the solution to one and the same problem, namely, What is the nature of reality? Philosophy approaches this problem from a more general point of view, by examining the most basic concepts of the human mind. Science, on the other hand, chooses a more specific and detailed area of investigation.

(2) A philosopher who is not a scientist is in truth a person who speculates in a vacuum: he may say many things, but in most instances his utterances have nothing to do with reality. A scientist, on the other hand, who lacks a philosophical perspective is merely a technician of his field. He may also say and do many things, but they are usually unrelated to the fundamental problem of science, which is the elucidation of the problem of reality.

(3) Kant was, therefore, an advocate of the marriage between philosophy and science. This, of course, was also the case with Aristotle, Bacon, Descartes, and Schopenhauer.

(4) The process of philosophical and scientific progress must be the result of combining sense experience with intuition and imagination. The former without the latter can only yield a collection of unrelated and unorganized bits of information about the world. Intuition and imagination without sense

perception, on the other hand, can only lead to fruitless divagations.

(5) The world of experience or, as Kant would have said in 1755, the observable universe, is a reality which is thoroughly subjected to principles and laws. Nothing in the universe is random; nothing is the result of chance occurrences.

After 1755, Kant became more and more concerned with strictly philosophical problems. As he tell us in his *Prolegomena*, it was the influence of David Hume which led him away from the scientific dogmatism and philosophical optimism of his early days. He became, accordingly, interested in subjecting to the most severe *criticism*, not merely this or that philosophical or scientific contention, but the very capacity of the human mind to know reality. Thus, the prime goal of his *Critique of Pure Reason* was to examine the intellectual mechanism which makes knowledge possible. The *Prolegomena* was Kant's attempt to clarify some of the statements of the *Critique* which had given rise to much controversy.

The chief conclusions reached in his *Critique of Pure Reason* are these:

(1) The world of reality is not independent of the human consciousness. It is the result of man's awareness of the world as well as of the world-as-it-is-in-itself. In this sense, then, all knowledge is relative to the human mind.

(2) Space and time are not, as Newton had maintained, independent realities of existence which have little or nothing to do with the human mind. On the contrary, space and time are, according to Kant, pure forms of intuition which belong to the mind. In the absence of a knowing mind, therefore, there is neither time nor space.

(3) Knowledge is possible through the application of certain a priori concepts or categories which, like time and space, are part of the human field of consciousness. These categories are notions like unity, limitation, reality, causality, possibility, necessity, and others.

(4) Knowledge of the world-as-it-is-in-itself (that is, independent of the human mind) is, according to Kant, absolutely impossible. Equally impossible is knowledge about what Kant regarded as the fundamental problems of metaphysics: the existence of God, the immortality of the human soul, and the reality of freedom. This really amounts to saying that as a system of knowledge metaphysics is an impossible dream of the human mind. We can only know, so to speak, the surface of reality, the world-as-it-appears-to-us. We are forever forbidden to know reality, as this is independent of the human mind, inasmuch as the very tools by means of which we come to know anything are relative to the human consciousness: time, space, and the categories of the understanding.

This is, at least according to some interpreters, the chief message of the *Critique of Pure Reason*. Other interpretations of Kant have been advanced by scholars, but it would be useless in this context to go into the matter any further. At any rate, one point should be emphasized: the proud young astronomer of 1755 became the cautious philosopher of 1781, as he realized, after a long period of reflection, that the universe with its countless island-universes and its multitude of objects is, after all, nothing but a representation in the human mind. This does not mean, however, that Kant came to share the subjective idealism of George Berkeley according to whom, as we saw, "to be is to be perceived." Beneath the world of representation, which is, according to Kant, nothing but a phenomenon arising in the human consciousness, there is a real world, a noumenal world, which transcends our knowing limitations but which exists in itself nevertheless.

Kant felt, especially as he expressed his ideas in his moral writings (*Critique of Practical Reason* for example), that the only possible avenue through which we could gain some grasp of the real world was through a religious faith sustained by moral behavior. It was due to this contention, then, that as the great philosopher of Konigsberg approached death, he became more and more convinced that science and philosophy, our knowledge of the galaxies and our analyses of experience, are of secondary importance in human life. What truly counts in a person's life is his commitment to a moral and holy life: the rest is, as in Plato's parable of the cave, a child's game.

What a very strange journey of ideas! What a moving pilgrimage of the spirit! Schopenhauer, as we will see later, reconstructed the Kantian journey, and came to a similar, yet more pessimistic, conviction about the world which most of us call real. According to Schopenhauer, the only way to salvation is to abandon the world of physical experience by (1) recognizing the limitations of our cognitive consciousness, and (2) renouncing the world of appearances.

The influence of Kant is, as we said above, still very powerful. In science, especially in astronomy and cosmology, we are still verifying the amazing fruitfulness of his speculations: (1) We are more and more convinced that his nebular hypothesis of the formation of the solar system is the most adequate explanation of planetary formation; (2) we know that outside the Milky Way there are innumerable "island-universes" which float in endless space; (3) we know that, as Kant stated, the axial rotation of the earth has been slowed by the gravitational force of the moon; and (4) some of us are beginning to suspect, although in defiance of most cosmological ideas of the present, that the galaxies of our cosmic vicinity are all rotating around a tremendous center of attraction, as Kant already suspected in 1755.

In philosophy, Kant's influence is equally great, although many philosophers and scientists have forgotten the Kantian admonition that philosophy and science cannot be meaningfully separated from each other and from a moral attitude. Kant's analysis of the nature of time and space, of the process of knowledge, of the structure of consciousness, and of the problems entailed by unwarranted metaphysical assertions, lives among us.

Kant's writings are, as the student will discover, extremely difficult and obscure. For some reason he lacked the brillances of Schopenhauer, the forcefulness of Nietzsche, the clarity of Hume, and the precision of Aristotle. But he made up amply for the defects of his style by being endowed with an almost superhuman power to penetrate into the most complex issues of human existence: this is, perhaps, the reason for his obscurity.

The world of modern philosophy after both Hume and Kant may be represented as follows:

The arrow from the subject to the experience in both Hume and Kant is meant to stress the contribution of the knowing subject to our knowledge. Kant was alone in appreciating this aspect of Hume's philosophy.

Yet a tremendous difference still exists. The point which Kant makes is that the contribution of the mind, what he called the noumenal self, is absolute and unchanging. In Kant, this accounts for certainty and moral absoluteness, since in his ethical theory the self will be the origin of moral commands. The self, for Kant, is outside of the world process and thus immune to change. For Hume, the self is part of the process and therefore subject to change. As Hume put it, the contribution of the mind is the same as long as human nature remains the same. But human nature might change. As Kant pointed out with respect to Hume, if the self is biologically based, then there is no permanent frame of reference. In opting for a permanent frame of reference, Kant is more truly a modern Platonist than a Copernican. Hume remains more consistently a Copernican.

Kant admits Hume's critique against a priori reasoning in the old Platonic theories. Yet Kant argues for the permanence of the first principles as well as the fact that they are not derived from experience.

Critique of Pure Reason

PREFACE TO THE FIRST EDITION (1781)

Our reason has this peculiar fate that, with reference to one class of its knowledge, it is always troubled with questions which cannot be ignored, because they spring from the very nature of reason, and which cannot be answered, because they transcend the powers of human reason.

Nor is human reason to be blamed for this. It begins with principles which, in the course of experience, it *must* follow, and which are sufficiently confirmed by experience. With these again, according to the necessities of its nature, it rises higher and higher to more remote conditions. But when it perceives that in this way its work remains for ever incomplete, because the questions never cease, it finds itself constrained to take refuge in principles which exceed every possible experimental application, and nevertheless seem so unobjectionable that even ordinary common sense agrees with them. Thus, however, reason becomes involved in darkness and contradictions, from which, no doubt, it may conclude that errors must be lurking somewhere, but without being able to discover them, because the principles which it follows transcend all the limits of experience and therefore withdraw themselves from all experimental tests. It is the battle-field of these endless controversies which is called *Metaphysic.*

There was a time when Metaphysic held a royal place among all the sciences, and, if the will were taken for the deed, the exceeding importance of her subject might well have secured to her that place of honour. At present it is the fashion to despise Metaphysic, and the poor matron, forlorn and forsaken, complains like Hecuba, *Modo maxima rerum, tot generis natisque potens—nunc trahor exul, inops* (Ovid, Metam. xiii. 508).

At first the rule of Metaphysic, under the dominion of the dogmatists, was despotic. But as the laws still bore the traces of an old barbarism, intestine wars and complete anarchy broke out, and the sceptics, a kind of nomads, despising all settled culture of the land, broke up from time to time all civil society. Fortunately their number was small, and they could not prevent the old settlers from returning to cultivate the ground afresh, though without any fixed plan or agreement. Not long ago one might have thought, indeed, that all these quarrels were to have been settled and the legitimacy of her claims decided once for all through a certain physiology of the human understanding, the work of the celebrated *Locke.* But, though the descent of that royal pretender, traced back as it had been to the lowest mob of common experience, ought to have rendered her claims very suspicious, yet, as that genealogy turned out to be in reality a false invention, the old queen (Metaphysic) continued to maintain her claims, everything fell back into the old rotten dogmatisim, and the contempt from which metaphysical science was to have been rescued, remained the same as ever. At present, after everything has been tried, so they say, and tried in vain, there reign in philosophy weariness and complete indifferentism, the mother of chaos and night in all sciences but, at the same time, the spring or, at least, the prelude of their near reform and of a new light, after an ill-applied study has rendered them dark, confused, and useless.

It is in vain to assume a kind of artificial indifferentism in respect to enquiries the object of which cannot be indifferent to human nature. Nay, those pretended indifferentists (however they may try to disguise themselves by changing scholastic terminology into popular language), if they think at all, fall back inevitably into those very metaphysical dogmas which they profess to despise. Nevertheless this indifferentism, showing itself in the very midst of the most flourishing state of all sciences, and affecting those very sciences the teachings of which, if they could be had, would be the last to be surrendered, is a phenomenon well worthy of our attention and consideration. It is clearly the result, not of the carelessness, but of the matured judgment of our age, which will no longer rest satisfied with the mere appearance of knowledge. It is, at the same time, a powerful appeal to reason to undertake anew the most difficult of its duties, namely, self-knowledge, and to institute a court of appeal which should protect the just rights of reason, but dismiss all groundless claims, and should do this not by means of irresponsible decrees, but according to the eternal and unalterable laws of reason. This court of appeal is no other than the *Critique of Pure Reason.*

I do not mean by this a criticism of books and systems, but of the faculty of reason in general, touching that whole class of knowledge which it may strive after, unassisted by experience. This must decide the question of the possibility or impossibility of metaphysic in general, and the determination of its sources, its extent, and its limits—and all this according to fixed principles.

This, the only way that was left, I have followed, and I flatter myself that I have thus removed all those errors which have hitherto brought reason, whenever it was unassisted by experience, into conflict with itself. I have not evaded its questions by pleading the insufficiency of human reason, but I have classified them according to principles, and, after showing the point where reason begins to misunderstand itself, solved them satisfactorily. It is true that the answer of those questions is not such as a dogma-enamoured curiosity might wish for, for such curiosity could not have been satisfied except by juggling tricks in which I am not adept. But this was not the intention of the natural destiny of our reason, and it

became the duty of philosophy to remove the deception which arose from a false interpretation, even though many a vaunted and cherished dream should vanish at the same time. In this work I have chiefly aimed at completeness, and I venture to maintain that there ought not to be one single metaphysical problem that has not been solved here, or to the solution of which the key at least has not been supplied. In fact Pure Reason is so perfect a unity that, if its principle should prove insufficient to answer any one of the many questions started by its very nature, one might throw it away altogether, as insufficient to answer the other questions with perfect certainty.

While I am saying this I fancy I observe in the face of my readers an expression of indignation, mixed with contempt, at pretensions apparently so self-glorious and extravagant; and yet they are in reality far more moderate than those made by the writer of the commonest essay professing to prove the simple nature of the soul or the necessity of a first beginning of the world. For, while he pretends to extend human knowledge beyond the limits of all possible experience, I confess most humbly that this is entirely beyond my power. I mean only to treat of reason and its pure thinking, a knowledge of which is not very far to seek, considering that it is to be found within myself. Common logic gives an instance how all the simple acts of reason can be enumerated completely and systematically. Only between the common logic and my work there is this difference, that my question is,—what can we hope to achieve with reason, when all the material and assistance of experience is taken away?

So much with regard to the completeness in our laying hold of every single object, and the thoroughness in our laying hold of all objects, as the material of our critical enquiries—a completeness and thoroughness determined, not by a casual idea, but by the nature of our knowledge itself.

Besides this, certainty and clearness with regard to form are two essential demands that may very properly be addressed to an author who ventures on so slippery an undertaking.

First, with regard to certainty, I have pronounced judgment against myself by saying that in this kind of enquiries it is in no way permissible to propound mere opinions, and that everything looking like a hypothesis is counterband, that must not be offered for sale at however low a price, but must, as soon as it has been discovered, be confiscated. For every kind of knowledge which professes to be certain *a priori*, proclaims itself that it means to be taken for absolutely necessary. And this applies, therefore, still more to a definition of all pure knowledge *a priori*, which is to be the measure, and therefore also an example, of all apodictic philosophical certainty. Whether I have fulfilled what I have here undertaken to do, must be left to the judgment of the reader; for it only behoves the author to propound his arguments, and not to determine beforehand the effect which they ought to produce on his judges. But, in order to prevent any unnecessary weakening of those arguments, he may be allowed to point out himself certain passages, which, though they refer to collateral objects only, might occasion some mistrust, and thus to counteract in time the influence which the least hesitation of the reader in respect to these minor points might exercise with regard to the principal object.

I know of no enquiries which are more important for determining that faculty which we call understanding and for fixing its rules and its limits, than those in the Second Chapter of my Transcendental Analytic, under the title of 'Deduction of the Pure Concepts of the Understanding.' They have given me the greatest but, I hope, not altogether useless trouble. This enquiry, which rests on a deep foundation, has two sides. The one refers to the objects of the pure understanding, and is intended to show and explain the objective value of its concepts *a priori*. It is, therefore, of essential importance for my purposes. The other is intended to enquire into the pure understanding itself, its possibility, and the powers of knowledge on which it rests, therefore its subjective character; a subject which, though important for my principal object, yet forms no essential part of it, because my principal problem is and remains, What and how much may understanding and reason know without all experience? and not, How is the faculty of thought possible? The latter would be an enquiry into a cause of a given effect; it would, therefore, be of the nature of an hypothesis (though, as I shall show elsewhere, this is not quite so); and it might seem as

if I had here allowed myself to propound a mere opinion, leaving the reader free to hold another opinion also. I therefore warn the reader, in case my subjective deduction should not produce that complete conviction which I expect, that the objective deduction, in which I am here chiefly concerned, must still retain its full strength. . . .

Surely it should be an attraction to the reader if he is asked to join his own efforts with those of the author in order to carry out a great and important work, according to the plan here proposed, in a complete and lasting manner. Metaphysic, according to the definitions here given, is the only one of all sciences which, through a small but united effort, may count on such completeness in a short time, so that nothing will remain for posterity but to arrange everything according to its own views for didactic purposes, without being able to add anything to the subject itself. For it is in reality nothing but an inventory of all our possessions acquired through Pure Reason, systematically arranged. Nothing can escape us, because whatever reason produces entirely out of itself, cannot hide itself, but is brought to light by reason itself, so soon as the common principle has been discovered. This absolute completeness is rendered not only possible, but necessary, through the perfect unity of this kind of knowledge, all derived from pure concepts, without any influence from experience, or from special intuitions leading to a definite kind of experience, that might serve to enlarge and increase it. . . .

PREFACE TO THE SECOND EDITION
(1787)

Whether the treatment of that class of knowledge with which reason is occupied follows the secure method of a science or not, can easily be determined by the result. If, after repeated preparations, it comes to a standstill, as soon as its real goal is approached, or is obliged, in order to reach it, to retrace its steps again and again, and strike into fresh paths; again, if it is impossible to produce unanimity among those who are engaged in the same work, as to the manner in which their common object should be obtained, we may be convinced that such a study is far from having attained to the secure method of a science, but is groping only in the dark. In that case we are conferring a great benefit on reason, if we only find out the right method, though many things should have to be surrendered as useless, which were comprehended in the original aim that had been chosen without sufficient reflection.

That *Logic,* from the earliest times, has followed that secure method, may be seen from the fact that since *Aristotle* it has not had to retrace a single step, unless we choose to consider as improvements the removal of some unnecessary subtleties, or the clearer definition of its matter, both of which refer to the elegance rather than to the solidity of the science. It is remarkable also, that to the present day, it has not been able to make one step in advance, so that, to all appearance, it may be considered as completed and perfect. If some modern philosophers thought to enlarge it, by introducing *psychological* chapters on the different faculties of knowledge (faculty of imagination, wit, etc.), or *metaphysical* chapters on the origin of knowledge, or the different degrees of certainty according to the difference of objects (idealism, scepticism, etc.), or lastly, *anthropological* chapters on prejudices, their causes and remedies, this could only arise from their ignorance of the peculiar nature of logical science. We do not enlarge, but we only disfigure the sciences, if we allow their respective limits to be confounded: and the limits of logic are definitely fixed by the fact, that it is a science which has nothing to do but fully to exhibit and strictly to prove all formal rules of thought (whether it be *a priori* or empirical, whatever be its origin or its object, and whatever be the impediments, accidental or natural, which it has to encounter in the human mind).

That logic should in this respect have been so successful, is due entirely to its limitation, whereby it has not only the right, but the duty, to make abstraction of all the objects of knowledge and their differences, so that the understanding has to deal with nothing beyond itself and its own forms. It was, of course, far more difficult for reason to enter on the secure method of science, when it has to deal not with itself only, but also with objects. Logic, therefore, as a kind of preparation (*propaedeutic*) forms, as it were, the vestibule of the sciences only, and where real knowledge is concerned, is presupposed for critical purposes only, while the acquisition of knowledge must be sought

for in the sciences themselves, properly and objectively so called.

If there is to be in those sciences an element of reason, something in them must be known *a priori*, and knowledge may stand in a twofold relation to its object, by either simply *determining* it and its concept (which must be supplied from elsewhere), or by making it *real* also. The former is *theoretical*, the latter *practical knowledge* of reason. In both the *pure* part, namely, that in which reason determines its object entirely *a priori* (whether it contain much or little), must be treated first, without mixing up with it what comes from other sources; for it is bad economy to spend blindly whatever comes in, and not to be able to determine, when there is a stoppage, which part of the income can bear the expenditure, and where reductions must be made.

Mathematics and *physics* are the two theoretical sciences of reason, which have to determine their *objects a priori*; the former quite purely, the latter partially so, and partially from other sources of knowledge besides reason.

Mathematics, from the earliest times to which the history of human reason can reach, has followed, among that wonderful people of the Greeks, the safe way of a science. But it must not be supposed that it was as easy for mathematics as for logic, in which reason is concerned with itself alone, to find, or rather to make for itself that royal road. I believe, on the contrary, that there was a long period of tentative work (chiefly still among the Egyptians), and that the change is to be ascribed to a *revolution*, produced by a happy thought of a single man, whose experiment pointed unmistakably to the path that had to be followed, and opened and traced out for the most distant times the safe way of a science. The history of that intellectual revolution, which was far more important than the discovery of the passage round the celebrated Cape of Good Hope, and the name of its fortunate author, have not been preserved to us. But the story preserved by Diogenes Laertius, who names the reputed author of the smallest elements of ordinary geometrical demonstration, even of such as, according to general opinion, do not require to be proved, shows, at all events, that the memory of the revolution, produced by the very first traces of the discovery of a new method, appeared extremely important to the mathematicians, and thus remained unforgotten. A new light flashed on the first man who demonstrated the properties of the isosceles triangle (whether his name was *Thales* or any other name), for he found that he had not to investigate what he saw in the figure, or the mere concept of that figure, and thus to learn its properties; but that he had to produce (by construction) what he had himself according to concepts *a priori,* placed into that figure and represented in it, so that, in order to know anything with certainty *a priori,* he must not attribute to that figure anything beyond what necessarily follows from what he has himself placed into it, in accordance with the concept.

It took a much longer time before physics entered on the high way of science: for no more than a century and a half has elapsed, since Bacon's ingenious proposal partly initiated that discovery, partly, as others were already on the right track, gave a new impetus to it,—a discovery which, like the former, can only be explained by a rapid intellectual revolution. In what I have to say, I shall confine myself to natural science, so far as it is founded on *empirical* principles.

When Galileo let balls of a particular weight, which he had determined himself, roll down an inclined plain, or Torricelli made the air carry a weight, which he had previously determined to be equal to that of a definite volume of water; or when, in later times, Stahl changed metal into lime, and lime again into metals, by withdrawing and restoring something, a new light flashed on all students of nature. They comprehended that reason has insight into that only, which she herself produces on her own plan, and that she must move forward with the principles of her judgments, according to fixed laws, and compel nature to answer her questions, but not let herself be led by nature, as it were in leading strings, because otherwise accidental observations, made on no previously fixed plan, will never converge towards a necessary law, which is the only thing that reason seeks and requires. Reason, holding in one hand its principles, according to which concordant phenomena alone can be admitted as laws of nature, and in the other hand the experiment, which it has devised according to those principles, must approach nature, in order to be taught by it: but not in the character of a pupil, who agrees to everything the master likes, but as an appointed judge, who compels the witnesses to answer the questions which he himself proposes. Therefore even the science of physics entirely owes the beneficial revolution in its character to the happy thought, that we ought to seek in nature (and not import into it by means of fiction) whatever reason must learn from nature, and could not know by itself, and that we must do this in accordance with what reason itself has originally placed into nature. Thus only has the study of nature entered on the secure method of a science, after having for many centuries done nothing but grope in the dark.

Metaphysic, a completely isolated and speculative science of reason, which declines all teaching of experience, and rests on concepts only (not on their application to intuition, as mathematics), in which reason therefore is meant to be her own pupil, has hitherto not been so fortunate as to enter on the secure path of a science, although it is older than all other sciences, and would remain, even if all the rest were swallowed up in the abyss of an all-destroying barbarism. In metaphysic, reason, even if it tries only to understand *a priori* (as it pretends to do) those laws which are confirmed by the commonest experience, is constantly brought to a standstill, and we are obliged again and again to retrace our steps, because they do not lead us where we want to go; while as to any unanimity among those who are engaged in the same work, there is so little of it in metaphysic, that it has rather become an arena, specially destined, it would seem, for those who wish to exercise themselves in mock fights, and where no combatant has, as yet, succeeded in gaining an inch of ground that he could call permanently his own. It cannot be denied, therefore, that the method of metaphysic has hitherto consisted in groping only, and, what is the worst, in groping among mere concepts.

What then can be the cause that hitherto no secure method of science has been discovered? Shall we say that it is impossible? Then why should nature have visited our reason with restless aspiration to look for it, as if it were its most important concern? Nay more, how little should we be justified in trusting our reason if, with regard to one of the most important objects we wish to know, it not only abandons us, but lures us on by vain hopes, and in the end betrays us! Or, if hitherto we have only failed to meet with the right path, what indications are there to make us hope that, if we renew our researches, we shall be more successful than others before us?

The examples of mathematics and natural sciences, which by one revolution have become what they now are, seem to me sufficiently remarkable to induce us to consider, what may have been the essential element in that intellectual revolution which has proved so beneficial to them, and to make the experiment, at least, so far as the analogy between them, as sciences of reason, with metaphysic allows it, of imitating them. Hitherto it has been supposed that all our knowledge must conform to the objects: but, under this supposition, all attempts to establish anything about them *a priori* by means of concepts, and thus to enlarge our knowledge, have come to nothing. The experiment therefore ought to be made, whether we should not succeed better with the problems of metaphysic, by assuming that the objects must conform to our mode of cognition, for this would better agree with the demanded possibility of an *a priori* knowledge of them, which is to settle something about objects, before they are given us. We have here the same case as with the first thought of Copernicus, who, not being able to get on in the explanation of the movements of the heavenly bodies, as long as he assumed that all the stars turned around the spectator, tried, whether he could not succeed better, by assuming the spectator to be turning round, and the stars to be at rest. A similar experiment may be tried in metaphysic, so far as the *intuition* of objects is concerned. If the intuition had to conform to the constitution of objects, I do not see how we could know anything of it *a priori*; but if the object (as an object of the senses) conforms to the constitution of our faculty of intuition, I can very well conceive such a possibility. As, however, I cannot rest in these intuitions, if they are to become knowledge, but have to refer them, as representations, to something as their object, and must determine that object by them, I have the choice of admitting, either that the *concepts*, by which I carry out that determination, conform to the object, being then again in the same perplexity on account of the manner how I can know anything about it *a priori;* or that the objects, or what is the same, the experience in which alone they are known (as given objects), must conform to those concepts. In the latter case, the solution becomes more easy, because experience, as a kind of knowledge, requires understanding, and I must therefore, even before objects are given to me, presuppose the rules of the understanding as existing within me *a priori*, these rules being expressed in concepts *a priori*, to which all objects of experience must necessarily conform, and with which they must agree. With regard to objects, so far as they are conceived by reason only, and conceived as necessary, and which can never be given in experience, at least in that form in which they are conceived by reason, we shall find that the attempts at conceiving them (for they must admit of being conceived) will furnish afterwards an excellent test of our new method of thought, according to which we do not know of things anything *a priori* except what we ourselves put into them.

This experiment succeeds as well as we could desire, and promises to metaphysic, in its first part, which deals with concepts *a priori*, of which the corresponding objects may be given in experience, the secure method of a science. For by thus changing our point of view, the possibility of knowledge *a priori* can well be explained, and, what is still more, the laws which *a priori* lie at the foundation of nature, as the sum total of the objects of experience, may be supplied with satisfactory proofs, neither of which was possible with the procedure hitherto adopted. But there arises from this deduction of our faculty of knowing *a priori*, as given in the first part of metaphysic, a somewhat startling result, apparently most detrimental to the objects of metaphysic that have to be treated in the second part, namely, that impossibility of going with it beyond the frontier of possible experience, which is precisely the most essential purpose of metaphysical science. But here we have exactly the experiment which, by disproving the opposite, establishes the truth of our first estimate of the knowledge of reason *a priori*, namely, that it can refer to phenomena only, but must leave the thing by itself as unknown to us, though as existing by itself. For that which impels us necessarily to go beyond the limits of experience and of all phenomena, is the *unconditioned*, which reason postulates in all things by themselves, by necessity and by right, for everything conditioned, so that the series of conditions should thus become complete. If then we find that, under the supposition of our experience conforming to the objects as things by themselves, it is *impossible to conceive* the unconditioned *without contradiction*, while, under the supposition of our representation of things, as they are given to us, not conforming to them as things by themselves, but, on the contrary, of the objects conforming to our mode of representation, that *contradiction vanishes*. Therefore the unconditioned must not be looked for in things, so far as we know them (so far as they are given to us), but only so far as we do not know them (as things by themselves), we clearly perceive that, what we at first assumed tentatively only, is fully confirmed. But, after all progress in the field of the supersensuous has thus been denied to speculative reason, it is still open to us to see, whether in the practical knowledge of reason *data* may not be found which enable us to determine that transcendent concept of the unconditioned which is demanded by reason, in order thus, according to the wish of metaphysic, to get beyond the limits of all possible experience, by means of our knowledge *a priori*, which is possible to us for practical purposes only. In this case, speculative reason has at least gained for us room for such an extension of knowledge, though it had to leave it empty, so that we are not only at liberty, but are really called upon to fill it up, if we are able, by *practical* data of reason.

The very object of the critique of pure speculative reason consists in this attempt at changing the old procedure of metaphysic, and imparting to it the secure method of a science, after having completely revolutionized it, following the example of geometry and physical science. That critique is a treatise on the method (*Traité de la méthode*), not a system of the science itself; but it marks out nevertheless the whole plan of that science, both with regard to its limits, and to its internal organisation. For pure speculative reason has this peculiar advantage that it is able, nay, bound to measure its own powers, according to the different ways in which it chooses its own objects, and to completely enumerate the different ways of choosing problems; thus tracing a complete outline of a system of metaphysic. This is due to the fact that, with regard to the first point, nothing can be attributed to objects in knowl-

edge *a priori*, except what the thinking subject takes from within itself; while, with regard to the second point, reason, so far as its principles of cognition are concerned, forms a separate and independent unity, in which, as in an organic body, every member exists for the sake of all others, and all others exist for the sake of the one, so that no principle can be safely applied in *one relation*, unless it has been carefully examined in *all* its relations, to the whole employment of pure reason. Hence, too, metaphysic has this singular advantage, an advantage which cannot be shared by any other science, in which reason has to deal with objects (for *Logic* deals only with the form of thought in general) that, if it has once attained, by means of this critique, to the secure method of a science, it can completely comprehend the whole field of knowledge pertaining to it, and thus finish its work and leave it to posterity, as a capital that can never be added to, because it has only to deal with principles and the limits of their employment, which are fixed by those principles themselves. And this completeness becomes indeed an obligation, if it is to be a fundamental science, of which we must be able to say, '*nil actum reputans, si quid superesset agendum.*'

But it will be asked, what kind of treasure is it which we mean to bequeath to posterity in this metaphysic of ours, after it has been purified by criticism, and thereby brought to a permanent condition? After a superficial view of this work, it may seem that its advantage is *negative* only, warning us against venturing with speculative reason beyond the limits of experience. Such is no doubt its primary use: but it becomes *positive*, when we perceive that the principles with which speculative reason ventures beyond its limits, lead inevitably, not to an *extension*, but, if carefully considered, to a *narrowing* of the employment of reason, because, by indefinitely extending the limits of sensibility, to which they properly belong, they threaten entirely to supplant the pure (practical) employment of reason. Hence our *critique*, by limiting sensibility to its proper sphere, is no doubt *negative*; but by thus removing an impediment, which threatened to narrow, or even entirely to destroy its practical employment, it is in reality of *positive*, and of very important use, if only we are convinced that there is an absolutely necessary practical use of pure reason (the moral use), in which reason must inevitably go beyond the limits of speculative reason. To deny that this service, which is rendered by criticism, is a *positive* advantage, would be the same as to deny that the police confers upon us any positive advantage, its principal occupation being to prevent violence, which citizens have to apprehend from citizens, so that each may pursue his vocation in peace and security. We had established in the analytical part of our critique the following points:—First, that space and time are only forms of sensuous intuition, therefore conditions of the existence of things, as phenomena only; Secondly, that we have no concepts of the understanding, and therefore nothing whereby we can arrive at the knowledge of things, except in so far as an intuition corresponding to these concepts can be given, and consequently that we cannot have knowledge of any object, as a thing by itself, but only in so far as it is an object of sensuous intuition, that is, a phenomenon. This proves no doubt that all speculative knowledge of reason is limited to objects of *experience*; but it should be carefully borne in mind, that this leaves it perfectly open to us, to *think* the same objects as things by themselves, though we cannot *know* them. For otherwise we should arrive at the absurd conclusion, that there is phenomenal appearance without something that appears. Let us suppose that the necessary distinction, established in our critique, between things as objects of experience and the same time by themselves, had not been made. In that case, the principle of causality, and with it the mechanism of nature, as determined by it, would apply to all things in general, as efficient causes. I should then not be able to say of one and the same being, for instance the human soul, that its will is free, and, at the same time, subject to the necessity of nature, that is, not free, without involving myself in a palpable contradiction: and this because I had taken the soul, in both propositions, in *one and the same sense*, namely, as a thing in general (as something by itself), as, without previous criticism, I could not but take it.

If, however, our criticism was true, in teaching us to take an object in two senses, namely, either as a phenomenon, or as a thing by itself, and if the deduction of our concepts of the understanding was correct, and the principle of causality applies to things only, if taken in the first sense, namely, so far as they are objects of experience, but not to things, if taken in their second sense, we can, without any contradiction, think the same will when phenomenal (in visible actions) as necessarily conforming to the law of nature, and so far, *not free*, and yet, on the other hand, when belonging to a thing by itself, as not subject to that law of nature, and therefore *free*. Now it is quite true that I may not *know* my soul, as a thing by itself, by means of speculative reason (still less through empirical observation), and consequently may not know freedom either, as the quality of a being to which I attribute effects in the world of sense, because, in order to do this, I should have to know such a being as determined in its existence, and yet as not determined in time (which, as I cannot provide my concept with any intuition, is impossible). This, however, does not prevent me from *thinking* freedom; that is, my representation of it contains at least no contradiction within itself if only our critical distinction of the two modes of representation (the sensible and the intelligible), and the consequent limitation of the concepts of the pure understanding, and of the principles based on them, has been properly carried out. If, then, morality necessarily presupposed freedom (in the strictest sense) as a property of our will, producing, as *a priori data* of it, practical principles, belonging originally to our reason, which, without freedom, would be absolutely impossible, while speculative reasons had proved that such a freedom cannot even be thought, the former supposition, namely, the moral one, would necessarily have to yield to another, the opposite of which involves a palpable contradiction, so that *freedom*, and with it morality (for its opposite contains no contradiction, unless freedom is presupposed), would have to make room for the *mechanism* of nature. Now, however, as morality requires nothing but that freedom should only not contradict itself and that, though unable to understand, we should at least be able to think it, there being no reason why freedom should interfere with the natural mechanism of the same act (if only taken in a different sense), the doctrine of morality may well hold its place, and the doctrine of nature may hold its place too, which would have been impossible, if our critique had not previously taught us our inevitable ignorance with regard to things by themselves, and limited everything, which we are able to *know* theoretically, to mere phenomena. The same discussion as to the positive advantage to be derived from the critical principles of pure reason might be repeated with regard to the concept of *God,* and of the *simple nature* of our *soul*; but, for the sake of brevity, I shall pass this by. I am not allowed therefore even to *assume,* for the sake of the necessary practical employment of my reason, *God, freedom,* and *immortality,* if I cannot *deprive* speculative reason of its pretensions to transcendent insights, because reason, in order to arrive at these, must use principles which are intended, originally for objects of possible experience only, and which, if in spite of this, they are applied to what cannot be an object of experience, really changes this into a phenomenon, thus rendering all *practical extension* of pure reason impossible. I had therefore to remove *knowledge,* in order to make room for *belief.* For the dogmatism of metaphysic, that is, the presumption that it is possible to achieve anything in metaphysic without a previous criticism of pure reason, is the source of all that unbelief, which is always very dogmatical, and wars against all morality. . . .

INTRODUCTION

I

THE IDEA OF TRANSCENDENTAL PHILOSOPHY

Experience is no doubt the first product of our understanding, while employed in fashioning the raw material of our sensations. It is therefore our first instruction, and in its progress so rich in new lessons that the chain of all future generations will never be in want of new information that may be gathered on that field. Nevertheless, experience is by no means the only field to which our understanding can be confined. Experience tells us what is, but not that it must be necessarily as it is, and not otherwise. It therefore never gives us any really general truths, and our reason, which is particularly anxious for that class of knowledge, is roused by it rather than satisfied. General truths, which at the same time bear the character of an inward necessity, must be independent of experience,—clear and certain by

themselves. They are therefore called knowledge *a priori*, while what is simply taken from experience is said to be, in ordinary parlance, known *a posteriori* or empirically only.

Now it appears, and this is extremely curious, that even with our experiences different kinds of knowledge are mixed up, which must have their origin *a priori*, and which perhaps serve only to produce a certain connection between our sensuous representations. For even if we remove from experience everything that belongs to the senses, there remain nevertheless certain original concepts, and certain judgments derived from them, which must have had their origin entirely *a priori*, and independent of all experience, because it is owing to them that we are able, or imagine we are able to predicate more of the objects of our senses than can be learnt from mere experience, and that our propositions contain real generality and strict necessity, such as mere empirical knowledge can never supply.

But what is still more extraordinary is this, that certain kinds of knowledge leave the field of all possible experience, and seem to enlarge the sphere of our judgments beyond the limits of experience by means of concepts to which experience can never supply any corresponding objects.

And it is in this very kind of knowledge which transcends the world of the senses, and where experience can neither guide nor correct us, that reason prosecutes its investigations, which by their importance we consider far more excellent and by their tendency far more elevated than anything the understanding can find in the sphere of phenomena. Nay, we risk rather anything, even at the peril of error, than that we should surrender such investigations, either on the ground of their uncertainty, or from any feeling of indifference or contempt.

Now it might seem natural that, after we have left the solid ground of experience, we should not at once proceed to erect an edifice with knowledge which we possess without knowing whence it came, and trust to principles the origin of which is unknown, without having made sure of the safety of the foundations by means of careful examination. It would seem natural, I say, that philosophers should first of all have asked the question how the mere understanding could arrive at all this knowledge *a priori*, and what extent, what truth, and what value it could possess. If we take natural to mean what is just and reasonable, then indeed nothing could be more natural. But if we understand by natural what takes place ordinarily, then, on the contrary, nothing is more natural and more intelligible than that this examination should have been neglected for so long a time. For one part of this knowledge, namely, the mathematical, has always been in possession of perfect trustworthiness; and thus produces a favourable presumption with regard to other parts also, although these may be of a totally different nature. Besides, once beyond the precincts of experience, we are certain that experience can never contradict us, while the charm of enlarging our knowledge is so great that nothing will stop our progress until we encounter a clear contradiction. This can be avoided if only we are cautious in our imaginations, which nevertheless remain what they are, imaginations only. How far we can advance independent of all experience in *a priori* knowledge is shown by the brilliant example of mathematics. It is true they deal with objects and knowledge so far only as they can be represented in intuition. But this is easily overlooked, because that intuition itself may be given *a priori*, and be difficult to distinguish from a pure concept. Thus inspirited by a splendid proof of the power of reason, the desire of enlarging our knowledge sees no limits. The light dove, piercing in her easy flight the air and perceiving its resistance, imagines that flight would be easier still in empty space. It was thus that Plato left the world of sense, as opposing so many hindrances to our understanding, and ventured beyond on the wings of his ideas into the empty space of pure understanding. He did not perceive that he was making no progress by these endeavours, because he had no resistance as a fulcrum on which to rest or to apply his powers, in order to cause the understanding to advance. It is indeed a very common fate of human reason first of all to finish its speculative edifice as soon as possible, and then only to enquire whether the foundation be sure. Then all sorts of excuses are made in order to assure us as to its solidity, or to decline altogether such a late and dangerous enquiry. The reason why during the time of building we feel free from all anxiety and suspicion and believe in the apparent solidity of our foundation, is this:—A great,

perhaps the greatest portion of what our reason finds to do consists in the analysis of our concepts of objects. This gives us a great deal of knowledge which, though it consists in no more than in simplifications and explanations of what is comprehended in our concepts (though in a confused manner), is yet considered as equal, at least in form, to new knowledge. It only separates and arranges our concepts, it does not enlarge them in matter or contents. As by this process we gain a kind of real knowledge *a priori*, which progresses safely and usefully, it happens that our reason, without being aware of it, appropriates under that pretence propositions of a totally different character, adding to given concepts new and strange ones *a priori*, without knowing whence they come, nay without even thinking of such a question. I shall therefore at the very outset treat of the distinction between these two kinds of knowledge.

Of the Distinction between Analytical and Synthetical Judgments

In all judgments in which there is a relation between subject and predicate (I speak of affirmative judgments only, the application to negative ones being easy), that relation can be of two kinds. Either the predicate B belongs to the subject A as something contained (though covertly) in the concept A; or B lies outside the sphere of the concept A, though somehow connected with it. In the former case I call the judgment analytical, in the latter synthetical. Analytical judgments (affirmative) are therefore those in which the connection of the predicate with the subject is conceived through identity, while others in which the connection is conceived without identity, may be called synthetical. The former might be called illustrating, the latter expanding judgments, because in the former nothing is added by the predicate to the concept of the subject, but the concept is only divided into its constituent concepts which were always conceived as existing within it, though confusedly; while the latter add to the concept of the subject a predicate not conceived as existing within it, and not to be extracted from it by any process of mere analysis. If I say, for instance, All bodies are extended, this is an analytical judgment. I need not go beyond the concept connected with the name of body, in order to find that extension is connected with it. I have only to analyse that concept and become conscious of the manifold elements always contained in it, in order to find that predicate. This is therefore an analytical judgment. But if I say, All bodies are heavy, the predicate is something quite different from what I think as the mere concept of body. The addition of such a predicate gives us a synthetical judgment.

It becomes clear from this.

1. That our knowledge is in no way extended by analytical judgments, but that all they effect is to put the concepts which we possess into better order and render them more intelligible.

2. That in synthetical judgments I must have besides the concept of the subject something else (*x*) on which the understanding relies in order to know that a predicate, not contained in the concept, nevertheless belongs to it.

In empirical judgments this causes no difficulty, because that *x* is here simply the complete experience of an object which I conceive by the concept A, that concept forming one part only of my experience. For though I do not include the predicate of gravity in the general concept of body, that concept nevertheless indicates the complete experience through one of its parts, so that I may add other parts also of the same experience, all belonging to that concept. I may first, by an analytical process, realise the concept of body through the predicates of extension, impermeability, form, etc., all of which are contained in it. Afterwards I expand my knowledge, and looking back to the experience from which my concept of body was abstracted, I find gravity always connected with the before-mentioned predicates. Experience therefore is the *x* which lies beyond the concept A, and on which rests the possibility of a synthesis of the predicate of gravity B with the concept A.

In synthetical judgments *a priori*, however, that help is entirely wanting. If I want to go beyond the concept A in order to find another concept B connected with it, where is there anything on which I may rest and through which a synthesis might become possible, considering that I cannot have the advantage of looking about in the field of experience? Take the proposition that all which happens has its cause. In the concept of something that happens I no doubt conceive of something ex-

isting preceded by time, and from this certain analytical judgments may be deduced. But the concept of cause is entirely outside that concept, and indicates something different from that which happens, and is by no means contained in that representation. How can I venture then to predicate of that which happens, something totally different from it, and to represent the concept of cause, though not contained in it, as belonging to it, and belonging to it by necessity? What is here the unknown *x*, on which the understanding may rest in order to find beyond the concept A a foreign predicate B, which nevertheless is believed to be connected with it? It cannot be experience, because the proposition that all which happens has its cause represents this second predicate as added to the subject not only with greater generality than experience can ever supply, but also with a character of necessity, and therefore purely *a priori*, and based on concepts. All our speculative knowledge *a priori* aims at and rests on such synthetical, i.e. expanding propositions, for the analytical are no doubt very important and necessary, yet only in order to arrive at that clearness of concepts which is requisite for a safe and wide synthesis, serving as a really new addition to what we possess already.

We have here a certain mystery before us, which must be cleared up before any advance into the unlimited field of a pure knowledge of the understanding can become safe and trustworthy. We must discover on the largest scale the ground of the possibility of synthetical judgments *a priori*; we must understand the conditions which render every class of them possible, and endeavour not only to indicate in a sketchy outline, but to define in its fulness and practical completeness, the whole of that knowledge, which forms a class by itself, systematically arranged according to its original sources, its divisions, its extent and its limits. So much for the present with regard to the peculiar character of synthetical judgments.

It will now be seen how there can be a special science serving as a critique of pure reason. Every kind of knowledge is called pure, if not mixed with anything heterogeneous. But more particularly is that knowledge called absolutely pure, which is not mixed up with an experience or sensation, and is therefore possible entirely *a priori*. Reason is the faculty which supplies the principles of knowledge *a priori*. Pure reason therefore is that faculty which supplies the principles of knowing anything entirely *a priori*. An Organum of pure reason ought to comprehend all the principles by which pure knowledge *a priori* can be acquired and fully established. A complete application of such an Organum would give us a System of Pure Reason. But as that would be a difficult task, and as at present it is still doubtful whether and when such an expansion of our knowledge is here possible, we may look on a mere criticism of pure reason, its sources and limits, as a kind of preparation for a complete system of pure reason. Its usefulness would be negative only, serving for a purging rather than for an expansion of our reason, and, what after all is a considerable gain, guarding reason against errors.

I call all knowledge *transcendental* which is occupied not so much with objects, as with our *a priori* concepts of objects. A system of such concepts might be called Transcendental Philosophy. But for the present this is again too great an undertaking. We should have to treat therein completely both of analytical knowledge, and of synthetical knowledge *a priori,* which is more than we intend to do, being satisfied to carry on the analysis so far only as is indispensably necessary in order to recognise in their whole extent the principles of synthesis *a priori*, which alone concern us. This investigation which should be called a transcendental critique, but not a systematic doctrine, is all we are occupied with at present. It is not meant to extend our knowledge, but only to rectify it, and to become the test of the value of all *a priori* knowledge. Such a critique therefore is a preparation for a New Organum, or, if that should not be possible, for a Canon at least, according to which hereafter a complete system of a philosophy of pure reason, whether it serve for an expansion or merely for a limitation of it, may be carried out, both analytically and synthetically. That such a system is possible, nay that it need not be so comprehensive as to prevent the hope of its completion, may be gathered from the fact that it would have to deal, not with the nature of things, which is endless, but with the understanding which judges of the nature of things, and this again so far only as its knowledge *a priori* is concerned. Whatever the understanding possesses *a priori*, as it has not to be looked for without, can

hardly escape our notice, nor is there any reason to suppose that it will prove too extensive for a complete inventory, and for such a valuation as shall assign to it its true merits or demerits.

II

DIVISION OF TRANSCENDENTAL PHILOSOPHY

Transcendental Philosophy is with us an idea (of a science) only, for which the critique of pure reason should trace, according to fixed principles, an architectonic plan, guaranteeing the completeness and certainty of all parts of which the building consists. (It is a system of all principles of pure reason.) The reason why we do not call such a critique a transcendental philosophy in itself is simply this, that in order to be a complete system, it ought to contain likewise a complete analysis of the whole of human knowledge *a priori*. It is true that our critique must produce a complete list of all the fundamental concepts which constitute pure knowledge. But it need not give a detailed analysis of these concepts, nor a complete list of all derivative concepts. Such an analysis would be out of place, because it is not beset with the doubts and difficulties which are inherent in synthesis, and which alone necessitate a critique of pure reason. Nor would it answer our purpose to take the responsibility of the completeness of such an analysis, however, and the derivation from such *a priori* concepts as we shall have to deal with presently, may easily be supplied, if only they have first been laid down as perfect principles of synthesis, and nothing is wanting to them in that respect.

All that constitutes transcendental philosophy belongs to the critique of pure reason, nay it is the complete idea of transcendental philosophy, but not yet the whole of that philosophy itself, because it carries the analysis so far only as is requisite for a complete examination of synthetical knowledge *a priori*.

The most important consideration in the arrangement of such a science is that no concepts should be admitted which contain anything empirical, and that the *a priori* knowledge shall be perfectly pure. Therefore, although the highest principles of morality and their fundamental concepts are *a priori* knowledge, they do not belong to transcendental philosophy, because the concepts of pleasure and pain, desire, inclination, free-will, etc., which are all of empirical origin, must here be presupposed. Transcendental philosophy is the wisdom of pure speculative reason. Everything practical, so far as it contains motives, has reference to sentiments, and these belong to empirical sources of knowledge.

If we wish to carry out a proper division of our science systematically, it must contain first *a doctrine of the elements,* secondly, *a doctrine of the method* of pure reason. Each of these principal divisions will have its subdivisions, the grounds of which cannot however be explained here. So much only seems necessary for previous information, that there are two stems of human knowledge, which perhaps may spring from a common root, unknown to us, viz. *sensibility* and the *understanding*, objects being given by the former and thought by the latter. If our sensibility should contain *a priori* representations, constituting conditions under which alone objects can be given, it would belong to transcendental philosophy, and the doctrine of this transcendental sense-perception would necessarily form the first part of the doctrine of elements, because the conditions under which alone objects of human knowledge can be given must precede those under which they are thought. . . .

Results of this Deduction of the Concepts of the Understanding

We cannot *think* any object except by means of the categories; we cannot *know* any subject that has been thought, except by means of intuitions, corresponding to those concepts. Now all our intuitions are sensuous, and this knowledge, so far as its object is given, is empirical. But empirical knowledge is experience, and therefore no *knowledge a priori* is possible to us, except of *objects* of possible *experience* only.

This knowledge, however, though limited to objects of experience, is not, therefore, entirely derived from experience, for both the pure intuitions and the pure concepts of the understanding are elements of knowledge which exist in us *a priori*. Now there are only two ways in which a necessary harmony of experience with the concepts of its objects can be conceived; either experience makes these concepts possible or these concepts make experience possible. The former will not hold good with respect to the categories (nor with pure sensuous intuition), for they are concepts *a priori*, and therefore independent of experience. To ascribe to them an empirical origin, would be to admit a kind of *generatio aequivoca*. There remains, therefore, the second alternative only (a kind of system of the *epigenesis* of pure reason), namely, that the categories, on the part of the understanding, contain the grounds of the possibility of all experience in general. How they render experience possible, and what principles of the possibility of experience they supply in their employment on phenomena, will be shown more fully in the following chapter on the transcendental employment of the faculty of judgment.

Some one might propose to adopt a middle way between the two, namely, that the categories are neither *self-produced* first principles *a priori* of our knowledge, nor derived from experience, but subjective dispositions of thought, implanted in us with our existence, and so arranged by our Creator that their employment should accurately agree with the laws of nature, which determine experience (a kind of *system of preformation* of pure reason). But, in that case, not only would there be no end of such an hypothesis, so that no one could know how far the supposition of predetermined dispositions to future judgments might be carried, but there is this decided objection against that middle course that, by adopting it, the categories would lose that necessity which is essential to them. Thus the concept of cause, which asserts, under a presupposed condition, the necessity of an effect, would become false, if it rested only on some subjective necessity implanted in us of connecting certain empirical representations according to the rule of causal relation. I should not be able to say that the effect is connected with the cause in the object (that is, by necessity), but only, I am so constituted that I cannot think these representations as connected in any other way. This is exactly what the sceptic most desires, for in that case all our knowledge, resting on the supposed objective validity of our judgments, is nothing but mere illusion, nor would there be wanting people to say they know nothing of such subjective necessity (which can only be felt); and at all events we could not quarrel with anybody about what depends only on the manner in which his own subject is organised. . . .

Of the Pure Concepts of the Understanding, or of the Categories

General logic, as we have often said, takes no account of the contents of our knowledge, but expects that representations will come from elsewhere in order to be turned into concepts by an analytical process. Transcendental logic, on the contrary, has before it the manifold contents of sensibility *a priori*, supplied by transcendental aesthetic as the material for the concepts of the pure understanding, without which those concepts would be without any contents, therefore entirely empty. It is true that space and time contain what is manifold in the pure intuition *a priori*, but they belong also to the conditions of the receptivity of our mind under which alone it can receive representations of objects and which therefore must affect the concepts of them also. The spontaneity of our thought requires that what is manifold in the pure intuition should first be in a certain way examined, received, and connected, in order to produce a knowledge of it. This act I call *synthesis*.

In its most general sense, I understand by synthesis the act of arranging different representations together and of comprehending what is manifold in them under one form of knowledge. Such a synthesis is pure, if the manifold is not given empirically, but *a priori* (as in time and space). Before we can proceed to an analysis of our representations, these must first be given, and as far as their contents are concerned, no concepts can arise analytically. Knowledge is first produced by the synthesis of what is manifold (whether given empirically or *a priori*). That knowledge may at first be crude and confused and in need of analysis, but it is synthesis which really collects the elements of knowledge, and unites them to a certain extent. It is therefore the first thing which we have to consider, if we want to form an opinion on the first origin of our knowledge.

We shall see hereafter that synthesis in general is the mere result of what I call the faculty of imagination, a blind but indispen-sable function of the soul, without which we should have no knowledge whatsoever, but of the existence of which we are scarcely conscious. But to reduce this synthesis to concepts is a function that belongs to the understanding, and by which the understanding supplies us for the first time with knowledge properly so called. . . .

By means of analysis different representations are brought under one concept, a task treated of in general logic; but how to bring, not the representations, but the pure synthesis of representations, under concepts, that is what transcendental logic means to teach. The first that must be given us *a priori* for the sake of knowledge of all objects, is the manifold in pure intuition. The second is, the synthesis of the manifold by means of imagination. but this does not yet produce true knowledge. The concepts which impart unity to this pure synthesis and consist entirely in the representation of this necessary synthetical unity, add the third contribution towards the knowledge of an object, and rest on the understanding.

The same function which imparts unity to various representations in one judgment imparts unity likewise to the mere synthesis of various representations in one intuition, which in a general way may be called the pure concept of the understanding. The same understanding, and by the same operations by which in concepts it achieves through analytical unity the logical form of a judgment, introduces also, through the synthetical unity of the manifold in intuition, a transcendental element into its representations. They are therefore called pure concepts of the understanding, and they refer *a priori* to objects, which would be quite impossible in general logic.

In this manner there arise exactly so many pure concepts of the understanding which refer *a priori* to objects of intuition in general, as there were in our table logical functions in all possible judgments, because those functions completely exhaust the understanding, and comprehend every one of its faculties. Borrowing a term of Aristotle, we shall call these concepts *categories*, our intention being originally the same as his, though widely diverging from it in its practical application.

TABLE OF CATEGORIES

I

Of Quantity
Unity
Plurality
Totality

II

Of Quality
Reality
Negation
Limitation

III

Of Relation
Inherence and Subsistence
(*Substantia et accidens*)
Causality and Depend-
ence (cause and effect)
Community (reciprocity
between the active and the
passive)

IV

Of Modality

Possibility
Existence
Necessity

Impossibility
Non-existence
Contingency

This then is a list of all original pure concepts
of synthesis, which belong to the understanding
a priori.

Prolegomena to Any Future Metaphysic

INTRODUCTION

There are learned men, to whom the history of philosophy (both ancient and modern) is philosophy itself; for such the present Prolegomena are not written. They must wait till those who endeavor to draw from the fountain of reason itself have made out their case; it will then be the historians' turn to inform the world of what has been done. Moreover, nothing can be said, which in their opinion has not been said already, and indeed this may be applied as an infallible prediction to all futurity; for as the human reason has for many centuries pursued with ardour infinitely various objects in various ways, it is hardly to be expected that we should not be able to match every new thing with some old thing not unlike it.

My object is to persuade all who think Metaphysics worth studying, that it is absolutely necessary to adjourn for the present this (historical) labour, to consider all that has been done as undone, and to start first of all with the question, 'Whether such a thing as metaphysic be at all possible?'

If it be a science, how comes it that it cannot, like other sciences, obtain for itself an universal and permanent recognition? If not, how is it ever making constant pretensions, under this supposition, and keeping the human mind in suspense with hopes that never fade, and yet are never fulfilled? Whether then, as a result, we demonstrate our knowledge or our ignorance, we must come once for all to a definite conclusion about the nature of this pretended science, which cannot possibly remain on its present footing. It seems almost ridiculous, while every other science is continually advancing, that in this, which would be very Wisdom, at whose oracle all men inquire, we should perpetually revolve round the same point, without gaining a single step. And so its followers having melted away, we do not find men who feel able to shine in other sciences venturing their reputation here, where everybody, however ignorant in other matters, pretends to deliver a final verdict, as in this domain there is as yet no certain weight and measure to distinguish sound knowledge from shallow talk.

But after long elaboration of a science, when men begin to wonder how far it has advanced, it is not without precedent that the question should at last occur, whether and how such a science be even possible? For the human reason is so constructive, that it has already several times built up a tower, and then razed it to examine the nature of the foundation. It is never too late to mend; but if the change comes late, there is always more difficulty in setting it going.

The question whether a science be possible, presupposes a doubt as to its actuality. But such a doubt offends the men whose whole possessions consist of this supposed jewel; hence he who raises the doubt must expect opposition from all sides. Some, in the proud consciousness of their possessions, which are ancient, and therefore considered legitimate, will take their metaphysical compendia in their hands, and look down on him with contempt; others, who never see anything except it be identical with what they have seen before, will not understand him, and everything will remain for a time, as if nothing had happened to excite the concern, or the hope, for an impending change.

Nevertheless, I venture to predict that the

independent reader of these Prolegomena will not only doubt his previous science, but ultimately be fully persuaded, that it cannot exist without satisfying the demands here stated, on which its possibility depends; and, as this has never been done, that there is, as yet, no such thing as Metaphysic. But as it can never cease to be in demand—

'Rusticus expectat, dum defluat amnis, at ille
Labitur et labetur in omne volubilis aevum;'—

since the interests of mankind are interwoven with it so intimately, he must confess that a radical reform, or rather a new birth of the science after an original plan, must be unavoidably at hand, however men may struggle against it for a while.

Since the Essays of Locke and Leibnitz, or rather since the origin of metaphysic so far as we know its history, nothing has ever happened which might have been more decisive to the fortunes of the science than the attack made upon it by David Hume. He threw no light on this species of knowledge, but he certainly struck a spark from which light might have been obtained, had it caught a proper substance to nurture and develop the flame.

Hume started chiefly from a single but important concept in Metaphysic—that of Cause and Effect (including the deduced notions of action and power). He calls on reason, which pretends to have generated this notion from itself, to answer him with what right it thinks anything to be so constituted, that if granted, something else must necessarily be granted thereby; for this is the meaning of the concept of cause. He demonstrated irresistibly that it was perfectly impossible for reason to think such a combination by means of concepts and *a priori*—a combination that contains necessity. We cannot at all see why, in consequence of the existence of one thing, another must necessarily exist, or how the concept of one thing, another must necessarily exist, or how the concept of such a combination can arise *a priori*. Hence he inferred, that reason was altogether deluded by this concept, which it considered erroneously as one of its children, whereas in reality the concept was nothing but the bastard offspring of the imagination, impregnated by experience, and so bringing certain representations under the Law of Association. The subjective necessity, that is, the custom which so arises, is then substituted for an objective necessity from real knowledge. Hence he inferred that reason had no power to think such combinations, even generally, because its concepts would then be mere inventions, and all its pretended *a priori* cognitions nothing but common experiences marked with a false stamp. In plain language there is not, and cannot be, any such thing as metaphysic at all. This conclusion, however hasty and mistaken, was at least founded upon investigation, and the investigation deserved to have suggested to the brighter spirits of his day a combined attempt at a happy solution of the problem proposed by him, if such solution were possible. Thus a complete reform of the science must have resulted.

But the perpetual hard fate of metaphysic would not allow him to be understood. We cannot without a certain sense of pain consider how utterly his opponents, Reid, Oswald, Beattie, and even Priestley, missed the point of the problem. For while they were ever assuming as conceded what he doubted, and demonstrating with eagerness and often with arrogance what he never thought of disputing, they so overlooked his indication towards a better state of things, that everything remained undisturbed in its old condition.

The question was not whether the concept of cause was right, useful, and even indispensable with regard to our knowledge of nature, for this Hume had never doubted. But the question to which Hume expected an answer was this, whether that concept could be thought by reason *a priori*, and whether it consequently possesses an inner truth, independent of all experience, and therefore applied more widely than to the mere objects of experience. It was surely a question concerning the *origin*, not concerning the *indispensable use* of the concept. Had the former question been determined, the conditions of the use and valid application of the concept would have been given *ipso facto*.

But the opponents of the greater thinker should have probed very deeply into the nature of reason, so far as it concerns pure thinking, if they would satisfy the conditions of the problem—a task which did not suit them. They therefore discovered a more convenient means of putting on a bold face without any proper insight into the question, by appealing to the *common sense of mankind.* It is indeed a great gift of God, to possess right, or (as they now call it) plain common sense. But this common sense must be shown practically, by well-considered and reasonable thoughts and words, not by appealing to it as an oracle, when you can advance nothing rational in justification of yourself. To appeal to common sense, when insight and science fail, and no sooner—this is one of the subtle discoveries of modern times, by means of which the most vapid babbler can safely enter the lists with the most thorough-going thinker, and hold his own. But as long as a particle of insight remains, no one would think of having recourse to this subterfuge. For what is it, but an appeal to the opinion of the multitude, of whose applause the philosopher is ashamed, while the popular and superficial man glories and confides in it? I should think Hume might fairly have laid as much claim to sound sense as Beattie, and besides to a critical understanding (such as the latter did not possess), which keeps common sense within such limits as to prevent it from speculating, or, if it does speculate, keeps it from wishing to decide when it cannot satisfy itself concerning its own principles. By this means alone can common sense remain sound sense. Chisels and hammers may suffice to work a piece of wood, but for steel-engraving we require a special instrument. Thus common sense and speculative understanding are each serviceable in their own way, the former in judgments which apply immediately to experience, the latter when we judge universally from mere concepts, as in metaphysic, where that which calls itself (often *per antiphrasin*) sound common sense has no right to judge at all.

I honestly confess, the suggestion of David Hume was the very thing, which many years ago first interrupted my dogmatic slumber, and gave my investigations in the field of speculative philosophy quite a new direction. I am far from following him in all his conclusions, which only resulted from his regarding not the whole of his problem, but a part, which by itself can give us no information. If we start from a well-founded, but undeveloped, thought, which another has bequeathed to us, we may well hope by continued reflection to advance farther than the acute man, to whom we owe the first spark of light.

I therefore first tried whether Hume's objec-

tion could not be put into a general form, and soon found that the concept of the connexion of cause and effect was by no means the only one by which the understanding thinks the connexion of things *a priori*, but rather that metaphysic consists altogether of such connexions. I sought to make certain of their number, and when I had succeeded in this to my expectation, by starting from a single principle, I proceeded to the deduction of these concepts, which I was now certain were not deduced from experience, as Hume had apprehended, but sprang from the pure understanding. This deduction, which seemed impossible to my acute predecessor, which had never even occurred to any one else, though they were all using the concepts unsuspiciously without questioning the basis of their objective validity —this deduction was the most difficult task ever undertaken in aid of metaphysic. More especially, no existing metaphysic could assist me in the least, because this deduction must prove the very possibility of metaphysic. But as soon as I had succeeded in solving Hume's problem not merely in a particular case, but with respect to the whole faculty of pure reason. I could proceed safely, though slowly, to determine the whole sphere of pure reason completely and from general principles, in its bounds, as well as in its contents. This was what metaphysic required, in order to construct its system safely.

But I fear that the *carrying out* of Hume's problem in its widest extent (see my Critique of the Pure Reason) will fare as the *problem* itself fared, when first proposed. It will be misjudged because it is misunderstood, and misunderstood because men choose to skim through the book, and not to *think* through it—a disagreeable task, because the work is dry, obscure, opposed to all ordinary notions, and moreover voluminous. I confess, however, I did not expect to hear from philosophers complaints of want of popularity, entertainment, and facility, when the existence of a highly esteemed and to us indispensable cognition is at stake, which cannot be established otherwise than by the strictest rules of scholastic accuracy. Popularity may follow, but is inadmissible at the commencement. Yet as regards a certain obscurity, arising partly from the extent of the plan, in which the principal points of the investigation cannot be easily gathered into view, the complaint is partly just, and I intend to remove it by the present Prolegomena.

The work which represents the pure faculty of reason in its whole compass and bounds will always remain the groundwork to which the Prolegomena, as a preliminary exercise, refer; for we must have that Critique completed as a science, systematically, in its minutest details, before we can think of letting Metaphysics appear on the scene, or even have the most distant hope of attaining it.

We have been long accustomed to seeing antiquated knowledge produced as new by being taken out of its former context, and fitted into a suit of any fancy pattern under new titles. Most readers will set out by expecting nothing else from the Critique; but these Prolegomena may persuade him that it is a perfectly new science, of which no one has ever even thought, the very idea of which was unknown, and for which nothing hitherto accomplished can be of the smallest use, except it be the indication suggested by Hume's doubts. Yet even he did not suspect such a formal science, but ran his ship ashore, for safety's sake, on scepticism, there to let it lie and rot; whereas my object is rather to give it a pilot, who, by means of safe astronomical principles drawn from a knowledge of the globe, and provided with a complete chart and compass, may steer the ship safely, whither he listeth.

If we proceed to a perfectly isolated and peculiar new science, with the presupposition that we can judge it by means of a supposed science that has been already acquired, whereas the reality of this latter must be first of all thoroughly questioned—if we do this, it will make men think they merely recognize old knowledge. For the terms are similar, with this difference, that everything must appear distorted, absurd, and unintelligible, because men start from a mental attitude not the author's, but their own, which through long habit has become a second nature. But the voluminous character of the work, so far as it depends on the subject, and not the exposition, its consequent unavoidable dryness, and its scholastic accuracy—these are qualities which can only benefit the science, though they may damage the book.

Few writers are gifted with the subtlety, and at the same time with the grace of David Hume,

or with the depth, as well as the elegance, of Moses Mendelssohn. Yet I flatter myself I might have made my own exposition popular, had my object been merely to sketch out a plan, and leave its completion to others, instead of having my heart in the welfare of the science that I had so long pursued; in truth, it required no little constancy, and even self-denial, to postpone the sweets of an immediate success to the prospect of a slower, but more lasting reputation.

Making plans is often the occupation of a luxurious and boastful mind, which thus obtains the reputation of a creative genius, by demanding what it cannot itself supply; by censuring, what it cannot improve; and by proposing, what it knows not where to find. And yet something more should belong to a sound plan of a general Critique of the Pure Reason than mere conjectures, if this plan is to be other than the usual declamation of pious aspirations. But pure reason is a sphere so separate and self-contained, that we cannot touch a part without affecting all the rest. We can therefore do nothing without first determining the position of each part, and its relation to the rest; for, as our judgment cannot be corrected by anything without, the validity and use of every part depends upon the relation in which it stands to all the rest within reason.

So in the structure of an organized body, the end of each member can only be deduced from the full conception of the whole. It may, then, be said of such a Critique, that it is never trustworthy except it be *perfectly complete,* down to the smallest elements of the reason. In the sphere of this faculty you can determine either *everything* or *nothing.*

But altogether a mere sketch, preceding the Critique of Pure Reason, would be unintelligible, unreliable and useless, it is all the more useful as a sequel. For so we are able to grasp the whole, to examine in detail the chief points of importance in the science, and to improve in many respects our exposition, as compared with the first execution of the work.

Such is the plan sketched out in the following pages, which, after the completion of the work, may be carried out *analytically,* though the work itself must absolutely be executed in the *synthetical* method, in order that the science may present all its articulations, as the structure of a peculiar cognitive faculty, in their natural combination. But should any reader find this plan, which I publish as the Prolegomena to any future Metaphysics, itself difficult, let him consider that every one is not bound to study Metaphysics, that there are many minds which succeed very well, in genuine and even deep sciences more closely allied to intuition, while they cannot succeed in investigations proceeding only by means of abstract concepts. In such cases men should apply their talents to other subjects. But he that undertakes to judge, or still more to construct a system of Metaphysics, must satisfy the demands here made, either by adopting my solution, or by thoroughly refuting it, and substituting another. To evade it is impossible.

In conclusion, let it be remembered that this much-abused obscurity—a very common cloak for men's own laziness or stupidity—has its uses, since all who in other sciences observe a prudent silence, in this speak authoritatively, and decide boldly, because their ignorance is not here contrasted with the knowledge of others. . . .

This is the proper place to remove Hume's difficulty. He justly maintains, that we can by no means see by reason the possibility of Causality, that is, of the reference of the existence of one thing to the existence of another, which is necessitated by the former. I add, that we comprehend just as little the concept of Subsistence, that is, the necessity that at the foundation of the existence of things there lies a subject which cannot itself be a predicate of any other thing; nay, we cannot even form a notion of the possibility of such a thing (though we can point out examples of its use in experience). The very same incomprehensibility affects the Community of things, as we cannot comprehend how from the state of one thing an inference to the state of quite another thing beyond it, and *vice versa*, can be drawn, and how substances which have each their own separate existence should depend upon one another necessarily. But I am very far from holding these concepts to be derived merely from experience, and the necessity represented in them, to be imaginary and a mere illusion produced in us by long habit. On the contrary, I have amply shown, that the principles [derived] from them are firmly established *a*

priori, or before all experience, and have their undoubted objective value, though only with regard to experience.

I have indeed no notion of such a connexion of things in themselves, that they can either exist as substances, or act as causes, or stand in community with others (as parts of a real whole), and I can just as little conceive such properties in phenomena as such, because those concepts contain nothing that lies in the phenomena, but what the understanding alone must think. But we have a concept of such connexion of representations in our understanding, and in judgments generally—a concept that representations appear in one sort of judgments as subject in relation to predicate, in another as reason in relation to consequence, and in a third as parts, which constitute together a total possible cognition. Besides we cognise *a priori* that without considering the representation of an object as determined in some of these respects, we can have no valid cognition of the object, and, if we should occupy ourselves about the object *per se*, there is no possible attribute, by which I could know that it is determined under any of these aspects, that is, under the concept either of substance, or of cause, or (in relation to other substances) of community, for I have no notion of the possibility of such a connexion of existence [*per se*]. But the question is not how things in themselves, but how the empirical cognition of things is determined, as regards the above aspects of judgments in general, that is, how things, as objects of experience, can and shall be subsumed under these concepts of the understanding. And then it is clear, that I completely comprehend not only the possibility, but also the necessity of subsuming all phenomena under these concepts, that is, of using them for principles of the possibility of experience.

Let us make an experiment with Hume's problematical concept (his *crux metaphysicorum*), the concept of cause. In the first place I am given *a priori*, by means of logic, the form of a conditional judgment in general, that is, one given cognition as antecedent and another as consequent. But it is possible, that in perception we may meet with a rule of relation, which runs thus: that a certain phenomenon is constantly followed by another (though not conversely), and this is a case for me to use the hypothetical judgment, and, for instance, to say, if the sun shines long enough upon a body, it grows warm. Here there is indeed as yet no necessity of connexion, or concept of cause. But I proceed and say, that if the [above] proposition, which is merely a subjective connexion of perceptions, is to be a judgment of experience, it must be considered as necessary and universally valid. Such a proposition would be, 'the sun is by its light the cause of heat.' The empirical rule is now considered as a law, and as valid not merely of phenomena, but valid of them for the purposes of a possible experience which requires thoroughly and therefore necessarily valid rules. I therefore easily comprehend the concept of cause, as a concept necessarily belonging to the mere form of experience, and its possibility as a synthetical union of perceptions in consciousness generally; but I do not at all comprehend the possibility of a thing generally as a cause, because the concept of cause denotes a condition not at all belonging to things, but to experience. It is nothing in fact but an objectively valid cognition of phenomena and of their succession, so far as the antecedent can be conjoined with the consequent according to the rule of hypothetical judgments.

Hence to the pure concepts of the understanding, if they quit objects of experience and would refer to things in themselves, (*noumena*) have no signification whatever. They serve, as it were, only to spell phenomena, that we may be able to read them as experience; the principles which arise from their reference to the sensible world, only serve our understanding for empirical use. Beyond this they are arbitrary combinations, without objective reality, and we can neither cognise their possibility *a priori*, nor verify their reference to objects or make it intelligible by any example; because examples can be borrowed from some possible experience, consequently the objects of these concepts can be found nowhere but in a possible experience.

This complete (though to its originator unexpected) solution of Hume's problem preserves therefore to the pure concepts of the understanding their *a priori* origin, and to the universal laws of nature their validity, as laws of the understanding, yet so that their use is limited to experience, because their possibility depends solely on the reference of the understanding to experience; but not by deriving them from experience, but by deriving it from

them, a completely reversed mode of connexion which never occurred to Hume.

This is therefore the result of all our foregoing inquiries: all synthetical principles *a priori* are nothing more than principles of possible experience, and can never be referred to things in themselves, but to phenomena as objects of experience. And hence pure mathematic as well as pure physic can never be referred to anything more than mere phenomena, and can only represent either that which makes experience generally possible, or else that which, as it is derived from these principles, must always be capable of being represented in some possible experience. . . .

SECOND PART OF THE GENERAL TRANSCENDENTAL PROBLEM

How is the Pure Science of Nature possible?

Nature is the *existence* of things, so far as it is determined according to universal laws. Should nature signify the existence of things *in themselves,* we could never cognise nature either *a priori* or *a posteriori.* Not *a priori,* for how can we know what belongs to things in themselves, since this never can be done by the dissection of our concepts (analytical judgments)? For we do not want to know what is contained in our concept of a thing (for this [content] belongs to its logical being), but what is in the actuality of the thing superadded to our concept, and by what the thing itself is determined in its existence outside the concept. Our understanding, and the conditions on which alone it can connect the determinations of things in their existence, do not prescribe any rule to things themselves; these do not conform to our understanding, but it must conform itself to them; they must therefore be first given us in order to gather these determinations from them, wherefore they would not be cognised *a priori.*

A cognition of the nature of things in themselves *a posteriori* would be equally impossible. For, if experience is to teach us *laws,* to which the existence of things is subject, these laws, if they regard things in themselves, must belong to them *of necessity* even outside our experience. But experience teaches us what exists and how it exists, but never that it must necessarily exist so and not otherwise. Experience therefore can never teach us the nature of things in themselves. . . .

How is Nature itself possible?

This question—the highest point that transcendental philosophy can ever reach, and to which, as its boundary and completion, it must proceed—properly contains two [subordinate] questions.

First: How is nature at all possible in the *material* sense, as to intuition, [I mean nature] considered as the complex of phenomena; how are space, time, and that which fills both—the object of sensation, in general possible? The answer is: By means of the constitution of our Sensibility, according to which it is specifically affected by objects, which are in themselves unknown to it, and totally distinct from those phenomena. This answer is given in the *Critique* itself in the transcendental Aesthetic, and in these *Prolegomena* by the solution of the first general problem.

Secondly: How is nature possible in the formal sense, nature as the complex of the rules, under which all phenomena must come, in order to be thought as connected in experience? The answer must be this: It is only possible by means of the constitution of our Understanding, according to which all the above representations of the sensibility are necessarily referred to a consciousness, and by which the peculiar way in which we think (that is, by rules), and hence experience also, are possible, but must be clearly distinguished from an insight into the objects in themselves. This answer is given in the *Critique* itself in the transcendental Logic, and in these *Prolegomena,* in the course of the solution of the second main problem.

But how this peculiar property of our sensibility itself is possible, or that of our understanding and of the apperception which is necessarily its basis and that of all thinking—this cannot be further resolved or answered, because we require these [faculties] for all our answers and for all our thinking about objects.

There are many laws of nature, which we can only know by means of experience; but conformity to law in the connexion of phenomena, that is, nature in general, we cannot discover by any experience, because experience itself requires laws, which are *a priori* at the basis of

its possibility.

The possibility of experience in general is therefore at the same time the universal law of nature, and the principles of the former (experience) are the very laws of the latter (nature). For we do not know nature but as the complex of the phenomena, that is, of representations in us, and hence can only derive the laws of its connexion from the principles of their connexion in us, that is, from the conditions of their necessary union in consciousness, which union constitutes the possibility of experience.

Even the main proposition expounded throughout this section—that universal laws of nature can be distinctly cognised *a priori*—leads naturally to the proposition: that the highest legislation of nature must lie in ourselves (that is, in our understanding), and that we must not seek the universal laws of nature in nature by means of experience, but conversely must seek nature, as to its universal conformity to law, in the conditions of the possibility of experience, which lie in our sensibility and in our understanding. For how were it otherwise possible to know *a priori* these laws, as they are not rules of analytical cognition, but really synthetical extensions of it? Such a necessary agreement of the principles of possible experience with the laws of the possibility of nature, can only proceed from one of two reasons: either these laws are drawn from nature by means of experience, or conversely nature is derived from the laws of the possibility of experience in general, and is quite the same as the mere universal conformity to law of the latter. The former is self-contradictory, for the universal laws of nature can and must be cognised *a priori* (that is, independent of all experience), and be the foundation of all empirical use of the understanding; the latter alternative therefore alone remains.

But we must distinguish the empirical laws of nature, which always presuppose particular perceptions, from the pure or universal laws of nature, which, without being based on particular perceptions, contain merely the conditions of their necessary union in experience. In relation to the latter, nature and *possible* experience are quite the same, and as the conformity to law here depends upon the necessary connexion of phenomena in experience (without which we cannot cognise any object whatever in the sensible world), consequently upon the original laws of the understanding, it seems at first strange, but is not the less certain, to says as regards the latter: *The understanding does not draw its laws (a priori) from nature, but prescribes them to it.*

We shall illustrate this apparently daring proposition by an example which will show that laws, which we discover in objects of sensuous intuition (especially when these laws are cognised as necessary), are commonly held to be such as the understanding has placed in them, though they are similar in all points to the laws of nature, which we ascribe to experience.

If we consider the properties of the circle, by which this figure unites so many arbitrary determinations of space in itself, and therefore in a universal rule, we cannot avoid attributing a nature to this geometrical thing. Two right lines, for example, which intersect one another and the circle, however they may be drawn, are always divided so that the rectangle under the segments of the one is equal to that under the segments of the other. The question now is: Does this law lie in the circle or in the understanding? Does this figure, independently of the understanding, contain in itself the ground of the law, or does the understanding, having constructed according to its concepts (according to the equality of the radii) the figure itself, introduce into it this law of the chords cutting one another in geometrical proportion? When we follow the proofs of this law, we soon perceive, that it can only be derived from the condition on which the understanding founds the construction of this figure, and which is that of the equality of the radii. But, if we enlarge this concept, to pursue further the unity of various properties of geometrical figures under common laws, and consider the circle as a conic section, which of course is subject to the same fundamental conditions of construction as other conic sections, we shall find, that all the chords, which intersect within the ellipse, parabola, and hyperbola, always intersect so that the rectangles under their segments are not indeed equal, but always bear a constant ratio to one another [the directions of the chords being fixed]. If we proceed still farther, to the fundamental laws of physical astronomy, we find a physical law of reciprocal attraction diffused over all material nature, the rule of which attraction is: 'that it decreases inversely as the square of the distance

from each attracting point, that is, as the spherical surfaces, over which this power diffuses itself—increase,' which law seems to be necessarily inherent in the very nature of things, and hence is usually propounded as cognisable *a priori*. Simple as the sources of this law are, merely resting upon the relation of spherical surfaces of different radii, its consequences are so valuable with regard to the variety of their agreement and its regularity, that not only are all possible orbits of the celestial bodies conic sections, but such a relation of these orbits to each other results, that no other law of attraction, than that of the inverse square of the distance, can be imagined as fit for a cosmical system.

Here then is a Nature that rests upon laws which the understanding cognises *a priori*, and chiefly from the universal principles of the determination of space. And the question now is: Do the laws of nature lie in space, and does the understanding learn them by merely endeavouring to find out the fruitful meaning that lies in space; or do they inhere in the understanding and in the way in which it determines space according to the conditions of the synthetical unity in which its concepts are all centred? Space is something so uniform and as to all particular properties so indeterminate, that we should certainly not seek a store of laws of nature in it. Whereas that which determines space to the form of a circle or to the figures of a sphere, is the understanding, so far as it contains the ground of the unity of their constructions. The mere universal form of intuition, called space, must therefore be the substream of all intuitions determinable to particular objects, and in it of course the condition of the possibility and of the variety of these intuitions lies. But the unity of the objects is entirely determined by the understanding, and on conditions which lie in its own nature; and thus the understanding is the origin of the universal order of nature, in that it comprehends all appearances under its own law, and thereby first constructs, *a priori*, experience (as to its form), by means of which whatever is to be cognised only by experience, is subjected to its laws necessarily. For we are not now concerned with the nature of things in themselves, which is independent of the conditions both of our sensibility and our understanding, but with nature, as an object of possible experience, and in this case the understanding, whilst it makes experience possible, thereby insists that the sensuous world is either not an object of experience at all, or must be Nature.

Copernicanism

As opposed to the two great philosophical perspectives of the classical world, Platonism and Aristotelianism, the modern world has seen the rise of a third perspective which will be called Copernicanism. This does not mean that all modern and contemporary philosophers are Copernicans. On the contrary, most are not. Many still operate with sophisticated refurbishings of both Platonism and Aristotelianism. Many would argue that their views defy classification by this scheme.

Copernicanism arises from the conflict between the Copernican and Ptolemaic theories of astronomy. The presence of two theories, both of which are mathematically coherent and both of which "fit" the known facts, reveals the inadequacy of both Platonic and Aristotelian views. We cannot choose among theories by consulting experience, hence the inadequacy of the empiricism inherent in the Aristotelian view. In fact, the way in which experience is interpreted depends as much on our theory as our theory depends upon experience. The possibility of alternative mathematical systems or alternative ideals is equally as destructive to the Platonic view.

Inherent in both classical views is the notion of knowledge being totally independent of mankind. On the contrary, the Copernican would argue that knowledge is the product of the interaction of mankind and the world. Hence any analysis of science and rationality must take into account the activities and interests of men. Science and rationality cannot be mere correspondence to a structure that is independent of mankind.

369

In the oldest version of Copernicanism, that is, in Hume, the model science was Newtonian mechanics. Hume followed Newton in emphasizing that theories must relate to experience, that they must be universal as far as possible, and that they must avoid meaningless abstractions. All of these rules are easily interpretable as saying that theories serve as suggestions for extending our knowledge and control over the universe. Even the element of predictability and determinism that one finds in Newton's mechanics are understandable in Copernican terms as instruments for control. No doubt the Aristotelian would interpret the replacement of one theory by a more general or comprehensive theory as showing that we are getting closer to the truth. But the Copernican would insist on the permanently hypothetical character of all science. In the contemporary period, instrumentalism and pragmatism can be construed as versions of Copernicanism. A good explanation is not one which follows a deductive or demonstrative pattern but rather one which leads to successful prediction. In this sense the rules of human reasoning are neither a priori nor derived from experience; they are derived from hypotheses.

In social science, if we continue to follow Newton, we end up with *psychologism*. This is the view that human behavior can be understood in terms of fundamental psychological laws which are analogous to the laws of motion. History can reveal how these laws have operated in the past, but the laws are fundamentally psychological, not historical. Mechanistically viewed, individual behavior is a kind of vector-resolution of the multiple drives or passions. Social phenomena represent a vector-resolution of the more fundamental behavior of individuals. Values are thus explainable as the product of individuals interacting with the environment and with other individuals, with each individual seeking to maximize his self-interest. Social cooperation results from the realization that our needs are best served in a socially cooperative setting.

The fundamental point of controversy, or flaw as others would say, in Copernicanism is whether determinism can be consistently held in such a theory. If all behavior is really determined, does it really make sense to have policies or so-called rational practices? In response to this criticism and other technical issues, contemporary Copernicans have shifted away from deterministic Newtonian mechanics and have adopted instead, as their model science, the evolutionary biological perspective. These developments, however, are beyond the scope of the present chapter.

Chapter VI—Political Philosophy

Introduction

Political philosophy is such a vast subject with so many ramifications that it would be impossible to do justice to it within the confines of a single chapter of a book, or even perhaps in a single course. Rather than attempt anything like a comprehensive treatment, we have decided to focus on the extent to which fundamental philosophical perspectives such as the ones we have identified, play a role in the formation of political philosophies. Our emphasis and our treatment are necessarily selective; thus, we make no pretense to covering even the most important issues.

One problem that the new student of political philosophy will likely have is the difficulty of seeing that political issues and philosophies are much more diverse than he initially realized. We are all the products of our time and place, and if we have no background we are likely to think that our problems are the only pro lems, that our questions are the only questions, that our way of answering questions (even where we disagree) is the only way to answer questions, and so forth. Hopefully, our selections will try to show the different directions from which philosophers have approached political issues.

From the philosophical point of view there are three fundamental issues that must be faced by any political philosophy: (1) What is the source or origin of our values, specifically our political or social rules? (2) What is the source or origin of human motivation; that is, why do people behave as they do? (3) What is the relationship between our rules and our behavior? Presumably behind these questions is the concern for having the "right" rules and getting ourselves to follow them.

With regard to the first issue, the source of values, there is one traditional, nonphilosophical answer, namely God. That is, we may identify all rules as originating with the deity. This kind of answer is only relevant to our present concern insofar as someone attempts to provide a philosophical rationale for interpreting God's rules. This leads into the question of what ways have been offered in philosophy for understanding rules. There is, of course, the *Platonic* answer that the rules are a priori, independent of experience including history, and are given only to some. Either you see or you do not. There is also the *Aristotelian* answer that the rules are first principles or derivations from first principles abstracted from experience, including the possibility of historical experience. Here it is argued that there are certain fundamental facts about the world or man or both, from which we may deduce what the rules ought to be. Sometimes this is identified as the *natural law* tradition. Finally, we may tentatively identify the third or *Copernican* answer, that rules are hypotheses to be revised as we proceed.

With regard to the second issue, the origin of human motivation, we may likewise identify three possibilities. Within the Platonic tradition we may identify belief as the source of motivation. That is, we act according to our beliefs including our beliefs about what we want. We may be right or wrong about the means and the ends as well. For the Aristotelian, the issue is more complex. Motivation depends upon our *habits* as well as our beliefs, and our habits in turn depend upon the institutions responsible for shaping them, including the family, the schools, jobs, and so on. The issue is further complicated because some Aristotelians adhere to a belief in free will, whereas some subscribe to a belief in determinism. Still, reason plays an important role in overcoming those pressures, both individual and social, which deflect us from pursuing our end. There is a firm belief that some end or consistent set of ends directs us. For the Copernican there is no permanent set of ends. Either we pursue ends because we are determined to do so in a specific context, and this is to be discovered psychologically, or we pursue ends we have freely chosen from what we imagine to be the possible alternatives available to us.

Issue three, the relationship of rules to motivation or behavior, likewise reveals three alternative views. For Platonists the relationship is logical. We are logically determined to do what we believe to be the case. If we really understand the rules and their truth, then we automatically act in accordance with them. Hence, it is easy to see that the Platonist is almost exclusively concerned with the first issue, since everything hinges upon it. The Aristotelian describes the relationship between rules in a quasi-legal fashion. Here the mediation of the institutions of society requires a sort of legal connection between our values enshrined in our rules and our behavior. For the Copernican, the relationship between rules and behavior is purely natural; either it is psychologically determined or the question of such a relationship is rejected as artificial. For the latter there is no conflict of ideal and actual, so there can be no special problem of relating theory to practice.

Let us look at a few issues to see how these perspectives emerge. To begin with, Is there a distinction between moral and political philosophy or values? If we are to be strict Aristotelians there can be no such dichotomy, for all values emerge only in a social setting. Either the society is healthy, in which case moral and social values are equivalent, or the society is unhealthy, in which case no values are presently actualized; they are only potential. The religious orthodox or the Platonist who wishes to criticize a given society may speak in terms of an independent and absolute standard of which our society is but an imperfect manifestation. But in a sense the question is artificial, since all of these views can accommodate ways of speaking that permit us to criticize the status quo. Finally, it is always open to the Copernican to suggest a new hypothesis.

Then there is the perennial question of *who* should be the ruler or rulers. For a Platonist, those who know should rule. For an Aristotelian, those who can best help us achieve our end should rule. If we know the end or ends, then who or how many hardly seems important. One person, or a few, or many may be involved in the actual rule. And Aristotle himself recognized that there are good and bad forms of rule by any number. Hobbes argued for the benefits of one man rule; Locke pointed out the possibilities of corruption and advocated majority rule; Mill just as easily could point to the possibilities of corruption in a majority. For the Copernican, ruling is not a special kind of knowledge.

There are questions which are also meaningful only to certain kinds of theories. If you are an Aristotelian you may disagree on the ends. Are men basically materialistic and selfish, or are they only happy and productive in a nonmaterialistic society? If you are an Aristotelian with a quasi-legal model, you must raise questions about the limits of the rulers. You must raise questions about what ends the state may pursue. But essential to Aristotelianism is the need to define what is basic to man and what, therefore, has to be protected from violation.

Finally, there is the issue of how one goes about changing the rules of the game. Does Platonism offer a clear cut theory of what to do if you think that you "know" and that the current leaders do not know? Does Platonism encourage people to become romantic revolutionaries? Is there a meaningful role for the individual in Aristotelian theories? By this we mean, What do we do if we do not agree with the stated end? Must we use channels to change the rules? What about "Catch-22"? Is the majority always right, and is their consent alone the only valuable frame of reference? Is the development of history beyond the participation of individuals? That is, do I have a real choice other than following history's inevitable course?

One might be tempted to argue, as some have, that our basic philosophies do not provide any clear cut policies and that they can be used to justify anything. Hence all political philosophy is mere rhetoric. Others would reply that they have to be correctly interpreted. Still others, like the Copernican, might argue that these philosophies are only hypotheses, that many of these hypotheses may no longer be useful, and that what we need are new ones. Perhaps those who cry that all thought is mere rationalization are like the sceptics.

Thomas Hobbes

Like his continental counterpart Machiavelli, Hobbes (1588-1679) is identified as the first to break away from discussing political theory in a theological context. He opposed the appeal to conscience (Platonic absolute) and revelation as socially disruptive, and he despised democracies as unstable. But he did not advocate divine right. Hobbes' most important theoretical contribution was the description of the state of nature. Hobbes does not claim that such a state ever existed, but he does abstract from our experience of international affairs the reality of such a state. Moreover, he does not claim that the ensuing social contract, which allows for the security in which we can pursue our ends, was actually a historical fact. Yet he does believe in tacit consent as the experiential basis on which we can abstract the living reality of a social contract.

The fundamental theoretical difficulty in Hobbes' view is the conflict between his natural-law position (Aristotelian) and his belief in determinism. We are led to ask if it makes sense to really expect men with the characteristics Hobbes describes, ever to form a stable community. If we are moved by determining forces beyond our control, the appeal to reason hardly seems adequate. Finally, we might ask if tacit consent is a meaningful concept. Can there be tacit dissent?

Leviathan

OF THE DIFFERENCE OF MANNERS

By *manners,* I mean not here, decency of be-havior; as how one should salute another, or how a man should wash his mouth, or pick his teeth before company, and such other points of the *small morals;* but those qualities of man-kind, that concern their living together in peace, and unity. To which end we are to consider, that the felicity of this life, consisteth not in the repose of a mind satisfied. For there is no such *finis ultimus,* utmost aim, nor *sum-mum bonum,* greatest good, as is spoken of in the books of the old moral philosophers. Nor can a man any more live, whose desires are at an end, than he, whose senses and imaginations are at a stand. Felicity is a continual progress of the desire, from one object to another; the attaining of the former, being still but the way to the latter. The cause whereof is, that the object of man's desire, is not to enjoy once only, and for one instant of time; but to assure for ever, the way of his future desire. And therefore the voluntary actions, and inclinations of all men, tend, not only to the procuring, but also to the assuring of a contented life; and differ only in the way: which ariseth partly from the diver-sity of passions in diverse men; and partly from the difference of the knowledge, or opinion each one has of the causes, which produce the effect desired.

So that in the first place, I put for a general inclination of all mankind, a perpetual and restless desire of power after power, that ceaseth only in death. And the cause of this, is not always that a man hopes for a more inten-sive delight, than he has already attained to; or that he cannot be content with a moderate power: but because he cannot assure the power and means to live well, which he hath present, without the acquisition of more. And from hence it is, that kings, whose power is greatest, turn their endeavors to the assuring it at home by laws, or abroad by wars; and when that is done, there succeedeth a new desire; in some, of fame from new conquest; in others, of ease and sensual pleasure; in others, of admiration, or being flattered for excellence in some art, or other ability of the mind. . . .

OF THE NATURAL CONDITION OF MANKIND AS CONCERNING THEIR FELICITY, AND MISERY

Nature hath made men so equal, in the facul-ties of the body and mind; as that, though there be found one man sometimes manifestly stronger in body or of quicker mind than another, yet when all is reckoned together, the difference between man and man is not so con-siderable, as that one man can thereupon claim to himself any benefit, to which another may not pretend as well as he. For as to the strength of body, the weakest has strength enough to kill the strongest, either by secret machination, or by confederacy with others that are in the same danger with himself.

And as to the faculties of the mind—setting aside the arts grounded upon words, and especially that skill of proceeding upon general and infallible rules, called science; which very few have, and but in few things; as being not a native faculty, born with us; nor attained, as prudence, while we look after somewhat else—I find yet a greater equality amongst men, than that of strength. For prudence is but experience which equal time equally bestows on all men, in those things they equally apply themselves unto. That which may perhaps make such equality incredible, is but a vain conceit of one's own wisdom, which almost all men think they have in a greater degree than the vulgar; that is, than all men but themselves, and a few others, whom by fame, or for concurring with themselves, they approve. For such is the nature of men, that howsoever they may acknowledge many others to be more witty, or more eloquent, or more learned, yet they will hardly believe there be many so wise as themselves; for they see their own wit at hand, and other men's at a distance. But this proveth rather that men are in that point equal, than unequal. For there is not ordinarily a greater sign of the equal distribution of anything, than that every man is contented with his share.

From this equality of ability, ariseth equality of hope in the attaining of our ends. And therefore if any two men desire the same thing, which nevertheless, they cannot both enjoy, they become enemies; and in the way to their end, which is principally their own conservation, and sometimes their delectation only, endeavour to destroy, or subdue one another. And from hence it comes to pass that where an invader hath no more to fear than another man's single power; if one plant, sow, build, or possess a convenient seat, others may probably be expected to come prepared with forces united, to dispossess and deprive him, not only of the fruit of his labor, but also of his life or liberty. And the invader again is in the like danger of another.

And from this diffidence of one another, there is no way for any man to secure himself so reasonable as anticipation; that is, by force or wiles to master the persons of all men he can, so long, till he see no other power great enough to endanger him: and this is no more than his own conservation requireth, and is generally allowed. Also because there be some, that taking pleasure in contemplating their own power in the acts of conquest, which they pursue farther than their security requires; if others, that otherwise would be glad to be at ease within modest bounds, should not by invasion increase their power, they would not be able long time, by standing only on their defense, to subsist. And by consequence, such augmentation of dominion over men being

necessary to a man's conservation, it ought to be allowed him.

Again, men have no pleasure, but on the contrary a great deal of grief, in keeping company, where there is no power able to overawe them all. For every man looketh that his companion should value him at the same rate he sets upon himself; and upon all signs of contempt, or undervaluing, naturally endeavors as far as he dares (which amongst them that have no common power to keep them in quiet, is far enough to make them destroy each other), to extort a greater value from his contemners by damage, and from others by the example.

So that in the nature of man, we find three principal causes of quarrel. First, competition; second, diffidence; thirdly, glory.

The first maketh men invade for gain; the second, for safety; and the third, for reputation. The first use violence to make themselves masters of other men's persons, wives, children, and cattle; the second, to defend them; the third, for trifles, as a word, a smile, a different opinion, and any other sign of undervalue, either direct in their persons, or by reflection in their kindred, their friends, their nation, their profession, or their name.

Hereby it is manifest that during the time men live without a common power to keep them all in awe, they are in that condition which is called war; and such a way as is of every man against every man. For *war* consisteth not in battle only, or the act of fighting, but in a tract of time wherein the will to contend by battle is sufficiently known, and therefore the notion of *time* is to be considered in the nature of war, as it is in the nature of weather. For as the nature of foul weather lieth not in a shower or two of rain, but in an inclination thereto of many days together; so the nature of war consisteth not in actual fighting, but in the known disposition thereto, during all the time there is no assurance to the contrary. All other time is *peace*.

Whatsoever therefore is consequent to a time of war, where every man is enemy to every man; the same is consequent to the time, wherein men live without other security than what their own strength and their own invention shall furnish them withal. In such condition there is no place for industry, because the fruit thereof is uncertain: and consequently no culture of the earth; no navigation, nor use of the commodities that may be imported by sea; no commodious building; no instruments of moving, and removing, such things as require much force; no knowledge of the face of the earth; no account of time; no arts; no letters; no society; and which is worst of all, continual fear, and danger of violent death; and the life of man, solitary, poor, nasty, brutish, and short.

It may seem strange to some man that has not well weighted these things, that nature should thus dissociate, and render men apt to invade and destroy one another; and he may, therefore, not trusting to this inference, made from the passions, desire perhaps to have the same confirmed by experience. Let him therefore consider with himself, when taking a journey, he arms himself and seeks to go well accompanied; when going to sleep, he locks his doors; when even in his house he locks his chests; and this when he knows there be laws, and public officers, armed, to revenge all injuries shall be done him: what opinion he has of his fellow-subjects, when he rides armed; of his fellow-citizens, when he locks his doors; and of his children, and servants, when he locks his chests. Does he not there as much accuse mankind by his actions, as I do by my words? But neither of us accuse man's nature in it. The desires, and other passions of man, are in themselves no sin. No more are the actions that proceed from those passions, till they know a law that forbids them: which till laws be made they cannot know; nor can any law be made, till they have agreed upon the person that shall make it.

It may peradventure be thought, there was never such a time nor condition of war as this; and I believe it was never generally so, over all the world: but there are many places where they live so now. For the savage people in many places of America, except the government of small families, the concord whereof dependeth on natural lust, have no government at all; and live at this time in that brutish manner, as I said before. Howsoever, it may be perceived what manner of life there would be, where there were no common power to fear; by the manner of life which men that have formerly lived under a peaceful government, use to degenerate into in a civil war.

But though there had never been any time wherein particular men were in a condition of war one against another; yet in all times, kings, and persons of sovereign authority, because of their independency, are in continual jealousies,

and in the state and posture of gladiators; having their weapons pointing, and their eyes fixed on one another; that is, their forts, garrisons, and guns upon the frontiers of their kingdoms; and continual spies upon their neighbors; which is a posture of war. But because they uphold thereby the industry of their subjects, there does not follow from it that misery which accompanies the liberty of particular men.

To this war of every man against every man, this also is consequent: *that nothing can be unjust*. The notions of right and wrong, justice and injustice, have there no place. Where there is no common power, there is no law; where no law, no injustice. Force and fraud are in war the two cardinal virtues. Justice and injustice are none of the faculties neither of the body nor mind. If they were, they might be in a man that were alone in the world, as well as his senses and passions. They are qualities that relate to men in society, not in solitude. It is consequent also to the same condition, that there be no propriety, no dominion, no *mine* and *thine* distinct; but only that to be every man's, that he can get; and for so long as he can keep it. And thus much for the ill condition which man by mere nature is actually placed in; though with a possibility to come out of it, consisting partly in the passions, partly in his reason.

The passions that incline men to peace are fear of death, desire of such things as are necessary to commodious living, and a hope by their industry to obtain them. And reason suggesteth convenient articles of peace, upon which men may be drawn to agreement. These articles are they which otherwise are called the Laws of Nature whereof I shall speak more particularly in the two following chapters.

OF THE FIRST AND SECOND NATURAL LAWS, AND OF CONTRACTS

The right of nature, which writers commonly call *jus naturale,* is the liberty each man hath to use his own power, as he will himself, for the preservation of his own nature; that is to say, of his own life; and consequently, of doing anything, which in his own judgment and reason, he shall conceive to be the aptest means thereunto.

By *liberty,* is understood, according to the

proper signification of the word, the absence of external impediments: which impediments, may oft take away part of a man's power to do what he would; but cannot hinder him from using the power left him, according as his judgment and reason shall dictate to him.

A *law of nature, lex naturalis,* is a precept or general rule, found out by reason, by which a man is forbidden to do that which is destructive of his life, or taketh away the means of preserving the same; and to omit that by which he thinketh it may be best preserved. For though they that speak of this subject, use to confound *jus* and *lex, right* and *law;* yet they ought to be distinguished: because *right* consisteth in liberty to do or to forbear, whereas *law* determineth and bindeth to one of them; so that law, and right differ as much as obligation and liberty; which in one and the same matter are inconsistent.

And because the condition of man, as hath been declared in the precedent chapter, is a condition of war of everyone against everyone; in which case everyone is governed by his own reason, and there is nothing he can make use of that may not be a help unto him in preserving his life against his enemies: it followeth, that in such a condition every man has a right to everything; even to one another's body. And therefore, as long as this natural right of every man to everything endureth, there can be no security to any man, how strong or wise soever he be, of living out the time which nature ordinarily alloweth men to live. And consequently it is a precept, or general rule of reason, *that every man ought to endeavor peace, as far as he has hope of obtaining it; and when he cannot obtain it, that he may seek and use all helps and advantages of war.* The first branch of which rule containeth the first and fundamental law of nature; which is, *to seek peace and follow it.* The second, the sum of the right of nature; which is, *by all means we can, to defend ourselves.*

From this fundamental law of nature, by which men are commanded to endeavor peace, is derived this second law: *that a man be willing, when others are so too, as far forth as for peace and defense of himself he shall think it necessary, to lay down this right to all things; and be contented with so much liberty against other men, as he would allow other men against himself.* For as long as every man

holdeth this right, of doing anything he liketh, so long are all men in the condition of war. But if other men will not lay down their right, as well as he, then there is no reson for anyone to divest himself of his: for that were to expose himself to prey, which no man is bound to, rather than to dispose himself to peace. This is that law of the Gospel: *whatsoever you require that others should do to you, that do ye to them.* And that law of all men, *quod tibi fieri non vis, alteri ne feceris* (do not do unto others what you do not wish them to do unto you).

To *lay down* a man's *right* to anything, is to *divest* himself of the *liberty,* of hindering another of the benefit of his own right to the same. For he that renounceth or passeth away his right, giveth not to any other man a right which he had not before; because there is nothing to which every man had not right by nature: but only standeth out of his way, that he may enjoy his own original right, without hindrance from him, not without hindrance from another. So that the effect which redoundeth to one man, by another man's defect of right, is but so much diminution of impediments to the use of his own right original.

Right is laid aside, either by simple renouncing it, or by transferring it to another. By *simply renouncing,* when he cares not to whom the benefit thereof redoundeth. By *transferring,* when he intendeth the benefit thereof to some certain person or persons. And when a man hath in either manner abandoned or granted away his right; then is he said to be *obliged,* or bound, not to hinder those to whom such right is granted or abandoned, from the benefit of it; and that he *ought,* and it is his *duty,* not to make void that voluntary act of his own; and that such hindrance is *injustice,* and *injury,* as being *sine jure;* the right being before renounced, or transferred. So that injury, or injustice, in the controversies of the world, is somewhat like to that, which in the disputations of scholars is called *absurdity.* For as it is there called an absurdity to contradict what one maintained in the beginning; so in the world, it is called injustice, and injury, voluntarily to undo that which from the beginning he had voluntarily done. The way by which a man either simply renounceth, or transferreth his right, is a declaration, or signification, by some voluntary and sufficient sign or signs, that he doth so renounce or transfer, or hath so renounced or transferred the same, to him that accepteth it. And these signs are either words only, or actions only, as it happeneth most often, both words and actions. And the same are the *bonds,* by which men are bound and obliged—bonds that have their strength, not from their own nature, for nothing is more easily broken than a man's word, but from fear of some evil consequence upon the rupture.

Whensoever a man transferreth his right, or renounceth it; it is either in consideration of some right reciprocally transferred to himself; or for some other good he hopeth for thereby. For it is a voluntary act; and of the voluntary act of every man, the object is some *good to himself.* And therefore there be some rights which no man can be understood by any words, or other signs, to have abandoned or transferred. As first a man cannot lay down the right of resisting them that assault him by force, to take away his life; because he cannot be understood to aim thereby, at any good to himself. The same may be said of wounds, and chains, and imprisonment: both because there is no benefit consequent to such patience, as there is to the patience of suffering another to be wounded or imprisoned; as also because a man cannot tell, when he seeth men proceed against him by violence, whether they intend his death or not. And lastly the motive, an end for which this renouncing and transferring of right is introduced, is nothing else but the security of a man's person, in his life, and in the means of so preserving life as not of to be weary of it. And therefore if a man by words, or others signs, seem to despoil himself of the end for which those signs were intended, he is not to be understood as if he meant it, or that it was his will, but that he was ignorant of how such words and actions were to be interpreted.

The mutual transferring of right, is what men call *contract.*

There is difference between transferring of right to the thing, and transferring, or tradition—that is delivery—of the thing itself. For the thing may be delivered together with the translation of the right, as in buying and selling with ready money, or exchange of goods, or lands; and it may be delivered sometime after.

Again, one of the contractors may deliver the thing contracted for on his part, and leave the other to perform his part at some determinate time after, and in the meantime be trusted; and

then the contract on his part is called *pact,* or *covenant:* or both parts may contract now to perform hereafter; in which cases, he that is to perform in time to come, being trusted, his performance is called *keeping of promise,* or faith; and the failing of performance, if it be voluntary, *violation of faith.*

When the transferring of right is not mutual; but one of the parties transferreth, in hope to gain thereby friendship, or service from another, or from his friends; or in hope to gain the reputation of charity, or magnanimity; or to deliver his mind from the pain of compassion; or in hope of reward in heaven; this is not contract, but *gift, free-gift, grace:* which words signify one and the same thing.

Signs of contract, are either *express,* or *by inference.* Express, are words spoken with understanding of what they signify: and such words are either of the time *present,* or *past;* as, *I give, I grant, I have given, I have granted, I will that this be yours:* or of the future; as, *I will give, will grant:* which words of the future are called *promise.*

Signs by inference are sometimes the consequence of words; sometimes the consequence of silence; sometimes the consequence of actions; sometimes the consequence of forbearing an action; and generally a sign by inference, of any contract, is whatsoever sufficiently argues the will of the contractor.

Words alone, if they be of the time to come, and contain a bare promise, are an insufficient sign of a free-gift, and therefore not obligatory. For if they be of the time to come, as *tomorrow I will give,* they are a sign I have not given yet, and consequently that my right is not transferred, but remaineth till I transfer it by some other act. But if the words be of the time present, or past, as, *I have given, or, do give to be delivered tomorrow,* then is my tomorrow's right given away today; and that by the virtue of the words, though there were no other argument of my will. And there is a great difference in the signification of these words, *volo hoc tuum esse cras,* and *cras dabo;* that is, between *I will that this be thine tomorrow,* and, *I will it thee tomorrow:* for the word *I will,* in the former manner of speech, signifies an act of the will present; but in the latter, it signifies a promise of an act of the will to come: and therefore the former words, being of the present, transfer a future right; the latter, that be of the future, transfer nothing. But if there be other signs of the will to transfer a right, besides words; then, though the gift be free, yet may the right be understood to pass by words of the future: as if a man propound a prize to him that comes first to the end of a race, the gift is free; and though the words be of the future, yet the right passeth: for if he would not have his words so be understood, he should not have let them run.

In contracts, the right passeth, not only where the words are of the time present, or past, but also where they are of the future: because all contract is mutual translation, or change or right; and therefore he that promiseth only, because he hath already received the benefit for which he promiseth, is to be understood as if he intended the right should pass: for unless he had been content to have his words so understood, the other would not have performed his part first. And for that cause, in buying, and selling, and other acts of contract, a promise is equivalent to a convenant; and therefore obligatory.

He that performeth first in the case of a contract, is said to *merit* that which he is to receive by the performance of the other; and he hath it as *due*. Also when a prize is propounded to many, which is to be given to him only that winneth; or money is thrown amongst many, to be enjoyed by them that catch it; though this be a free gift; yet so to win, or so to catch, is to *merit*, and to have it as *due*. For the right is transferred in the propounding of the prize, and in throwing down the money; though it be not determined to whom, but by the event of the contention. But there is between these two sorts of merit, this difference, that in contract, I merit by virtue of my own power, and the contractor's need; but in this case of free gift, I am enabled to merit only by the benignity of the giver: in contract, I merit at the contractor's hand that he should depart with his right; in this case of gift, I merit not that the giver should part with his right; but that when he has parted with it, it should be mine, rather than another's. And this I think to be the meaning of that distinction of the Schools, between *meritum congrui*, and *meritum condigni*. For God Almighty, having promised Paradise to those men, hoodwinked with carnal desires, that can walk through this world according to the precepts, and limits prescribed by him; they

say, he that shall so walk, shall merit Paradise *ex congruo*. But because no man can demand a right to it, by his own righteousness, or any other power in himself, but by the free grace of God only; they say, no man can merit Paradise *ex condigno*. This I say, I think is the meaning of that distinction; but because disputers do not agree upon the signification of their own terms of art, longer than it serves their turn; I will not affirm anything of their meaning: only this I say; when a gift is given indefinitely, as a prize to be contended for, he that winneth meriteth, and may claim the prize as due.

If a convenant be made, wherein neither of the parties perform presently, but trust one another; in the condition of mere nature, which is a condition of war of every man against every man, upon any reasonable suspicion, it is void: but if there be a common power set over them both, with right and force sufficient to compel performance, it is not void. For he that performeth first, has no assurance the other will perform after; because the bonds of words are too weak to bridle men's ambition, avarice, anger, and other passions, without the fear of some coercive power; which in the condition of mere nature, where all men are equal, and judges of the justness of their own fears, cannot possibly be supposed. And therefore he which performeth first, does but betray himself to his enemy; contrary to the right, he can never abandon, of defending his life, and means of living.

But in a civil estate, where there is a power set up to constrain those that would otherwise violate their faith, that fear is no more reasonable; and for that cause, he which by the covenant is to perform first, is obliged so to do.

OF THE RIGHTS OF SOVEREIGNS BY INSTITUTION

A commonwealth is said to be *instituted,* when a multitude of men do agree and covenant, everyone with everyone, that to whatsoever man, or assembly of men, shall be given by the major part the right to present the person of them all, that is to say, to be their *representative;* everyone, as well he that voted for it as he that voted against it, shall authorize all the actions and judgments of that man, or assembly of men, in the same manner as if they were his own, to the end to live peaceably amongst themselves and be protected against other men.

From this institution of a commonwealth are derived all the *rights* and *faculties* of him, or them, on whom sovereign power is conferred by the consent of the people assembled.

First, because they covenant, it is to be understood they are not obliged by former covenant to anything repugnant hereunto. And consequently they that have already instituted a commonwealth, being thereby bound by covenant to own the actions and judgments of one, cannot lawfully make a new covenant amongst themselves, to be obedient to any other, in anything whatsoever, without his permission. And therefore, they that are subject to a monarch, cannot without his leave cast off monarchy, and return to the confusion of a disunited multitude; not transfer their person from him that beareth it, to another man, or other assembly of men: for they are bound, every man to every man, to own, and be reputed author of all, that he that already is their sovereign shall do and judge fit to be done; so that any one man dissenting, all the rest should break their covenant made to that man, which is injustice: and they have also every man given the sovereignty to him that beareth their person; and therefore if they depose him, they take from him that which is his own, and so again it is injustice. Besides, if he that attempteth to depose his sovereign, be killed or punished by him for such attempt, he is author of his own punishment, as being by the institution, author of all his sovereign shall do; and because it is injustice for a man to do anything for which he may be punished by his own authority, he is also upon that title, unjust. And whereas some men have pretended for their disobedience to their sovereign, a new covenant, made not with men but with God, this also is unjust: for there is no covenant with God, but by mediation of somebody that representeth God's person; which none doth but God's lieutenant, who hath the sovereignty under God. But this pretense of covenant with God, is so evident a lie, even in the pretenders' own consciences, that it is not only an act of an unjust, but also of a vile and unmanly disposition.

Secondly, because the right of bearing a person of them all, is given to him they make sovereign, by covenant only of one to another, and not of him to any of them; there can happen no breach of covenant on the part of the sovereign; and consequently none of his subjects, by any pretense of forfeiture, can be freed from his subjection. That he which is made sovereign maketh no covenant with his subjects beforehand, is manifest; because either he must make it with the whole multitude, as one party to the covenant, or he must make a several covenant with every man. With the whole, as one party, it is impossible, because as yet they are not one person: and if he make so many several covenants as there be men, those covenants after he hath the sovereignty are void; because what act soever can be pretended by any one of them for breach thereof, is the act both of himself and of all the rest, because done in the person, and by the right of every one of them in particular. Besides, if any one, or more of them, pretend a breach of the covenant made by the sovereign at his institutions; and others; as one other of his subjects, or himself alone, pretend there was no such breach: there is in this case, no judge to decide the controversy; it returns therefore to the sword again; and every man recovereth the right of protecting himself by his own strength, contrary to the design they had in the institution. It is therefore in vain to grant sovereignty by way of precedent covenant. The opinion that any monarch receiveth his power by covenant, that is to say, on condition, proceedeth from want of understanding this easy truth, that convenants being but words and breath, have no force to oblige, contain, constrain, or protect any man, but what it has from the public sword; that is, from the untied hands of that man, or assembly of men that hath the sovereignty of them all, in him united. But when an assembly of men is made sovereign, then no man imagineth any such covenant to have passed in the institution; for no man is so dull as to say, for example, the people of Rome made a covenant with the Romans, to hold the sovereignty on such or such conditions; which not performed, the Romans might lawfully depose the Roman people. That men see not the reason to be alike in a monarchy and in a popular government, proceedeth from the ambition of some that are kinder to the government of an assembly, whereof they may hope to participate, than of monarchy, which they despair to enjoy,

Thirdly, because the major part hath by consenting voices declared a sovereign, he that dissented must now consent with the rest; that is, be contented to avow all the actions he shall do, or else justly be destroyed by the rest. For if he voluntarily entered into the congregation of them that were assembled, he sufficiently declared thereby his will, and therefore tacitly covenanted to stand to what the major part should ordain; and therefore if he refuse to stand thereto, or make protestation against any of their decrees, he does contrary to his covenant, and therefore unjustly. And whether he be of the congregation or not, and whether his consent be asked or not, he must either submit to their decrees, or be left in the condition of war he was in before; wherein he might without injustice be destroyed by any man whatsoever.

Fourthly, because every subject is by this institution author of all the actions and judgments of the sovereign instituted; it follows that whatsoever he doth, it can be no injury to any of his subjects, nor ought he to be by any of them accused to injustice. For he that doth anything by authority from another, doth therein no injury to him by whose authority he acteth: but by this institution of a commonwealth, every particular man is author of all the sovereign doth: and consequently he that complaineth of injury from his sovereign, complaineth of that whereof he himself is author; and therefore ought not to accuse any man but himself; nor himself of injury, because to do injury to one's self, is impossible. It is true that they that have sovereign power may commit iniquity, but not injustice, or injury, in the proper signification.

Fifthly, and consequently to that which was said last, no man that hath sovereign power can justly be put to death, or otherwise in any manner by his subjects punished. For seeing every subject is author of the actions of his sovereign, he punisheth another for the actions committed by himself.

And because the end of this institution, is the peace and defense of them all, and whosoever has right to the end has right to the means; it belongeth of right, to whatsoever man or assembly that hath the sovereignty, to be judge both of the means of peace and defense, and also of the hindrances and disturbances of the same; and to do whatsoever he shall think necessary to be done, both beforehand, for the preserving of peace and security, by prevention of discord at home and hostility from abroad.

and, when peace and security are lost, for the recovery of the same. And therefore,

Sixthly, it is annexed to the sovereignty, to be judge of what opinions and doctrines are averse, and what conducing to peace; and consequently, on what occasions, how far, and what men are to be trusted withal, in speaking to multitudes of people; and who shall examine the doctrines of all books before they be published. For the actions of men proceed from their opinions; and in the well-governing of opinions consisteth the well-governing of men's actions, in order to their peace and concord. And though in matter of doctrine nothing ought to be regarded but the truth, yet this is not repugnant to regulating the same by peace. For doctrine repugnant to peace can no more be true, than peace and concord can be against the law of nature. It is true that in a commonwealth, where, by the negligence or unskillfulness of governors and teachers, false doctrines are by time generally received; the contrary truths may be generally offensive. Yet the most sudden and rough bursting in of a new truth that can be, does never break the peace, but only sometimes awake the war. For those men that are so remissly governed, that they dare take up arms to defend or introduce an opinion, are still in war; and their condition not peace, but only a cessation of arms for fear of one another; and they live, as it were, in the precincts of battle continually. It belongeth therefore to him that hath the sovereign power, to be judge, or constitute all judges of opinions and doctrines, as a thing necessary to peace; thereby to prevent discord and civil war.

Seventhly, is annexed to the sovereignty, the whole power of prescribing the rules, whereby every man may know what goods he may enjoy, and what actions he may do, without being molested by any of his fellow-subjects; and this is it men call *propriety*. For before constitution of sovereign power, as hath already been shown, all men had right to all things; which necessarily causeth war: and therefore this propriety, being necesary to peace, and depending on sovereign power, is the act of that power, in order to the public peace. These rules of propriety, or *meum* and *tuum*, and of good, evil, lawful, and unlawful in the actions of subjects, are the civil laws; that is to say the laws of each commonwealth in particular: though the name of civil law be now restrained to the ancient civil laws of the city of Rome; which being the head of a great part of the world, her laws at that time were in these parts the civil law.

Eighthly, is annexed to the sovereignty, the right of judicature; that is to say, of hearing and deciding all controversies which may arise concerning law, either civil or natural, or concerning fact. For without the decision of controversies, there is no protection of one subject against the injuries of another: the laws concerning *meum* and *tuum* are in vain; and to every man remaineth, from the natural and necessary appetite of his own conservation, the right of protecting himself by his private strength, which is the condition of war, and contrary to the end for which every commonwealth is instituted.

Ninthly, is annexed to the sovereignty, the right of making way and peace with other nations and commonwealths; that is to say, of judging when it is for the public good, and how great forces are to be assembled, armed, and paid for that end; and to levy money upon the subjects, to defray the expenses thereof. For the power by which the people are to be defended, consisteth in their armies; and the strength of an army, in the union of their strength under one command: which command the sovereign instituted, therefore hath; because the command of the militia, without other institution, maketh him that hath it sovereign. And therefore whosoever is made general of any army, he that hath the sovereign power is always generalissimo.

Tenthly, is annexed to the sovereignty, the choosing of all counsellors, ministers, magistrates, and offices, both in peace and war. For seeing the sovereign is charged with the end, which is the common peace and defense, he is understood to have power to use such means as he shall think most fit for his discharge.

Eleventhly, to the sovereign is committed the power of rewarding with riches, or honor, and of punishing with corporal or pecuniary punishment, or with ignominy, every subject according to the law he hath formerly made; or if there be no law made, according as he shall judge most to conduce to the encouraging of men to serve the commonwealth, or deterring of them from doing disservice to the same.

Lastly, considering what value men are naturally apt to set upon themselves, what respect they look for from others, and how little they value other men; from whence continually arise amongst them, emulation, quarrels, factions, and at last war, to the destroying of one another and diminution of their strength against a common enemy; it is necessary that there be laws of honor, and a public rate of the worth of such men as have deserved or are able to deserve well of the commonwealth; and that there be force in the hands of some or other, to put those laws in execution. But it hath already been shown, that not only the whole militia, or foces of the commonwealth, but also the judicature of all controveries, is annexed to the sovereignty. To the sovereign therefore it belongeth also to give titles of honor; and to appoint what order of place and dignity each man shall hold; and what signs of respect, in public or private meetings, they shall give to one another.

These are the rights which make the essence of sovereignty, and which are the marks whereby a man may discern in what man, or assembly of men, the sovereign power, is placed and resideth. For these are incommunicable and inseparable. The power to coin money, to dispose of the estate and persons of infant heirs, to have pre-emption in markets, and all other statute prerogatives, may be transferred by the sovereign; and yet the power to protect his subjects be retained. But if he transfer the militia, he retains the judicature in vain, for want of execution the laws; or if he gives away the power of raising money, the militia is in or if he give away the government of doctrines, men will be frighted into rebellion with the fear of spirits. And so if we consider any one of the said rights, we shall presently see that the holding of all the rest will produce no effect in the conservation of peace and justice, the end for which all commonwealths are instituted. And this division is it whereof it is said, *a kingdom divided in itself cannot stand:* for unless this division precede, division into opposite armies can never happen. If there had not first been an opinion received of the greatest part of England, that these powers were divided between the King and the Lords and the House of Commons, the people had never been divided and fallen into this civil war; first between those that disagreed in politics, and after between the dissenters about the liberty of religion: which have so instructed men in this point of sovereign right; and there be few now in England that do not see that these rights are inseparable, and will be so generally acknowledged at the next return of peace; and so continue till their miseries are forgotten; and no longer, except the vulgar be better taught than they have hitherto been.

And because they are essential and inseparable rights, it follows necessarily that in whatsoever words any of them seem to be granted away, yet if the sovereign power itself be not in direct terms renounced, and the name of sovereign no more given by the grantees to him that grants them, the grant is void: for when he has granted all he can, if we grant back the sovereignty, all is restored, as inseparably annexed thereunto.

This great authority being indivisible, and inseparably annexed to the sovereignty, there is little ground for the opinion of them that say of sovereign kings, though they be *singulis majores,* of greater power than every one of their subjects, yet they be *universis minores,* of less power than them all together. For if by 'all together' they mean not the collective body as one person, then 'all together' and 'every one' signify the same, and the speech is absurd. But if by 'all together' they understand them as one person, which person the sovereign bears, then the power of all together is the same with the sovereign's power, and so again the speech is absurd; which absurdity they see well enough when the sovereignty is in an assembly of the people, but in a monarch they see it not; and yet the power of sovereignty is the same in whomsoever it be placed.

And as the power, so also the honor of the sovereign, ought to be greater than that of any or all the subjects. For in the sovereignty is the fountain of honor. The dignities of lord, earl, duke, and prince are his creatures. As in the presence of the master, the servants are equal and without any honor at all; so are the subjects, in the presence of the sovereign. And though they shine some more, some less, when they are out of his sight; yet in his presence, they shine no more than the stars in the presence of the sun.

But a man may here object that the condition of subjects is very miserable, as being obnoxious to the lusts, and other irregular passions, of him or them that have so unlimited a power in their hands. And commonly they that live under a monarch, think it the fault of monarchy; and they that live under the government of democracy, or other sovereign assembly, attribute all the inconvenience to that form of commonwealth; whereas the power in all forms, if they be perfect enough to protect them, is the same: not considering that the state of man can never be without some incommodity or other; and that the greatest that in any form of government can possibly happen to the people in general, is scarce sensible, in respect to the miseries and horrible calamities that accompany a civil war, or that dissolute condition of masterless men, without subjection to laws and a coercive power to tie their hands from rapine and revenge; nor considering that the greatest pressure of sovereign governors, proceedeth not from any delight or profit they can expect in the damage or weakening of their subjects, in whose vigor consisteth their own strength and glory; but in the restiveness of themselves, that unwillingly contributing to their own defense, make it necessary for their governors to draw from them what they can in time of peace, that they may have means on any emergent occasion or sudden need, to resist or take advantage on their enemies. For all men are by nature provided of notable multiplying glasses, that is their passions and self-love, through which every little payment appeareth a great grievance; but are destitute of those prospective glasses, namely moral and civil science, to see afar off the miseries that hang over them, and cannot without such payment be avoided.

John Locke

Locke's background in general was discussed in a previous section. With regard to his political philosophy the following should be noted. Locke's *Second Treatise of Civil Government*, from which our selection is taken, was composed in 1679 and 1680. It is the classic statement of Whig constitutionalism and government by consent, and along with the views of the Frenchman Montesquieu, was the model for American government. On the surface, Locke's argument is directed against the divine right theory of kings as it was articulated by Sir Robert Filmer.

When compared to Hobbes' doctrine of the social contract there is an important difference. Locke may be said to be arguing for two contracts, a first contract for the establishment of society and a second contract for the establishment of a government. Sovereignty rests ultimately with the people in society who may dispose of their government if the government does not live up to its contract. This is the right of revolution. Since there is a separate contract for the establishment of society, the dissolution of government does not dissolve society as in the case of Hobbes.

The reader might ask if Locke's argument for the power of majorities is any better than Hobbes' for a monarchy. Also, why was Locke unsympathetic to representative democracy? Finally, does it help or hinder Hobbes and Locke to have a contract theory as a framework for their views?

Concerning Civil Government

OF THE BEGINNING OF POLITICAL SOCIETIES

95. Men being, as has been said, by nature free, equal, and independent, no one can be put out of this estate, and subjected to the political power of another, without his own consent, which is done by agreeing with other men to join and unite into a community for their comfortable, safe, and peaceable living one amongst another, in a secure enjoyment of their properties, and a greater security against any that are not of it. This any number of men may do, because it injures not the freedom of the rest; they are left as they were in the liberty of the state of nature. When any number of men have so consented to make one community or government, they are thereby presently incorporated, and make one body politic, wherein the majority have a right to act and conclude the rest.

96. For when any number of men have, by the consent of every individual, make a community, they have thereby made that community one body, with a power to act as one body, which is only by the will and determination of the majority. For that which acts any community being only the consent of the individuals of it, and it being one body must move one way, it is necessary the body should move that way whither the greater force carries it, which is the consent of the majority; or else it is impossible it should act or continue one body, one community which the consent of every individual that united into it agreed that it should; and so everyone is bound by that consent to be concluded by the majority. And therefore we see that in assemblies empowered to act by positive laws, where no number is set by that positive law which empowers them, the act of the majority passes for the act of the whole, and of course determines, as having by the law of nature and reason the power of the whole.

97. And thus every man, by consenting with others to make one body politic under one government, puts himself under an obligation to every one of that society, to submit to the determination of the majority, and to be concluded by it; or else this original compact, whereby he with others incorporates into one society, would signify nothing, and be no compact, if he be left free and under no other ties than he was in before in the state of nature. For what appearance would there be of any compact? What new engagement if he were no farther tied by any decrees of the society, than he himself thought fit, and did actually consent to? This would be still as great a liberty as he himself had before his compact, or anyone else in the state of nature hath, who may submit himself and consent to any acts of it if he thinks fit.

98. For if the consent of the majority shall not in reason be received as the act of the whole and conclude every individual, nothing but the consent of every individual can make anything to be the act of the whole, which considering the infirmities of health and avocations of business, which in a number, though much less than that of a commonwealth, will necessarily keep many away from the public assembly, and the variety of opinions, and contrariety of interest, which unavoidably happen in all collections of men, 'tis next to impossible ever to be had. And therefore if the coming into society

be upon such terms it will be only like Cato's coming into the theater, *tantum ut exiret.* Such a constitution as this would make the mighty leviathan of a shorter duration that the feeblest creatures, and not let it outlast the day it was born in; which cannot be supposed till we can think that rational creatures should desire and constitute societies only to be dissolved. For where the majority cannot conclude the rest, there they cannot act as one body, and consequently will be immediately dissolved again.

99. Whosoever therefore out of a state of nature unite into a community must be understood to give up all the power necessary to the ends for which they unite into society, to the majority of the community, unless they expressly agreed in any number greater than the majority. And this is done by barely agreeing to unite into one political society, which is all the compact that is, or needs be, between the individuals that enter into or make up a commonwealth. And thus that which begins and actually constitutes any political society is nothing but the consent of any number of freemen capable of a majority to unite and incorporate into such a society. And this is that, and that only, which did or could give beginning to any lawful government in the world.

OF THE ENDS OF POLITICAL SOCIETY AND GOVERNMENT

123. If man in the state of nature be so free, as has been said, if he be absolute lord of his own person and possessions, equal to the greatest, and subject to nobody, why will he part with his freedom, this empire, and subject himself to the dominion and control of any other power? To which, it is obvious to answer, that though in the state of nature he hath such a right, yet the enjoyment of it is very uncertain, and constantly exposed to the invasions of others. For all being kings as much as he, every man his equal, and the greater part no strict observers of equity and justice, the enjoyment of the property he has in this state is very unsafe, very unsecure. This makes him willing to quit this condition, which, however free, is full of fears and continual dangers; and it is not without reason that he seeks out and is willing to join in society with others, who are already united, or have in mind to unite, for the mutual preservation of their lives, liberties, and estates, which I

call by the general name, property.

124. The great and chief end, therefore, of men's uniting into commonwealths, and putting themselves under government, is the preservation of their property; to which in the state of nature there are many things wanting.

First, There wants an established, settled, known law, received and allowed by common consent to be the standard of right and wrong, and the common measure to decide all controversies between them. For though the law of nature be plain and intelligible to all rational creatures; yet men, being biased by their interest, as well as ignorant for want of study of it, are not apt to allow of it as a law binding to them in the application of it to their particular cases.

125. Secondly, In the state of nature there wants a known and indifferent judge, with authority to determine all differences according to the established law. For everyone in that state, being both judge and executioner of the law of nature, men being partial to themselves, passion and revenge is very apt to carry them too far, and with too much heat in their own cases, as well as negligence and unconcernedness, to make them too remiss in other men's.

126. Thirdly, In the state of nature there often wants power to back and support the sentence when right, and to give it due execution. They who by any injustice offend, will seldom fail, where they are able to force to make good their injustice; such resistance many times makes the punishment dangerous, and frequently destructive to those who attempt it.

127. Thus mankind, notwithstanding all the privileges of the state of nature, being but in an ill condition, while they remain in it, are quickly driven into society. Hence it comes to pass that we seldom find any number of men live any time together in this state. The inconveniences that they are therein exposed to by the irregular and uncertain exercise of the power every man has of punishing the transgressions of others, make them take sanctuary under the established laws of government, and therein seek the preservation of their property. It is this makes them so willingly give up everyone his single power of punishing, to be exercised by such alone, as shall be appointed to it amongst them; and by such rules as the community, or those authorized by them to that

purpose, shall agree on. And in this we have the original right and rise of both the legislative and executive power, as well as of the governments and societies themselves.

128. For in the state of nature, to omit the liberty he has of innocent delights, a man has two powers.

The first is to do whatsoever he thinks fit for the preservation of himself, and others within the permission of the law of nature, by which law, common to them all, he and all the rest of mankind are of one community, make up one society, distinct from all other creatures. And were it not for the corruption and viciousness of degenerate men there would be no need of any other, no necessity that men should separate from this great and natural community, and associate into lesser combinations.

The other power a man has in the state of nature is the power to punish the crimes committed against that law. Both these he gives up when he joins in a private, if I may so call it, or particular political society, and incorporates into any commonwealth separate from the rest of mankind.

129. The first power, viz., of doing whatsoever he thought fit for the preservation of himself and the rest of mankind, he gives up to be regulated by laws made by the society, so far forth as the preservation of himself and the rest of that society shall require; which laws of the society in many things confine the liberty he had by the law of nature.

130. Secondly, The power of punishing he wholly gives up, and engages his natural force (which he might before employ in the execution of the law of nature, by his own single authority as he thought fit), to assist the executive power of the society, as the law thereof shall require. For being now in a new state, wherein he is to enjoy many conveniences, from the labor, assistance, and society of others in the same community, as well as protection from its whole strength; he has to part also with as much of his natural liberty, in providing for himself, as the good, property and safety of the society shall require; which is not only necessary but just, since the other members of the society do the like.

131. But though men when they enter into society give up the equality, liberty and executive power they had in the state of nature into the hands of the society, to be so far disposed of

by the legislative as the good of the society shall require; yet it being only with an intention in everyone the better to preserve himself, his liberty and property (for no rational creature can be supposed to change his condition with an intention to the worse), the power of the society, or legislative constituted by them, can never be supposed to extend farther than the common good, but is obliged to secure everyone's property by providing against those three defects above-mentioned that made the state of nature so unsafe and uneasy. And so whoever has the legislative or supreme power of any commonwealth is bound to govern by established standing laws; promulgated and known to the people, and not by extemporary decrees; by indifferent and upright judges, who are to decide controversies by those laws; and to employ the force of the community at home only in the execution of such laws, or abroad, to prevent or redress foreign injuries, and secure the community from inroads and invasion. And all this to be directed to no other end but the peace, safety, and public good of the people.

OF THE FORMS OF A COMMONWEALTH

132. The majority having, as has been shown, upon men's first uniting into society, the whole power of the community, naturally in them, may employ all that power in making laws for the community from time to time, and executing those laws by officers of their own appointing: and then the form of the government is a perfect democracy; or else may put the power of making laws into the hands of a few select men, and their heirs or successors, and then it is an oligarchy; or else into the hands of one man and then it is a monarchy; if to him and his heirs, it is an hereditary monarchy; if to him only for life, but upon his death the power only of nominating a successor to return to them, an elective monarchy. And so accordingly of these, the community may make compounded and mixed forms of government, as they think good. And if the legislative power be at first given by the majority to one or more persons only for their lives, or any limited time, and then the supreme power to revert to them again; when it is so reverted, the community may dispose of it again anew into what hands they please, and so constitute a new form of government. For the form of government

depending upon the placing of the supreme power, which is the legislative, it being impossible to conceive that an inferior power should prescribe to a superior, or any but the supreme make laws, according as the power of making laws is placed, such is the form of the commonwealth.

133. By commonwealth, I must be understood all along to mean, not a democracy, or any form of government, but any independent community which the Latins signified by the word *civitas*, to which the word which best answers in our language is commonwealth, and most properly expresses such a society of men, which community does not, for there may be subordinate communities in a government; and city much less. And therefore to avoid ambiguity I crave leave to use the word commonwealth in that sense, in which I find it used by King James himself, which I think to be its genuine signification; which if anybody dislike, I consent with him to change it for a better.

OF THE SUBORDINATION OF THE POWERS OF THE COMMONWEALTH

149. Though in a constituted commonwealth, standing upon its own basis, and acting according to its own nature, that is, acting for the preservation of the community, there can be but one supreme power, which is the legislative, to which all the rest are and must be subordinate, yet the legislative being only of fiduciary power to act for certain ends, there remains still in the people a supreme power to remove or alter the legislative when they find the legislative act contrary to the trust reposed in them; for all power given with trust for the attaining an end, being limited by that end, wherever that end is manifestly neglected or opposed, the trust must necessarily be forfeited, and the power devolve into the hands of those that gave it who may place it anew where they shall think best for their safety and security. And thus the community perpetually retains a supreme power of saving themselves from the attempts and designs of anybody, even of their legislators wherever they shall be so foolish or so wicked as to lay and carry on designs against the liberties and properties of the subject; for no man or society of men, having a power to deliver up their preservation, or consequently the means of it to the absolute will and arbitrary dominion of another, whenever anyone shall go about to bring them into such a slavish, condition they will always have a right to preserve what they have not a power to part with; and to rid themselves of those who invade this fundamental, sacred and unalterable law of self-preservation for which they entered into society; and thus the community may be said in this resepct to be always the supreme power, but not as considered under any form of government, because this power of the people can never take place till the government be dissolved.

OF THE DISSOLUTION OF GOVERNMENT

211. He that will with any clearness speak of the dissolution of government ought, in the first place, to distinguish between the dissolution of the society and the dissolution of the government. That which makes the community, and brings men out of the loose state of nature into one politic society, is the agreement which everyone has with the rest to incorporate and act one body, and so be one distinct commonwealth. The usual and almost only way whereby this union is dissolved, is the inroad of foreign force making a conquest upon them. For in that case (not being able to maintain and support themselves as one entire and independent body) the union belonging to that body which consisted therein must necessarily cease, and so everyone return to the state he was in before, with a liberty to shift for himself and provide for his own safety as he thinks fit in some other society. Wherever the society is dissolved, it is certain the government of that society cannot remain. Thus conqueror's swords often cut up governments by the roots, and mangle societies to pieces, separating the subdued or scattered multitude from the protection of and dependence on that society which ought to have preserved them from violence. The world is too well instructed in, and too forward to allow of this way of dissolving of, governments to need any more to be said of it; and there wants not much argument to prove that where the society is dissolved, the government cannot remain—that being as impossible as for the frame of a house to subsist when the materials of it are scattered and displaced by a whirlwind, or jumbled into a confused heap by

an earthquake.

212. Besides this overturning from without, governments are dissolved from within.

First, When the legislative is altered. Civil society being a state of peace amongst those who are of it, from whom the state of war is excluded by the umpirage which they have provided in their legislative for the ending all differences that may arise amongst any of them, it is in their legislative that the members of a commonwealth are united and combined together in one coherent living body. This is the soul that gives form life, and unity to the commonwealth. From hence the several members have their mutual influence, sympathy, and connection. And, therefore, when the legislative is broken or dissolved, dissolution and death follow. For the essence and union of the society consisting in having one will, the legislative, when once established by the majority, has the declaring and, as it were, keeping of, that will. The constitution of the legislative is the first and fundamental act of the society, whereby provision is made for the continuation of their union, under the direction of persons and bonds of laws made by persons authorized thereunto by the consent and appointment of the people, without which no one man or number of men amongst them can have authority of making laws that shall be binding to the rest. When any one or more shall take upon them to make laws, whom the people have not appointed so to do, they make laws without authority, which the people are not therefore bound to obey; by which means they come again to be out of subjection, and may constitute to themselves a new legislative, as they think best, being in full liberty to resist the force of those who without authority would impose anything upon them. Everyone is at the disposure of his own will when those who had by the delegation of the society the declaring of the public will, are excluded from it, and others usurp the place who have no such authority or delegation.

213. This being usually brought about by such in the commonwealth who misuse the power they have, it is hard to consider it aright, and know at whose door to lay it, without knowing the form of government in which it happens. Let us suppose, then, the legislative placed in the concurrance of three distinct persons.

(1) A single hereditary person having the constant supreme executive power, and with it the power of convoking and dissolving the other two within certain periods of time.

(2) An assembly of hereditary nobility.

(3) An assembly of representatives chosen *pro tempore* by the people.

Such a form of government supposed, it is evident,

214. First, that when such a single person or prince sets up his own arbitrary will in place of the laws which are the will of the society, declared by the legislative, then the legislative is changed. For that being in effect the legislative whose rules and laws are put in execution and required to be obeyed when other laws set up, and other rules pretended and enforced, than what the legislative constituted by the society have enacted, it is plain that the legislative is changed. Whoever introduces new laws, not being thereunto authorized by the fundamental appointment of the society, or subverts the old, disowns and overturns the power by which they were made, and so sets up a new legislative.

215. Secondly, When the prince hinders the legislative from assembling in its due time, or from acting freely, pursuant to those ends for which it was constituted, the legislative is altered. For it is not a certain number of men, no, nor their meeting, unless they have also freedom of debating and lesiure of perfecting what is for the good of the society, wherein the legislative consists. When these are taken away or altered so as to deprive the society of the due exercise of their power, the legislative is truly altered. For it is not names that constitute governments, but the use and exercise of those powers that were intended to accompany them; so that he who takes away the freedom, or hinders the acting of the legislative in its due seasons, in effect takes away the legislative, and puts an end to the government.

216. Thirdly, When, by the arbitrary power of the prince, the electors or ways of elections are altered, without the consent and contrary to the common interest of the people, there also the legislative is altered. For if others than those whom the society hath authorized thereunto, do choose, or in another way than what the society hath prescribed, those chosen are not the legislative appointed by the people.

217. Fourthly, The delivery also of the people into the subjection of foreign power, either by

the prince, or by the legislative, is certainly a change of the legislative, and so a dissolution of the government. For the end why people entered into society being to be preserved one entire, free, independent society, to be governed by its own laws, this is lost whenever they are given up into the power of another.

218. Why, in such a constitution as this, the dissolution of the government in these cases is to be imputed to the prince is evidence, because he, having the force, treasure, and offices of the State to employ, and often persuading himself or being flattered by others, that, as supreme magistrate, he is incapable of control; he alone is in a condition to make great advances towards such changes under pretense of lawful authority, and has it in his hands to terrify or suppress oppressors as factious, seditious, and enemies to the government; whereas no other part of the legislative, or people, is capable by themselves to attempt any alteration of the legislative without open and visible rebellion, apt enough to be taken notice of, which when it prevails , produces effects very little different from foreign conquest. Besides, the prince, in such a form of government, having the power of dissolving the other parts of the legislative, and thereby rendering them private persons, they can never, in opposition to him, or without his concurrence, alter the legislative by a law, his consent being necessary to give any of their decrees that sanction. But yet so far as the other parts of the legislative any way contribute to any attempt upon the government, and do either promote, or not, what lies in them, hinder such designs, they are guilty, and partake in this, which is certainly the greatest crime men can be guilty of one towards another.

219. There is one way more whereby such a government may be dissolved, and that is, when he who has the supreme executive power neglects and abandons that charge, so that the laws already made can no longer be put in execution. This is demonstratively to reduce all to anarchy, and so effectually to dissolve the government. For laws not being made for themselves, but to be by their execution the bonds of the society, to keep every part of the body politic, in its due place and function, when that totally ceases, the government visibly ceases, and the people become a confused multitude without order or connection. Where

there is no longer the administration of justice, for the securing of men's rights, nor any remaining power within the community to direct the force, or provide for the necessities of the public, there certainly is no government left. Where the laws cannot be executed, it is all one as if there were no laws; and a government without laws is, I suppose, a mystery in politics, inconceivable to human capacity, and inconsistent with human society.

220. In these and the like cases, when the government is dissolved, the people are at liberty to provide for themselves by erecting a new legislative, different from the other, by the change of persons, or form, or both, as they shall find it for their safety and good. For the society can never, by the fault of another, lose the native and original right it has to preserve itself, which can only be done by a settled legislative, and a fair and impartial execution of the laws made by it. But the state of mankind is not so miserable that they are not capable of using this remedy, till it be too late to look for any. To tell people they may provide for themselves by erecting a new legislative, when by oppression, artifice, or being delivered over to a foreign power, their old one is gone, is only to tell them they may expect relief when it is too late, and the evil is past cure. This is in effect no more than to bid them first be slaves, and then to take care of their liberty; and when their chains are on tell them they may act like free men. This, if barely, so, is rather mockery than relief; and men can never be secure from tyranny if there be no means to escape it till they are perfectly under it. And therefore it is that they have not only a right to get out of it, but to prevent it.

221. There is therefore secondly another way whereby governments are dissolved, and that is when the legislative or the prince, either of them, acts contrary to their trust.

First, The legislative acts against the trust reposed in them when they endeavor to invade the property of the subject, and to make themselves or any part of the community masters or arbitrary disposers of the lives, liberties, or fortunes of the people.

222. The reason why men enter into society is the preservation of their property; and the end why they choose and authorize a legislative is that there may be laws made, and rules set, as guards and fences to the properties of all the

members of the society to limit the power and moderate the dominion of every part and member of the society. For since it can never be supposed to be the will of the society that the legislative should have a power to destroy that which everyone designs secure by entering into society, and for which the people submitted themselves to legislators of their own making, whenever the legislators endeavor to take away and destroy the property of the people, or to reduce them to slavery under arbitrary power, they put themselves into a state of war with the people, who are thereupon absolved from any further obedience, and are left to the common refuge which God hath provided for all men against force and violence. Whensoever, therefore, the legislative shall transgress this fundamental rule of society, and either by ambition, fear, folly, or corruption, endeavor to grasp themselves or put into the hands of any other an absolute power over the lives, liberties, and estates of the people, by this breach of trust they forfeit the power the people had put into their hands, for quite contrary ends, and it devolves to the people, who have a right to resume their original liberty, and by the establishment of the new legislative (such as they shall think fit) provide for their own safety and security, which is the end for which they are in society. What I have said here concerning the legislative in general, holds true also concerning the supreme executor, who having a double trust put in him, both to have a part in the legislative and the supreme execution of the law, acts against both when he goes about to set up his own arbitrary will as the law of the society. He acts also contrary to his trust when he either employs the force, treasure, and offices of the society, to corrupt the representatives, and gain them to his purposes; or openly pre-engages the electors, and prescribes to their choice such whom he has by solicitations, threats, promises, or otherwise won to his designs, and employs them to bring in such, who have promised beforehand what to vote and what to enact. Thus to regulate candidates and electors, and new-model the ways of election, what is it but to cut up the government by the roots, and poison the very fountain of public security? For the people having reserved to themselves the choice of their representatives as the fence to their properties, could do it for no other end but that they might always be freely chosen, and, so chosen, freely act and advise as the necessity of the commonwealth and the public good should upon examination and mature debate be judged to require. This those who give their votes before they hear the debate, and have weighed the reason on all sides, are not capable of doing. To prepare such an assembly as this, and endeavor to set up the declared abettors of his own will for the true representatives of the people and the lawmakers of the society, is certainly as great a breach of trust and as perfect a declaration of a design to subvert the government as is possible to be met with. To which if one shall add rewards and punishments visibly employed to the same end and all the arts of perverted law made use of to take off and destroy all that stand in the way of such a design, and will not comply and consent to betray the liberties of their country, it will be past doubt what is doing. What power they ought to have in the society who thus employ it contrary to the trust that went along with it in its first institution is easy to determine; and one cannot but see that he who has once attempted any such thing as this cannot any longer be trusted.

J. J. Rousseau

Although frequently linked with the philosophers of Enlightenment France, Rousseau (1712-1778) did not really share their outlook. In the *Social Contract* (1762), he went even further in attenuating the concept of a contract. The individual was related to society by will, not by an agreement. In his description of the state of nature, Rousseau argued against Hobbes, against the mechanistic view of human nature, and he argued that inequality was the result of the corruption caused by private property. Rousseau also developed further the notion of the "general will" which he had described in an earlier work *Discourse on Inequality* (1754), as "the voice of God." Finally, Rousseau introduced the concept of freedom not as having the ability to satisfy one's appetites —for appetite is slavery—but as the willing obedience to law.

Rousseau went out of his way to distinguish the general will from the majority will and, in fact, from the will of all. This is a consistent development of his notion of freedom. The general will is a kind of ideal in terms of which we may judge any society. In this respect it is, in Rousseau, a Platonic notion.

The Social Contract

SUBJECT OF THE FIRST BOOK

Man is born free, and everywhere he is in chains. Many a one believes himself the master of others, and yet he is a greater slave than they. How has this change come about? I do not know. What can render it legitimate? I believe that I can settle this question.

If I considered only force and the results that proceed from it, I should say that so long as a people is compelled to obey and does obey, it does well; but that, so soon as it can shake off the yoke and does shake it off, it does better; for, if men recover their freedom by virtue of the same right by which it was taken away, either they are justified in resuming it, or there was no justification for depriving them of it. But the social order is a sacred right which serves as a foundation for all others. This right, however, does not come from nature. It is therefore based on conventions. The question is to know what these conventions are. Before coming to that, I must establish what I have just laid down.

THE SOCIAL PACT

I assume that men have reached a point at which the obstacles that endanger their preservation in the state of nature overcome by their resistance the forces which each individual can exert with a view to maintaining himself in that state. Then this primitive condition cannot longer subsist, and the human race would perish unless it changed its mode of existence.

Now as men cannot create any new forces, but only combine and direct those that exist, they have no other means of self-preservation than to form by aggregation a sum of forces which may overcome the resistance, to put them in action by a single motive power, and to make them work in concert.

This sum of forces can be produced only by the combination of many; but the strength and freedom of each man being the chief instruments of his preservation, how can he pledge them without injuring himself, and without neglecting the cares which he owes to himself? This difficulty, applied to my subject, may be expressed in these terms:—

"To find a form of association which may defend and protect with the whole force of the community, the person and property of every associate, and by means of which, coalescing with all, may nevertheless obey only himself, and remain as free as before." Such is the fundamental problem of which the social contract furnishes the solution.

The clauses of this contract are so determined by the nature of the act that the slightest modification would render them vain and ineffectual; so that, although they have never perhaps been formally enunciated, they are everywhere the same, everywhere tacitly admitted and recognized, until, the social pact being violated, each man regains his original rights and recovers his natural liberty while losing the conventional liberty for which he renounced it.

These clauses, rightly understood, are reducible to one only, viz, the total alienation to the whole community of each associate with all his rights; for, in the first place, since each gives himself up entirely, the conditions are equal for all; and, the conditions being equal for all, no one has any interest in making them burdensome to others.

Further, the alienation being made without reserve, the union is as perfect as it can be, and an individual associate can no longer claim anything; for, if any rights were left to individuals, since there would be no common superior who could judge between them and the public, each, being on some point his own judge, would soon claim to be so on all; the state of nature would still subsist, and the association would necessarily become tyrannical or useless.

In short, each giving himself to all, gives himself to nobody; and as there is no one associate over whom we do not acquire the same rights which we concede to him over ourselves, we gain the equivalent of all that we lose, and more power to preserve what we have.

If, then, we set aside what is not of the essence of the social contract, we shall find that it is reducible to the following terms: "Each of us puts in common his person and his whole power under the supreme direction of the general will; and in return we receive every member as an indivisible part of the whole."

Forthwith, instead of the individual personalities of all the contracting parties, this act of association produces a moral and collective body, which is composed of as many members as the assembly has voices, and which receives from this same act its unity, its common self (*moi*), its life, and its will. This public person, which is thus formed by the union of all the individual members, formerly took the name of *city,* and now takes that of *republic* or *body politic*, which is called by its members *State* when it is passive, *sovereign* when it is active, *power* when it is compared to similar bodies. With regard to the associates, they take collectively the name of *people*, and are called individually *citizens,* as participating in the sovereign power, and *subjects*, as subjected to the laws of the State. But these terms are often confused and are mistaken one for another; it is sufficient to know how to distinguish them when they are used with complete precision.

THE SOVEREIGN

We see from this formula that the act of association contains a reciprocal engagement between the public and individuals, and that every individual, contracting so to speak with himself, is engaged in a double relation, viz, as a member of the sovereign toward individuals, and as a member of the State toward the sovereign. But we cannot apply here the maxim of civil law that no one is bound by engagements made with himself; for there is a great difference between being bound to oneself and to a whole of which one forms part.

We must further observe that the public resolution which can bind all subjects to the sovereign in consequence of the two different relations under which each of them is regarded cannot, for a contrary reason, bind the sovereign to itself; and that accordingly it is contrary to the nature of the body politic for the sovereign to impose on itself a law which it cannot transgress. As it can only be considered under one and the same relation, it is in the position of an individual contracting with himself; whence we see that there is not, nor can be, any kind of fundamental law binding upon the body of the people, not even the social contract. This does not imply that such a body cannot perfectly well enter into engagements with others in what does not derogate from this contract; for, with regard to foreigners, it becomes a simple being, an individual.

But the body politic or sovereign, deriving its existence only from the sanctity of the contract, can never bind itself, even to others, in anything that derogates from the original act, such as alienation of some portion of itself, or submission to another sovereign. To violate the act by which it exists would be to annihilate itself; and what is nothing produces nothing.

So soon as the multitude is thus united in one body, it is impossible to injure one of the members without attacking the body, still less to injure the body without the members feeling the effects. Thus duty and interest alike oblige the two contracting parties to give mutual assistance; and the men themselves should seek to combine in this twofold relationship all the advantages which are attendant on it.

Now, the sovereign, being formed only of the individuals that compose it, neither has nor can have any interest contrary to theirs; consequently the sovereign power needs no guarantee toward its subjects, because it is impossible that the body should wish to injure all its members; and we shall see hereafter that it can injure no one as an individual. The sovereign, for the simple reason that it is so, is always everything that it ought to be.

But this is not the case as regards the relation

of subjects to the sovereign, which, notwithstanding the common interest, would have no security for the performance of their engagements, unless it found means to ensure their fidelity.

Indeed, every individual may, as a man, have a particular will contrary to, or divergent from, the general will which he has as a citizen; his private interest may prompt him quite differently from the common interest; his absolute and naturally independent existence may make him regard what he owes to the common cause as a gratuitous contribution, the loss of which will be less harmful to others than the payment of it will be burdensome to him; and, regarding the moral person that constitutes the State as an imaginary being because it is not a man, he would be willing to enjoy the rights of a citizen without being willing to fulfill the duties of a subject. The progress of such injustice would bring about the ruin of the body politic.

In order, then, that the social pact may not be a vain formulary, it tacitly includes this engagement, which can alone give force to the others, that whoever refuses to obey the general will shall be constrained to do so by the whole body; which means nothing else than that he shall be forced to be free; for such is the condition which, uniting every citizen to his native land, guarantees him from all personal dependence, a condition that insures the control and working of the political machine, and alone renders legitimate civil engagements, which, without it, would be absurd and tyrannical, and subject to the most enormous abuses.

THE CIVIL STATE

The passage from the state of nature to the civil state produces in man a very remarkable change, by substituting in his conduct justice for instinct, and by giving his actions the moral quality that they previously lacked. It is only when the voice of duty succeeds physical impulse, and law succeeds appetite, that man, who till then had regarded only himself, sees that he is obliged to act on other principles, and to consult his reason before listening to his inclinations. Although, in this state, he is deprived of many advantages that he derives from nature, he acquires equally great ones in return; his faculties are exercised and developed; his ideas are expanded; his feelings

are ennobled; his whole soul is exalted to such a degree that, if the abuses of this new condition did not often degrade him below that from which he has emerged, he ought to bless without ceasing the happy moment that released him from it for ever, and transformed him from a stupid and ignorant animal into an intelligent being and a man.

Let us reduce this whole balance to terms easy to compare. What man loses by the social contract is his natural liberty and an unlimited right to anything which tempts him and which he is able to attain: what he gains is civil liberty and property in all that he possesses. In order that we may not be mistaken about these compensations, we must clearly distinguish natural liberty, which is limited only by the powers of the individual, from civil liberty, which is limited by the general will; and possession, which is nothing but the result of force or the right of first occupancy, from property, which can be based only on a positive title.

Besides the preceding, we might add to the acquisitions of the civil state moral freedom, which alone renders man truly master of himself; for the impulse of mere appetite is slavery, while obedience to a self-prescribed law is liberty. But I have already said too much on this head, and the philosophical meaning of the term *liberty* does not belong to my present subject.

THAT SOVEREIGNTY IS INALIENABLE

The first and most important consequence of the principles above established is that the general will alone can direct the forces of the State according to the object of its institution, which is the common good; for if the opposition of private interests has rendered necessary the establishment of societies, the agreement of these same interests has rendered it possible. That which is common to these different interests forms the social bond; and unless there were some point in which all interests agree, no society could exist. Now, it is solely with regard to this common interest that the society should be governed.

I say, then, that sovereignty, being nothing but the exercise of the general will, can never be alienated, and that the sovereign power, which is only a collective being, can be represented by itself alone; power indeed can be transmitted, but not will.

In fact, if it is not impossible that a particular will should agree on some point with the general will, it is at least impossible that this agreement should be lasting and constant; for the particular will naturally tends to preferences, and the general will to equality. It is still more impossible to have a security for this agreement; even though it should always exist, it would not be a result of art, but of chance. The sovereign may indeed say: "I will now what a certain man wills, or at least what he says that he wills"; but he cannot say: "What that man wills to-morrow, I shall also will," since it is absurd that the will should bind itself as regards the future, and since it is not incumbent on any will to consent to anything contrary to the welfare of the being that wills. If then, the nation simply promises to obey, it dissolves itself by that act and loses its character as a people; the moment there is a master, there is no longer a sovereign, and forthwith the body politic is destroyed.

This does not imply that the orders of the chiefs cannot pass for decisions of the general will, so long as the sovereign, free to oppose them, refrains from doing so. In such a case the consent of the people should be inferred from the universal silence. This will be explained at greater length.

THAT SOVEREIGNTY IS INDIVISIBLE

For the same reason that sovereignty is inalienable it is indivisible; for the will is either general, or it is not; it is either that of the body of the people, or that of only a portion. In the first case, this declared will is an act of sovereignty and constitutes law; in the second case, it is only a particular will, or an act of magistracy —it is at most a decree.

But our publicists, being unable to divide sovereignty in its principle, divide it in its object. They divide it into force and will, into legislative power and executive power; into rights of taxation, of justice, and of war; into internal administration and power of treating with foreigners—sometimes confounding all these departments, and sometimes separating them. They make the sovereign a fantastic being, formed of connected parts; it is as if they composed a man of several bodies, one with eyes, another with arms, another with feet, and nothing else. The Japanese conjurers, it is said, cut up a child before the eyes of the spectators; then, throwing all its limbs into the air, they make the child come down again alive and whole. Such almost are the juggler's tricks of our publicists; after dismembering the social body by a deception worthy of the fair, they recombine its parts, nobody knows how.

This error arises from their not having formed exact notions about the sovereign authority, and from their taking as parts of this authority what are only emanations from it. Thus, for example, the acts of declaring war and making peace have been regarded as acts of sovereignty, which is not the case, since neither of them is a law, but only an application of the law, a particular act which determines the case of the law, as will be clearly seen when the idea attached to the word *law* is fixed.

By following out the other divisions in the same way it would be found that, whenever the sovereignty appears divided, we are mistaken in our supposition; and that the rights which are taken as parts of that sovereignty are all subordinate to it, and always suppose supreme wills of which these rights are merely executive.

It would be impossible to describe the great obscurity in which this want of precision has involved the conclusions of writers on the subject of political right when they have endeavored to decide upon the respective rights of kings and peoples on the principles that they had established. Every one can see in chapters III and IV of the first book of Grotius, how that learned man and his translator Barbeyrac became entangled and embarrassed in their sophisms, for fear of saying too much or not saying enough according to their views, and so offending the interests that they had to conciliate. Grotius, having taken refuge in France through discontent with his own country, and wishing to pay court to Louis XIII, to whom his book is dedicated, spares no pains to despoil the people of all their rights, and, in the most artful manner, bestow them on kings. This also would clearly have been the inclination of Barbeyrac, who dedicated his translation to the king of England, George I. But unfortunately the expulsion of James II, which he calls an abdication, forced him to be reserved and to equivocate and evade in order not to make William appear a usurper. If these two writers had adopted true principles, all difficulties would have been removed, and they would have been always consistent; but they would have spoken the truth with regret, and would have paid court only to the people. Truth, however, does not lead to fortune, and the people confer neither embassies, nor professorships, nor pensions.

WHETHER THE GENERAL WILL CAN ERR

It follows from what precedes that the general will is always right and always tends to the public advantage; but it does not follow that the resolutions of the people have always the same rectitude. Men always desire their own good, but do not always discern it; the people are never corrupted, though often deceived, and it is only then that they seem to will what is evil.

There is often a great deal of difference between the will of all and the general will; the latter regards only the common interest, while the former has regard to private interests, and is merely a sum of particular wills; but take away from these same wills the pluses and minuses which cancel one another, and the general will remains as the sum of the differences.

If the people come to a resolution when adequately informed and without any communication among the citizens, the general will would always result from the great number of slight differences, and the resolution would always be good. But when factions, partial associations, are formed to the detriment of the whole society the will of each of these associations becomes general with reference to its members, and particular with reference to the State; it may then be said that there are no longer as many voters as there are men, but only as many voters as there are associations. The differences become less numerous and yield a less general result. Lastly, when one of these associations becomes so great that it predominates over all the rest, you no longer have as the result a sum of small differences, but a single difference; there is then no longer a general will, and the opinion which prevails is only a particular opinion.

It is important, then, in order to have a clear declaration of the general will, that there should be no partial association in the State,

and that every citizen should express only his own opinion. Such was the unique and sublime institution of the great Lycurgus. But if there are partial associations, it is necessary to multiply their number and prevent inequality, as Solon, Numa, and Servius did. These are the only proper precautions for insuring that the general will may always be enlightened, and that the people may not be deceived.

THAT THE GENERAL WILL IS INDESTRUCTIBLE

So long as a number of men in combination are considered as a single body, they have but one will, which relates to the common preservation and to the general well-being. In such a case all the forces of the State are vigorous and simple, and its principles are clear and luminous; it has no confused and conflicting interests; the common good is everywhere plainly manifest and only good sense is required to perceive it. Peace, union, and equality are foes to political subtleties. Upright and simpleminded men are hard to deceive because of their simplicity; allurements and refined pretexts do not impose upon them; they are not even cunning enough to be dupes. When, in the happiest nation in the world, we see troops of peasants regulating the affairs of the State under an oak and always acting wisely, can we refrain from despising the refinements of other nations, who make themselves illustrious and wretched with so much art and mystery?

A State thus governed needs very few laws; and in so far as it becomes necessary to promulgate new ones, this necessity is universally recognized. The first man to propose them only gives expression to what all have previously felt, and neither factions nor eloquence will be needed to pass into law what every one has already resolved to do, so soon as he is sure that the rest will act as he does.

What deceives reasoners is that, seeing only States that are ill-constituted from the beginning, they are impressed with the impossibility of maintaining such a policy in those States; they laugh to think of all the follies to which a cunning knave, an insinuating speaker, can persuade the people of Paris or London. They know not that Cromwell would have been put in irons by the people of Berne, and the Duke of Beaufort imprisoned by the Genevese.

But when the social bond begins to be relaxed and the State weakened, when private interests begin to make themselves felt and small associations to exercise an influence on the State, the common interest is injuriously affected and finds adversaries, unanimity no longer reigns in the voting; the general will is no longer the will of all; opposition and disputes arise, and the best counsel does not pass uncontested.

Lastly, when the State, on the verge of ruin, no longer subsists except in a vain and illusory form, when the social bond is broken in all hearts, when the basest interest shelters itself impudently under the sacred name of the public welfare, the general will becomes dumb; all, under the guidance of secret motives, no more express their opinions as citizens than if the State had never existed; and, under the name of laws, they deceitfully pass unjust decrees which have only private interest as their end.

Does it follow from this that the general will is destroyed or corrupted? No; it is always constant, unalterable, and pure; but it is subordinated to others which get the better of it. Each, detaching his own interest from the common interest, sees clearly that he cannot completely separate it; but his share in the injury done to the State appears to him as nothing in comparison with the exclusive advantage which he aims at appropriating to himself. This particular advantage being excepted, he desires the general welfare for his own interests quite as strongly as any other. Even in selling his vote for money, he does not extinguish in himself the general will, but eludes it. The fault that he commits is to change the state of the question, and to answer something different from what he was asked; so that, instead of saying by a vote: "It is beneficial to the State," he says: "It is beneficial to a certain man or a certain party that such or such a motion should pass." Thus the law of public order in assemblies is not so much to maintain in them the general will as to insure that it shall always be consulted and always respond.

I might in this place make many reflections on the simple right of voting in every act of sovereignty—a right which nothing can take away from the citizens—and on that of speaking, proposing, dividing, and discussing, which the government is always very careful to leave to its members only; but this important matter would require a separate treatise, and I cannot say everything in this one.

G. W. F. Hegel

Hegel (1770-1831) was a German philosopher who formulated a highly influential theory known as *absolute idealism*. It is idealistic in the philosophical sense of believing that reality is spiritual, not material. It is absolute in the sense that it asserts the world to be in a process of continual historical development progressing to the full development of the Absolute. Every aspect of human existence is a manifestation of progress from lower to higher forms of the Absolute.

Every social collective, whether the family, or civil society, or the state is a manifestation of objective spirit, and the state is the highest manifestation. Since the individual can only be understood as part of a social institution, there can be no ethics apart from politics, no morality apart from social good. The individual is only fully developed, and therefore free, in the social whole. This view directly contradicts the individualistic tendencies of the Anglo-Saxon political philosophers. Hence, Hegel opposes the notion of representative democracies wherein representation is of mere individuals. Instead he proposes a corporate society in which the various institutions are representative bodies.

The Philosophy of Right

75 . . . It is a popular view in modern times that the state is a contract of all with all. All conclude, so the doctrine runs, a compact with the prince, and he in turn with the subjects. According to this superficial view, there is in contract only one unity of different wills; but in fact there are two identical wills, both of which are persons, and wish to remain possessors. Contract, besides, arises out of the spontaneous choice of the persons. Marriage, indeed, has that point in common with contract, but with the state it is different. An individual cannot enter or leave the social condition at his option, since every one is by his very nature a citizen of a state. The characteristic of man as rational is to live in a state; if there is no state, reason claims that one should be founded. A state, it is true, must grant permission either to enter or to leave it; but this permission is not given in deference to the arbitrary choice of the individual, nor is the state founded upon a contract which presupposes this choice. It is false to say that it rests with the arbitrary will of all to establish a state; rather it is absolutely necessary for every one to be in a state. The great progress of the modern state is due to the fact that it has and keeps an absolute end, and no man is now at liberty to make private arrangements in connection with this end, as they did 'n the middle ages. . . .

THE CIVIC COMMUNITY

182. The concrete person, who as particular is an end to himself, is a totality of wants and a mixture of necessity and caprice. As such he is one of the principles of the civic community. But the particular person is essentially connected with others. Hence each establishes and satisfies himself by means of others, and so must call in the assistance of the form of universality. This universality is the other principle of the civic community.

Addition. —The civic community is the realm of difference, intermediate between the family and the state, even if its construction folowed in point of time the construction of the state. It, as the difference, must presuppose the state. On the self-dependent 'state it must rely for its subsistence. Further, the creation of the civic community belongs to the modern world which alone has permitted every element of the idea to receive its due. When the state is represented as a union of different persons, that is, a unity which is merely a community, it is only the civic community which is meant. Many modern teachers of political science have not been able to develop any other view of the state. In this society every one is an end to himself; all others are for him nothing. And yet without coming into relation with others he cannot realize his ends. Hence to each particular person others are a means to the attainment of his end. But the particular purpose gives itself through reference to others the form of universality, and in satisfying itself accomplishes at the same time the well-being of others. Since particularity is bound up with the conditioning universal, the joint whole is the ground of adjustment or mediation, upon which all individualities, all talents, all accidents of birth or fortune disport themselves. Here the foundations of all the passions are let loose, being merely governed by reason. Particularity limited by universality is the only standard to which the particular person conforms in promoting his well-being.

183. The self-seeking end is conditioned in its realization by the universal. Hence is formed a system of mutual dependence, a system which interweaves the subsistence, happiness, and rights of the individual with the subsistence, happiness, and right of all. The general right and well-being form the basis of the individual's right and well-being, which only by this connection receives actuality and security. This system we may in the first instance call the external state, the state which satisfies one's needs, and meets the requirements of the understanding.

187. Individuals in the civic community are private persons, who pursue their own interests. As these interests are occasioned by the universal, which appears as a means, they can be obtained only in so far as individuals in their desire, will, and conduct, conform to the universal, and become a link in the chain of the whole. The interest of the idea as such does not, it is true, lie in the consciousness of the citizens; yet it is not wholly wanting. It is found in the process, by means of which the individual, through necessity of nature and the caprice of his wants, seeks to raise his individual natural existence into formed freedom and the formal universality of knowing and willing. Thus, without departing from its particular nature, the individual's character is enlarged.

Note.—The view that civilization is an external and degenerate form of life is allied to the idea that the natural condition of uncivilized peoples is one of unsophisticated innocence. So also the view that civilization is a mere means for the satisfaction of one's needs, and for the enjoyment and comfort of one's particular life, takes for granted that these selfish ends are absolute. Both theories manifest ignorance of the nature of spirit and the end of reason. Spirit is real only when (by its own motion) it divides itself, gives itself limit and finitude in the natural needs and the region of external necessity, and then, by moulding and shaping itself in them, overcomes them, and secures for itself an objective embodiment. It works away from the condition of simple nature, in which there is either no self or a crude state of consciousness and will, and transcends the naive individuality, in which spirit is submerged. . . .

. . . Culture or education is, as we may thus, conclude, in its ultimate sense a liberation, and

that of a high kind. Its task is to make possible the infintely subjective substantiality of the ethical life. In the process we pass upwards from the direct and natural existence to what is spiritual and has the form of the universal.—In the individual agent this liberation involves a struggle against mere subjectivity, immediate desire, subjective vanity, and capricious liking. The hardness of the task is in part the cause of the disfavour under which it falls. None the less is it through the labour of education that the subjective will itself wins possession of the objectivity, in which alone it is able and worthy to be the embodiment of the idea. . . .

188. The civic community contains three elements:

A. The recasting of want, and the satisfaction of the individual through his work, through the work of all others, and through the satisfaction of their wants. This is a system of wants.

B. Actualization of the general freedom required for this, *i.e.,* the protection of property by the administration of justice.

C. Provision against possible mischances, and care for the particular interest as a common interest, by means of police and the corporation.

THE STATE

257. The state is the realized ethical idea or ethical spirit. It is the will which manifests itself clear and visible, substantiates itself. It is the will which thinks and knows itself, and carries out what it knows, and in so far as it knows. The state finds in ethical custom its direct and unreflected existence, and its indirect and reflected existence in the self-consciousness of the individual and in his knowledge and activity. Self-consciousness in the form of social disposition has its substantive freedom in the state, as the essence, purpose, and produce of its activity. . . .

258. The state, which is the realized substantive will, having its reality in the particular self-consciousness raised to the plane of the universal, is absolutely rational. This substantive unity is its own motive and absolute end. In this end freedom attains its highest right. This end has the highest right over the individual, whose highest duty in turn is to be a member of the state.

Note.—Were the state to be considered as exchangeable with the civic society, and were its decisive features to be regarded as the security, and protection of property and personal freedom, the interest of the individual as such would be the ultimate purpose of the social union. It would then be at one's option to be a member of the state.—But the state has a totally different relation to the individual. It is the objective spirit, and he has his truth, real existence, and ethical status only in being a member of it. Union, as such, is itself the true content and end, since the individual is intended to pass into a universal life. His particular satisfactions, activities, and way of life have in this authenticated substantive principle their origin and result....

To Rousseau is to be ascribed the merit of discovering and presenting a principle, which comes up to the standard of the thought, and is indeed thinking itself, not only in its form, such as would be a social impulse or divine authority but in its very essence. This principle of Rousseau is will. But he conceives of the will only in the limited form of the individual will, as did also Fichte afterwards, and regards the universal will not as the absolutely reasonable will, but only as the common will, proceeding out of the individual will as conscious. Thus the union of individuals in a state becomes a contract, which is based upon caprice, opinion, and optional, explicit consent. Out of this view the understanding deduces consequences, which destroy the absolutely divine, and its absolute authority and majesty. Hence, when these abstractions attained to power, there was enacted the most tremendous spectacle which the human race has ever witnessed. All the usages and institutions of a great state were swept away. It was then proposed to begin over again, starting from the thought, and as the basis of the state to will only what was judged to be rational. But as the undertaking was begun with abstractions void of all ideas, it ended in scenes of tragic cruelty and horror.

260. The state is the embodiment of concrete freedom. In this concrete freedom, personal individuality and its particular interests, as found in the family and civic community, have their complete development. In this concrete freedom, too, the rights of personal individuality receive adequate recognition. These interests and rights pass partly of their own accord into the interest of the universal. Partly, also, do the individuals recognize by their own knowledge and will the universal as their own substantive spirit, and work for it as their own end. Hence, neither is the universal completed without the assistance of the particular interest, knowledge, and will, nor, on the other hand, do individuals, as private persons, live merely for their own special concern. They regard the general end, and are in all their activities conscious of this end. The modern state has enormous strength and depth, in that it allows the principle of subjectivity to complete itself to an independent extreme of personal particularity, and yet at the same time brings it back into the substantive unity, and thus preserves particularlity in the principle of the state.

Addition.—The peculiarity of the idea of the modern state is that it is the embodimenet of freedom, not according to subjective liking, but to the conception of the will, the will, that is, in its universal and divine character. Incomplete states are they, in which this idea is still only a germ, whose particular phases are not permitted to mature into self-dependence. In the republics of classical antiquity universality, it is true, is to be found. But in those ages particularity had not as yet been released from its fetters, and led back to universality or the universal purpose of the whole. The essence of the modern state binds together the universal and the full freedom of particularity, including the welfare of individuals. It insists that the interests of the family and civic community shall link themselves to the state, and yet is aware that the universal purpose can make no advance without the private knowledge and will of a particularity, which must adhere to its right. The universal must be actively furthered, but, on the other side, subjectivity must be wholly and vitally developed. Only when both elements are present in force is the state to be regarded as articulate and truly organized.

261. In contrast with the spheres of private right and private good, of the family and of the civic community, the state is on one of its sides an external necessity. It is thus a higher authority, in regard to which the laws and interests of the family and community are subject and dependent. On the other side, however, the state is the indwelling end of these things, and is strong in its union of the universal end with the particular interests of individuals. Thus,

273. Here it is natural to put a second question:—Who shall frame the constitution? This question seems intelligible at first glance, but on closer examination turns out to be meaningless. It presupposes that no constitution exists, but merely a collection of atomic individuals. How a heap of individuals is to obtain a constitution, whether by its own efforts or by means of others, whether by goodness, thought, or force, must be left to itself to decide, for with a mere mass the conception has nothing to do. If the question, however, takes for granted the existence of an actual constitution, then to make a constitution means only to modify it, the previous existence of the constitution implying that any change must be made constitutionally. But it is strictly essential that the constitution, though it is begotten in time, should not be contemplated as made. It is rather to be thought of as above and beyond what is made, as self-begotten and self-centred, as divine and perpetual.

Addition.—The principle of the modern world as a whole is freedom of subjectivity, the principle that all essential aspects of the spiritual whole should attain their right by self-development. From this standpoint one can hardly raise the idle question, as to which form is the better, monarchy or democracy. We venture to reply simply that the forms of all constitutions of the state are one-sided, if they are not able to contain the principle of free subjectivity, and do not know how to correspond to completed reason.

279. The phrase "sovereignty of the people," can be used in the sense that a people is in general self-dependent in its foreign relations, and constitutes its own state. Such are the people of Great Britain, for example. But the people of England, Scotland, Ireland, Venice, Genoa, or Ceylon, have ceased to be a sovereign people, since they no longer have independent princes, and the chief government is not exclusively their own. Further, it may be said that internal sovereignty resides in the people if, as was already pointed out, we speak in general terms, and mean that sovereignty of the people is usually in moderns times opposed to the sovereignty of the monarch. This view of the sovereignty of the people may be traced to a just so far as people have duties to fulfill towards it, they have also rights.

confused idea of what is meant by "the people." The people apart from their monarch, and the common membership necessarily and directly associated with him, is a formless mass. It is no longer a state. In it occur none of the characteristic features of an equipped whole, such as sovereignty, government, law-courts, magistrates, professions, etc., etc. When these elements of an organized national life make their appearance in a people, it causes to be that undefined abstraction, which is indicated by the mere general notion "people."

If by the phrase "sovereignty of the people" is to be understood a republic, or more precisely a democracy, for by a republic we understand various empirical mixtures which do not belong to a philosophic treatise, all that is necessary has already been said. There can no longer be any defense of such a notion in contrast with the developed idea.—When a people is not a patriarchal tribe, having passed from the primitive condition, which made the forms of aristocracy and democracy possible, and is represented not as in a wilful and unorganized condition, but as a self-developed truly organic totality, in such a people sovereignty is the personality of the whole, and exists, too, in a reality, which is proportionate to the conception, the person of the monarch.

281. If we are to apprehend the idea of the monarch, it is not sufficient for us to say that God has established kings, since God has made everything, even the worst of things. Nor can we proceed very far under the guidance of the principle of utility, since it is always open to point out disadvantages. Just as little are we helped by regarding monarchy as positive right. That I should have property is necessary, but this specific possession is accidental. Accidental also appears to be the right that one man should stand at the helm of state, if this right, too, be regarded as abstract and positive. But this right is present absolutely, both as a felt want and as a need of the thing itself. A monarch is not remarkable for bodily strength or intellect, and yet millions permit themselves to be ruled by him. To say that men permit themselves to be governed contrary to their interests, ends, and intentions is preposterous, since men are not so stupid. It is their need and the inner power of the idea which urge them to this in opposition to their seeming consciousness, and retain them in this relation. . . .

301. There are found in current opinion so

unspeakable many perverted and false notions and sayings concerning the people the constitution, and the classes, that it would be a vain task to specify, explain, and correct them. When it is argued that an assembly of estates is necessary and advantageous, it is meant that the people's deputies, or, indeed, the people itself, must best understand their own interest, and that it has undoubtedly the truest desire to secure this interest. But it is rather true that the people, is so far as this term signifies a special part of the citizens, does not know what it wills. To know what we will, and further what the absolute will, namely reason, wills, is the fruit of deep knowledge and insight, and is therefore not the property of the people. . . .

General well-being does not therefore depend upon the particular insight of the classes, but is rather the achievement of the official deputies. They can inspect the work of the officers who are farthest removed from the observation of the chief functionaries of state. They too, have a concrete perception of the more urgent special needs and defects. But to this intelligent oversight must be added the possibility of public censure. This possibility has the effect of calling out the best insight upon public affairs and projects, and also, the purest motives; its influence is felt by the members of the classes themselves. . . .

308. It is held that all should share individually in the counsels and decisions regarding the general affairs of state. The reason assigned is that all are members of the state, its affairs are the affairs of all, and for the transaction of these affairs all with their knowledge and will have a right to be present. This is a notion which, although it has no reasonable form, the democratic element would insert into the organism of state, notwithstanding the fact that the state is an organism only because of its reasonable form. This superficial view fastens upon and adheres to the abstraction "member of the state." But the rational method, the consciousness of the idea, is concrete and is combined with the true practical sense, which is itself nothing else than the rational sense or the sense for the idea. Yet this sense is not to be confounded with mere business routine, or bounded by the horizon of a limited sphere. The concrete state is the whole, articulated into its particular circles, and the member of the state is the member of a circle or class. Only his objective character can be recognized in the

state. His general character contains the twofold element, private person and thinking person, and thinking is the consciousness and willing of the universal. But consciousness and will cease to be empty only when they are filled with particularity, and by particularity is meant the characteristic of a particular class. The individual is species, let us say, but has his intrinsic general actuality in the species next above it. He attains actual and vital contact with the universal in the sphere of the corporations and societies. It remains open to him by means of his skill to make his way into any class, for which he has the capacity, including the universal class. Another assumption, found in the current idea that all should have a sphere in the business of state, is that all understand this business. This is as absurd as it, despite its absurdity, is widespread. However, through the channel of public opinion every one is free to express and make good his subjective opinion concerning the universal.

316. Formal subjective freedom, implying that individuals as such should have and express their own judgment, opinion, and advice concerning affairs of state, makes its appearance in that aggregate, which is called public opinion. In it what is absolutely universal, substantive, and true is joined with its opposite, the independent, peculiar, and particular opinions of the many. This phase of existence is therefore the actual contradiction of itself; knowledge is appearance, the essential exists directly as the unessential.

Addition.—Public opinion is the unorganized means through which what a people wills and thinks is made known. That which is effective in the state must indeed be in organic relation to it; and in the constitution this is the case. But at all times public opinion has been a great power, and it is especially so in our time, when the principle of subjective freedom has such importance and significance. What now shall be confirmed is confirmed no longer through force, and but little through use and wont, but mainly by insight and reasons.

317. Public opinion contains therefore the eternal substantive principles of justice, the true content and result of the whole constitution, of legislation, and of the universal condition in general. It exists in the form of sound human understanding, that is, of an ethical principle which in the shape of prepossessions runs through everything. It contains the true

wants and right tendencies of actuality.

But when this inner phase comes forth into consciousness, it appears to imaginative thinking in the form of general propositions. It claims to be of interest partly on its own separate account; but it also comes to the assistance of concrete reasoning upon felt wants and upon the events, arrangements, and relations of the state. When this happens, there is brought forward also the whole range of accidental opinion, with its ignorance and perversion, its false knowledge and incorrect judgment. Now, as to the consciousness of what is peculiar in thought and knowledge, with which the present phenomenon has to do, it may be said that the worse an opinion is, the more peculiar and unique it is. The bad is in its content wholly particular and unique.; the rational on the contrary, is the absolutely universal. Yet it is the unique upon which opinion founds its exalted self-esteem. . . .

319. The liberty of taking part in state affairs, the pricking impulse to say and to have said one's opinion, is directly secured by police laws and regulations, which, however, hinder and punish the exceed of this liberty. Indirect security is based upon the government's strength, which lies mainly in the rationality of its constitution and the stability of its measure, but partly also in the publicity given to the assemblies of the classes. Security is guaranteed by publicity in so far as the assemblies voice the mature and educated insight into the interests of the state, and pass over to others what is less significant, especially if they are disabused of the idea that the utterances of these others are peculiarly important and efficacious. Besides, a broad guarantee is found in the general differences and contempt, with which shallow and malicious utterances are quickly and effectually visited.

Note.—One means of freely and widely participating in public affairs is the press, which, in its more extended range, is superior to speech, although inferior in vivacity.—To define liberty of the press as liberty to speak and write what one pleases is parallel to the definitions of liberty in general, as liberty to do what one pleases. These views belong to the undeveloped crudity and superficiality of fanciful theorizing. . . But it thus comes into contact with the freedom of others, upon whom it depends whether the act is actually an injury or not.

The fact remains that injury to the honour of individuals generally, as libel, abuse, disdainful treatment of the government, its officials and officers, especially the person of the prince, contempt for the laws, incitement to civil broil etc., are all crimes or faults of different magnitudes. The greater indefiniteness of these acts, due to the element in which they find utterance, does not annul their real character.

324. It is a very distorted account of the matter when the state, in demanding sacrifices from the citizens, is taken to be simply the civic community, whose object is merely the security of life and property. Security cannot possibly be obtained by the sacrifice of what is to be secured.

Herein is to be found the ethical element in war. War is not to be regarded as an absolute evil. It is not a merely external accident, having its accidental ground in the passions of powerful individuals or nations, in acts of injustice, or in anything which ought not to be. Accident befalls that which is by nature accidental, and this fate is a necessity. So from the standpoint of the conception and in philosophy the merely accidental vanishes, because in it, as it is a mere appearance, is recognized its essence, namely, necessity. It is necessary that what is finite, such as life and property, should have its contingent nature exposed, since contingency is inherent in the conception of the finite. This necessity has in one phase of it the form of a force of nature, since all that is finite is mortal and transient. But in the ethical life, that is to say, the state, this force and nature are separated. Necessity becomes in this way exalted to the work of freedom, and becomes a force which is ethical. What from the standpoint of nature is transient, is now transient because it is willed to be so; and that, which is fundamentally negative, becomes substantive and distinctive individuality in the ethical order. . . .

342. Moreover, world history is not a court of judgment, whose principle is force, nor is it the abstract and irrational necessity of a blind fate. It is self-caused and self-realized reason, and its actualized existence in spirit is knowledge. Hence, its development issuing solely out of the conception of its freedom is a necessary development of the elements of reason. It is, therefore, an unfolding of the spirit's self-consciousness and freedom. It is the exhibition and actualization of the universal spirit.

Karl Marx

It is difficult to separate the real Marx (1818-83), German-born social philosopher, from the mythology which inevitably develops around an influential figure. In 1843 he moved to Paris where he established a life-long friendship and collaboration with Friedrich Engels, and in 1848 they completed the *Communist Manifesto* reprinted below. From 1850 until his death, Marx lived in London and wrote his monumental *Das Kapital*.

Marx began with Hegel's concept of the dialectic of history and, like him, worked out a theory of progressive social and historical change culminating in a specific end. However, Marx explained change in terms of material factors, not spiritual factors as in Hegel, and that is why Marx's philosophy is sometimes spoken of as *dialectical materialism*. The specific material factors responsible for historical development were, according to Marx, economic.

Marx was thus concerned with the laws of economic-historical development in which one era passes into another, with those forces and conditions within present bourgeois society leading to its alleged inevitable replacement, and with some speculation about the next and final stage. While the overall process is rational, men are not, in the old sense. Our political views are mere reflections of our present economic position. Hence, violence and revolution are necessary. Finally, in the future classless society, the result of changes in economic conditions, there would be no state, in the sense of a special institution necessary for maintaining order, or in practice, of oppressing one class for the benefit of another.

413

Manifesto of the Communist Party

A spectre is haunting Europe—the spectre of Communism. All the Powers of old Europe have entered into a holy alliance to exorcise this spectre: Pope and Czar, Metternich and Guizot, French Radicals and German police-spies.

Where is the party in opposition that has not been decried as Communistic by its opponents in power? Where the Opposition that has not hurled back the branding reproach of Communism, against the more advanced opposition parties, as well as against its reactionary adversaries?

Two things result from this fact.

I. Communism is already acknowledged by all European Powers to be itself a Power.

II. It is high time that Communists should openly, in the face of the whole world, publish their views, their aims, their tendencies, and meet this nursery tale of the Spectre of Communism with a Manifesto of the party itself.

To this end, Communists of various nationalities have assembled in London, and sketched the following Manifesto, to be published in the English, French, German, Italian, Flemish and Danish languages.

The history of all hitherto existing society is the history of class struggles.

Freeman and slave, patrician and plebeian, lord and serf, guildmaster and journeyman, in a word, oppressor and oppressed, stood in constant opposition to one another, carried on an uninterrupted, now hidden, now open fight, a fight that each time ended, either in a revolutionary reconstitution of society at large, or in the common ruin of the contending classes.

In the earlier epochs of history, we find almost everywhere a complicated arrangement of society into various orders, a manifold gradation of social rank. In ancient Rome we have patricians, knights, plebeians, slaves; in the Middle Ages, feudal lords, vassals, guildmasters, journeymen, apprentices, serfs; in almost all of these classes, again, subordinate gradations.

The modern bourgeois society that has sprouted from the ruins of feudal society has not done away with class antagonisms. It has but established new classes, new conditions of oppression, new forms of struggle in place of the old ones.

Our epoch, the epoch of the bourgeoisie, possesses, however, this distinctive feature: It has simplified the class antagonisms. Society as a whole is more and more splitting up into two great hostile camps, into two great classes directly facing each other—bourgeoisie and proletariat.

From the serfs of the Middle Ages sprang the chartered burghers of the earliest towns. From these burgesses the first elements of the bourgeoisie were developed.

The discovery of America, the rounding of the Cape, opened up fresh ground for the rising bourgeoisie. The East-Indian and Chinese markets, the colonization of America, trade with the colonies, the increase in the means of exchange and in commodities generally, gave to commerce, to navigation, to industry, an impulse never before known, and thereby, to the revolutionary element in the tottering feudal society, a rapid development.

The feudal system of industry, in which industrial production was monopolized by closed guilds, now no longer sufficed for the growing wants of the new markets. The manufacturing system took its place. The guildmasters were pushed aside by the manufacturing middle class; division of labor between the different corporate guilds vanished in the face of division of labor in each single workshop.

Meantime the markets kept ever growing, the demand ever rising. Even manufacturing no longer sufficed. Thereupon, steam and machinery revolutionized industrial production. The place of manufacture was taken by the giant, modern industry, the place of the industrial middle class, by industrial millionaires—the leaders of whole industrial armies, the modern bourgeois.

Modern industry has established the world market, for which the discovery of America paved the way. This market has given an immense development to commerce, to navigation, to communication by land. This development has, in its turn, reacted on the extension of industry; and in proportion as industry, commerce, navigation, railways extended, in the same proportion the bourgeoisie developed, increased its capital, and pushed into the background every class handed down from the Middle Ages.

We see, therefore, how the modern bourgeoisie is itself the product of a long course of development, of a series of revolutions in the modes of production and of exchange.

Each step in the development of the bourgeoisie was accompanied by the corresponding political advance of that class. An oppressed class under the sway of the feudal nobility, it became an armed and self-governing association in the medieval commune; here independent urban republic (as in Italy and Germany), there taxable "third estate" of the monarchy (as in France); afterwards, in the period of manufacture proper, serving either the semi-feudal or the absolute monarchy as a counterpoise against the nobility, and, in fact, cornerstone of the great monarchies in general—the bourgeoisie has at last, since the establishment of modern industry and of the world market, conquered for itself, in the modern representative state, exclusive political sway. The executive of the modern state is but a committee for managing the common affairs of the whole bourgeoisie.

The bourgeoisie has played a most revolutionary role in history.

The bourgeoisie, wherever it has got the upper hand, has put an end to all feudal, patriarchal, idyllic relations. It has pitilessly torn asunder the motley feudal ties that bound man to his "natural superiors," and has left no other bond between man and man than naked self-interest, than callous "cash payment." It has drowned the most heavenly ecstasies of religious fervor, of chivalrous enthusiasm, of philistine sentimentalism, in the icy water of egotistical calculation. It has resolved personal worth into exchange value, and in place of the numberless indefeasible chartered freedoms, has set up that single, unconscionable freedom—Free Trade. In one word, for exploitation, veiled by religious and political illusions, it has substituted naked, shameless, direct, brutal exploitation. . . .

The bourgeoisie cannot exist without constantly revolutionizing the instruments of production, and thereby the relations of production, and with them the whole relations of society. Conservation of the old modes of production in unaltered form, was, on the contrary, the first condition of existence for all earlier industrial classes. Constant revolutionizing of production, uninterrupted disturbance of all social conditions, everlasting uncertainty and agitation distinguish the bourgeois epoch from all earlier ones. All fixed, fast-frozen relations, with their train of ancient and venerable prejudices and opinions, are swept away, all new-formed ones become antiquated before they can ossify. All that is solid melts into air, all that is holy is profaned, and man is at last compelled to face with sober senses his real conditions of life and his relations with his kind. . . .

The bourgeoisie, by the rapid improvements of all instruments of production, by the immensely facilitated means of communication, draws all nations, even the most barbarian, into civilization. The cheap prices of its commodities are the heavy artillery with which it batters down all Chinese walls, with which it forces the barbarians' intensely obstinate hatred of foreigners to capitulate. It compels all nations, on pain of extinction, to adopt the bourgeois mode of production, it compels them to introduce what it calls civilization into their midst, *i.e.*, to become bourgeois themselves. In a word, it creates a world after its own image. . . .

The bourgeoisie, during its rule of scarce one hundred years, has created more massive and more colossal productive forces than have all preceding generations together. Subjection of nature's forces to man, machinery, application of chemistry to industry and agriculture, steam-navigation, railways, electric telegraphs, clearing of whole continents for cultivation, canalization of rivers, whole populations conjured out of the ground—what earlier century had even a presentiment that such productive forces slumbered in the lap of social labor?

We see then that the means of production and of exchange, which served as the foundation for the growth of the bourgeoisie, were generated in feudal society. At a certain stage in the development of these means of production and of exchange, the conditions under which feudal society produced and exchanged, the feudal organization of agriculture and manufacturing industry, in a word, the feudal relations of property became no longer compatible with the already developed productive forces; they became so many fetters. They had to be burst asunder; they were burst asunder.

Into their place stepped free competition, accompanied by a social and political constitution adapted to it, and by the economic and political sway of the bourgeois class.

A similar movement is going on before our own eyes. Modern bourgeois society with its relations of production, of exchange and of property, a society that has conjured up such gigantic means of production and of exchange, is like the sorcerer who is no longer able to control the powers of the nether world whom he has called up by his spells. For many a decade past the history of industry and commerce is but the history of the revolt of modern productive forces against modern conditions of production, against the property relations that are the conditions for the existence of the bourgeoisie and of its rule. It is enough to mention the commercial crises that by their periodical return put the existence of the entire bourgeois society on trial, each time more threateningly. In these crises a great part not only of the existing products, but also of the previously created productive forces, are periodically destroyed. In these crises there breaks out an epidemic that, in all earlier epochs, would have seemed an absurdity—the epidemic of over-production. Society suddenly finds itself put back into a state of momentary barbarism; it appears as if a famine, a universal war of devastation had cut off the supply of every means of

subsistence; industry and commerce seem to be destroyed. And why? Because there is too much civilization, too much means of subsistence, too much industry, too much commerce. The productive forces at the disposal of society no longer tend to further the development of the conditions of bourgeois property; on the contrary, they have become too powerful for these conditions, by which they are fettered, and no sooner do they overcome these fetters than they bring disorder into the whole of bourgeois society, endanger the existence of bourgeois property. The conditions of bourgeois society are too narrow to comprise the wealth created by them. And how does the bourgeoisie get over these crises? On the one hand by enforced destruction of a mass of productive forces; on the other, by the conquest of new markets, and by the more thorough exploitation of the old ones. That is to say, by paving the way for more extensive and more destructive crises, and by diminishing the means whereby crises are prevented.

The weapons with which the bourgeoisie felled feudalism to the ground are now turned against the bourgeoisie itself.

But not only has the bourgeoisie forged the weapons that bring death to itself; it has also called into existence the men who are to wield those weapons—the modern working class—the proletarians.

In proportion as the bourgeoisie, *i.e.,* capital, is developed, in the same proportion is the proletariat, the modern working class, developed—a class of laborers, who live only so long as they find work, and who find work only so long as their labor increases capital. These laborers, who must sell themselves piecemeal, are a commodity, like every other article of commerce, and are consequently exposed to all the vicissitudes of competition, to all the fluctuations of the market.

Owing to the extensive use of machinery and to division of labor, the work of the proletarians has lost all individual character, and, consequently, all charm for the workman. He becomes an appendage of the machine, and it is only the most simple, most monotonous, and most easily acquired knack, that is required of him. Hence, the cost of production of a workman is restricted, almost entirely, to the means of subsistence that he requires for his maintenance, and for the propagation of his race.

But the price of a commodity, and therefore also of labor, is equal to its costs of production. In proportion, therefore, as the repulsiveness of the work increases, the wage decreases. Nay more, in proportion as the use of machinery and division of labor increases, in the same proportion the burden of toil also increases, whether by prolongation of the working hours, by increase of the work exacted in a given time, or by increased speed of the machinery, etc.

Modern industry has converted the little workshop of the patriarchal master into the great factory of the industrial capitalist. Masses of laborers, crowded into the factory, are organized like soldiers. As privates of the industrial army they are placed under the command of a perfect hierarchy of officers and sergeants. Not only are they slaves of the bourgeois class, and of the bourgeois state; they are daily and hourly enslaved by the machine, by the supervisor, and, above all, by the individual bourgeois manufacturer himself. The more openly this despotism proclaims gain to be its end and aim, the more petty, the more hateful and the more embittering it is. . . .

The proletariat goes through various stages of development. With its birth begins its struggle with the bourgeoisie. At first the contest is carried on by individual laborers, then by the work people of a factory, then by the operatives of one trade, in one locality, against the individual bourgeois who directly exploits them. They direct their attacks not against the bourgeois conditions of production, but against the instruments of production themselves; they destroy imported wares that compete with their labor, they smash machinery to pieces, they set factories ablaze, they seek to restore by force the vanished status of the workman of the Middle Ages.

At this stage the laborers still form an incoherent mass scattered over the whole country, and broken up by their mutual competition. If anywhere they unite to form more compact bodies, this is not yet the consequence of their own active union, but of the union of the bourgeoisie, which class, in order to attain its own political ends, is compelled to set the whole proletariat in motion, and is moreover still able to do so for a time. At this stage, therefore, the proletarians do not fight their enemies, but the enemies of their enemies, the remnants of absolute monarchy, the landowners, the nonin-

dustrial bourgeois, the petty bourgeoisie. Thus the whole historical movement is concentrated in the hands of the bourgeoisie; every victory so obtained is a victory for the bourgeoisie.

But with the development of industry the proletariat not only increases in number; it becomes concentrated in greater masses, its strength grows, and it feels that strength more. The various interests and conditions of life within the ranks of the proletariat are more and more equalized, in proportion as machinery obliterates all distinctions of labor and nearly everywhere reduces wages to the same low level. The growing competition among the bourgeois, and the resulting commercial crises, make the wages of the workers ever more fluctuating. The unceasing improvement of machinery, ever more rapidly developing, makes their livelihood more and more precarious; the collisions between individual workmen and individual bourgeois take more and more the character of collisions between two classes. Thereupon the workers begin to form combinations (trade unions) against the bourgeoisie; they club together in order to keep up the rate of wages; they found permanent associations in order to make provision beforehand for these occasional revolts. Here and there the contest breaks out into riots.

Now and then the workers are victorious, but only for a time. The real fruit of their battle lies, not in the immediate results, but in the ever expanding union of the workers. This union is furthered by the improved means of communication which are created by modern industry, and which place the workers of different localities in contact with one another. It was just this contact that was needed to centralize the numerous local struggles, all of the same character, into one national struggle between classes. But every class struggle is a political struggle. And that union, to attain which the burghers of the Middle Ages, with their miserable highways, required centuries, the modern proletarians, thanks to railways, achieve in a few years.

This organization of the proletarians into a class, and consequently into a political party, is continually being upset again by the competition between the workers themselves, But it ever rises up again, stronger, firmer, mightier. It compels legislative recognition of particular interests of the workers, by taking advantage of the divisions among the bourgeoisie itself.

Thus the ten-hour bill in England was carried. . . .

Finally, in times when the class struggle nears the decisive hour, the process of dissolution going on within the ruling class, in fact within the whole range of old society, assumes such a violent, glaring character, that a small section of the ruling class cuts itself adrift, and joins the revolutionary class, the class that holds the future in its hands. Just as, therefore, at an earlier period, a section of the nobility went over to the bourgeoisie, so now a portion of the bourgeoisie goes over to the proletariat, and in particular, a portion of the bourgeois ideologists, who have raised themselves to the level of comprehending theoretically the historical movement as a whole.

Of all the classes that stand face to face with the bourgeoisie today, the proletariat alone is a really revolutionary class. The other classes decay and finally disappear in the face of modern industry; the proletariat is its special and essential product. . . .

The social conditions of the old society no longer exist for the proletariat. The proletarian is without property; his relation to his wife and children has no longer anything in common with bourgeois family relations; modern industrial labor, modern subjection to capital, the same in England as in France, in America as in Germany, has stripped him of every trace of national character. Law, morality, religion, are to him so many bourgeois prejudices, behind which lurk in ambush just as many bourgeois interests.

All the preceding classes that got the upper hand, sought to fortify their already acquired status by subjecting society at large to their conditions of appropriation. The proletarians cannot become masters of the productive forces of society, except by abolishing their own previous mode of appropriation, and thereby also every other previous mode of appropriation. They have nothing of their own to secure and to fortify; their mission is to destroy all previous securities for, and insurances of, individual property.

All previous historical movements were movements of minorities, or in the interest of minorities. The proletarian movement is the self-conscious, independent movement of the immense majority, in the interest of the immense majority. The proletariat, the lowest stratum of our present society, cannot stir, cannot raise itself up, without the whole superincumbent strata of official society being sprung into the air. . . .

Hitherto, every form of society has been based, as we have already seen, on the antagonism of oppressing and oppressed classes. But in order to oppress a class, certain conditions must be assured to it under which it can, at least, continue its slavish existence. The serf, in the period of serfdom, raised himself to membership in the commune, just as the petty bourgeois, under the yoke of feudal absolutism, managed to develop into a bourgeois. The modern laborer, on the contrary, instead of rising with the progress of industry, sinks deeper and deeper below the conditions of existence of his own class. He becomes a pauper, and pauperism develops more rapidly than population and wealth. And here it becomes evident, that the bourgeoisie is unfit any longer to be the ruling class in society, and to impose its conditions of existence upon society as an overriding law. It is unfit to rule because it is incompetent to assure an existence to its slave within his slavery, because it cannot help letting him sink into such a state, that it has to feed him, instead of being fed by him. Society can no longer live under this bourgeoisie, in other words, its existence is no longer compatible with society.

The essential condition for the existence and sway of the bourgeois class, is the formation and augmentation of capital; the condition for capital is wage-labor. Wage-labor rests exclusively on competition between the laborers. The advance of industry, whose involuntary promoter is the bourgeoisie, replaces the isolation of the laborers, due to competition, by their revolutionary combination, due to association. The development of modern industry, therefore, cuts from under its feet the very foundation on which the bourgeoisie produces and appropriates products. What the bourgeoisie therefore produces, above all, are its own gravediggers. Its fall and the victory of the proletariat are equally inevitable. . . .

All property relations in the past have continually been subject to historical change consequent upon the change in historical conditions.

The French Revolution, for example, abolished feudal property in favor of bourgeois property.

The distinguishing feature of communism is not the abolition of property generally, but the abolition of bourgeois property. But modern bourgeois private property is the final and most complete expression of the system of producing and appropriating products that is based on class antagonisms, on the exploitation of the many by the few.

In this sense, the theory of the Communists may be summed up in the single sentence: Abolition of private property.

We Communists have been reproached with the desire of abolishing the right of personally acquiring property as the fruit of a man's own labor, which property is alleged to be the groundwork of all personal freedom, activity and independence.

Hard-won, self-acquired, self-earned property! Do you mean the property of the petty artisan and of the small peasant, a form of property that preceded the bourgeois form? There is no need to abolish that; the development of industry has to a great extent already destroyed it, and is still destroying it daily.

Or do you mean modern bourgeois private property?

But does wage-labor create any property for the laborer? Not a bit. It creates capital, *i.e.*, that kind of property which exploits wage-labor and which cannot increase except upon condition of begetting a new supply of wage-labor for fresh exploitation. Property, in its present form, is based on the antagonism of capital and wage-labor. Let us examine both sides of this antagonism.

To be a capitalist, is to have not only a purely personal but a social *status* in production. Capital is a collective product, and only by the united action of many members, nay, in the last resort, only by the united action of all members of society, can it be set in motion.

Capital is therefore not a personal, it is a social, power.

When, therefore, capital is converted into common property, into the property of all members of society, personal property is not thereby transformed into social property. It is only the social character of the property that is changed. It loses its class character.

Let us now take wage-labor.

The average price of wage-labor is the minimum wage, *i.e.*, that quantum of the means of subsistence which is absolutely requisite to keep the laborer in bare existence as a laborer. What, therefore, the wage-laborer appropriates by means of his labor, merely suffices to prolong and reproduce a bare existence. We by no means intend to abolish this personal appropriation of the products of labor, an appropriation that is made for the maintenance and reproduction of human life, and that leaves no surplus wherewith to command the labor of others. All that we want to do away with is the miserable character of this appropriation, under which the laborer lives merely to increase capital and is allowed to live only insofar as the interest of the ruling class requires it.

In bourgeois society, living labor is but a means to increase accumulated labor. In Communist society, accumulated labor is but a means to widen, to enrich, to promote the existence of the laborer.

In bourgeois society, therefore, the past dominates the present; in Communist society, the present dominates the past. In bourgeois society capital is independent and has individuality, while the living person is dependent and has no individuality.

And the abolition of this state of things is called by the bourgeois, abolition of individuality, bourgeois independence, and bourgeois freedom is undoubtedly aimed at.

By freedom is meant, under the present bourgeois conditions of production, free trade, free selling and buying.

But if selling and buying disappears, free selling and buying disappears also. This talk about free selling and buying, and all the other "brave words" of our bourgeoisie about freedom in general, have a meaning, if any, only in contrast with restricted selling and buying, with the fettered traders of the Middle Ages, but have no meaning when opposed to the Communist abolition of buying and selling, of the bourgeois conditions of production, and of the bourgeoisie itself.

You are horrified at our intending to do away with private property. But in your existing society, private property is already done away with for nine-tenths of the population; its existence for the few is solely due to its nonexistence in the hands of those nine-tenths. You reproach us, therefore, with intending to do away with a form of property, the necessary condition for whose existence is the nonexistence of any property for the immense majority of society.

In a word, you reproach us with intending to do away with your property. Precisely so; that is just what we intend.

From the moment when labor can no longer be converted into capital, money, or rent, into a social power capable of being monopolized, *i.e.,* from the moment when individual property can no longer be transformed into bourgeois property, into capital, from that moment, you say, individuality vanishes.

You must, therefore, confess that by "individual" you mean no other person than the bourgeois, than the middle-class owner of property. This person must, indeed, be swept out of the way, and made impossible.

Communism deprives no man of the power to appropriate the products of society; all that it does is to deprive him of the power to subjugate the labor of others by means of such appropriation. . . .

All objections urged against the Communist mode of producing and appropriating material products, have, in the same way, been urged against the Communist modes of producing and appropriating intellectual products. Just as, to the bourgeois, the disappearance of class property is the disappearance of production itself, so the disappearance of class culture is to him identical with the disappearance of all culture.

That culture, the loss of which he laments, is, for the enormous majority, a mere training to act as a machine.

But don't wrangle with us so long as you apply, to our intended abolition of bourgeois property, the standard of your bourgeois notions of freedom, culture, law, etc. Your very ideas are but the outgrowth of the conditions of your bourgeois production and bourgeois property, just as your jurisprudence is but the will of your class made into a law for all, a will whose essential character and direction are determined by the economic conditions of existence of your class.

The selfish misconception that induces you to transform into eternal laws of nature and of reason, the social forms springing from your present mode of production and form of property—historical relations that rise and disappear in the progress of production—this misconception you share with every ruling class that has preceded you. What you see clearly in the case of ancient property, what you admit in the case of feudal property, you are of course forbidden to admit in the case of your own bourgeois form of property. . . .

The charges against communism made from a religious, a philosophical, and, generally, from an ideological standpoint, are not deserving of serious examination.

Does it require deep intuition to comprehend that man's ideas, views, and conceptions, in one word, man's consciousness, changes with every change in the conditions of his material existence, in his social relations and in his social life?

What else does the history of ideas prove, than that intellectual production changes its character in proportion as material production is changed? The ruling ideas of each age have ever been the ideas of its ruling class.

When people speak of ideas that revolutionize society, they do but express the fact that within the old society the elements of a new one have been created, and that the dissolution of the old ideas keeps even pace with the dissolution of the old conditions of existence.

When the ancient world was in its last throes, the ancient religions were overcome by Christianity. When Christian ideas succumbed in the eighteenth century to rationalist ideas, feudal society fought its death-battle with the then revolutionary bourgeoisie. The ideas of religious liberty and freedom of conscience, merely gave expression to the sway of free competition within the domain of knowledge.

"Undoubtedly," it will be said, "religion, moral, philosophical and juridical ideas have been modified in the course of historical development. But religion, morality, philosophy, political science, and law, constantly survived this change."

"There are, besides, eternal truths, such as Freedom, Justice, etc., that are common to all states of society. But communism abolishes eternal truths, it abolished all religion, and all morality, instead of constituting them on a new basis; it therefore acts in contradiction to all past historical experience."

What does this accusation reduce itself to? The history of all past society has consisted in the development of class antagonisms, antagonisms that assumed different forms at different epochs.

But whatever form they may have taken, one

fact is common to all past ages, *viz.*, the exploitation of one part of society by the other. No wonder, then, that the social consciousness of past ages, despite all the multiplicity and variety it displays, moves within certain common forms, or general ideas, which cannot completely vanish except with the total disappearance of class antagonisms.

The Communist revolution is the most radical rupture with traditional property relations; no wonder that its development involves the most radical rupture with traditional ideas.

But let us have done with the bourgeois objections to communism.

We have seen above, that the first step in the revolution by the working class, is to raise the proletariat to the position of ruling class, to establish democracy.

The proletariat will use its political supremacy to west, by degrees, all capital from the bourgeoisie, to centralize all instruments of production in the hands of the state, *i.e.*, of the proletariat organized as the ruling class; and to increase the total of productive forces as rapidly as possible.

Of course, in the beginning, this cannot be effected except by means of despotic inroads on the rights of property, and on the conditions of bourgeois production; by means of measures, therefore, which appear economically insufficient and untenable, but which, in the course of the movement, outstrip themselves, necessitate further inroads upon the old social order, and are unavoidable as a means of entirely revolutionizing the mode of production. . . .

When, in the course of development, class distinctions have disappeared, and all production has been concentrated in the hands of a vast association of the whole nation, the public power will lose its political character. Political power, properly so called, is merely the organized power of one class for oppressing another. If the proletariat during its contest with the bourgeoisie is compelled, by the force of circumstances, to organize itself as a class, and, as such sweeps away by force the old conditions of production, then it will, along with these conditions, have swept away the conditions for the existence of class antagonisms, and of classes generally, and will thereby have abolished its own supremacy as a class.

In place of the old bourgeois society, with its classes and class antagonisms, we shall have an association, in which the free development of each is the condition for the free development of all.

J. S. Mill

The reader is reminded to reread the original selection on Mill in the section entitled "How to Read Philosophy." This piece and that one are from his essay On *Liberty* (1859). Mill is in many ways the culmination of the Anglo-Saxon tradition in political philosophy, and in his writings one may discern the emphasis on individualism shorn of its connection with the social contract theory, which he rejects.

The best way to understand Mill is to see him as rejecting the Aristotelian view of a built-in human nature. If there is no built-in human nature then there is no final end to be realized and no justification for social philosophies such as Hegel's, which argue that the institutional setting is necessary for human development. To be sure, there is the idea of development in Mill, but it is not a progress to a definite end. If there are no final ends, then there can be no absolute truths in politics, hence his opposition to censorship in any form. Mill seems to be arguing that humanity as a whole survives better when it allows individual variations, just as a species will prove more adaptable if it has many variations.

On Liberty

CHAPTER II

We have now recognized the necessity to the mental well-being of mankind (on which all their other well-being depends) of freedom of opinion, and freedom of the expression of opinion, on four distinct grounds, which we will now briefly recapitulate:

First, if any opinion is compelled to silence, that opinion may, for aught we can certainly know, be true. To deny this is to assume our own infallibility.

Secondly, though the silenced opinion be an error, it may, and very commonly does, contain a portion of truth; and since the general or prevailing opinion on any subject is rarely or never the whole truth, it is only by the collision of adverse opinions that the remainder of the truth has any chance of being supplied.

Thirdly, even if the received opinion be not only true, but the whole truth; unless it is suffered to be, and actually is, vigorously and earnestly contested, it will, by most of those who receive it, be held in the manner of a prejudice, with little comprehension or feeling of its rational grounds. And not only this, but, fourthly, the meaning of the doctrine of its vital effect on the character and conduct: the dogma becoming a mere formal profession, inefficacious for good, but cumbering the ground and preventing the growth of any real and heartfelt conviction from reason or personal experience. . . .

CHAPTER III

Such being the reasons which make it imperative that human beings should be free to form

opinions and to express their opinions without reserve; and such the baneful consequences to the intellectual, and through that to the moral nature of man, unless this liberty is either conceded or asserted in spite of prohibition; let us next examine whether the same reasons do not require that men should be free to act upon their opinions—to carry these out in their lives without hindrance, either physical or moral, from their fellow men, so long as it is at their own risk and peril. This last proviso is of course indispensable. No one pretends that actions should be as free as opinions. On the contrary, even opinions lose their immunity when the circumstances in which they are expressed are such as to constitute their expression a positive instigation to some mischievous act. An opinion that corn dealers are starvers of the poor, or that private property is robbery, ought to be unmolested when simply circulated through the press, but may justly incur punishment when delivered orally to an excited mob assembled before the house of a corn dealer, or when handed about among the same mob in the form of a placard. Acts, of whatever kind, which without justifiable cause do harm to others may be, and in the more important cases absolutely require to be, controlled by the unfavorable sentiments, and, when needful, by the active interference of mankind. The liberty of the individual must be thus far limited; he must not make himself a nuisance to other people. But if he refrains from molesting others in what concerns them, and merely acts according to his own inclination and judgment in things which concern himself, the same reasons which show that opinion should be free prove also that he should be allowed, without molestation, to carry his opinions into practice at his own cost. That mankind are not infallible; that their truths, for the most part, are only half-truths; that unity of opinion, unless resulting from the fullest and freest comparison of opposite opinions, is not desirable, and diversity not an evil, but a good, until mankind are much more capable than at present of recognizing all sides of the truth, are principles applicable to men's modes of action not less than to their opinions. As it is useful that while mankind are imperfect there should be different opinions, so it is that there should be given to varieties of character, short of injury to others; and that the worth of different modes of life should be proved practically, when anyone thinks fit to try them. It is desirable, in short, that in things which do not primarily concern others individuality should assert itself. Where not the person's own character but the traditions or customs of other people are the rule of conduct, there is wanting one of the principal ingredients of human happiness, and quite the chief ingredient of individual and social progress.

In maintaining this principle, the greatest difficulty to be encountered does not lie in the appreciation of means toward an acknowledged end, but in the indifference of persons in general to the end itself. If it were felt that the free development of individuality is one of the leading essentials of well-being; that it is not only a co-ordinate element with all that is designated by the terms civilization, instruction, education, culture, but is itself a necessary part and condition of all those things, there would be no danger that liberty should be undervalued, and the adjustment of the boundaries between it and social control would present no extraordinary difficulty. But the evil is that individual spontaneity is hardly recognized by the common modes of thinking as having any intrinsic worth, or deserving any regard on its own account. The majority, being satisfied with the ways of mankind as they now are (for it is they who make them what they are), cannot comprehend why those ways should not be good enough for everybody; and what is more, spontaneity forms no part of the ideal of the majority of moral, and social reformers, but is rather looked on with jealousy as a troublesome and perhaps rebellious obstruction to the general acceptance of what

these reformers, in their own judgment, think would be best for mankind. Few persons, out of Germany, even comprehend the meaning of the doctrine which Wilhelm von Humboldt, so eminent both as a *savant* and as a politician, made the text of a treatise—that "the end of man, or that which is prescribed by the eternal or immutable dictates of reason, and not suggested by vague and transient desires, is the highest and most harmonious development of his powers to a complete and consistent whole"; that, therefore, the object "toward which every human being must ceaselessly direct his efforts, and on which especially those who design to influence their fellow men must ever keep their eyes, is the individuality of power and development"; that for this there are two requisites, "freedom, and variety of situations"; and that from the union of these arise "individual vigor and manifold diversity," which combine themselves in "originality." . . .

Having said that the individuality is the same thing with development, and that it is only the cultivation of individuality which produces, or can produce, well-developed human beings, I might here close the argument: for what more or better can be said of any condition of human affairs than that it brings human beings themselves nearer to the best thing they can be? Or what worse can be said of any obstruction to good than that it prevents this? Doubtless, however, these considerations will not suffice to convince those who most need convincing; and it is necessary further to show that these developed human beings are of some use to the undeveloped—to point out to those who do not desire liberty, and would not avail themselves of it, that they may be in some intelligible manner rewarded for allowing other people to make use of it without hindrance.

In the first place, then, I would suggest that they might possibly learn something from them. It will not be denied by anybody that originality is a valuable element in human affairs. There is always need of persons not only to discover new truths and point out when what were once truths are true no longer, but also to commence new practices and set the example of more enlightened conduct and better taste and sense in human life. This cannot well be gainsaid by anybody who does not believe that the world has already attained perfection in all its ways and practices. It is true that this benefit is not capable of being rendered by everybody alike; there are but few persons, in comparison with the whole of mankind, whose experiments, if adopted by others, would be likely to be any improvement on established practice. But these few are the salt of the earth; without them, human life would become a stagnant pool. Not only is it they who introduce good things which did not before exist; it is they who keep the life in those which already exist. If there were nothing new to be done, would human intellect cease to be necessary? Would it be a reason why those who do the old things should forget why they are done, and do them like cattle, not like human beings? There is only too great a tendency in the best beliefs and practices to degenerate into the mechanical; and unless there were a succession of persons whose ever-recurring originality prevents the grounds of those beliefs and practices from becoming merely traditional, such dead matter would not resist the smallest shock from anything really alive, and there would be no reason why civilization should not die out, as in the Byzantine Empire. Persons of genius, it is true, are, and are always likely to be, a small minority; but in order to have them, it is necessary to preserve the soil in which they grow. Genius can only breathe freely in an *atmosphere* of freedom. Persons of genius are, *ex vi termini*, more individual than any other people—less capable, consequently, of fitting themselves, without hurtful compression, into any of the small number of molds which society provides in order to save its members the trouble of forming their own character. If from timidity they consent to be forced into one of these molds, and to let all that part of themselves which cannot expand

under the pressure remain unexpanded, society will be little the better of their genius. If they are of strong character and break their fetters, they become a mark for the society which has not succeeded in reducing them to commonplace, to point out with solemn warning as "wild," "erratic," and the like—much as if one should complain of the Niagara river for not flowing smoothly between its banks like a Dutch canal.

I insist thus emphatically on the importance of genius and the necessity of allowing it to unfold itself freely both in thought and in practice, being well aware that no one will deny the position in theory, but knowing also that almost everyone, in reality, is totally indifferent to it. People think genius a fine thing if it enables a man to write an exciting poem or paint a picture. But in its true sense, that of originality in thought and action, though no one says that it is not a thing to be admired, nearly all, at heart, think that they can do very well without it. Unhappily this is too natural to be wondered at. Originality is the one thing which unoriginal minds cannot feel the use of. They cannot see what it is to do for them; how should they? If they could see what it would do for them, it would not be originality. The first service which originality has to render them is that of opening their eyes: which being once fully done, they would have a chance of being themselves original. Meanwhile, recollecting that nothing was ever done which someone was not the first to do, and that all good things which exist are the fruits of originality, let them be modest enough to believe that there is something still left for it to accomplish, and assure themselves that they are more in need of originality, the less they are conscious of the want.

Chapter VII—Philosophy in Recent Times

Arthur Schopenhauer
and Friedrich Nietzsche

Few characters in the history of philosophy are as colorful and interesting as the German philosopher Arthur Schopenhauer (1788-1860). Endowed from his early days with a powerful intelligence and prodigious memory, Schopenhauer spent his entire life looking for the answer to what he regarded as the only real problem: What is the meaning of existence? He was a fervent disciple of Kant and held the curious view that his interpretation of Kant was the only valid one. Schopenhauer's views are all colored by a spirit of arrogance and conviction, which are not ideally associated with the spirit of Socratic humility that we learned from the *Apology*. But sometimes in reading Schopenhauer's writings, one is tempted to excuse his arrogance since the brilliance and depth of his philosophical analyses surpasses what most of us would hope to achieve.

Schopenhauer is often regarded as the father of pessimism, and is often depicted as an unhappy man for whom life brought only misery and pain. This is, however, only partly correct. There were surely many unhappy moments in his life, although he enjoyed abundantly those three gifts of nature which he regarded as essential to a happy life: mind, health, and money. His relationships with his fellow human beings were, however, always bad, since he looked upon most people (perhaps justifiably) as intellectually inferior to him. This led him into a life of solitude, and allowed him to cut his ties with the world of human involvements that often brings so much distraction and misery.

From the ivory tower of his solitude, and under the scrutiny of his keen understanding, Schopenhauer passed a merciless judgment on existence:

"Life," he said, "is a business which does not pay the costs." The world of experience in which all of us are so deeply immersed became for Schopenhauer a tedious farse from which it was essential to escape. Reason and thinking were his prime means of escaping the farse of existence.

The selections by Schopenhauer given in this last chapter are taken from his major work, *The World as Will and Idea*. In these selections the two basic themes in Scopenhauer's philosophy are beautifully developed: metaphysics and salvation.

Friedrich Nietzsche (1844-1900) was deeply influenced by Schopenhauer, even though, as in so many other historical instances, he came to reject entirely the pessimism of the latter's philosophy. The selection by Nietzsche does convey a philosophical atmosphere of spiritual energy in which, far from wishing to reject the will to life, the philosopher affirms this will, and finds in this affirmation the ultimate meaning of truth.

The Way of Salvation

There is only one inborn error, and that is, that we exist in order to be happy. It is inborn to us because it is one with our existence itself, and our whole being is only a paraphrase of it, nay, our body is its monogram. We are nothing more than will to live and the successive satisfaction of all our volitions is what we think in the conception of happiness.

As long as we persist in this inborn error, indeed even become rigidly fixed in it through optimistic dogmas, the world appears to us full of contradictions. For at every step, in great things as in small, we must experience that the world and life are by no means arranged with a view to containing a happy existence. While now by this the thoughtless man only finds himself tormented in reality, in the case of him who thinks there is added to his real pain the theoretical perplexity why a world and a life which exist in order that one may be happy in them answer their end so badly. First of all it finds expression in pious ejaculations, such as, "Ah! why are the tears on earth so many?" &c. &c. But in their train come disquieting doubts about the assumptions of those preconceived optimistic dogmas. One may try if one will to throw the blame of one's individual unhappiness now upon the circumstances, now upon other men, now upon one's own bad luck, or even upon one's own awkwardness, and may know well how all these have worked together to produce it; but this in no way alters the result that one has missed the real end of life, which consists indeed in being happy. The consideration of this is, then, often very depressing, especially if life is already on the wane; hence the countenances of almost all elderly persons wear the expression of that which in English is called disappointment. Besides this, however, hitherto every day of our life has taught us that joys and pleasures, even if attained, are in themselves delusive, do not perform what they promise, do not satisfy the heart, and finally their possession is at least embittered by the disagreeables that accompany them or spring from them; while, on the contrary, the pains and sorrows prove themselves very real, and often exceed all expectation. Thus certainly everything in life is calculated to recall us from that original error, and to convince us that the end of our existence is not to be happy. Indeed, if we regard it more closely and without prejudice, life rather presents itself as specially intended to be such that we shall not feel ourselves happy in it, for through its whole nature it bears the character of something for which we have no taste, which must be endured by us, and from which we have to return as from an error that our heart may be cured of the passionate desire of enjoyment, nay, of life, and turned away from the world. In this sense, it would be more correct to place the end of life in our woe than in our welfare. For the considerations at the conclusion of the preceding chapter have shown that the more one suffers the sooner one attains to the true end of life, and that the more happily one lives the longer this is delayed. . . . The peculiar effect of the tragic drama also ultimately depends upon the fact that it shakes that inborn error by vividly presenting in a great and striking example the vanity of human effort and the nothingness of this whole existence, and thus discloses the profound significance of life; hence it is recognised as the sublimest form of poetry. Whoever now has returned by one or other path from that error which dwells in us *a priori*, that great mistake of our existence, will soon see all in another light, and will now find the world in harmony with his insight, although not with his wishes. Misfortunes of every kind and magnitude, although they pain him, will no longer surprise him, for he has come to see that it is just pain and trouble that tend towards the true end of life, the turning away of the will from it. This will give him indeed a wonderful composedness in all that may happen, similar to that with which a sick person who undergoes a long and painful cure bears the pain of it as a sign of its efficacy. In the whole of human existence suffering expresses itself clearly enough as its true destiny. Life is deeply sunk in suffering, and cannot escape from it; our entrance into it takes place amid tears, its course is at bottom always tragic, and its end still more so. There is an unmistakable appearance of intention in this. As a rule man's destiny passes through his mind in a striking manner, at the very summit of his desires and efforts, and thus his life receives a tragic tendency by virtue of which it is fitted to free him from the passionate desires of which every individual existence is an example, and bring him into such a condition that he parts with life without retaining a single desire for it and its pleasures. Suffering, is, in fact, the purifying process through which alone, in most cases, the man is sanctified, *i.e.*, is led back from the path of error of the will to live. In accordance with this, the salutary nature of the cross and of suffering is so often explained in Christian books of edification, and in general the cross, an instrument of suffering, not of doing, is very suitably the symbol of the Christian religion. Nay, even the Preacher, who is still Jewish, but so very philosophical, rightly says: "Sorrow is better than laughter: for by the sadness of the countenance the heart is made better" (Eccles. vii. 3). Under the name of the alternate path I have presented suffering as to a certain extent a substitute for virtue and holiness; but here I must make the bold assertion that, taking everything into consideration, we have more to hope for our salvation and deliverance from what we suffer than from what we do.

If, then, suffering itself has such a sanctifying power, this will belong in an even higher degree to death, which is more feared than any suffering. Answering to this, a certain awe, kindred to that which great suffering occasions us, is felt in the presence of every dead person, indeed every case of death presents itself to a certain extent as a kind of apotheosis or canonisation; therefore we cannot look upon the dead body of even the most insignificant man without awe, and indeed, extraordinary as the remark may sound in this place, in the presence of every corpse the watch goes under arms. Dying is certainly to be regarded as the real aim of life: in the moment of death all that is decided for which the whole course of life was only the preparation and introduction. Death is the result, the *Resume* of life, or the added up sum which expressed at once the instruction which life gave in detail, and bit by bit; this, that the whole striving whose manifestation is life was a vain, idle, and self-contradictory effort, to have returned from which is a deliverance. As the whole, slow vegetation of the plant is related to the fruit, which now at a stroke achieves a hundredfold what the plant achieved gradually and bit by bit, so life, with its obstacles, deluded hopes, frustrated plans, and constant suffering, is related to death, which at one stroke destroys all, all that the man has willed, and so crowns the instruction which life gave him. The completed course of life upon which the dying man looks back has an effect upon the whole will that objectifies itself in this perishing individuality, analogous to that which a motive exercises upon the conduct of the man. It gives it a new direction, which accordingly is the moral and essential result of the life. Just because a sudden death makes this retrospect impossible, the Church regards such a death as a misfortune, and prays that it should be averted. Since this retrospect, like the distinct foreknowledge of death, as conditioned by the reason, is possible only in man, not in the brute, and accordingly man alone really drinks the cup of death, humanity is the only material in which the will can deny itself and entirely turn away from life. To the will that does not deny itself every birth imparts a new and different intellect still it has learned the true nature of life, and in consequence of this wills it no more.

In the natural course, in age the decay of the body coincides with that of the will. The desire for pleasures soon vanishes with the capacity to enjoy them. The occasion of the most vehement willing, the focus of the will, the sexual impulse, is first extinguished, whereby the man is placed in a position which resembles the state of innocence which existed before the development of the genital system. The illusions, which set up chimeras as exceedingly desirable benefits, vanish, and the knowledge of the vanity of all early blessings takes their place. Selfishness is repressed by the love of one's children, by means of which the man already begins to live more in the ego of others than in his own, which now will soon be no more. This course of life is at least the desirable one; it is the euthanasia of the will. In hope of this the Brahman is ordered, after he has passed the best years of his life, to foresake possessions and family, and lead the life of a hermit. But if, conversely, the desire outlives the capacity for enjoyment, and we now regret particular pleasures in life which we miss, instead of seeing the emptiness and vanity of all; and if then gold, the abstract representative of the objects of desire for which the sense is dead, takes the place of all these objects themselves, and now excites the same vehement passions which were formerly more pardonably awakened by the objects of actual pleasure, and thus now with deadened senses a lifeless but indestructible object is desired with equally indestructible eagerness; or, also, if, in the same way, existence in the opinion of others takes the place of existence and action in the real world, and now kindles the same passions; —then the will has become sublimated and etherealised into avarice or ambition; but has thereby thrown itself into the last fortress, in which it can only now be besieged by death. The end of existence has been missed.

All these considerations afford us a fuller explanation of that purification, conversion of the will and deliverance, denoted in the preceding chapter by the expression alternate path which is brought about by the suffering of life, and without doubt is the most frequent. For it is the way of sinners such as we all are. The other way, which leads to the same goal, by means of mere knowledge and the consequent appropriation of the suffering of a whole world, is the narrow path of the elect, the saints, and therefore to be regarded as a rare exception. Therefore without that first way for most of us there would be no salvation to hope for. However, we struggle against entering upon it, and strive rather to procure for ourselves a safe and agreeable existence, whereby we chain our will

ever more firmly to life. The conduct of the ascetics is the opposite of this. They make their life intentionally as poor, hard, and empty of pleasure as possible, because they have their true and ultimate welfare in view. But fate and the course of things care for us better than we ourselves, for they frustrate on all sides our arrangements for an utopian life, the folly of which is evident enough from its brevity, uncertainty, and emptiness, and its conclusion by bitter death; they strew thorns upon thorns in our path, and meet us everywhere with healing sorrow, the panacea of our misery. What really gives its wonderful and ambiguous character to our life is this, that two diametrically opposite aims constantly cross each other in it; that of the individual will directed to chimerical happiness in an ephemeral, dream-like, and delusive existence, in which, with reference to the past, happiness and unhappiness are a matter of indifference, and the present is every moment becoming the past; and that of fate visibly enough directed to the destruction of our happiness, and thereby to the mortification of our will and the abolition of the illusion that holds us chained in the bonds of this world.

The prevalent and peculiarly Protestant view that the end of life lies solely and immediately in the moral virtues, thus in the practice of justice and benevolence, betrays its insufficiency even in the fact that so miserably little real and pure morality is found among men. I am not speaking at all of lofty virtue, nobleness, magnanimity, and self-sacrifice, which one hardly finds anywhere but in plays and novels, but only of those virtues which are the duty of every one. Let whoever is old think of all those with whom he has had to do; how many persons will he have met who were merely really and truly *honest?* Were not by far the greater number, in spite of their shameless indignation at the slightest suspicion of dishonesty or even untruthfulness, in plain words, the precise opposite? Were not abject selfishness, boundless avarice, well-concealed knavery, and also poisonous envy and fiendish delight in the misfortunes of others so universally prevalent that the slightest exception was met with surprise? And benevolence, how very rarely it extends beyond a gift of what is so superfluous that one never misses it. And is the whole end of existence to lie in such exceedingly rare and weak traces of morality? If we place it, on the contrary, in the entire reversal of this nature of ours (which bears the evil fruits just mentioned) brought about by suffering, the matter gains an appearance of probability and is brought into agreement with what actually lies before us.

Life presents itself then as a purifying process, of which the purifying lye is pain. If the process is carried out, it leaves behind it the previous immorality and wickedness as refuse. . . .

On Truth and Falsity in Their Ultramoral Sense

In some remote corner of the universe, effused into innumerable solar-systems, there was once a star upon which clever animals invented cognition. It was the haughtiest, most mendacious moment in the history of this world, but yet only a moment. After Nature had taken breath awhile the star congealed and the clever animals had to die.—Someone might write a fable after this style, and yet he would not have illustrated sufficiently, how wretched, shadow-like, transitory, purposeless and fanciful the human intellect appears in Nature. There were eternities during which this intellect did not exist, and when it has once more passed away there will be nothing to show that it has existed. For this intellect is not concerned with any further mission transcending the sphere of human life. No, it is purely human and none but its owner and procreator regards it so pathetically as to suppose that the world revolves around it. If, however, we and the gnat could understand each other we should learn that even the gnat swims through the air with the same pathos, and feels within itself the flying centre of the world. Nothing in Nature is so bad or so insignificant that it will not, at the smallest puff of that force cognition, immediately swell up like a balloon, and just as a mere porter wants to have his admirer, so the very proudest man, the philosopher, imagines he sees from all sides the eyes of the universe telescopically directed upon his actions and thoughts.

It is remarkable that this is accomplished by the intellect, which after all has been given to the most unfortunate, the most delicate, the most transient beings only as an expedient, in order to detain them for a moment in existence, from which without that extra-gift they would have every cause of flee as swiftly as Lessing's son. That haughtiness connected with cognition and sensation, spreading blinding fogs before the eyes and over the senses of men, deceives itself therefore as to the value of existence owing to the fact that it bears within itself the most flattering evaluation of cognition. Its most general effect is deception; but even its most particular effects have something of deception in their nature.

The intellect, as a means for the preservation of the individual, develops its chief power in dissimulation; for it is by dissimulation that the feebler, and less robust individuals preserve themselves, since it has been denied them to fight the battle of existence with horns or the sharp teeth of beasts of prey. In man this art of dissimulation reaches its acme of perfection: in him deception, flattery, falsehood and fraud, slander, display, pretentiousness, disguise, cloaking convention, and acting to others and to himself in short, the continual fluttering to and fro around the *one* flame—Vanity: all these things are so much the rule, and the law, that few things are more incomprehensible than the way in which an honest and pure impulse to truth could have arisen among men. They are deeply immersed in illusions and dream-fancies; their eyes glance only over the surface of things and see "forms"; their sensation nowhere leads to truth, but contents itself with receiving stimuli and, so to say, with playing hide-and-seek on the back of things. In addition to that, at night man allows his dreams to lie to him a whole life-time long, without his moral sense ever trying to prevent him; whereas men are said to exist who by the exercise of a strong will have overcome the habit of snoring. What indeed *does* man know about himself? Oh! that he could but once see himself complete, placed as it were in an illuminated glass-case! Does not nature keep secret from him most things, even about his body, *e.g.*, the convolutions of the intestines, the quick flow of the blood-currents, the intricate vibrations of the fibres, so as to banish and lock him up in proud, delusive knowledge? Nature threw away the key; and woe to the fateful curiosity which might be able for a moment to look out and down through a crevice in the chamber of consciousness, and discover that man, indifferent to his own ignorance, is resting on the pitiless, the greedy, the insatiable, the murderous, and, as it were, hanging in dreams on the back of a tiger. Whence, in the wide world, with this state of affairs, arises the impulse to truth?

As far as the individual tries to preserve himself against other individuals, in the natural state of things he uses the intellect in most cases only for dissimulation; since, however, man both from necessity and boredom wants to exist socially and gregariously, he must needs make peace and at least endeavour to cause the greatest *bellum omnium contra omnes* to disappear from this world. This first conclusion of peace brings with it a something which looks like the first step towards the attainment of that enigmatical bent for truth. For that which henceforth is to be "truth" is now fixed; that is to say, a uniformly valid and binding designation of things is invented and the legislature of language also gives the first laws of truth: since here, for the first time, originates the contrast between truth and falsity. The liar uses the valid designations, the words, in order to make the unreal appear as real; *e.g.*, he says, "I am rich," whereas the right designation for his state would be "poor." He abuses the fixed conventions by convenient substitution or even inversion of terms. If he does this in a selfish and moreover harmful fashion, society will no longer trust him but will even exclude him. In this way men avoid not so much being defrauded, but being injured by fraud. At bottom, at this juncture too, they hate not deception, but the evil, hostile consequences of certain species of deception. And it is in a similarly limited sense only that man desires truth: he covets the agreeable, life-preserving conse-quences of truth; he is indifferent towards pure, ineffective knowledge; he is even inimical towards truths which possibly might prove harmful or destroying. And, moreover, what after all are those conventions of language? Are they possibly products of knowledge, of the love of truth; do the designations and the things coincide? Is language the adequate expression of all realities?

Only by means of forgetfulness can man ever arrive at imagining that he possesses "truth" in that degree just indicated. If he does not mean to content himself with truth in the shape of tautology, that is, with empty husks, he will always obtain illusions instead of truth. What is a word? The expression of a nerve-stimulus in sounds. But to infer a cause outside us from the nerve-stimulus is already the result of a wrong and unjustifiable application of the proposition of causality. How should we dare, if truth with the genesis of language, if the point of view of certainty with the designations had alone been decisive; how indeed should we dare to say: the stone is hard; as if "hard" was known to us otherwise; and not merely as an entirely sub-jective stimulus! We divide things according to genders; we designate the tree as masculine, the plant as feminine: what arbitrary meta-phors! How far flown beyond the canon of cer-tainty! We speak of a "serpent"; the desig-nation fits nothing but the sinuosity, and could therefore also appertain to the worm. What ar-bitrary demarcations! what one-sided prefer-ences given sometimes to this, sometimes to that quality of a thing! The different languages placed side by side show that with words truth or adequate expression matters little: for otherwise there would not be so many lan-guages. The "Thing-in-itself" (it is just this which would be the pure ineffective truth) is also quite incomprehensible to the creator of language and not worth making any great en-deavour to obtain. He designates only the relations of things to men and for their expres-sion he calls to his help the most daring meta-phors. A nerve-stimulus, first transformed into a percept! First metaphor! The percept again copied into a sound! Second metaphor! And each time he leaps completely out of one sphere right into the midst of an entirely different one. One can imagine a man who is quite deaf and has never had a sensation of tone and of music; just as this man will possibly marvel at Chladni's sound figures in the sand, will discover their cause in the vibrations of the string, and will then proclaim that now he knows what man calls "tone"; even so does it happen to us all with language. When we talk about trees, colours, snow and flowers, we believe we know something about the things themselves, and yet we only possess metaphors of the things, and these metaphors do not in the least correspond to the original essentials. Just as the sound shows itself, as a sand-figure, in the same way the enigmatical x of the Thing-in-itself is seen first as nerve-stimulus, then as percept, and finally as sound. At any rate the genesis of language did not therefore proceed on logical lines, and the whole material in which and with which the man of truth, the investigator, the philosopher works and builds, originates, if not from Nephelococcygia, cloud-land, at any rate not from the essence of things.

Let us especially think about the formation of ideas. Every word becomes at once an idea not by having, as one might presume, to serve as a reminder for the original experience happening but once and absolutely individualised, to which experience such word owes its origin, no, but by having simultaneously to fit innumerable, more or less similar (which really means never equal, therefore altogether unequal) cases. Every idea originates through equating the unequal. As certainly as no one leaf is exactly similar to any other, so certain is it that the idea "leaf" has been formed through an arbitrary omission of these individual differences, through a forgetting of the differentiating qualities, and this idea now awakens the notion that in nature there is, besides the leaves, a something called *the* "leaf," perhaps a primal form according to which all leaves were woven, drawn, accurately measured, coloured, crinkled, painted, but by unskilled hands, so that no copy had turned out correct and trustworthy as a true copy of the primal form. We call a man "honest"; we ask, why has he acted so honestly to-day? Our customary answer runs, "On account of his honesty." *The* Honesty! That means again: the "leaf" is the cause of the leaves. We really and truly do not know anything at all about an essential quality which might be called *the* honesty, but we do know about numerous individualised, and therefore unequal actions, which we equate by omission of the unequal, and now designate as honest actions; finally out of them we formulate a *qualitas occulta* with the name "Honesty." The disregarding of the individual and real furnishes us with the idea, as it likewise also gives us the form; whereas nature knows of no forms and ideas, and therefore knows no species but only an x, to us inaccessible and indefinable. For our antithesis of individual and species is anthropomorphic too and does not come from the essence of things, although on the other hand we do not dare to say that it does not correspond to it; for that would be a dogmatic assertion and as such just as undemonstrable as its contrary.

What therefore is truth? A mobile army of metaphors, metonymies, anthropomorphisms: in short a sum of human relations which became poetically and rhetorically intensified, metamorphosed, adorned, and after long usage seem to a nation fixed, canonic and binding; truths are illusions of which one has forgotten that they *are* illusions; worn-out metaphors which have become powerless to affect the senses; coins which have their observe effaced and now are no longer of account as coins but merely as metal.

Still we do not yet know whence the impulse to truth comes, for up to now we have heard only about the obligation which society imposes in order to exist: to be truthful, that is, to use the usual metaphors, therefore expressed morally: we have heard only about the obligation to lie according to a fixed convention, to lie gregariously in a style binding for all. Now man of course forgets that matters are going thus with him; he therefore lies in that fashion pointed out unconsciously and according to habits of centuries' standing—and by *this very unconsciousness*, by this very forgetting, he arrives at a sense for truth. Through this feeling of being obliged to designate one thing as "red," another as "cold," a third one as 'dumb," awakes a moral emotion relating to truth. Out of the antithesis "liar" whom nobody trusts, whom all exclude, man demonstrates to himself the venerableness, reliability, usefulness of truth. Now as a *"rational"* being he submits his actions to the sway of abstractions; he no longer suffers himself to be carried away by sudden impressions, by sensations, he first generalises all these impressions into paler cooler ideas, in order to attach to them the ship of his life and actions. Everything which makes man stand out in bold relief against the animal depends on this faculty of volatilising the concrete metaphors into a schema, and therefore resolving a perception into an idea. For within the range of those schemata a something becomes possible that never could succeed under the first perceptual impressions: to build up a pyramidal order with castes and grades, to create a new world of laws, privileges, suborders, delimitations, which now stands opposite the other perceptual world of first impressions and assumes the appearance of being the more fixed, general, known, human of the two and therefore the regulating and imperative one. Whereas every metaphor of perception is individual and without its equal and therefore knows how to escape all attempts to classify it, the great edifice of ideas shows the rigid regularity of a Roman Columbarium and in logic breathes forth the sternness and coolness which we find in mathematics. He who has been breathed upon by this coolness will scarcely believe, that the idea too, bony and hexahedral, and permutable as a die, remains however only as the *residuum of a metaphor*, and that the illusion of the artistic metamorphosis of a nerve-stimulus into percepts is, if not the mother, then the grandmother of every idea. Now in this game of dice, "Truth" means to use every die as it is designated, to count its points carefully, to forms exact classifications, and never to violate the order of castes and the sequences of rank. Just as the Romans and Etruscans for their benefit cut up the sky by means of strong mathematical lines and banned a god as it were into a *templum,* into a space limited in this fashion, so every nation has above its head such a sky of ideas divided up mathematically, and it understands the demand for truth to mean that every conceptual god is to be looked for only in *his* own sphere. One may here well admire man, who succeeded in piling up an infinitely complex dome of ideas on a movable foundation and as it were on running water, as a powerful genius of architecture. Of course in order to obtain hold on such a foundation it must be as an edifice piled up out of cobwebs, so fragile, as to be carried away by the waves: so firm, as not to be blown asunder by every wind. In this way man as an architectural genius rises high above the bee; she builds with wax, which she brings together out of nature; he with the much more

delicate material of ideas, which he must first manufacture within himself. He is very much to be admired here—but not on account of his impulse for truth, his bent for pure cognition of things. If somebody hides a thing behind a bush, seeks it again and finds it in the self-same place, then there is not much to boast of, respecting this seeking and finding; thus, however, matters stand with the seeking and finding of "truth" within the realm of reason. If I make the definition of the mammal and then declare after inspecting a camel, "Behold a mammal," then no doubt a truth is brought to light thereby, but it is of very limited value, I mean it is anthropomorphic through and through, and does not contain one single point which is "true-in-itself," real and universally valid, apart from man. The seeker after such truths seeks at the bottom only the metamorphosis of the world in man, he strives for an understanding of the world as a human-like thing and by his battling gains at best the feeling of an assimilation. Similarly, as the astrologer contemplated the stars in the service of man and in connection with their happiness and unhappiness, such a seeker contemplates the whole world as related to man, as the infinitely protracted echo of an original sound: man; as the multiplied copy of the one archtype: man. His procedure is to apply man as the measure of all things, whereby he starts from the error of believing that he has these things immediately before him as pure objects. He therefore forgets that the original metaphors of perception *are* metaphors, and takes them for the things themselves.

Only by forgetting that primitive world of metaphors, only by the congelation and coagulation of an original mass of similes and percepts pouring forth as a fiery liquid out of the primal faculty of human fancy, only by the invincible faith, that *this* sun, *this* window, *this* table is a truth in itself: in short only by the fact that man forgets himself as subject; and what is more as an *artistically creating* subject: only by all this does he live with some repose, safely and consequence. If he were able to get out of the prison walls of this faith, even for an instant only, his "self-consciousness" would be destroyed at once. Already it costs him some trouble to admit to himself that the insect and the bird perceive a world different from his own, and that the question, which of the two world-perceptions is more accurate, is quite a senseless one, since to decide this question it would be necessary to apply the standard of *right perception*, i.e., to apply a standard which *does not exist*. On the whole it seems to me that the "right perception"—which would mean the adequate expression of an object in the subject —is a nonentity full of contradictions: for between two utterly different spheres, as between subject and object, there is no causality, no accuracy, no expression, but at the utmost an *aesthetical* relation, I mean a suggestive metamorphosis, a stammering translation into quite a distinct foreign language, for which purpose however there is needed at any rate an intermediate sphere, an intermediate force, freely composing and freely inventing. The word "phenomenon" contains many seductions, and on that account I avoid it as much as possible, for it is not true that the essence of things appears in the empiric world. A painter who had no hands and wanted to express the picture distinctly present to his mind by the agency of song, would still reveal much more with this permutation of spheres, than the empiric world reveals about the essence of things. The very relation of a nerve-stimulus to the product percept is in itself no necessary one; but if the same percept has been reproduced millions of times and has been the inheritance of many successive generations of man, and in the end appears each time to all mankind as the result of the same cause, then it attains finally for man the same importance as if it were *the* unique, necessary percept and as if that relation between the original nerve-stimulus and the percept produced were a close relation of causality: just as a dream eternally repeated, would be perceived and judged as though real. But the congelation and coagulation of a metaphor does not at all guarantee the necessity and exclusive justification of that metaphor.

Surely every human being who is at home with such contemplations has felt a deep distrust against any idealism of that kind, as often as he has distinctly convinced himself of the eternal rigidity, omnipresence, and infallibility of nature's laws: he has arrived at the conclusion that as far as we can penetrate the heights of the telescopic and the depths of the microscopic world, everything is quite secure, complete, infinite, determined, and continuous.

Science will have to dig in these shafts eternally and successfully and all things found are sure to have to harmonise and not to contradict one another. How little does this resemble a product of fancy, for if it were one it would necessarily betray somewhere its nature of appearance and unreality. Against this it may be objected in the first place that if each of us had for himself a different sensibility, if we ourselves were only able to perceive sometimes as a bird, sometimes as a worm, sometimes as a plant, or if one of us saw the same stimulus as red, another as blue, if a third person even perceived it as a tone, then nobody would talk of such an orderliness of nature, but would conceive of her only as an extremely subjective structure. Secondly, what is, for us in general, a law of nature? It is not known in itself but only in its effects, that is to say in its relations to other laws of nature, which again are known to us only as sums of relations. Therefore all these relations refer only one to another and are absolutely incomprehensible to us in their essence; only that which we add: time, space, *i.e.*, relations of sequence and numbers, are really known to us in them. Everything wonderful however, that we marvel at in the laws of nature, everything that demands an explanation and might seduce us into distrusting idealism, lies really and solely in the mathematical rigour and inviolability of the conceptions of time and space. These however we produce within ourselves and throw them forth with that necessity with which the spider spins; since we are compelled to conceive all things under these forms only, then it is no longer wonderful that in all things we actually conceive none but these forms: for they all must bear within themselves the laws of number, and this very idea of number is the most marvellous in all things. All obedience to law which impresses us so forcibly in the orbits of stars and in chemical processes coincides at the bottom with those qualities which we ourselves attach to those things, so that it is we who thereby make the impression upon ourselves. Whence it clearly follows that that artistic formation of metaphors, with which every sensation in us begins, already presupposes those forms, and is therefore only consummated within them; only out of the persistency of these primal forms the possibility explains itself, how afterwards out of the metaphors themselves a structure of ideas could again be compiled. For the latter is an imitation of the relations of time, space and number in the realm of metaphors.

2

As we saw, it is *language* which has worked originally at the construction of ideas; in later times it is *science.* Just as the bee works at the same time at the cells and fills them with honey, thus science works irresistibly at that great columbarium of ideas, the cemetery of perceptions, builds ever newer and higher storeys; supports, purifies, renews the old cells, and endeavours above all to fill that gigantic framework and to arrange within it the whole of the empiric world, *i.e.,* the anthropomorphic world. And as the man of action binds his life to reason and its ideas, in order to avoid being swept away and losing himself, so the seeker after truth builds his hut close to the towering edifice of science in order to collaborate with it and to find protection. And he needs protection. For there are awful powers which continually press upon him, and which hold out against the "truth" of science "truths" fashioned in quite another way, bearing devices of the most heterogeneous character.

That impulse towards the formation of metaphors, that fundamental impulse of man, which we cannot reason away for one moment—for thereby we should reason away man himself— is in truth not defeated nor even subdued by the fact that out of its evaporated products, the ideas, a regular and rigid new world has been built as a stronghold for it. This impulse seeks for itself a new realm of action and another river-bed, and finds it in *Mythos* and more generally in *Art.* This impulse constantly confuses the rubrics and cells of the ideas, by putting up new figures of speech, metaphors, metonymies; it constantly shows its passionate longing for shaping the existing world of waking man as motley, irregular, inconsequentially incoherent, attractive, and eternally new as the world of dreams is. For indeed, waking man *per se* is only clear about his being awake through the rigid and orderly woof of ideas, and it is for this very reason that he sometimes comes to believe that he was dreaming when that woof of ideas has for a moment been torn by Art. Pascal is quite right, when he asserts, that if the same dream came to us every night

we should be just as much occupied by it as by the things which we see every day; to quote his words, "If an artisan were certain that he would dream every night for fully twelve hours that he was a king, I believe that he would be just as happy as a king who dreams every night for twelve hours that he is an artisan." The wide-awake day of a people mystically excitable, let us say of the earlier Greeks, is in fact through the continually-working wonder, which the mythos presupposes, more akin to the dream than to the day of the thinker sobered by science. If every tree may at some time talk as a nymph, or a god under the disguise of a bull, carry away virgins, if the goddess Athene herself be suddenly seen as, with a beautiful team, she drives, accompanied by Pisistratus, through the markets of Athens—and every honest Athenian did believe this—at any moment, as in a dream, everything is possible; and all nature swarms around man as if she were nothing but the masquerade of the gods, who found it a huge joke to deceive man by assuming all possible forms.

Man himself, however, has an invincible tendency to let himself be deceived, and he is like one enchanted with happiness when the rhapsodist narrates to him epic romances in such a way that they appear real or when the actor on the stage makes the king appear more kingly than reality shows him. Intellect, that master of dissimulation, is free and dismissed from his service as slave, so long as it is able to deceive without *injuring*, and then it celebrates its Saturnalia. Never is it richer, prouder, more luxuriant, more skillful and daring; with a creator's delight it throws metaphors into confusion, shifts the boundary-stones of the abstractions, so that for instance it designates the stream as the mobile way which carries man to that place whither he would otherwise go. Now it has thrown off its shoulders the emblem of servitude. Usually with gloomy officiousness it endeavours to point out the way to a poor individual coveting existence, and it fares forth for plunder and booty like a servant for his master, but now it itself has become a master and may wipe from its countenance the expression of indigence. Whatever it now does, compared with its former doings, bears within itself dissimulation, just as its former doings bore the character of distortion. It copies human life, but takes it for a good thing and seems to rest quite satisfied with it. That enormous framework and hoarding of ideas, by clinging to which needy man saves himself through life, is to the freed intellect only a scaffolding and a toy for its most daring feats, and when it smashes it to pieces, throws it into confusion, and then puts it together ironically, pairing the strangest, separating the nearest items, then it manifests that it has no use for those makeshifts of misery, and that it is now no longer led by ideas but by intuitions. From these intuitions no regular road leads into the land of the spectral schemata, the abstractions; for them the word is not made, when man sees them he is dumb, or speaks in forbidden metaphors and in unheard-of combinations of ideas, in order to correspond creatively with the impression of the powerful present intuition at least by destroying and jeering at the old barriers of ideas.

There are ages, when the rational and the intuitive man stand side by side, the one full of fear of the intuition, the other full of scorn for the abstraction; the latter just as irrational as the former is inartistic. Both desire to rule over life; the one by knowing how to meet the most important needs with foresight, prudence, regularity; the other as an "over-joyous" hero by ignoring those needs and taking that life only as real which stimulates appearance and beauty. Wherever intuitive man, as for instance in the earlier history of Greece, brandishes his weapons more powerfully and victoriously than his opponent, there under favorable conditions, a culture can develop and art can establish her rule over life. That dissembling, that denying of neediness, that splendour of metaphorical notions and especially that directness of dissimulation accompany all utterances of such a life. Neither the house of man, nor his way of walking, nor his clothing, nor his earthen jug suggest that necessity invented them; it seems as if they all were intended as the expressions of a sublime happiness, an Olympic cloudlessness, and as it were a playing at seriousness. Whereas the man guided by ideas and abstractions only wards off misfortune by means of them, without even enforcing for himself happiness out of the abstractions; whereas he strives after the greatest possible freedom from pains, the intuitive man dwelling in the midst of culture has from his intuitions a harvest: besides the warding off of evil, he attains a continuous in-pouring of enlightenment, enlivenment and redemption. Of course when he *does* suffer, he suffers more: and he even suffers more frequently since he cannot learn from experience, but again and again falls into the same ditch into which he has fallen before. In suffering he is just as irrational as in happiness; he cries aloud and finds no consolation. How different matters are in the same misfortune with the Stoic, taught by experience and ruling himself by ideas! He who otherwise only looks for uprightness, truth, freedom from deceptions and shelter from ensnaring and sudden attack, in his misfortune performs the masterpiece of dissimulation, just as the other did in his happiness; he shows no twitching mobile human face, but a mask with dignified, harmonious features; he does not cry out or even alter his voice; when a heavy thundercloud bursts upon him, he wraps himself up in his cloak and with slow and measured steps walks away from beneath it.

William James

William James (1842-1910) one of the best known and most influential American thinkers, was a distinguished member of a distinguished family. His brother was the famous novelist Henry James. William's reputation was first established in the field of psychology, and his work *Psychology* is still a classic in the field. Later he taught at Harvard in a brilliant philosophy department which included Josiah Royce and George Santayana.

James is known for formulating the philosophy called *pragmatism*. Pragmatism has always been a disputed doctrine, but James' formulation of it in practice has always remained fairly consistent. In those decisions where incontestable evidence is not available, we need another criterion for making up our minds. In addition, James was aware of the fact that certain hypotheses were not only reactions to the world but ways of changing the world—including the agent who first formulated the hypothesis. Pragmatism was meant to take this element into account.

"The will to believe" is not a rationalization licensing us to believe whatever we want. In fact, it is a moral and a metaphysical position derived from James' insight into the nature of science as experimentalism. James is opposed to the cautions of Bacon and the demands of Descartes. Every hypothesis is initially uncertain and its formulation an act of daring. Just as science progresses by believing in the efficacy of action or experiment, so all of life's decisions are possible only on the assumption that we are free to choose and that our decisions make a difference. Finally, James is always reminding us that we are fallible, that even our successes can be viewed only as tentative and are subject to further revision or to replacement by other daring hypotheses.

The Will to Believe

In the recently published Life by Leslie Stephen of his brother, Fitz-James, there is an account of a school to which the latter went when he was a boy. The teacher, a certain Mr. Guest, used to converse with his pupils in this wise: "Gurney, what is the difference between justification and sanctification?—Stephen, prove the omnipotence of God!" etc. In the midst of our Harvard freethinking and indifference we are prone to imagine that here at your good old orthodox College conversation continues to be somewhat upon this order; and to show you that we at Harvard have not lost all interest in these vital subjects, I have brought with me tonight something like a sermon on justification by faith to read to you—I mean an essay in justification of faith, a defence of our right to adopt a believing attitude in religious matters, in spite of the fact that our merely logical intellect may not have been coerced. "The Will to Believe," accordingly, is the title of my paper.

I have long defended to my own students the lawfulness of voluntarily adopted faith; but as soon as they have got well imbued with the logical spirit, they have as a rule refused to admit my contention to be lawful philosophically, even though in point of fact they were personally all the time chock-full of some faith or other themselves. I am all the while, however, so profoundly convinced that my own position is correct, that your invitation has seemed to me a good occasion to make my statements more clear. Perhaps your minds will be more open than those with which I have hitherto had to deal. I will be as little technical as I can, though I must begin by setting up some technical distinctions that will help us in the end.

1

Let us give the name of *hypothesis* to anything that may be proposed to our belief; and just as the electricians speak of live and dead wires, let us speak of any hypothesis as either *live* or *dead*. A live hypothesis is one which appeals as a real possibility to him to whom it is proposed. If I ask you to believe in the Mahdi, the notion makes no electric connection with your name— it refuses to scintillate with any credibility at all. As an hypothesis it is completely dead. To an Arab, however (even if he be not one of the Mahdi's followers), the hypothesis is among the mind's possibilities: it is alive. This shows that deadness and liveness in an hypothesis are not intrinsic properties, but relations to the individual thinker. They are measured by his willingness to act. The maximum of liveness in an hypothesis means willingness to act irrevocably. Practically, that means belief; but there is some believing tendency wherever there is willingness to act at all.

Next, let us call the decision between two hypotheses an *option*. Options may be of several kinds. They may be—first, *living* or *dead*; secondly, *forced* or *avoidable*; thirdly, *momentous* or *trivial*; and for our purposes we may call an option a *genuine* option when it is of the forced, living, and momentous kind.

1. A living option is one in which both hypotheses are live ones. If I say to you: "Be a theosophist or be a Mohammedan," it is probably a dead option, because for you neither hypothesis is likely to be alive. But if I say: "Be an agnostic or be a Christian," it is otherwise: trained as you are, each hypothesis makes some appeal, however small, to your belief.

2. Next, if I say to you: "Choose between going out with your umbrella or without it," I do not offer you a genuine option, for it is not forced. You can easily avoid it by not going out at all. Similarly, if I say, "Either love me or hate me," "Either call my theory true or call it false," your option is avoidable. You may remain indifferent to me, neither loving nor hating, and you may decline to offer any judgment as to my theory. But if I say, "Either accept this truth or go without it," I put on you a forced option, for there is no standing place outside of the alternative. Every dilemma based on a complete logical disjunction, with no possibility of not choosing, is an option of this forced kind.

3. Finally, if I were Dr. Nansen and proposed to you to join my North Pole expedition, your option would be momentous; for this would probably be your only similar opportunity, and your choice now would either exclude you from the North Pole sort of immortality altogether or put at least the chance of it into your hands. He who refuses to embrace a unique opportunity loses the prize as surely as if he tried and failed. *Per contra,* the option is trivial when the opportunity is not unique, when the stake is insignificant, or when the decision is reversible if it later proves unwise. Such trivial options abound in the scientific life. A chemist finds an hypothesis live enough to spend a year in its verification: he believes in it to that extent. But if his experiments prove inconclusive either way, he is quit for his loss of time, no vital harm being done.

It will facilitate our discussion if we keep all these distinctions well in mind.

2

The next matter to consider is the actual psychology of human opinion. When we look at certain facts, it seems as if our passional and volitional nature lay at the root of all our convictions. When we look at others, it seems as if they could do nothing when the intellect had once said its say. Let us take the latter facts up first.

Does it not seem preposterous on the very fact of it to talk of our opinions being modifiable at will? Can our will either help or hinder our intellect in its perceptions of truth? Can we, by just willing it, believe that Abraham Lin-

coln's existence is a myth, and that the portraits of him in *McClure's Magazine* are all of some one else: Can we, by any effort of our will, or by any strength of wish that it were true, believe outselves well and about when we are roaring with rheumatism in bed, or feel certain that the sum of the two one-dollar bills in our pocket must be a hundred dollars? We can say any of these things, but we are absolutely impotent to beleive them; and of just such things is the whole fabric of the truths that we do believe in made up—matters of fact, immediate or remote, as Hume said, and relations between ideas, which are either there or not there for us if we see them so, and which if not there cannot be put there by any action of our own.

In Pascal's *Thoughts* there is a celebrated passage known in literature as Pascal's wager. In it he tries to force us into Christianity by reasoning as if our concern with truth resembled our concern with the stakes in a game of chance. Translated freely his words are these: You must either believe or not believe that God is—which will you do? Your human reason cannot say. A game is going on between you and the nature of things which at the day of judgment will bring out either heads or tails. Weigh what your gains and your losses would be if you should stake all you have on heads, or God's existence: if you win in such case, you gain eternal beatitude; if you lose, you lose nothing at all. If there were an infinity of chances, and only one of God in this wager, still you ought to stake your all on God; for though you surely risk a finite loss by this procedure, any finite loss is reasonable, even a certain one is reasonable, if there is but the possibility of infinite gain. Go, then, and take holy water, and have masses said; belief will come and stupefy your scruples—*Cela vous fera croire et vous abetira.* Why should you not? At bottom, what have you to lose?

You probably feel that when religious faith expresses itself thus, in the language of the gaming-table, it is put to its last trumps. Surely Pascal's own personal belief in masses and holy water had far other springs; and this celebrated page of his is but an argument for others, a last desperate snatch at a weapon against the hardness of the unbelieving heart. We feel that a faith in masses and holy water adopted wilfully after such a mechanical calculation would lack the inner soul of faith's reality; and if we were ourselves in the place of the Deity, we should probably take particular pleasure in cutting off believers of this pattern from their infinite reward. It is evident that unless there be some pre-existing tendency to believe in masses and holy water, the option offered to the will by Pascal is not a living option. Certainly no Turk ever took to masses and holy water on its account; and even to us Protestants these means of salvation seem such foregone impossibilities that Pascal's logic, invoked for them specifically, leaves us unmoved. As well might the Mahdi write to us, saying, "I ar the Expected One whom God has created in his effulgence. You shall be infinitely happy if you confess me; otherwise you shall be cut off from the light of the sun. Weigh, then, your infinite gain if I am genuine against your finite sacrifice if I am not!" His logic would be that of Pascal; but he would vainly use it on us, for the hypothesis he offers us is dead. No tendency to act on it exists in us to any degree.

The talk of believing by our volition seems, then, from one point of view, simply silly. From another point of view it is worse than silly, it is vile. When one turns to the magnificent edifice of the physical sciences, and sees how it was reared; what thousands of disinterested moral lives of men lie buried in its mere foundations; what patience and postponement, what choking down of preference, what submission to the icy laws of outer fact are wrought into its very stones and mortar; how absolutely impersonal it stands in its vast augustness—then how besotted and contemptible seems every little sentimentalist who comes blowing his voluntary smoke-wreaths, and pretending to decide things from out of his private dream! Can we wonder if those bred in the rugged and manly school of science should feel like spewing such subjectivism out of their mouths? The whole system of loyalties which grow up in the schools of science go dead against its toleration; so that it is only natural that those who have caught the scientific fever should pass over to the opposite extreme, and write sometimes as if the incorruptibly truthful intellect ought positively to prefer bitterness and unacceptableness to the heart in its cup.

It fortifies my soul to know
That though I perish, Truth is so—

sings Clough, while Huxley exclaims: "My own consolation lies in the reflection that, however bad our posterity may become, so far as they hold by the plain rule of not pretending to believe what they have no reason to believe, because it may be to their advantage so to pretend [the word 'pretend' is surely here redundant], they will not have reached the lowest depth of immorality." And that delicious *enfant terrible* Clifford writes: "Belief is desecrated when given to unproved and unquestioned statements for the solace and private pleasure of the believer. . . . Whoso would deserve well of his fellows in this matter will guard the purity of his belief with a very fanaticism of jealous care, lest at any time it should rest on an unworthy object, and catch a stain which can never be wiped away. . . . If [a] belief has been accepted on insufficient evidence [even though the beleif be true, as Clifford on the same page explains] the pleasure is a stolen one. . . . It is sinful because it is stolen in defiance of our duty to mankind. That duty is to guard ourselves from such beliefs as from a pestilence which may shortly master our own body and then spread to the rest of the town. . . . It is wrong always, everywhere, and for every one, to believe anything upon insufficient evidence."

3

All this strikes one as healthy, even when expressed, as by Clifford, with somewhat too much of robustious pathos in the voice. Free will and simple wishing do seem, in the matter of our credences, to be only fifth wheels to the coach. Yet if any one should thereupon assume that intellectual insight is what remains after wish and will and sentimental preference have taken wing, or that pure reason is what then settles our opinions, he would fly quite as directly in the teeth of the facts.

It is only our already dead hypotheses that our willing nature is unable to bring to life again. But what has made them dead for us is for the most part a previous action of our willing nature of an antagonistic kind. When I say "willing nature," I do not mean only such deliberate volitions as may have set up habits of belief that we cannot now escape from—I mean all such factors of belief as fear and hope, prejudice and passion, imitation and partisanship the circumpressure of our caste and set. As a matter of fact we find ourselves believing, we hardly know how or why. Mr. Balfour gives the name of "authority" to all those influences, born of the intellectual climate, that make hypotheses possible or impossible for us, alive or dead. Here in this room, we all of us believe in molecules and the conservation of energy, in democracy and necessary progress, in Protestant Christianity and the duty of fighting for "the doctrine of the immortal Monroe," all for no reasons worthy of the name. We see into these matters with no more inner clearness, and probably with much less, than any disbeliever in them might possess. His unconventionality would probably have some grounds to show for its conclusions; but for us, not insight, but the *prestige* of the opinions, is what makes the spark shoot from them and light up our sleeping magazines of faith. Our reason is quite satisfied, in nine hundred and ninety-nine cases out of every thousand of us, if it can find a few arguments that will do to recite in case our credulity is criticized by some one else. Our faith is faith in some one else's faith, and in the greatest matters this is most the case. Our belief in truth itself, for instance, that there is a truth, and that our minds and it are made for each other—what is it but a passionate affirmation of desire, in which our social system backs us up? We want to have a truth; we want to beleive that our experiments and studies and discussions must put us in a continually better and better position towards it; and on this line we agree to fight out our thinking lives. But if a Pyrrhonistic sceptic asks us *how we know* all this, can our logic find a reply? No! certainly it cannot. It is just one volition against another— we willing to go in for life upon a trust or assumption which he, for his part, does not care to make.

As a rule we disbelieve all facts and theories for which we have no use. Clifford's cosmic emotions find no use for Christian feelings. Huxley belabors the bishops because there is no use for sacerdotalism in his scheme of life. Newman, on the contrary, goes over to Romanism, and finds all sorts of reasons good for staying there, because a priestly system is for him an organic need and delight. Why do so few "scientists" even look at the evidence for telepathy, so called? Because they think, as a

leading biologist, now dead, once said to me, that even if such a thing were true, scientists ought to band together to keep it suppressed and concealed. It would undo the uniformity of Nature and all sorts of other things without which scientists cannot carry on their pursuits. But if this very man had been shown something which as a scientist he might *do* with telepathy, he might not only have examined the evidence, but even have found it good enough. This very law which the logicians would impose upon us —if I may give the name of logicians to those who would rule out our willing nature here—is based on nothing but their own natural wish to exclude all elements for which they, in their professional quality of logicians, can find no use.

Evidently, then, our non-intellectual nature does influence our convictions. There are passional tendencies and volitions which run before and others which come after belief, and it is only the latter that are too late for the fair; and they are not too late when the previous passional work has been already in their own direction. Pascal's argument, instead of being powerless, then seems a regular clincher, and is the last stroke needed to make our faith in masses and holy water complete. The state of things is evidently far from simple; and pure insight and logic, whatever they might do ideally, are not the only things that really do produce our creeds.

4

Our next duty, having recognized this mixed-up state of affairs, is to ask whether it be simply reprehensible and pathological, or whether, on the contrary, we must treat it as a normal element in making up our minds. The thesis I defend is, briefly stated, this: *Our passional nature not only lawfully may, but must, decide an option between propositions, whenever it is a genuine option that cannot by its nature be decided on intellectual grounds; for to say, under such circumstances, "Do not decide, but leave the question open," is itself a passional decision—just like deciding yes or no—and is attended with the same risk of losing the truth.* The thesis thus abstractly expressed will, I trust, soon become quite clear. But I must first indulge in a bit more of preliminary work.

5

It will be observed that for the purposes of this discussion we are on "dogmatic" ground—ground, I mean, which leaves systematic philosophical scepticism altogether out of account. The postulate that there is truth, and that it is the destiny of our minds to attain it, we are deliberately resolving to make, though the sceptic will not make it. We part company with him, therefore, absolutely, at this point. But the faith that truth exists, and that our minds can find it, may be held in two ways. We may talk of the *empiricist* way and of the *absolutist* way of believing in truth. The absolutists in this matter say that we not only can attain to knowing truth, but we can *know when* we have attained to knowing it; while the empiricists think that although we may attain it, we cannot infallibly know when. To *know* is one thing, and to know for certain *that* we know is another. One may hold to the first being possible without the second; hence the empiricists and the absolutists, although neither of them is a sceptic in the usual philosophic sense of the term, show very different degrees of dogmatism in their lives.

If we look at the history of opinions, we see that the empiricist tendency has largely prevailed in science, while in philosophy the absolutist tendency has had everything its own way. The characteristic sort of happiness, indeed, which philosophies yield has mainly consisted in the conviction felt by each successive school or system that by it bottom-certitude had been attained. "Other philosophies are collections of opinions, mostly false; *my* philosophy gives standing-ground forever"—who does not recognize in this the key-note of every system worthy of the name? A system, to be a system at all, must come as a *closed* system, reversible in this or that detail, perchance, but in its essential features never!

Scholastic orthodoxy, to which one must always go when one wishes to find perfectly clear statement, has beautifully elaborated this absolutist conviction in a doctrine which it calls that of "objective evidence." If, for example, I am unable to doubt that I now exist before you, that two is less than three, or that if all men are mortal then I am mortal too, it is because these things illumine my intellect irresistibly. The final ground of this objective evidence possessed by certain propositions is the *adaequatio intellectus nostri cum re.* The certitude it brings involves an *aptitudinem ad extorquendum certum assensum* on the part of the truth envisaged, and on the side of the subject a *quietem in cognitione*, when once the object is mentally received, that leaves no possibility of doubt behind; and in the whole transaction nothing operates but the *entitas ipsa* of the object and the *entitas ipsa* of the mind. We slouchy modern thinkers dislike to talk in Latin,—indeed, we dislike to take in set terms at all; but at bottom our own state of mind is very much like this whenever we uncritically abandon ourselves: You believe in objective evidence, and I do. Of some things we feel that we are certain: we know, and we know that we do know. There is something that gives a click inside of us, a bell that strikes twelve, when the hands of our mental clock have swept the dial and meet over the meridian hour. The greatest empiricists among us are only empiricists on reflection: when left to their instincts, they dogmatize like infallible popes. When the Cliffords tell us how sinful it is to be Christians on such "insufficient evidence," insufficiency is really the last thing they have in mind. For them the evidence is absolutely sufficient, only it makes the other way. They believe so completely in an anti-Christian order of the universe that there is no living option: Christianity is a dead hypothesis from the start.

6

But now, since we are all such absolutists by instinct, what in our quality of students of philosophy ought we to do about the fact? Shall we espouse and indorse it? Or shall we treat it as a weakness of our nature from which we must free ourselves, if we can?

I sincerely believe that the latter course is the only one we can follow as reflective men. Objective evidence and certitude are doubtless very fine ideals to play with, but where on this moonlit and dream-visited planet are they found? I am, therefore, myself a complete empiricist so far as my theory of human knowledge goes. I live, to be sure, by the practical faith that we must go on experiencing and thinking over our experience, for only thus can our opinions grow more true; but to hold any one of them—I absolutely do not care which—as if it never could be reinterpretable or corrigible, I believe to be a tremendously mistaken attitude, and I think that the whole history of philosophy will bear me out. There is but one indefectibly certain truth, and that is the truth that Pyrrhonistic scepticism itself leaves standing—the truth that the present phenomenon of consciousness exists. That, however, is the bare starting-point of knowledge, the mere admission of a stuff to be philosophized about. The various philosophies are but so many attempts at expressing what this stuff really is. And if we repair to our libraries what disagreement do we discover! Where is a certainly true answer found? Apart from abstract propositions of comparison (such as two and two are the same as four), propositions which tell us nothing by themselves about concrete reality, we find no proposition ever regarded by any one as evidently certain that has not either been called a falsehood, or at least had its truth sincerely questioned by some one else. The transcending of the axioms of geometry, not in play but in earnest, by certain of our contemporaries (as Zollner and Charles H. Hinton), and the rejection of the whole Aristotelian logic by the Hegelians, are striking instances in point.

No concrete test of what is really true has ever been agreed upon. Some make the criterion external to the moment of perception, putting it either in revelation, the *consensue gentium*, the instincts of the heart, or the systematized experience of the race. Others make the perceptive moment its own test—Descartes, for instance, with his clear and distinct ideas guaranteed by the veracity of God; Reid with his "commonsense"; and Kant with his forms of synthetic judgment *a priori*. The inconceivability of the opposite; the capacity to be vertified by sense; the possession of complete organic unity or self-relation, realized when a thing is its own other—are standards which, in turn, have been used. The much lauded objective evidence is never triumphantly there; it is a mere aspiration or *Grenzhegriff*, marking the infinitely remote ideal of our thinking life. To claim that certain truths now possess it, is simply to say that when you think them true and they *are* true, then their evidence is objective, otherwise it is not. But practically one's conviction that the evidence one goes by is of the real objective brand, is only one more subjective opinion added to the lot. For what a contradictory array of opinions have objective evidence and absolute certitude been claimed! The world is rational through and through—its existence is an utlimate brute fact; there is a personal God—a personal God is inconceivable; there is an extra-mental physical world immediately known—the mind can only know its own ideas; a moral imperative exists—obligation is only the resultant of desires; a permanent spiritual principle is in every one—there are only shifting states of mind; there is an endless chain of causes—there is an absolute first cause; an eternal necessity—a freedom; a purpose—no purpose; a primal One—a primal Many; a universal continuity—an essential discontinuity in things; an infinity—no infinity. There is this—there is that; there is indeed nothing which some one has not thought absolutely true, while his neighbor deemed it absolutely false; and not an absolutist among them seems ever to have considered that the trouble may all the time be essential, and that the intellect, even with truth directly in its grasp, may have no infallible signal for knowing whether it be truth or no. When one remembers that the most striking practical application to life of the doctrine of objective certitude has been the conscientious labors of the Holy Office of the Inquisition, one feels less tempted than ever to lend the doctrine a respectful ear.

But please observe, now, that when as empiricists we give up the doctrine of objective certitude, we do not thereby give up the quest or hope of truth itself. We still pin our faith on its existence, and still believe that we gain an even better position towards it by systematically continuing to roll up experiences and think. Our great difference from the scholastic lies in the way we face. The strength of his system lies in the principles, the origin, the *terminus a quo* of his thought; for us the strength is in the outcome, the upshot, the *terminus ad quem*. Not where it comes from but what it leads to is to decide. It matters not to an empiricist from what quarter an hypothesis may come to him: he may have acquired it by fair means or by foul; passion may have whispered or accident suggested it; but if the total drift of thinking continues to confirm it, that is what he means by its being true.

7

One more point, small but important, and our preliminaries are done. There are two ways of looking at our duty in the matter of opinion—ways entirely different, and yet ways about whose difference the theory of knowledge seems hitherto to have shown very little concern. *We must know the truth;* and *we must avoid error*—these are our first and great commandments as would-be knowers; but they are not two ways of stating an identical commandment, they are two separable laws. Although it may indeed happen that when we believe the truth *A*, we escape as an incidental consequence from believing that falsehood *B*, it hardly ever happens that by merely disbelieving *B* we necessarily believe *A*. We may in escaping *B* fall into believing other falsehoods, *C* or *D*, just as bad as *B*; or we may escape *B* by not believing anything at all, not even *A*.

Believe truth! Shun error!—these, we see, are two materially different laws; and by choosing between them we may end by coloring differently our whole intellectual life. We may regard the chase for truth as paramount, and the avoidance of error as secondary; or we may, on the other hand, treat the avoidance of error as more imperative, and let truth take its chance. Clifford, in the instructive passage which I have quoted, exhorts us to the latter course. Believe nothing, he tells us, keep your mind in suspense forever, rather than by closing it on insufficient evidence incur the awful risk of believing lies. You, on the other hand, may think that the risk of being in error is a very small matter when compared with the blessings of real knowledge, and be ready to be duped many times in your investigation rather than postpone indefinitely the chance of guessing true. I myself find it impossible to go with Clifford. We must remember that these feelings of our duty about either truth or error are in any case only expressions of our passional life. Biologically considered, our minds are as ready to grind out falsehood as veracity, and he who says, "Better go without belief forever than believe a lie!" merely shows his own preponderant private horror of becoming a dupe. He may be critical of many of his desires and fears, but this fear he slavishly obeys. He cannot imagine any one questioning its binding force. For my own part, I have also a horror of being duped; but I can believe that worse things than being duped may happen to a man in this world: so Clifford's exhortation has to my ears a thoroughly fantastic sound. It is like a general informing his soldiers that it is better to keep out of battle forever than to risk a single wound. Not so are victories either over enemies or over nature gained. Our errors are surely not such awfully solemn things. In a world where we are so certain to incur them in spite of all our caution, a certain lightness of heart seems healthier than this excessive nervousness on their behalf. At any rate, it seems the fittest thing for the empiricist philosopher.

8

And now, after all this introduction, let us go straight at our question. I have said, and now repeat it, that not only as a matter of fact do we find our passional nature influencing us in our opinions, but that there are some options between opinions in which this influence must be regarded both as an inevitable and as a lawful determinant of our choice.

I fear here that some of you my hearers will begin to scent danger, and lend an inhospitable ear. Two first steps of passion you have indeed had to admit as necessary—we must think so as to avoid dupery, and we must think so as to gain truth; but the surest path to those ideal consummations, you will probably consider, if from now onwards to take no further passional step.

Well, of course, I agree as far as the facts will allow. Whether the option between losing truth and gaining it is not momentous, we can throw the chance of *gaining truth* away, and at any rate save ourselves from any chance of *believing falsehood*, by not making up our minds at all till objective evidence has come. In scientific questions, this is almost always the case; and even in human affairs in general, the need of acting is seldom so urgent that a false belief to act on is better than no belief at all. Law courts, indeed, have to decide on the best evidence attainable for the moment, because a judge's duty is to make law as well as to ascertain it, and (as a learned judge once said to me) few cases are worth spending much time over: the great thing is to have them decided on *any* acceptable principles, and got out of the way. But in our dealings with objective nature we obviously are recorders, not makers, of the truth; and decisions for the mere sake of deciding promptly and getting on to the next business would be wholly out of place. Throughout the breadth of physical nature facts are what they are quite independently of us, and seldom is there any such hurry about them that the risks of being duped by believing a premature theory need be faced. The questions here are always trivial options, the hypotheses are hardly living (at any rate not living for us spectators) the choice between believing truth or falsehood is seldom forced. The attitude of sceptical balance is therefore the absolutely wise one if we would escape mistakes. What difference, indeed, does it make to most of us whether we have or have not a theory of the Rontgen rays, whether we believe or not in mind-stuff, or have a conviction about the causality of conscious states? It makes no difference. Such options are not forced on us. On every account it is better not to make them, but still keep weighing reasons *pro et contra* with an indifferent hand.

I speak, of course, here of the purely judging mind. For purposes of discovery such indifference is to be less highly recommended, and science would be far less advanced than she is if the passionate desires of individuals to get their own faiths confirmed had been kept out of the game. See for example the sagacity which Spencer and Weismann now display. On the other hand, if you want an absolute duffer in an investigation, you must, after all, take the man, who has no interest whatever in its results: he is the warranted incapable, the positive fool. The most useful investigator, because the most sensitive observer, is always he whose eager interest in one side of the question is balanced by an equally keen nervousness lest he become deceived. Science has organized this nervousness into a regular *technique*, her so-called method of verification; and she has fallen so deeply in love with the method that one may even say she has ceased to care for truth by itself at all. It is only truth as technically verified that interests her. The truth of truths might come in merely affirmative form, and she would decline to touch it. Such truths as that, she might repeat with Clifford, would be stolen in defiance of her duty to mankind. Human passions, however, are stronger than technical rules. "*Le coeur a ses raisons,*" as Pascal says,

"*que la raison ne connait pas*"; and however indifferent to all but the bare rules of the game the umpire, the abstract intellect, may be, the concrete players who furnish him the materials to judge of are usually, each one of them, in love with some pet "live hypothesis" of his own. Let us agree, however, that wherever there is no forced option, the dispassionately judicial intellect with no pet hypothesis, saving us, as it does, from dupery at any rate, ought to be ideal.

The question next arises: Are there not somewhere forced options in our speculative questions, and can we (as men who may be interested at least as much in positively gaining truth as in merely escaping dupery) always wait with impunity till the coercive evidence shall have arrived? It seems *a priori* improbable that the truth should be so nicely adjusted to our needs and powers as that. In the great boarding-house of nature, the cakes and the butter and the syrup seldom come out so even and leave the plates so clean. Indeed, we should view them with scientific suspicion if they did.

ọ ,

Moral questions immediately present themselves as questions whose solution cannot wait for sensible proof. A moral question is a question not of what sensibly exists, but of what is good, or would be good if it did exist. Science can tell us what exists; but to compare the *worths*, both of what exists and of what does not exist, we must consult not science, but what Pascal calls our heart. Science herself consults her heart when she lays it down that the infinite ascertainment of fact and correction of false belief are the supreme goods for man. Challenge the statement, and science can only repeat it oracularly, or else prove it by showing that such ascertainment and correction bring man all sorts of other goods which man's heart in turn declares. The question of having moral beliefs at all or not having them is decided by our will. Are our moral preferences true or false, or are they only odd biological phenomena, making things good or bad for *us*, but in themselves indifferent? How can your pure intellect decide? If your heart does not *want* a world of moral reality, your head will assuredly never make you believe in one. Mephistophelian scepticism, indeed, will satisfy the head's play-instincts much better than any rigorous idealism can. Some men (even at the student age) are so naturally cool-hearted that the moralistic hypothesis never has for them any pungent life, and in their supercilious presence the hot young moralist always feels strangely ill at ease. The appearance of knowingness is on their side, of *naivete* and gullibility on his. Yet, in the inarticulate heart of him, he clings to it that he is not a dupe, and that there is a realm in which (as Emerson says) all their wit and intellectual superiority is no better than the cunning of a fox. Moral scepticism can no more be refuted or proved by logic than intellectual scepticism can. When we stick to it that there *is* truth (be it of either kind), we do so with our whole nature, and resolve to stand or fall by the results. The sceptic with his whole nature adopts the doubting attitude; but which of us is the wiser, Omniscience only knows.

Turn now from these wide questions of good to a certain class of questions of fact, questions concerning personal relations, states of mind between one man and another. *Do you like me or not?*—for example. Whether you do or not depends, in countless instances, on whether I meet you half-way, am willing to assume that you must like me, and show you trust and expectation. The previous faith on my part in your liking's existence is in such cases what makes your liking come. But if I stand aloof, and refuse to budge an inch until I have objective evidence, until you shall have done something apt, as the absolutists say, *ad extorquendum assensum meum*, ten to one your liking never comes. How many women's hearts are vanquished by the mere sanguine insistence of some man that they *must* love him! he will not consent to the hypothesis that they cannot. The desire for a certain kind of truth here brings about that special truth's existence; and so it is in innumerable cases of other sorts. Who gains promotions, boons, appointments, but the man in whose life they are seen to play the part of live hypotheses, who discounts them, sacrifices other things for their sake before they have come, and takes risks for them in advance? His faith acts on the power above him as a claim, and creates its own verification.

A social organism of any sort whatever, large or small, is what it is because each member proceeds to his own duty with a trust that the other members will simultaneously do theirs. Wherever a desired result is achieved by the co-operation of many independent persons, its existence as a fact is a pure consequence of the precursive faith in a commercial system, a ship, a college, an athletic team, all exist on this condition, without which not only is nothing achieved, but nothing is even attempted. A whole train of passengers (individually brave enough) will be looted by a few highwaymen, simply because the latter can count on one another, while each passenger fears that if he makes a movement of resistance, he will be shot before any one else backs him up. If we believed that the whole car-full would rise at once with us, we should each severally rise, and train-robbing would never even be attempted. There are, then, cases where a fact cannot come at all unless a preliminary faith exists in its coming. *And where faith in a fact can help create the fact,* that would be an insane logic which should say that faith running ahead of scientific evidence is the "lowest kind of immorality" into which a thinking being can fall. Yet such is the logic by which our scientific absolutists pretend to regulate our lives!

10

In truths dependent on our personal action, then, faith based on desire is certainly a lawful and possibly an indispensable thing.

But now, it will be said, these are all childish human cases, and have nothing to do with great cosmical matters, like the question of religious faith. Let us then pass on to that. Religions differ so much in their accidents that in discussing the religious question we must make it very generic and broad. What then do we now mean by the religious hypothesis? Science says things are; morality says some things are better than other things; and religion says essentially two things.

First, she says that the best things are the more eternal things, the overlapping things, the things in the universe that throw the last stone, so to speak, and say the final word. "Perfection is eternal"—this phrase of Charles Secrétan seems a good way of putting this first affirmation of religion, an affirmation which obviously cannot yet be verified scientifically at all.

The second affirmation of religion is that we are better off even now if we believe her first affirmation to be true.

Now, let us consider what the logical elements of this situation are *in case the religious hypothesis in both its branches be really true.* (Of course, we must admit that possibility at the outset. If we are to discuss the question at all, it must involve a living option. If for any of you religion be a hypothesis that cannot, by any living possibility, be true, then you need go no farther. I speak to the "saving remnant" alone.) So proceeding, we see, first, that religion offers itself as a *momentous* option. We are supposed to gain, even now, by our belief, and to lose by our non-belief a certain vital good. Secondly, religion is a *forced* option, so far as that good goes. We cannot escape the issue by remaining sceptical and waiting for more light, because, although we do avoid error in that way if *religion be untrue,* we lose the good, *if it be true,* just as certainly as if we positively chose to disbelieve. It is as if a man should hesitate indefinitely to ask a certain woman to marry him because he was not perfectly sure that she would prove an angel after he brought her home. Would he not cut himself off from that particular angel-possibility as decisively as if he went and married some one else? Scepticism, then, is not avoidance of option; it is option of a certain particular kind of risk. *Better risk loss of truth than chance of error*—that is your faith-vetoer's exact position. He is actively playing his stake as much as the believer is; he is backing the field against the religious hypothesis, just as the believer is backing the religious hypothesis against the field. To preach scepticism to us as a duty until "sufficient evidence" for religion be found, is tantamount therefore to telling us, when in presence of the religious hypothesis, that to yield to our fear of its being error is wiser and better than to yield to our hope that it may be true. It is not intellect against all passions, then; it is only intellect with one passion laying down its law. And by what, forsooth, is the supreme wisdom of this passion warranted? Dupery for dupery, what proof is there that dupery through hope is so much worse than dupery through fear? I, for one, can see no proof; and I simply refuse obedience to the scientists command to imitate his kind of option, in a case where my own sake is important enough to give me the right to choose my own form of risk. If religion be true and the evidence for it be still insufficient, I do not wish, by

putting your extinguisher upon my nature (which feels to me as if it had after all some business in this matter), to forfeit my sole chance in life of getting upon the winning side —that chance depending, of course, on my willingness to run the risk of acting as if my passional need of taking the world religiously might be prophetic and right.

All this is on the supposition that it really may be prophetic and right, and that, even to us who are discussing the matter, religion is a live hypothesis which may be true. Now, to most of us religion comes in a still further way that makes a veto on our active faith even more illogical. The more perfect and more eternal aspect of the universe is represented in our religions as having personal form. The universe is no longer a mere *It* to us, but a *Thou,* if we are religious; and any relation that may be possible from person to person might be possible here. For instance, although in one sense we are passive portions of the universe, in another we show a curious autonomy, as if we were small active centres on our own account. We feel, too, as if the appeal of religion to us were made to our own active good-will, as if evidence might be forever withheld from us unless we met the hypothesis half-way. To take a trivial illustration: just as a man who in a company of gentlemen made no advances, asked a warrant for every concession, and believed no one's word without proof, would cut himself off by such churlishness from all the social rewards that a more trusting spirit would earn—so here, one who should shut himself up in snarling logicality and try to make the gods extort his recognition willy-nilly, or not get it at all, might cut himself off forever from his only opportunity of making the gods' acquaintance. This feeling, forced on us we know not whence, that by obstinately believing that there are gods (although not to do so would be so easy both for our logic and our life) we are doing the universe the deepest service we can, seems part of the living essence of the religious hypothesis. If the hypothesis *were* true in all its part, including this one, then pure intellectualism, with its veto on our making willing advances, would be an absurdity; and some participation of our sympathetic nature would be logically required, I, therefore, for one, cannot see my way to accepting the agnostic rules for truth-seeking, or willfully agree to keep my willing nature out of the game. I cannot do so for this plain reason, that *a rule of thinking which would absolutely prevent me from acknowledging certain kinds of truth if those kinds of truth were really there, would be an irrational rule.* That for me is the long and short of the formal logic of the situation, no matter what the kinds of truth might materially be.

I confess I do not see how this logic can be escaped. But sad experience makes me fear that some of you may still shrink from radically saying with me, in *abstractor*, that we have the right to believe at our own risk any hypothesis that is live enough to tempt our will. I suspect, however, that if this is so, it is because you have got away from the abstract logical point of view altogether, and are thinking (perhaps without realizing it) of some particular religious hypothesis which for you is dead. The freedom to "believe what we will" you apply to the case of some patent superstition; and the faith you think of is the faith defined by the schoolboy when he said, "Faith is when you believe something that you know ain't true." I can only repeat that this is misapprehension. *In concreto,* the freedom to believe can only cover living options which the intellect of the individual cannot by itself resolve; and living options never seem absurdities to him who has them to consider. When I look at the religious question as it really puts itself to concrete men, and when I think of all the possibilities which both practically and theoretically it involves, then this command that we shall put a stopper on our heart, instincts, and courage, and *wait*— acting of course meanwhile more or less as if religion were *not* true—till doomsday, or till such time as our intellect and senses working together may have raked in evidence enough— this command, I say, seems to me the queerest idol ever manufactured in the philosophic cave. Were we scholastic absolutists, there might be more excuse. If we had an infallible intellect with its objective certitudes, we might feel ourselves disloyal to such a perfect organ of knowledge in not trusting to it exclusively, in not waiting for its releasing word. But if we are empiricists, if we believe that no bell in us tolls to let us know for certain when truth is in our grasp, then it seems a piece of idle fantasticality to preach so solemnly our duty of waiting for the bell. Indeed we *may* wait if we will—I hope you do not think that I am denying that— but if we do so, we do so at our peril as much as if we believed. In either case we *act,* taking our life in our hands. No one of us ought to issue vetoes to the other, nor should we bandy words of abuse. We ought, on the contrary, delicately and profoundly to respect one another's mental freedom: then only shall we bring about the intellectual republic; then only shall we have that spirit of inner intolerance without which all our outer tolerance is soulless, and which is empiricism's glory; then only shall we live and let live, in speculative as well as in practical things.

I began by a reference to Fitz-James Stephen; let me end by a quotation from him. "What do you think of yourself? What do you think of the world? ... These are questions with which all must deal as it seems good to them. They are riddles of the Sphinx, and in some way or other we must deal with them. ... In all important transactions of life we have to take a leap in the dark. ... If we decide to leave the riddles unanswered, that is a choice; if we waver in our answer, that, too, is a choice: but whatever choice we make, we make it at our peril. If a man chooses to turn his back altogether on God and the future, no one can prevent him; no one can show beyond reasonable doubt that he is mistaken. If a man thinks otherwise and acts as he thinks, I do not see that any one can prove that *he* is mistaken. Each must act as he thinks best; and if he is wrong, so much the worse for him. We stand on a mountain pass in the midst of whirling snow and blinding mist, through which we get glimpses now and then of paths which may be deceptive. If we stand still we shall be frozen to death. If we take the wrong road we shall be dashed to pieces. We do not certainly know whether there is any right one. What must we do? 'Be strong and of a good courage.' Act for the best, hope for the best, and take what comes. ... If death ends all, we cannot meet death better."

John Dewey

John Dewey (1859-1952) was perhaps America's most famous philosopher and educator. He was among the first to fully articulate the Copernican philosophy, but from the evolutionary, biological perspective, not the Newtonian, mechanical one. Since there is no fixed or eternal truth in his system, all forms of human activity, intellectual and otherwise, are instruments for solving human problems. Moreover, and herein lies Dewey's brilliance, the instruments used changed the problems themselves.

The selection below was originally entitled "The Reflex Arc Concept in Psychology," when it appeared in *The Psychological Review* (1896).

Dewey argues against the tendency to analyze an entity into parts and to try to explain the parts as if they could exist separately. This is the mechanical approach. Organic structures, like mankind, are not constructed piece by piece but grow; hence the history of their transformation is as important as the logic of their momentary structure. If we forget this, then we are apt to mistakenly treat human agents as if they are victims of totally external causes, or mistakenly try to reconstruct human behavorial models as sequences of discrete parts.

Human Beings Are Not Machines

That the greater demand for a unifying principle and controlling working hypothesis in psychology should come at just the time when all generalizations and classifications are most questioned and questionable is natural enough. It is the very cumulation of discrete facts creating the demand for unification that also breaks down previous lines of classification. The material is too great in mass and too varied in style to fit into existing pigeon-holes, and the cabinets of science break of their own dead weight. The idea of the reflex arc has upon the whole come nearer to meeting this demand for a general working hypothesis than any other single concept. It being admitted that the sensori-motor apparatus represents both the unit of nerve structure and the type of nerve function, the image of this relationship passed over into psychology, and became an organizing principle to hold together the multiplicity of fact.

In criticising this conception it is not intended to make a plea for the principles of explanation and classification which the reflex arc idea has replaced; but, on the contrary, to urge that they are not sufficiently displaced, and that in the idea of the sensori-motor circuit, conceptions of the nature of sensation and of action derived from the nominally displaced psychology are still in control.

The older dualism between sensation and idea is repeated in the current dualism of peripheral and central structures and functions; the older dualism of body and soul finds a distinct echo in the current dualism of stimulus and response. Instead of interpreting the character of sensation, idea and action from their place and function in the sensori-motor circuit, we still incline to interpret the latter from our preconceived and preformulated ideas of rigid distinctions between sensations, thoughts and acts. The sensory stimulus is one thing, the central activity, standing for the idea, is another thing, and the motor discharge, standing for the act proper, is a third. As a result, the reflex arc is not a comprehensive, or organic unity, but a patchwork of disjointed parts, a mechanical conjunction of unallied processes. What is needed is that the principle underlying the idea of the reflex arc as the fundamental psychical unity shall react into and determine the values of its constitutive factors. More specifically, what is wanted is that sensory stimulus, central connections and motor responses shall be viewed, not as separate and complete entities in themselves, but as divisions of labor, functioning factors, within the single concrete whole, now designated the reflex arc.

What is the reality so designated? What shall we term that which is not sensation-followed-by-idea-followed-by-movement, but which is primary; which is, as it were, the psychical organism of which sensation, idea and movement are the chief organs? Stated on the physiological side, this reality may most conveniently be termed coordination. This is the essence of the facts held together by and subsumed under the reflex arc concept. Let us take, for our example, the familiar child-candle instance (James, Psychology, Vol. I, p. 25). The ordinary interpretation would say the sensation of light is a stimulus to the grasping as a response, the burn resulting is a stimulus to withdrawing the hand as response and so on. There is, of course, no doubt that is a rough practical way of representing the process. But when we ask for its psychological adequacy, the case is quite different. Upon analysis, we find that we begin not with a sensory stimulus, but with a sensori-motor coordination, the optical-ocular, and that in a certain sense it is the movement which is primary, and the sensation which is secondary, the movement of body, head and eye muscles determining the quality of what is experienced. In other words, the real beginning is with the act of seeing; it is looking, and not a sensation of light. The sensory quale gives the value of the act, just as the movement furnishes its mechanism and control, but both sensation and movement lie inside, not outside the act.

Now if this act, the seeing, stimulates another act, the reaching, it is because both of these acts fall within a larger coordination; because seeing and grasping have been so often bound together to reinforce each other, to help each other out, that each may be considered practically a subordinate member of a bigger coordination. More specifically, the ability of the hand to do its work will depend, either directly or indirectly, upon its control, as well as its stimulation, by the act of vision. If the sight did not inhibit as well as excite the reaching, the latter would be purely indeterminate, it would be for anything or nothing, not for the particular object seen. The reaching, in turn, must both stimulate and control the seeing. The eye must be kept upon the candle if the arm is to do its work; let it wander and the arm takes up another task. In other words, we now have an enlarged and transformed coordination; the act is seeing no less than before, but it is now seeing-for-reaching purposes. There is still a sensori-motor circuit, one with more content or value, not a substitution of a motor response for a sensory stimulus.

Now take the affair at its next stage, that in which the child gets burned. It is hardly necessary to point out again that this is also a sensori-motor coordination and not a mere sensation. It is worth while, however, to note especially the fact that it is simply the completion, or fulfillment, of the previous eye-arm-hand coordination and not an entirely new occurrence. Only because the heat-pain quale enters into the same circuit of experience with the optical-ocular and muscular quales, does the child learn from the experience and get the ability to avoid the experience in the future.

More technically stated, the so-called response is not merely *to* the stimulus; it is *into* it. the burn is the original seeing, the original optical-ocular experience enlarged and transformed in its value. It is no longer mere seeing; it is seeing-of-a-light-that-means-pain-when-contact-occurs. The ordinary reflex arc theory proceeds upon the more or less tacit assumption that the outcome of the response is a totally new experience; that it is, say, the substitution of a burn sensation for a light sensation through the intervention of motion. The fact is that the sole meaning of the intervening movement is to maintain, reinforce or transform (as the case may be) the original quale; that we do not have the replacing of one sort of experience by another, but the development (or as it seems convenient to term it) the mediation of an experience. The seeing, in a word, remains to control the reaching, and is, in turn, interpreted by the burning.

The discussion up to this point may be summarized by saying that the reflex arc idea, as commonly employed, is defective in that it assumes sensory stimulus and motor response as distinct psychical existences, while in reality they are always inside a coordination and have their significance purely from the part played in maintaining or reconstituting the coordination; and (secondly) in assuming that the quale of experience which precedes the 'motor' phase and that which succeeds it are two different states, instead of the last being always the first reconstituted, the motor phase coming in only for the sake of such mediation. The result is that the reflex arc idea leaves us with a disjointed psychology, whether viewed from the standpoint of development in the individual or in the race, or from that of the analysis of the mature consciousness. As to the former, in its failure to see that the arc of which it talks is virtually a circuit, a continual reconstitution, it breaks continuity and leaves us nothing but a series of jerks, the origin of each jerk to be sought outside the process of experience itself, in either an external pressure of 'environment,' or else in an unaccountable spontaneous variation from within the 'soul' or the 'organism.' As to the latter, failing to see the unity of activity, no matter how much it may prate of unity, it still leaves us with sensation or peripheral stimulus; idea, or central process (the equivalent of attention); and motor response, or act, as three disconnected existences, having to be somehow adjusted to each other, whether through the intervention of an extra-experimental soul, or by mechanical push and pull.

Before proceeding to a consideration of the general meaning for psychology of the summary, it may be well to give another descriptive analysis, as the value of the statement depends entirely upon the universality of its range of application. For such an instance we may conveniently take Baldwin's analysis of the reactive consciousness. In this there are, he says (Feeling and Will, p. 60), "three elements corresponding to the three elements of the nervous arc. First, the receiving consciousness, the stimulus—say a loud, unexpected sound; second, the attention involuntarily drawn, the registering element; and, third, the muscular reaction following upon the sound—say flight from fancied danger." Now, in the first place, such an analysis is incomplete; it ignores the status prior to hearing the sound. Of course, if this status is irrelevant to what happens afterwards, such ignoring is quite legitimate. But is it irrelevant either to the quantity or the quality of the stimulus?

If one is reading a book, if one is hunting, if one is watching in a dark place on a lonely night, if one is performing a chemical experiment, in each case, the noise has a very different psychical value; it is a different experience. In any case, what proceeds the "stimulus' is a whole act, a sensori-motor coordination. What is more to the point, the 'stimulus' emerges out of this coordination; it is born from it as its matrix; it represents as it were an escape from it. I might here fall back upon authority, and refer to the widely accepted sensation continuum theory, according to which the sound cannot be absolutely *ex abrupto* from the outside, but is simply a shifting of focus of emphasis, a redistribution of tensions within the former act; and declare that unless the sound activity had been present to some extent in the prior coordination, it would be impossible for it now to come to prominence in consciousness. And such a reference would be only an amplification of what has already been said concerning the way in which the prior activity influences the value of the sound sensation. Or, we might point to cases of hypnotism, mono-ideaism and absent-mindedness, like that of Archimedes, as evidences that if the

previous coordination is such as rigidly to lock the door, the auditory disturbance will knock in vain for admission to consciousness. Or, to speak more truly in the metaphor, the auditory activity must already have one foot over the threshold, if it is ever to gain admittance.

But it will be more satisfactory, probably, to refer to the biological side of the case, and point out that as the ear activity has been evolved on account of the advantage gained by the whole organism, it must stand in the strictest histological and physiological connection with the eye, or hand, or leg, or whatever other organ has been the overt center of action. It is absolutely impossible to think of the eye center as monopolizing consciousness and the ear apparatus as wholly quiescent. What happens is a certain relative prominence and subsidence as between the various organs which maintain the organic equilibrium.

Furthermore, the sound is not a mere stimulus, or mere sensation; it again is an act, that of hearing. The muscular response is involved in this as well as sensory stimulus; that is, there is a certain definite set of the motor apparatus involved in hearing just as much as there is in subsequent running away. The movement and posture of the head, the tension of the ear muscles, are required for the 'reception' of the sound. It is just as true to say that the sensation of sound arises from a motor response as that the running away is a response to the sound. This may be brought out by reference to the fact that Professor Baldwin, in the passage quoted, has inverted the real order as between his first and second elements. We do not have first a sound and then activity of attention, unless sound is taken as mere nervous shock or physical event, not as conscious value. The conscious sensation of sound depends upon the motor response having already taken place; or, in terms of the previous statement (if stimulus is used as a conscious fact, and not as a mere physical event) it is the motor response or attention which constitutes that, which finally becomes the stimulus to another act. Once more, the final 'element,' the running away, is not merely motor, but is sensori-motor, having its sensory value and its muscular mechanism. It is also a coordination. And, finally, this sensori-motor coordination is not a new act, supervening upon what preceded. Just as the 'response' is necessary to constitute the stimulus, to determine it as sound and as this kind of sound, of wild beast or robber, so the sound experience must persist as a value in the running, to keep it up, to control it. The motor reaction involved in the running is, once more, into, not merely to, the sound. It occurs to change the sound, to get rid of it. The resulting quale, whatever it may be, has its meaning wholly determined by reference to the hearing of the sound. It is that experience mediated. What we have is a circuit, not an arc or broken segment of a circle. This circuit is more truly termed organic than reflex, because the motor response determines the stimulus, just as truly as sensory stimulus determines movement. Indeed, the movement is only for the sake of determining the stimulus, of fixing what kind of a stimulus it is, of interpreting it.

I hope it will not appear that I am introducing needless refinements and distinctions into what, it may be urged, is after all an undoubted fact, that movement as response follows sensation as stimulus. It is not a question of making the account of the process more complicated, though it is always wise to beware of that false simplicity which is reached by leaving out of account a large part of the problem. It is a question of finding out what stimulus or sensation, what movement and response mean; a question of seeing that they mean distinctions of flexible function only, not of fixed existence; that one and the same occurrence plays either or both parts, according to the shift of interest; and that balance of this functional distinction and relationship, the supposed problem of the adjustment of one to the other, whether by superior force in the stimulus or an agency *ad hoc* in the center or the soul, is a purely self-creating problem

We may see the disjointed character of the present theory, by calling to mind that it is impossible to apply the phrase 'sensori-motor' to the occurrence as a simple phrase of description; it has validity only as a term of interpretation, only, that is, as defining various functions exercised. In terms of description, the whole process may be sensory or it may be motor, but it cannot be sensori-motor. The 'stimulus,' the excitation of the nerve ending and of the sensory nerve, the central change, are just as much, or just as little, motion as the events taking place in the motor nerve and the muscles. It is one uninterrupted, continuous

redistribution of mass in motion. And there is nothing in the process, from the standpoint of description, which entitles us to call this reflex. It is redistribution pure and simple; as much so as the burning of a log, or the falling of a house or the movement of the wind. In the physical process, as physical, there is nothing which can be set off as stimulus, nothing which reacts, nothing which is response. There is just a change in the system of tensions.

The same sort of thing is true when we describe the process purely from the psychical side. It is now all sensation, all sensory quale; the motion, as psychically described, is just as much sensation as is sound or light or burn. Take the withdrawing of the hand from the candle flame as example. What we have is a certain visual-heat-pain-muscular-quale, transformed into another visual-touch-muscular-quale—the flame now being visible only at a distance, or not at all, the touch sensation being altered, etc. If we symbolize the original visual quale by v, the temperature by h, the accompanying muscular sensation by m, the whole experience may be stated as vhm-vh$m$-vhm'; m being the quale of withdrawing, m' the sense of the status after the withdrawal. The motion is not a certain kind of existence; it is a sort of sensory experience interpreted, just as is candle flame, or burn from candle flame. All are on a par.

But, in spite of all this, it will be urged, there is a distinction between stimulus and response, between sensation and motion. Precisely; but we ought now to be in a condition to ask of what nature is the distinction, instead of taking it for granted as a distinction somehow lying in the existence of the facts themselves. We ought to be able to see that the ordinary conception of the reflex arc theory, instead of being a case of plain science, is a survival of the metaphysical dualism, first formulated by Plato, according to which the sensation is an ambiguous dweller on the border land of soul and body, the idea (or central process) is purely psychical, and the act (or movement) purely physical. Thus the reflex arc formulation is neither physical (or physiological) nor psychological; it is a mixed materialistic-spiritualistic assumption.

If the previous descriptive analysis has made obvious the need of a reconsideration of the reflex arc idea, of the nest of difficulties and assumptions in the apparently simple statement, it is now time to undertake an explanatory analysis. The fact is that stimulus and response are not distinctions of existence, but teleological distinctions, that is, distinctions of function, or part played, with reference to reaching or maintaining an end. With respect to this teleological process two stages should be discriminated, as their confusion is one cause of the confusion attending the whole matter. In one case, the relation represents an organization of means with reference to a comprehensive end. It represents an accomplished adaptation. Such is the case in all well developed instincts, as when we say that the contact of eggs is a stimulus to the hen to set; or the sight of corn a stimulus to pick; such also is the case with all thoroughly formed habits, as when the contact with the floor stimulates walking. In these instances there is no question of consciousness of stimulus *as* stimulus, of response *as* response. There is simply a continuously ordered sequence of acts, all adapted in themselves and in the order of their sequence, to reach a certain objective end, the reproduction of the species, the preservation of life, locomotion to a certain place. The end has got thoroughly organized into the means. In calling one stimulus, another response we mean nothing more than that such an orderly sequence of acts is taking place. The same sort of statement might be made equally well with reference to the succession of changes in a plant, so far as these are considered with reference to their adaptation to, say, producing seed. It is equally applicable to the series of events in the circulation of the blood, or the sequence of acts occurring in a self-binding reaper.

Regarding such cases of organization viewed as already attained, we may say, positively, that it is only the assumed common reference to an inclusive end which marks each member off as stimulus and response, that apart from such reference we have only antecedent and consequent; in other words, the distinction is one of interpretation. Negatively, it must be pointed out that it is not legitimate to carry over, without change, exactly the same order of considerations to cases where it is a question of *conscious* stimulation and response. We may, in the above case, regard, if we please, stimulus and response each as an entire act, having an individuality of its own, subject even here to the qualification that individuality

means not an entirely independent whole, but a division of labor as regards maintaining or reaching an end. But in any case, it is an act, a sensori-motor coordination, which stimulates the response, itself in turn sensori-motor, not a sensation which stimulates a movement. Hence the illegitimacy of identifying, as is so often done, such cases of organized instincts or habits with the so-called reflex arc, or of transferring, without modification, considerations valid of this serial coordination of acts to the sensation-movement case.

The fallacy that arises when this is done is virtually the psychological or historical fallacy. A set of considerations which hold good only because of a completed process, is read into the content of the process which conditions this completed result. A state of things characterizing an outcome is regarded as a true description of events which led up to this outcome; when, actually, if this outcome had already been in existence, there would have been no necessity for the process. Or, to make the application to the case in hand, considerations valid of an attained organization or coordination, the orderly sequence of minor acts in a comprehensive coordination, are used to describe a process, viz., the distinction of mere sensation as stimulus and of mere movement as response, which takes place only because such an attained organization is no longer at hand, but is in process of constitution. Neither mere sensation, nor mere movement, can ever be either stimulus or response; only an act can be that; the *sensation* as stimulus means the lack of and search for such an objective stimulus, or orderly placing of an act; just as mere movement as response means the lack of and search for the right act to complete a given coordination.

A recurrence to our example will make these formulae clearer. As long as the seeing is an unbroken act, which is as experienced no more mere sensation than it is mere motion (though the onlooker or psychological observer can interpret it into sensation and movement), it is in no sense the sensation which stimulates the reaching; we have, as already sufficiently indicated, only the serial steps in a coordination of *acts*. But now take a child who, upon reaching for bright light (that is, exercising the seeing-reaching coordination) has sometimes had a delightful exercise, sometimes found something good to eat and sometimes burned himself. *Now the response is not only uncertain, but the stimulus is equally uncertain; one is uncertain only in so far as the other is.* The real problem may be equally well stated as either to discover the right stimulus, to constitute the stimulus, or to discover, to constitute, the response. The question of whether to reach or to abstain from reaching is the question what sort of a bright light have we here? Is it the one which means playing with one's hands, eating milk, or burning one's fingers? The stimulus must be constituted for the response to occur. Now it is at precisely this juncture and because of it that the distinction of sensation as stimulus and motion as response arises.

The sensation or conscious stimulus is not a thing or existence by itself; it is that phase of a coordination requiring attention because, by reason of the conflict within the coordination, it is uncertain how to complete it. It is the doubt as to the next act, whether to reach or no, which gives the motive to examining the act. The end to follow is, in this sense, the stimulus. It furnishes the motivation to attend to what has just taken place; to define it more carefully. From this point of view the discovery of the stimulus is the 'response' to possible movement as 'stimulus.' We must have an anticipatory sensation, an image, of the movements that may occur, together with their respective values, before attention will go to the seeing to break it up as a sensation of light, and of light of this particular kind. It is the initiated activities of reaching, which, inhibited by the conflict in the coordination, turn round, as it were, upon the seeing, and hold it from passing over into further act until its quality is determined. Just here the act as objective stimulus becomes transformed into sensation as possible, as conscious, stimulus. Just here also, motion as conscious response emerges.

In other words, sensation as stimulus does not mean any particular psychical *existence*. It means simply a function, and will have its value shift according to the special work requiring to be done. At one moment the various activities of reaching and withdrawing will be the sensation, because they are that phase of activity which sets the problem, or creates the demand for, the next act. At the next moment the previous act of seeing will furnish the sensation, being, in turn, that phase of activity which sets the pace upon which depends further action.

Generalized, sensation as stimulus, is always that phase of activity requiring to be defined in order that a coordination may be completed. What the sensation will be in particular at a given time, therefore, will depend entirely upon the way in which an activity is being used. It has no fixed quality of its own. The search for the stimulus is the search for exact conditions of action; that is, for the state of things which decided how a beginning coordination should be completed.

Similarly, motion, as response, has only a functional value. It is whatever will serve to complete the disintegrating coordination. Just as the discovery of the sensation marks the establishing of the problem, so the constitution of the response marks the solution of this problem. At one time, fixing attention, holding the eye fixed, upon the seeing and thus bringing out a certain quale of light is the response, because that is the particular act called for just then; at another time, the movement of the arm away from the light is the response. There is nothing in itself which may be labelled response. That one certain set of sensory quales should be marked off by themselves as 'motion' and put in antithesis to such sensory quales as those of color, sound and contact, as legitimate claimants to the title of sensation, is wholly inexplicable unless we keep the difference of function in view. It is the eye and ear sensations which fix for us the problem, report to us the conditions which have to be met if the coordination is to be successfully completed; and just the moment we need to know about our movements to get an adequate report, motion miraculously (from the ordinary standpoint) ceases to be motion and becomes 'muscular sensation.' On the other hand, take the change in values of experience, the transformation of sensory quales. Whether this change will or will not be interpreted as movement, whether or not any consciousness of movement will arise, will depend upon whether this change is satisfactory, whether or not it is regarded as a harmonious development of a coordination, or whether the change is regarded as simply a means in solving a problem, an instrument in reaching a more satisfactory coordination. So long as our experience runs smoothly we are no more conscious of motion as motion than we are of this or that color or sound by itself.

To sum up: the distinction of sensation and

movement as stimulus and response respectively is not a distinction which can be regarded as descriptive of anything which holds of psychical events or existences as such. The only events to which the terms stimulus and response can be descriptively applied are to minor acts serving by their respective positions to the maintenance of some organized coordination. The conscious stimulus or sensation, and the conscious response or motion, have a special genesis or motivation, and a special end or function. The reflex arc theory, by neglecting, by abstracting from, this genesis and this function gives us one disjointed part of a process as if it were the whole. It gives us literally an arc, instead of the circuit; and not giving us the circuit of which it is an arc, does not enable us to place, to center, the arc. This arc, again, falls apart into two separate existences having to be either mechanically or externally adjusted to each other.

The circle is a coordination, some of whose members have come into conflict with each other. It is the temporary disintegration and need of reconstitution which occasions, which affords the genesis of, the conscious distinction into sensory stimulus on one side and motor response on the other. The stimulus is that phase of the forming coordination which represents the conditions which have to be met in bringing it to a successful issue; the response is that phase of one and the same forming coordination which gives the key to meeting these conditions, which serves as instrument in effecting the successful coordination. They are therefore strictly correlative and contemporaneous. The stimulus is something to be discovered; to be made out; if the activity affords its own adequate stimulation, there is no stimulus save in the objective sense already referred to. As soon as it is adequately determined, then and then only is the response also complete. To attain either, means that the coordination has completed itself. Moreover, it is the motor response which assists in discovering and constituting the stimulus. It is the holding of the movement at a certain stage which creates the sensation, which throws it into relief.

It is the coordination which unifies that which the reflex arc concept gives us only in disjointed fragments. It is the circuit within which fall distinctions of stimulus and response as functional phases of its own mediation or completion. The point of this story is in its application; but the application of it to the question of the nature of psychical evolution, to the distinction between sensation and rational consciousness, and the nature of judgment must be deferred to a more favorable opportunity.

Bertrand Russell

Russell (1872-1970) was perhaps the best known philosopher of the twentieth century. Certainly he was the most notorious. Even in the first world war he was jailed by the British as a conscientious objector. Among professional philosophers he is best known for his monumental work on mathematical logic, *Principia Mathematica*, written at the turn of the century in conjunction with that other great British philosopher, Alfred North Whitehead.

Russell's message, in a nutshell, is that philosophy cannot be concerned with the universe as a whole, and it certainly cannot deal with problems of good and evil. This follows from Russell's views on what constitutes scientific philosophy. It is, of course, hard for many to reconcile this kind of assertion with Russell's own heroic activities. Russell claimed that his personal life could not be understood in terms of his conception of the right kind of philosophy. One may ask if Russell perhaps was a victim of the Aristotelian notion of knowledge for its own sake as opposed to knowledge for the sake of action. An Aristotelian would not consider this to be a victimization.

Mysticism and Logic

Metaphysics, or the attempt to conceive the world as a whole by means of thought, has been developed, from the first, by the union and conflict of two very different human impulses, the one urging men towards mysticism, the other urging them towards science. Some men have achieved greatness through one of these impulses alone, others through the other alone: in Hume, for example, the scientific impulse reigns quite unchecked, while in Blake a strong hostility to science co-exists with profound mystic insight. But the greatest men who have been philosophers have felt the need both of science and of mysticism: the attempt to harmonise the two was what made their life, and what always must, for all its arduous uncertainty, make philosophy, to some minds, a greater thing than either science or religion. . . .

Mystical philosophy, in all ages and in all parts of the world, is characterized by certain beliefs. . . .

There is, first, the belief in insight as against discursive analytic knowledge: the belief in a way of wisdom, sudden, penetrating, coercive, which is contrasted with the slow and fallible study of outward appearance by a science relying wholly upon the senses. All who are capable of absorption in an inward passion must have experienced at times the strange feeling of unreality in common objects, the loss of contact with daily things, in which the solidity of the outer world is lost, and the soul seems, in utter loneliness, to bring forth, out of its own depths, the mad dance of fantastic phantoms which have hitherto appeared as independently real and living. This is the negative side of the mystic's initiation: the doubt concerning common knowledge, preparing the way for the reception of what seems a higher wisdom. Many men to whom this negative experience is familiar do not pass beyond it, but for the mystic it is merely the gateway to an ampler world.

The mystic insight begins with the sense of a mystery unveiled, of a hidden wisdom now suddenly become certain beyond the possibility of a doubt. The sense of certainty and revelation comes earlier than any definite belief. The definite beliefs at which mystics arrive are the result of reflection upon the inarticulate experience gained in the moment of insight. Often, beliefs which have no real connection with this moment become subsequently attracted into the central nucleus; thus in addition to the convictions which all mystics share, we find, in many of them, other convictions of a more local and temporary character, which no doubt become amalgamated with what was essentially mystical in virtue of their subjective certainty. We may ignore such inessential accretions, and confine ourselves to the beliefs which all mystics share.

The first and most direct outcome of the moment of illumination is belief in the possibility of a way of knowledge which may be called revelation or insight or intuition, as contrasted with sense, reason, and analysis, which are regarded as blind guides leading to the morass of illusion. Closely connected with this belief is the conception of a Reality behind the world of appearance and utterly different from it. This Reality is regarded with an admiration often amounting to worship; it is felt to be always and everywhere close at hand, thinly veiled by the shows of sense, ready, for the receptive mind, to shine in its glory even through the apparent folly and wickedness of Man. The poet, the artist, and the lover are seekers after that glory: the haunting beauty that they pursue in the faint reflection of its sun. But the mystic lives in the full light of the vision: what others dimly seek he knows, with a knowledge beside which all other knowledge is ignorance.

The second characteristic of mysticism is its belief in unity, and its refusal to admit opposition or division anywhere. We found Heraclitus saying "good and ill are one"; and again he says, "the way up and the way down is one and the same." The same attitude appears in the simultaneous assertion of contradictory propositions, such as: "We step and do not step into the same rivers; we are and are not." The assertion of Parmenides, that reality is one and indivisible, comes from the same impulse towards unity. In Plato, this impulse is less prominent, being held in check by this theory of ideas; but it reappears; so far as his logic permits, in the doctrine of the primacy of the Good.

A third mark of almost all mystical metaphysics is the denial of the reality of Time. This is an outcome of the denial of division; if all is one, the distinction of past and future must be illusory. We have seen this doctrine prominent in Parmenides; and among moderns it is fundamental in the systems of Spinoza and Hegel.

The last of the doctrines of mysticism which we have to consider is its belief that all evil is mere appearance, an illusion produced by the divisions and oppositions of the analytic intellect. Mysticism does not maintain that such things as cruelty, for example, are good, but it denies that they are real: they belong to that lower world of phantoms from which we are to be liberated by the insight of the vision. Sometimes—for example in Hegel, and at least verbally in Spinoza—not only evil, but good also, is regarded as illusory, though nevertheless the emotional attitude towards what is held to be Reality is such as would naturally be associated with the belief that Reality is good. What is, in all cases, ethically characteristic of mysticism is absence of indignation or protest, acceptance with joy, disbelief in the ultimate truth of the division into two hostile camps, the good and the bad. This attitude is a direct outcome of the nature of the mystical

experience: with its sense of unity is associated a feeling of infinite peace. Indeed, it may be suspected that the feeling of peace produces, as feelings do in dreams, the whole system of associated beliefs which make up the body of mystic doctrine. But this is a difficult question, and one on which it cannot be hoped that mankind will reach agreement.

Four questions thus arise in considering the truth or falsehood of mysticism, namely:

I. Are there two ways of knowing, which may be called respectively reason and intuition? And if so, is either to be preferred to the other?

II. Is all plurality and division illusory?

III. Is time unreal?

IV. What kind of reality belongs to good and evil?

On all four of these questions, while fully developed mysticism seems to be mistaken, I yet believe that, by sufficient restraint, there is an element of wisdom to be learned from the mystical way of feeling, which does not seem to be attainable in any other manner. If this is the truth, mysticism is to be commended as an attitude towards life, not as a creed about the world. The metaphysical creed, I shall maintain, is a mistaken outcome of the emotion, although this emotion, as colouring and informing all other thoughts and feelings, is the inspirer of whatever is best in Man. Even the cautious and patient investigation of truth by science, which seems the very antithesis of the mystic's swift certainty, may be fostered and nourished by that very spirit of reverence in which mysticism lives and moves.

I. REASON AND INTUITION

Of the reality or unreality of the mystic's world I know nothing. I have no wish to deny it, nor even to declare that the insight which reveals it is not a genuine insight. What I do wish to maintain—and it is here that the scientific attitude becomes imperative—is that insight, untested and unsupported, is an insufficient guarantee of truth, in spite of the fact that much of the most important truth is first suggested by its means. It is common to speak of an opposition betwen instinct and reason; in the eighteenth century, the opposition was drawn in favour of reason, but under the influence of Rousseau and the romantic movement instinct was given the preference, first by those

who rebelled against artificial forms of government and thought, and then, as the purely
rationalistic defence of traditional theology
became increasingly difficult, by all who felt in
science a menace to creeds which they associated with a spiritual outlook on life and the
world. Bergson, under the name of "intuition,"
has raised instinct to the position of sole arbiter
of metaphysical truth. But in fact the opposition of instinct and reason is mainly illusory.
Instinct, intuition, or insight is what first leads
to the beliefs which subsequent reason confirms
or confutes; but the confirmation, where it is
possible, consists, in that last analysis, of
agreement with other beliefs no less instinctive.
Reason is a harmonising, controlling force
rather than a creative one. Even in the most
purely logical realm, it is insight that first
arrives at what is new.

Where instinct and reason do sometimes
conflict is in regard to single beliefs, held
instinctively, and held with such determination
that no degree of inconsistency with other
beliefs leads to their abandonment. Instinct,
like all human faculties, is liable to error. Those
in whom reason is weak are often unwilling to
admit this as regards themselves, though all
admit it in regard to others. Where instinct is
least liable to error is in practical matters as to
which right judgment is a help to survival:
friendship and hostility in others, for instance,
are often felt with extraordinary discrimination
through very careful disguises. But even in such
matters a wrong impression may be given by
reserve or flattery; and in matters less directly
practical, such as philosophy deals with, very
strong instinctive beliefs are sometimes wholly
mistaken, as we may come to know through
their perceived inconsistency with other equally
strong beliefs. It is such considerations that
necessitate the harmonising mediation of
reason, which tests our beliefs by their mutual
compatibility, and examines, in doubtful cases,
the possible sources of error on the one side and
on the other. In this there is no opposition to
instinct as a whole, but only to blind reliance
upon some one interesting aspect of instinct to
the exclusion of other more commonplace
but not less truthworthy aspects. It is such one-
sidedness, not instinct itself, that reason aims
at correcting. . . .

The theoretical understanding of the world,
which is the aim of philosophy, is not a matter of
great practical importance to animals, or to
savages, or even to most civilized men. It is
hardly to be supposed, therefore, that the
rapid, rough and ready methods of instinct or
intuition will find in this field a favourable
ground for their application. It is the older
kinds of activity, which bring out our kinship
with remote generations of animal and semi-
human ancestors, that show intuition at its
best. In such matters as self-preservation and
love, intuition will act sometimes (though not
always) with a swiftness and precision which are
astonishing to the critical intellect. But philosophy is not one of the pursuits which illustrate
our affinity with the past: it is a highly refined,
highly civilized pursuit, demanding, for its
success, a certain liberation from the life of
instinct, and even, at times, a certain aloofness
from all mundane hopes and fears. It is not in
philosophy, therefore, that we can hope to see
intuition at its best. On the contrary, since the
true objects of philosophy, and the habit of
thought demanded for their apprehension, are
strange, unusual, and remote, it is here, more
almost than anywhere else, that intellect proves
superior to intuition, and that quick unana-
lysed convictions are least deserving of uncriti-
cal acceptance.

In advocating the scientific restraint and
balance, as against the self-assertion of a confident reliance upon intuition, we are only
urging, in the sphere of knowledge, that largeness of contemplation, that impersonal disinterestedness, and that freedom from practical
preoccupations which have been inculcated by
all the great religions of the world. Thus our
conclusion, however it may conflict with the
explicit beliefs of many mystics, is, in essence,
not contrary to the spirit which inspires those
beliefs, but rather the outcome of this very
spirit as applied in the realm of thought.

II. UNITY AND PLURALITY

One of the most convincing aspects of the
mystic illumination is the apparent revelation
of the oneness of all things, giving rise to pan-
theism in religion and to monism in philosophy.
An elaborate logic, beginning with Parmenides,
and culminating in Hegel and his followers, has
been gradually developed, to prove that the
universe is one indivisible Whole, and that what
seem to be its parts, if considered as substantial

and self-existing, are mere illusion. The conception of a Reality quite other than the world of appearance, a reality one, indivisible, and unchanging, was introduced into Western philosophy by Parmenides, not, nominally at least, for mystical or religious reasons, but on the basis of a logical argument as to the impossibility of not-being, and most subsequent metaphysical systems are the outcome of this fundamental idea.

The logic used in defence of mysticism seems to be faulty as logic, and open to technical criticisms, which I have explained elsewhere. I shall not here repeat these criticisms, since they are lengthy and difficult, but shall instead attempt an analysis of the state of mind from which mystical logic has arisen.

Belief in a reality quite different from what appears to the senses arises with irresistible force in certain moods, which are the source of most mysticism, and of most metaphysics. While such a mood is dominant, the need of logic is not felt, and accordingly the more thoroughgoing mystics do not employ logic, but appeal directly to the immediate deliverance of their insight. But such fully developed mysticism is rare in the West. When the intensity of emotional conviction subsides, a man who is in the habit of reasoning will search for logical grounds in favour of the belief which he finds in himself. But since the belief already exists, he will be very hospitable to any ground that suggests itself. The paradoxes apparently proved by his logic are really the paradoxes of mysticism, and are the goals which he feels his logic must reach if it is to be in accordance with insight. The resulting logic has rendered most philosophers incapable of giving any account of the world of science and daily life. If they had been anxious to give such an account, they would probably have discovered the errors of their logic; but most of them were less anxious to understand the world of science and daily life than to convict it of unreality in the interests of a super-sensible "real" world. . . .

Such an attitude naturally does not tend to the best results. Everyone knows that to read an author simply in order to refute him is not the way to understand him; and to read the book of Nature with a conviction that it is all illusion is just as unlikely to lead to understanding. If our logic is to find the common world intelligible, it must not be hostile, but must be inspired by a genuine acceptance such as is not usually to be found among metaphysicians.

III. TIME

The unreality of time is a cardinal doctrine of many metaphysical systems, often nominally based, as already by Parmenides, upon logical arguments, but originally derived, at any rate in the founders of new systems, from the certainty which is born in a moment of a mystic insight. . . .

The belief that what is ultimately real must be immutable is a very common one: it gave rise to the metaphysical notion of substance, and finds, even now, a wholly illegitimate satisfaction in such scientific doctrines as the conservation of energy and mass.

It is difficult to disentangle the truth and the error in this view. The arguments for the contention that time is unreal and that the world of sense is illusory must, I think, be regarded as fallacious. Nevertheless there is some sense—easier to feel than to state—in which time is an unimportant and superficial characteristic of reality. Past and future must be acknowledged to be as real as the present, and a certain emancipation from slavery to time is essential to philosophic thought. The importance of time is rather practical than theoretical, rather in relation to our desires than in relation to truth. A truer image of the world, I think, is obtained by picturing things as entering into the stream of time from an eternal world outside, than from a view which regards time as the devouring tyrant of all that is. Both in thought and in feeling, even though time be real, to realise the unimportance of time is the gate of wisdom.

That this is the case may be seen at once by asking ourselves why our feelings towards the past are so different from our feelings towards the future. The reason for this difference is wholly practical; our wishes can affect the future but not the past, the future is to some extent subject to our power, while the past is unalterably fixed. But every future will some day be past: if we see the past truly now, it must, when it was still future, have been just what we now see it to be, and what is now future must be just what we shall see it to be when it has become past. The felt difference of quality between past and future, therefore, is not an intrinsic difference, but only a difference in relation to us; to impartial contemplation, it ceases to exist. And impartiality of contemplation is, in the intellectual sphere, that very same virtue of disinterestedness which, in the sphere of action, appears as justice and unselfishness. Whoever wishes to see the world truly, to rise in thought above the tyranny of practical desires, must learn to overcome the difference of attitude towards past and future, and to survey the whole stream of time in one comprehensive vision.

The kind of way in which, as it seems to me, time ought not to enter into our theoretic philosophical thought, may be illustrated by the philosophy which has become associated with the idea of evolution, and which is exemplified by Nietzsche, pragmatism, and Bergson. This philosophy, on the basis of the development which has led from the lowest forms of life up to man, sees in *progress* the fundamental law of the universe, and thus admits the difference between *earlier* and *later* into the very citadel of its contemplative outlook. With its past and future history of the world, conjectural as it is, I do not wish to quarrel. But I think that, in the intoxication of a quick success, much that is required for a true understanding of the universe has been forgotten. Something of Hellenism, something, too, of Oriental resignation, must be combined with its hurrying Western self-assertion before it can emerge from the ardour of youth into the mature wisdom of manhood. . . .

Life, in this [evolutionist] philosophy, is a continuous stream, in which all divisions are artificial and unreal. Separate things, beginnings and endings, are mere convenient fictions: there is only smooth unbroken transition. The beliefs of to-day may count as true to-day, if they carry us along the stream; but to-morrow they will be false, and must be replaced by new beliefs to meet the new situation. All our thinking consists of convenient fictions, imaginary congealings of the stream; reality flows on in spite of all our fictions, and though it can be lived, it cannot be conceived in thought. Somehow, without explicit statement, the assurance is slipped in that the future, though we cannot foresee it, will be better than the past or the present; the reader is like the child which expects a sweet because it has been told to open his mouth and shut its eyes. Logic, mathema-

tics, physics disappear in this philosophy, because they are too "static"; what is real is an impulse and movement towards a goal which, like the rainbow, recedes as we advance, and makes every place different when it reaches it from what it appeared to be at a distance.

I do not propose to enter upon a technical examination of this philosophy. I wish only to maintain that the motives and interests which inspire it are so exclusively practical, and the problems with which it deals are so special, that it can hardly be regarded as touching any of the questions that, to my mind, constitute genuine philosophy.

The predominant interest of evolutionism is in the question of human destiny, or at least of the destiny of Life. It is more interested in morality and happiness than in knowledge for its own sake. It must be admitted that the same may be said of many other philosophies, and that a desire for the kind of knowledge which philosophy can give is very rare. But if philosophy is to attain truth, it is necessary first and foremost that philosophers should acquire the disinterested intellectual curiosity which characterises the genuine man of science. Knowledge concerning the future—which is the kind of knowledge that must be sought if we are to know about human destiny—is possible within certain narrow limits. It is impossible to say how much the limits may be enlarged with the progress of science. But what is evident is that any proposition about the future belongs by its subject-matter to some particular science, and is to be ascertained, if at all, by the methods of that science. Philosophy is not a short cut to the same kind of results as those of the other sciences: if it is to be a genuine study, it must have a province of its own, and aim at results which the other sciences can neither prove nor disprove.

Evolutionism, in basing itself upon the notion of *progress*, which is change from the worse to the better, allows the notion of time, as it seems to me, to become its tyrant rather than its servant, and thereby loses that impartiality of contemplation which is the source of all that is best in philosophic thought and feeling. Metaphysicians, as we saw, have frequently denied altogether the reality of time. I do not wish to do this; I wish only to preserve the mental outlook which inspired the denial, the attitude which, in thought, regards the past as having the same reality as the present and the same importance as the future. "In so far," says Spinoza, "as the mind conceives a thing according to the dictate of reason, it will be equally affected whether the idea is that of a future, past, or present thing." It is this "conceiving according to the dictate of reason" that I find lacking in the philosophy which is based on evolution.

IV. GOOD AND EVIL

Mysticism maintains that all evil is illusory, and sometimes maintains the same view as regards good, but more often holds that all Reality is good. . . . The possibility of this universal love and joy in all that exists is of supreme importance for the conduct and happiness of life, and gives inestimable value to the mystic emotion, apart from any creeds which may be built upon it. But if we are not to be led into false beliefs, it is necessary to realise exactly *what* the mystic emotion reveals. It reveals a possibility of human nature—a possibility of a nobler, happier, freer life than any that can be otherwise achieved. But it does not reveal anything about the non-human, or about the nature of the universe in general. Good and bad, and even the higher good that mysticism finds everywhere, are the reflections of our own emotions on other things, not part of the substance of things as they are in themselves. And therefore an impartial contemplation, freed from all pre-occupation with Self, will not judge things good or bad, although it is very easily combined with that feeling of universal love which leads the mystic to say that the whole world is good. . . .

I believe . . . that the elimination of ethical considerations from philosophy is both scientifically necessary and—though this may seem a paradox—an ethical advance. Both these contentions must be briefly defended.

The hope of satisfaction to our more human desires—the hope of demonstrating that the world has this or that desirable ethical characteristic—is not one which, so far as I can see, a scientific philosophy can do anything whatever to satisfy. The difference between a good world and a bad one is a difference in the particular characteristics of the particular things that exist in these worlds: it is not a sufficiently abstract difference to come within the province of philosophy. Love and hate, for example, are ethical opposites, but to philosophy they are closely analogous attitudes toward objects. The general form and structure of those attitudes towards objects which constitute mental phenomena is a problem for philosophy, but the difference between love and hate is not a difference of form or structure, and therefore belongs rather to the special science of psychology than to philosophy. Thus the ethical interests which have often inspired philosophers must remain in the background: some kind of ethical interest may inspire the whole study, but none must obtrude in the detail or be expected in the special results which are sought.

If this view seems at first sight disappointing, we may remind ourselves that a similar change has been found necessary in all the other sciences. The physicist or chemist is not now required to prove the ethical importance of his ions or atoms; the biologist is not expected to prove the utility of the plants or animals which he dissects . . . In psychology, the scientific attitude is even more recent and more difficult than in the physical sciences; it is natural to consider that human nature is either good or bad, and to suppose that the difference between good and bad, so all-important in practice, must be important in theory also. It is only during the last century that an ethically neutral psychology has grown up; and here too, ethical neutrality has been essential to scientific success.

In philosophy, hitherto, ethical neutrality has been seldom sought and hardly ever achieved. Men have remembered their wishes, and have judged philosophies in relation to their wishes. Driven from the particular sciences, the belief that the notions of good and evil must afford a key to the understanding of the world has sought a refuge in philosophy. But even from this last refuge, if philosophy is not to remain a set of pleasing dreams, this belief must be driven forth. It is a commonplace that happiness is not best achieved by those who seek it directly; and it would seem that the same is true of the good. In thought, at any rate, those who forget good and evil and seek only to know the facts are more likely to achieve good than those who view the world through the distorting medium of their own desires.

We are thus brought back to our seeming

paradox, that a philosophy which does not seek to impose upon the world its own conceptions of good and evil is not only more likely to achieve truth, but is also the outcome of a higher ethical standpoint than one which, like evolutionism and most traditional systems, is perpetually appraising the universe and seeking to find in it an embodiment of present ideals. In religion, and in every deeply serious view of the world and of human destiny, there is an element of submission, a realisation of the limits of human power, which is somewhat lacking in the modern world, with its quick material successes and its insolent belief in the boundless possibilities of progress. "He that loveth his life shall lose it"; and there is danger lest, through a too confident love of life, life itself should lose much of what gives it its highest worth. The submission which religion inculcates in action is essentially the same in spirit as that which science teaches in thought; and the ethical neutrality by which its victories have been achieved is the outcome of that submission.

The good which it concerns us to remember is the good which it lies in our power to create—the good in our own lives and in our attitude towards the world. Insistence on belief in an external realisation of the good is a form of self-assertion, which, while it cannot secure the external good which it desires, can seriously impair the inward good which lies in our power, and destroy that reverence towards fact which

constitutes both what is valuable in humility and what is fruitful in the scientific temper.

Human beings cannot, of course, wholly transcend human nature; something subjective, if only the interest that determines the direction of our attention, must remain in all our thought. But scientific philosophy comes nearer to objectivity than any other human pursuit, and gives us, therefore, the closest constant and the most intimate relation with the outer world that it is possible to achieve. To the primitive mind, everything is either friendly or hostile; but experience has shown that friendliness and hostility are not the conceptions by which the world is to be understood. Scientific philosophy thus represents, though as yet only in a nascent condition, a higher form of thought than any pre-scientific belief or imagination, and, like every approach to self-transcendence, it brings with it a rich reward in increase of scope and breadth and comprehension. Evolutionism, in spite of its appeals to particular scientific facts, fails to be a truly scientific philosophy because of its slavery to time, its ethical preoccupations, and its predominant interest in our mundane concerns and destiny. A truly scientific philosophy will be more humble, more piecemeal, more arduous, offering less glitter of outward mirage to flatter fallacious hopes, but more indifferent to fate, and more capable of accepting the world without the tyrannous imposition of our human and temporary demands.

Translation Sources

The selections for Plato's *Dialogues* were taken from the English translation of B. Jowett. Aristotle's writings were translated as follows: The *Metaphysics* by John H. McMahon, *On Life* by W. A. Hammond, "How to Conduct a Philosophical Analysis" by William Ogle, and the *Ethics* by J. E. C. Welldon. The selections from St. Augustine's *City of God* were translated by M. Dods, G. Wilson, and J. J. Smith, and those from St. Thomas Aquinas by J. R. Rickaby. The passage from St. Anselm was translated by S. M. Deane.

The *Meditations* of Descartes was translated by John Veitch. Max Muller translated the passages from Kant's *Critique of Pure Reason,* and J. P. Mahaffy translated those which belong to the *Prolegomena.* Hegel's selection was taken from the translation of S. W. Dyde, and Schopenhauer's essay from the translation of R. B. Haldane and J. Kemp. Nietzsche's essay was translated by Maximilian A. Mugge.

The essay by Russell first appeared in July, 1914, in *The Hibbert Journal.*